THE ELEVENTH
Garfield
Fat Cat 3-Pack

JIM DAVIS

Ballantine Books • New York

A Ballantine Book
Published by The Ballantine Publishing Group

GARFIELD HAMS IT UP copyright © 1997 by Paws, Incorporated
GARFIELD THINKS BIG copyright © 1997 by Paws, Incorporated
GARFIELD THROWS HIS WEIGHT AROUND copyright © 1998 by Paws, Incorporated
GARFIELD Comic Strips copyright © 1996, 1997 by Paws, Incorporated

All rights reserved under International and Pan-American Copyright
Conventions. Published in the United States by The Ballantine Publishing
Group, a division of Random House, Inc., New York, and simultaneously
in Canada by Random House of Canada Limited, Toronto.

Ballantine and colophon are registered trademarks of Random House, Inc.

www.randomhouse.com/BB/

Library of Congress Catalog Card Number: 99-90502

ISBN: 0-345-43801-9

Manufactured in the United States of America

First Edition: September 1999

10 9 8 7 6 5 4 3 2 1

Garfield

hams it up

BY: JIM DAVIS

DEAR FLABBY

Snappy answers to sappy questions:
all your puny problems solved in 10 words or less!

Q: Dear Flabby,
   What can I do about my little brother? He's such a pest!
A: Have you tried a flyswatter?

Q: Dear Flabby,
   My boss is a mean, unappreciative slave driver who constantly belittles me. What can I do?
A: Shut up and get back to work!

Q: Dear Flabby,
   My dad insists I clean my room! How can I get out of this?
A: Get a new dad.

Q: Dear Flabby,
   Why are you so lazy?
A: Dear Loser,
   Why are you so stupid? Next question.

Q: Help! I need to lose weight! How can I stop eating all the fattening foods I love?
A: Send them to me and I'll eat them for you.

OUT

IN

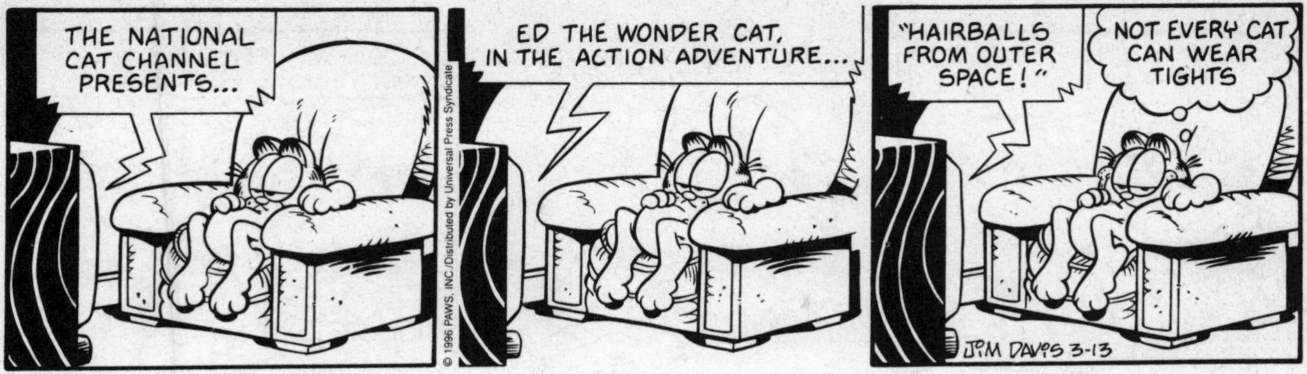
THE NATIONAL CAT CHANNEL PRESENTS...
© 1996 PAWS, INC./Distributed by Universal Press Syndicate
ED THE WONDER CAT, IN THE ACTION ADVENTURE...
"HAIRBALLS FROM OUTER SPACE!"
NOT EVERY CAT CAN WEAR TIGHTS
JIM DAVIS 3-13

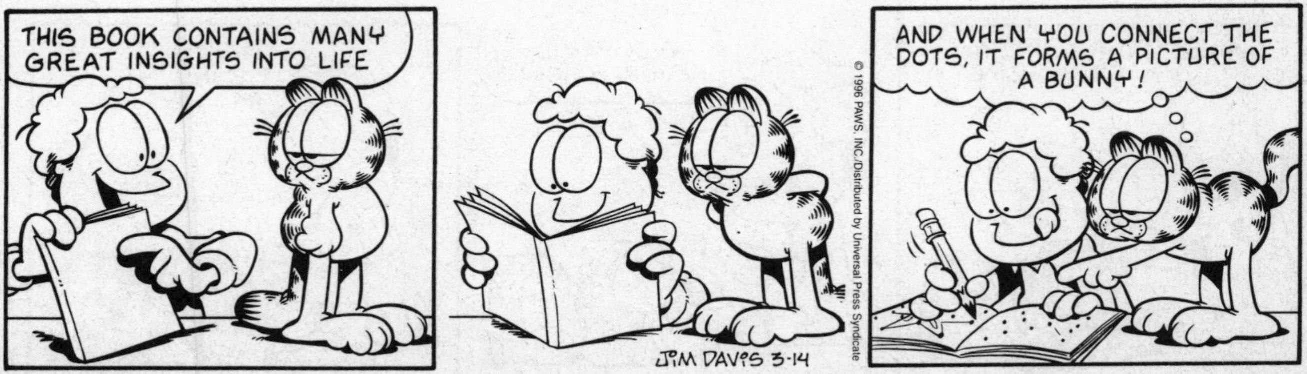
THIS BOOK CONTAINS MANY GREAT INSIGHTS INTO LIFE
JIM DAVIS 3-14
© 1996 PAWS, INC./Distributed by Universal Press Syndicate
AND WHEN YOU CONNECT THE DOTS, IT FORMS A PICTURE OF A BUNNY!

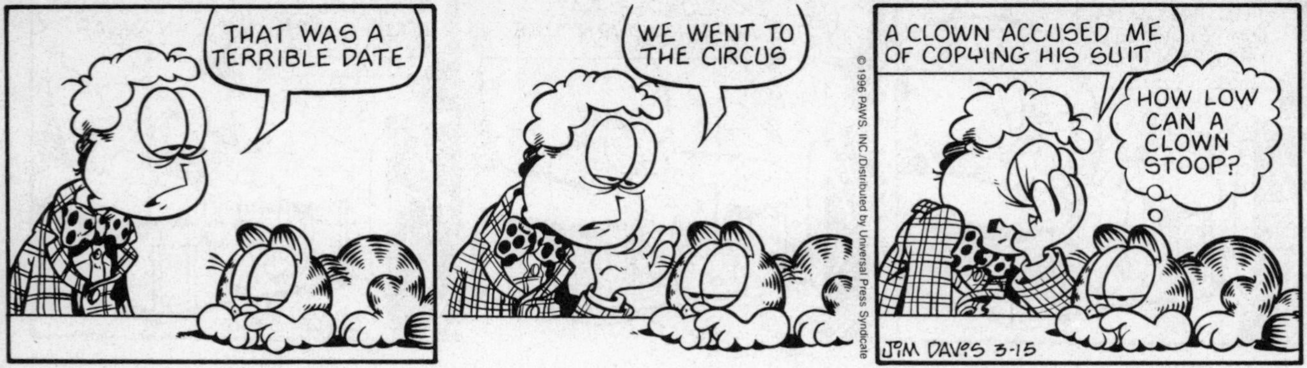
THAT WAS A TERRIBLE DATE
WE WENT TO THE CIRCUS
A CLOWN ACCUSED ME OF COPYING HIS SUIT
HOW LOW CAN A CLOWN STOOP?
JIM DAVIS 3-15

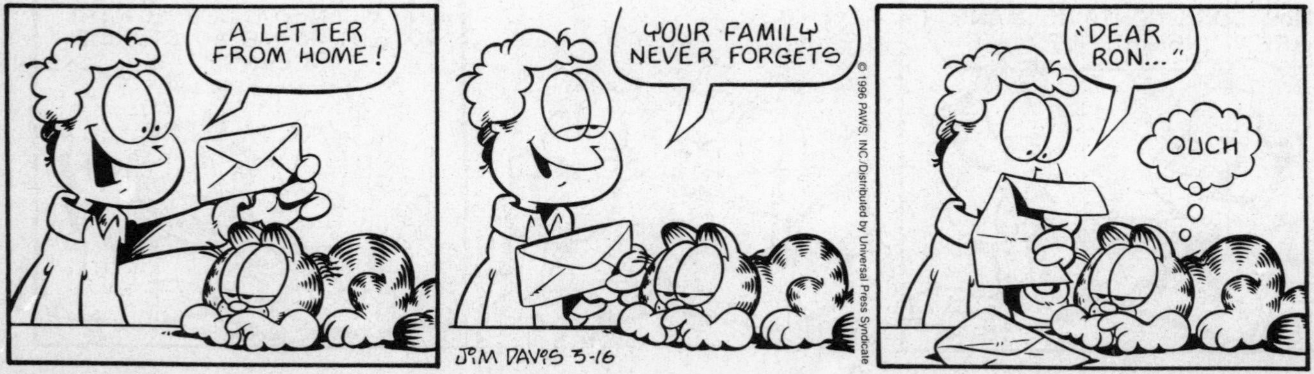
A LETTER FROM HOME!
YOUR FAMILY NEVER FORGETS
JIM DAVIS 3-16
"DEAR RON..."
OUCH

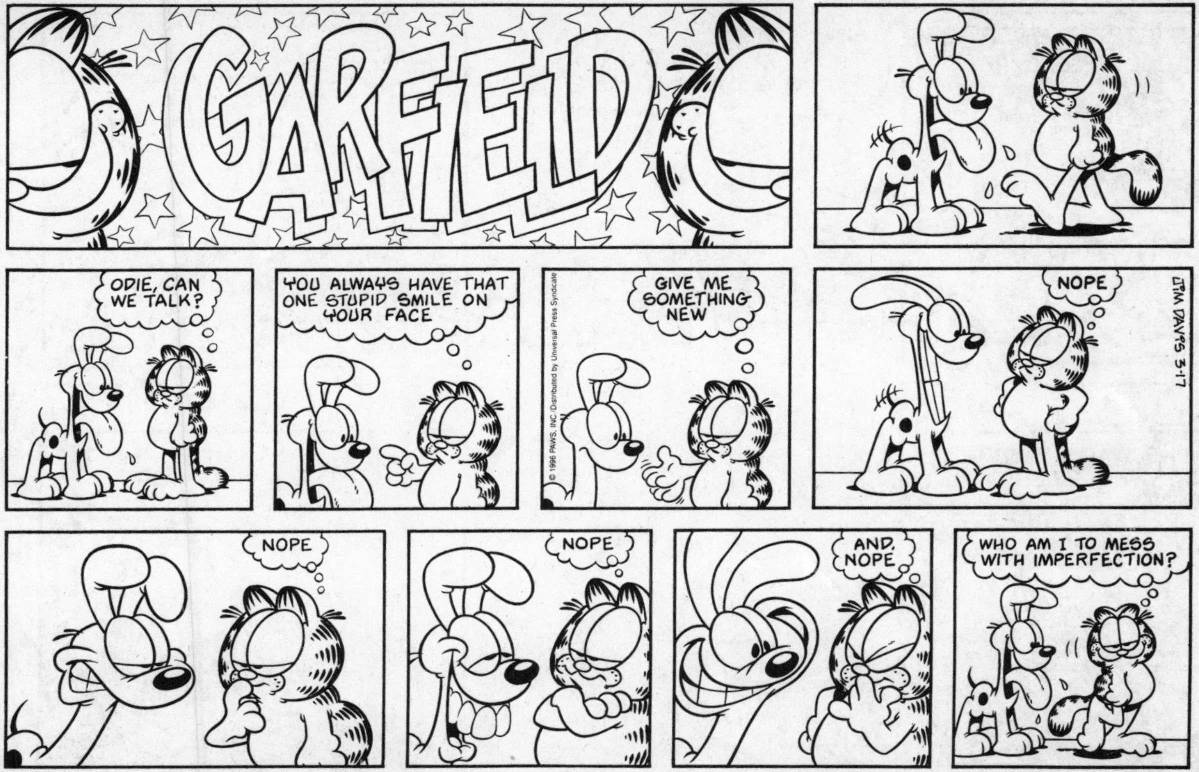
GARFIELD
ODIE, CAN WE TALK?
YOU ALWAYS HAVE THAT ONE STUPID SMILE ON YOUR FACE
© 1996 PAWS, INC./Distributed by Universal Press Syndicate
GIVE ME SOMETHING NEW
NOPE
JIM DAVIS 3-17
NOPE
NOPE
AND, NOPE
WHO AM I TO MESS WITH IMPERFECTION?

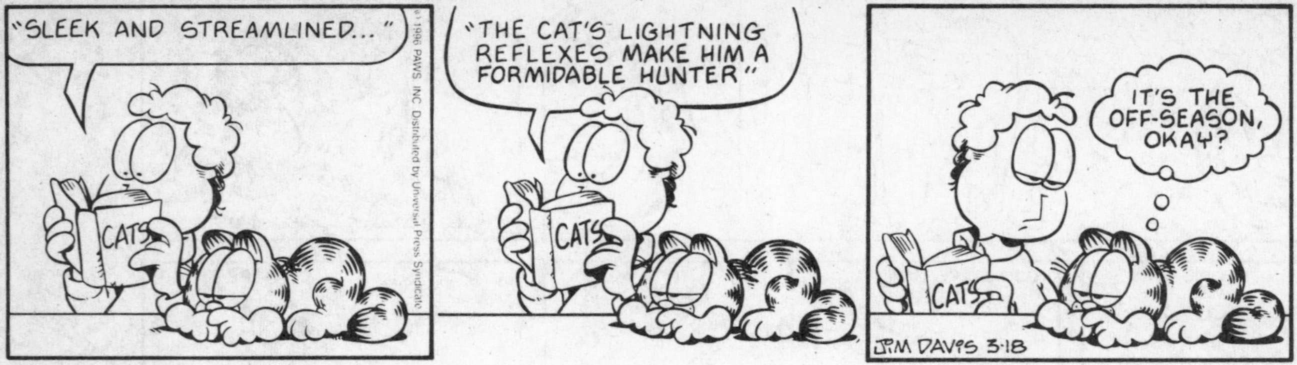
"SLEEK AND STREAMLINED..."
© 1996 PAWS INC Distributed by Universal Press Syndicate
"THE CAT'S LIGHTNING REFLEXES MAKE HIM A FORMIDABLE HUNTER"
IT'S THE OFF-SEASON, OKAY?
CATS
JIM DAVIS 3-18

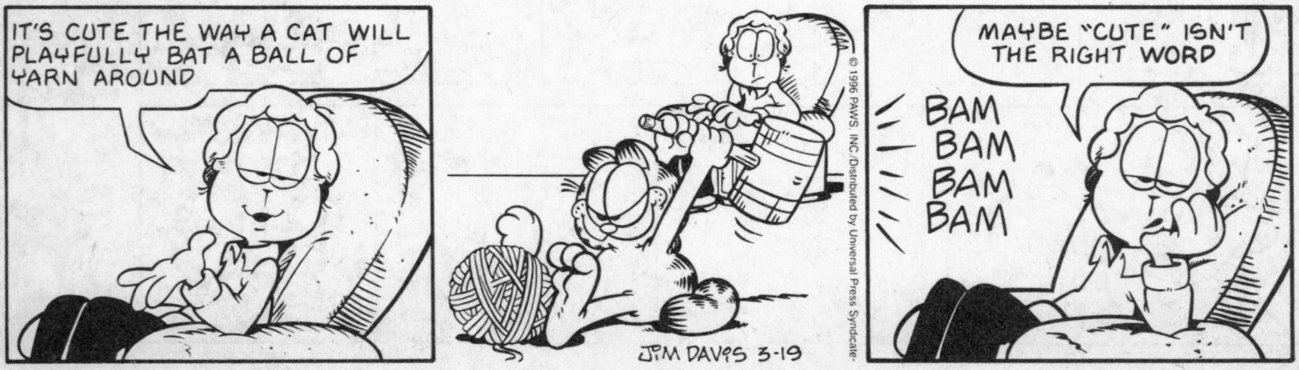
IT'S CUTE THE WAY A CAT WILL PLAYFULLY BAT A BALL OF YARN AROUND
JIM DAVIS 3-19
© 1996 PAWS, INC./Distributed by Universal Press Syndicate
MAYBE "CUTE" ISN'T THE RIGHT WORD
BAM BAM BAM BAM

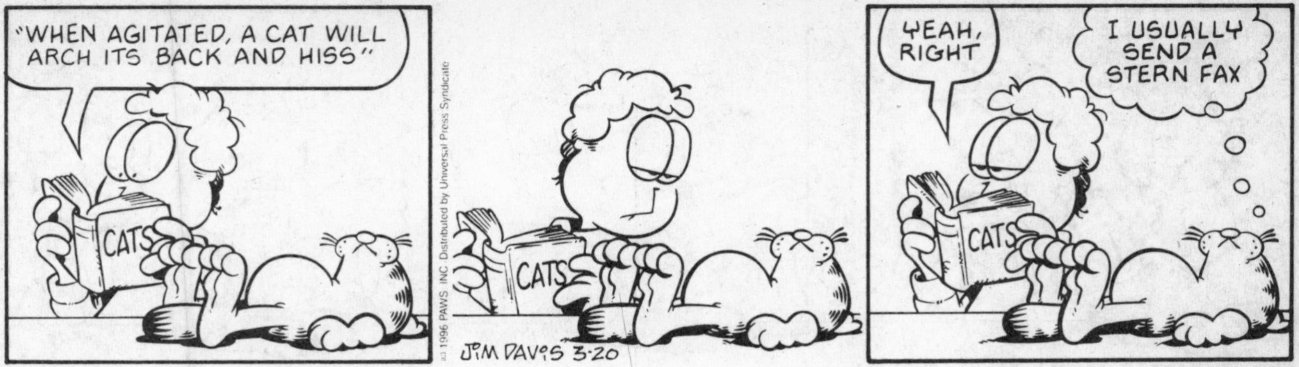
"WHEN AGITATED, A CAT WILL ARCH ITS BACK AND HISS"
© 1996 PAWS, INC. Distributed by Universal Press Syndicate
JIM DAVIS 3-20
YEAH, RIGHT
I USUALLY SEND A STERN FAX

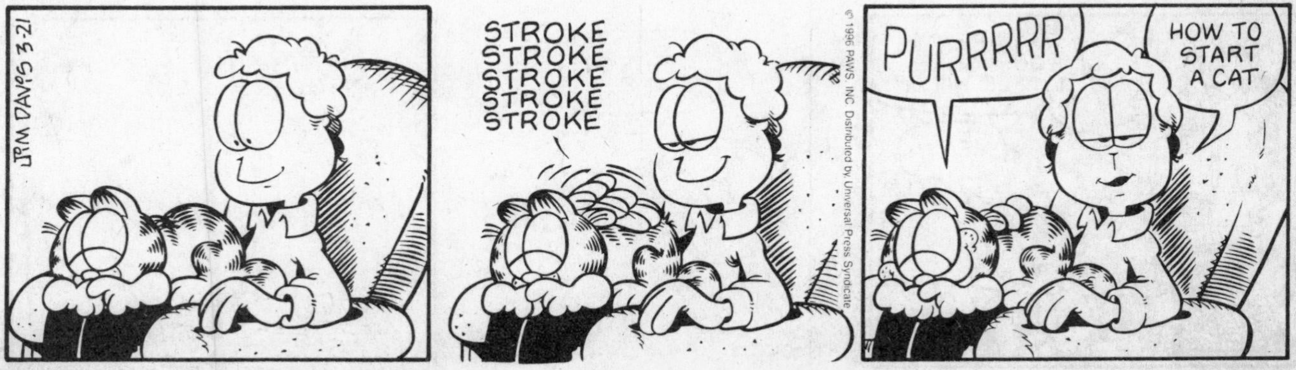
JIM DAVIS 3-21
STROKE STROKE STROKE STROKE STROKE
© 1996 PAWS, INC. Distributed by Universal Press Syndicate
PURRRRR
HOW TO START A CAT

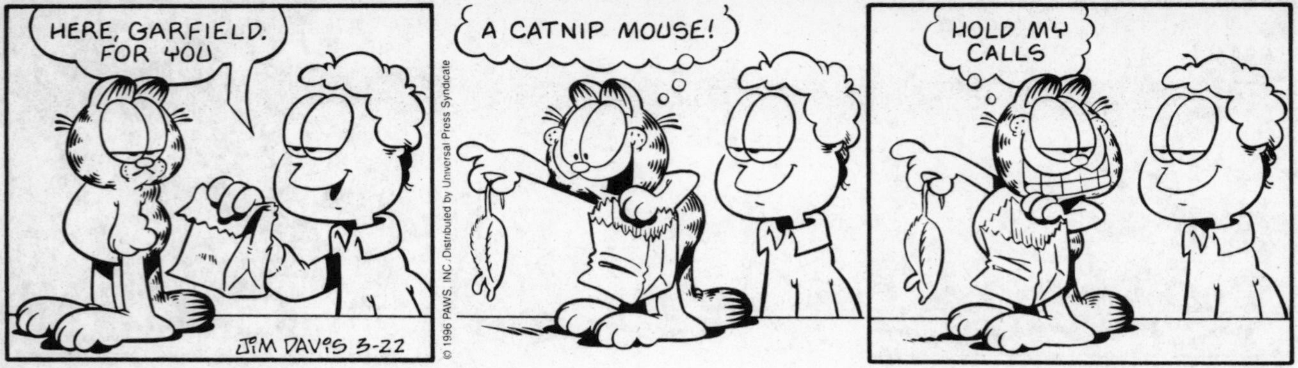
HERE, GARFIELD. FOR YOU
A CATNIP MOUSE!
HOLD MY CALLS
JIM DAVIS 3-22
© 1996 PAWS, INC. Distributed by Universal Press Syndicate

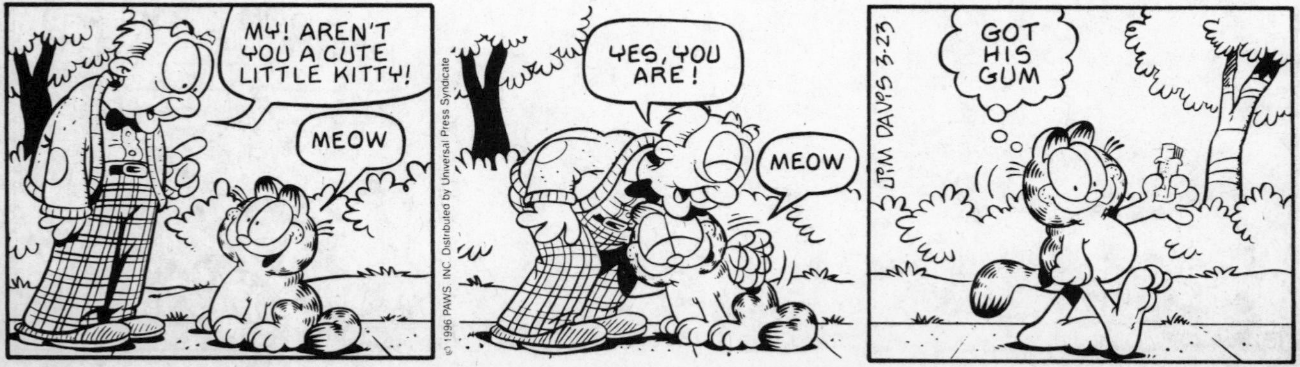
MY! AREN'T YOU A CUTE LITTLE KITTY!
MEOW
YES, YOU ARE!
MEOW
GOT HIS GUM
JIM DAVIS 3-23
© 1996 PAWS, INC. Distributed by Universal Press Syndicate

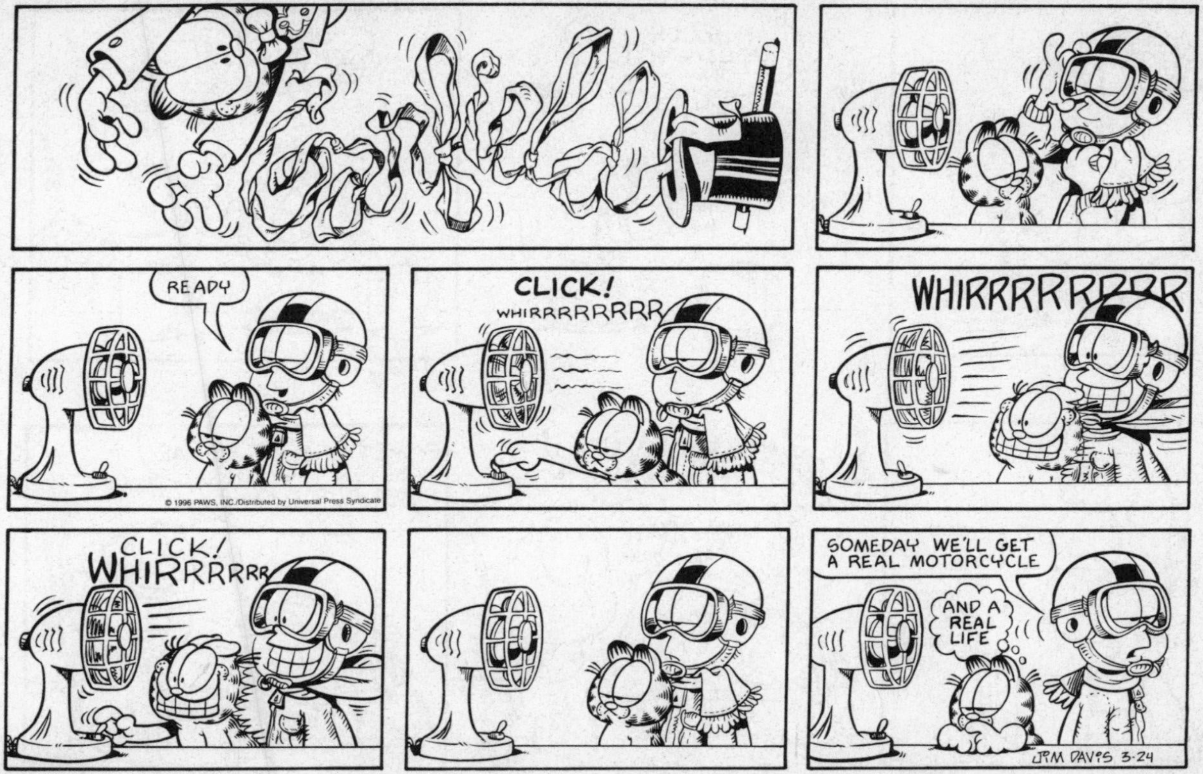

READY
CLICK!
WHIRRRRRRRR
WHIRRRRRRRR
CLICK!
WHIRRRRRR
SOMEDAY WE'LL GET A REAL MOTORCYCLE
AND A REAL LIFE
JIM DAVIS 3-24

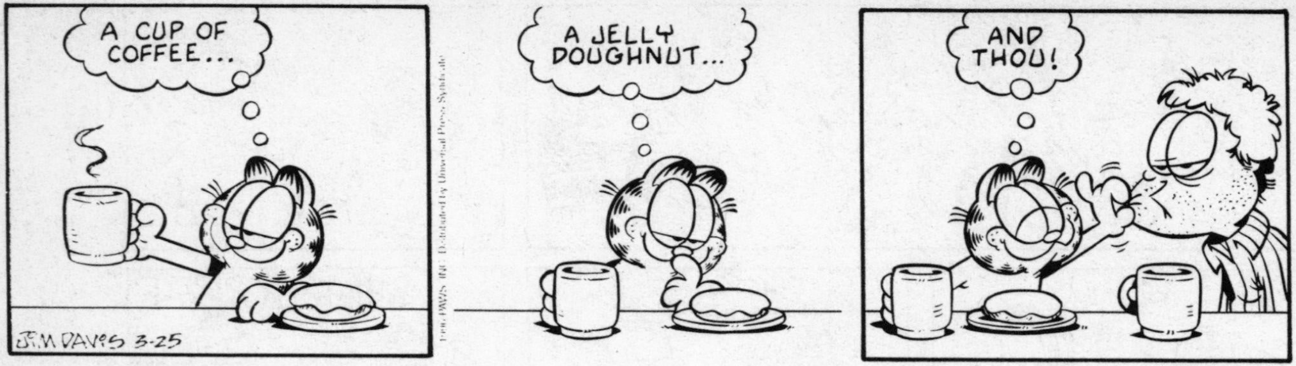
A CUP OF COFFEE...
A JELLY DOUGHNUT...
AND THOU!
JIM DAVIS 3-25

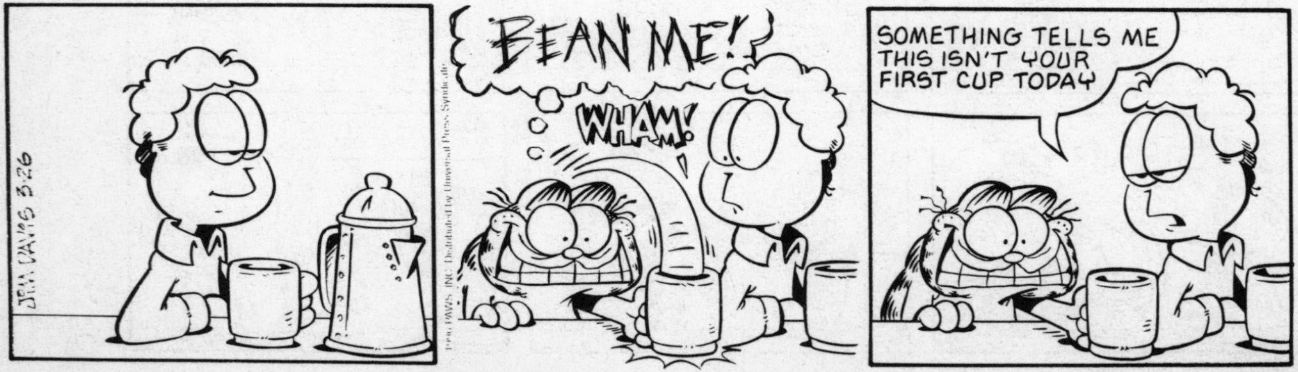
JIM DAVIS 3-26
BEAN ME!
WHAM!
SOMETHING TELLS ME THIS ISN'T YOUR FIRST CUP TODAY

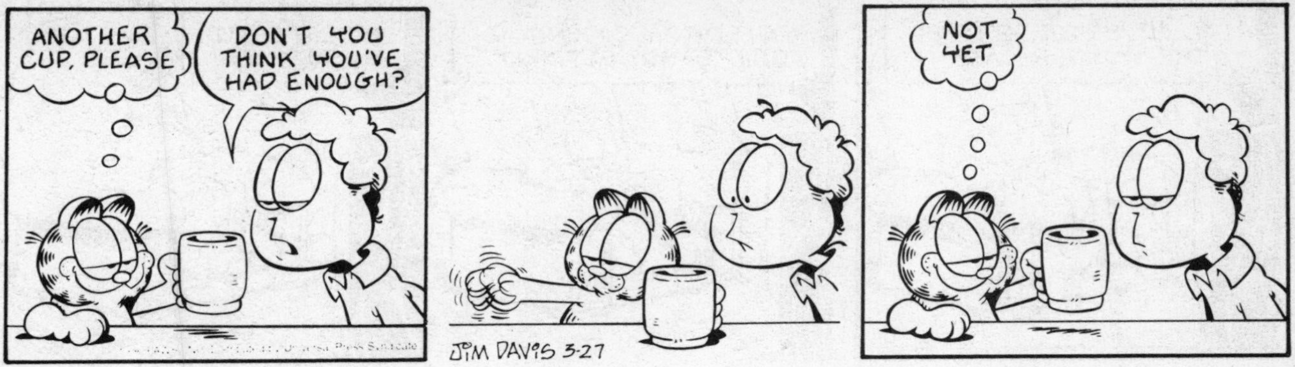
ANOTHER CUP, PLEASE
DON'T YOU THINK YOU'VE HAD ENOUGH?
NOT YET
JIM DAVIS 3-27

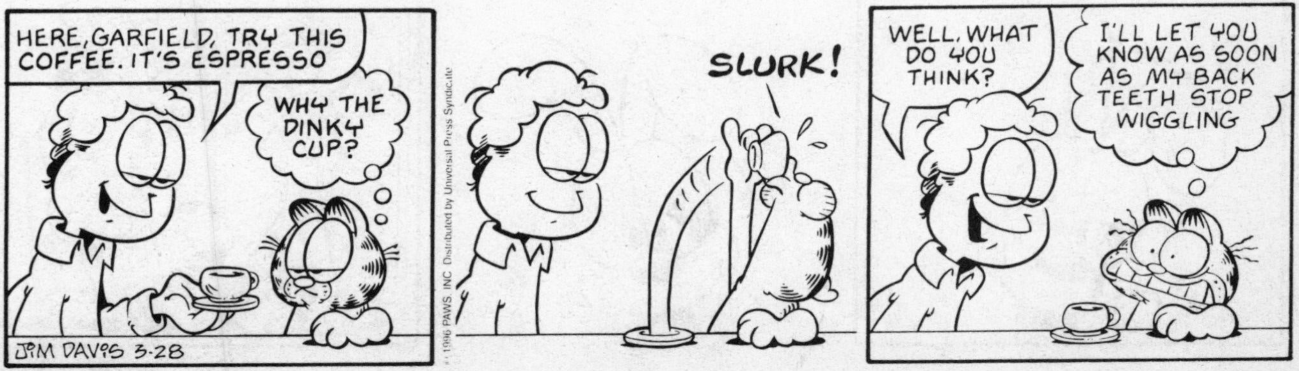
HERE, GARFIELD, TRY THIS COFFEE. IT'S ESPRESSO
WHY THE DINKY CUP?
JIM DAVIS 3-28
© 1986 PAWS, INC. Distributed by Universal Press Syndicate
SLURK!
WELL, WHAT DO YOU THINK?
I'LL LET YOU KNOW AS SOON AS MY BACK TEETH STOP WIGGLING

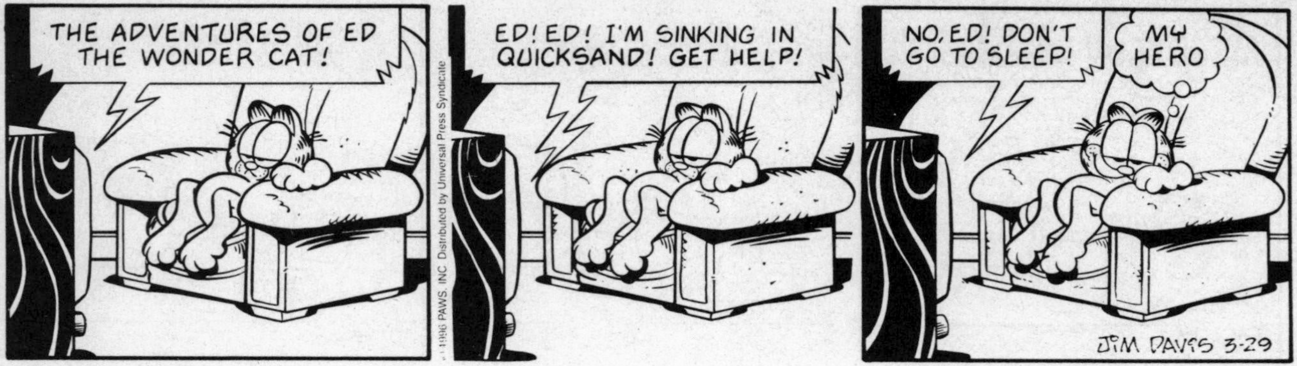
THE ADVENTURES OF ED THE WONDER CAT!
ED! ED! I'M SINKING IN QUICKSAND! GET HELP!
NO, ED! DON'T GO TO SLEEP!
MY HERO
JIM DAVIS 3-29
© 1996 PAWS, INC Distributed by Universal Press Syndicate

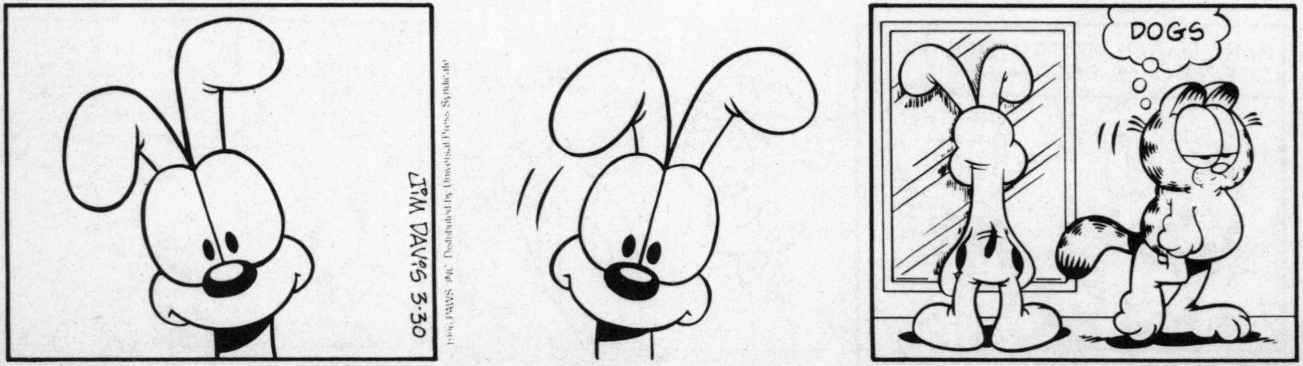
JIM DAVIS 3-30
DOGS

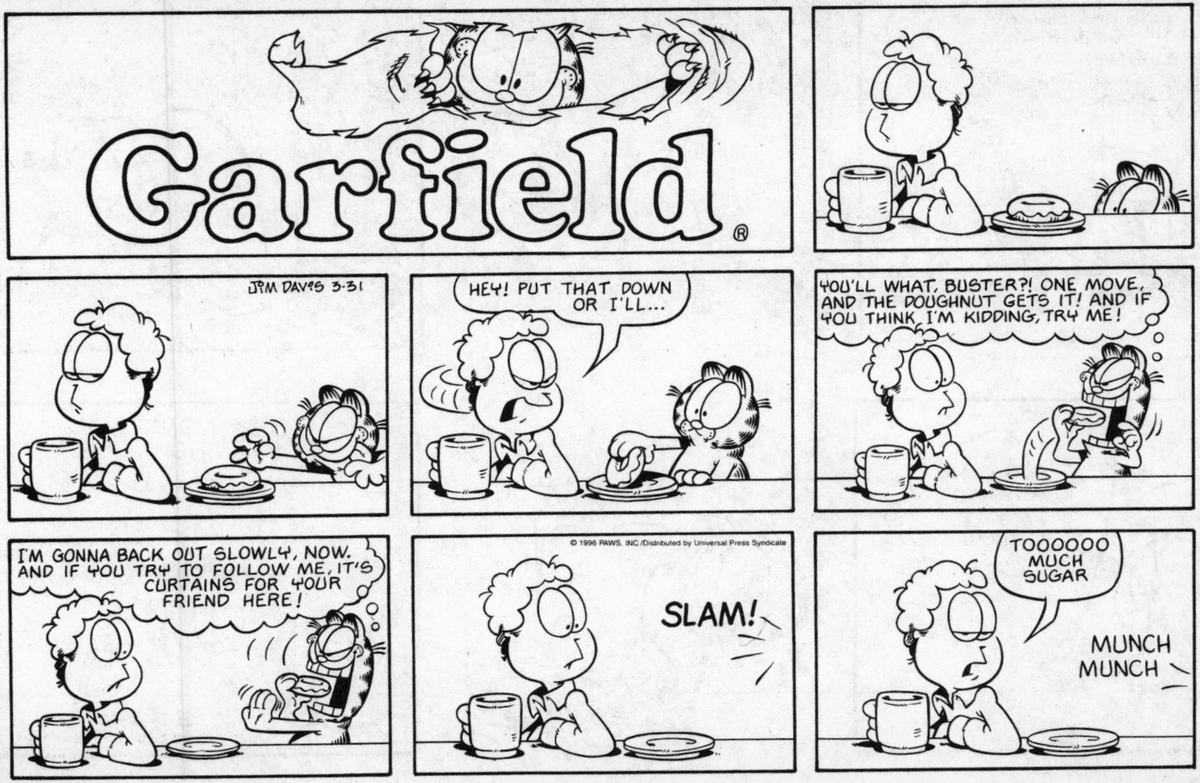
Garfield®
JIM DAVIS 3-31
HEY! PUT THAT DOWN OR I'LL...
YOU'LL WHAT, BUSTER?! ONE MOVE, AND THE DOUGHNUT GETS IT! AND IF YOU THINK I'M KIDDING, TRY ME!
I'M GONNA BACK OUT SLOWLY, NOW. AND IF YOU TRY TO FOLLOW ME, IT'S CURTAINS FOR YOUR FRIEND HERE!
© 1996 PAWS, INC./Distributed by Universal Press Syndicate
SLAM!
TOOOOOO MUCH SUGAR
MUNCH MUNCH

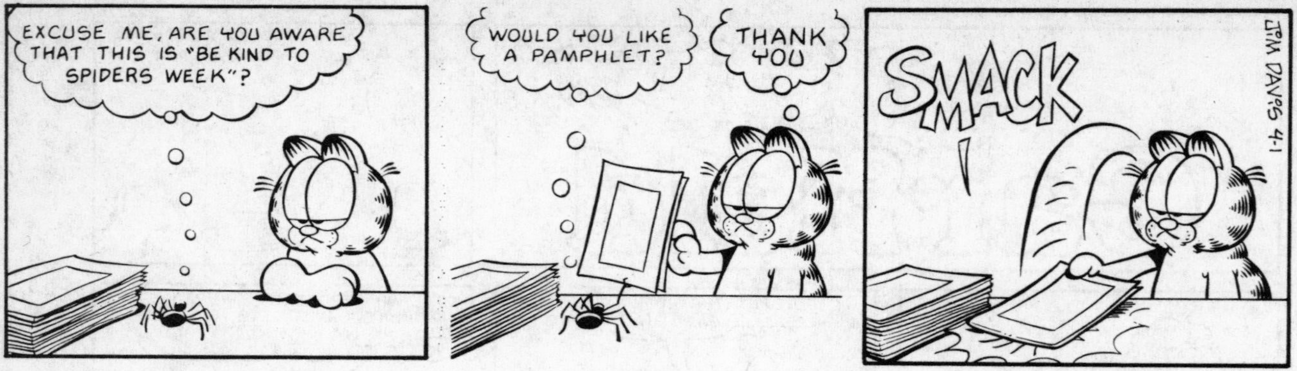
EXCUSE ME, ARE YOU AWARE THAT THIS IS "BE KIND TO SPIDERS WEEK"?
WOULD YOU LIKE A PAMPHLET?
THANK YOU
SMACK!
JIM DAVIS 4-1

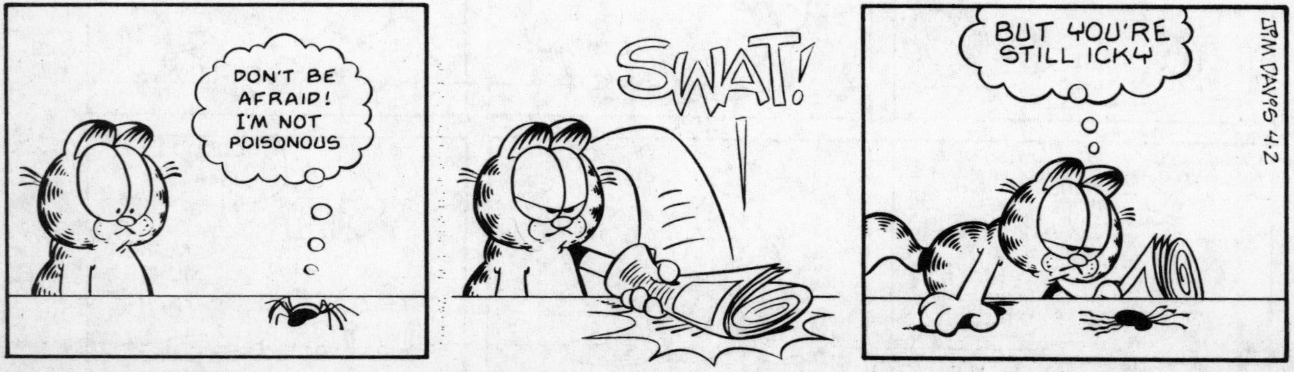
DON'T BE AFRAID! I'M NOT POISONOUS
SWAT!
BUT YOU'RE STILL ICKY
JIM DAVIS 4-2

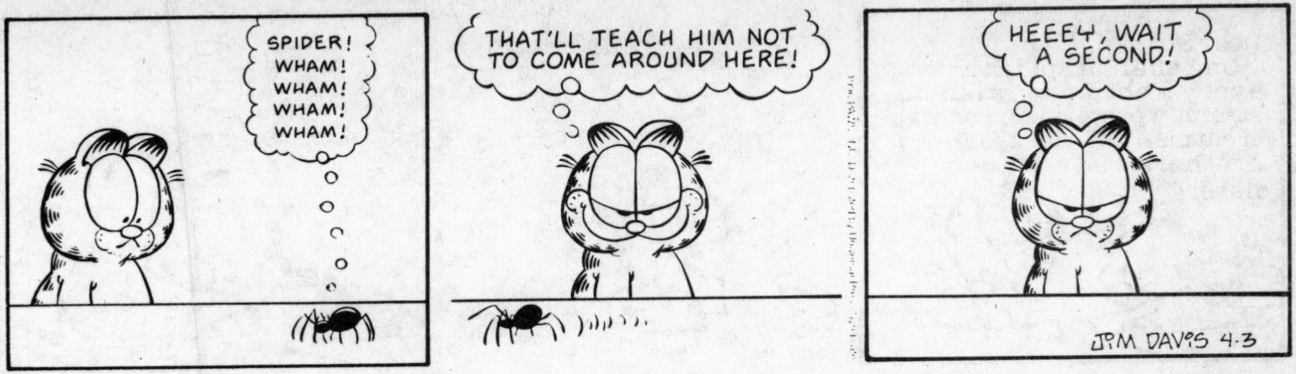
SPIDER! WHAM! WHAM! WHAM! WHAM!
THAT'LL TEACH HIM NOT TO COME AROUND HERE!
HEEEY, WAIT A SECOND!
JIM DAVIS 4-3

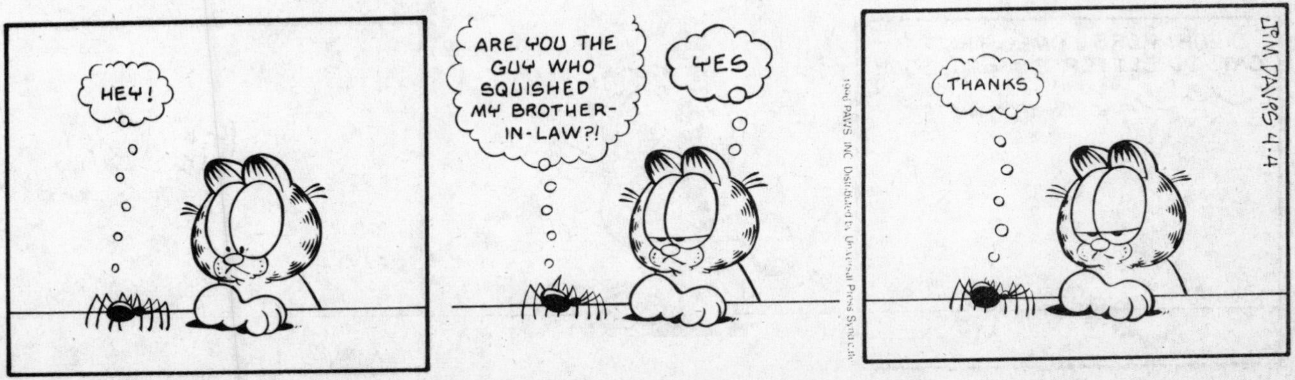
HEY!
ARE YOU THE GUY WHO SQUISHED MY BROTHER-IN-LAW?!
YES
THANKS
JIM DAVIS 4-4

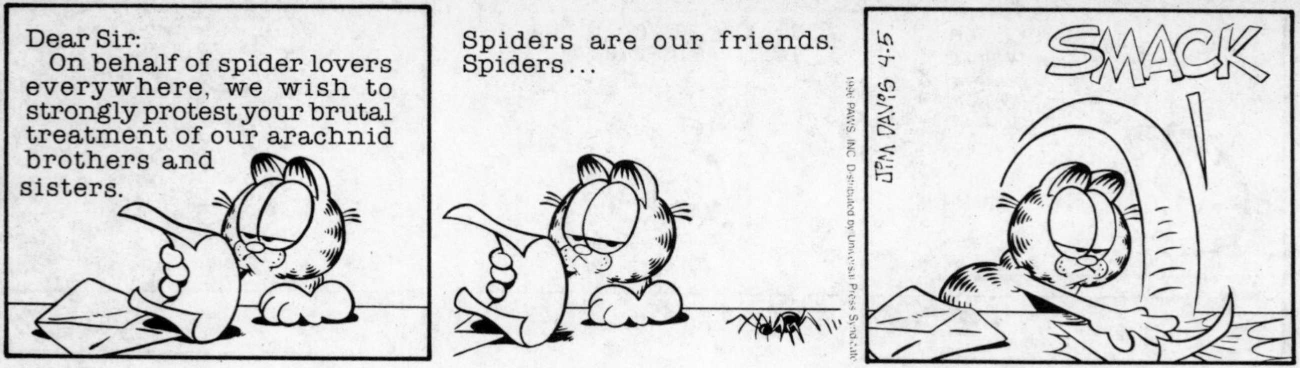
Dear Sir:
On behalf of spider lovers everywhere, we wish to strongly protest your brutal treatment of our arachnid brothers and sisters.
Spiders are our friends. Spiders...
PAWS INC Distributed by Universal Press Syndicate
JIM DAVIS 4-5
SMACK

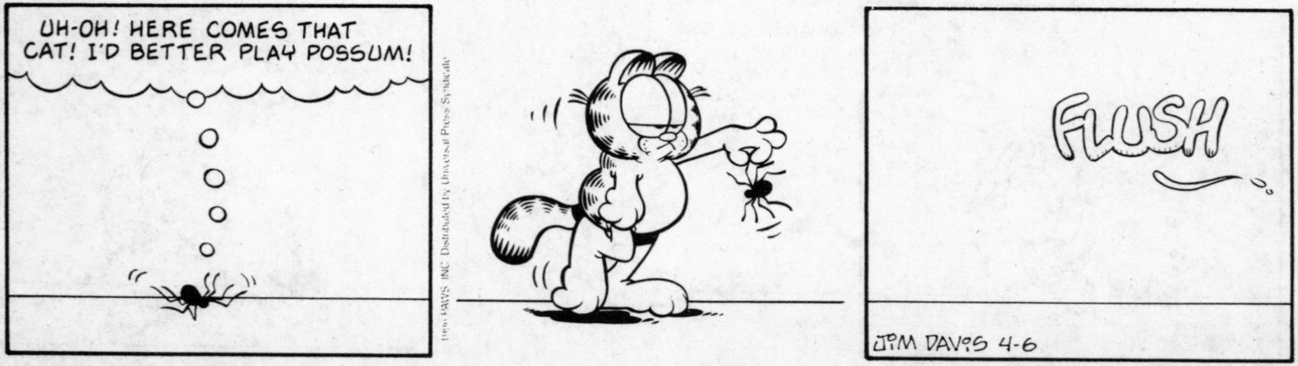
UH-OH! HERE COMES THAT CAT! I'D BETTER PLAY POSSUM!
PAWS INC Distributed by Universal Press Syndicate
FLUSH
JIM DAVIS 4-6

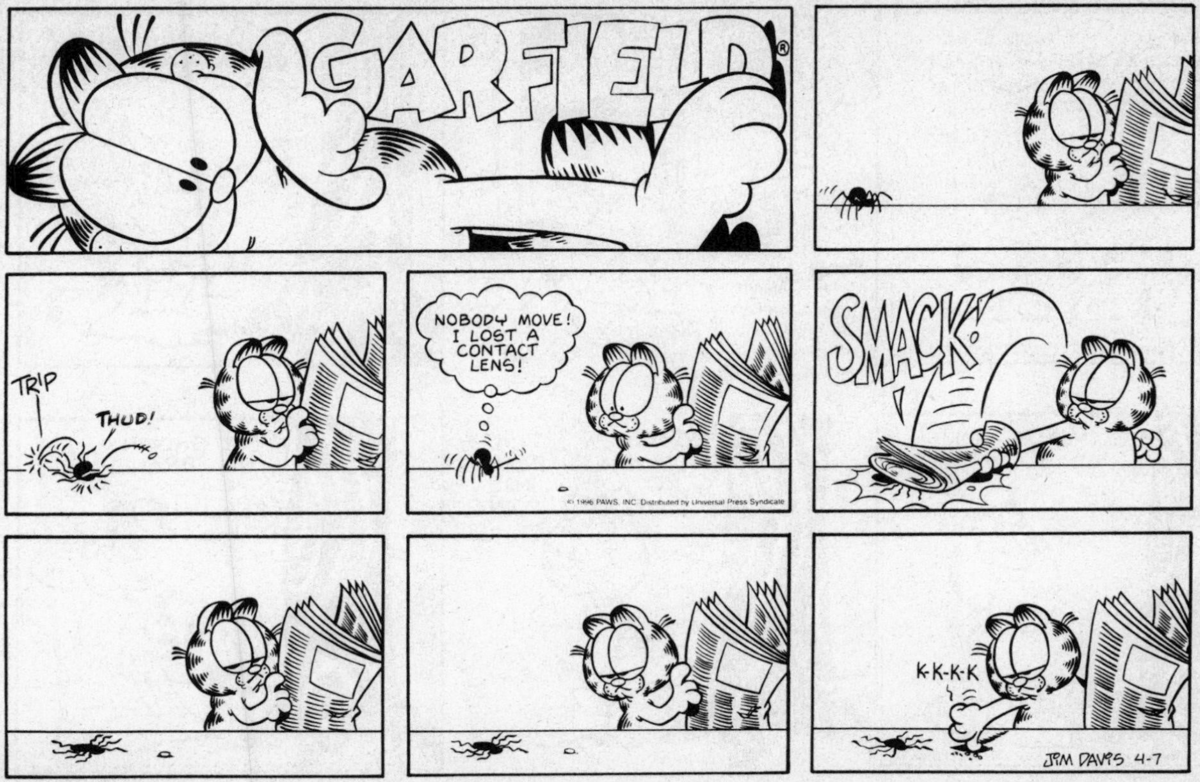
GARFIELD®
TRIP
THUD!
NOBODY MOVE! I LOST A CONTACT LENS!
© 1996 PAWS, INC. Distributed by Universal Press Syndicate
SMACK!
K-K-K-K
JIM DAVIS 4-7

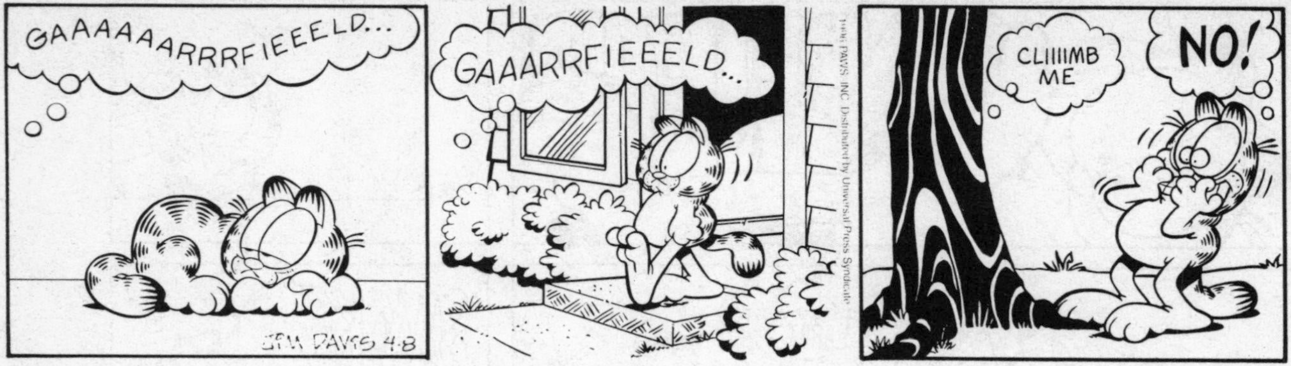
GAAAAAARRRRFIEEELD...
JIM DAVIS 4-8
GAAARRFIEEELD...
PAWS, INC Distributed by Universal Press Syndicate
CLIIIIMB ME
NO!

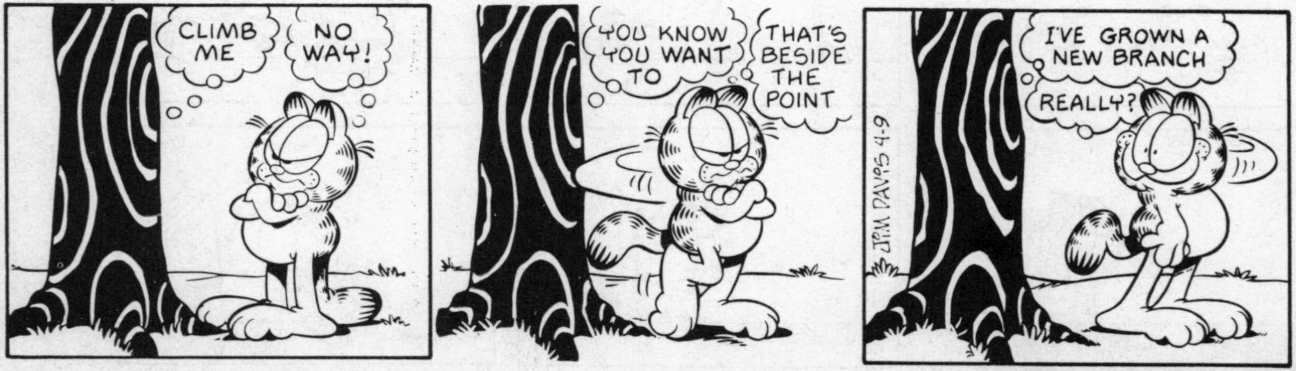
CLIMB ME
NO WAY!
YOU KNOW YOU WANT TO
THAT'S BESIDE THE POINT
JIM DAVIS 4-9
I'VE GROWN A NEW BRANCH
REALLY?

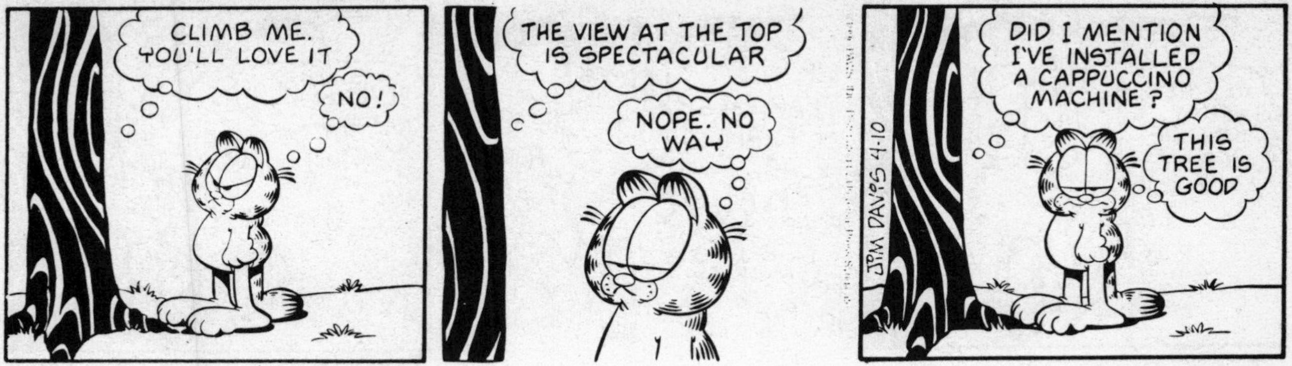
CLIMB ME. YOU'LL LOVE IT
NO!
THE VIEW AT THE TOP IS SPECTACULAR
NOPE. NO WAY
JIM DAVIS 4-10
DID I MENTION I'VE INSTALLED A CAPPUCCINO MACHINE?
THIS TREE IS GOOD

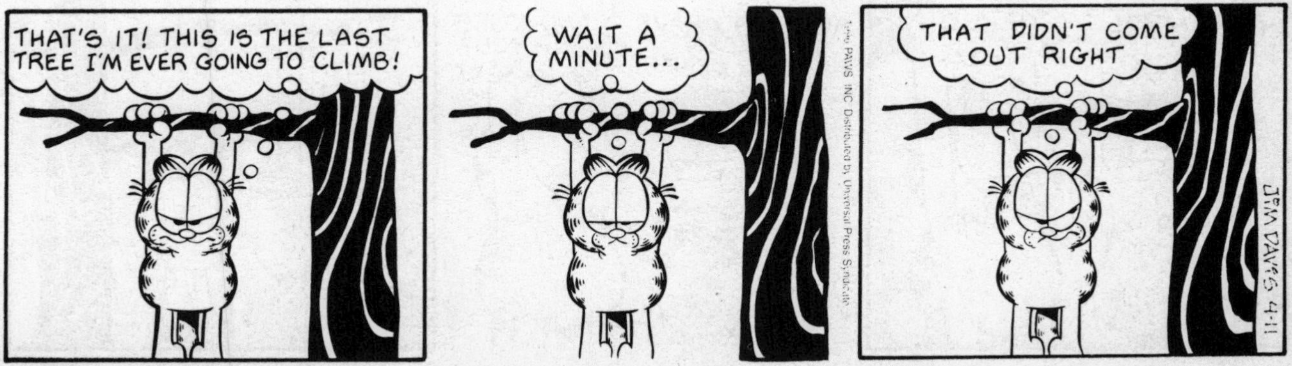
THAT'S IT! THIS IS THE LAST TREE I'M EVER GOING TO CLIMB!
WAIT A MINUTE...
PAWS INC Distributed by Universal Press Syndicate
THAT DIDN'T COME OUT RIGHT
JIM DAVIS 4-11

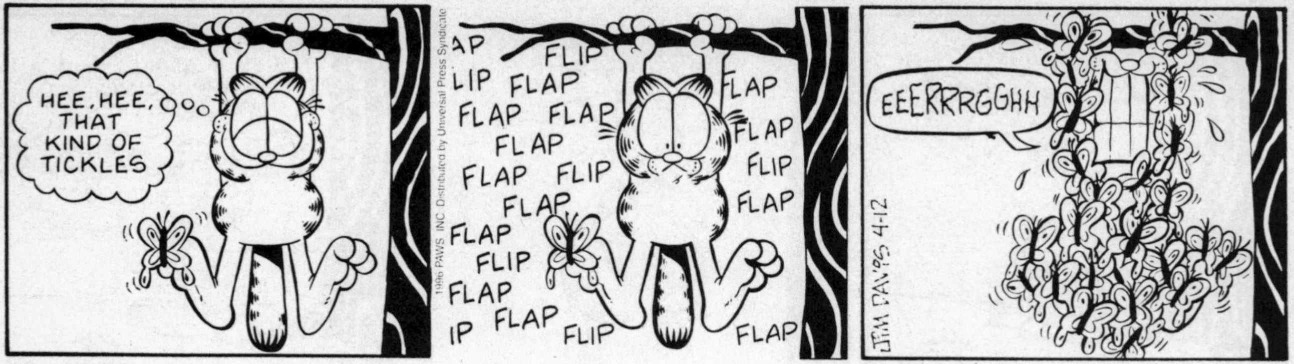
HEE, HEE, THAT KIND OF TICKLES
1996 PAWS, INC Distributed by Universal Press Syndicate
AP
FLIP
LIP FLAP
FLAP FLAP
FLAP
FLAP FLIP
FLAP
FLAP
FLIP
FLAP
IP FLAP
FLIP
FLAP
FLAP
FLIP
FLAP
FLAP
EEERRRGGHH
JIM DAVIS 4-12

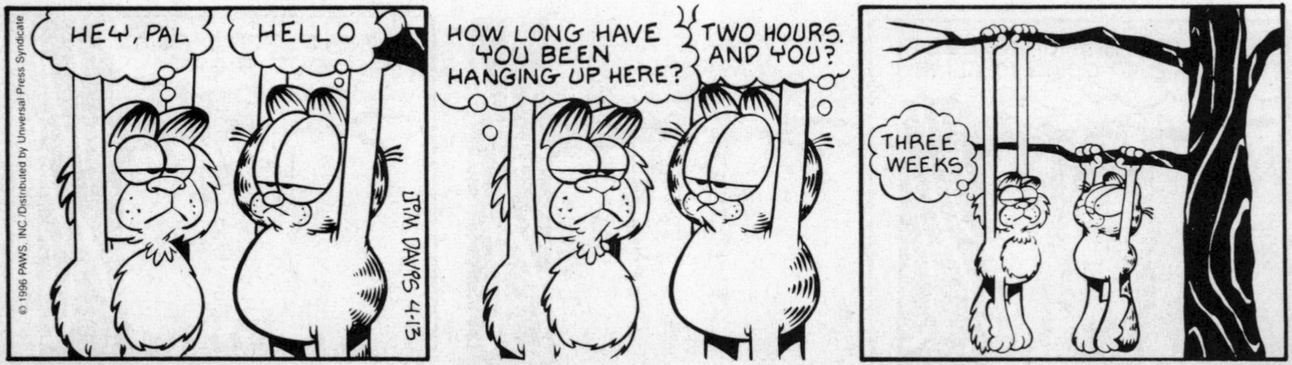
© 1996 PAWS, INC /Distributed by Universal Press Syndicate
HEY, PAL
HELLO
JIM DAVIS 4-13
HOW LONG HAVE YOU BEEN HANGING UP HERE?
TWO HOURS. AND YOU?
THREE WEEKS

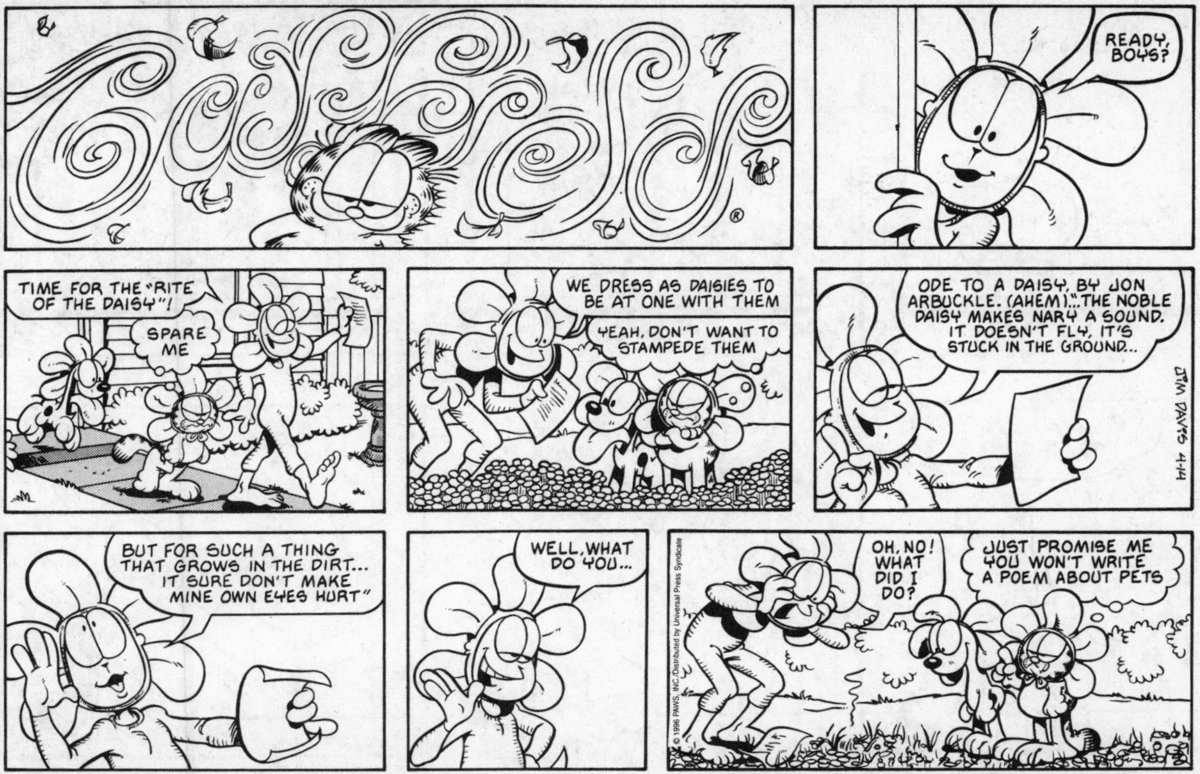
READY, BOYS?
TIME FOR THE "RITE OF THE DAISY"!
SPARE ME
WE DRESS AS DAISIES TO BE AT ONE WITH THEM
YEAH, DON'T WANT TO STAMPEDE THEM
ODE TO A DAISY, BY JON ARBUCKLE. (AHEM)..."THE NOBLE DAISY MAKES NARY A SOUND. IT DOESN'T FLY, IT'S STUCK IN THE GROUND...
JIM DAVIS 4-14
BUT FOR SUCH A THING THAT GROWS IN THE DIRT... IT SURE DON'T MAKE MINE OWN EYES HURT"
WELL, WHAT DO YOU...
© 1996 PAWS, INC./Distributed by Universal Press Syndicate
OH, NO! WHAT DID I DO?
JUST PROMISE ME YOU WON'T WRITE A POEM ABOUT PETS

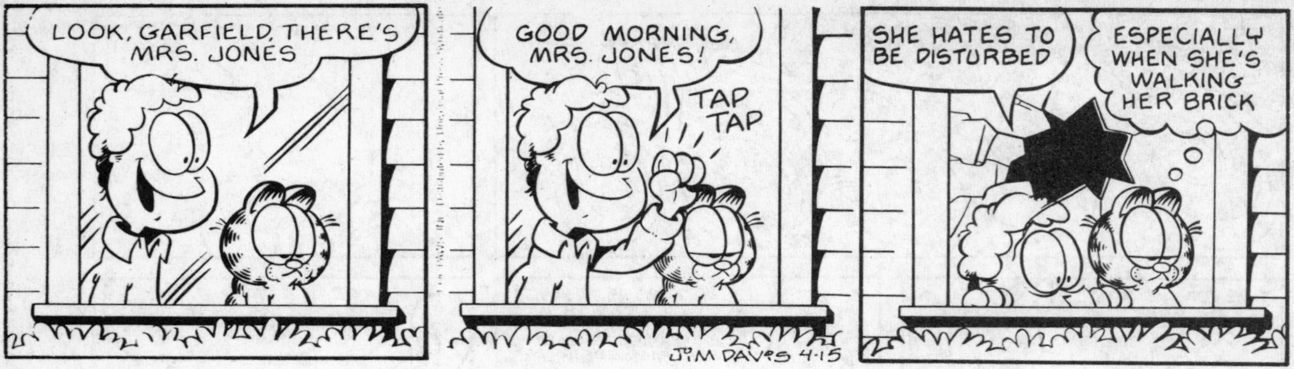
LOOK, GARFIELD, THERE'S MRS. JONES
GOOD MORNING, MRS. JONES!
TAP TAP
SHE HATES TO BE DISTURBED
ESPECIALLY WHEN SHE'S WALKING HER BRICK
JIM DAVIS 4-15

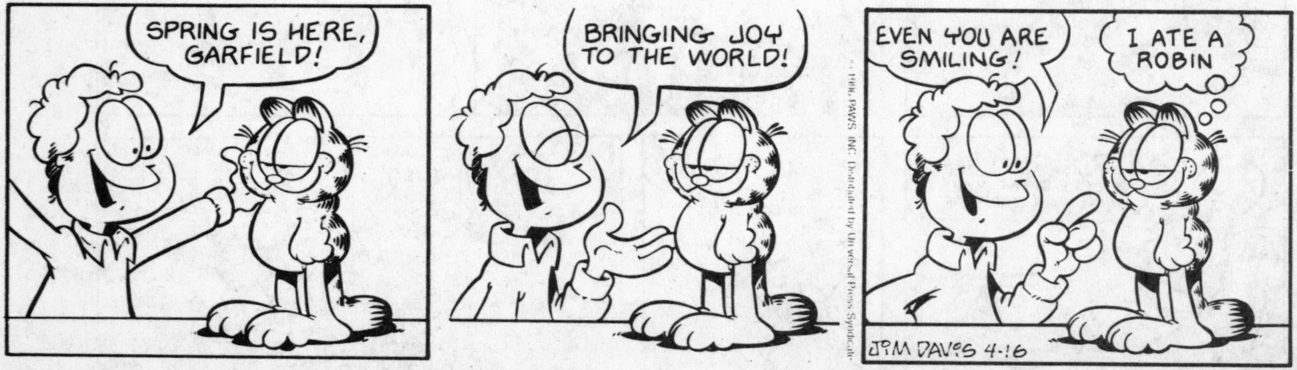
SPRING IS HERE, GARFIELD!
BRINGING JOY TO THE WORLD!
EVEN YOU ARE SMILING!
I ATE A ROBIN
JIM DAVIS 4-16
© 1986 PAWS, INC. Distributed by Universal Press Syndicate

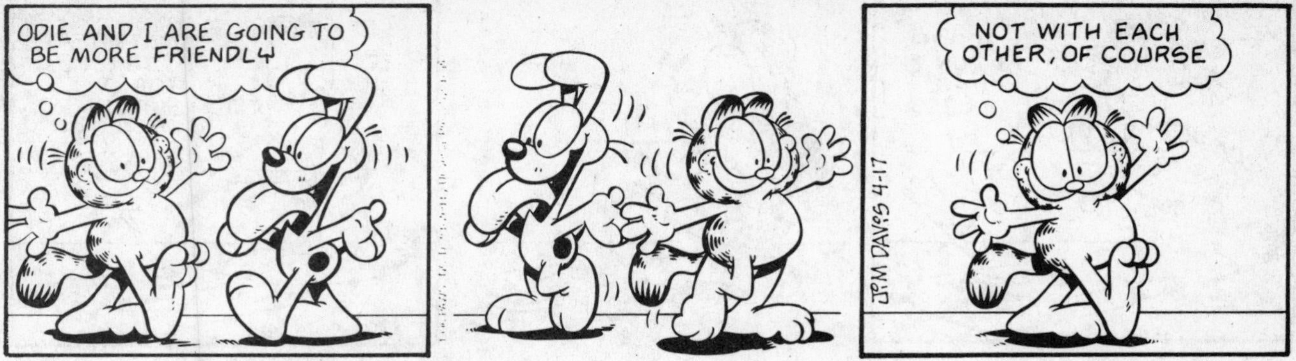
ODIE AND I ARE GOING TO BE MORE FRIENDLY
NOT WITH EACH OTHER, OF COURSE
JIM DAVIS 4-17

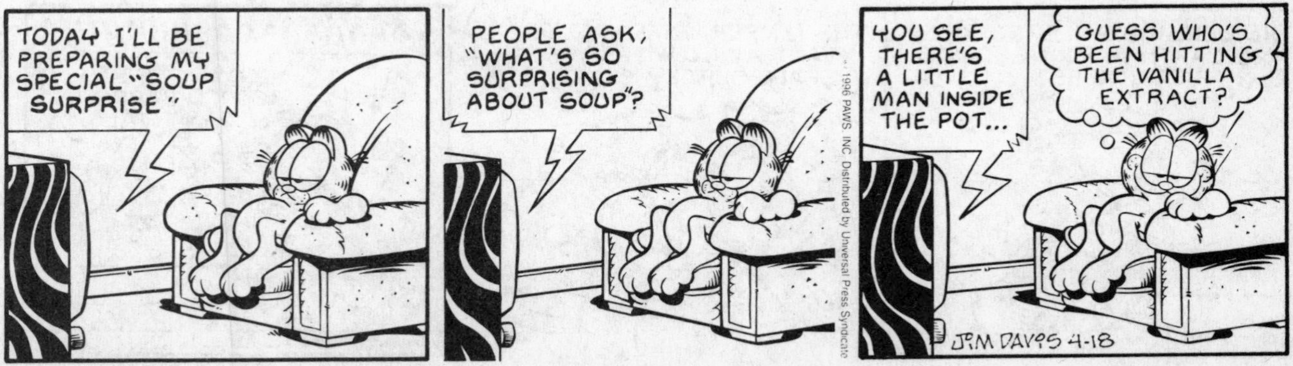
TODAY I'LL BE PREPARING MY SPECIAL "SOUP SURPRISE"
PEOPLE ASK, "WHAT'S SO SURPRISING ABOUT SOUP"?
YOU SEE, THERE'S A LITTLE MAN INSIDE THE POT...
GUESS WHO'S BEEN HITTING THE VANILLA EXTRACT?
© 1996 PAWS, INC. Distributed by Universal Press Syndicate
JIM DAVIS 4-18

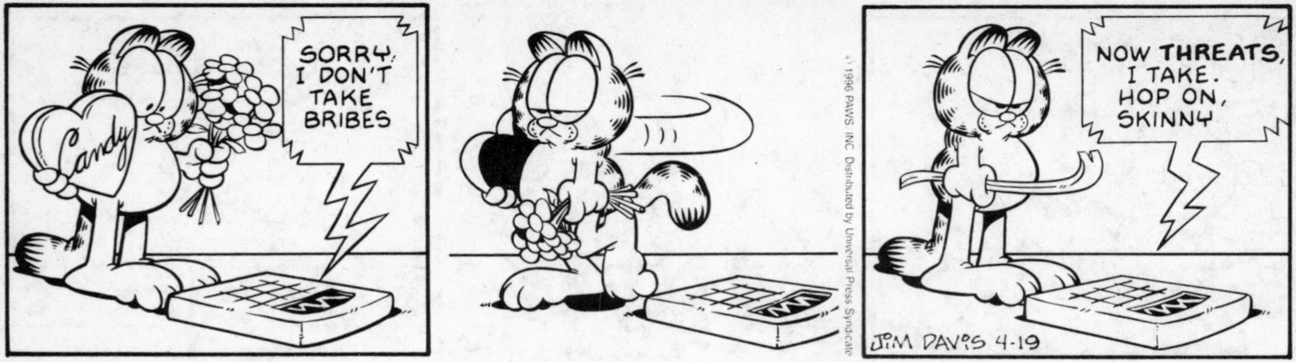
SORRY, I DON'T TAKE BRIBES
Candy
© 1996 PAWS, INC Distributed by Universal Press Syndicate
NOW THREATS, I TAKE. HOP ON, SKINNY
JIM DAVIS 4-19

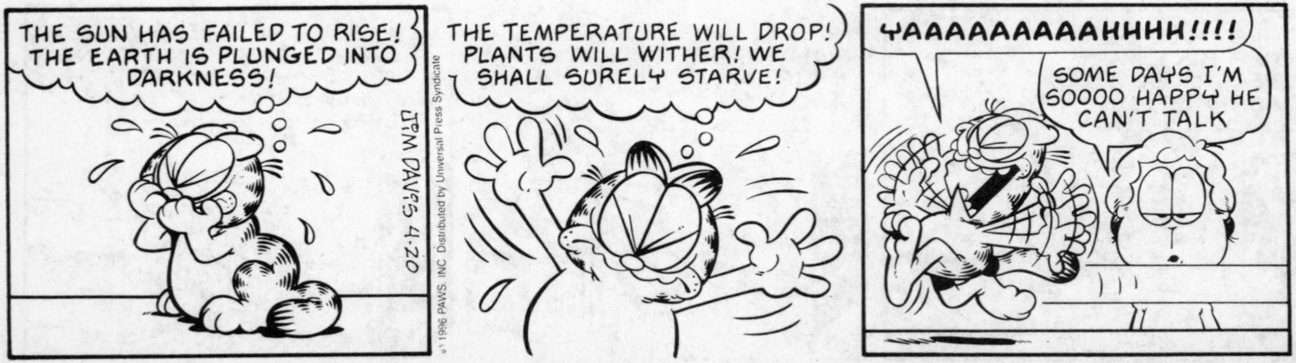
THE SUN HAS FAILED TO RISE! THE EARTH IS PLUNGED INTO DARKNESS!
JIM DAVIS 4-20
© 1996 PAWS, INC Distributed by Universal Press Syndicate
THE TEMPERATURE WILL DROP! PLANTS WILL WITHER! WE SHALL SURELY STARVE!
YAAAAAAAAAHHHH!!!!
SOME DAYS I'M SOOOO HAPPY HE CAN'T TALK

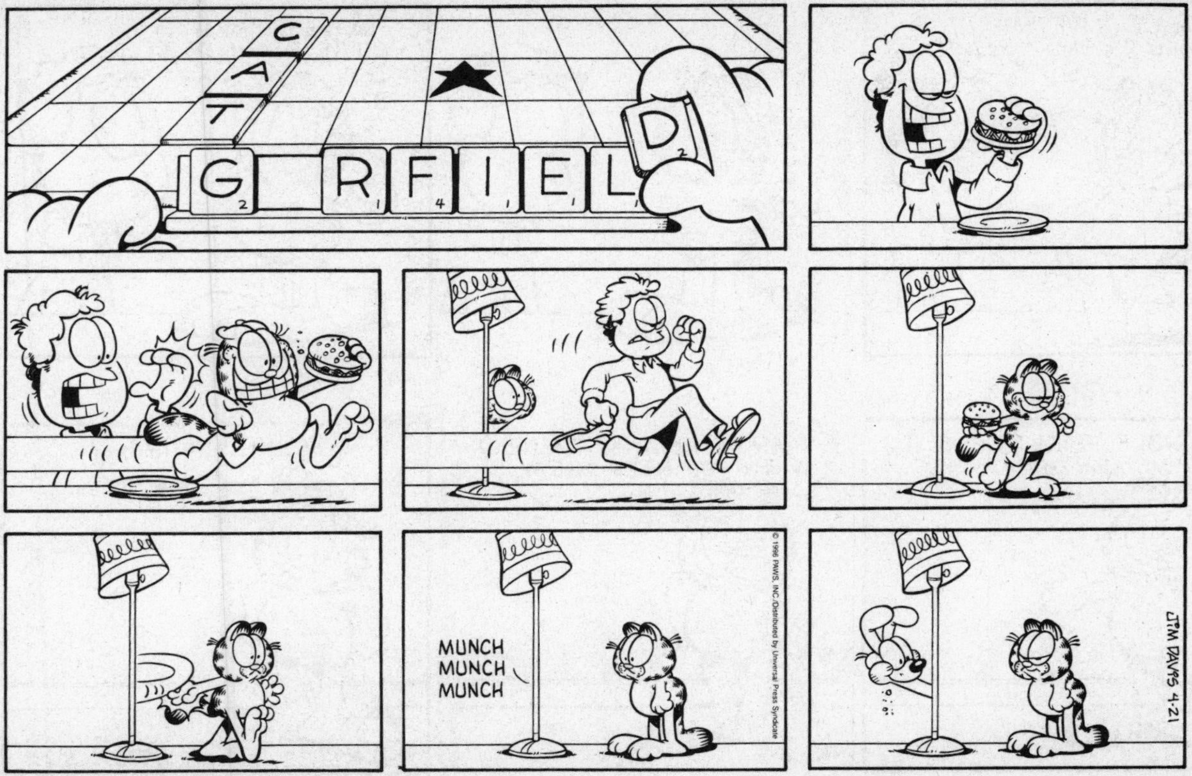
CAT
G RFIELD
MUNCH
MUNCH
MUNCH
© 1996 PAWS, INC./Distributed by Universal Press Syndicate
JIM DAVIS 4-21

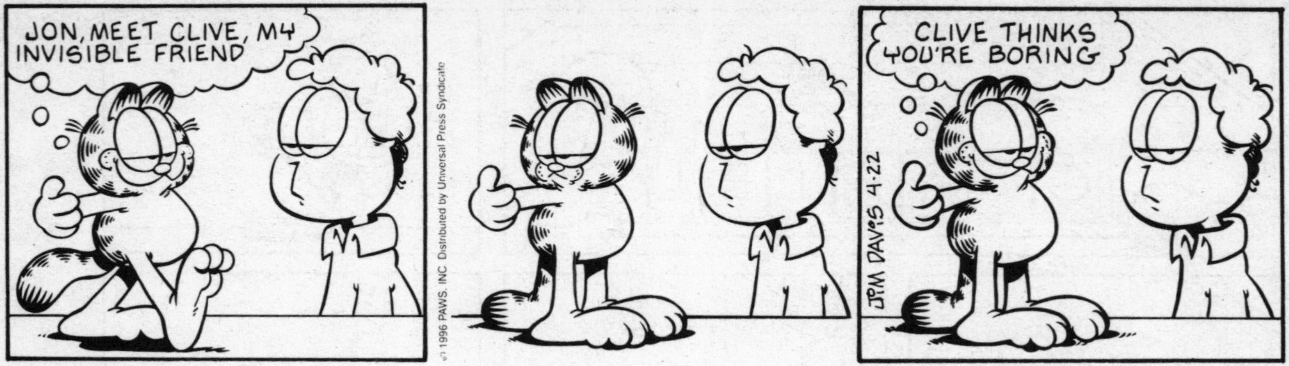
JON, MEET CLIVE, MY INVISIBLE FRIEND
CLIVE THINKS YOU'RE BORING
JIM DAVIS 4·22

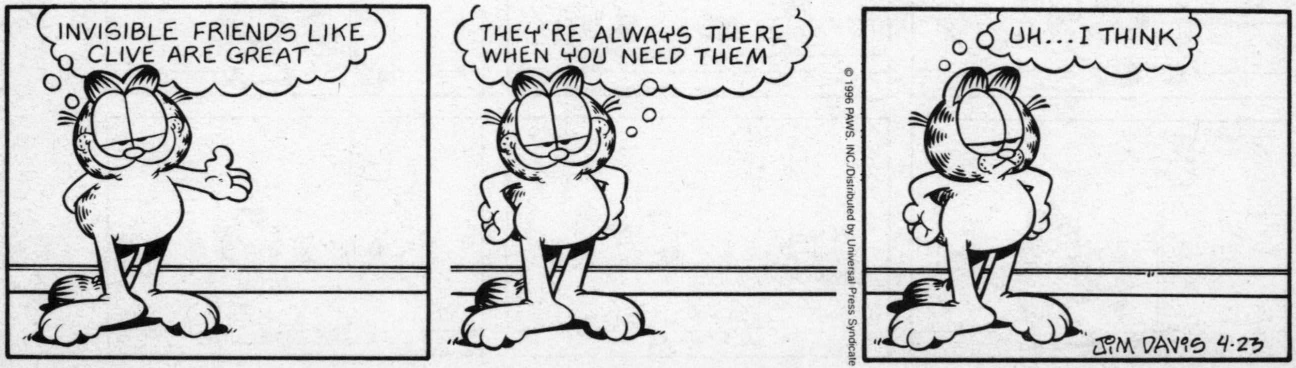
INVISIBLE FRIENDS LIKE CLIVE ARE GREAT
THEY'RE ALWAYS THERE WHEN YOU NEED THEM
UH...I THINK
JIM DAVIS 4·23

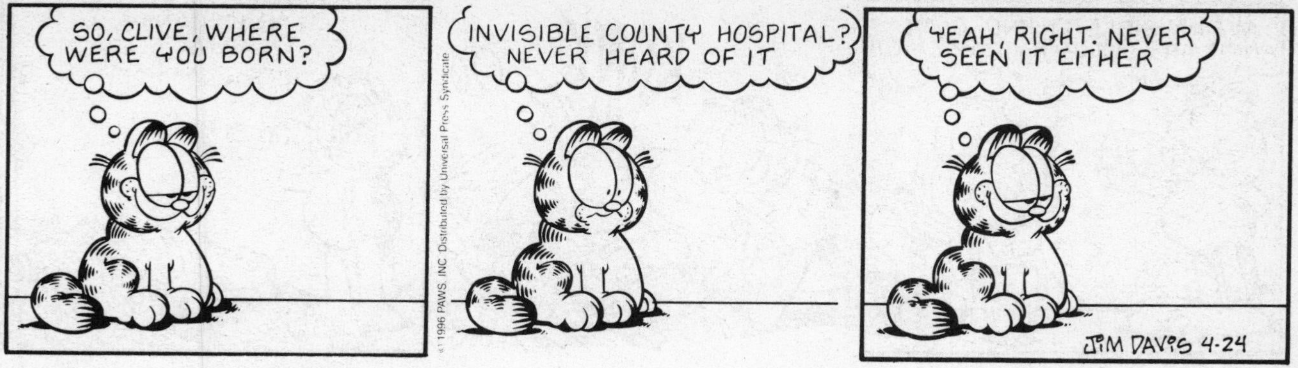
SO, CLIVE, WHERE WERE YOU BORN?
INVISIBLE COUNTY HOSPITAL? NEVER HEARD OF IT
YEAH, RIGHT. NEVER SEEN IT EITHER
© 1996 PAWS, INC. Distributed by Universal Press Syndicate
JIM DAVIS 4-24

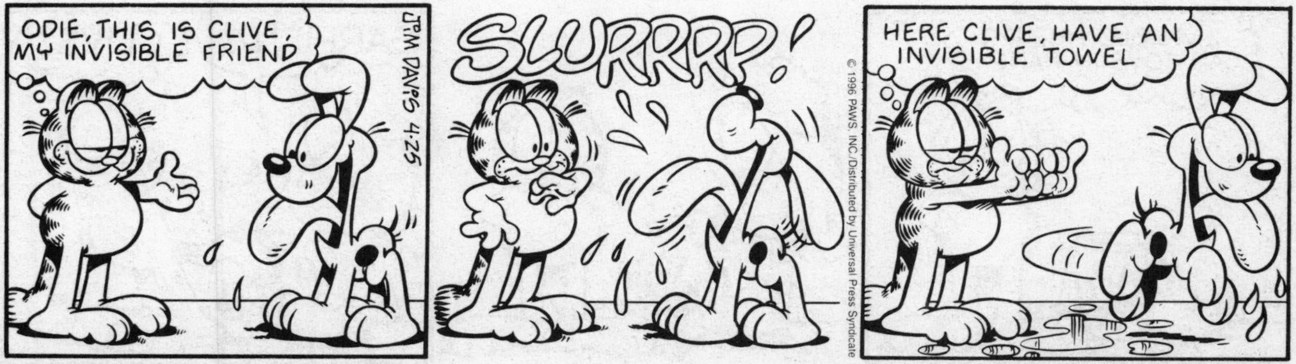
ODIE, THIS IS CLIVE, MY INVISIBLE FRIEND
JIM DAVIS 4-25
SLURRRP!
HERE CLIVE, HAVE AN INVISIBLE TOWEL
© 1996 PAWS, INC./Distributed by Universal Press Syndicate

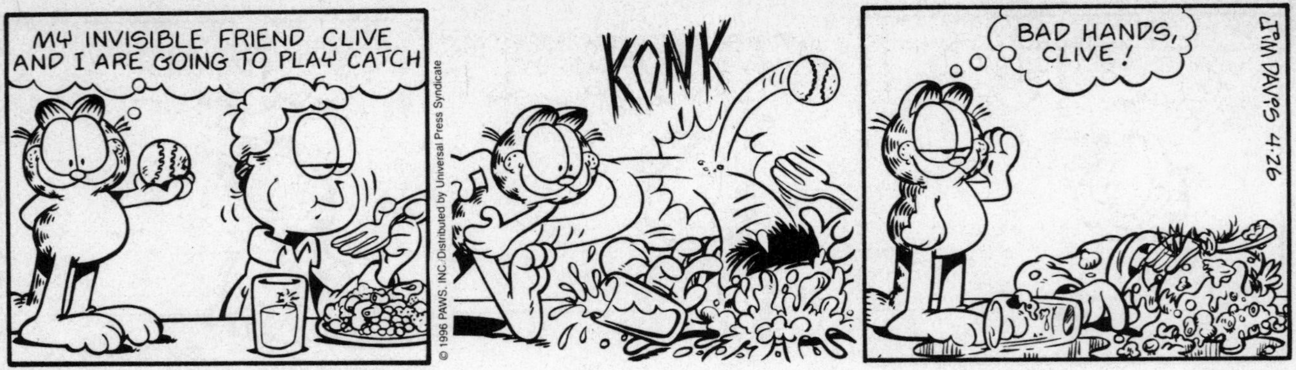
MY INVISIBLE FRIEND CLIVE AND I ARE GOING TO PLAY CATCH
© 1996 PAWS, INC. Distributed by Universal Press Syndicate
KONK
BAD HANDS, CLIVE!
JIM DAVIS 4·26

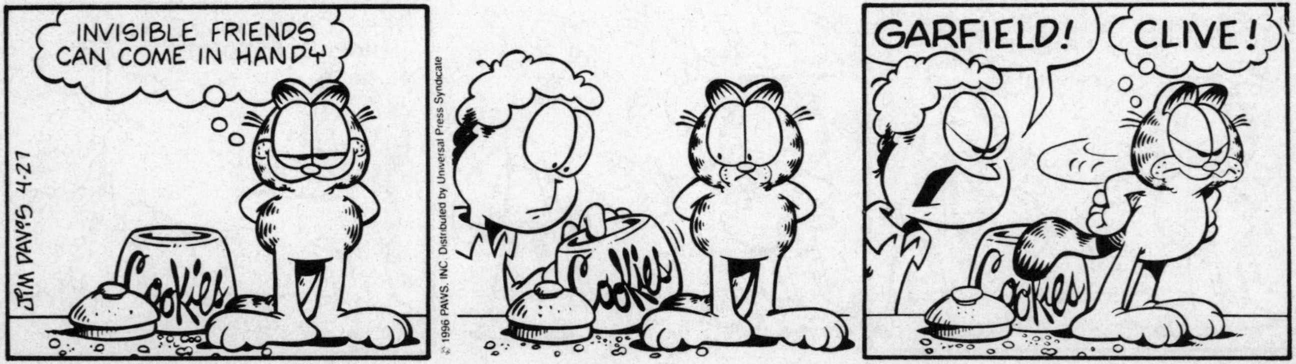
INVISIBLE FRIENDS CAN COME IN HANDY
Cookies
JIM DAVIS 4·27
© 1996 PAWS, INC. Distributed by Universal Press Syndicate
GARFIELD!
CLIVE!

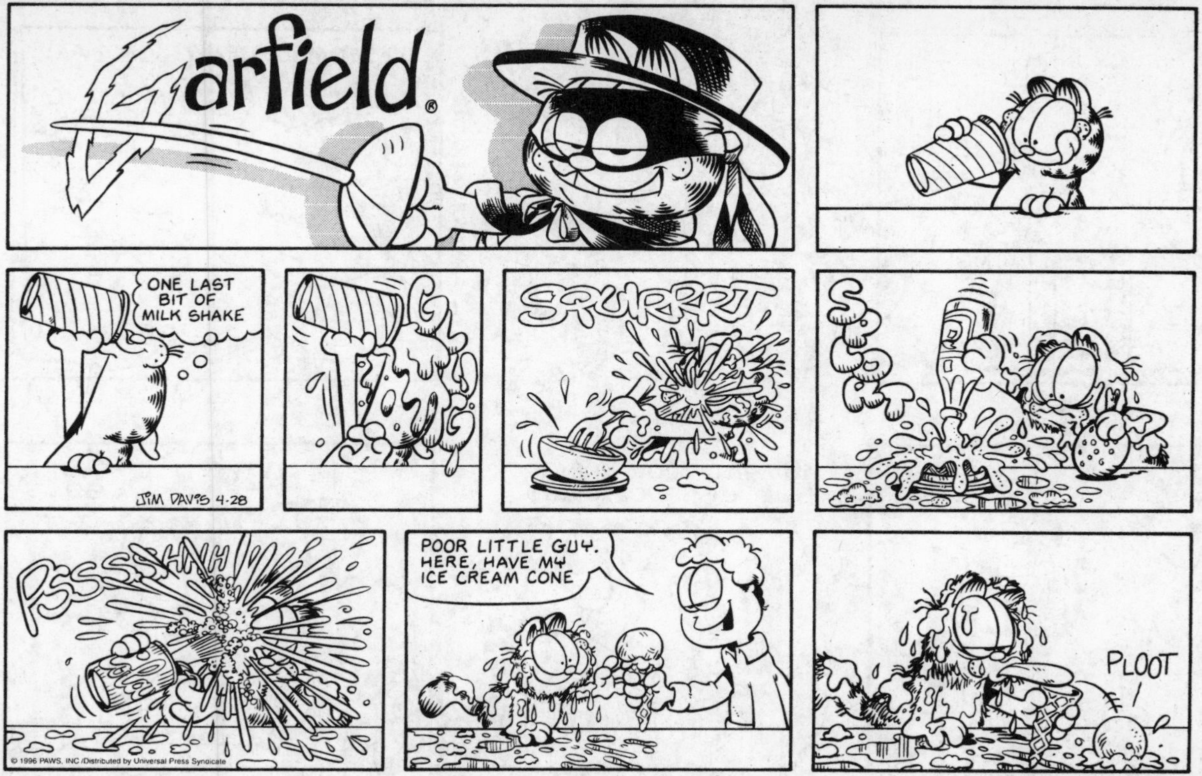
Garfield®
ONE LAST BIT OF MILK SHAKE
JIM DAVIS 4-28
SQUIRRRT
POOR LITTLE GUY. HERE, HAVE MY ICE CREAM CONE
PLOOT!
© 1996 PAWS, INC./Distributed by Universal Press Syndicate

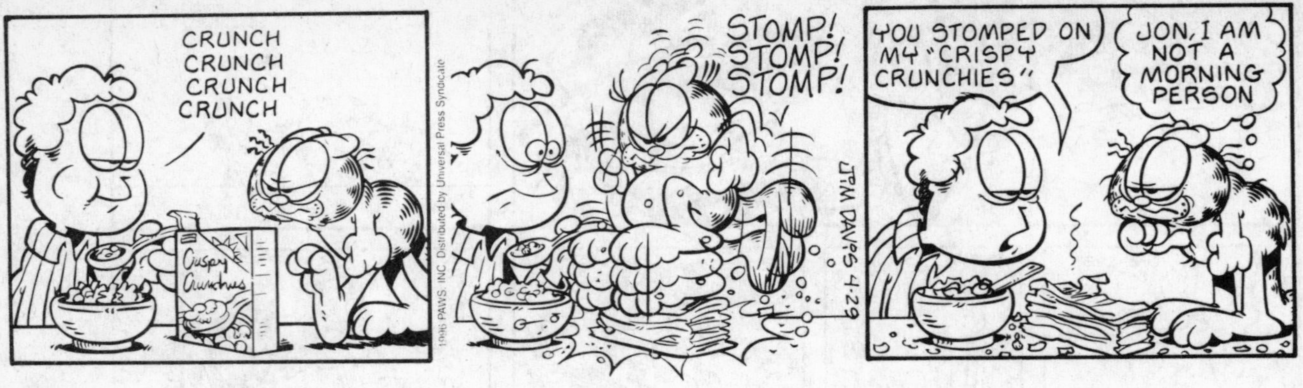
CRUNCH
CRUNCH
CRUNCH
CRUNCH
Crispy Crunchies
© 1996 PAWS, INC Distributed by Universal Press Syndicate
STOMP!
STOMP!
STOMP!
JIM DAVIS 4·29
YOU STOMPED ON MY "CRISPY CRUNCHIES"
JON, I AM NOT A MORNING PERSON

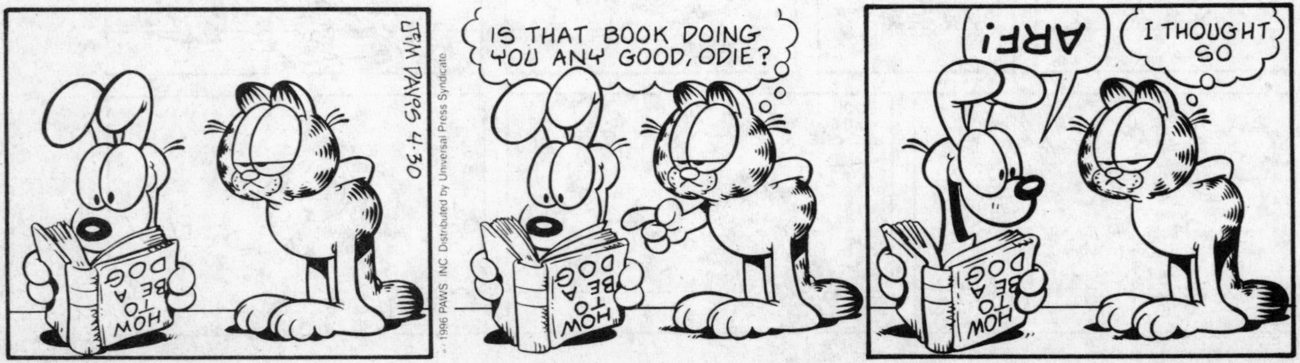
HOW TO BE A DOG
JIM DAVIS 4·30
© 1996 PAWS, INC Distributed by Universal Press Syndicate
IS THAT BOOK DOING YOU ANY GOOD, ODIE?
HOW TO BE A DOG
ARF!
I THOUGHT SO
HOW TO BE A DOG

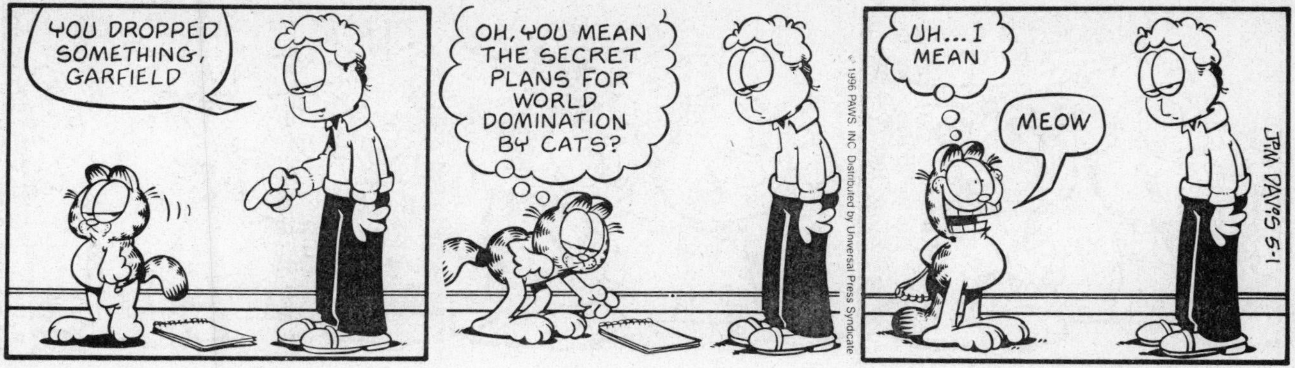
YOU DROPPED SOMETHING, GARFIELD
OH, YOU MEAN THE SECRET PLANS FOR WORLD DOMINATION BY CATS?
UH... I MEAN
MEOW
JIM DAVIS 5-1
© 1996 PAWS, INC. Distributed by Universal Press Syndicate

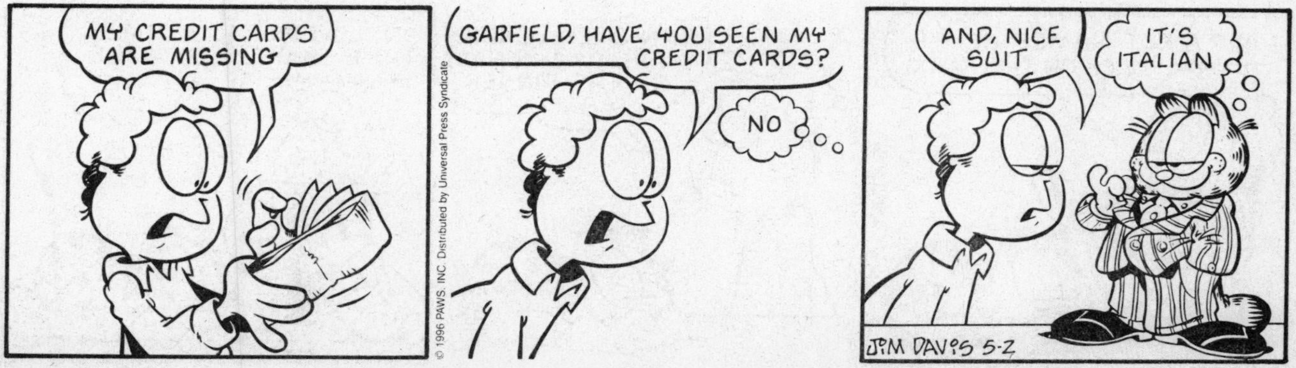
MY CREDIT CARDS ARE MISSING
GARFIELD, HAVE YOU SEEN MY CREDIT CARDS?
NO
AND, NICE SUIT
IT'S ITALIAN
JIM DAVIS 5-2
© 1996 PAWS, INC. Distributed by Universal Press Syndicate

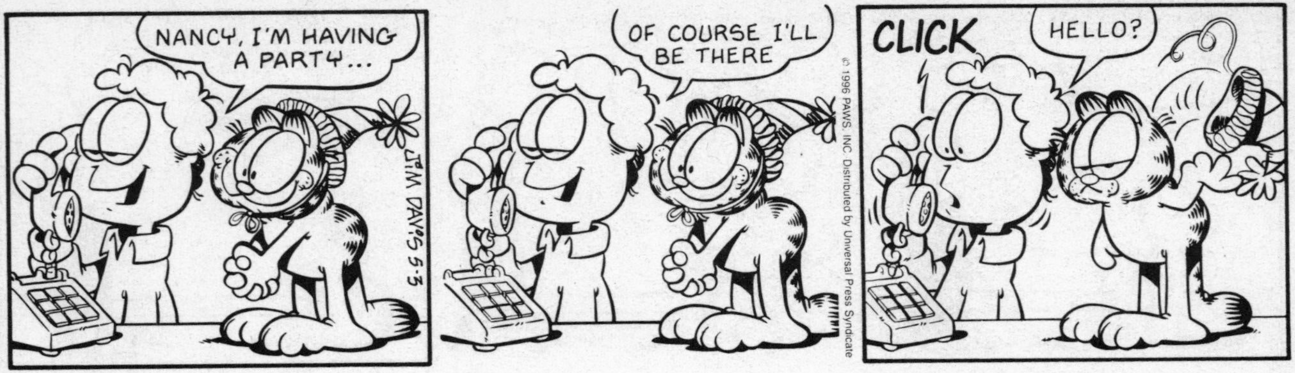
NANCY, I'M HAVING A PARTY...
JIM DAVIS 5-3
OF COURSE I'LL BE THERE
© 1996 PAWS, INC. Distributed by Universal Press Syndicate
CLICK
HELLO?

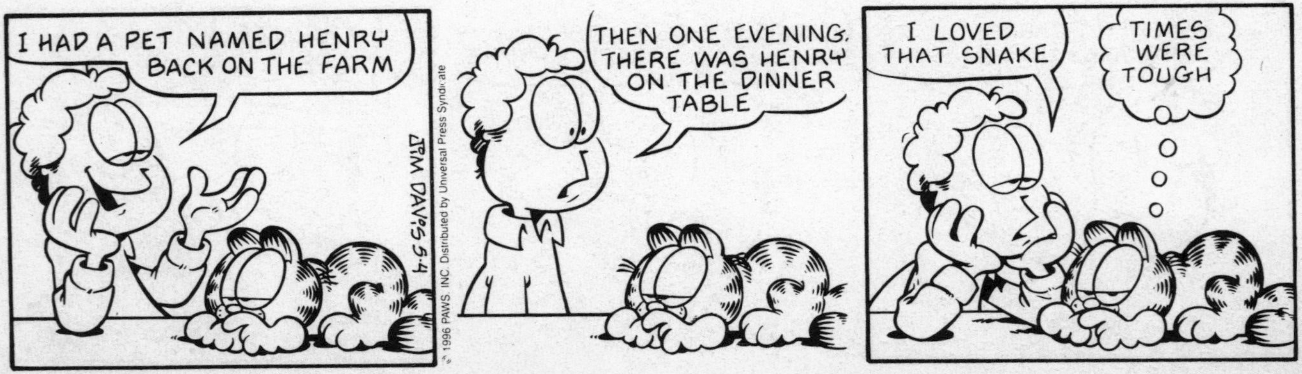
I HAD A PET NAMED HENRY BACK ON THE FARM
JIM DAVIS 5-4
© 1996 PAWS, INC. Distributed by Universal Press Syndicate
THEN ONE EVENING, THERE WAS HENRY ON THE DINNER TABLE
I LOVED THAT SNAKE
TIMES WERE TOUGH

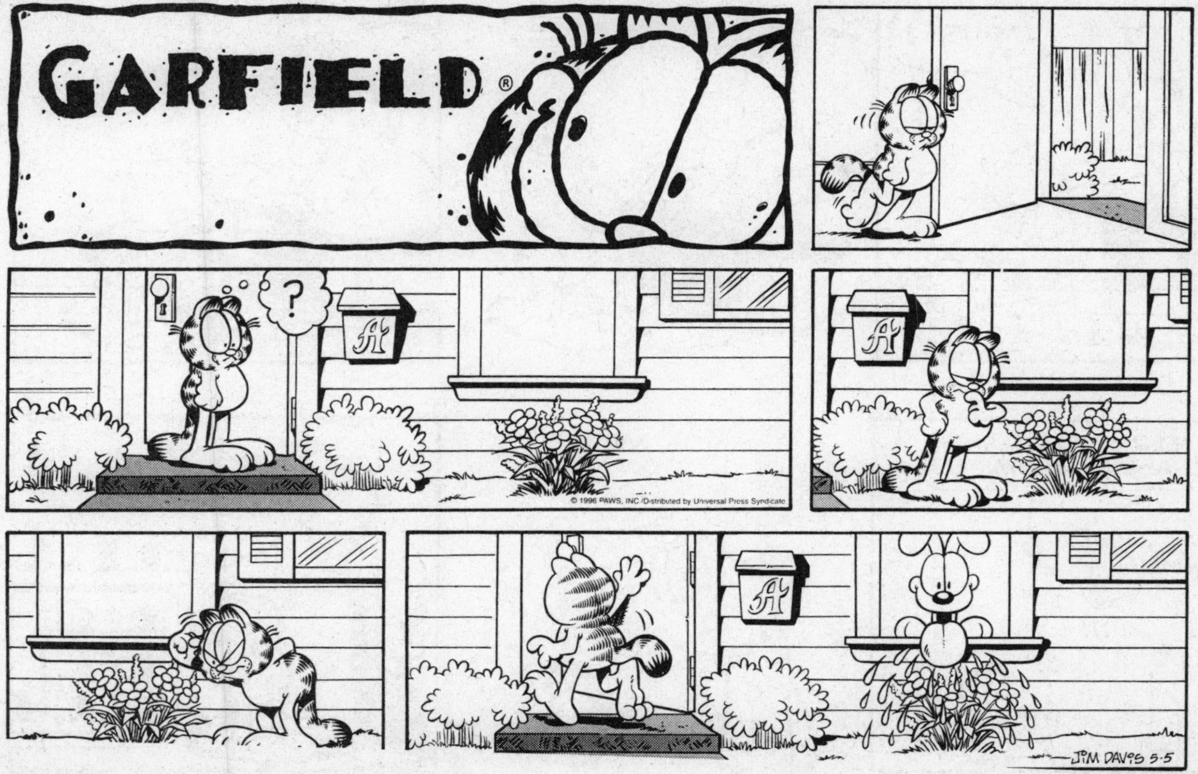
GARFIELD®
?
© 1996 PAWS, INC./Distributed by Universal Press Syndicate
JIM DAVIS 5-5

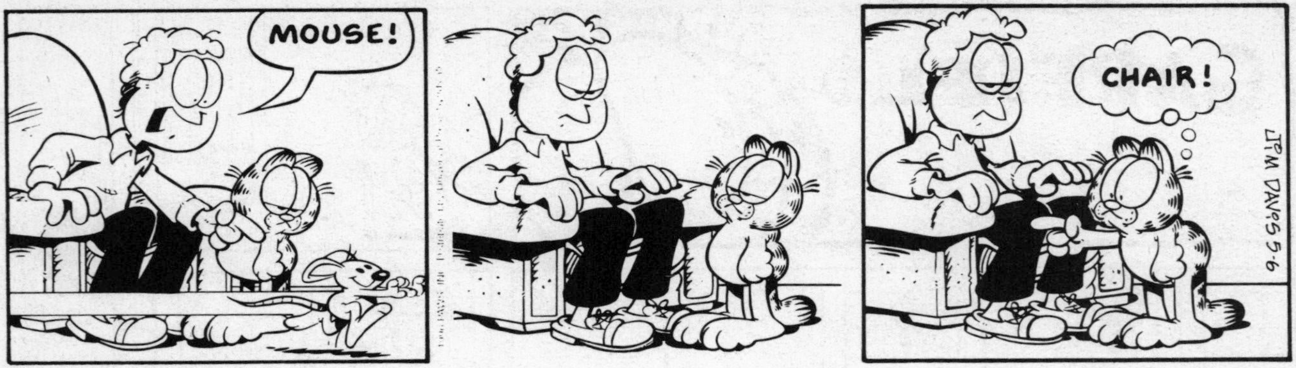
MOUSE!
CHAIR!
JIM DAVIS 5-6

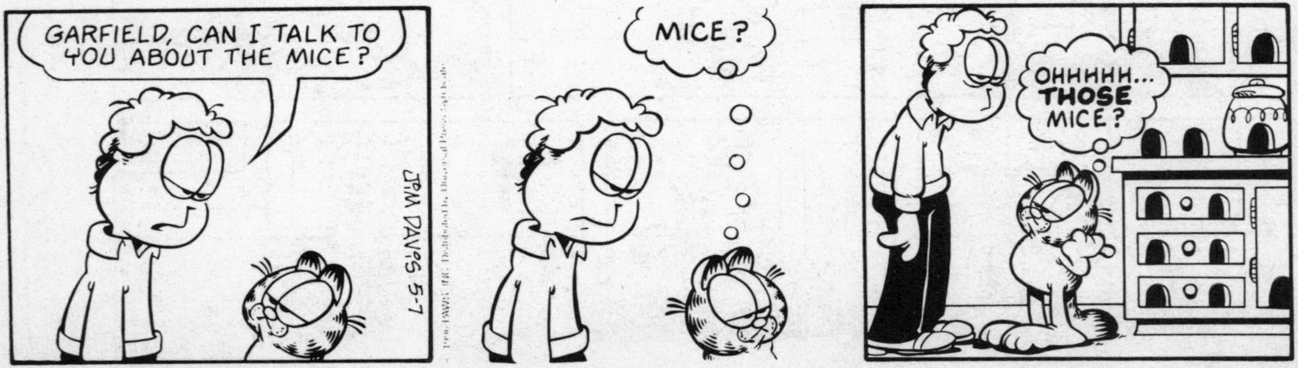
GARFIELD, CAN I TALK TO YOU ABOUT THE MICE?
MICE?
OHHHHH... **THOSE** MICE?
JIM DAVIS 5-7

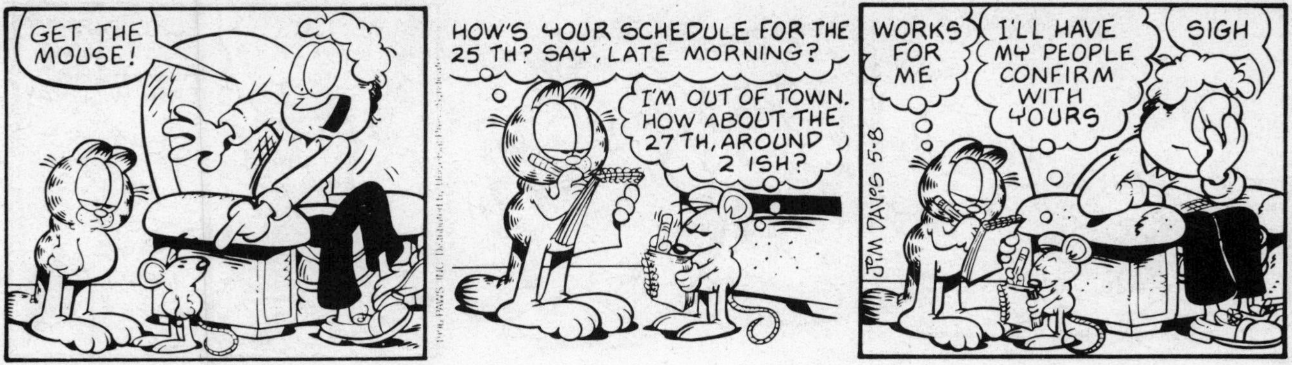
GET THE MOUSE!
HOW'S YOUR SCHEDULE FOR THE 25 TH? SAY, LATE MORNING?
I'M OUT OF TOWN. HOW ABOUT THE 27TH, AROUND 2 ISH?
JIM DAVIS 5-8
WORKS FOR ME
I'LL HAVE MY PEOPLE CONFIRM WITH YOURS
SIGH

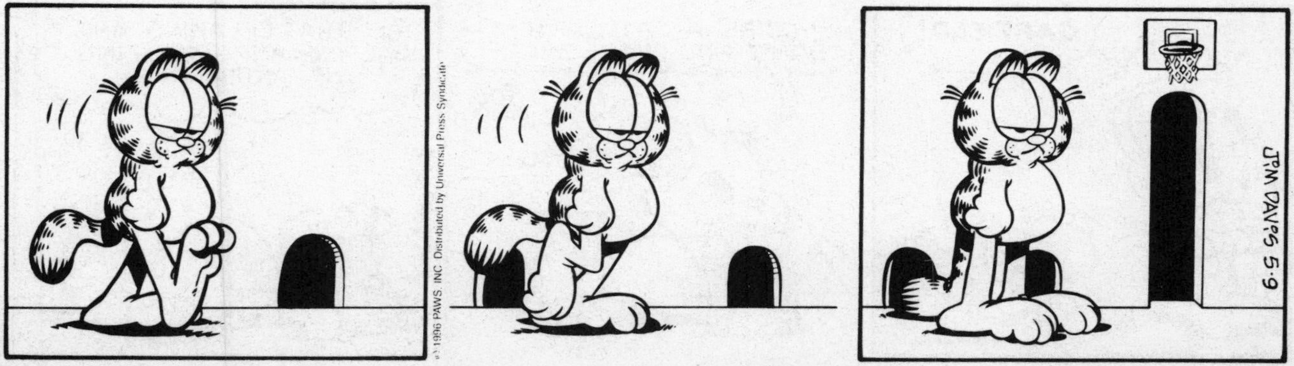
© 1996 PAWS, INC. Distributed by Universal Press Syndicate
JIM DAVIS 5-9

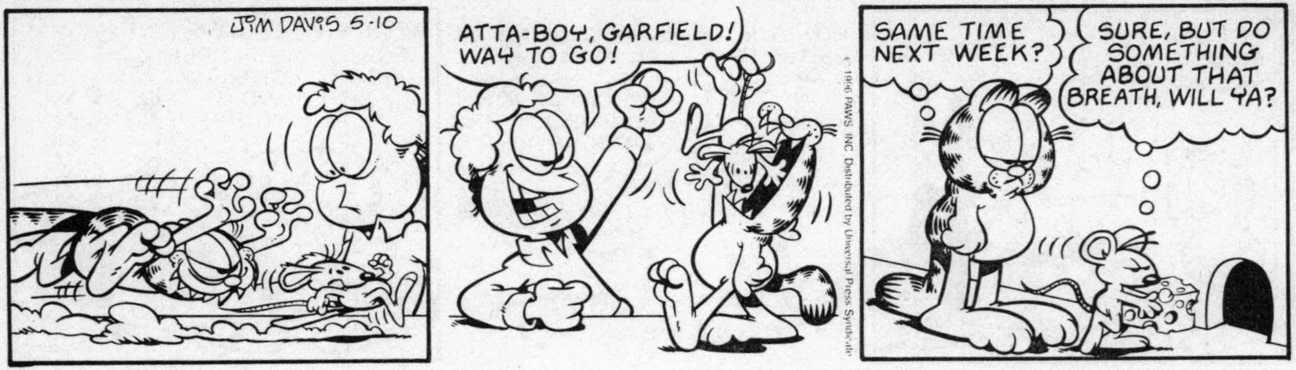
JIM DAVIS 5-10
ATTA-BOY, GARFIELD! WAY TO GO!
SAME TIME NEXT WEEK?
SURE, BUT DO SOMETHING ABOUT THAT BREATH, WILL YA?
© 1986 PAWS, INC. Distributed by Universal Press Syndicate

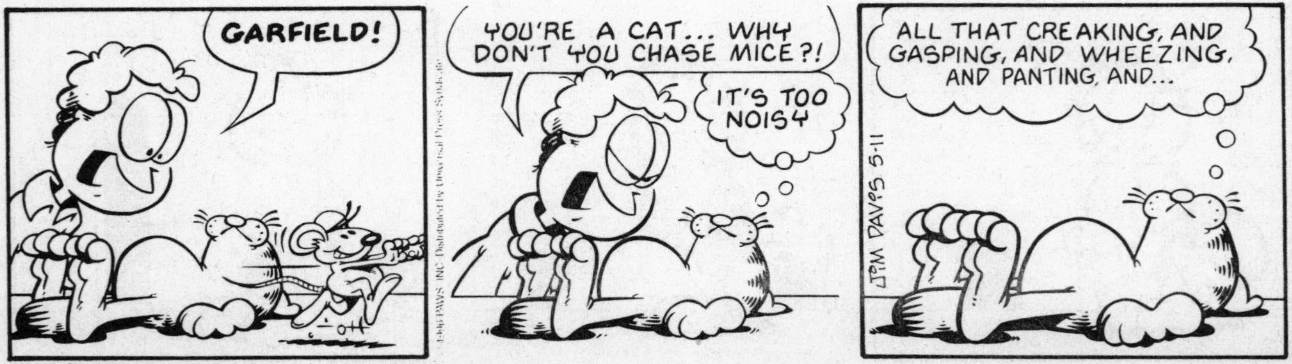
GARFIELD!
YOU'RE A CAT... WHY DON'T YOU CHASE MICE?!
IT'S TOO NOISY
JIM DAVIS 5-11
ALL THAT CREAKING, AND GASPING, AND WHEEZING, AND PANTING, AND...
© 1986 PAWS, INC. Distributed by Universal Press Syndicate

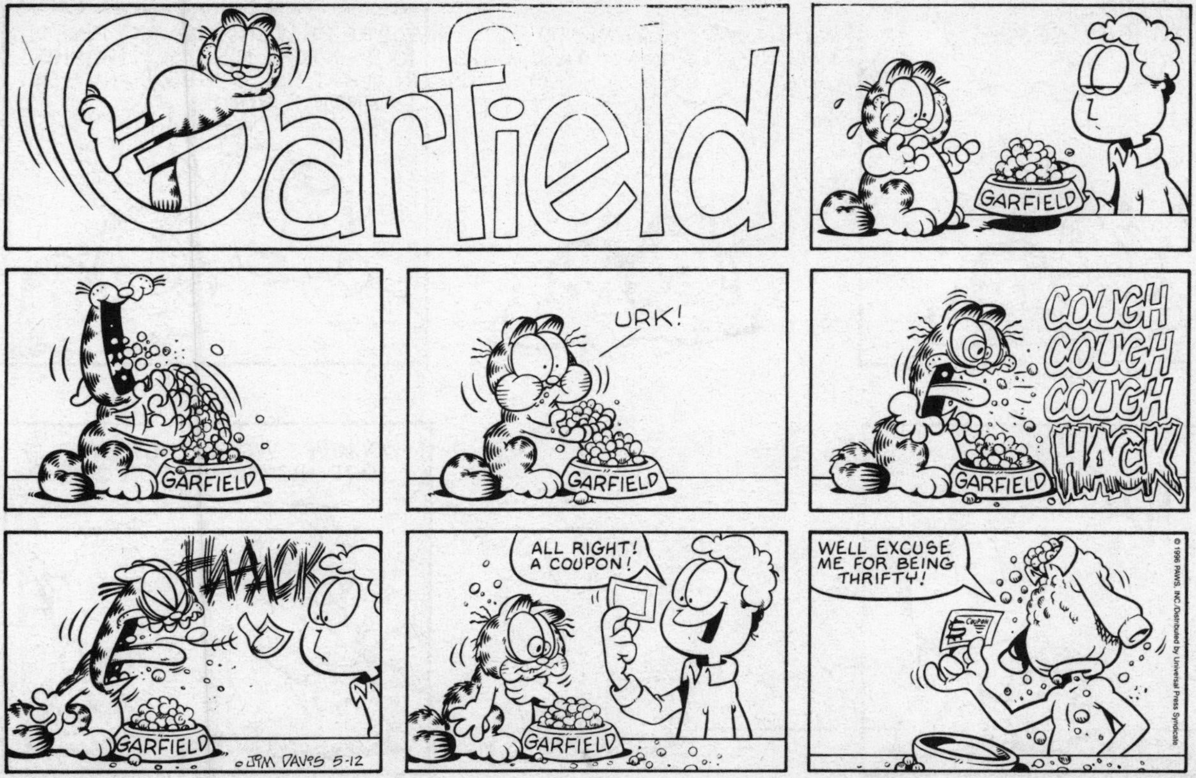

Garfield
URK!
COUGH
COUGH
COUGH
HACK
HACK
©JIM DAVIS 5-12
ALL RIGHT! A COUPON!
WELL EXCUSE ME FOR BEING THRIFTY!
COUPON
© 1996 PAWS, INC./Distributed by Universal Press Syndicate

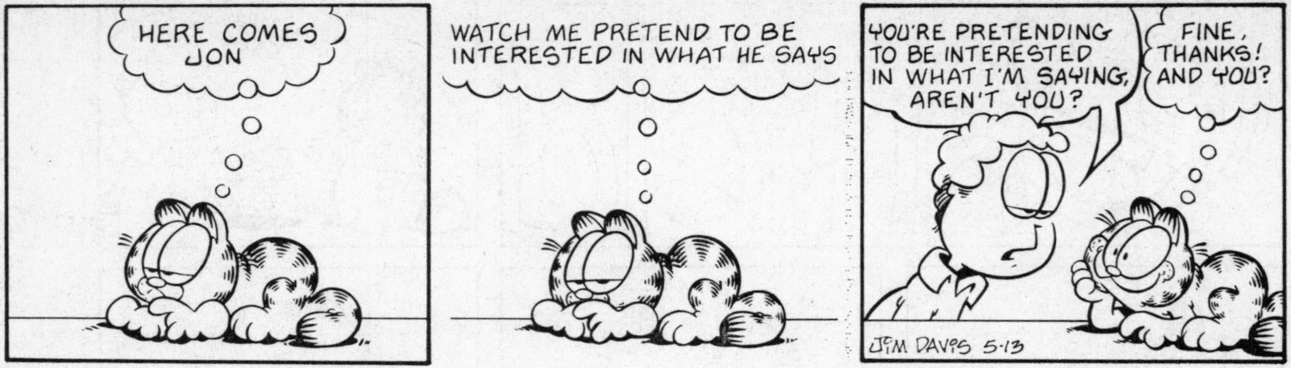
HERE COMES JON
WATCH ME PRETEND TO BE INTERESTED IN WHAT HE SAYS
YOU'RE PRETENDING TO BE INTERESTED IN WHAT I'M SAYING, AREN'T YOU?
FINE, THANKS! AND YOU?
JIM DAVIS 5-13

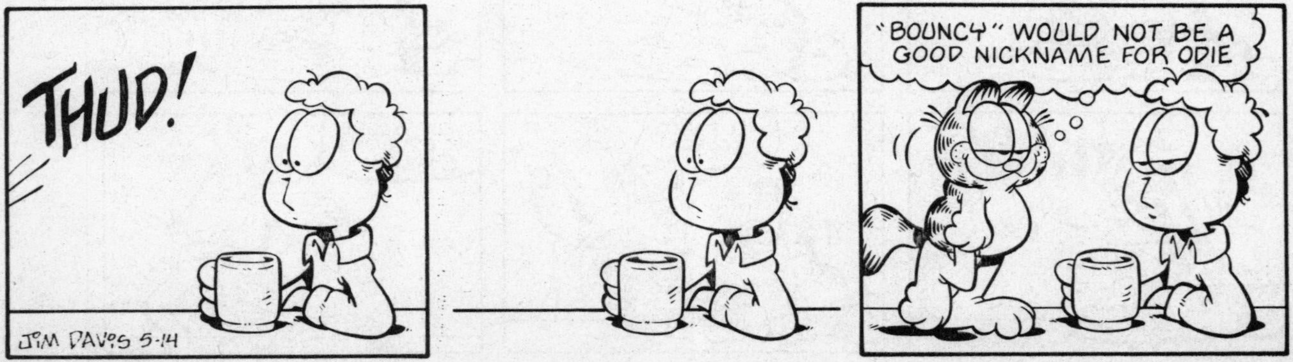
THUD!
JIM DAVIS 5-14
"BOUNCY" WOULD NOT BE A GOOD NICKNAME FOR ODIE

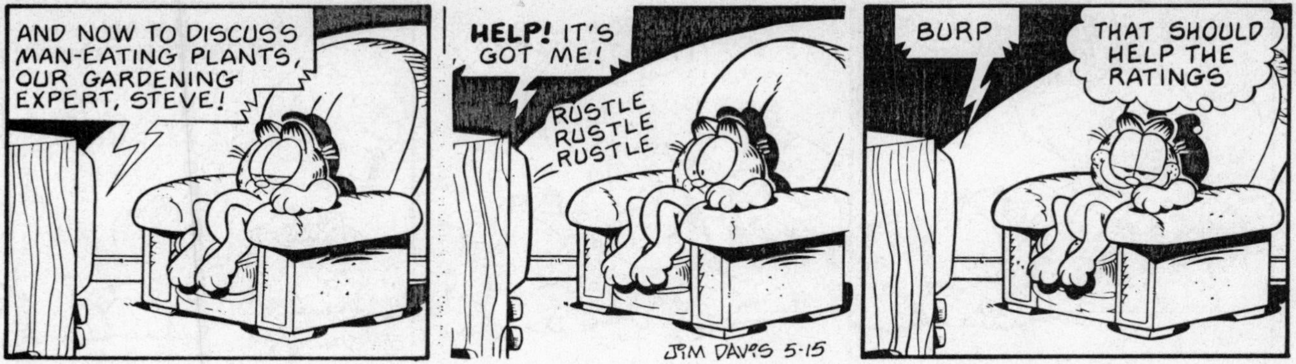
AND NOW TO DISCUSS MAN-EATING PLANTS, OUR GARDENING EXPERT, STEVE!
HELP! IT'S GOT ME!
RUSTLE RUSTLE RUSTLE
BURP
THAT SHOULD HELP THE RATINGS
JIM DAVIS 5-15

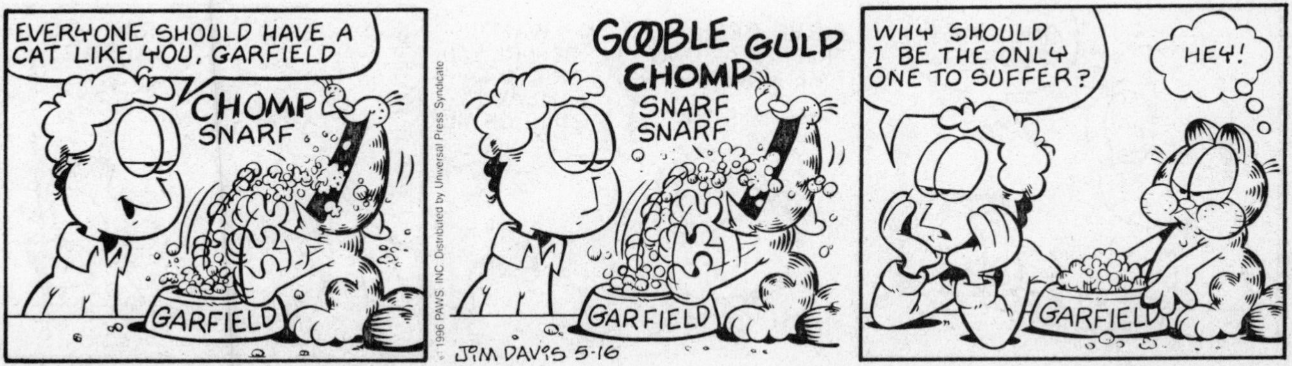
EVERYONE SHOULD HAVE A CAT LIKE YOU, GARFIELD
CHOMP SNARF
GARFIELD
GOOBLE GULP CHOMP
SNARF SNARF
GARFIELD
JIM DAVIS 5-16
WHY SHOULD I BE THE ONLY ONE TO SUFFER?
HEY!
GARFIELD
© 1996 PAWS, INC. Distributed by Universal Press Syndicate

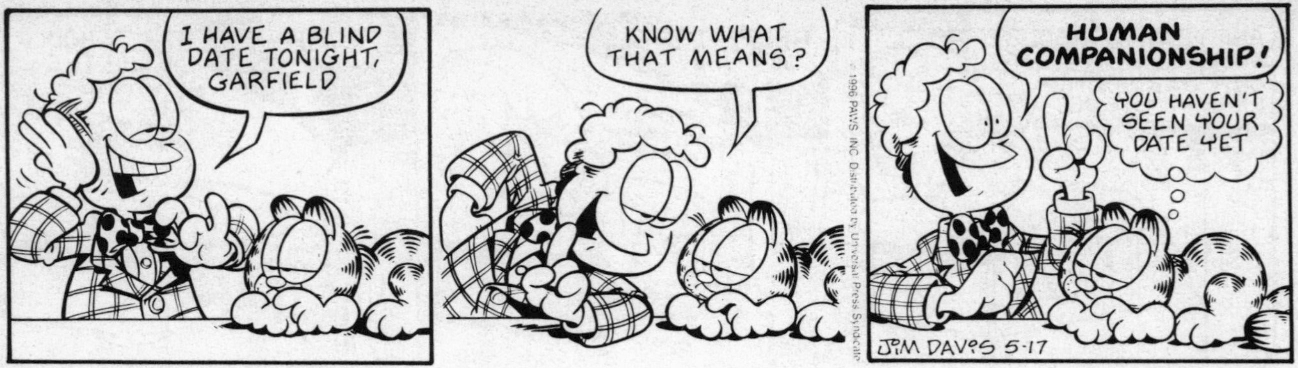
I HAVE A BLIND DATE TONIGHT, GARFIELD
KNOW WHAT THAT MEANS?
HUMAN COMPANIONSHIP!
YOU HAVEN'T SEEN YOUR DATE YET
© 1996 PAWS, INC. Distributed by Universal Press Syndicate
JIM DAVIS 5-17

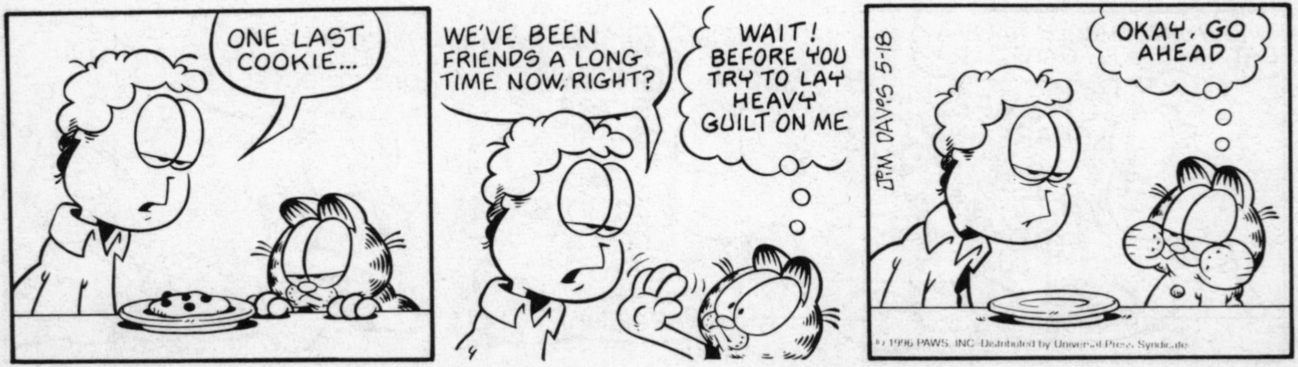
ONE LAST COOKIE...
WE'VE BEEN FRIENDS A LONG TIME NOW, RIGHT?
WAIT! BEFORE YOU TRY TO LAY HEAVY GUILT ON ME
JIM DAVIS 5-18
OKAY, GO AHEAD
© 1996 PAWS, INC. Distributed by Universal Press Syndicate

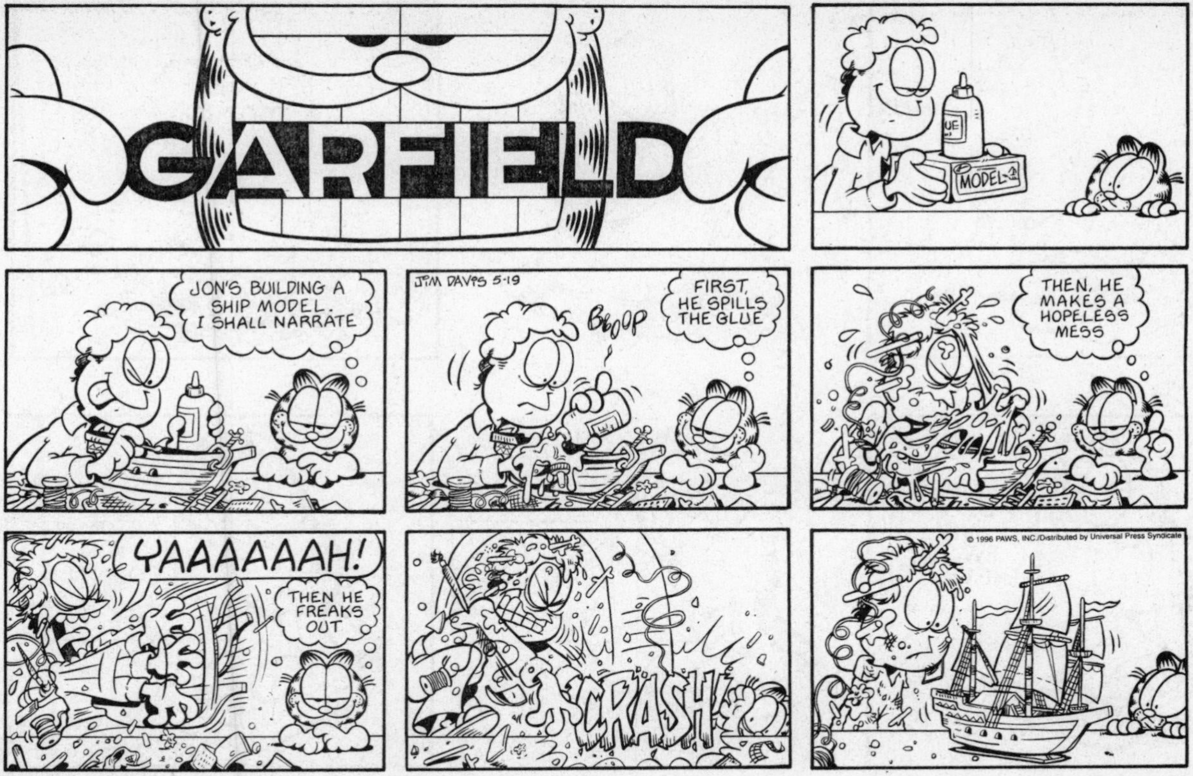
GARFIELD
MODEL
JON'S BUILDING A SHIP MODEL. I SHALL NARRATE
JIM DAVIS 5-19
BLOOP
FIRST, HE SPILLS THE GLUE
THEN, HE MAKES A HOPELESS MESS
YAAAAAAH!
THEN HE FREAKS OUT
CRASH!
© 1996 PAWS, INC./Distributed by Universal Press Syndicate

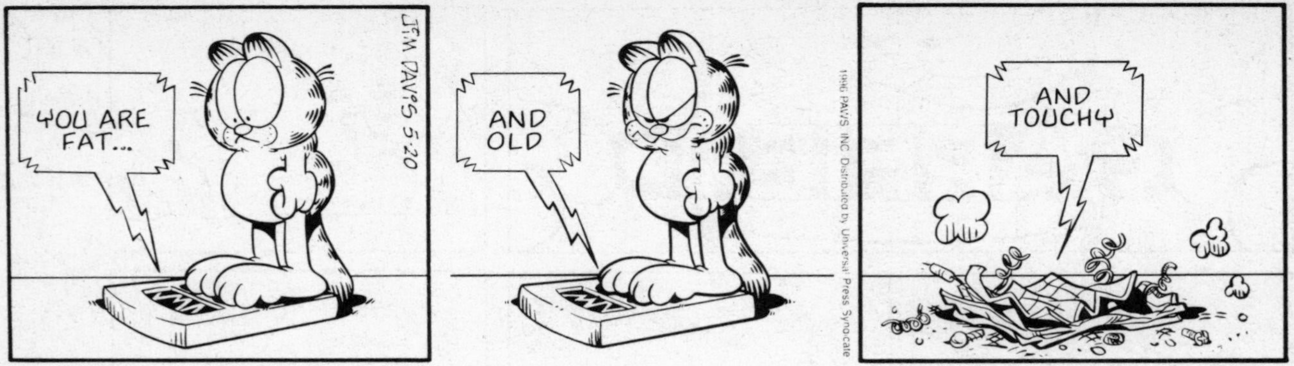
YOU ARE FAT...
JIM DAVIS 5-20
AND OLD
1986 PAWS INC Distributed by Universal Press Syndicate
AND TOUCHY

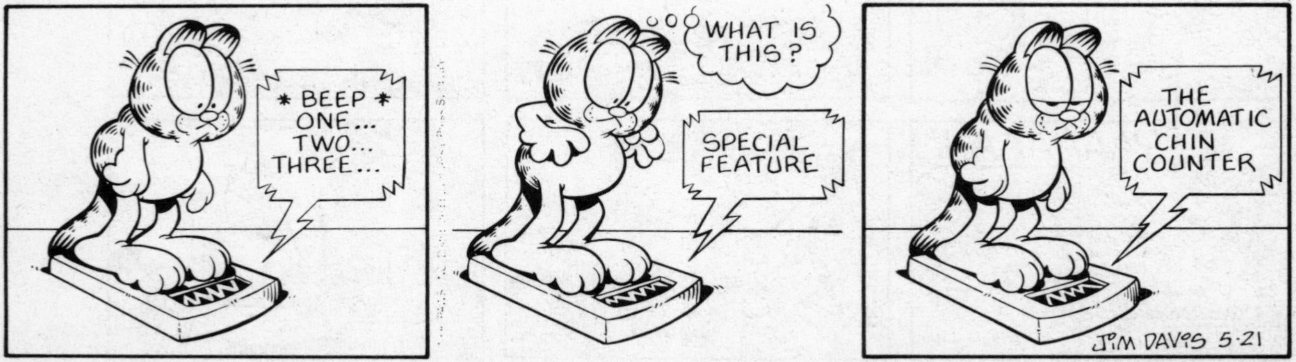
* BEEP * ONE... TWO... THREE...
WHAT IS THIS?
SPECIAL FEATURE
THE AUTOMATIC CHIN COUNTER
JIM DAVIS 5-21

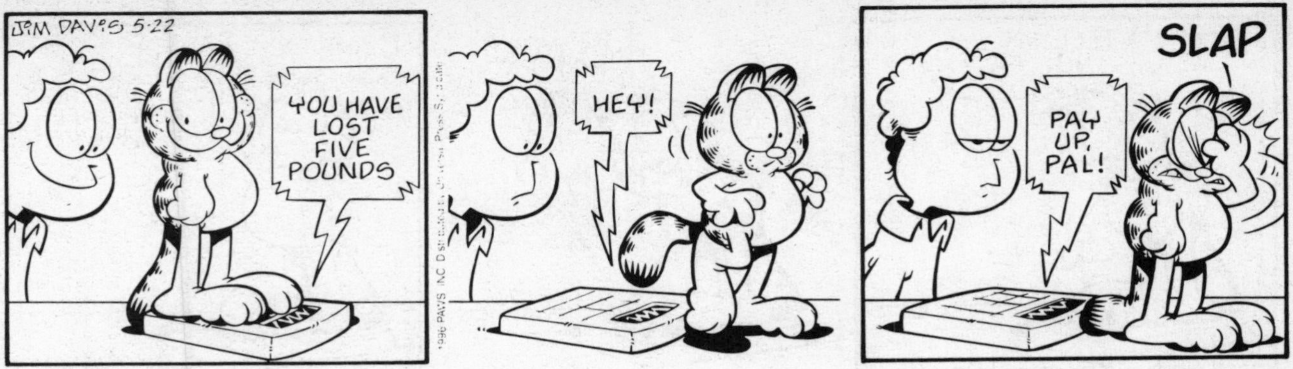
JIM DAVIS 5-22
YOU HAVE LOST FIVE POUNDS
HEY!
PAY UP, PAL!
SLAP

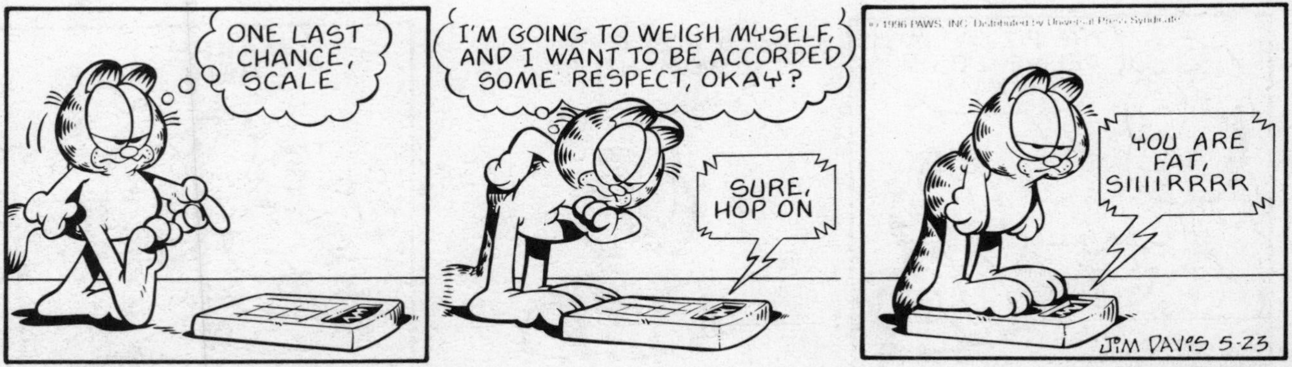
ONE LAST CHANCE, SCALE
I'M GOING TO WEIGH MYSELF, AND I WANT TO BE ACCORDED SOME RESPECT, OKAY?
SURE, HOP ON
© 1996 PAWS, INC Distributed by Universal Press Syndicate
YOU ARE FAT, SIIIIRRRR
JIM DAVIS 5-23

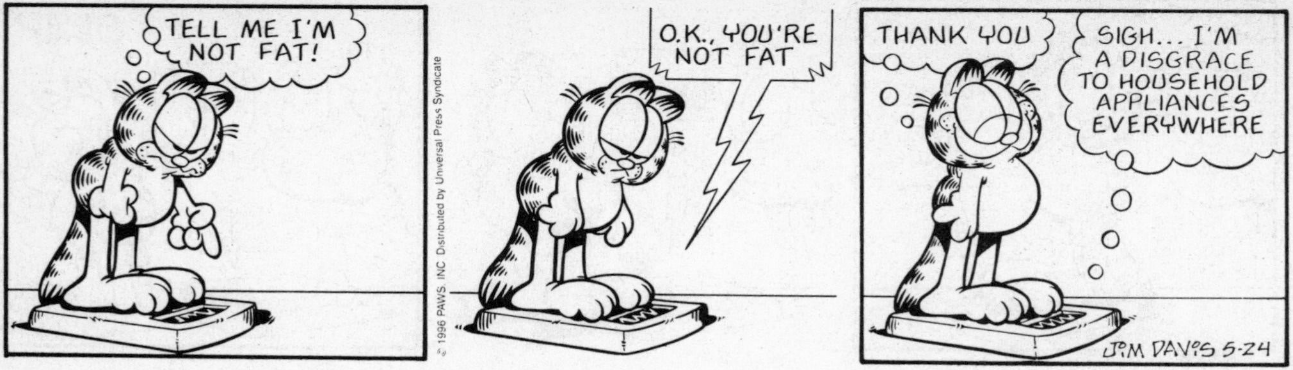
TELL ME I'M NOT FAT!
O.K., YOU'RE NOT FAT
THANK YOU
SIGH... I'M A DISGRACE TO HOUSEHOLD APPLIANCES EVERYWHERE
JIM DAVIS 5-24
© 1996 PAWS, INC. Distributed by Universal Press Syndicate

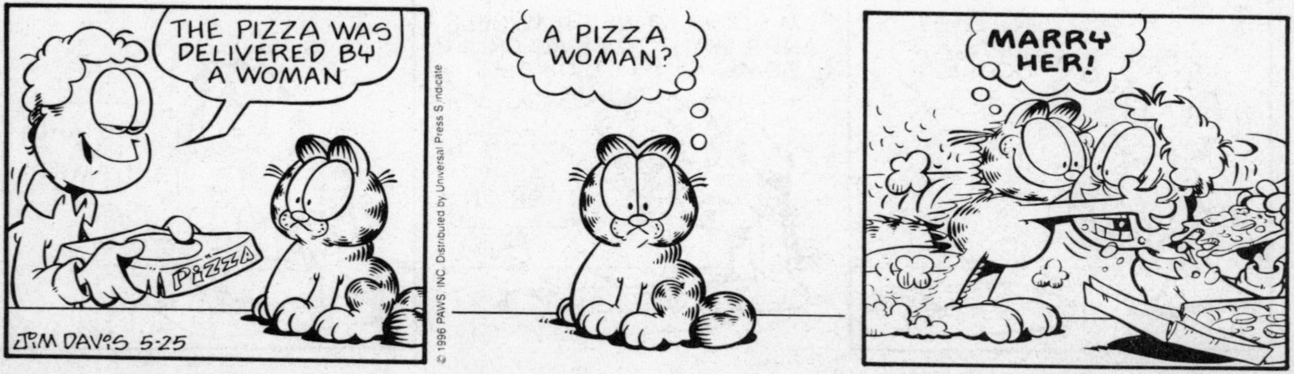
THE PIZZA WAS DELIVERED BY A WOMAN
PIZZA
A PIZZA WOMAN?
MARRY HER!
JIM DAVIS 5-25
© 1996 PAWS, INC. Distributed by Universal Press Syndicate

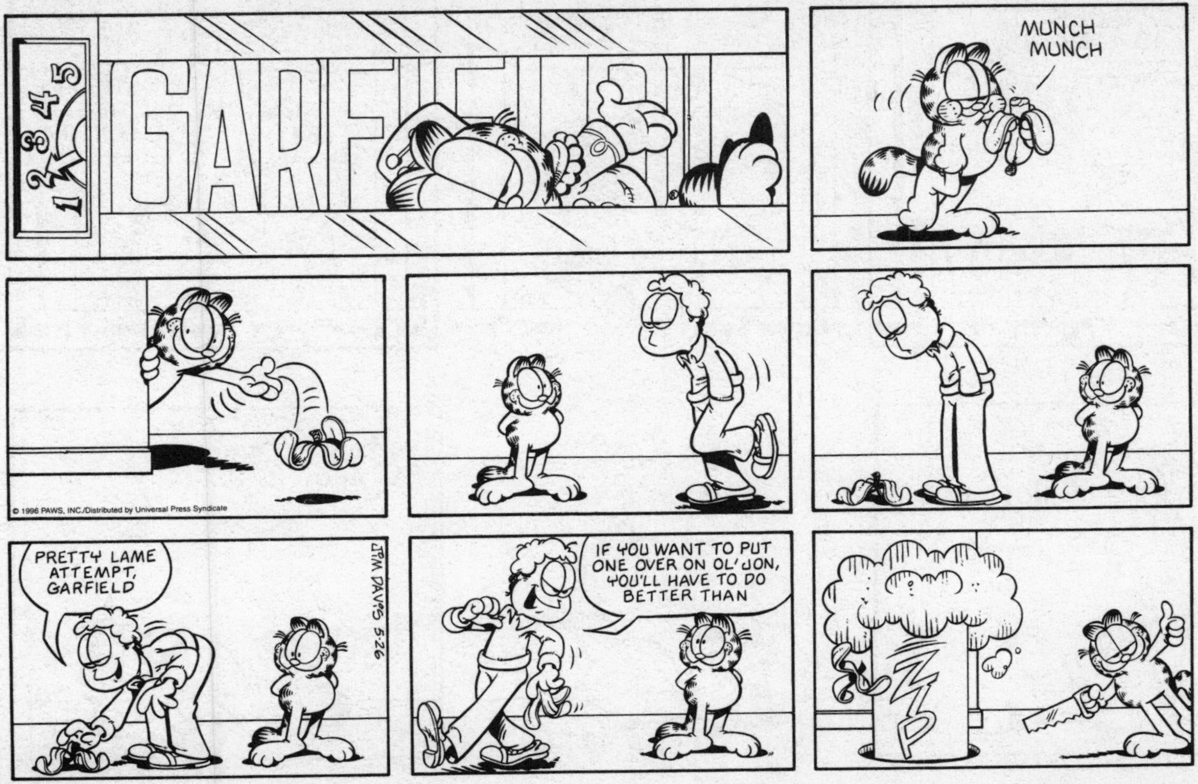
1 2 3 4 5
GARFIELD
MUNCH
MUNCH
PRETTY LAME ATTEMPT, GARFIELD
JIM DAVIS 5-26
IF YOU WANT TO PUT ONE OVER ON OL' JON, YOU'LL HAVE TO DO BETTER THAN
ZZZIP

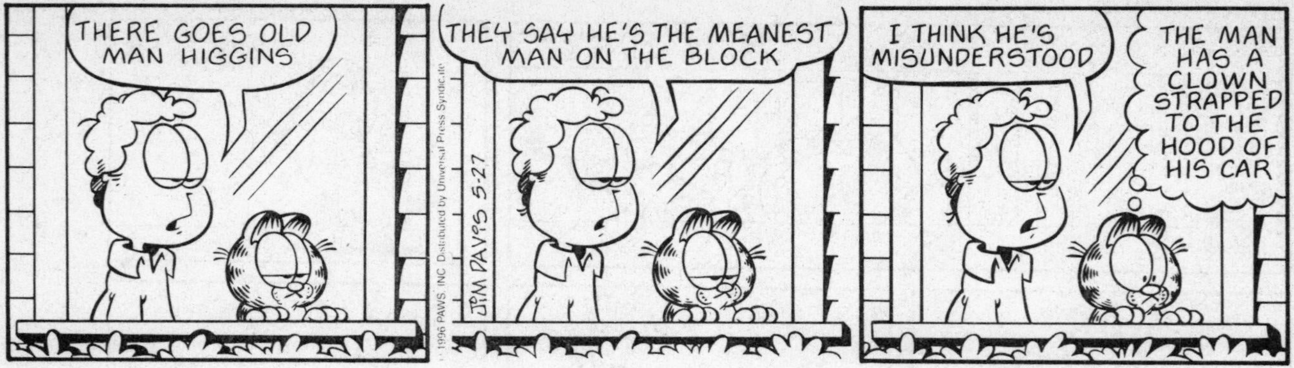
THERE GOES OLD MAN HIGGINS
THEY SAY HE'S THE MEANEST MAN ON THE BLOCK
I THINK HE'S MISUNDERSTOOD
THE MAN HAS A CLOWN STRAPPED TO THE HOOD OF HIS CAR
JIM DAVIS 5-27
© 1996 PAWS, INC. Distributed by Universal Press Syndicate

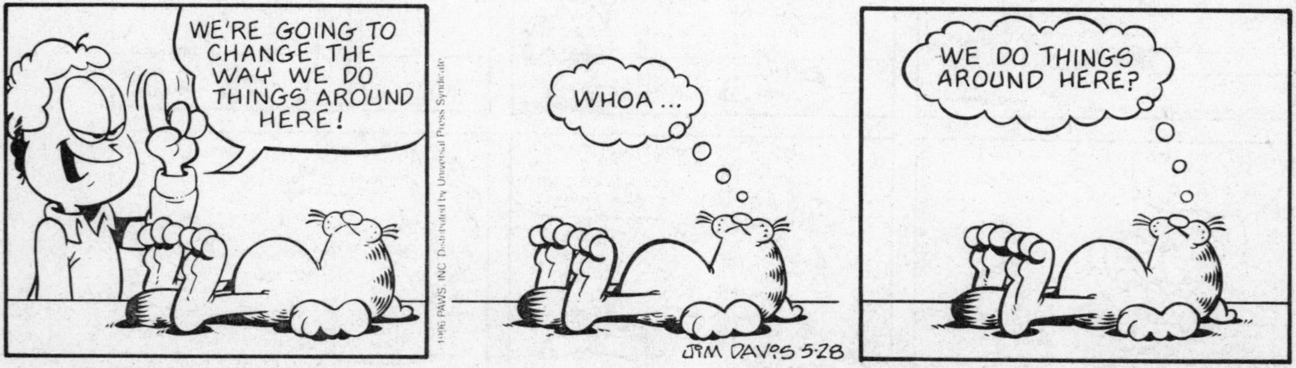
WE'RE GOING TO CHANGE THE WAY WE DO THINGS AROUND HERE!
WHOA ...
WE DO THINGS AROUND HERE?
JIM DAVIS 5-28
© 1996 PAWS, INC. Distributed by Universal Press Syndicate

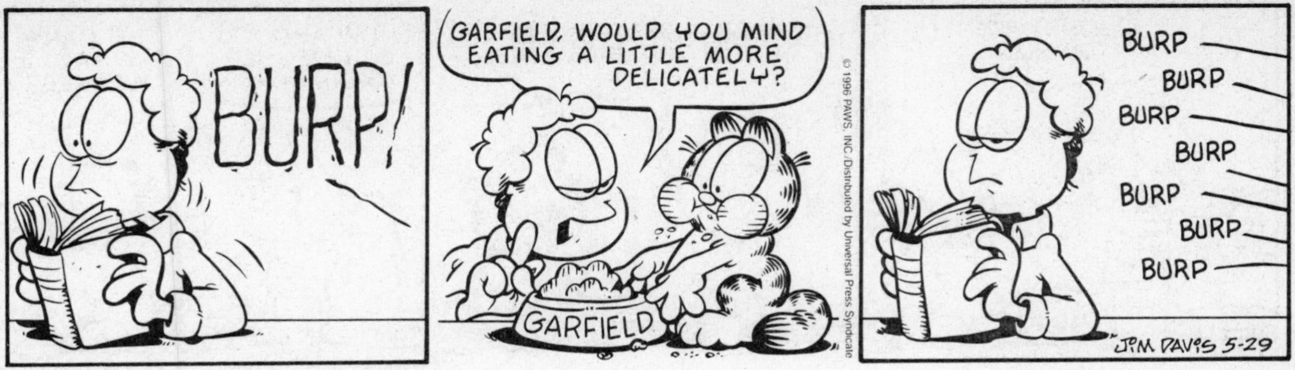
BURP!
GARFIELD, WOULD YOU MIND EATING A LITTLE MORE DELICATELY?
GARFIELD
BURP
BURP
BURP
BURP
BURP
BURP
BURP
JIM DAVIS 5-29

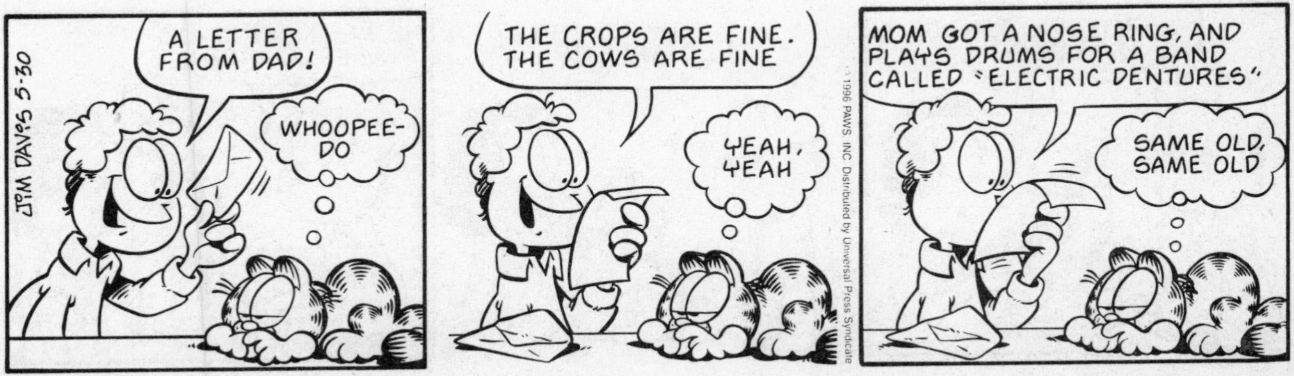
JIM DAVIS 5-30
A LETTER FROM DAD!
WHOOPEE-DO
THE CROPS ARE FINE. THE COWS ARE FINE
YEAH, YEAH
MOM GOT A NOSE RING, AND PLAYS DRUMS FOR A BAND CALLED "ELECTRIC DENTURES"
SAME OLD, SAME OLD

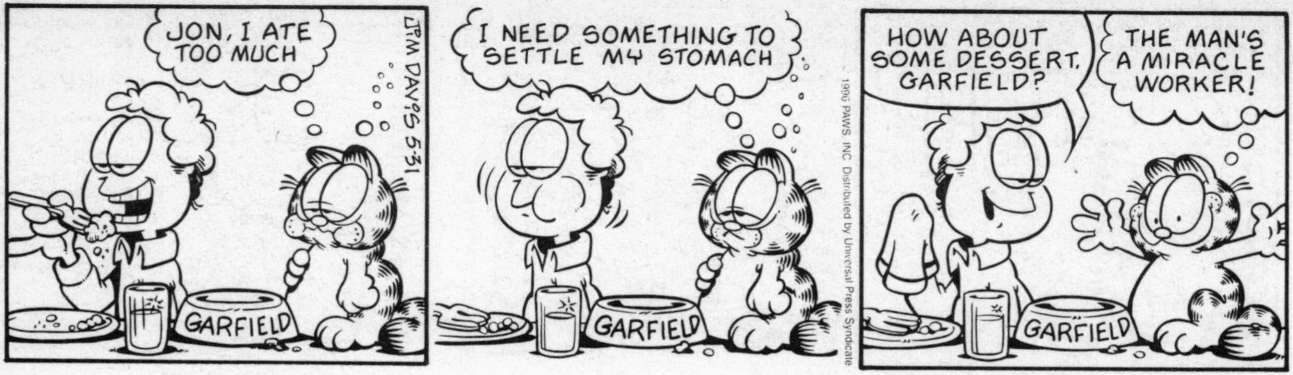
JON, I ATE TOO MUCH
JIM DAVIS 5-31
I NEED SOMETHING TO SETTLE MY STOMACH
HOW ABOUT SOME DESSERT, GARFIELD?
THE MAN'S A MIRACLE WORKER!
GARFIELD

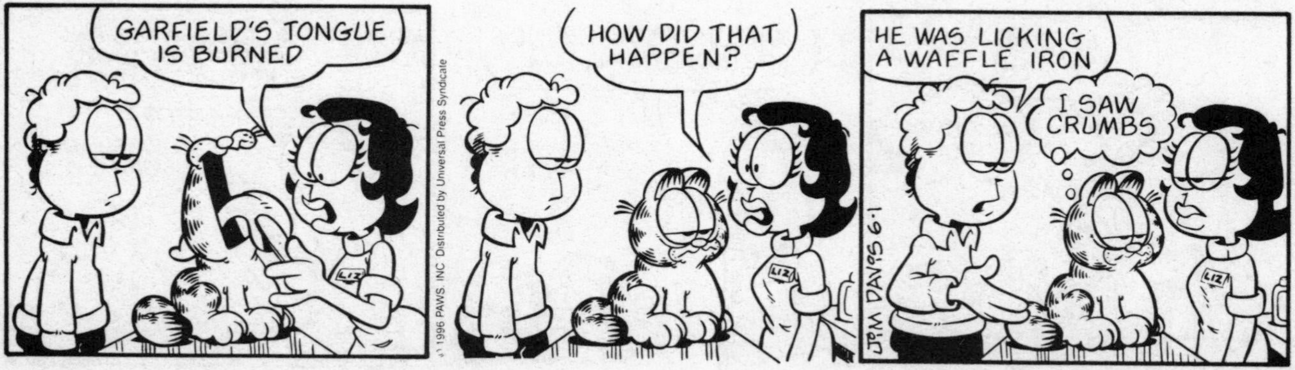
GARFIELD'S TONGUE IS BURNED
HOW DID THAT HAPPEN?
HE WAS LICKING A WAFFLE IRON
I SAW CRUMBS
JIM DAVIS 6-1
LIZ

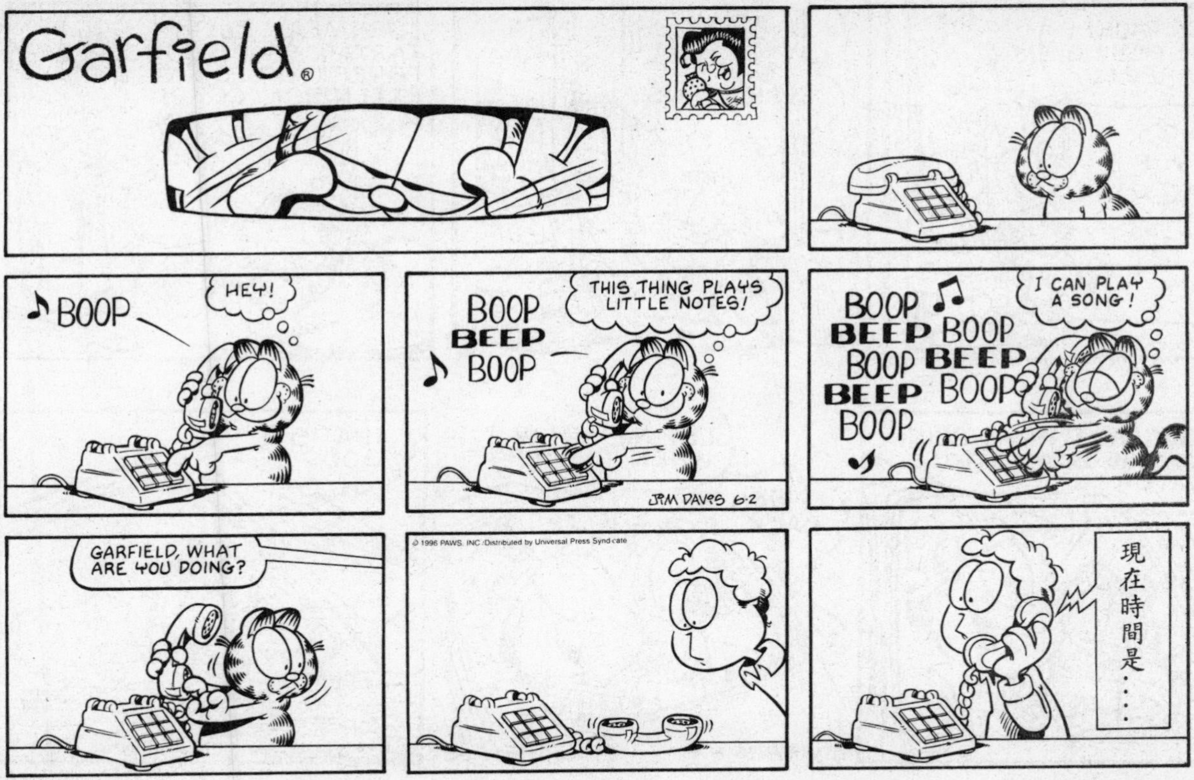
Garfield®
BOOP
HEY!
BOOP
BEEP
BOOP
THIS THING PLAYS LITTLE NOTES!
JIM DAVIS 6-2
BOOP
BEEP
BOOP
BEEP
BOOP
BOOP
BEEP
BOOP
I CAN PLAY A SONG!
GARFIELD, WHAT ARE YOU DOING?
© 1996 PAWS, INC./Distributed by Universal Press Syndicate
現在時間是....

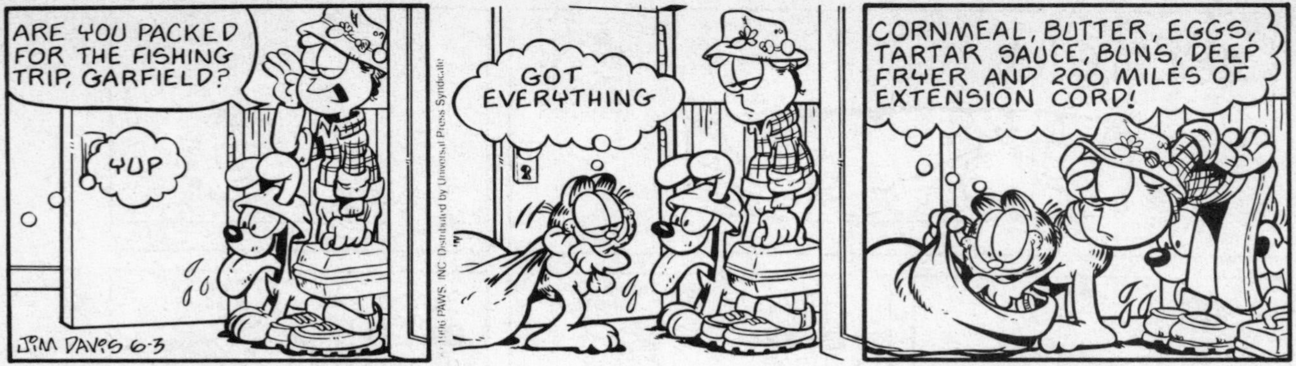
ARE YOU PACKED FOR THE FISHING TRIP, GARFIELD?
YUP
JIM DAVIS 6-3
© 1996 PAWS, INC. Distributed by Universal Press Syndicate
GOT EVERYTHING
CORNMEAL, BUTTER, EGGS, TARTAR SAUCE, BUNS, DEEP FRYER AND 200 MILES OF EXTENSION CORD!

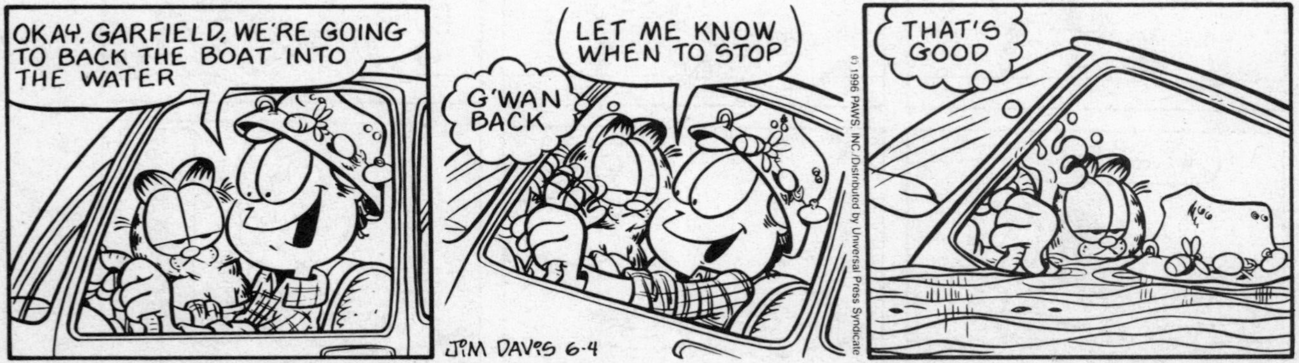
OKAY, GARFIELD, WE'RE GOING TO BACK THE BOAT INTO THE WATER
LET ME KNOW WHEN TO STOP
G'WAN BACK
JIM DAVIS 6-4
© 1996 PAWS, INC./Distributed by Universal Press Syndicate
THAT'S GOOD

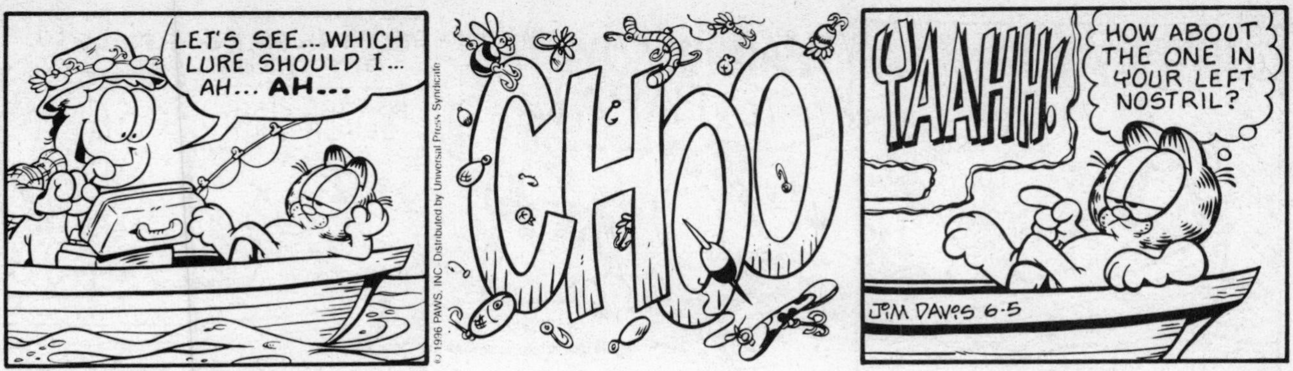
LET'S SEE... WHICH LURE SHOULD I... AH... **AH...**
CHOO
YAAHH!
HOW ABOUT THE ONE IN YOUR LEFT NOSTRIL?
JIM DAVIS 6-5

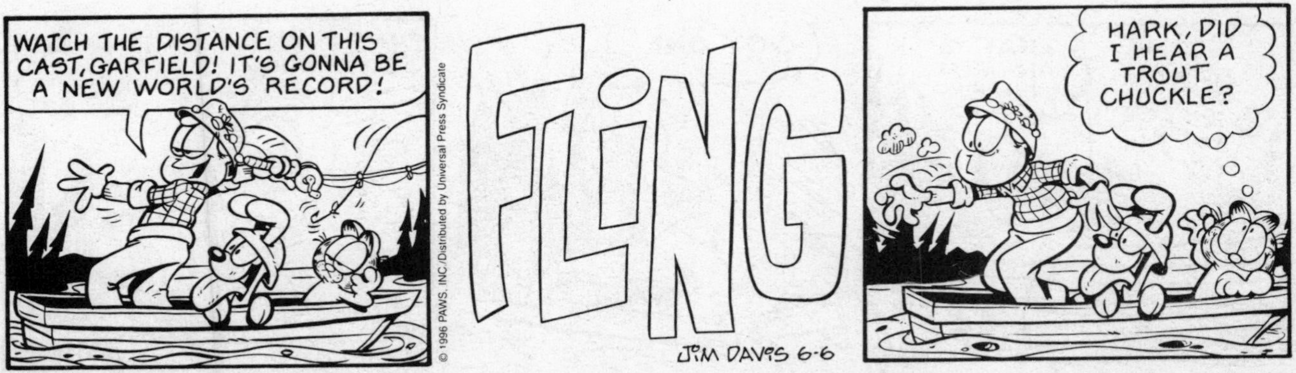
WATCH THE DISTANCE ON THIS CAST, GARFIELD! IT'S GONNA BE A NEW WORLD'S RECORD!
FLING
HARK, DID I HEAR A TROUT CHUCKLE?
JIM DAVIS 6-6

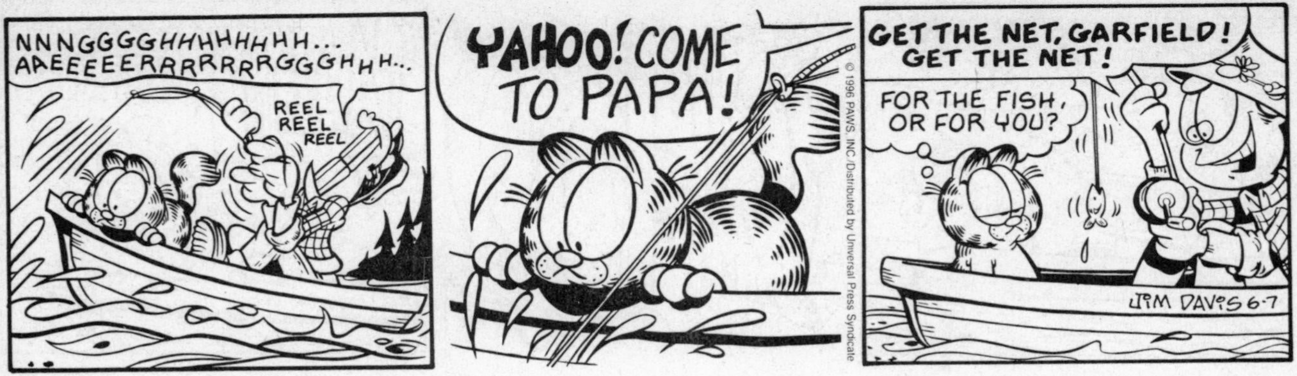
NNNGGGGHHHHHHHH...
AAEEEEEERRRRRRRGGGHHH...
REEL
REEL
REEL
YAHOO! COME TO PAPA!
GET THE NET, GARFIELD! GET THE NET!
FOR THE FISH, OR FOR YOU?
JIM DAVIS 6-7
© 1996 PAWS, INC./Distributed by Universal Press Syndicate

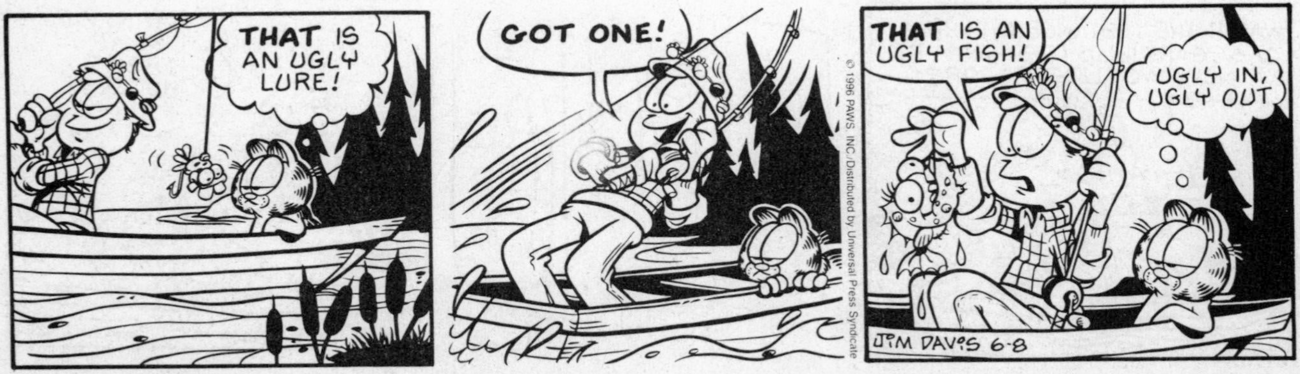
THAT IS AN UGLY LURE!
GOT ONE!
THAT IS AN UGLY FISH!
UGLY IN, UGLY OUT
JIM DAVIS 6-8
© 1996 PAWS, INC./Distributed by Universal Press Syndicate

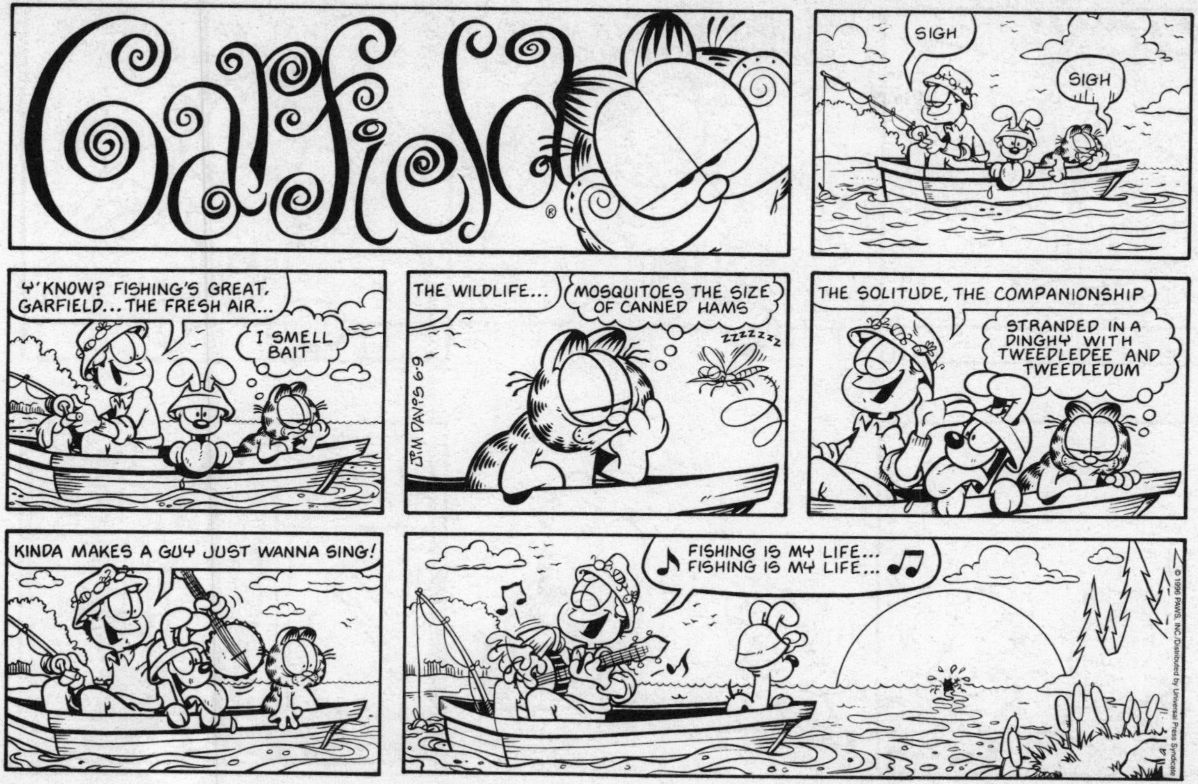
GARFIELD®
SIGH
SIGH
Y'KNOW? FISHING'S GREAT, GARFIELD... THE FRESH AIR...
I SMELL BAIT
THE WILDLIFE...
MOSQUITOES THE SIZE OF CANNED HAMS
ZZZZZZZ
JIM DAVIS 6-9
THE SOLITUDE, THE COMPANIONSHIP
STRANDED IN A DINGHY WITH TWEEDLEDEE AND TWEEDLEDUM
KINDA MAKES A GUY JUST WANNA SING!
FISHING IS MY LIFE...
FISHING IS MY LIFE...
© 1996 PAWS, INC./Distributed by Universal Press Syndicate

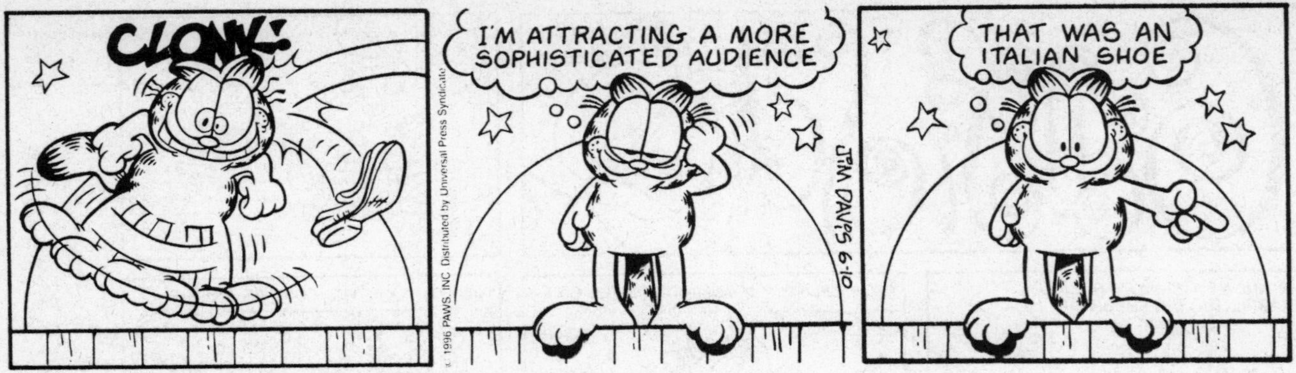
CLONK!
I'M ATTRACTING A MORE SOPHISTICATED AUDIENCE
THAT WAS AN ITALIAN SHOE
© 1996 PAWS, INC Distributed by Universal Press Syndicate
JIM DAVIS 6-10

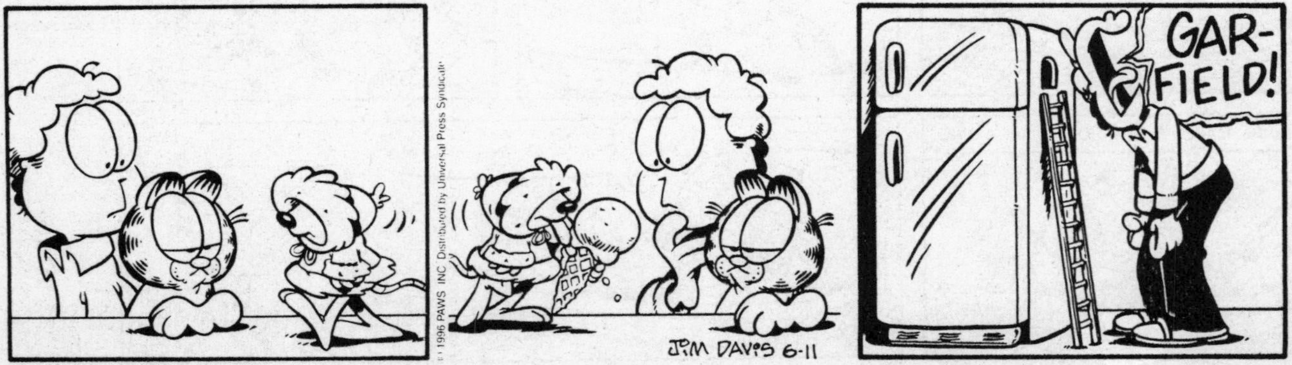
GAR-FIELD!
© 1996 PAWS, INC Distributed by Universal Press Syndicate
JIM DAVIS 6-11

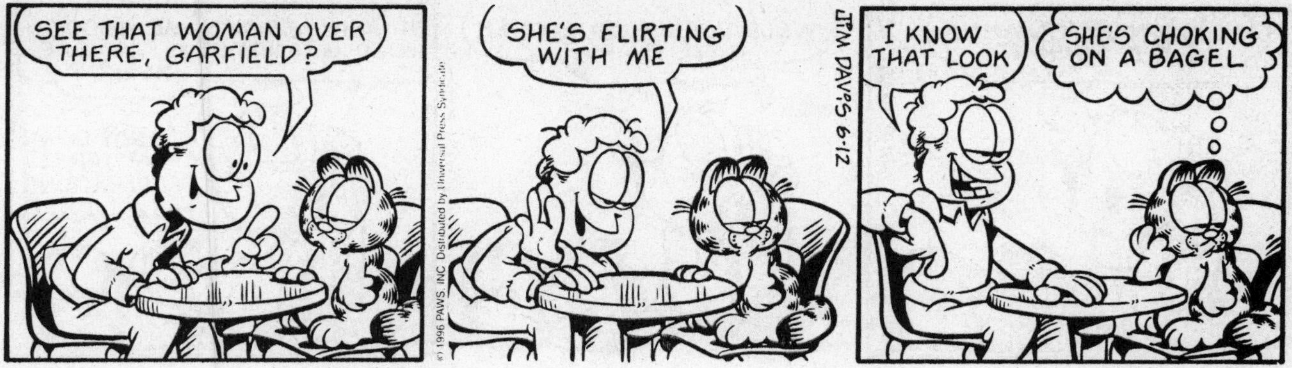
SEE THAT WOMAN OVER THERE, GARFIELD?
SHE'S FLIRTING WITH ME
© 1996 PAWS, INC Distributed by Universal Press Syndicate
JIM DAVIS 6-12
I KNOW THAT LOOK
SHE'S CHOKING ON A BAGEL

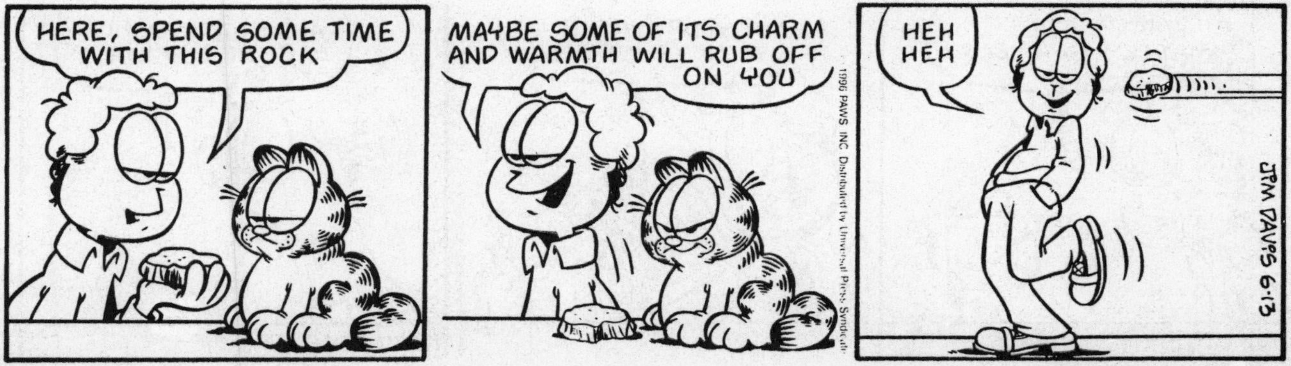
HERE, SPEND SOME TIME WITH THIS ROCK
MAYBE SOME OF ITS CHARM AND WARMTH WILL RUB OFF ON YOU
© 1996 PAWS, INC Distributed by Universal Press Syndicate
HEH HEH
JIM DAVIS 6-13

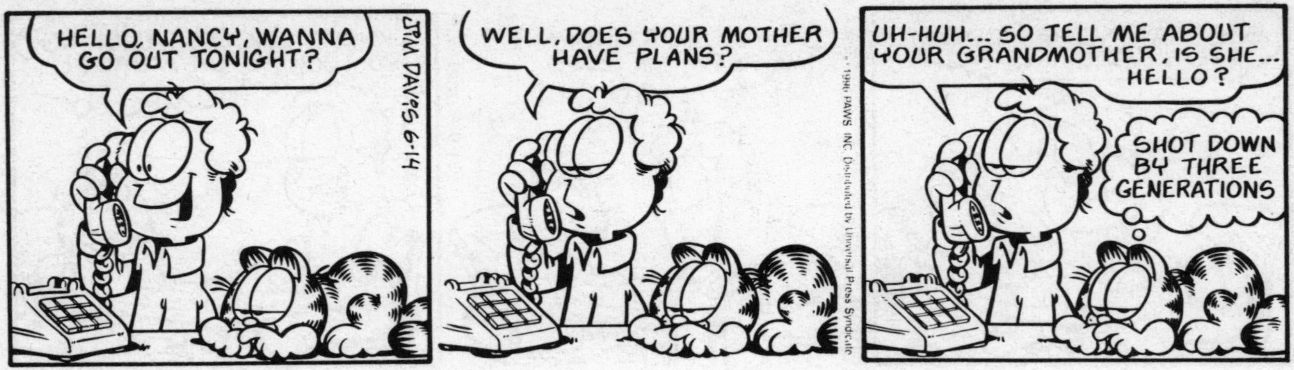
HELLO, NANCY, WANNA GO OUT TONIGHT?
JIM DAVIS 6-14
WELL, DOES YOUR MOTHER HAVE PLANS?
© 1986 PAWS INC Distributed by Universal Press Syndicate
UH-HUH... SO TELL ME ABOUT YOUR GRANDMOTHER, IS SHE... HELLO?
SHOT DOWN BY THREE GENERATIONS

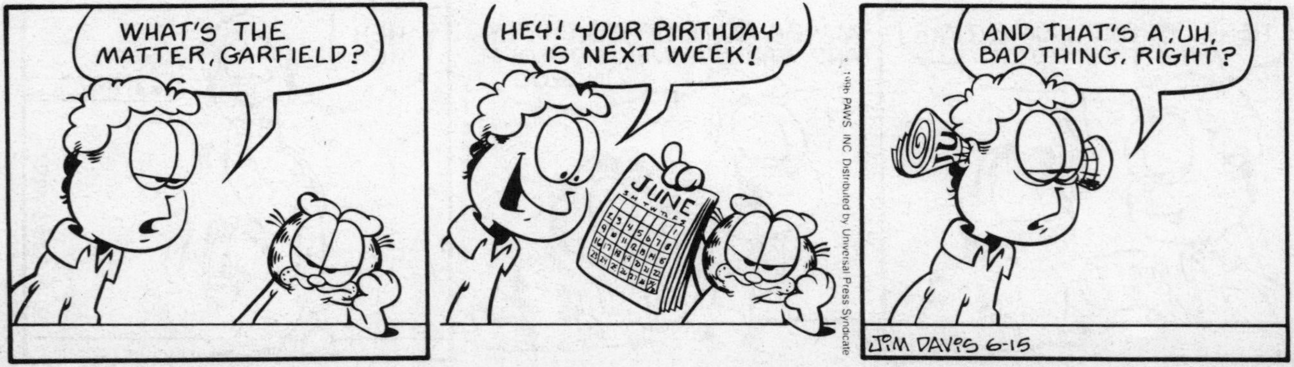
WHAT'S THE MATTER, GARFIELD?
HEY! YOUR BIRTHDAY IS NEXT WEEK!
JUNE
© 1986 PAWS INC Distributed by Universal Press Syndicate
AND THAT'S A, UH, BAD THING, RIGHT?
JIM DAVIS 6-15

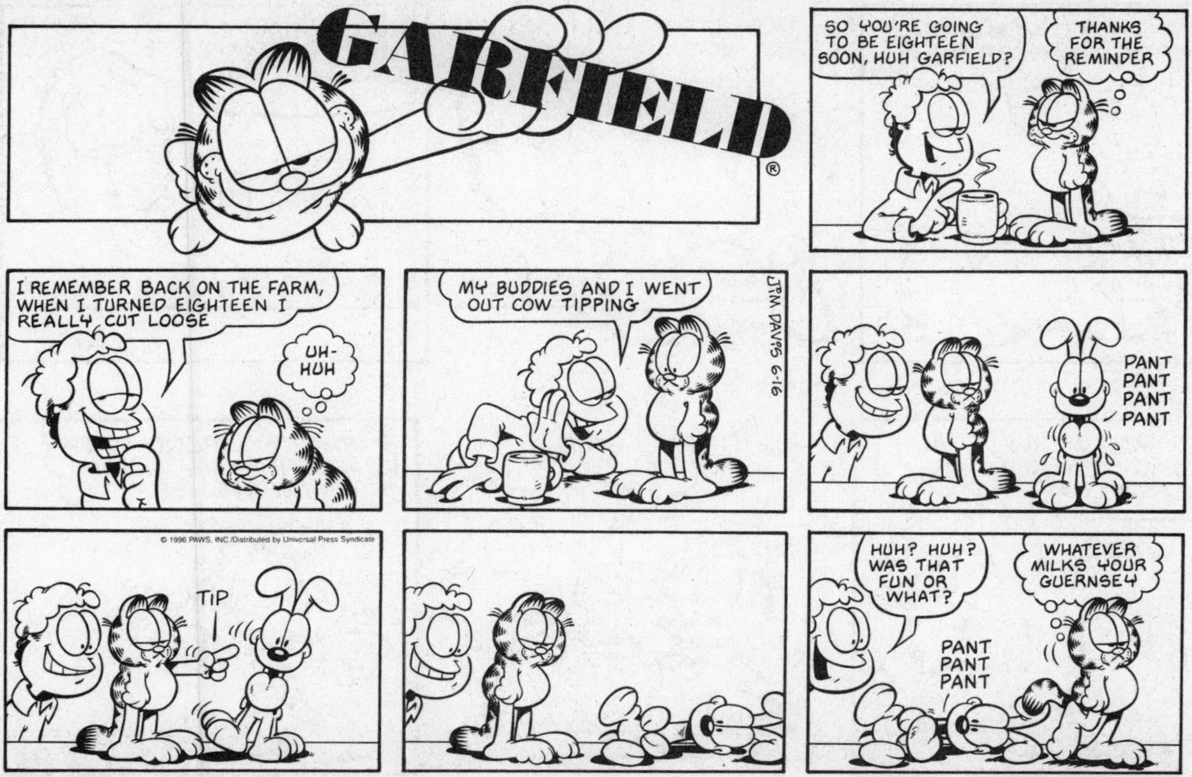
GARFIELD
SO YOU'RE GOING TO BE EIGHTEEN SOON, HUH GARFIELD?
THANKS FOR THE REMINDER
I REMEMBER BACK ON THE FARM, WHEN I TURNED EIGHTEEN I REALLY CUT LOOSE
UH-HUH
MY BUDDIES AND I WENT OUT COW TIPPING
JIM DAVIS 6-16
PANT PANT PANT PANT
© 1996 PAWS, INC./Distributed by Universal Press Syndicate
TIP
HUH? HUH? WAS THAT FUN OR WHAT?
WHATEVER MILKS YOUR GUERNSEY
PANT PANT PANT

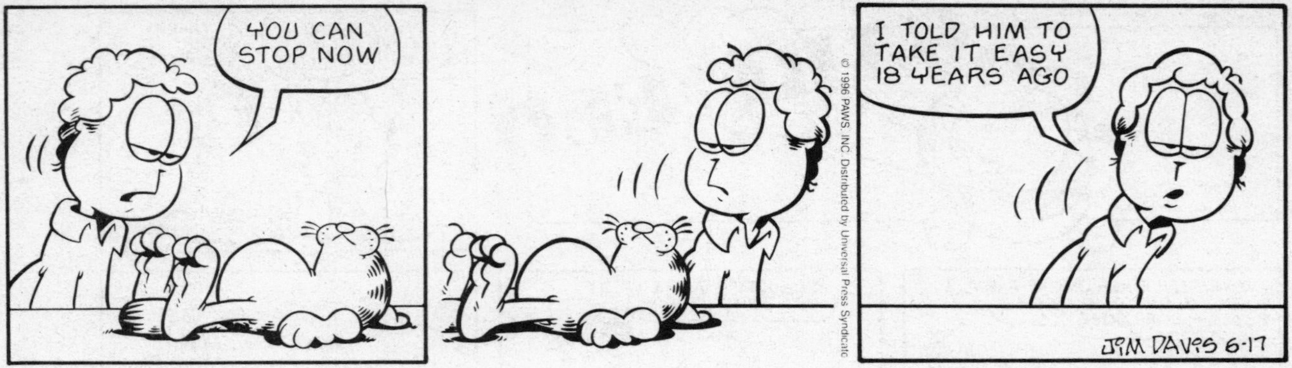
YOU CAN STOP NOW
I TOLD HIM TO TAKE IT EASY 18 YEARS AGO
JIM DAVIS 6-17
© 1996 PAWS, INC. Distributed by Universal Press Syndicate

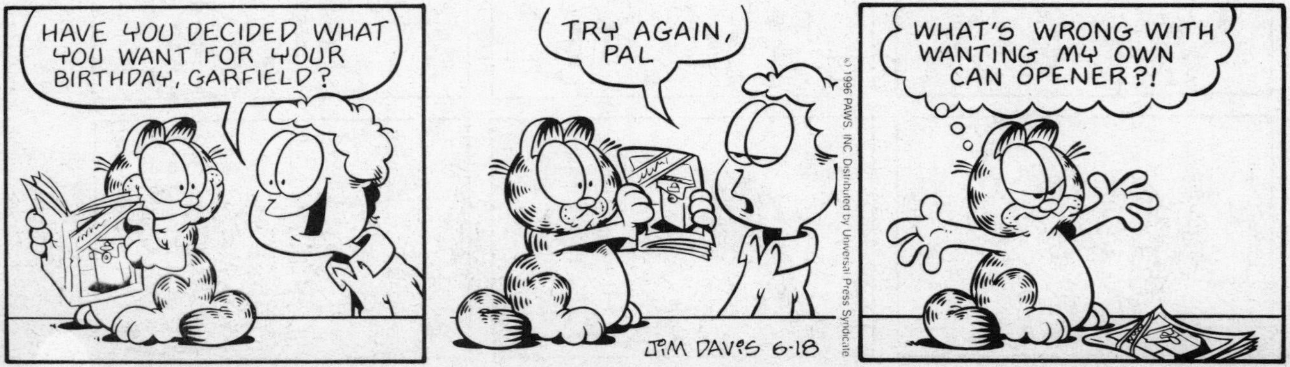
HAVE YOU DECIDED WHAT YOU WANT FOR YOUR BIRTHDAY, GARFIELD?
TRY AGAIN, PAL
WHAT'S WRONG WITH WANTING MY OWN CAN OPENER?!
JIM DAVIS 6-18
© 1996 PAWS, INC. Distributed by Universal Press Syndicate

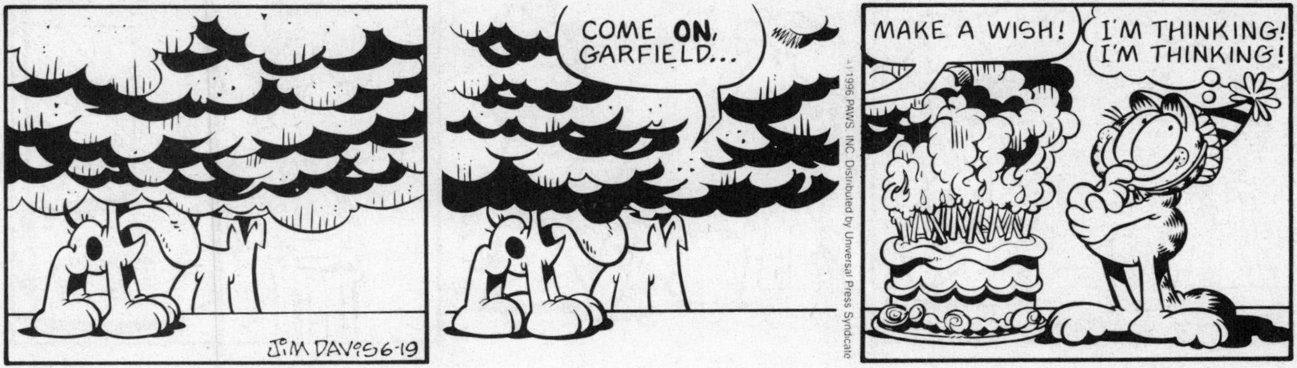
JIM DAVIS 6-19
COME ON, GARFIELD...
© 1996 PAWS, INC. Distributed by Universal Press Syndicate
MAKE A WISH!
I'M THINKING! I'M THINKING!

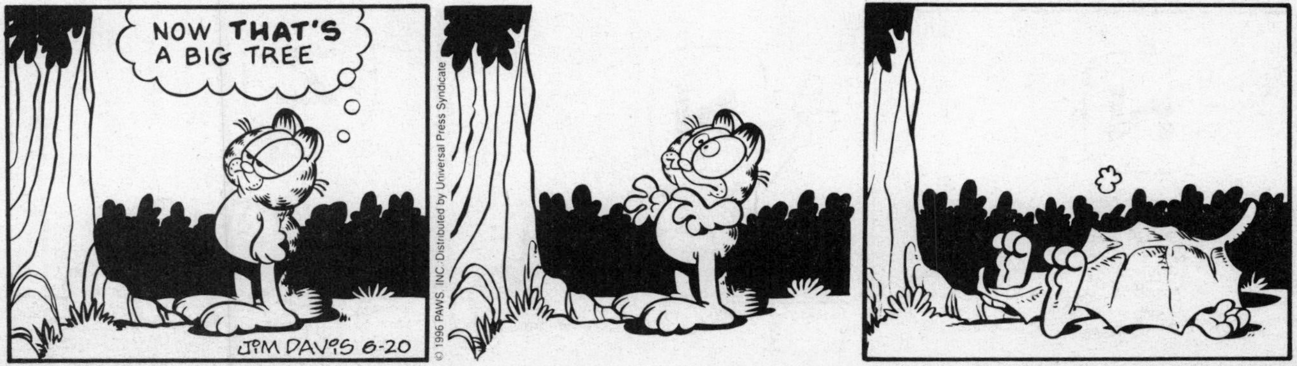
NOW THAT'S A BIG TREE
JIM DAVIS 6-20
© 1996 PAWS, INC. Distributed by Universal Press Syndicate

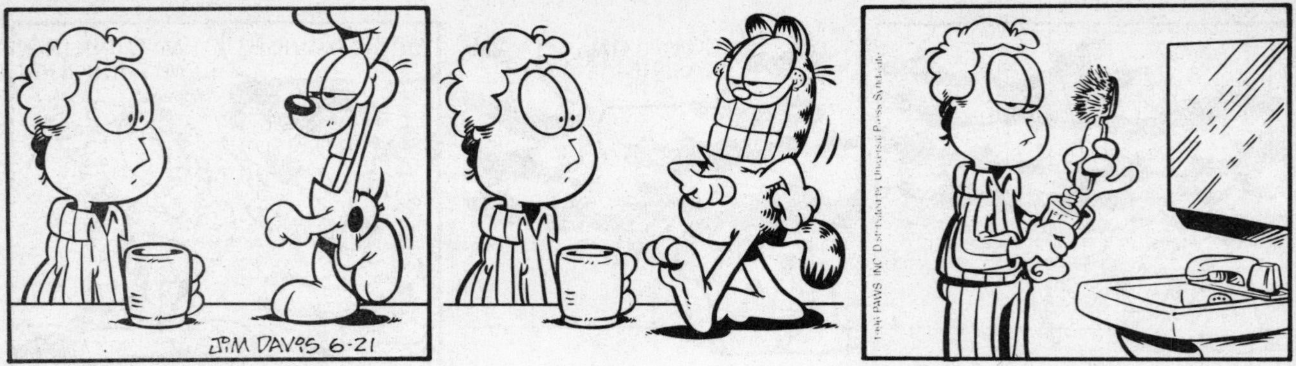
JIM DAVIS 6-21

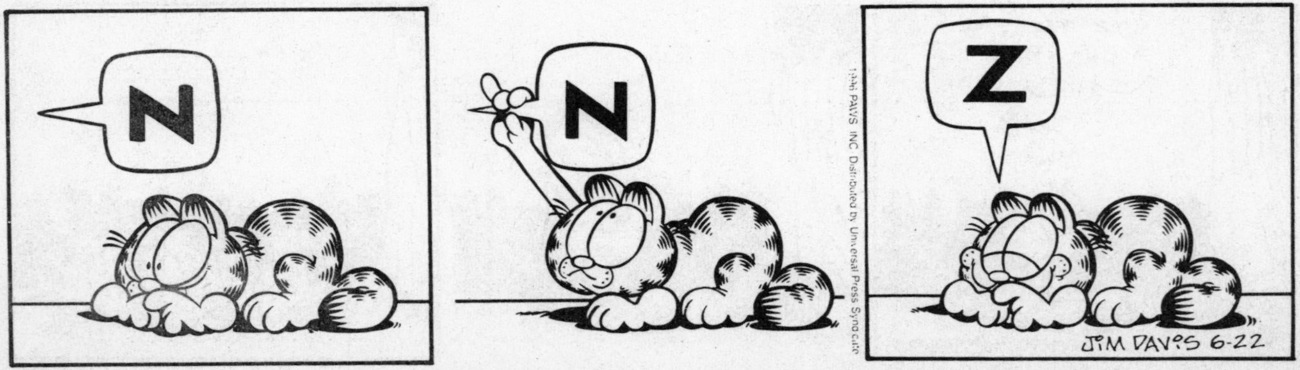
N
N
Z
JIM DAVIS 6-22

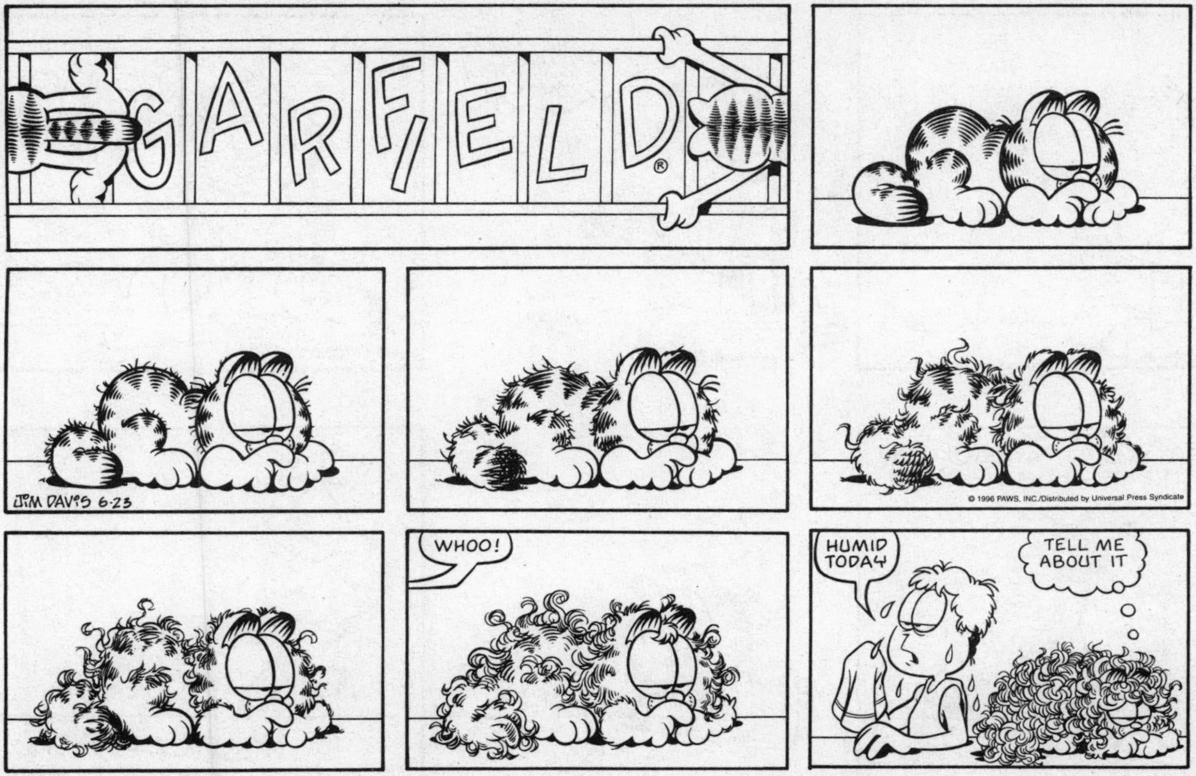
GARFIELD®
JIM DAVIS 6-23
© 1996 PAWS, INC./Distributed by Universal Press Syndicate
WHOO!
HUMID TODAY
TELL ME ABOUT IT

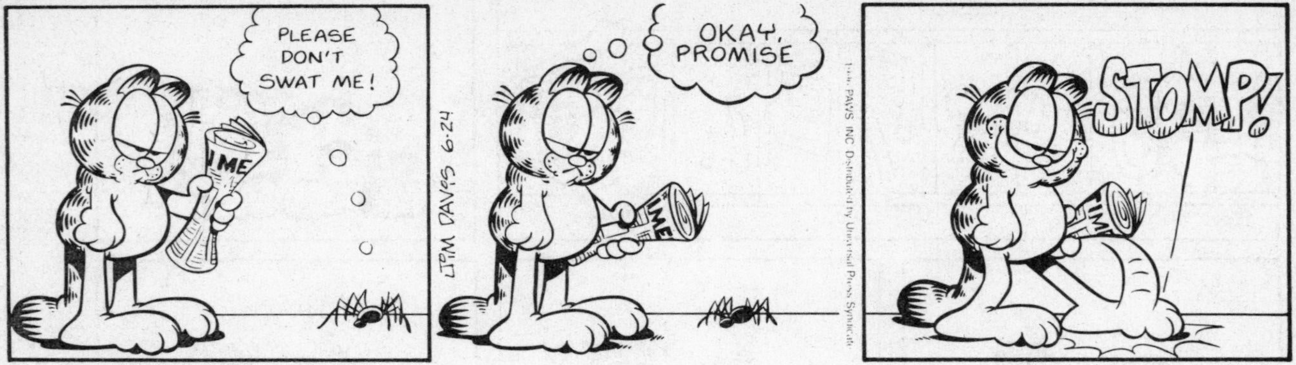
PLEASE DON'T SWAT ME!
JIM DAVIS 6·24
OKAY, PROMISE
STOMP!

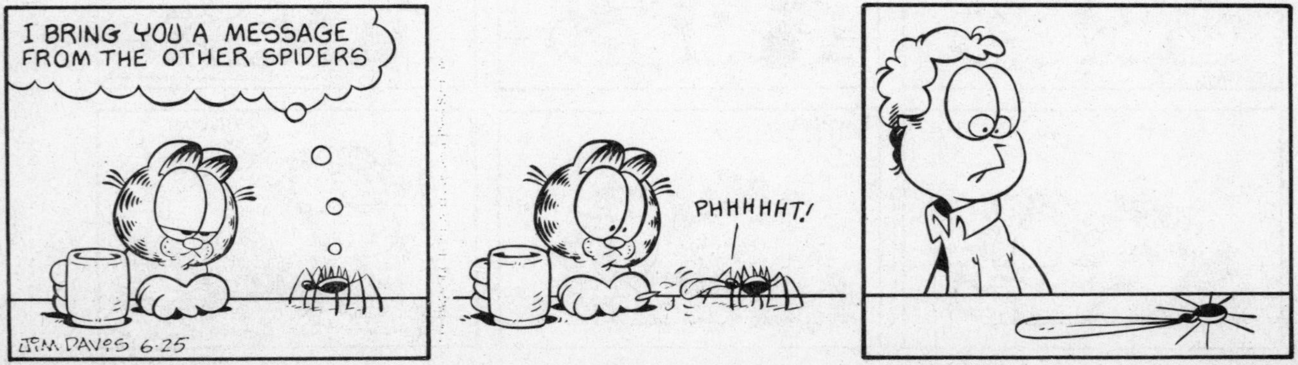
I BRING YOU A MESSAGE FROM THE OTHER SPIDERS
JIM DAVIS 6·25
PHHHHHT!

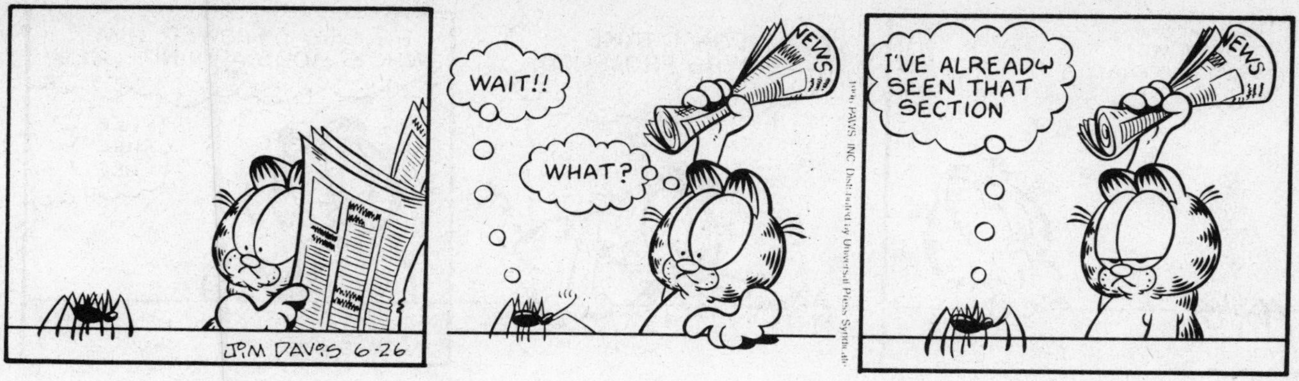
JIM DAVIS 6-26
WAIT!!
WHAT?
1990 PAWS INC Distributed by Universal Press Syndicate
NEWS
I'VE ALREADY SEEN THAT SECTION
NEWS

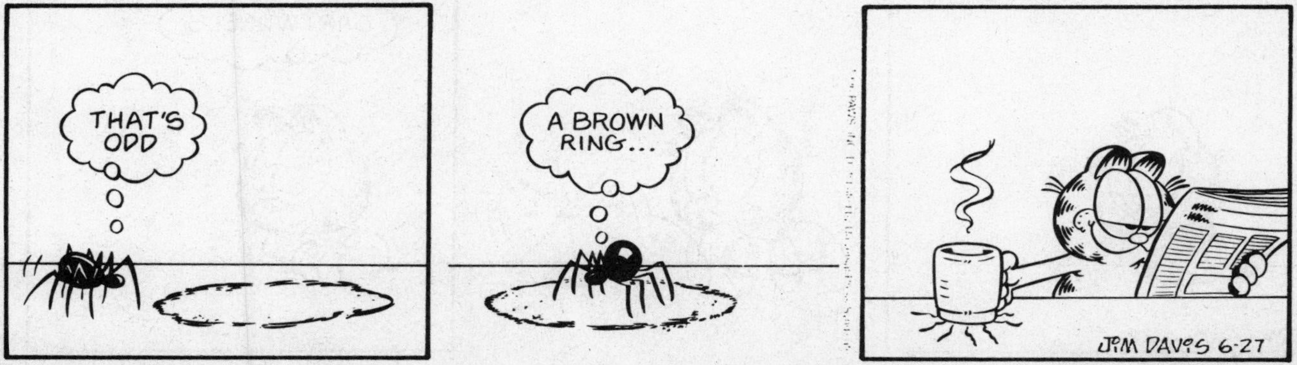
THAT'S ODD
A BROWN RING...
JIM DAVIS 6-27

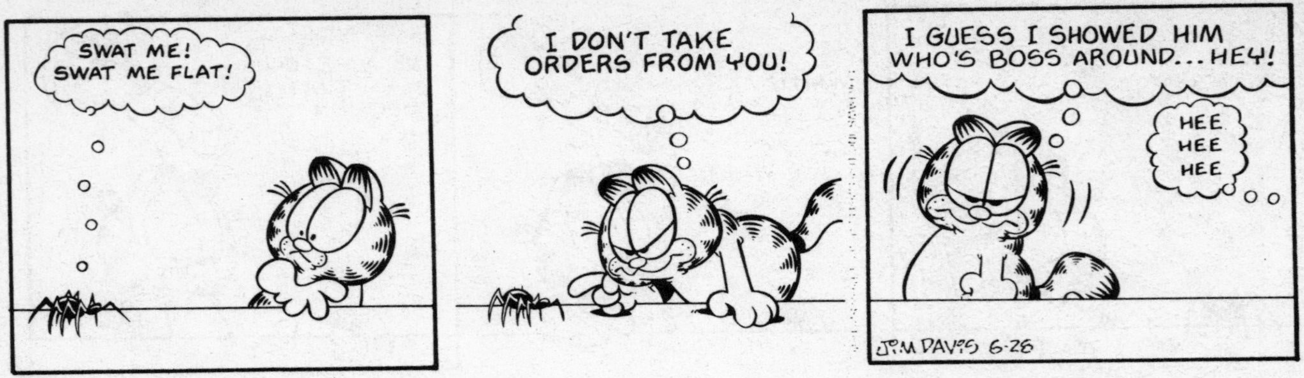
SWAT ME! SWAT ME FLAT!
I DON'T TAKE ORDERS FROM YOU!
I GUESS I SHOWED HIM WHO'S BOSS AROUND... HEY!
HEE HEE HEE
JIM DAVIS 6-28

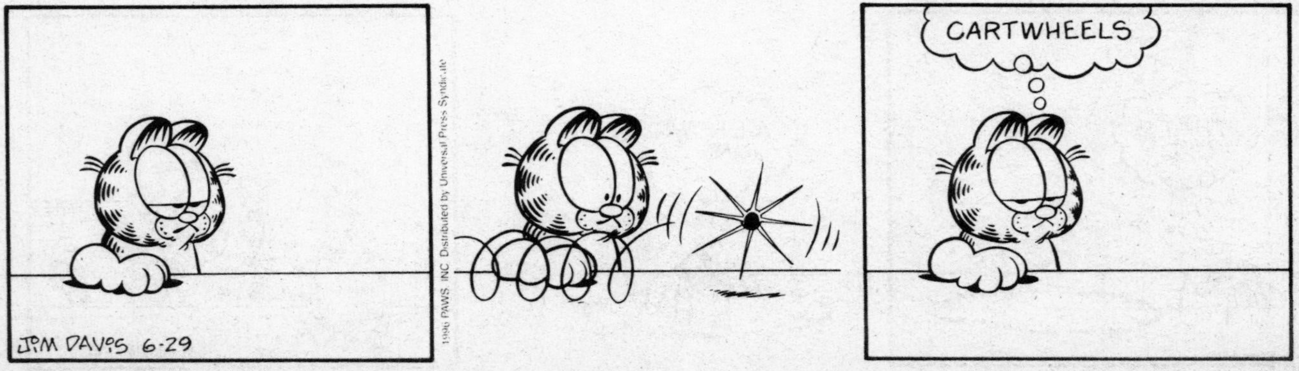
JIM DAVIS 6-29
1996 PAWS, INC Distributed by Universal Press Syndicate
CARTWHEELS

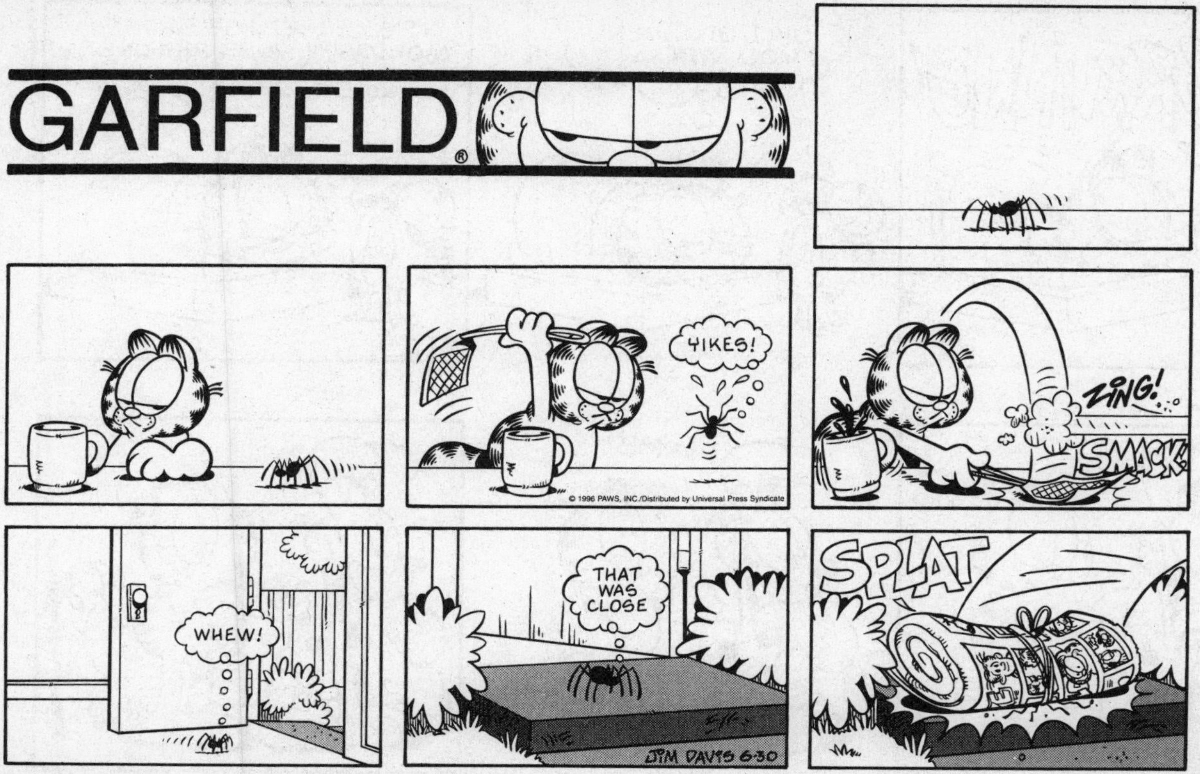
GARFIELD
YIKES!
© 1996 PAWS, INC./Distributed by Universal Press Syndicate
ZING!
SMACK!
WHEW!
THAT WAS CLOSE
JIM DAVIS 6-30
SPLAT

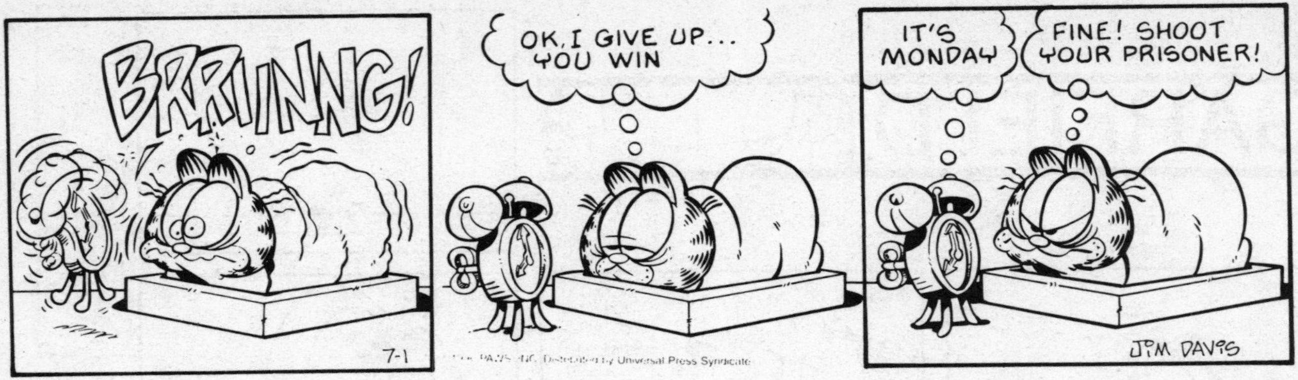
BRRIINNG!
OK, I GIVE UP... YOU WIN
IT'S MONDAY
FINE! SHOOT YOUR PRISONER!
7-1
PAWS, INC. Distributed by Universal Press Syndicate
JIM DAVIS

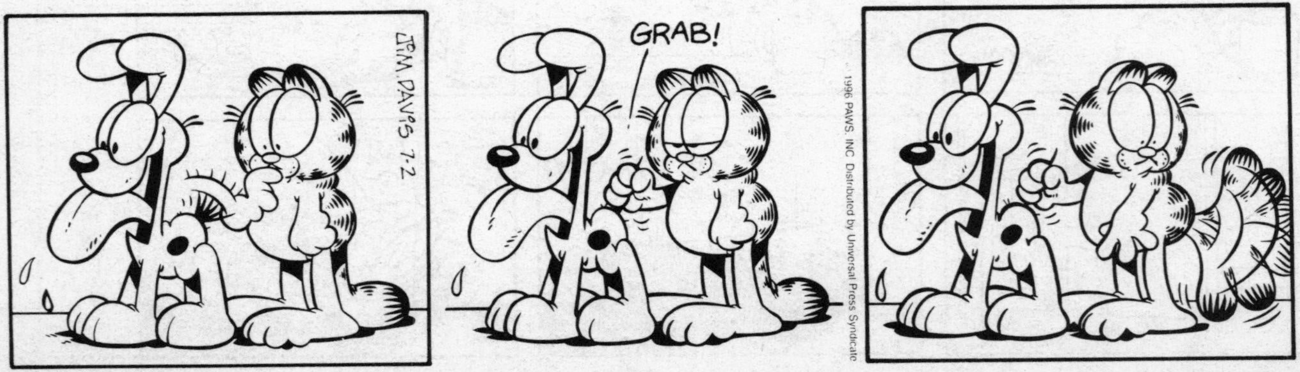
JIM DAVIS 7-2
GRAB!
© 1996 PAWS, INC. Distributed by Universal Press Syndicate

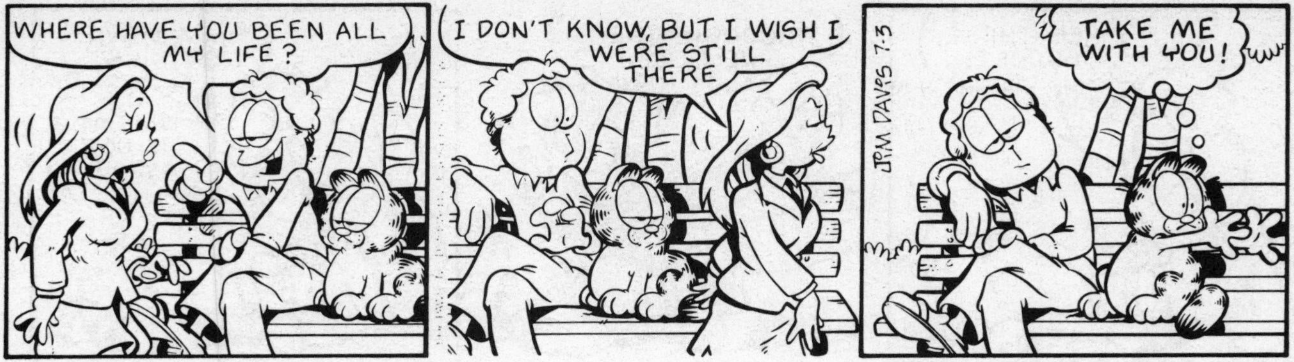
WHERE HAVE YOU BEEN ALL MY LIFE?
I DON'T KNOW, BUT I WISH I WERE STILL THERE
JIM DAVIS 7-3
TAKE ME WITH YOU!

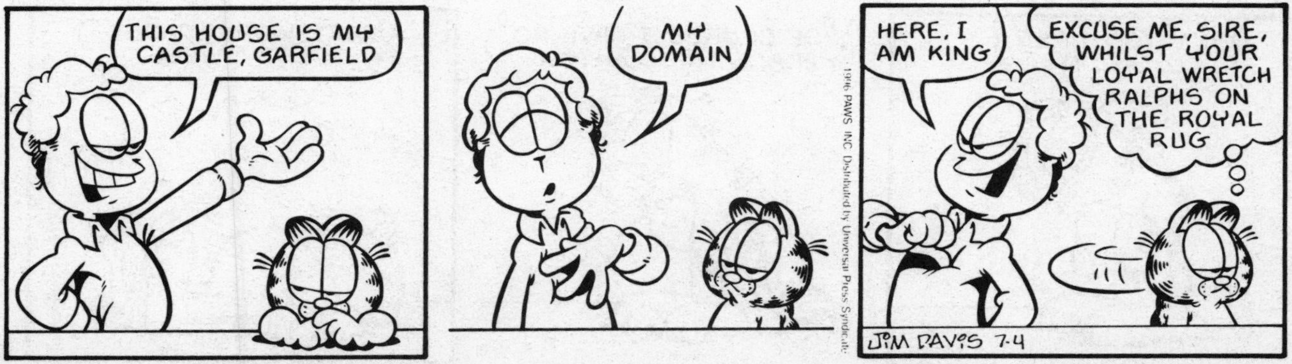
THIS HOUSE IS MY CASTLE, GARFIELD
MY DOMAIN
HERE, I AM KING
EXCUSE ME, SIRE, WHILST YOUR LOYAL WRETCH RALPHS ON THE ROYAL RUG
JIM DAVIS 7-4

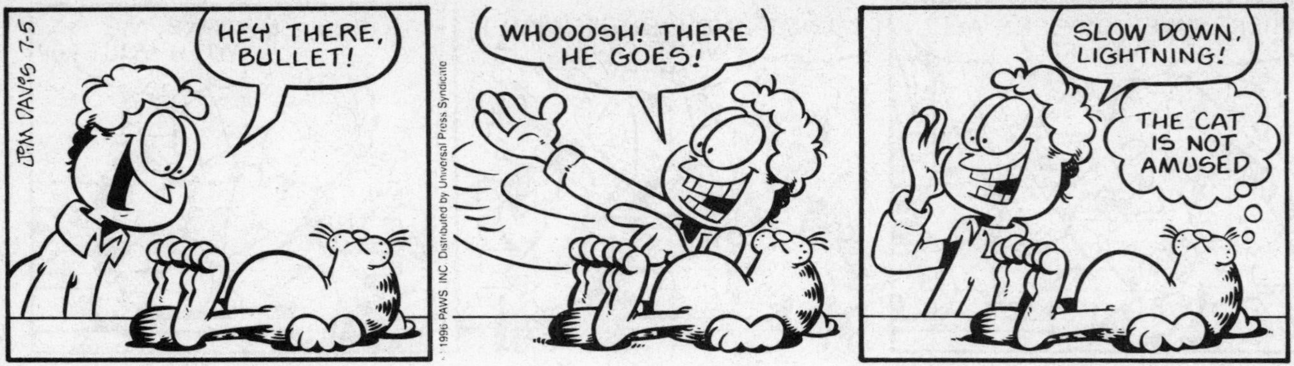
JIM DAVIS 7-5
© 1996 PAWS INC Distributed by Universal Press Syndicate
HEY THERE, BULLET!
WHOOOSH! THERE HE GOES!
SLOW DOWN, LIGHTNING!
THE CAT IS NOT AMUSED

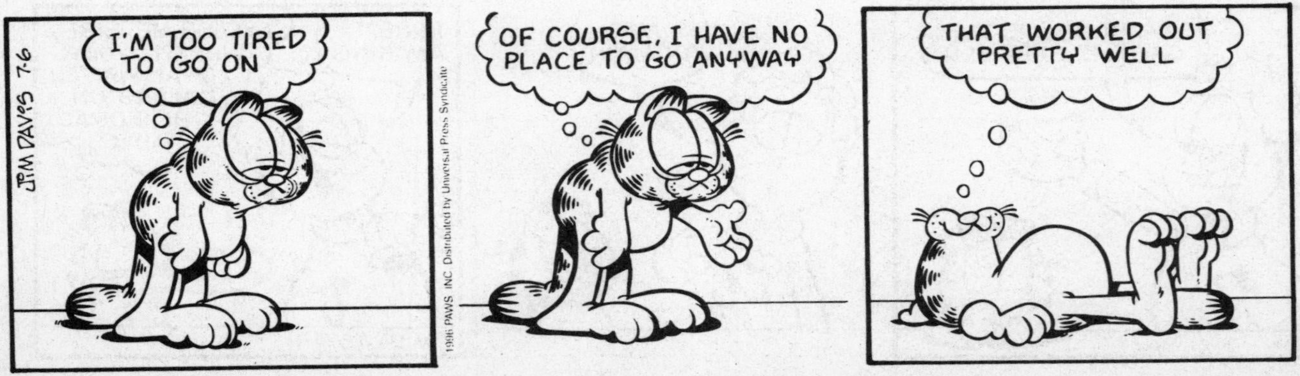
JIM DAVIS 7-6
1996 PAWS INC Distributed by Universal Press Syndicate
I'M TOO TIRED TO GO ON
OF COURSE, I HAVE NO PLACE TO GO ANYWAY
THAT WORKED OUT PRETTY WELL

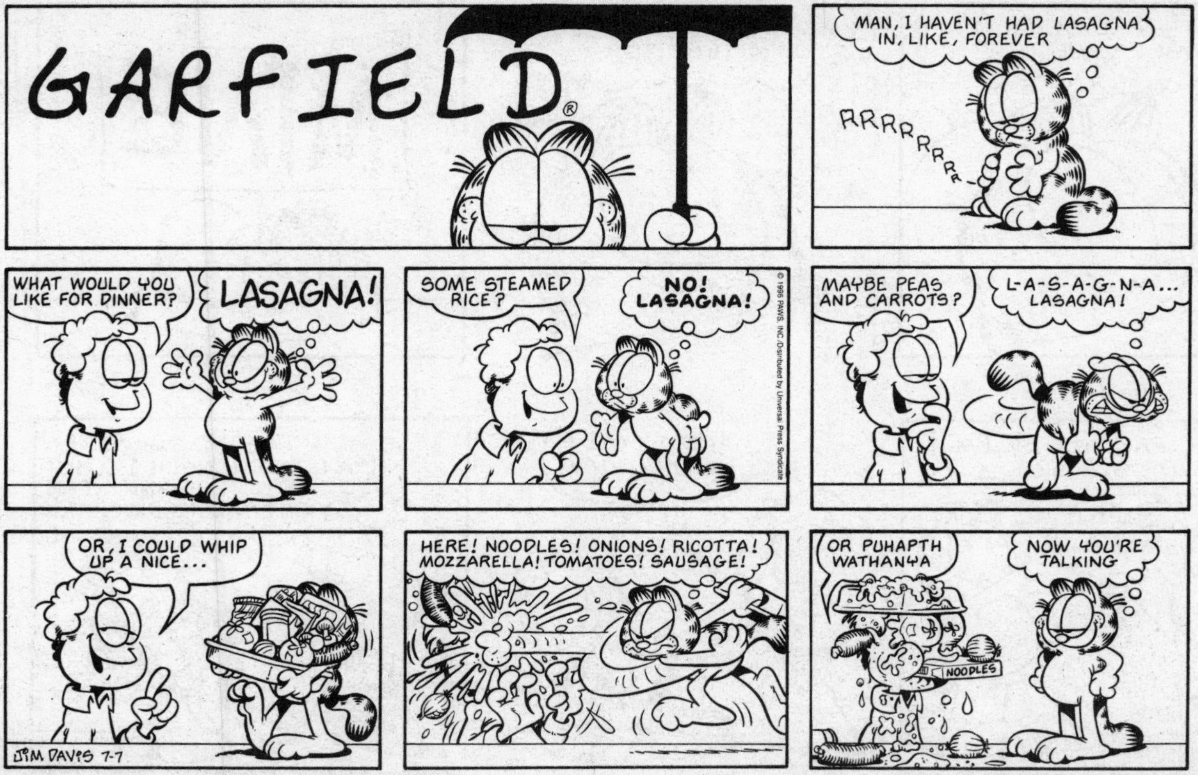
GARFIELD®
MAN, I HAVEN'T HAD LASAGNA IN, LIKE, FOREVER
RRRRRRRRR—
WHAT WOULD YOU LIKE FOR DINNER?
LASAGNA!
SOME STEAMED RICE?
NO! LASAGNA!
© 1995 PAWS, INC./Distributed by Universal Press Syndicate
MAYBE PEAS AND CARROTS?
L-A-S-A-G-N-A... LASAGNA!
OR, I COULD WHIP UP A NICE...
HERE! NOODLES! ONIONS! RICOTTA! MOZZARELLA! TOMATOES! SAUSAGE!
OR PUHAPTH WATHANYA
NOODLES
NOW YOU'RE TALKING
JIM DAVIS 7-7

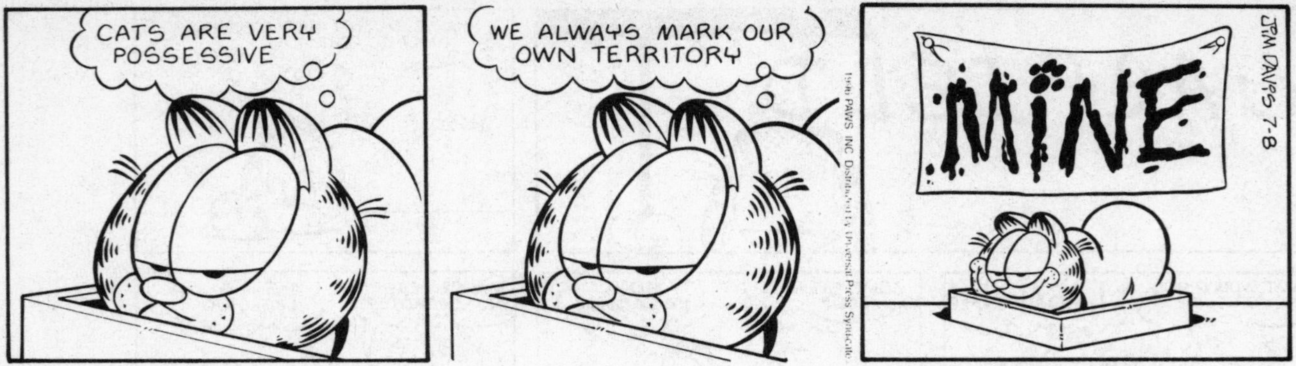
CATS ARE VERY POSSESSIVE
WE ALWAYS MARK OUR OWN TERRITORY
MINE
JIM DAVIS 7-8

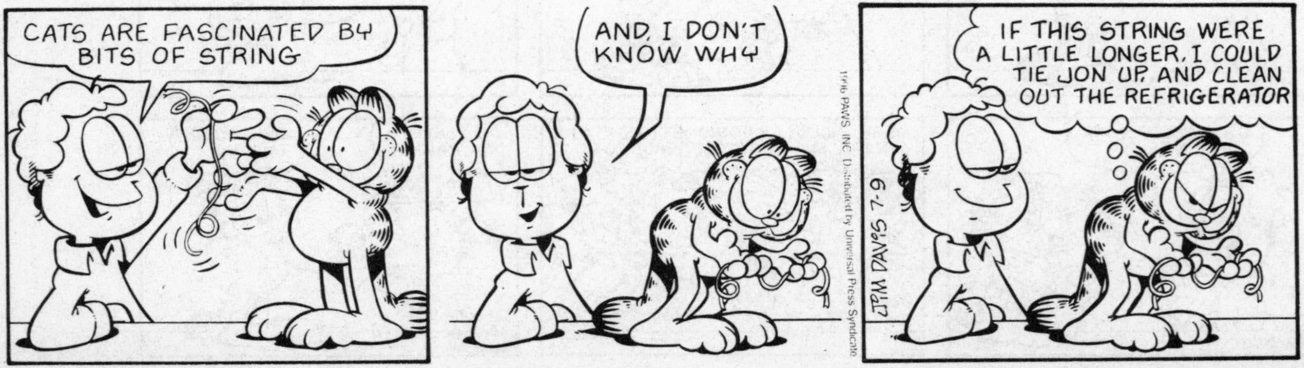
CATS ARE FASCINATED BY BITS OF STRING
AND, I DON'T KNOW WHY
IF THIS STRING WERE A LITTLE LONGER, I COULD TIE JON UP, AND CLEAN OUT THE REFRIGERATOR
JIM DAVIS 7-9

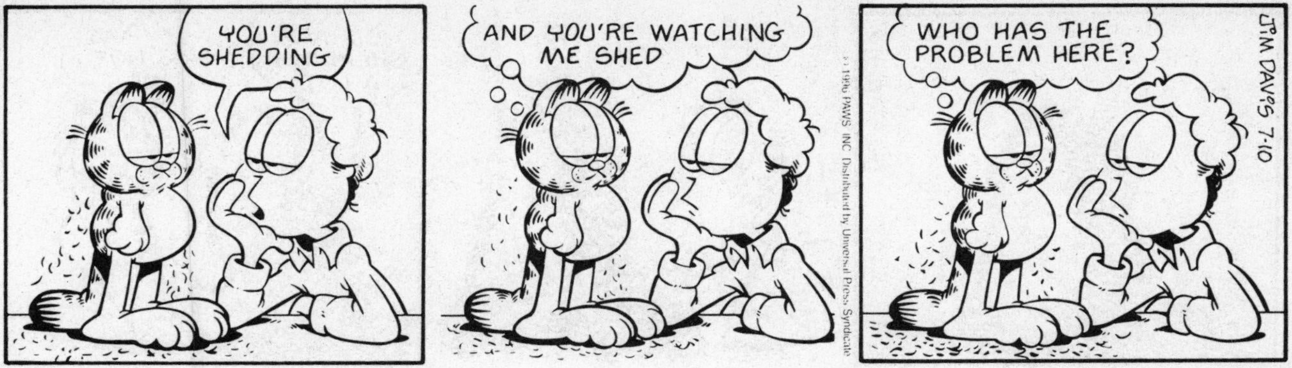
YOU'RE SHEDDING
AND YOU'RE WATCHING ME SHED
WHO HAS THE PROBLEM HERE?
JIM DAVIS 7-10
© 1996 PAWS INC Distributed by Universal Press Syndicate

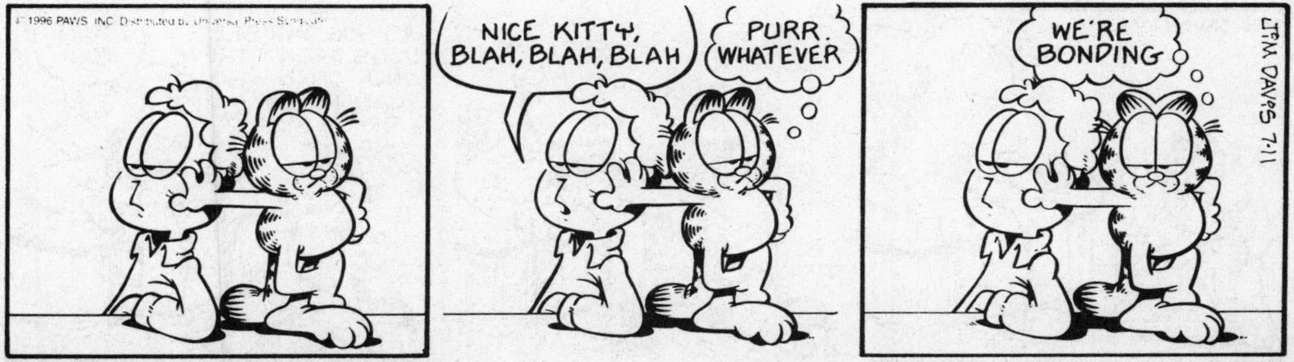
NICE KITTY, BLAH, BLAH, BLAH
PURR. WHATEVER
WE'RE BONDING
JIM DAVIS 7-11

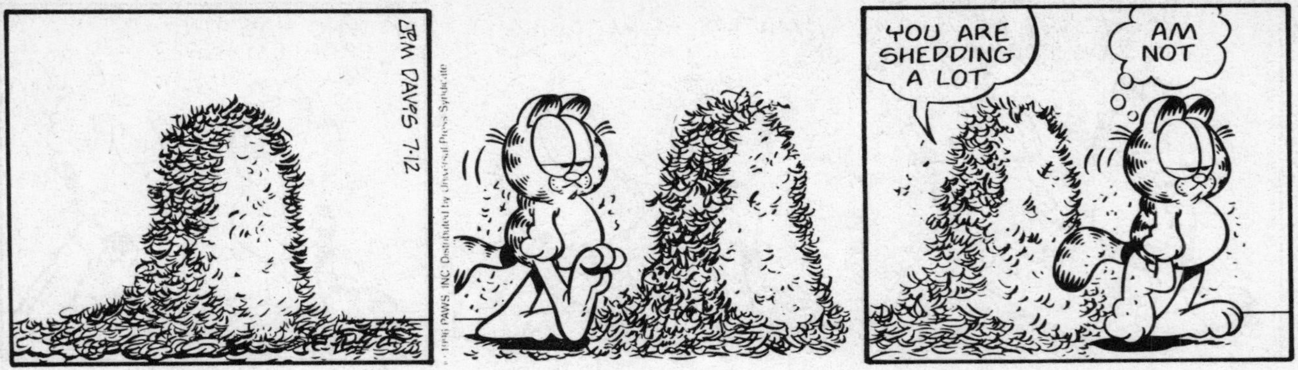
JIM DAVIS 7-12
YOU ARE SHEDDING A LOT
AM NOT

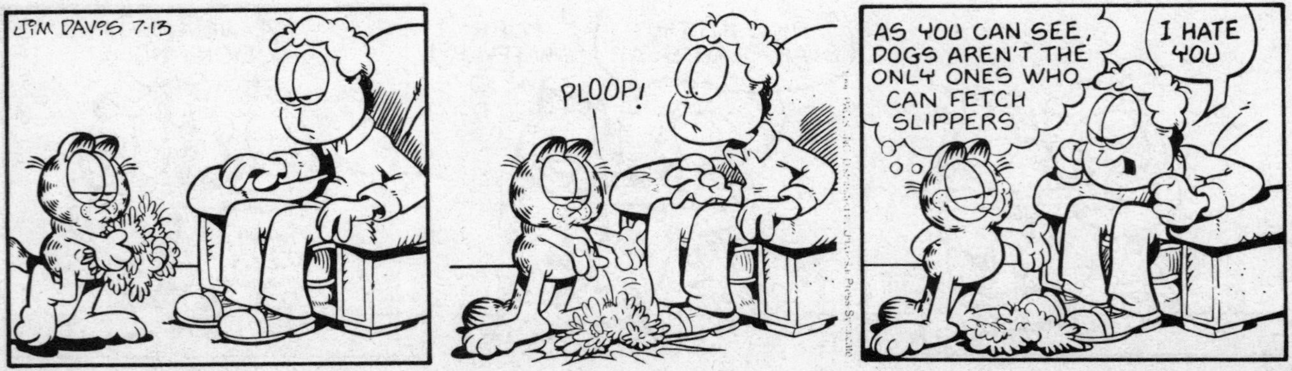
JIM DAVIS 7-13
PLOOP!
AS YOU CAN SEE, DOGS AREN'T THE ONLY ONES WHO CAN FETCH SLIPPERS
I HATE YOU

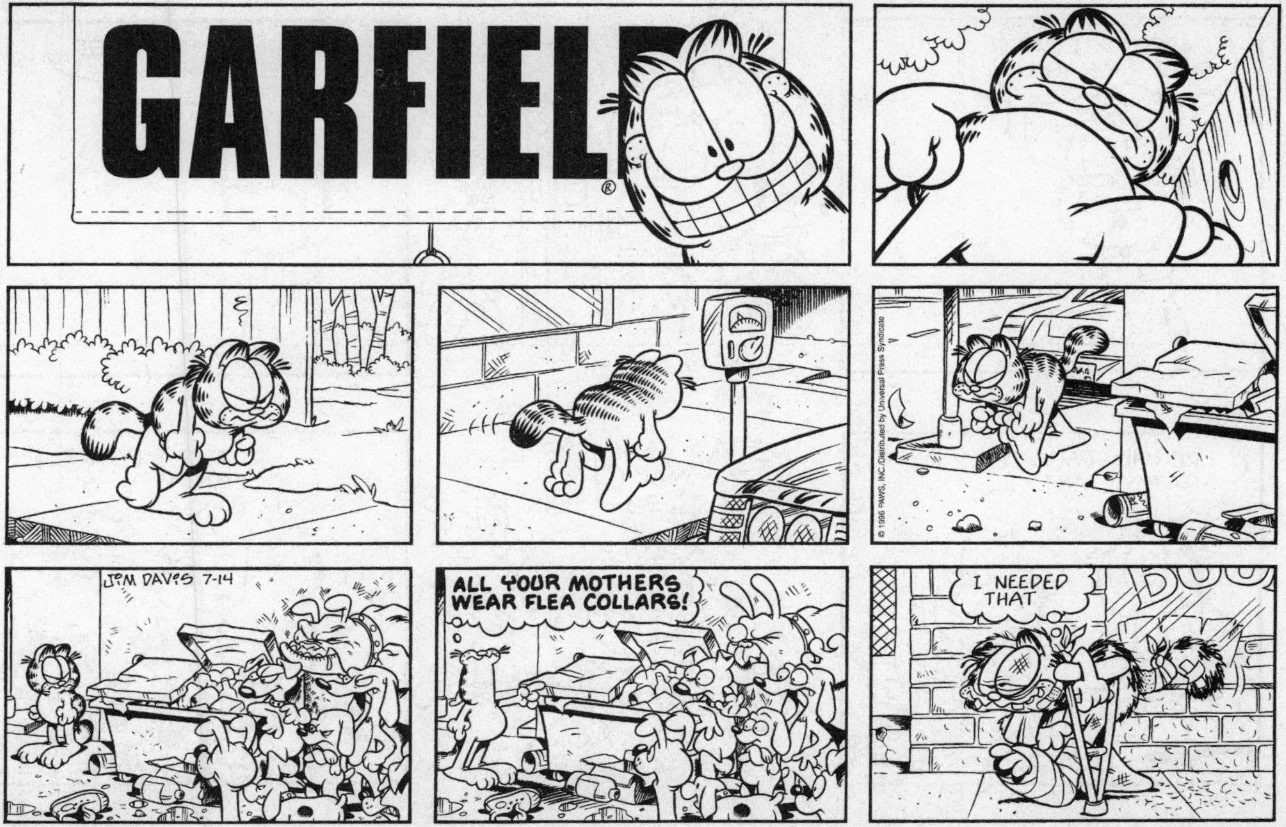
GARFIELD
© 1996 PAWS, INC./Distributed by Universal Press Syndicate
JIM DAVIS 7-14
ALL YOUR MOTHERS WEAR FLEA COLLARS!
I NEEDED THAT

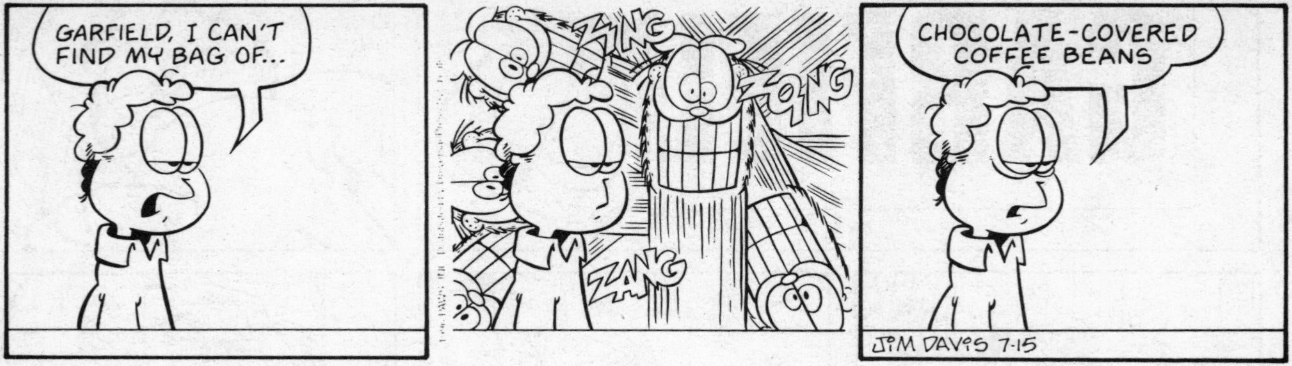
GARFIELD, I CAN'T FIND MY BAG OF...
ZING
ZONG
ZANG
CHOCOLATE-COVERED COFFEE BEANS
JIM DAVIS 7-15

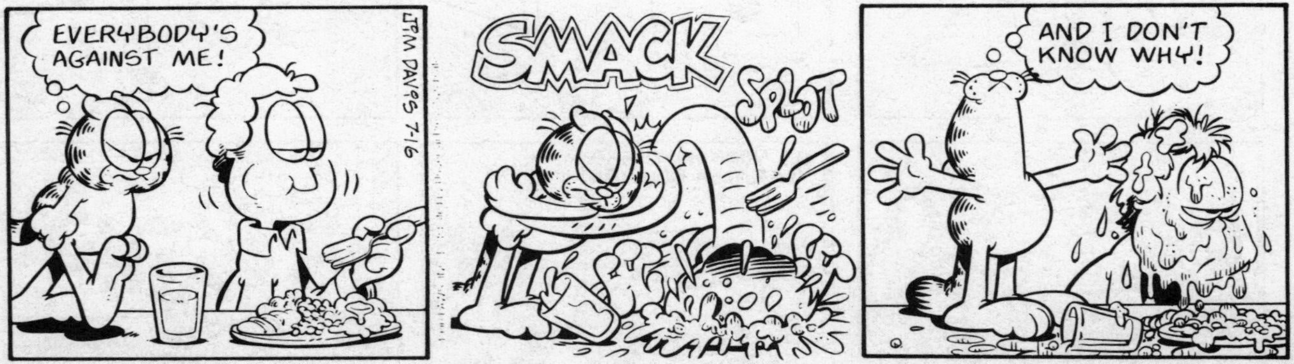
EVERYBODY'S AGAINST ME!
JIM DAVIS 7-16
SMACK
SPLOT
AND I DON'T KNOW WHY!

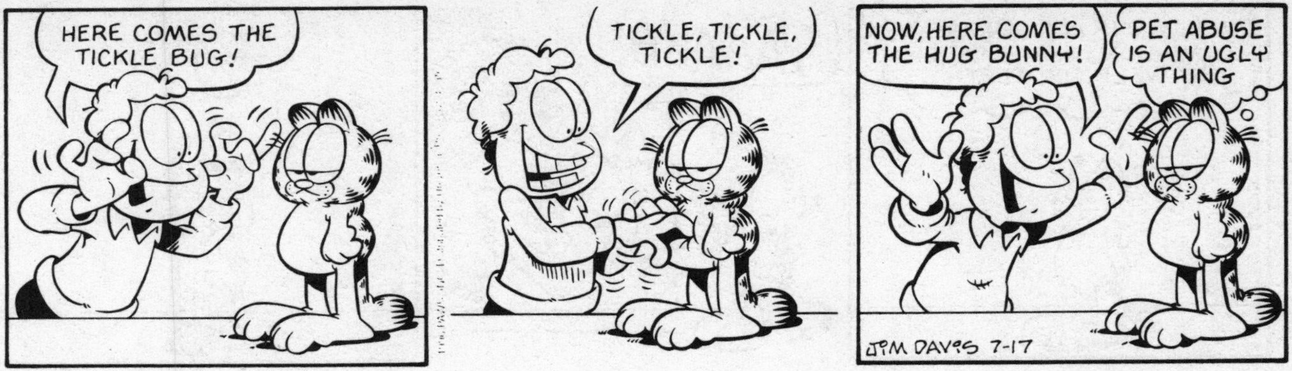
HERE COMES THE TICKLE BUG!
TICKLE, TICKLE, TICKLE!
NOW, HERE COMES THE HUG BUNNY!
PET ABUSE IS AN UGLY THING
JIM DAVIS 7-17

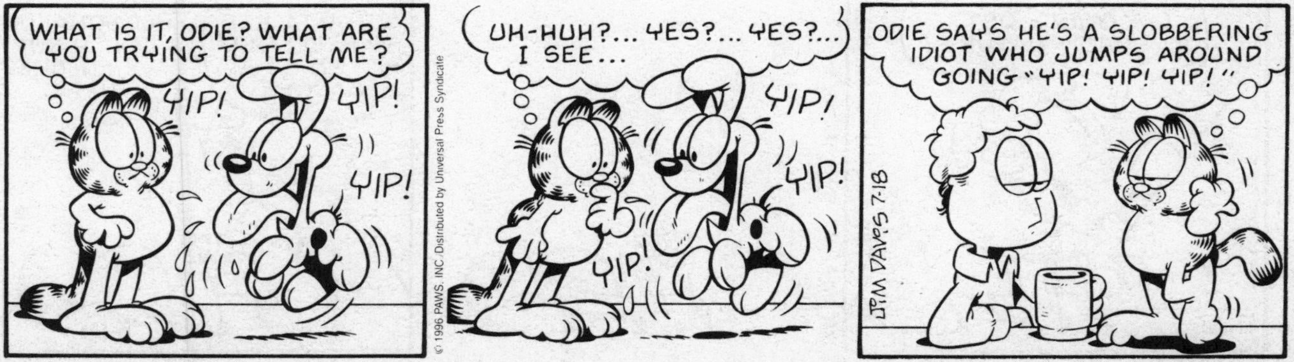
WHAT IS IT, ODIE? WHAT ARE YOU TRYING TO TELL ME?
YIP!
YIP!
YIP!
UH-HUH?... YES?... YES?... I SEE...
YIP!
YIP!
YIP!
ODIE SAYS HE'S A SLOBBERING IDIOT WHO JUMPS AROUND GOING "YIP! YIP! YIP!"
JIM DAVIS 7-18

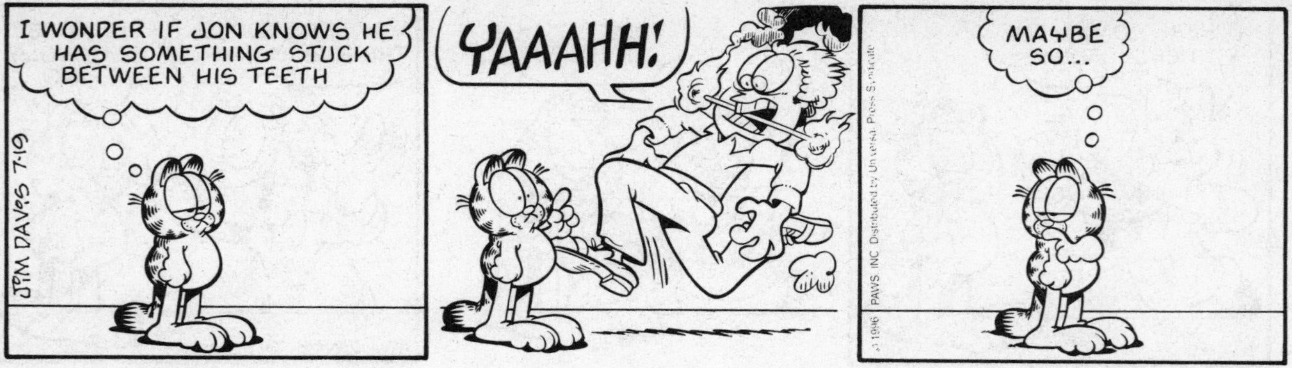
I WONDER IF JON KNOWS HE HAS SOMETHING STUCK BETWEEN HIS TEETH
YAAAHH!
MAYBE SO...
© 1996 PAWS INC Distributed by Universal Press Syndicate

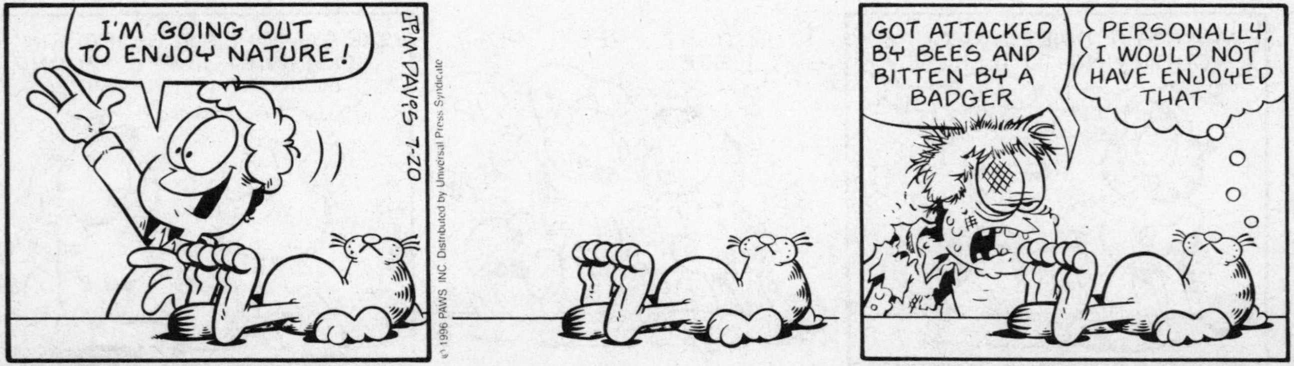
I'M GOING OUT TO ENJOY NATURE!
© 1996 PAWS INC Distributed by Universal Press Syndicate
GOT ATTACKED BY BEES AND BITTEN BY A BADGER
PERSONALLY, I WOULD NOT HAVE ENJOYED THAT

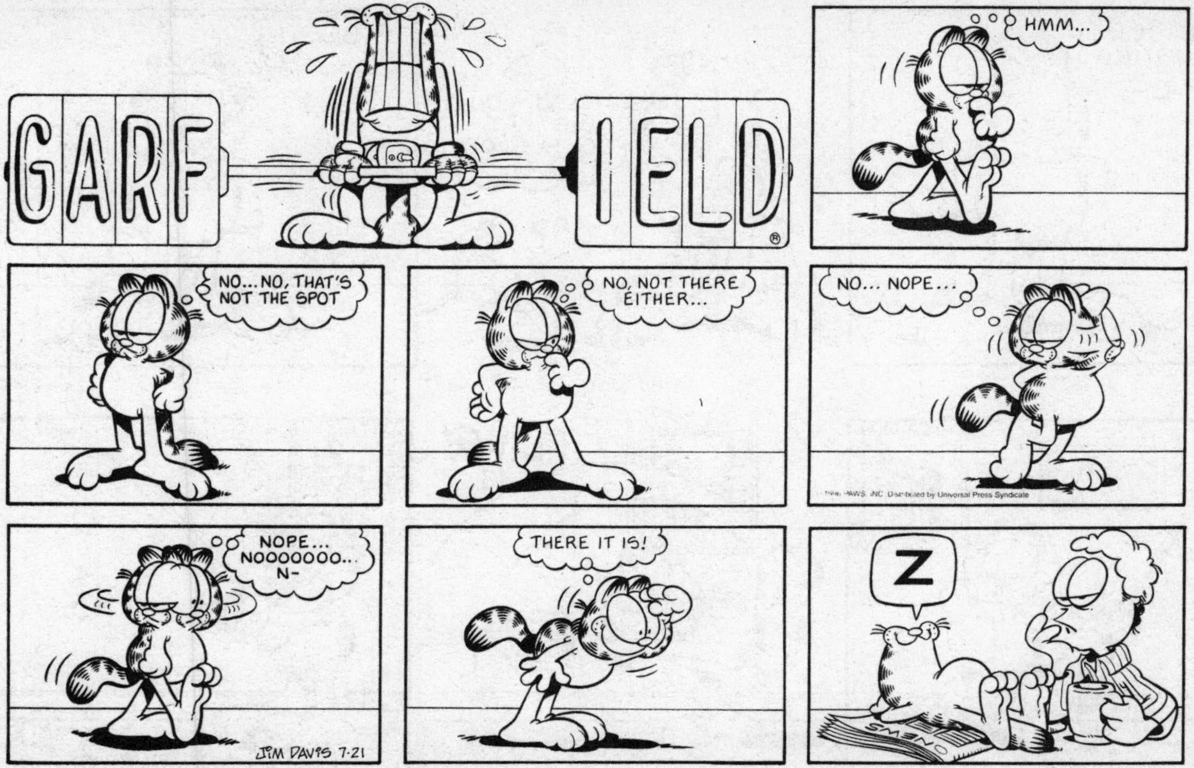
GARF
IELD
HMM...
NO...NO, THAT'S NOT THE SPOT
NO, NOT THERE EITHER...
NO... NOPE...
PAWS, INC. Distributed by Universal Press Syndicate
NOPE... NOOOOOOO... N-
JIM DAVIS 7-21
THERE IT IS!
Z
NEWS

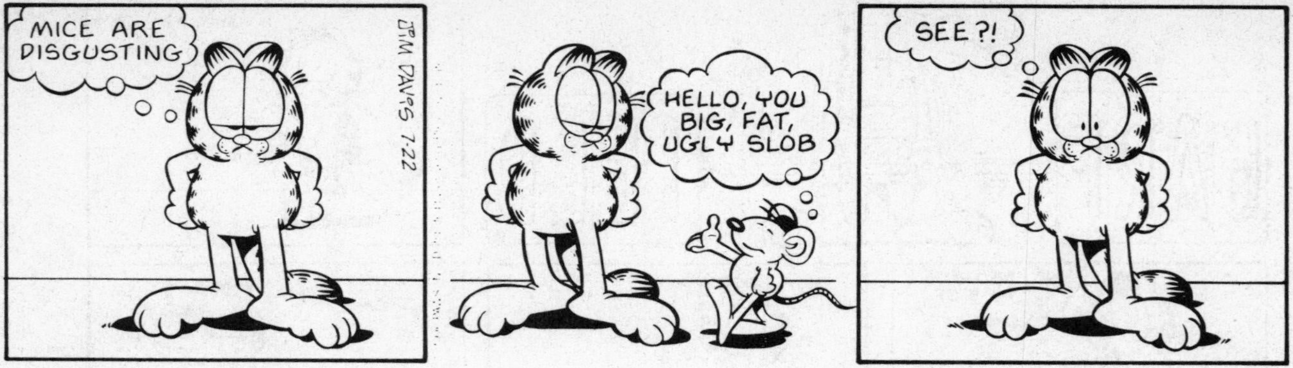
MICE ARE DISGUSTING
JIM DAVIS 7-22
HELLO, YOU BIG, FAT, UGLY SLOB
SEE?!

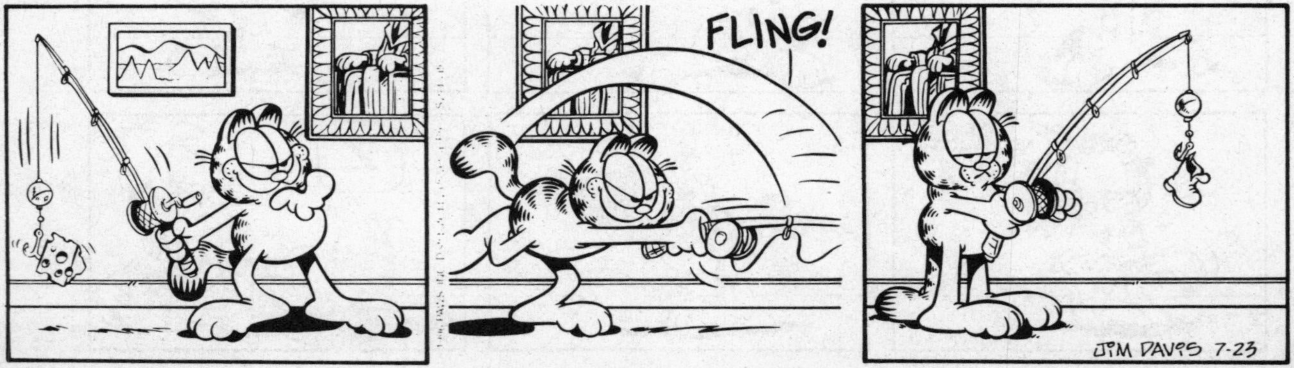
FLING!
JIM DAVIS 7-23

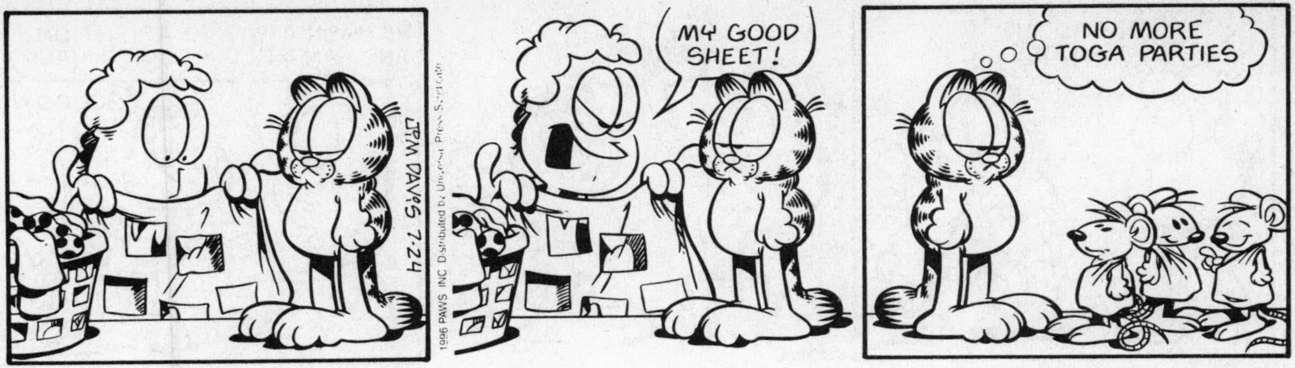
JIM DAVIS 7-24
1996 PAWS INC Distributed by Universal Press Syndicate
MY GOOD SHEET!
NO MORE TOGA PARTIES

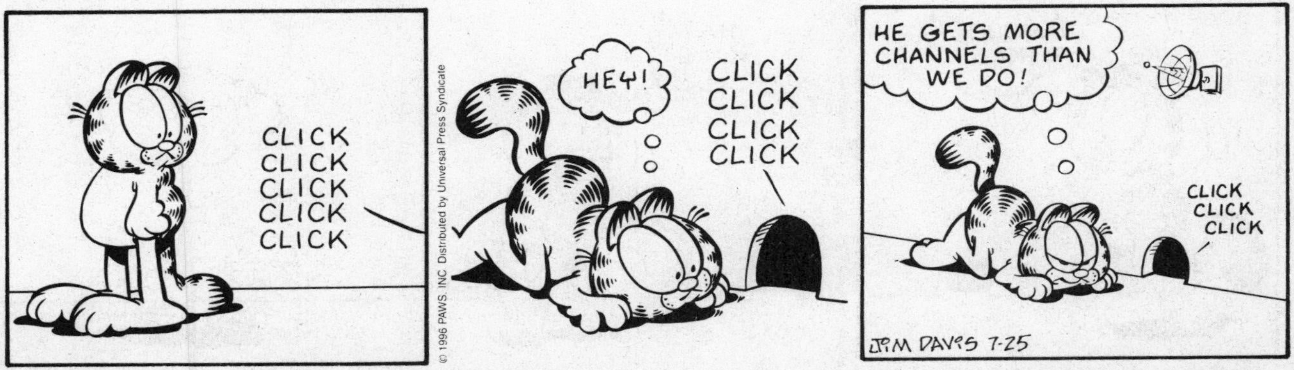
CLICK CLICK CLICK CLICK CLICK
© 1996 PAWS, INC Distributed by Universal Press Syndicate
HEY!
CLICK CLICK CLICK CLICK
HE GETS MORE CHANNELS THAN WE DO!
CLICK CLICK CLICK
JIM DAVIS 7-25

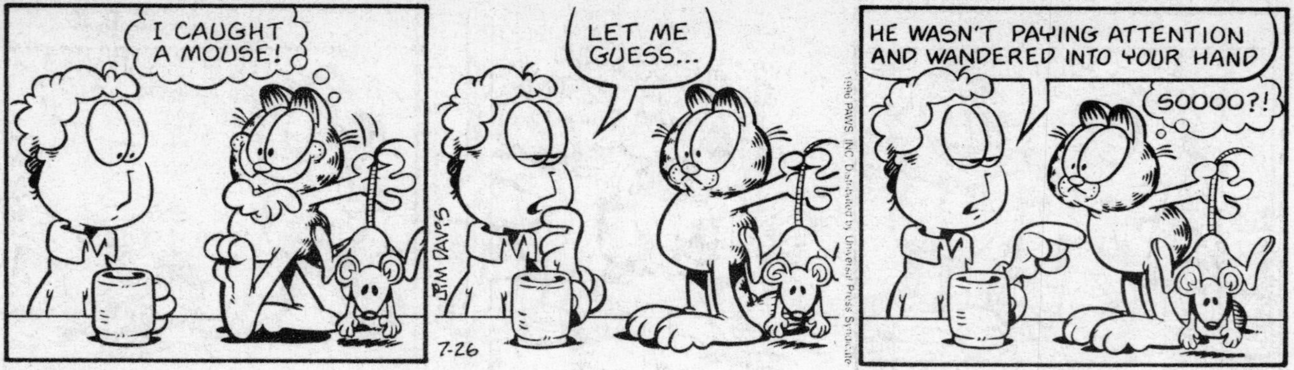
I CAUGHT A MOUSE!
LET ME GUESS...
HE WASN'T PAYING ATTENTION AND WANDERED INTO YOUR HAND
SOOOO?!
JIM DAVIS
7-26

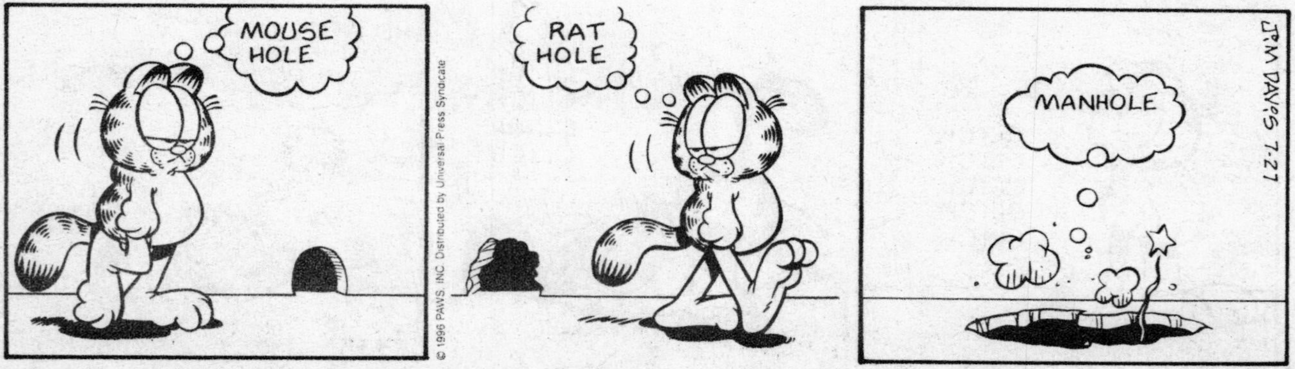
MOUSE HOLE
RAT HOLE
MANHOLE
JIM DAVIS 7-27

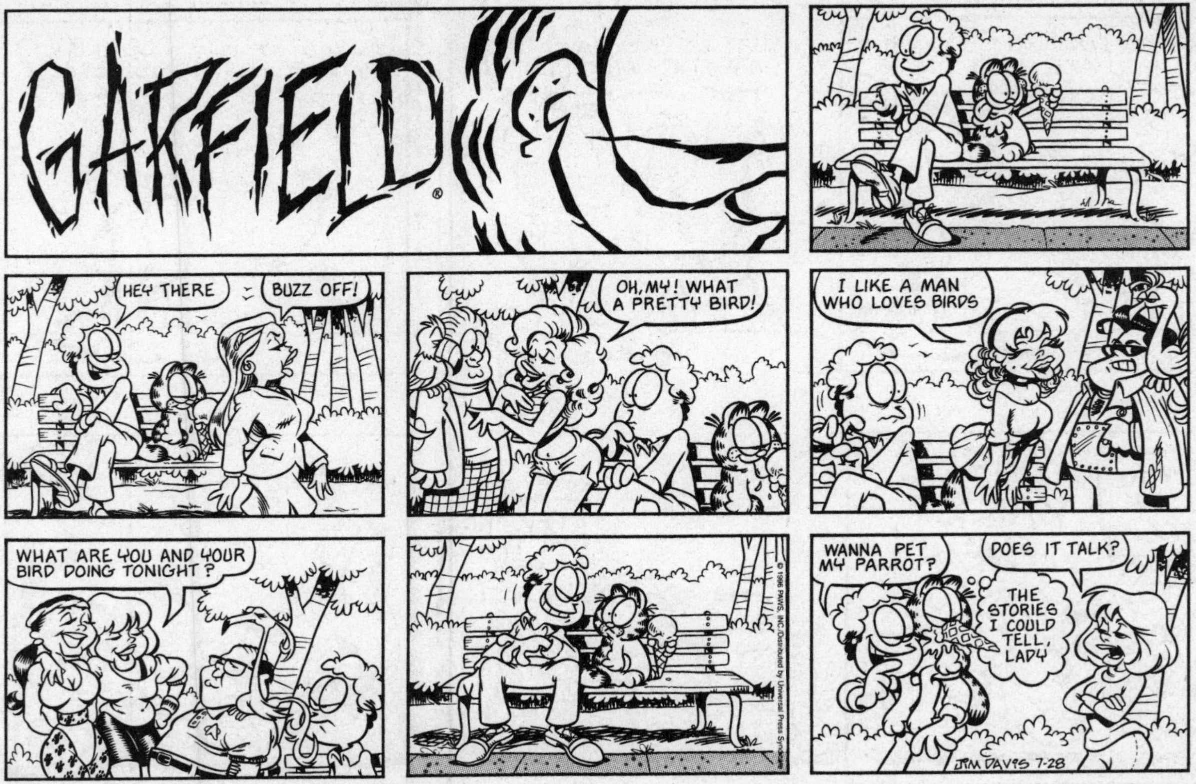
GARFIELD®
HEY THERE
BUZZ OFF!
OH, MY! WHAT A PRETTY BIRD!
I LIKE A MAN WHO LOVES BIRDS
WHAT ARE YOU AND YOUR BIRD DOING TONIGHT?
© 1996 PAWS, INC./Distributed by Universal Press Syndicate
WANNA PET MY PARROT?
DOES IT TALK?
THE STORIES I COULD TELL, LADY
JIM DAVIS 7-28

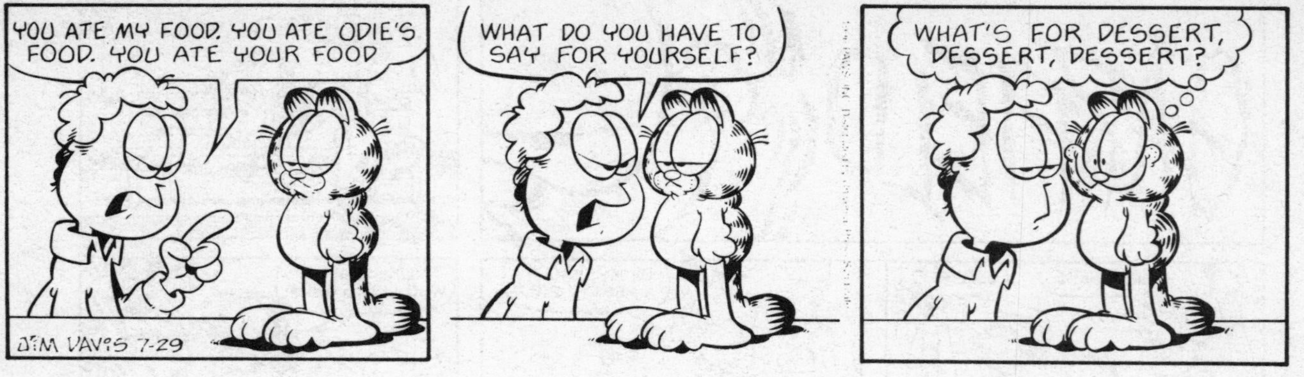
YOU ATE MY FOOD. YOU ATE ODIE'S FOOD. YOU ATE YOUR FOOD
JIM DAVIS 7-29
WHAT DO YOU HAVE TO SAY FOR YOURSELF?
WHAT'S FOR DESSERT, DESSERT, DESSERT?

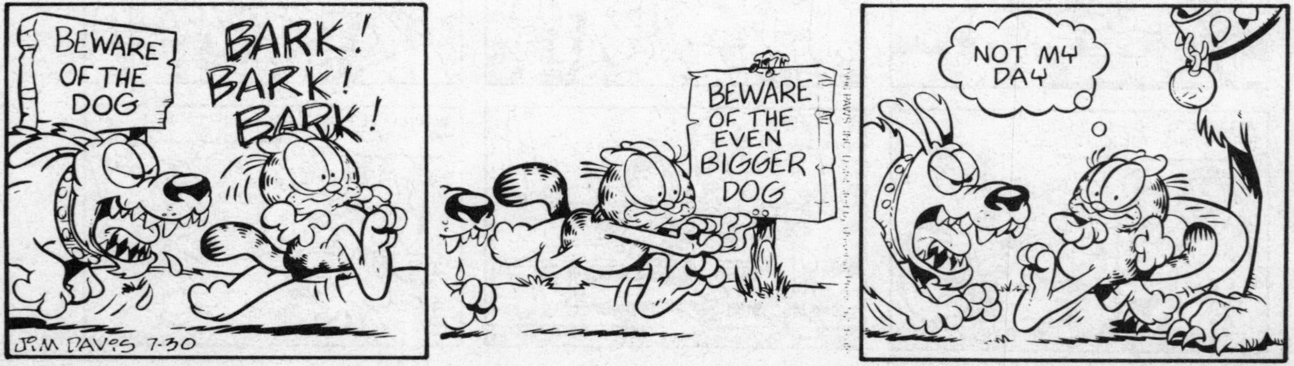
BEWARE OF THE DOG
BARK! BARK! BARK!
JIM DAVIS 7-30
BEWARE OF THE EVEN BIGGER DOG
NOT MY DAY

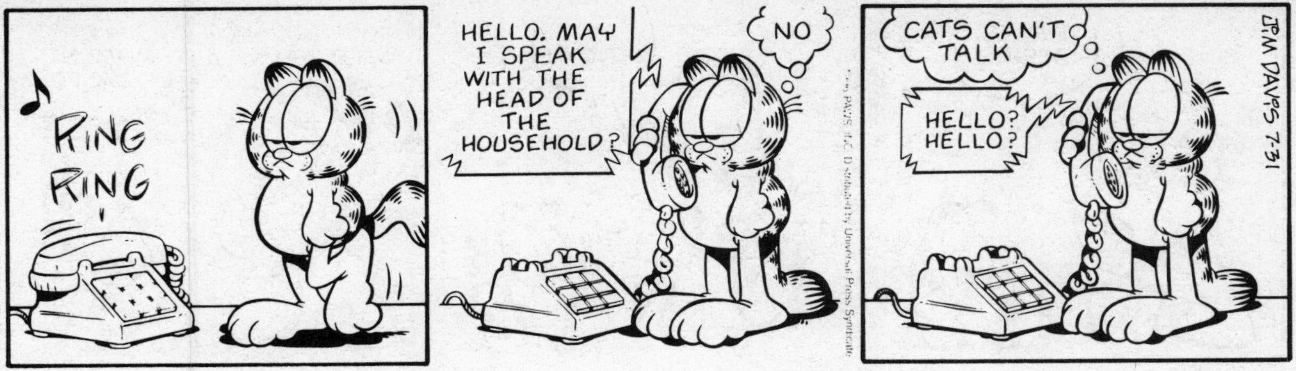
RING
RING
HELLO. MAY I SPEAK WITH THE HEAD OF THE HOUSEHOLD?
NO
HELLO? HELLO?
CATS CAN'T TALK
JIM DAVIS 7-31

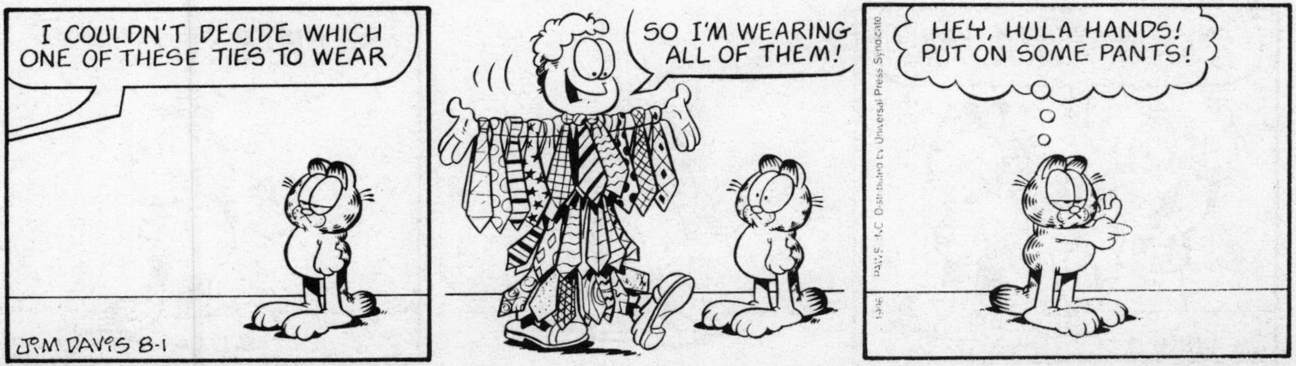
I COULDN'T DECIDE WHICH ONE OF THESE TIES TO WEAR
SO I'M WEARING ALL OF THEM!
HEY, HULA HANDS! PUT ON SOME PANTS!
JIM DAVIS 8-1

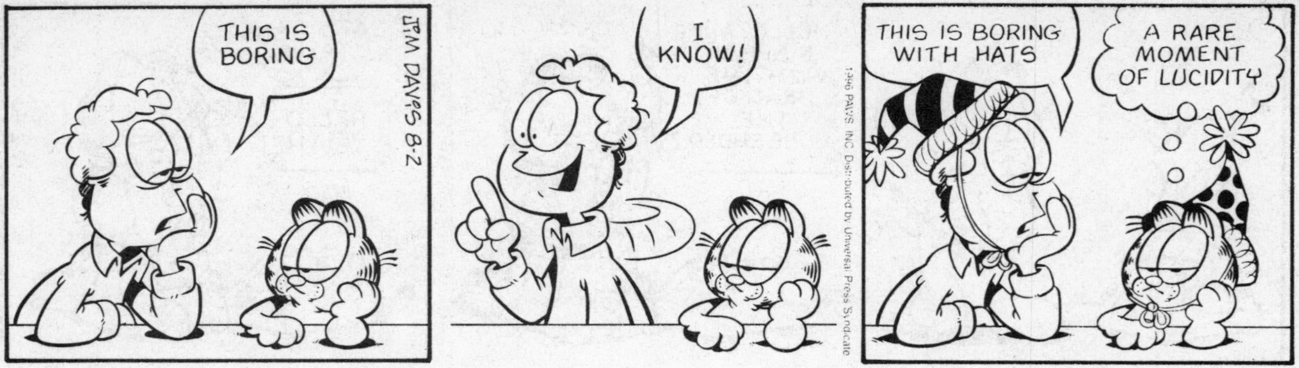
THIS IS BORING
JIM DAVIS 8-2
I KNOW!
THIS IS BORING WITH HATS
A RARE MOMENT OF LUCIDITY

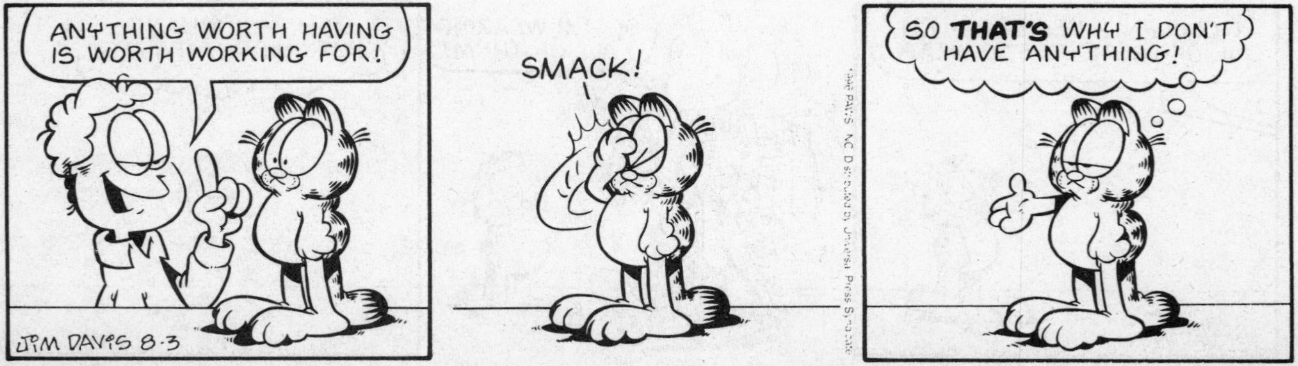
ANYTHING WORTH HAVING IS WORTH WORKING FOR!
JIM DAVIS 8-3
SMACK!
SO **THAT'S** WHY I DON'T HAVE ANYTHING!

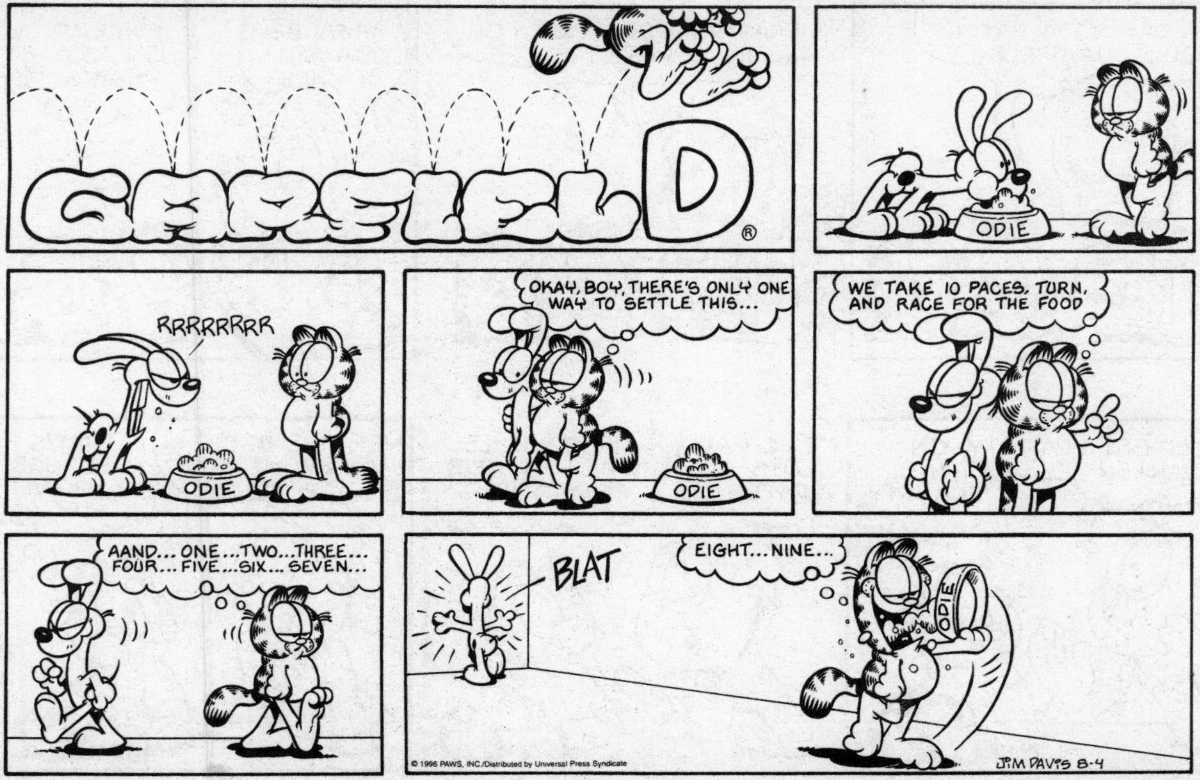
GARFIELD
ODIE
RRRRRRRR
ODIE
OKAY, BOY, THERE'S ONLY ONE WAY TO SETTLE THIS...
ODIE
WE TAKE 10 PACES, TURN, AND RACE FOR THE FOOD
AAND... ONE...TWO...THREE... FOUR... FIVE...SIX... SEVEN...
BLAT
EIGHT... NINE...
ODIE
© 1996 PAWS, INC./Distributed by Universal Press Syndicate
JIM DAVIS 8-4

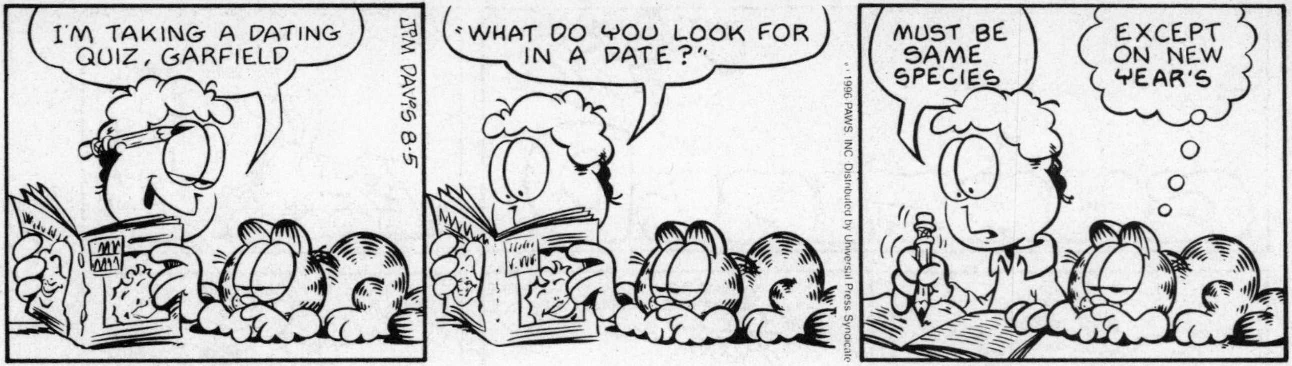
I'M TAKING A DATING QUIZ, GARFIELD
JIM DAVIS 8-5
"WHAT DO YOU LOOK FOR IN A DATE?"
© 1996 PAWS, INC Distributed by Universal Press Syndicate
MUST BE SAME SPECIES
EXCEPT ON NEW YEAR'S

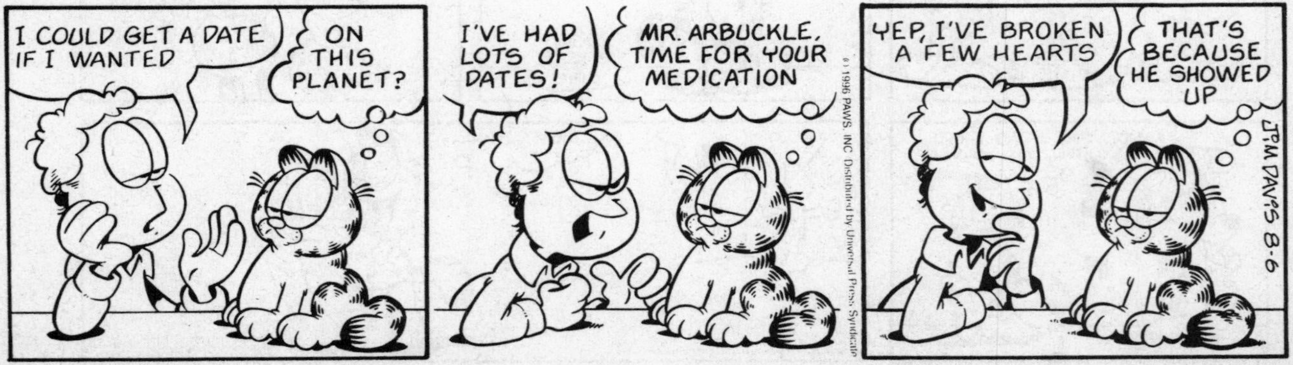
I COULD GET A DATE IF I WANTED
ON THIS PLANET?
I'VE HAD LOTS OF DATES!
MR. ARBUCKLE, TIME FOR YOUR MEDICATION
© 1996 PAWS, INC Distributed by Universal Press Syndicate
YEP, I'VE BROKEN A FEW HEARTS
THAT'S BECAUSE HE SHOWED UP
JIM DAVIS 8-6

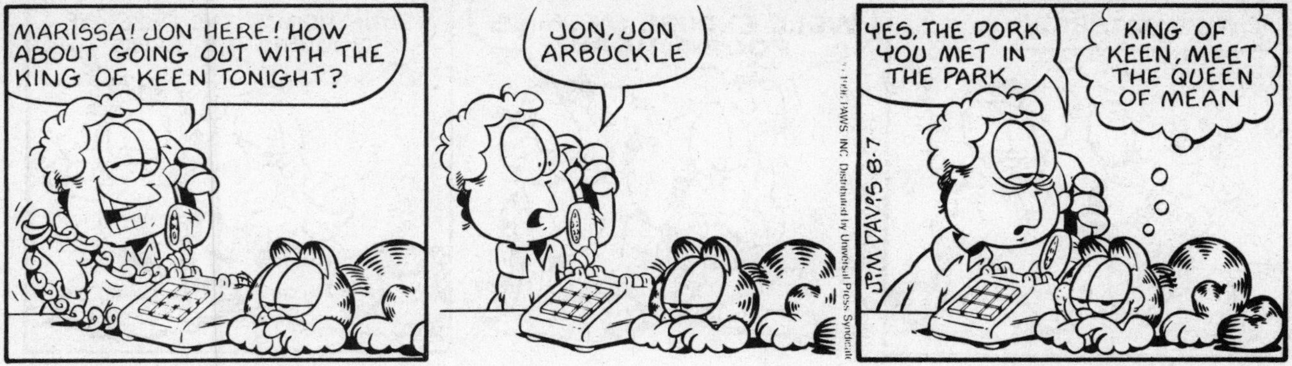
MARISSA! JON HERE! HOW ABOUT GOING OUT WITH THE KING OF KEEN TONIGHT?
JON, JON ARBUCKLE
YES, THE DORK YOU MET IN THE PARK
KING OF KEEN, MEET THE QUEEN OF MEAN
JIM DAVIS 8·7

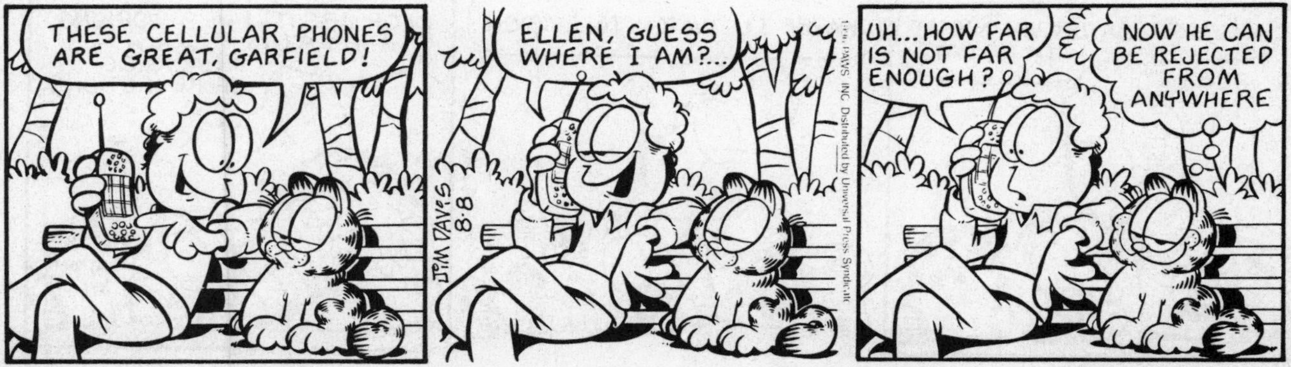
THESE CELLULAR PHONES ARE GREAT, GARFIELD!
ELLEN, GUESS WHERE I AM?...
UH... HOW FAR IS NOT FAR ENOUGH?
NOW HE CAN BE REJECTED FROM ANYWHERE
JIM DAVIS 8·8

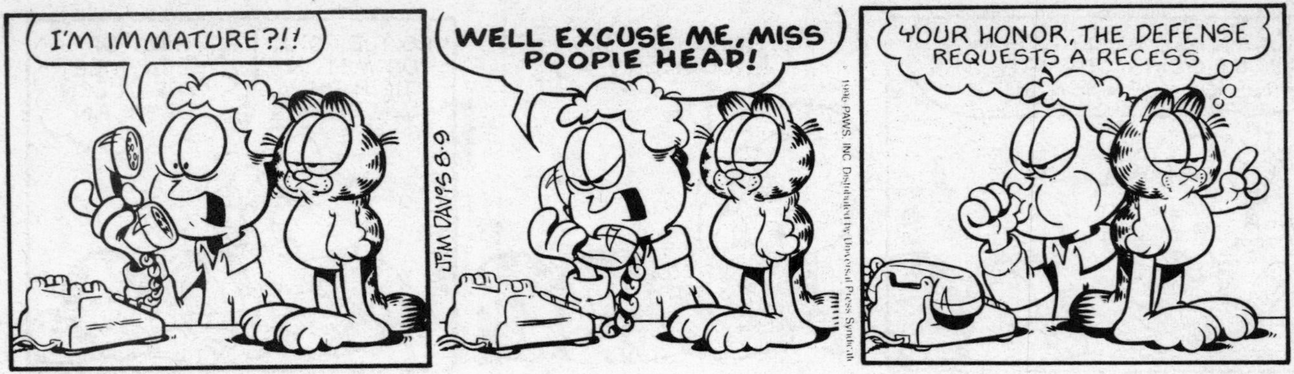
I'M IMMATURE?!!
JIM DAVIS 8-9
WELL EXCUSE ME, MISS POOPIE HEAD!
© 1986 PAWS, INC. Distributed by Universal Press Syndicate
YOUR HONOR, THE DEFENSE REQUESTS A RECESS

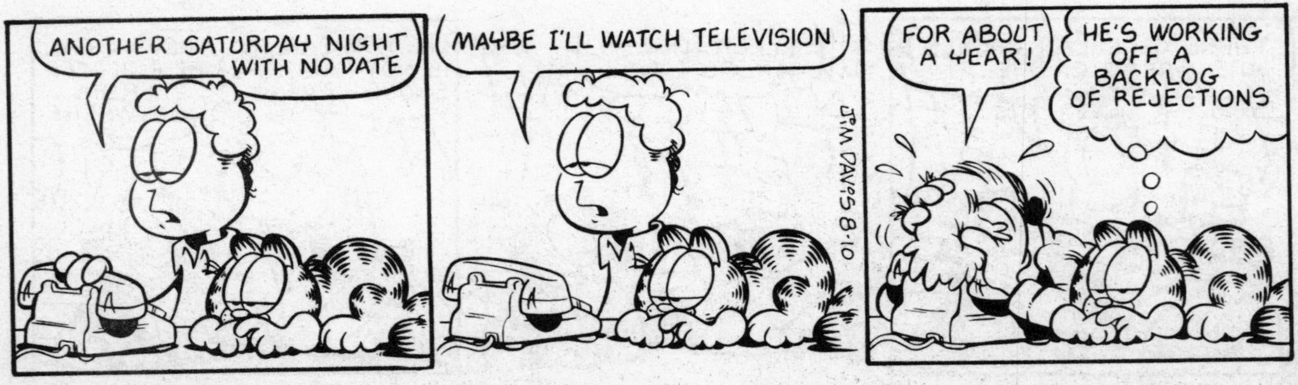
ANOTHER SATURDAY NIGHT WITH NO DATE
MAYBE I'LL WATCH TELEVISION
JIM DAVIS 8-10
FOR ABOUT A YEAR!
HE'S WORKING OFF A BACKLOG OF REJECTIONS

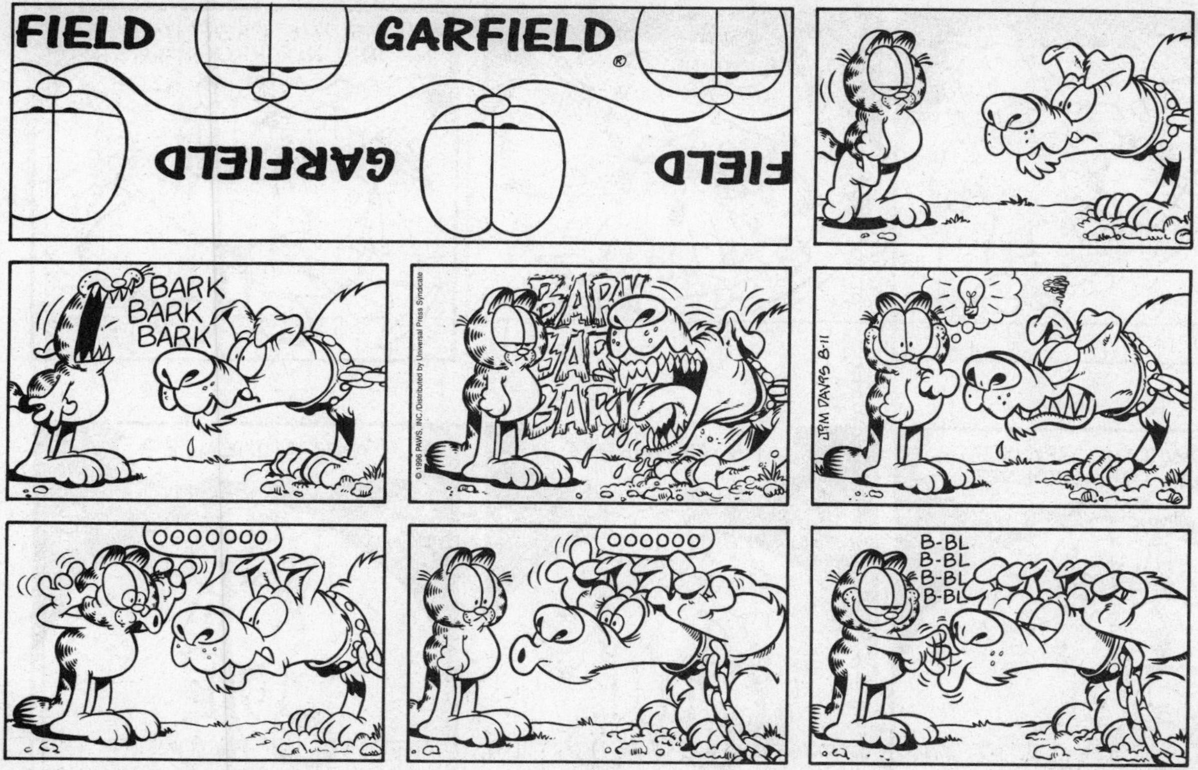
FIELD
GARFIELD
BARK
BARK
BARK
BARK
BARK
BARK
© 1996 PAWS, INC./Distributed by Universal Press Syndicate
JPM DAVPS 8-11
OOOOOOO
OOOOOO
B-BL
B-BL
B-BL
B-BL

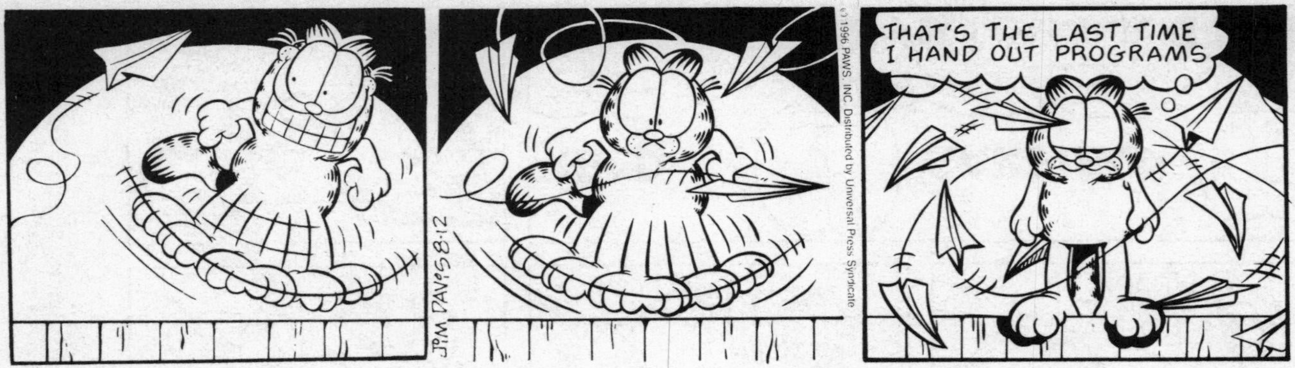
JIM DAVIS 8·12
© 1996 PAWS, INC. Distributed by Universal Press Syndicate
THAT'S THE LAST TIME I HAND OUT PROGRAMS

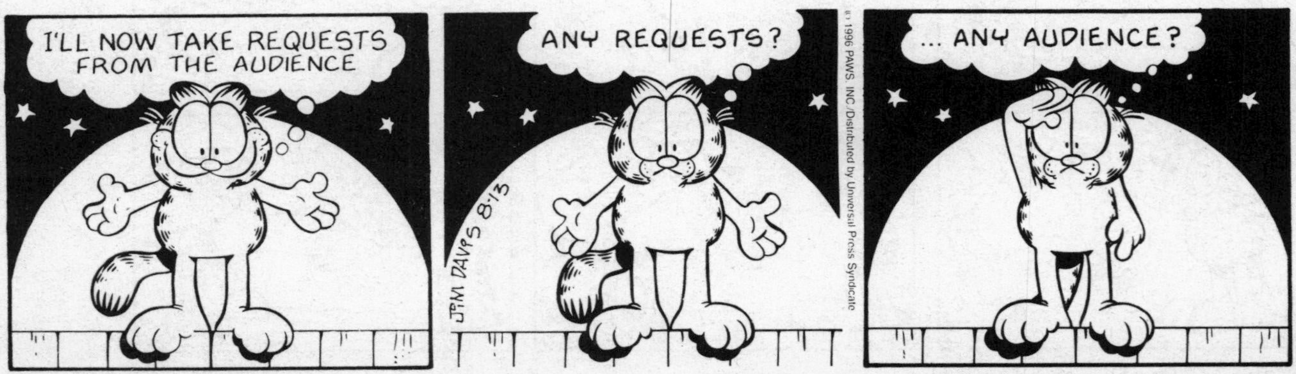
I'LL NOW TAKE REQUESTS FROM THE AUDIENCE
JIM DAVIS 8·13
ANY REQUESTS?
© 1996 PAWS, INC./Distributed by Universal Press Syndicate
... ANY AUDIENCE?

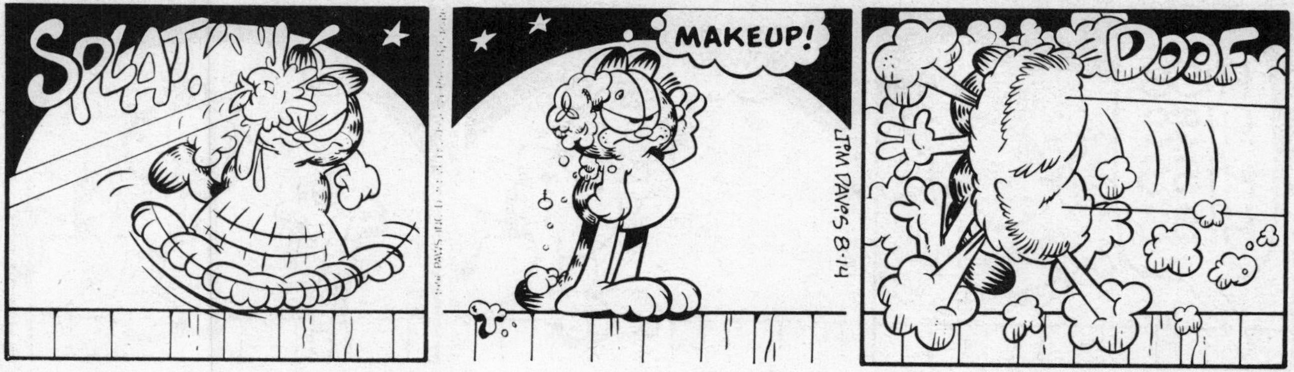
SPLAT!
MAKEUP!
JIM DAVIS 8-14
DOOF

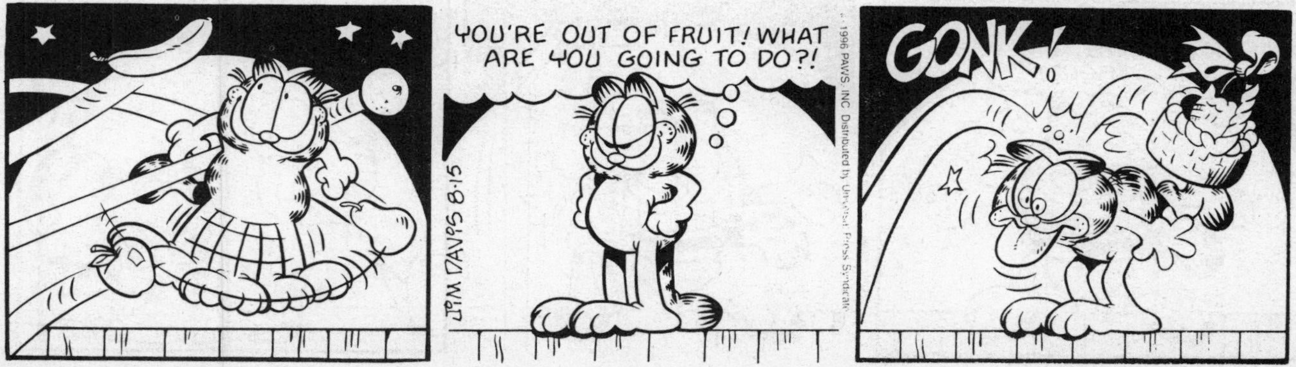
JIM DAVIS 8-15
YOU'RE OUT OF FRUIT! WHAT ARE YOU GOING TO DO?!
© 1996 PAWS, INC Distributed by Universal Press Syndicate
GONK!

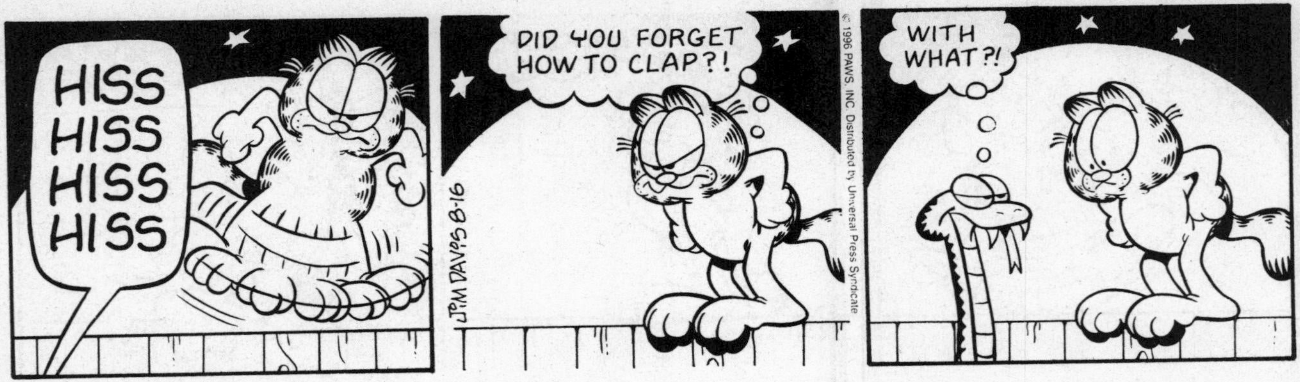
HISS HISS HISS HISS
DID YOU FORGET HOW TO CLAP?!
WITH WHAT?!
JIM DAVIS 8-16
© 1996 PAWS, INC. Distributed by Universal Press Syndicate

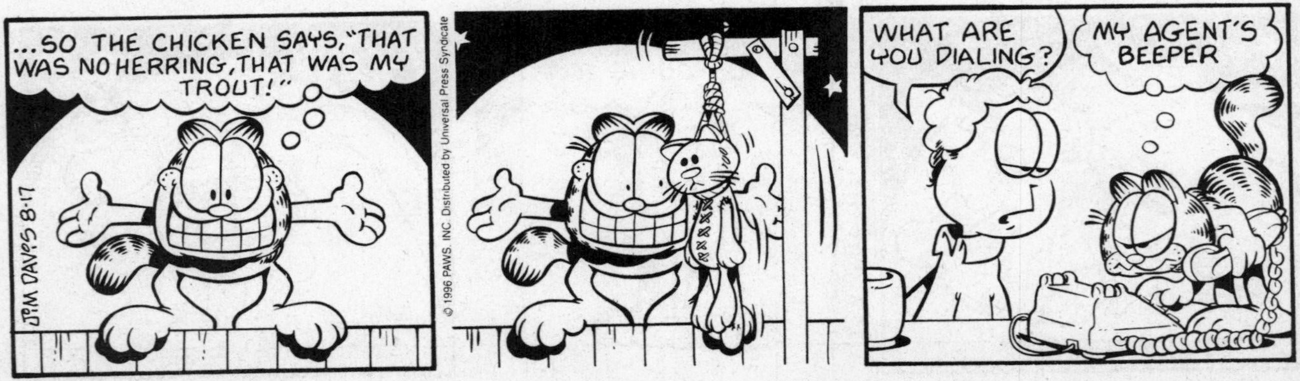
...SO THE CHICKEN SAYS, "THAT WAS NO HERRING, THAT WAS MY TROUT!"
WHAT ARE YOU DIALING?
MY AGENT'S BEEPER
JIM DAVIS 8-17
© 1996 PAWS, INC. Distributed by Universal Press Syndicate

DON'T EAT THAT POOR, DEFENSELESS DOUGHNUT!

DON'T LISTEN TO HIM! CHOW DOWN, PAL!

DO WHAT IS RIGHT! DO WHAT'S IN YOUR HEART!

© 1996 PAWS, INC./Distributed by Universal Press Syndicate

JIM DAVIS 8-18

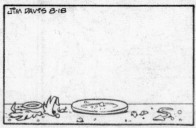

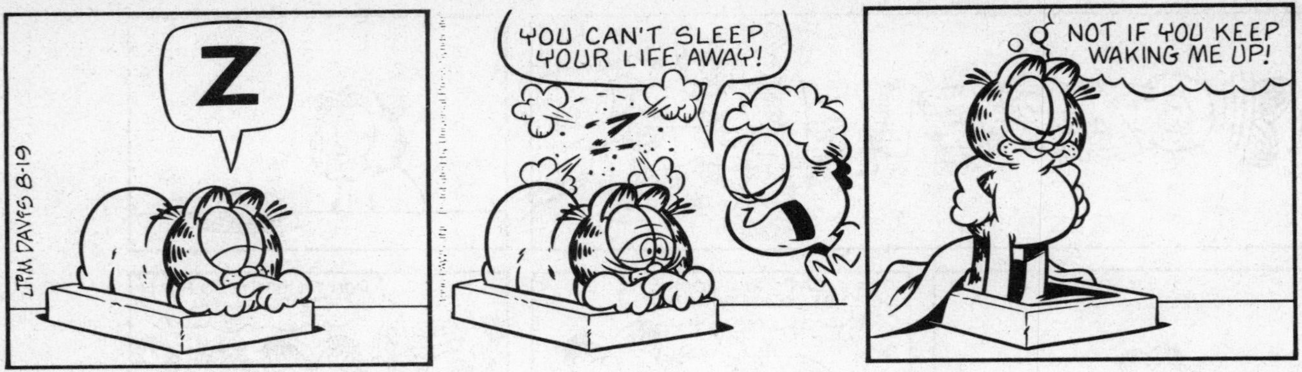
Z
JIM DAVIS 8-19
YOU CAN'T SLEEP YOUR LIFE AWAY!
NOT IF YOU KEEP WAKING ME UP!

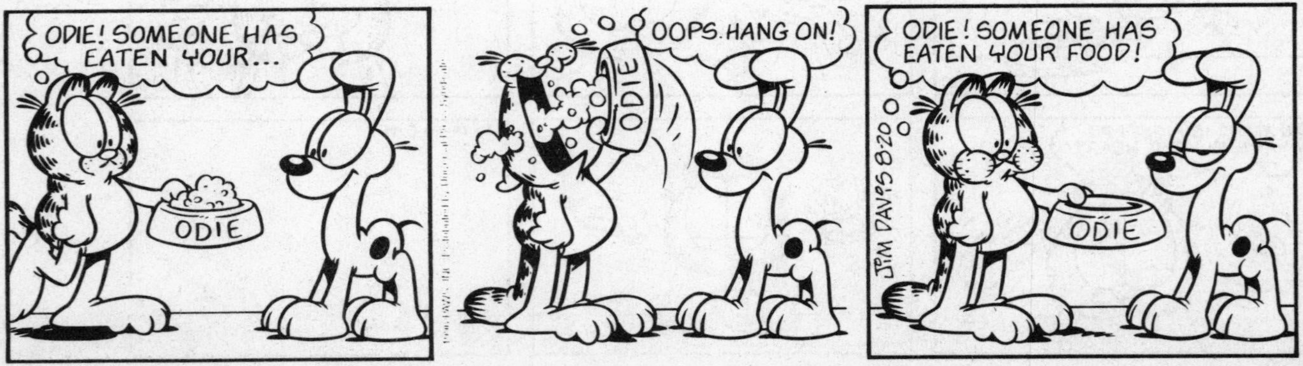
ODIE! SOMEONE HAS EATEN YOUR...
ODIE
OOPS. HANG ON!
ODIE
ODIE! SOMEONE HAS EATEN YOUR FOOD!
JIM DAVIS 8-20
ODIE

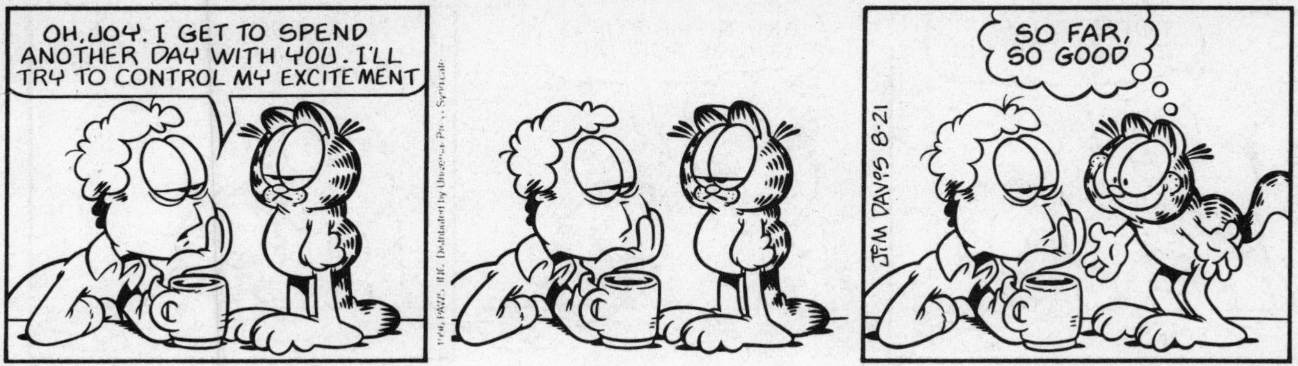
OH, JOY. I GET TO SPEND ANOTHER DAY WITH YOU. I'LL TRY TO CONTROL MY EXCITEMENT
SO FAR, SO GOOD
JIM DAVIS 8-21

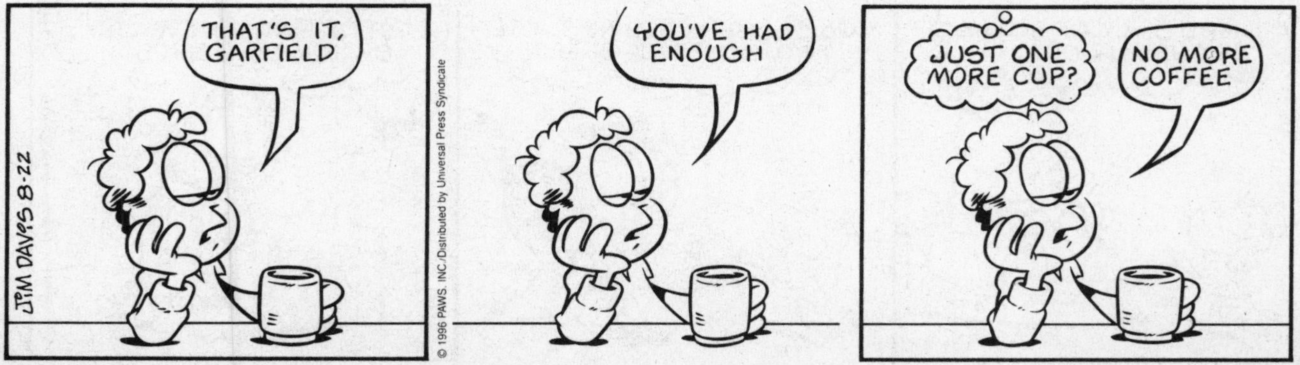
JIM DAVIS 8-22
THAT'S IT, GARFIELD
YOU'VE HAD ENOUGH
JUST ONE MORE CUP?
NO MORE COFFEE
© 1996 PAWS. INC./Distributed by Universal Press Syndicate

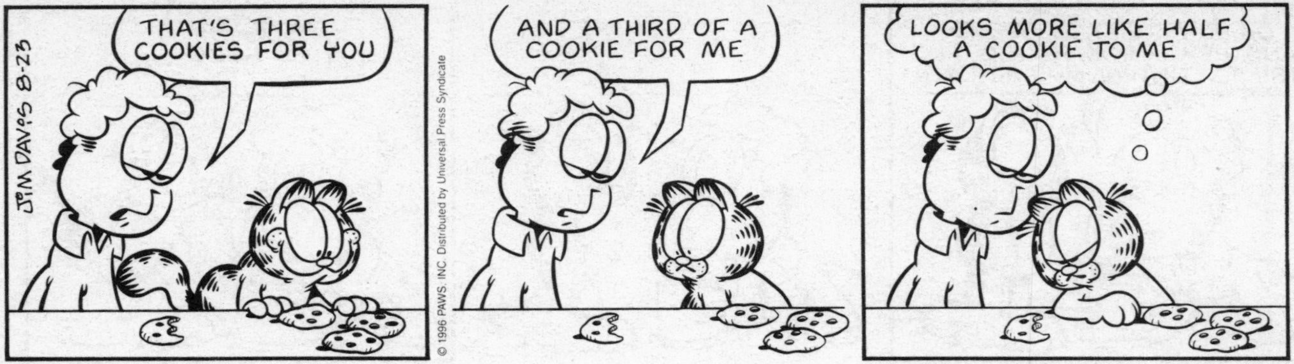
JIM DAVIS 8-23
THAT'S THREE COOKIES FOR YOU
AND A THIRD OF A COOKIE FOR ME
LOOKS MORE LIKE HALF A COOKIE TO ME
© 1996 PAWS, INC Distributed by Universal Press Syndicate

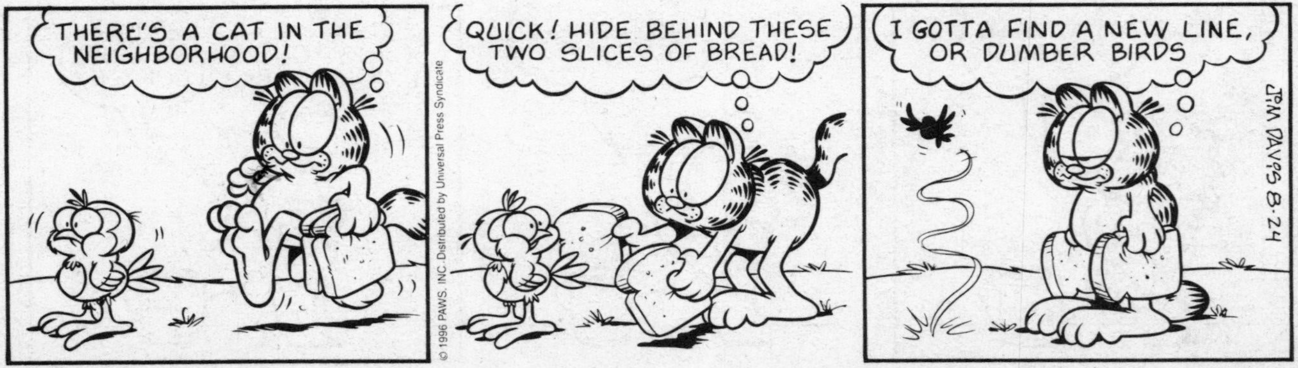
THERE'S A CAT IN THE NEIGHBORHOOD!
QUICK! HIDE BEHIND THESE TWO SLICES OF BREAD!
I GOTTA FIND A NEW LINE, OR DUMBER BIRDS
JIM DAVIS 8-24
© 1996 PAWS, INC. Distributed by Universal Press Syndicate

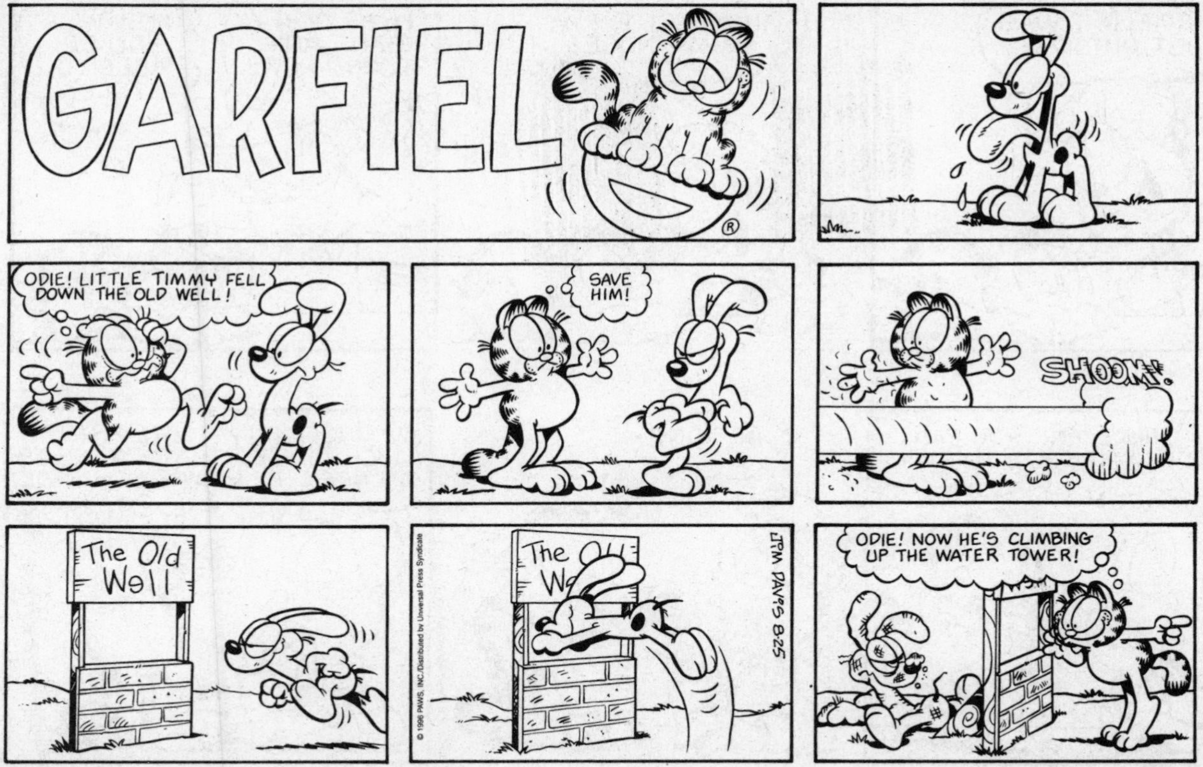
GARFIEL
ODIE! LITTLE TIMMY FELL DOWN THE OLD WELL!
SAVE HIM!
SHOOM!
The Old Well
© 1996 PAWS, INC./Distributed by Universal Press Syndicate
JPM DAVIS 8-25
ODIE! NOW HE'S CLIMBING UP THE WATER TOWER!

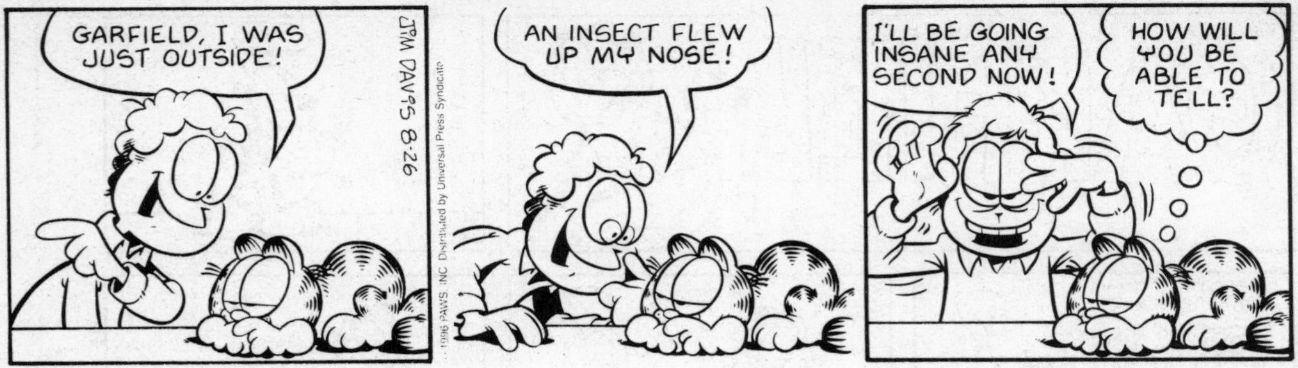
GARFIELD, I WAS JUST OUTSIDE!
JIM DAVIS 8-26
© 1996 PAWS, INC. Distributed by Universal Press Syndicate
AN INSECT FLEW UP MY NOSE!
I'LL BE GOING INSANE ANY SECOND NOW!
HOW WILL YOU BE ABLE TO TELL?

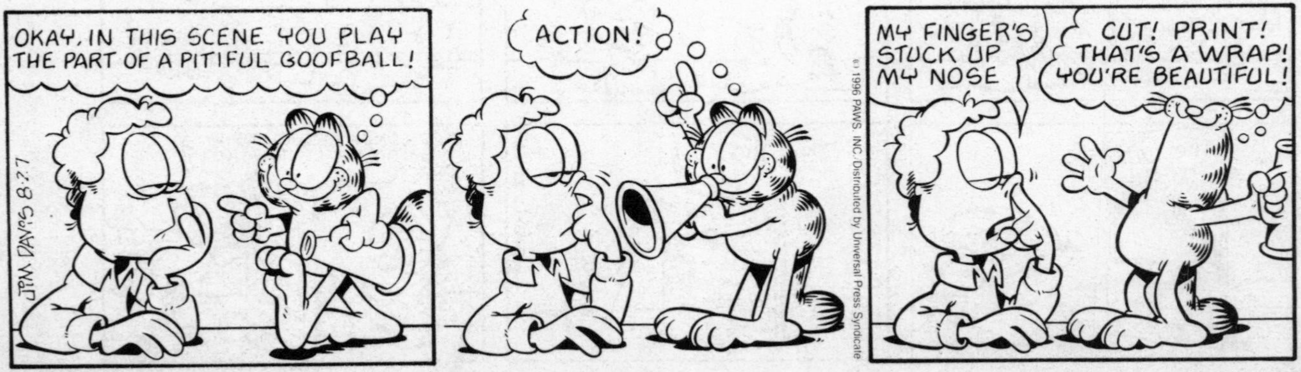
OKAY, IN THIS SCENE YOU PLAY THE PART OF A PITIFUL GOOFBALL!
JIM DAVIS 8-27
ACTION!
© 1996 PAWS, INC. Distributed by Universal Press Syndicate
MY FINGER'S STUCK UP MY NOSE
CUT! PRINT! THAT'S A WRAP! YOU'RE BEAUTIFUL!

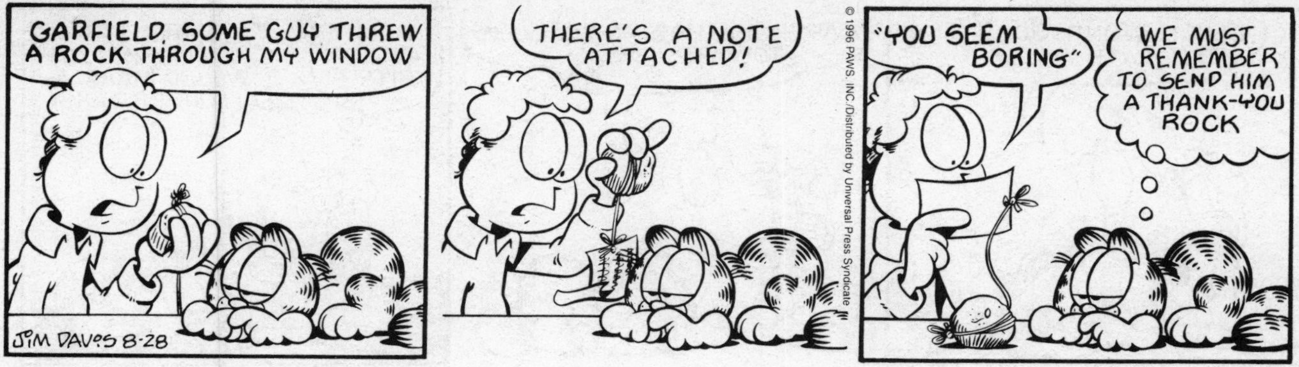
GARFIELD, SOME GUY THREW A ROCK THROUGH MY WINDOW
JIM DAVIS 8-28
THERE'S A NOTE ATTACHED!
© 1996 PAWS, INC./Distributed by Universal Press Syndicate
"YOU SEEM BORING"
WE MUST REMEMBER TO SEND HIM A THANK-YOU ROCK

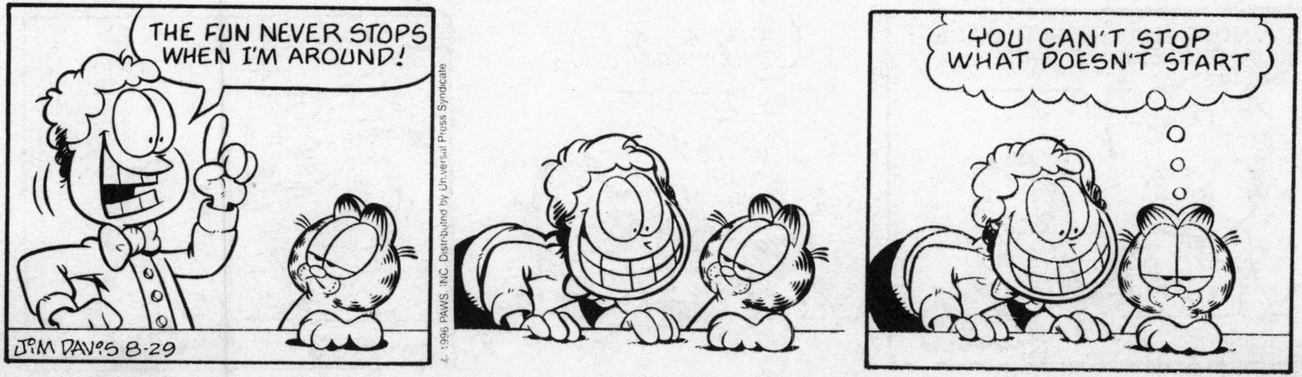
THE FUN NEVER STOPS WHEN I'M AROUND!
JIM DAVIS 8-29
© 1996 PAWS, INC. Distributed by Universal Press Syndicate
YOU CAN'T STOP WHAT DOESN'T START

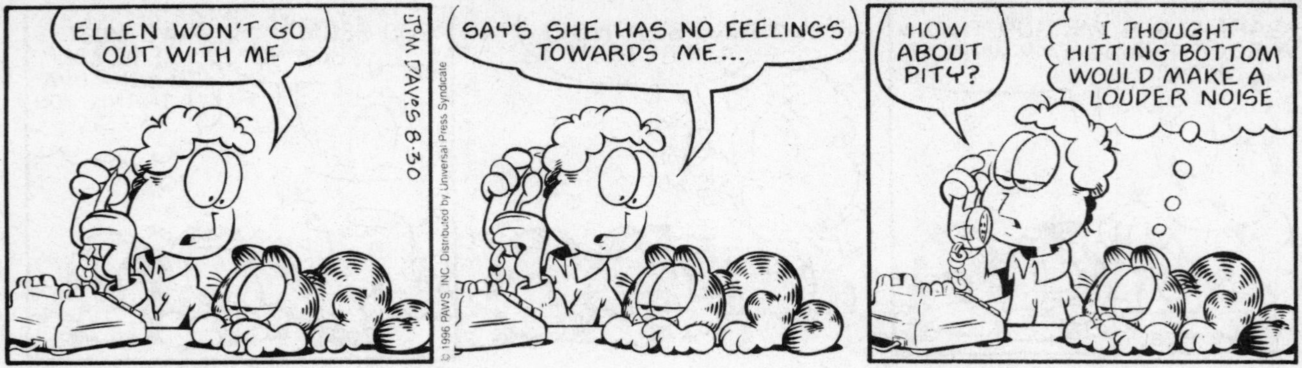
ELLEN WON'T GO OUT WITH ME
JIM DAVIS 8-30
SAYS SHE HAS NO FEELINGS TOWARDS ME...
HOW ABOUT PITY?
I THOUGHT HITTING BOTTOM WOULD MAKE A LOUDER NOISE

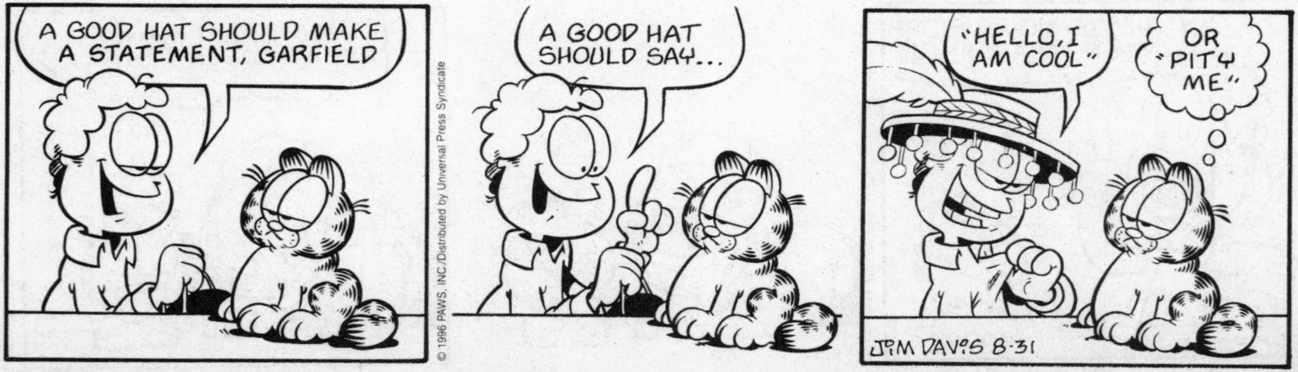
A GOOD HAT SHOULD MAKE A STATEMENT, GARFIELD
A GOOD HAT SHOULD SAY...
"HELLO, I AM COOL"
OR "PITY ME"
JIM DAVIS 8-31

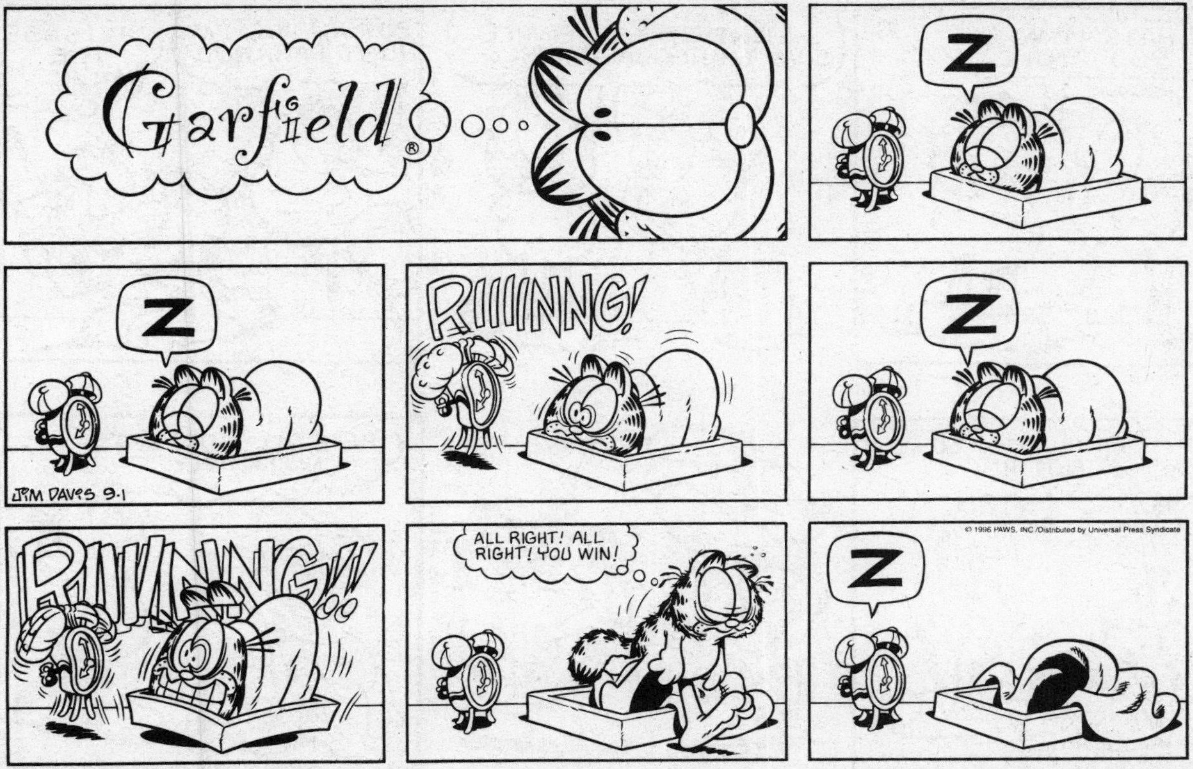

Garfield®
Z
Z
JIM DAVIS 9-1
RIIIINNG!
Z
RIIIINNG!!
ALL RIGHT! ALL RIGHT! YOU WIN!
© 1996 PAWS, INC./Distributed by Universal Press Syndicate
Z

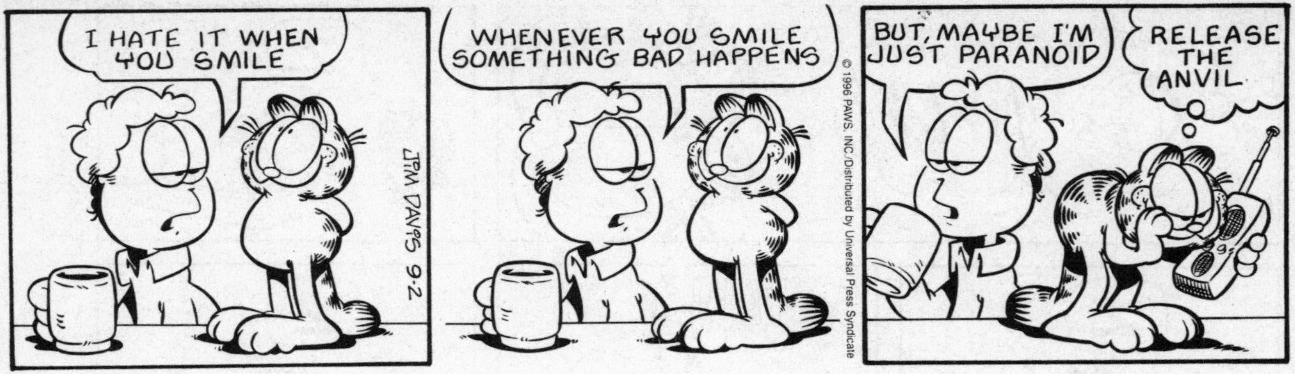
I HATE IT WHEN YOU SMILE
JIM DAVIS 9-2
WHENEVER YOU SMILE SOMETHING BAD HAPPENS
© 1996 PAWS, INC./Distributed by Universal Press Syndicate
BUT, MAYBE I'M JUST PARANOID
RELEASE THE ANVIL

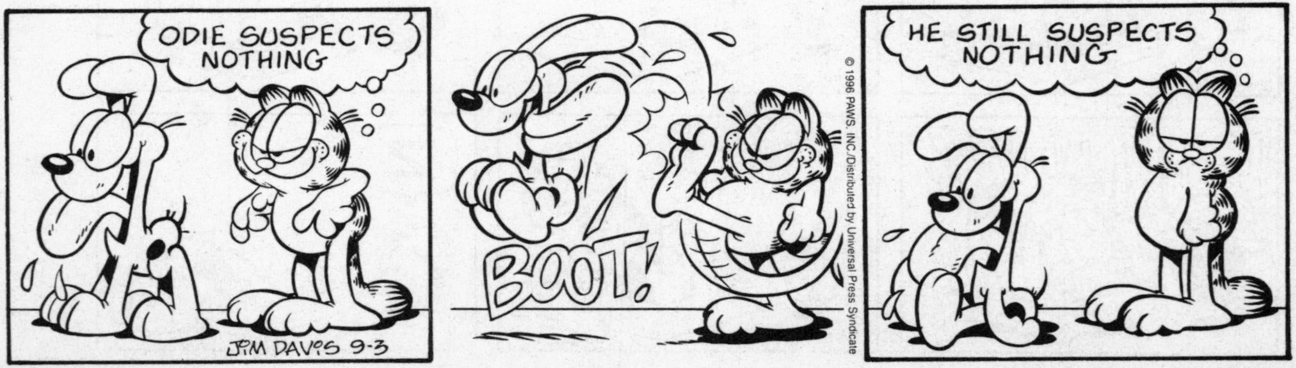
ODIE SUSPECTS NOTHING
JIM DAVIS 9-3
BOOT!
© 1996 PAWS, INC./Distributed by Universal Press Syndicate
HE STILL SUSPECTS NOTHING

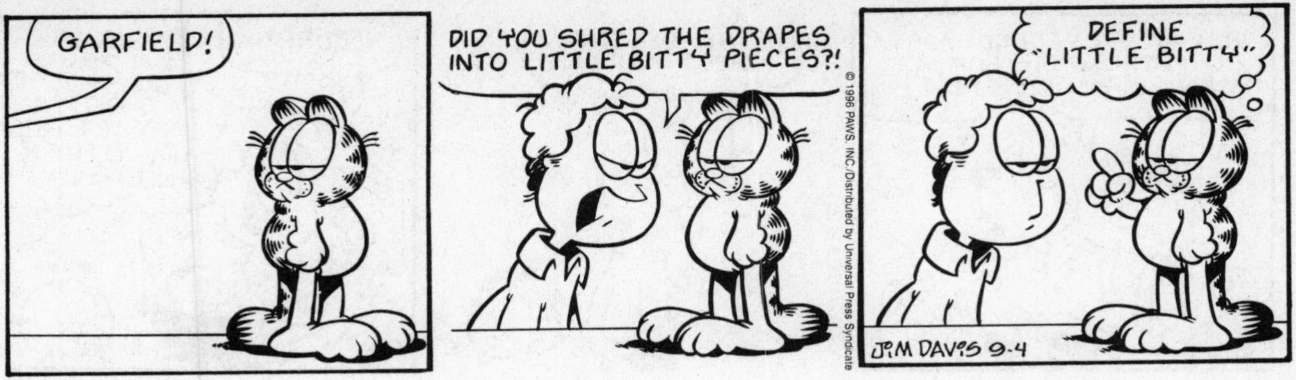
GARFIELD!
DID YOU SHRED THE DRAPES INTO LITTLE BITTY PIECES?!
© 1996 PAWS, INC./Distributed by Universal Press Syndicate
DEFINE "LITTLE BITTY"
JIM DAVIS 9-4

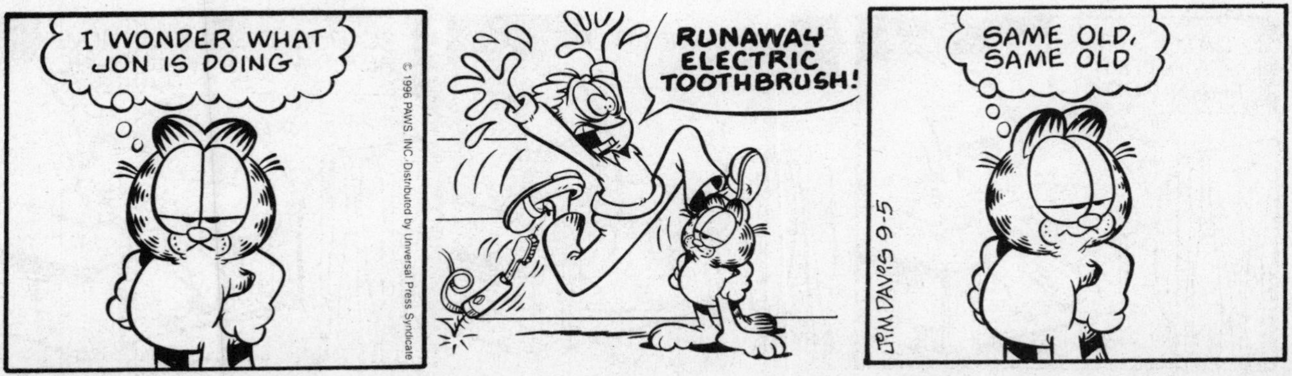
I WONDER WHAT JON IS DOING
© 1996 PAWS, INC./Distributed by Universal Press Syndicate
RUNAWAY ELECTRIC TOOTHBRUSH!
JIM DAVIS 9-5
SAME OLD, SAME OLD

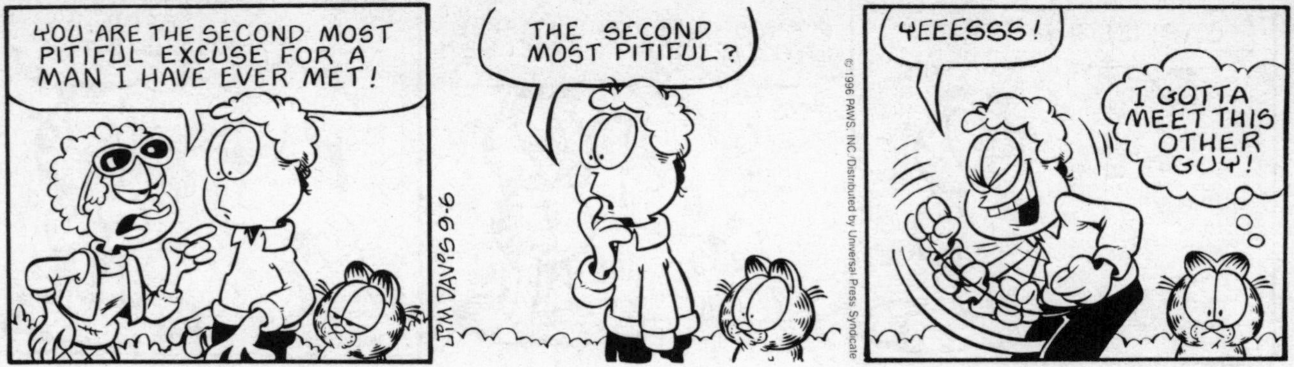

YOU ARE THE SECOND MOST PITIFUL EXCUSE FOR A MAN I HAVE EVER MET!
JIM DAVIS 9-6
THE SECOND MOST PITIFUL?
© 1996 PAWS, INC./Distributed by Universal Press Syndicate
YEEESSS!
I GOTTA MEET THIS OTHER GUY!

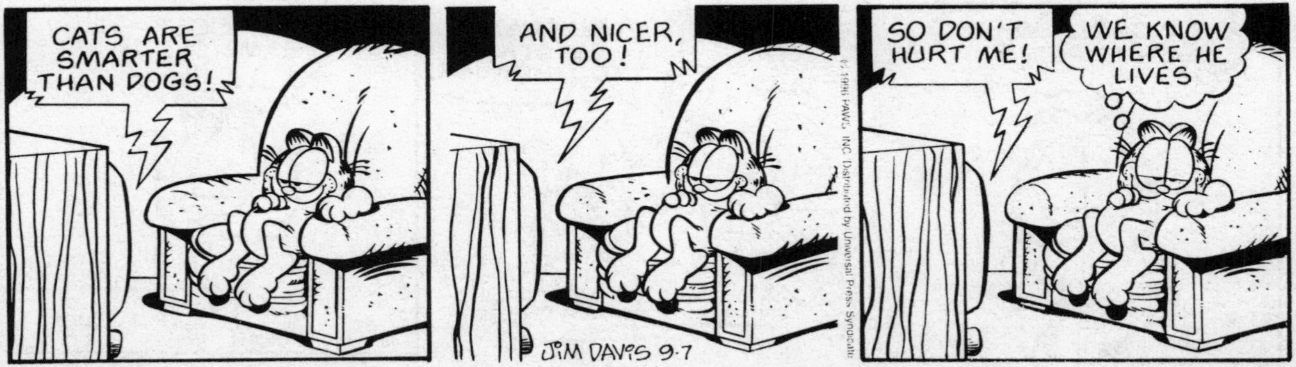

CATS ARE SMARTER THAN DOGS!
AND NICER, TOO!
JIM DAVIS 9-7
SO DON'T HURT ME!
WE KNOW WHERE HE LIVES

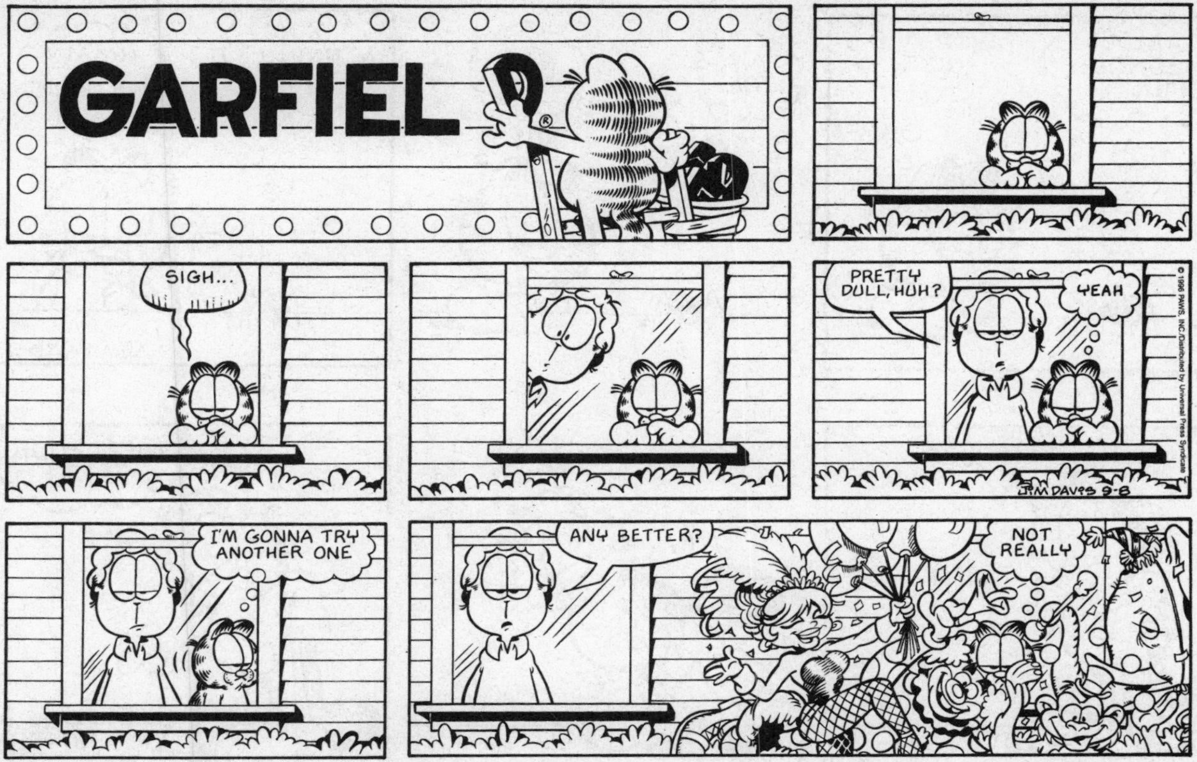
GARFIELD
SIGH...
PRETTY DULL, HUH?
YEAH
© 1996 PAWS, INC./Distributed by Universal Press Syndicate
JIM DAVIS 9-8
I'M GONNA TRY ANOTHER ONE
ANY BETTER?
NOT REALLY

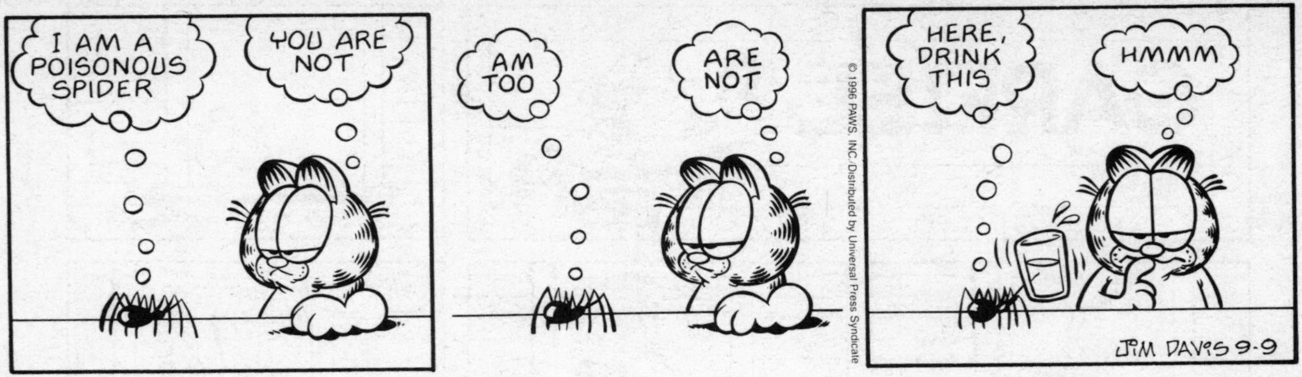
I AM A POISONOUS SPIDER
YOU ARE NOT
AM TOO
ARE NOT
© 1996 PAWS, INC./Distributed by Universal Press Syndicate
HERE, DRINK THIS
HMMM
JIM DAVIS 9-9

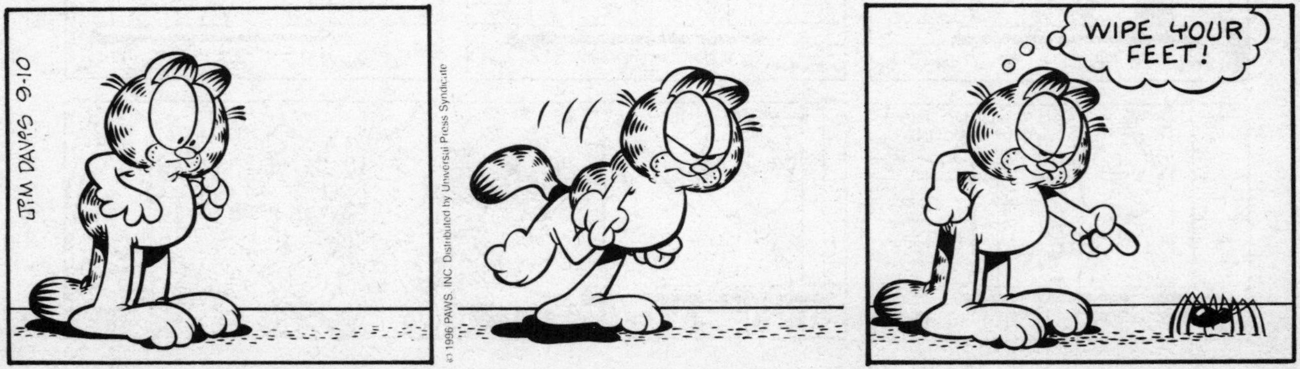
JIM DAVIS 9-10
© 1996 PAWS, INC Distributed by Universal Press Syndicate
WIPE YOUR FEET!

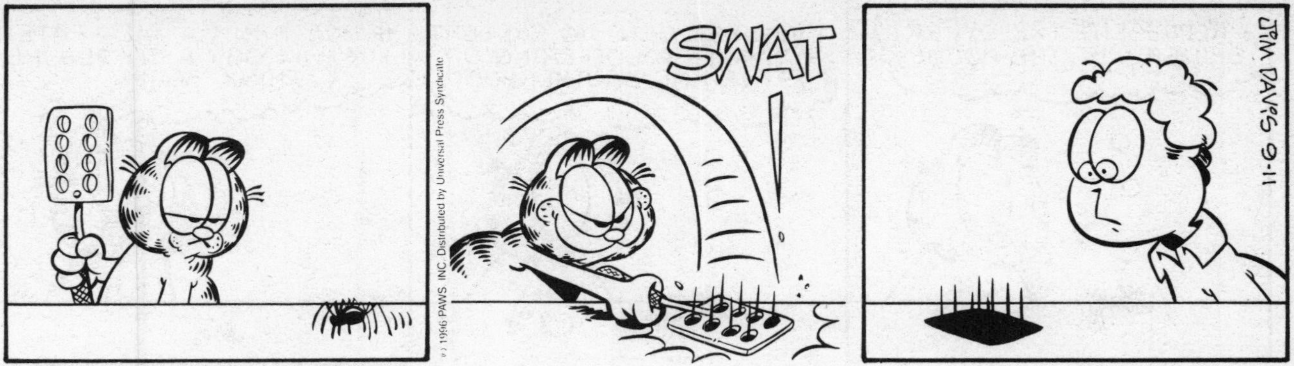
© 1996 PAWS, INC. Distributed by Universal Press Syndicate
SWAT
JPM DAVIS 9-11

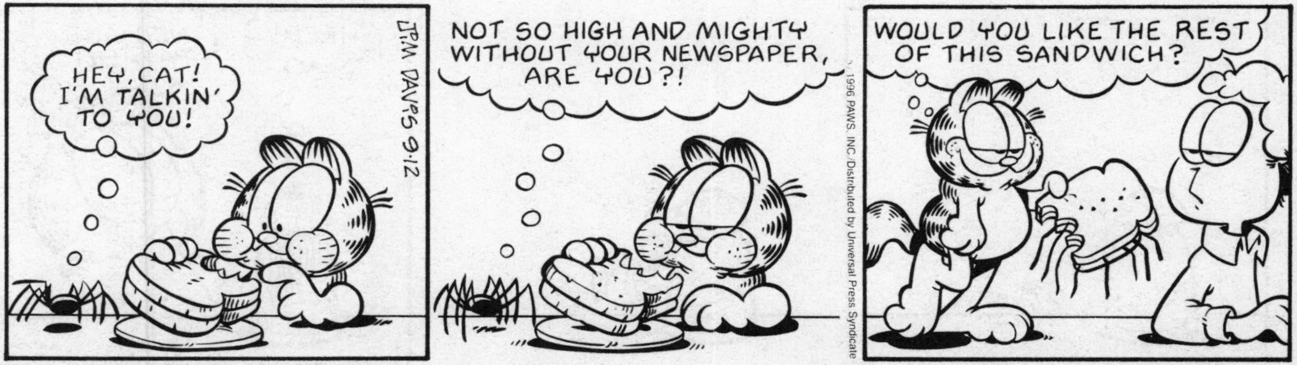
JPM DAVIS 9-12
HEY, CAT! I'M TALKIN' TO YOU!
NOT SO HIGH AND MIGHTY WITHOUT YOUR NEWSPAPER, ARE YOU?!
© 1996 PAWS, INC./Distributed by Universal Press Syndicate
WOULD YOU LIKE THE REST OF THIS SANDWICH?

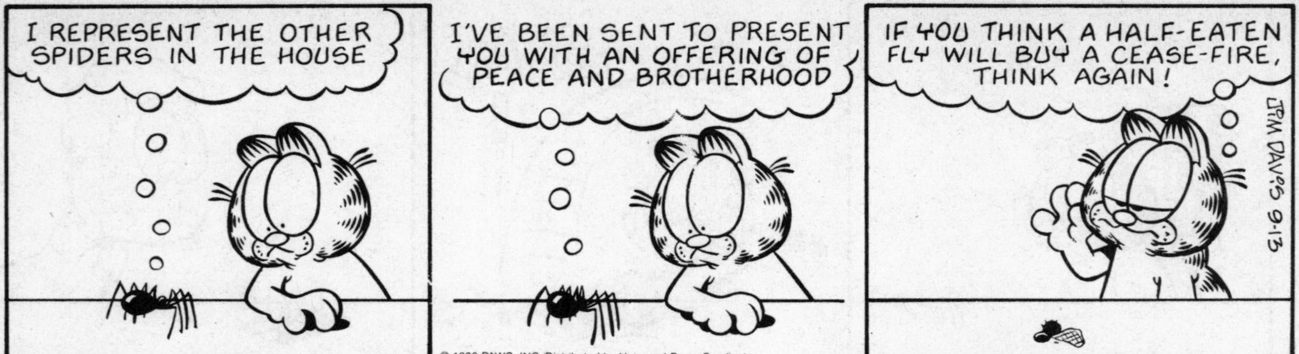
I REPRESENT THE OTHER SPIDERS IN THE HOUSE
I'VE BEEN SENT TO PRESENT YOU WITH AN OFFERING OF PEACE AND BROTHERHOOD
IF YOU THINK A HALF-EATEN FLY WILL BUY A CEASE-FIRE, THINK AGAIN!
JIM DAVIS 9-13

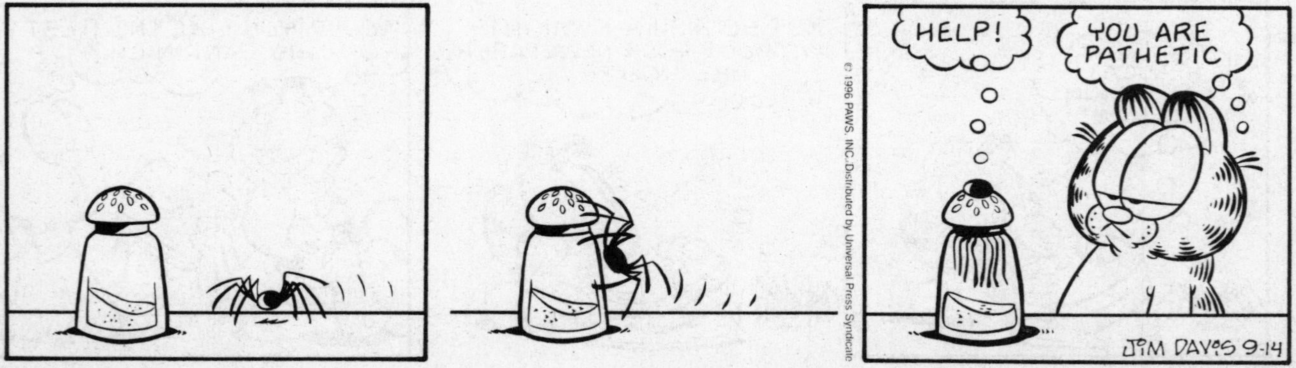
HELP!
YOU ARE PATHETIC
JIM DAVIS 9-14

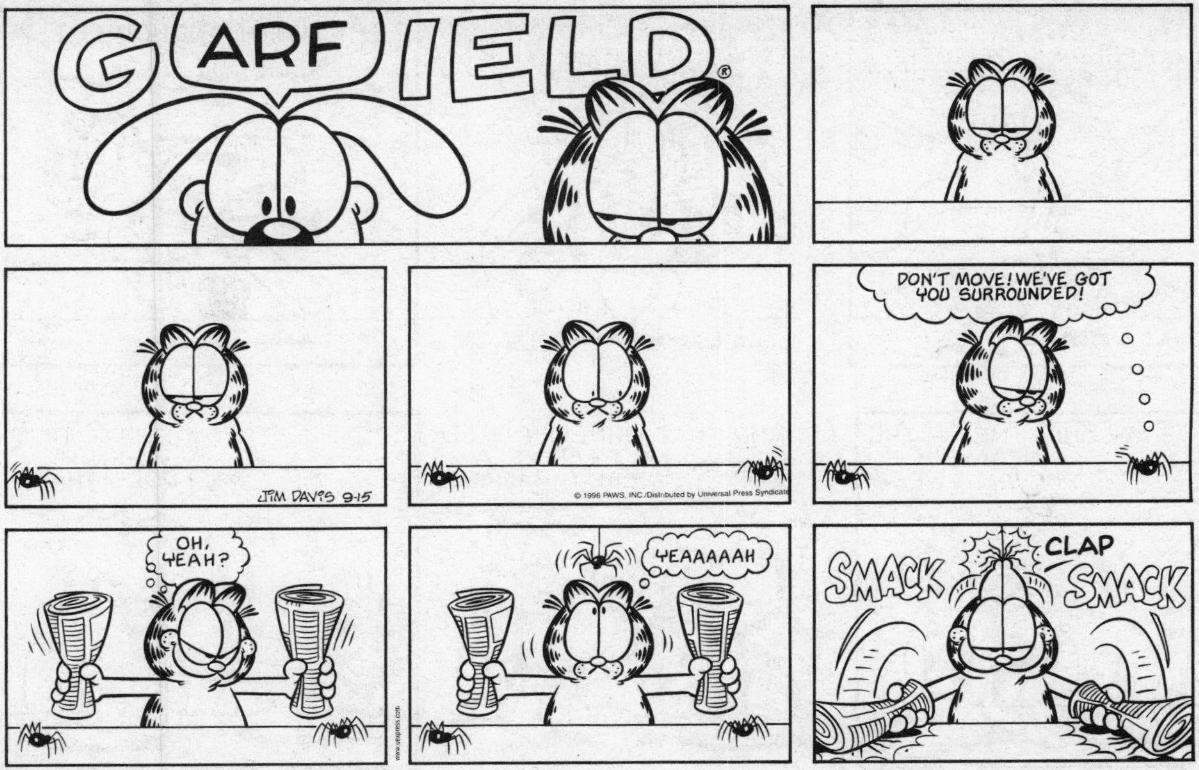
GARFIELD
ARF
JIM DAVIS 9-15
© 1996 PAWS, INC./Distributed by Universal Press Syndicate
DON'T MOVE! WE'VE GOT YOU SURROUNDED!
OH, YEAH?
www.uexpress.com
YEAAAAAH
SMACK
CLAP
SMACK

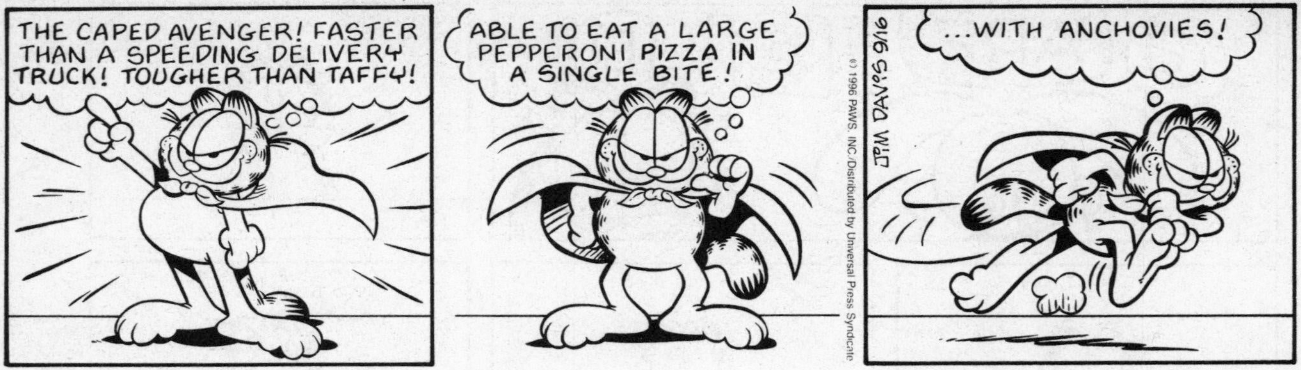
THE CAPED AVENGER! FASTER THAN A SPEEDING DELIVERY TRUCK! TOUGHER THAN TAFFY!
ABLE TO EAT A LARGE PEPPERONI PIZZA IN A SINGLE BITE!
© 1996 PAWS, INC./Distributed by Universal Press Syndicate
JIM DAVIS 9/16
...WITH ANCHOVIES!

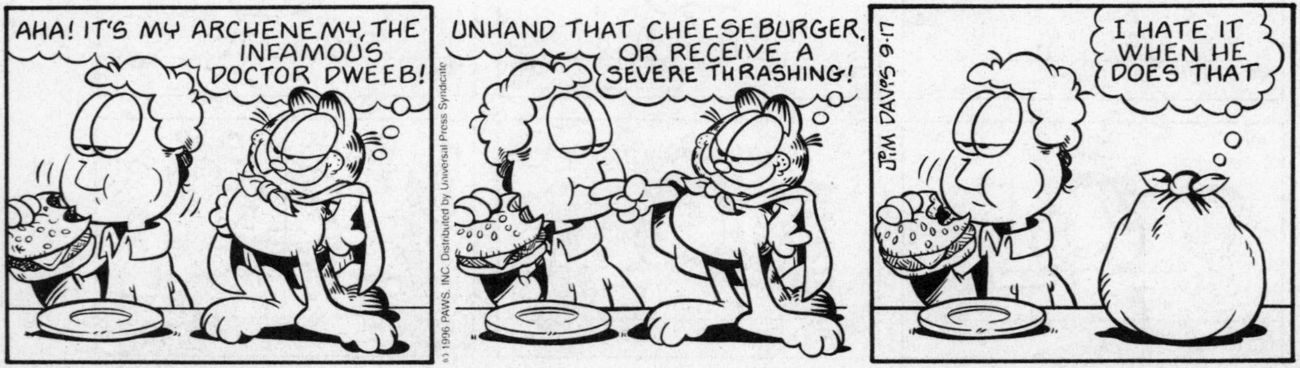
AHA! IT'S MY ARCHENEMY, THE INFAMOUS DOCTOR DWEEB!
© 1996 PAWS, INC. Distributed by Universal Press Syndicate
UNHAND THAT CHEESEBURGER, OR RECEIVE A SEVERE THRASHING!
JIM DAVIS 9-17
I HATE IT WHEN HE DOES THAT

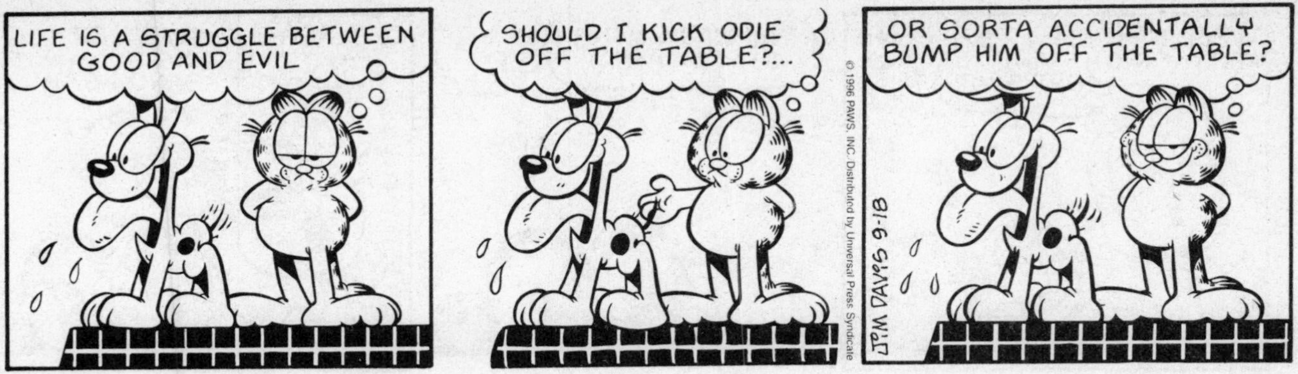
LIFE IS A STRUGGLE BETWEEN GOOD AND EVIL
SHOULD I KICK ODIE OFF THE TABLE?...
OR SORTA ACCIDENTALLY BUMP HIM OFF THE TABLE?
JIM DAVIS 9-18
© 1996 PAWS, INC. Distributed by Universal Press Syndicate

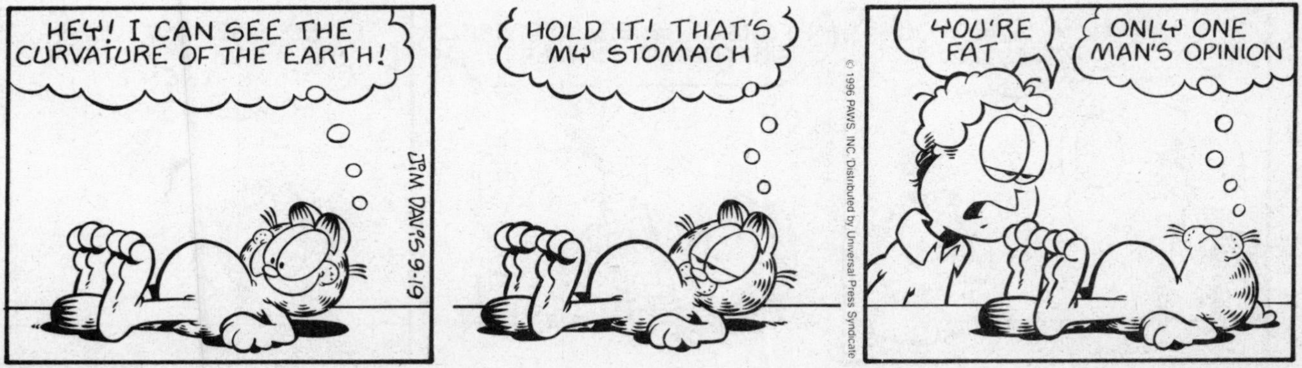
HEY! I CAN SEE THE CURVATURE OF THE EARTH!
HOLD IT! THAT'S MY STOMACH
YOU'RE FAT
ONLY ONE MAN'S OPINION
JIM DAVIS 9-19
© 1996 PAWS, INC. Distributed by Universal Press Syndicate

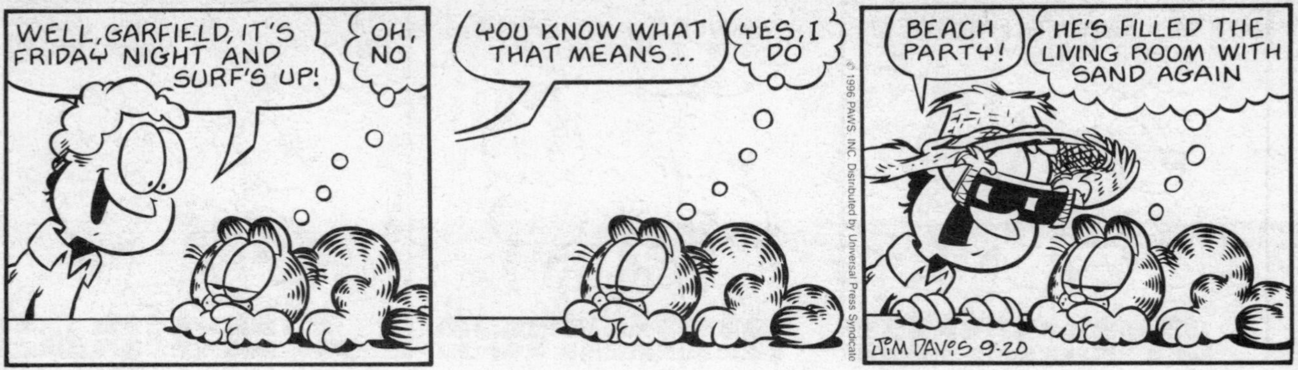
WELL, GARFIELD, IT'S FRIDAY NIGHT AND SURF'S UP!
OH, NO
YOU KNOW WHAT THAT MEANS...
YES, I DO
BEACH PARTY!
HE'S FILLED THE LIVING ROOM WITH SAND AGAIN
JIM DAVIS 9-20

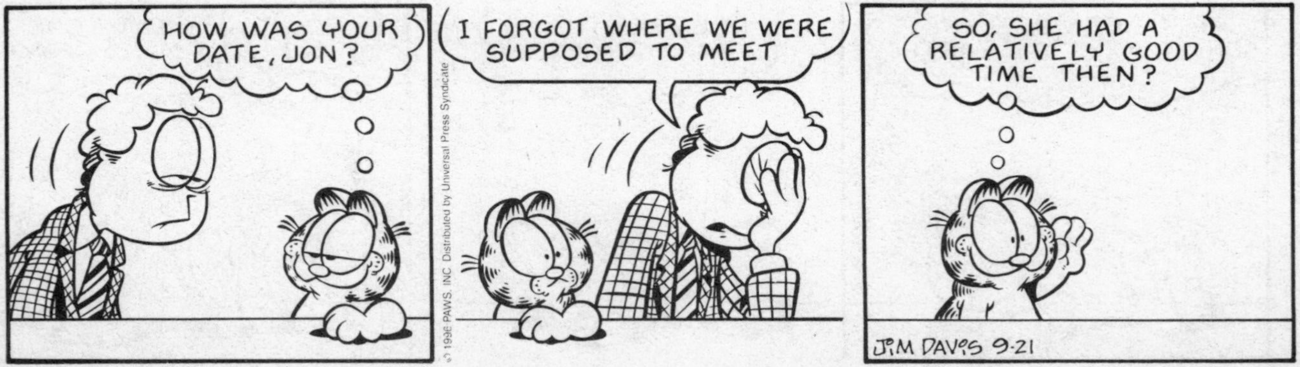
HOW WAS YOUR DATE, JON?
I FORGOT WHERE WE WERE SUPPOSED TO MEET
SO, SHE HAD A RELATIVELY GOOD TIME THEN?
JIM DAVIS 9-21

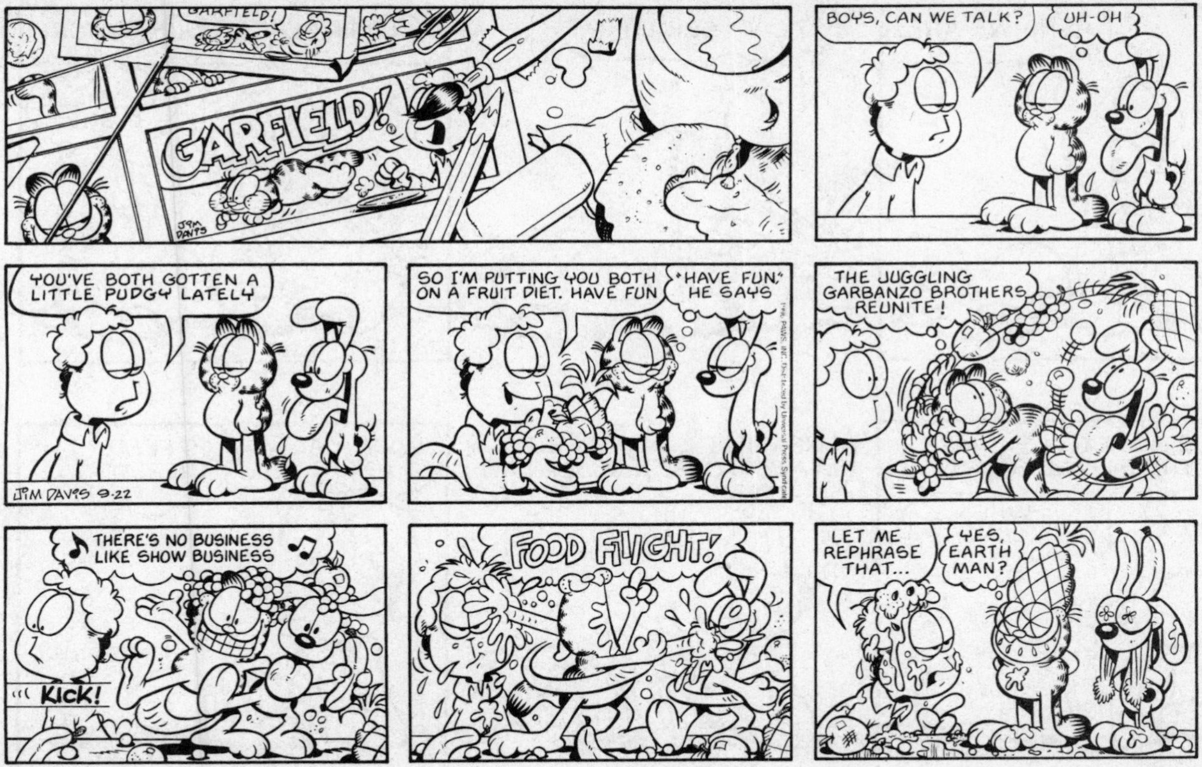
GARFIELD!
GARFIELD!
JIM DAVIS
BOYS, CAN WE TALK?
UH-OH
YOU'VE BOTH GOTTEN A LITTLE PUDGY LATELY
JIM DAVIS 9-22
SO I'M PUTTING YOU BOTH ON A FRUIT DIET. HAVE FUN
"HAVE FUN," HE SAYS
THE JUGGLING GARBANZO BROTHERS REUNITE!
THERE'S NO BUSINESS LIKE SHOW BUSINESS
KICK!
FOOD FLIGHT!
LET ME REPHRASE THAT...
YES, EARTH MAN?

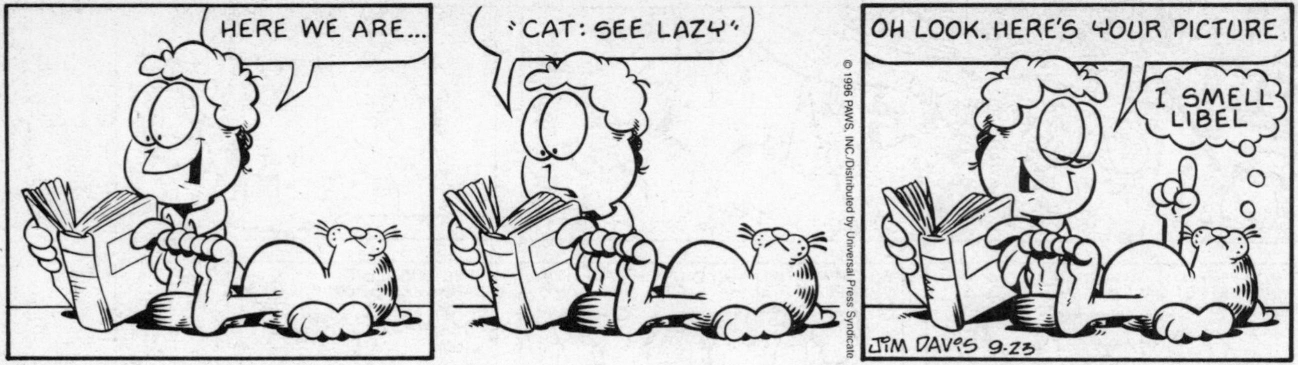
HERE WE ARE...
"CAT: SEE LAZY"
OH LOOK. HERE'S YOUR PICTURE
I SMELL LIBEL
JIM DAVIS 9-23
© 1996 PAWS, INC./Distributed by Universal Press Syndicate

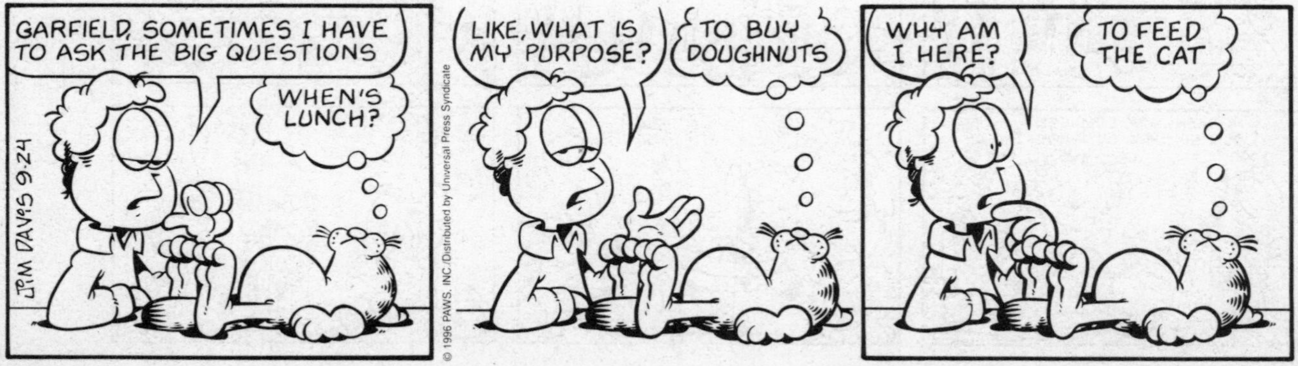
GARFIELD, SOMETIMES I HAVE TO ASK THE BIG QUESTIONS
WHEN'S LUNCH?
JIM DAVIS 9-24
© 1996 PAWS, INC./Distributed by Universal Press Syndicate
LIKE, WHAT IS MY PURPOSE?
TO BUY DOUGHNUTS
WHY AM I HERE?
TO FEED THE CAT

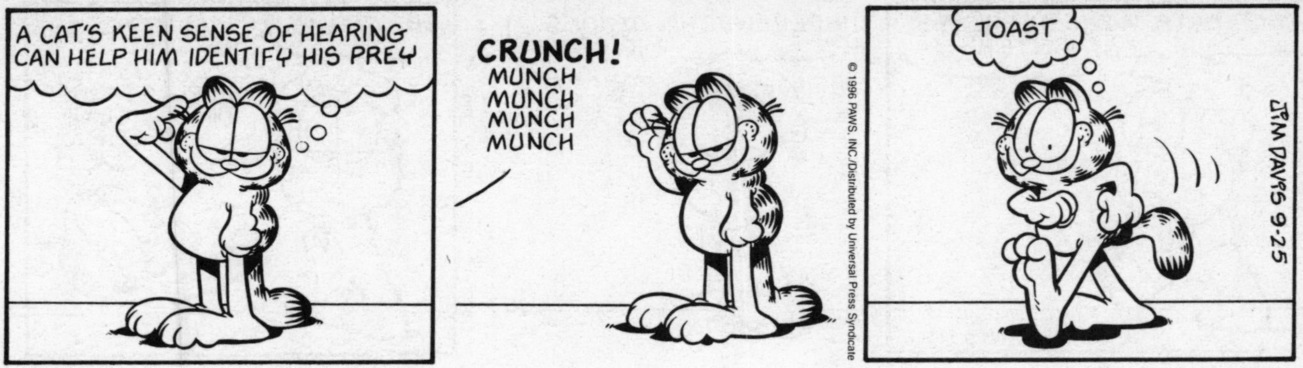
A CAT'S KEEN SENSE OF HEARING CAN HELP HIM IDENTIFY HIS PREY
CRUNCH!
MUNCH
MUNCH
MUNCH
MUNCH
TOAST
JIM DAVIS 9-25
© 1996 PAWS, INC./Distributed by Universal Press Syndicate

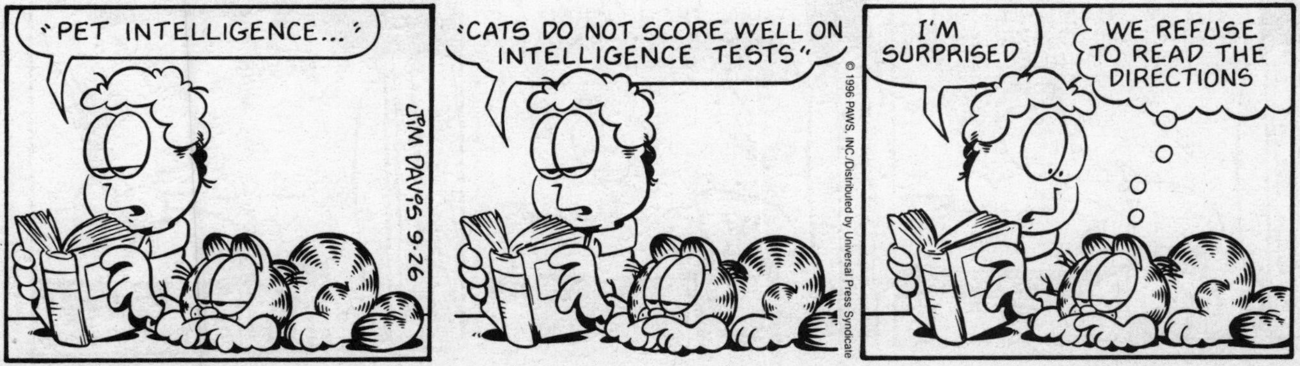
"PET INTELLIGENCE..."
JIM DAVIS 9-26
"CATS DO NOT SCORE WELL ON INTELLIGENCE TESTS"
I'M SURPRISED
WE REFUSE TO READ THE DIRECTIONS
© 1996 PAWS, INC./Distributed by Universal Press Syndicate

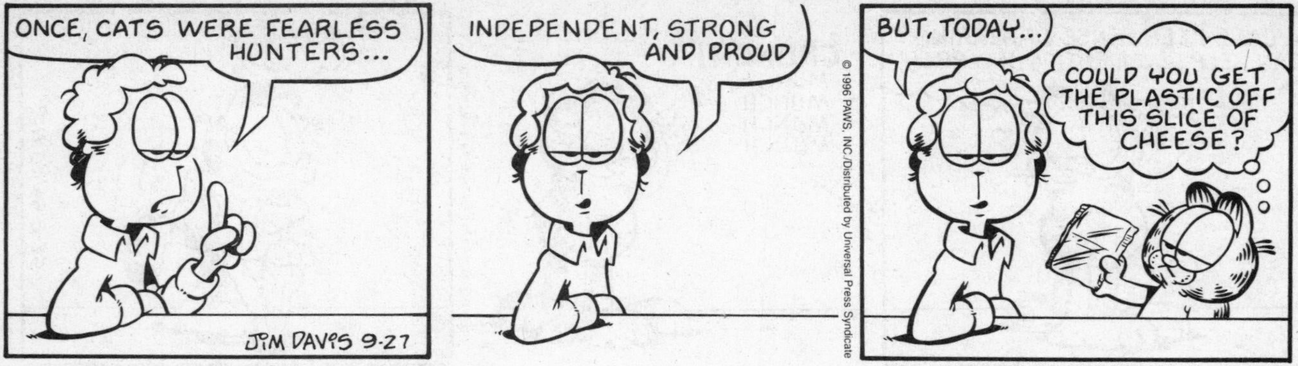
ONCE, CATS WERE FEARLESS HUNTERS...
JIM DAVIS 9-27
INDEPENDENT, STRONG AND PROUD
© 1996 PAWS, INC./Distributed by Universal Press Syndicate
BUT, TODAY...
COULD YOU GET THE PLASTIC OFF THIS SLICE OF CHEESE?

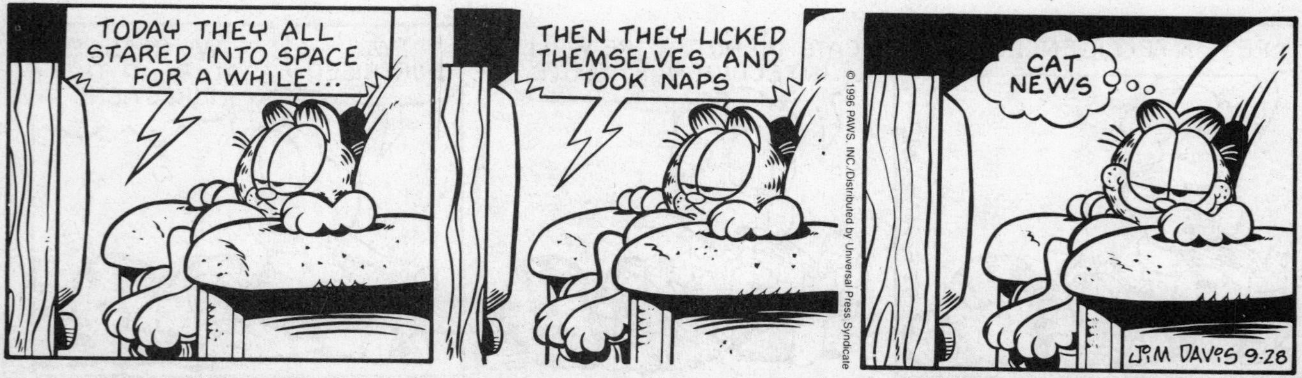
TODAY THEY ALL STARED INTO SPACE FOR A WHILE...
THEN THEY LICKED THEMSELVES AND TOOK NAPS
© 1996 PAWS, INC./Distributed by Universal Press Syndicate
CAT NEWS
JIM DAVIS 9-28

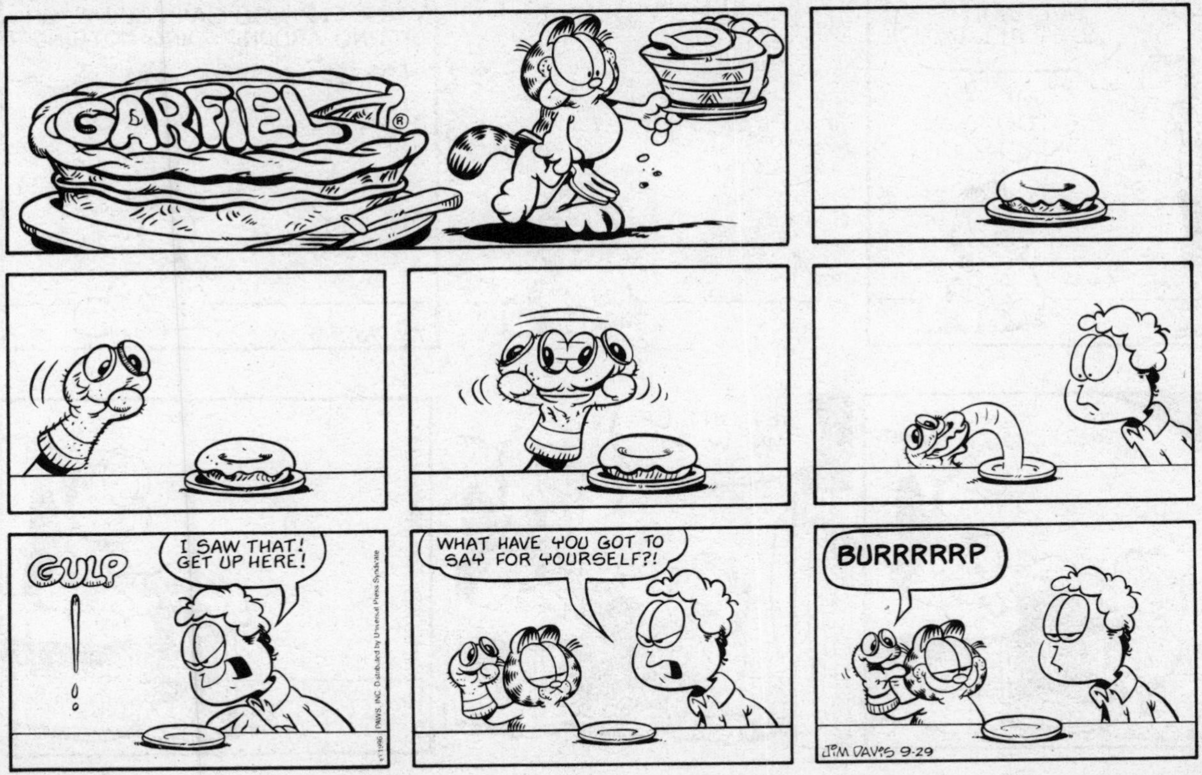
GARFIELD
GULP
I SAW THAT! GET UP HERE!
© 1986 PAWS, INC. Distributed by Universal Press Syndicate
WHAT HAVE YOU GOT TO SAY FOR YOURSELF?!
BURRRRRP
JIM DAVIS 9-29

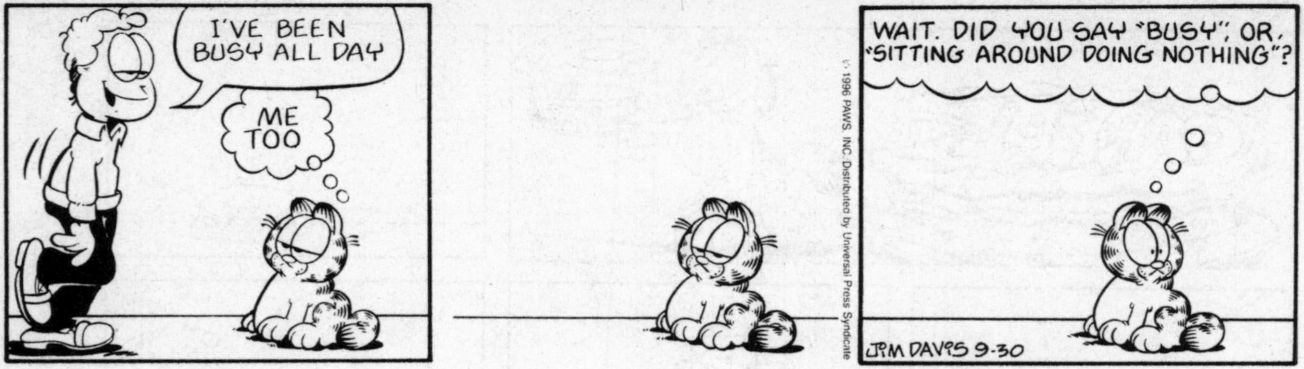
I'VE BEEN BUSY ALL DAY
ME TOO
WAIT. DID YOU SAY "BUSY", OR, "SITTING AROUND DOING NOTHING"?
JIM DAVIS 9-30
© 1996 PAWS, INC. Distributed by Universal Press Syndicate

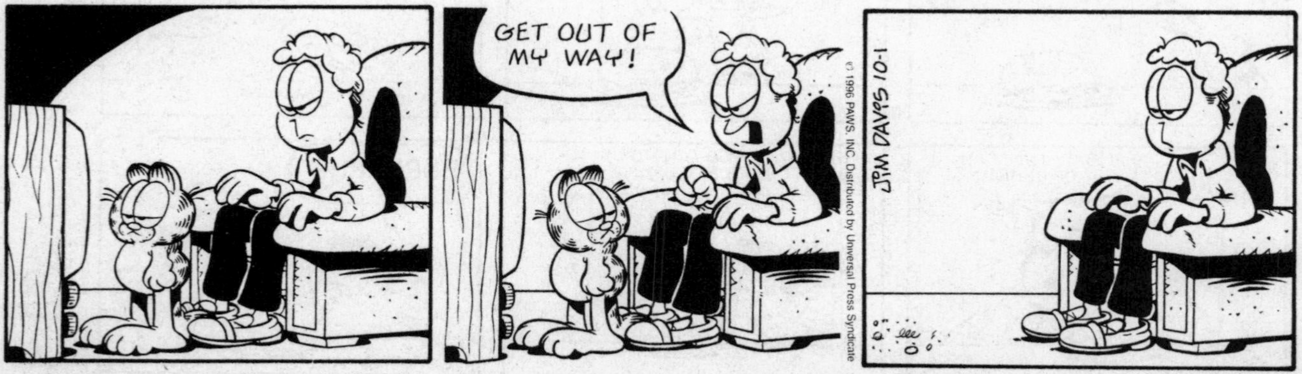
GET OUT OF MY WAY!
JIM DAVIS 10-1
© 1996 PAWS, INC. Distributed by Universal Press Syndicate

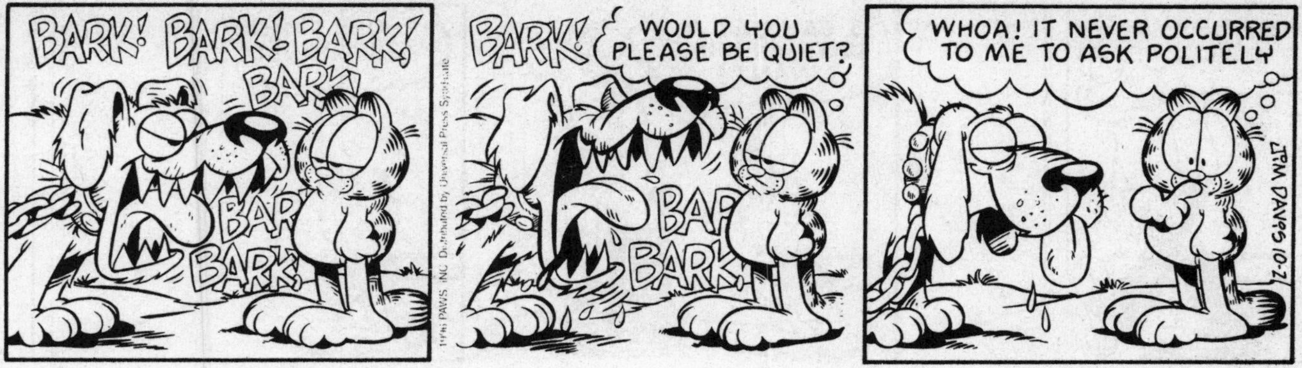
BARK! BARK! BARK!
BAR
BAR
BARK
© 1996 PAWS, INC. Distributed by Universal Press Syndicate
BARK!
WOULD YOU PLEASE BE QUIET?
BAR
BARK
WHOA! IT NEVER OCCURRED TO ME TO ASK POLITELY
JIM DAVIS 10-2

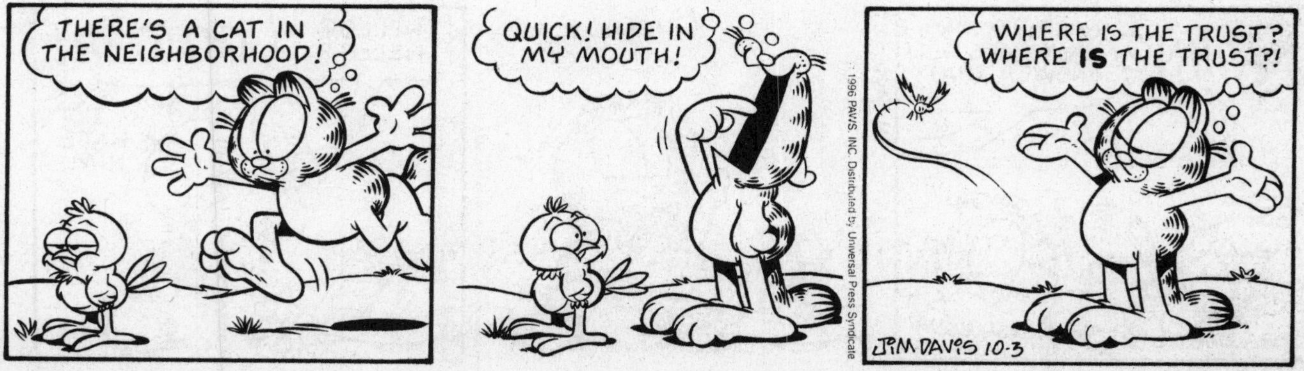
THERE'S A CAT IN THE NEIGHBORHOOD!
QUICK! HIDE IN MY MOUTH!
© 1996 PAWS, INC. Distributed by Universal Press Syndicate
WHERE IS THE TRUST? WHERE **IS** THE TRUST?!
JIM DAVIS 10-3

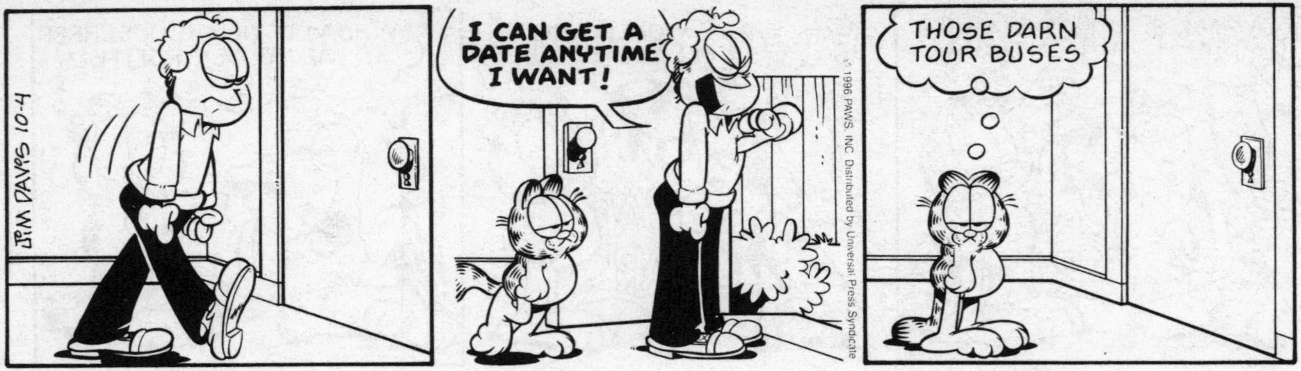
JIM DAVIS 10-4
I CAN GET A DATE ANYTIME I WANT!
© 1996 PAWS, INC. Distributed by Universal Press Syndicate
THOSE DARN TOUR BUSES

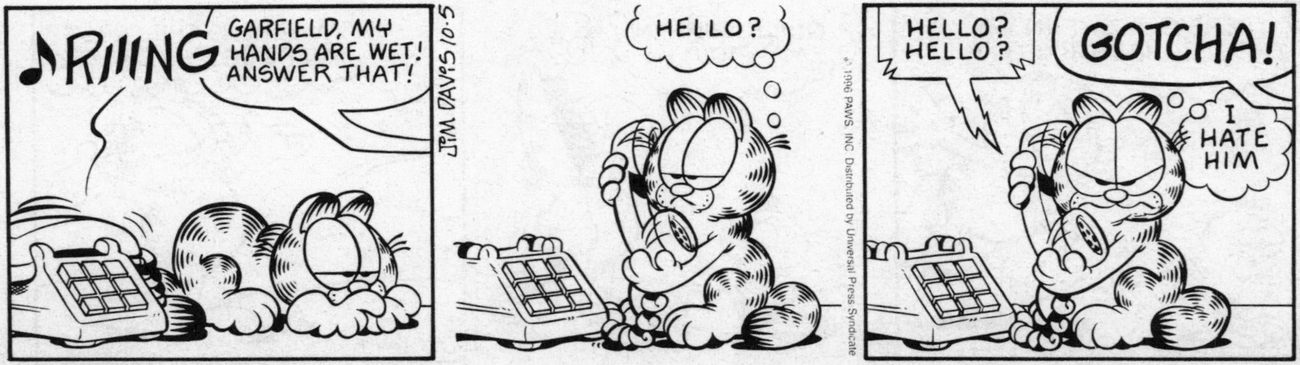
RIIING
GARFIELD, MY HANDS ARE WET! ANSWER THAT!
JIM DAVIS 10-5
HELLO?
© 1996 PAWS, INC. Distributed by Universal Press Syndicate
HELLO? HELLO?
GOTCHA!
I HATE HIM

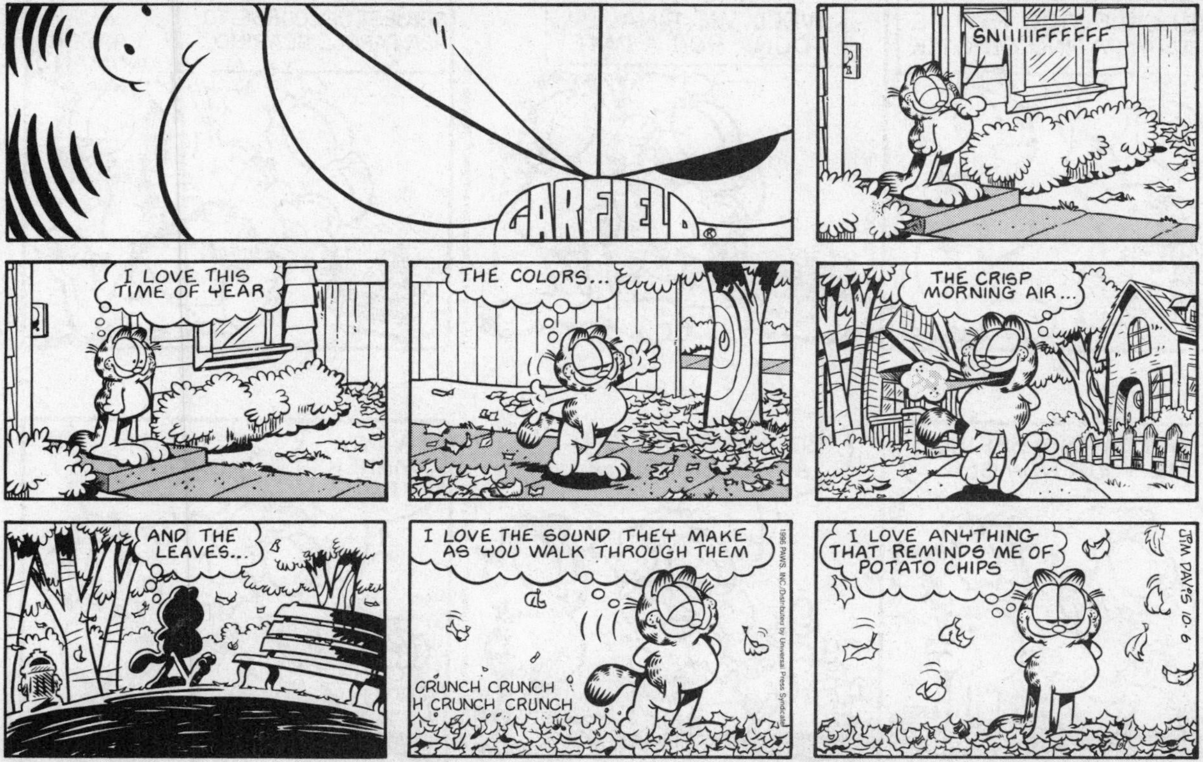
GARFIELD®
SNIIIIIFFFFFF
I LOVE THIS TIME OF YEAR
THE COLORS...
THE CRISP MORNING AIR...
AND THE LEAVES...
I LOVE THE SOUND THEY MAKE AS YOU WALK THROUGH THEM
CRUNCH CRUNCH
H CRUNCH CRUNCH
1996 PAWS, INC/Distributed by Universal Press Syndicate
I LOVE ANYTHING THAT REMINDS ME OF POTATO CHIPS
JPM DAVIS 10-6

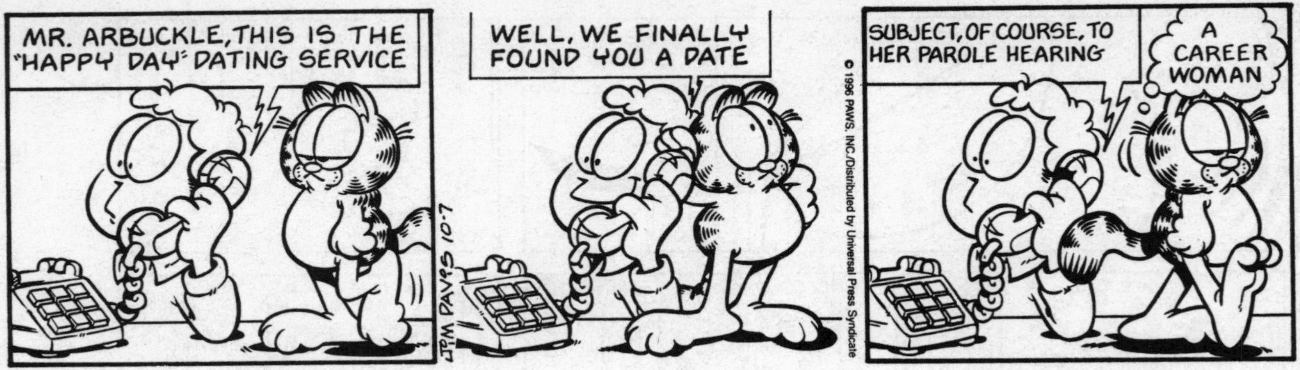
MR. ARBUCKLE, THIS IS THE "HAPPY DAY" DATING SERVICE
WELL, WE FINALLY FOUND YOU A DATE
SUBJECT, OF COURSE, TO HER PAROLE HEARING
A CAREER WOMAN
JIM DAVIS 10-7
© 1996 PAWS, INC./Distributed by Universal Press Syndicate

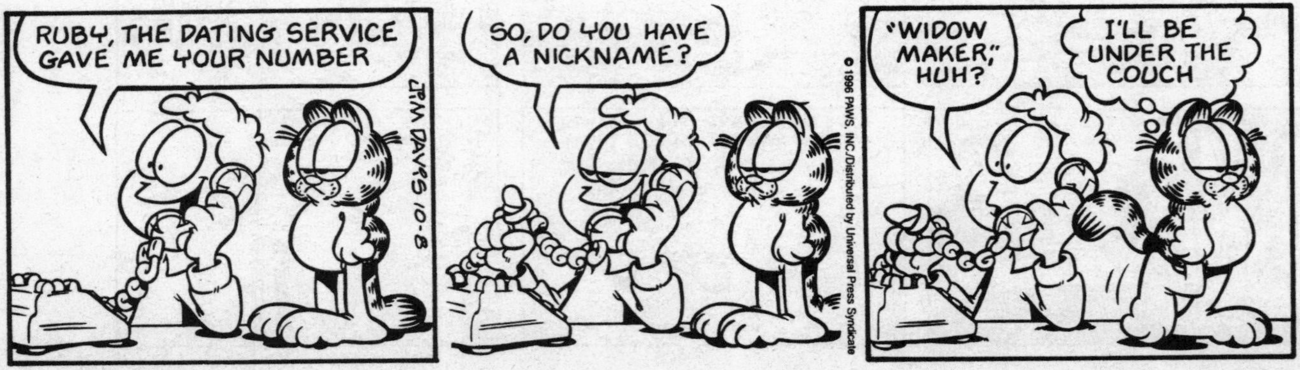
RUBY, THE DATING SERVICE GAVE ME YOUR NUMBER
SO, DO YOU HAVE A NICKNAME?
"WIDOW MAKER," HUH?
I'LL BE UNDER THE COUCH
JIM DAVIS 10-8
© 1996 PAWS, INC./Distributed by Universal Press Syndicate

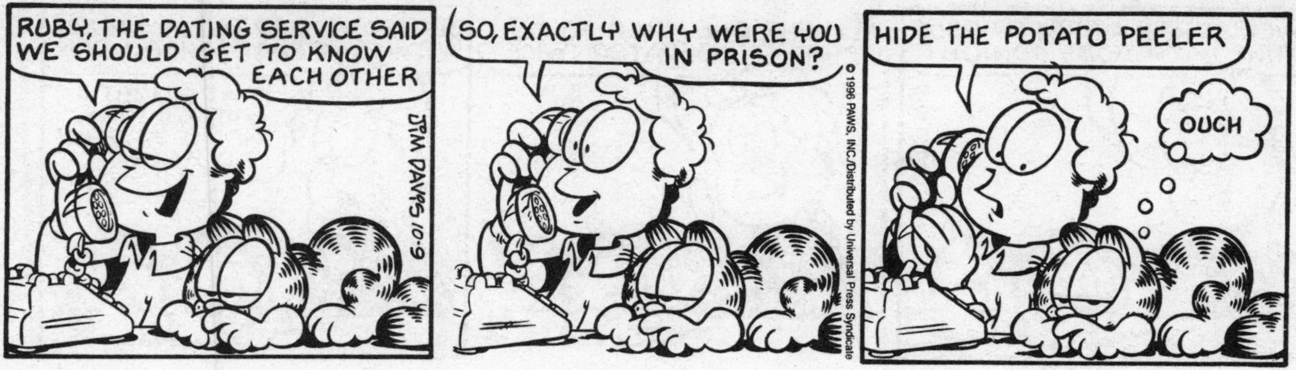
RUBY, THE DATING SERVICE SAID WE SHOULD GET TO KNOW EACH OTHER
JIM DAVIS 10-9
SO, EXACTLY WHY WERE YOU IN PRISON?
© 1996 PAWS, INC./Distributed by Universal Press Syndicate
HIDE THE POTATO PEELER
OUCH

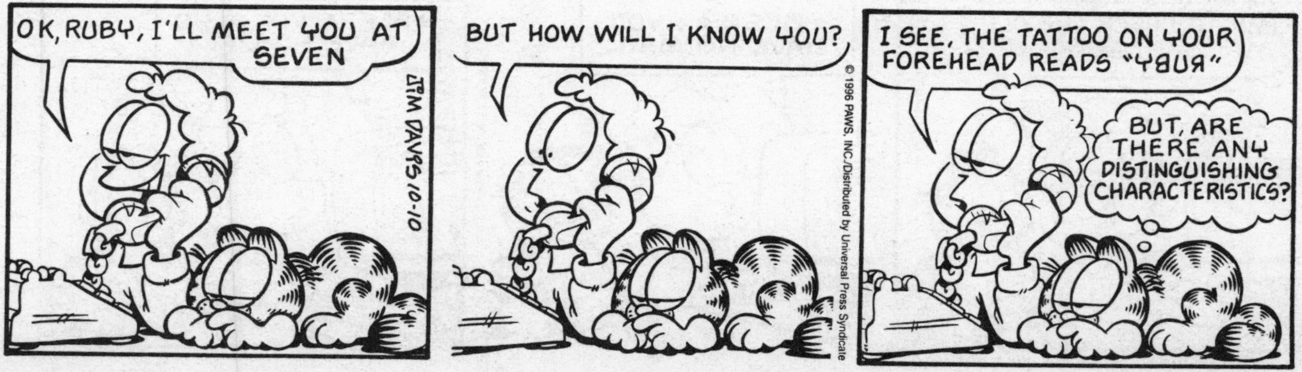
OK, RUBY, I'LL MEET YOU AT SEVEN
JIM DAVIS 10-10
BUT HOW WILL I KNOW YOU?
© 1996 PAWS, INC./Distributed by Universal Press Syndicate
I SEE, THE TATTOO ON YOUR FOREHEAD READS "YBUR"
BUT, ARE THERE ANY DISTINGUISHING CHARACTERISTICS?

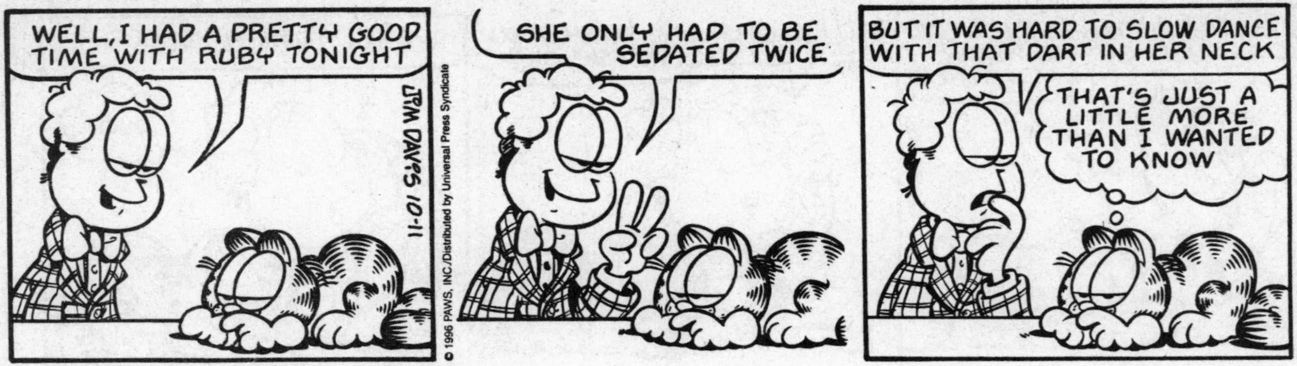
WELL, I HAD A PRETTY GOOD TIME WITH RUBY TONIGHT
JIM DAVIS 10-11
© 1996 PAWS, INC./Distributed by Universal Press Syndicate
SHE ONLY HAD TO BE SEDATED TWICE
BUT IT WAS HARD TO SLOW DANCE WITH THAT DART IN HER NECK
THAT'S JUST A LITTLE MORE THAN I WANTED TO KNOW

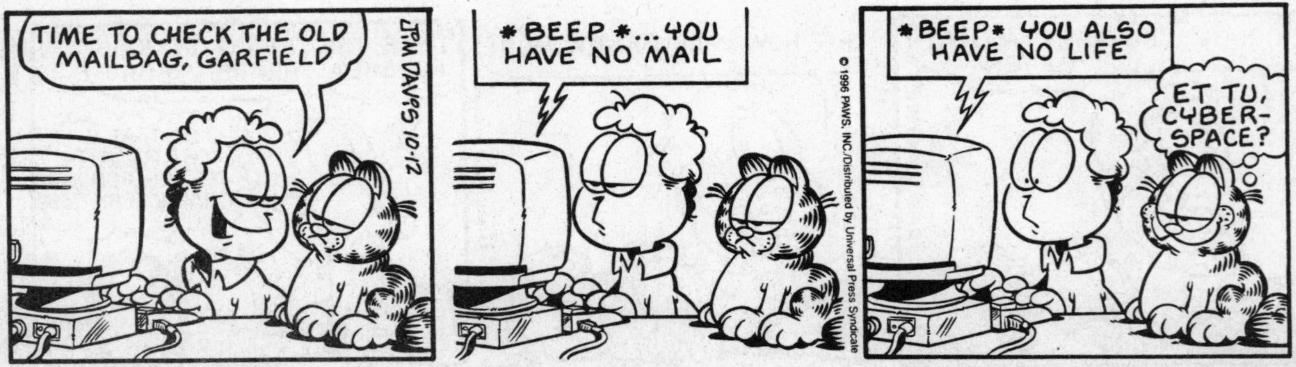
TIME TO CHECK THE OLD MAILBAG, GARFIELD
JIM DAVIS 10-12
BEEP... YOU HAVE NO MAIL
© 1996 PAWS, INC./Distributed by Universal Press Syndicate
BEEP YOU ALSO HAVE NO LIFE
ET TU, CYBER-SPACE?

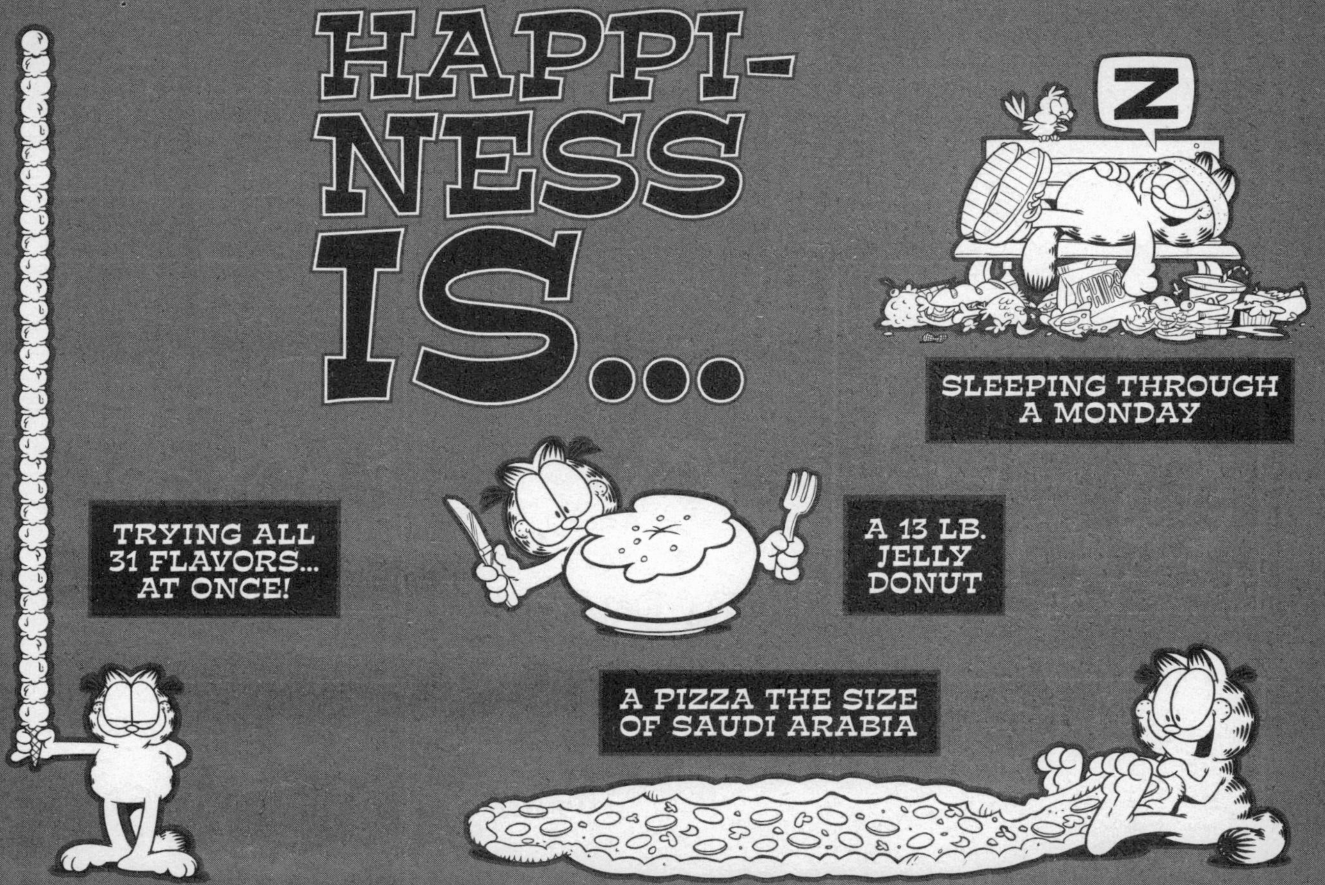
HAPPI-
NESS
IS...
Z
SLEEPING THROUGH A MONDAY
TRYING ALL 31 FLAVORS... AT ONCE!
A 13 LB. JELLY DONUT
CHIPS
A PIZZA THE SIZE OF SAUDI ARABIA

Garfield
thinks big

BY: JIM DAVIS

THINGS WE NEED MORE OF...

marathon naps
all-night smorgasbords
bacon
wrestling on TV
jelly donuts
back scratchers
scary movies
dog muzzles
fuzzy slippers
Elvis impersonators
cheese
roller coasters
teddy bears
weekends
pizza

THINGS WE CAN DO WITHOUT...

dogs
aerobics
brussel sprouts
decaf coffee
polka
spiders
bagpipes
fruitcakes
houseguests
lawyers
disco
tattoos
diets
Mondays
dog breath

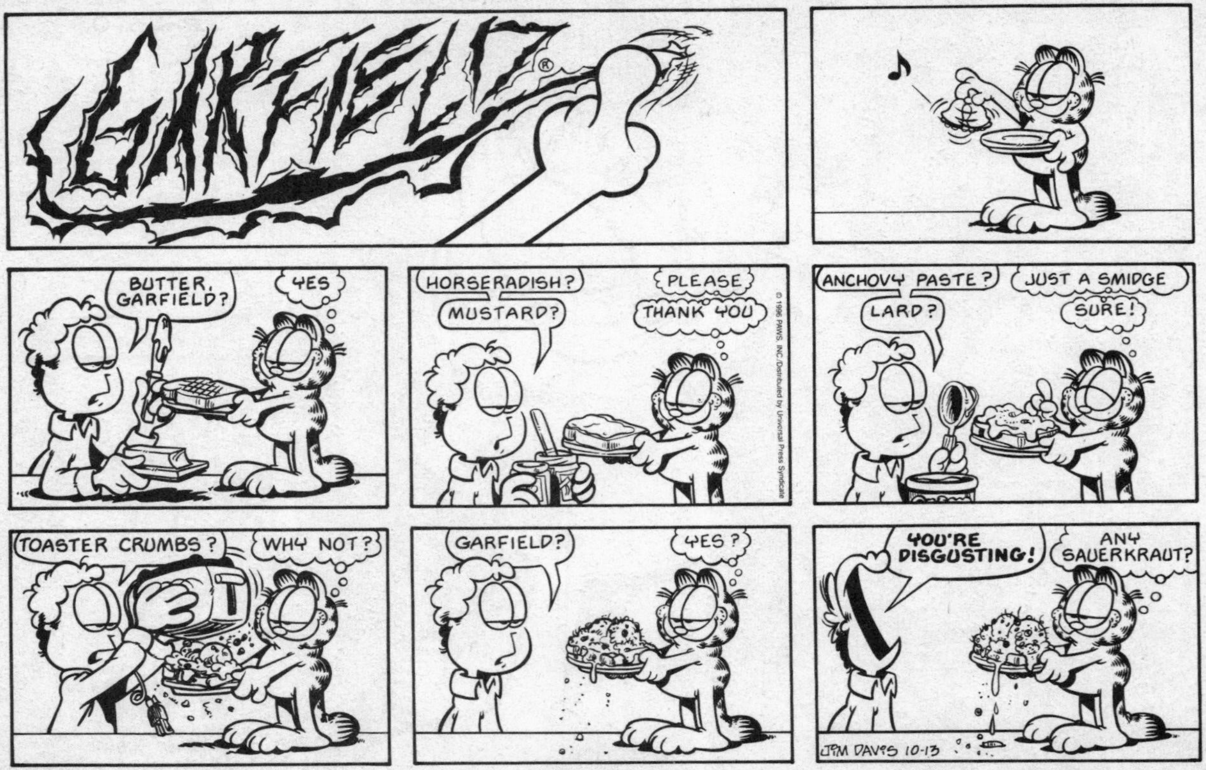
GARFIELD®
BUTTER, GARFIELD?
YES
HORSERADISH?
PLEASE
MUSTARD?
THANK YOU
© 1996 PAWS, INC./Distributed by Universal Press Syndicate
ANCHOVY PASTE?
JUST A SMIDGE
LARD?
SURE!
TOASTER CRUMBS?
WHY NOT?
GARFIELD?
YES?
YOU'RE DISGUSTING!
ANY SAUERKRAUT?
JPM DAVPS 10-13

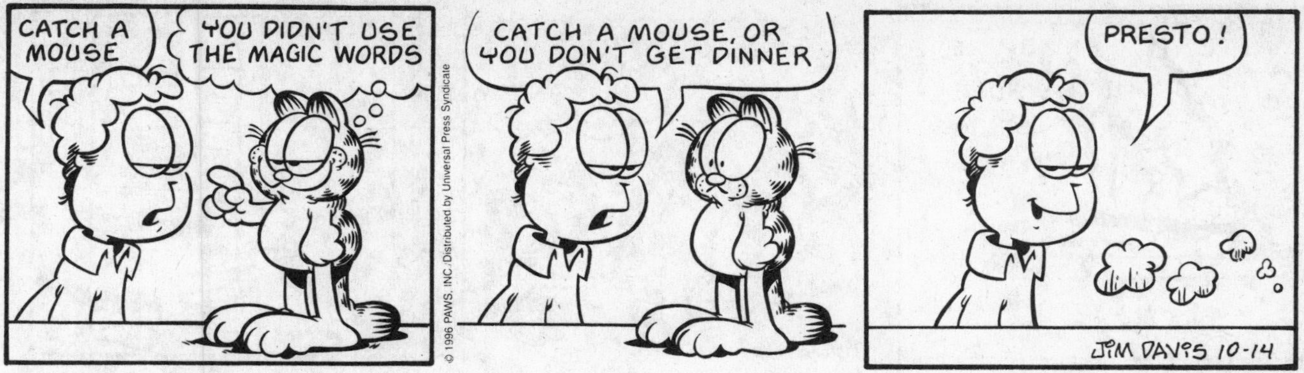
CATCH A MOUSE
YOU DIDN'T USE THE MAGIC WORDS
© 1996 PAWS. INC./Distributed by Universal Press Syndicate
CATCH A MOUSE, OR YOU DON'T GET DINNER
PRESTO!
JIM DAVIS 10-14

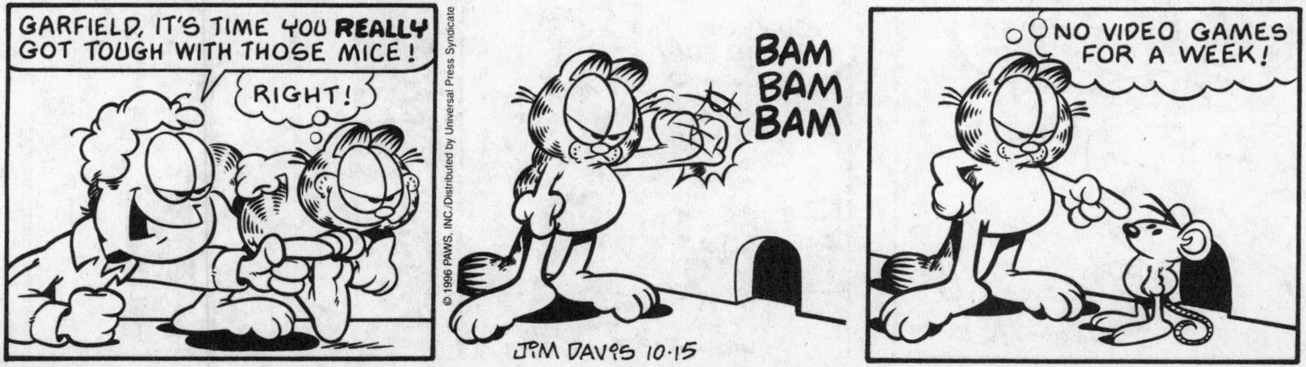
GARFIELD, IT'S TIME YOU **REALLY** GOT TOUGH WITH THOSE MICE!
RIGHT!
© 1996 PAWS. INC./Distributed by Universal Press Syndicate
BAM
BAM
BAM
JIM DAVIS 10-15
NO VIDEO GAMES FOR A WEEK!

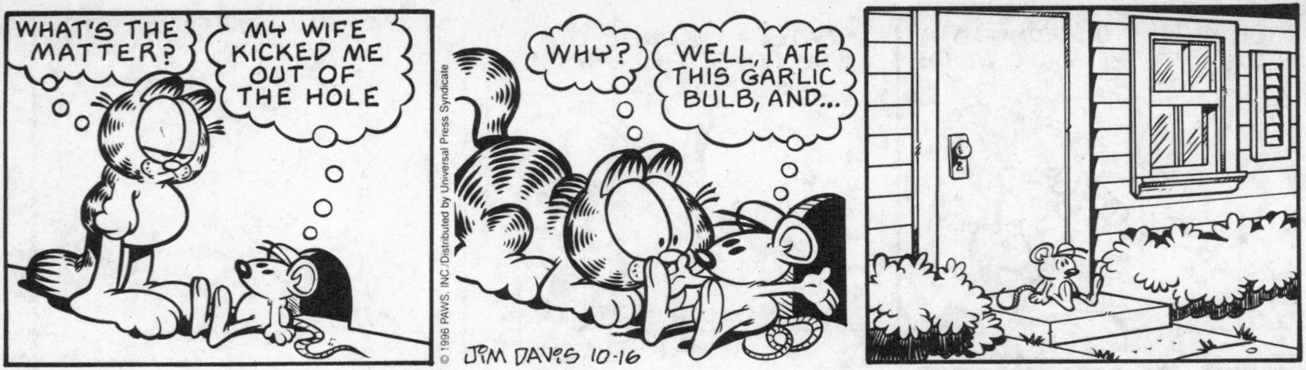
WHAT'S THE MATTER?
MY WIFE KICKED ME OUT OF THE HOLE
WHY?
WELL, I ATE THIS GARLIC BULB, AND...
© 1996 PAWS, INC./Distributed by Universal Press Syndicate
JIM DAVIS 10-16

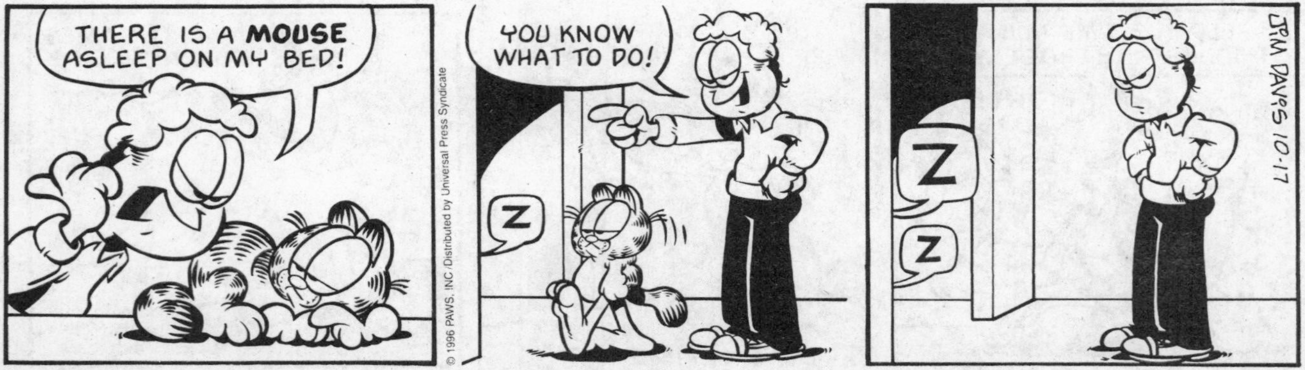
THERE IS A **MOUSE** ASLEEP ON MY BED!
© 1996 PAWS, INC./Distributed by Universal Press Syndicate
YOU KNOW WHAT TO DO!
Z
Z
Z
JIM DAVIS 10-17

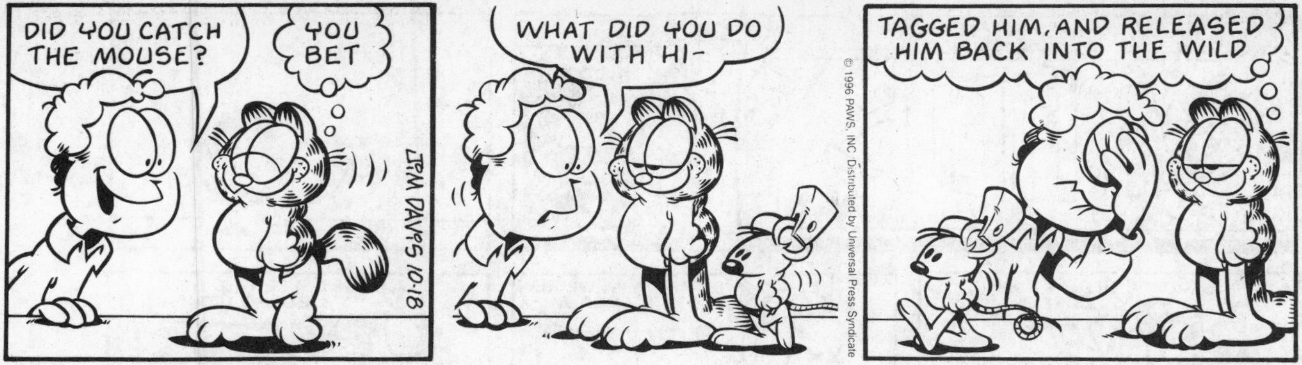
DID YOU CATCH THE MOUSE?
YOU BET
JIM DAVIS 10-18
WHAT DID YOU DO WITH HI-
TAGGED HIM, AND RELEASED HIM BACK INTO THE WILD

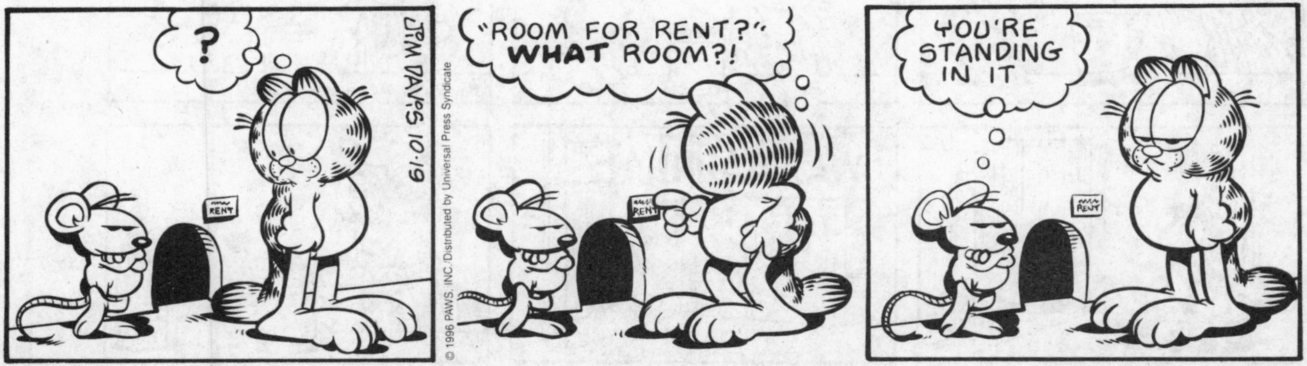
?
JIM DAVIS 10-19
"ROOM FOR RENT?" **WHAT** ROOM?!
YOU'RE STANDING IN IT

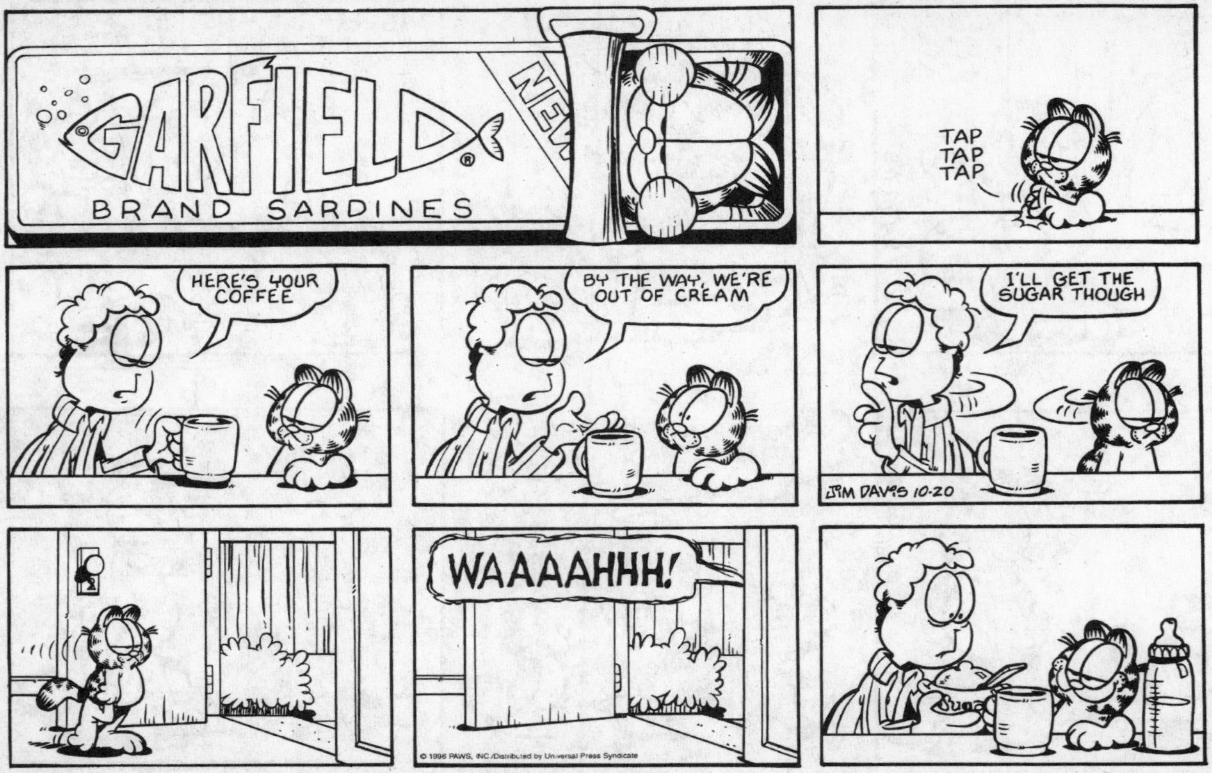
GARFIELD®
BRAND SARDINES
NEW
TAP
TAP
TAP
HERE'S YOUR COFFEE
BY THE WAY, WE'RE OUT OF CREAM
I'LL GET THE SUGAR THOUGH
JIM DAVIS 10-20
WAAAAHHH!
© 1996 PAWS, INC./Distributed by Universal Press Syndicate

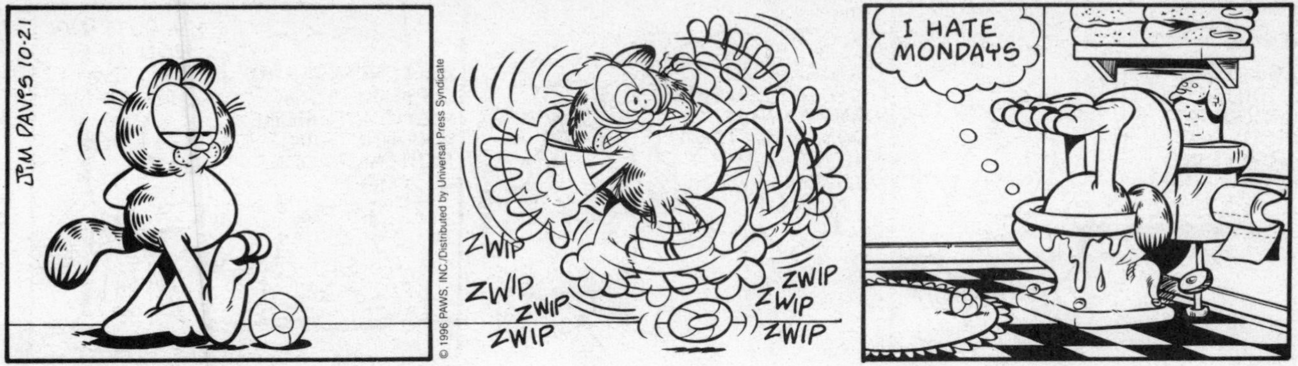
JIM DAVIS 10-21
© 1996 PAWS, INC./Distributed by Universal Press Syndicate
ZWIP
ZWIP
ZWIP
ZWIP
ZWIP
ZWIP
ZWIP
I HATE MONDAYS

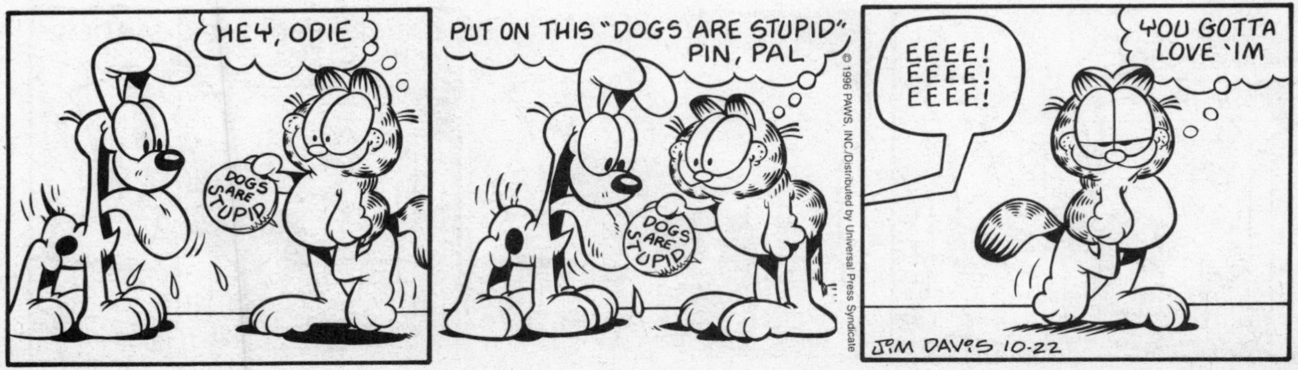
HEY, ODIE
DOGS ARE STUPID
PUT ON THIS "DOGS ARE STUPID" PIN, PAL
DOGS ARE STUPID
© 1996 PAWS, INC./Distributed by Universal Press Syndicate
EEEE!
EEEE!
EEEE!
YOU GOTTA LOVE 'IM
JIM DAVIS 10-22

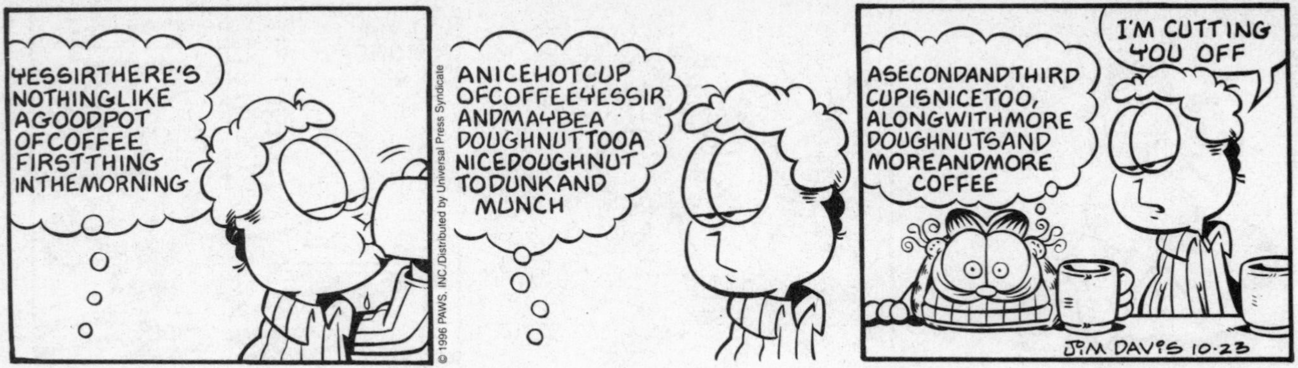
YESSIRTHERE'S NOTHINGLIKE AGOODPOT OFCOFFEE FIRSTTHING INTHEMORNING
ANICEHOTCUP OFCOFFEEYESSIR ANDMAYBEA DOUGHNUTTOOA NICEDOUGHNUT TODUNKAND MUNCH
ASECONDANDTHIRD CUPISNICETOO, ALONGWITHMORE DOUGHNUTSAND MOREANDMORE COFFEE
I'M CUTTING YOU OFF
JIM DAVIS 10-23

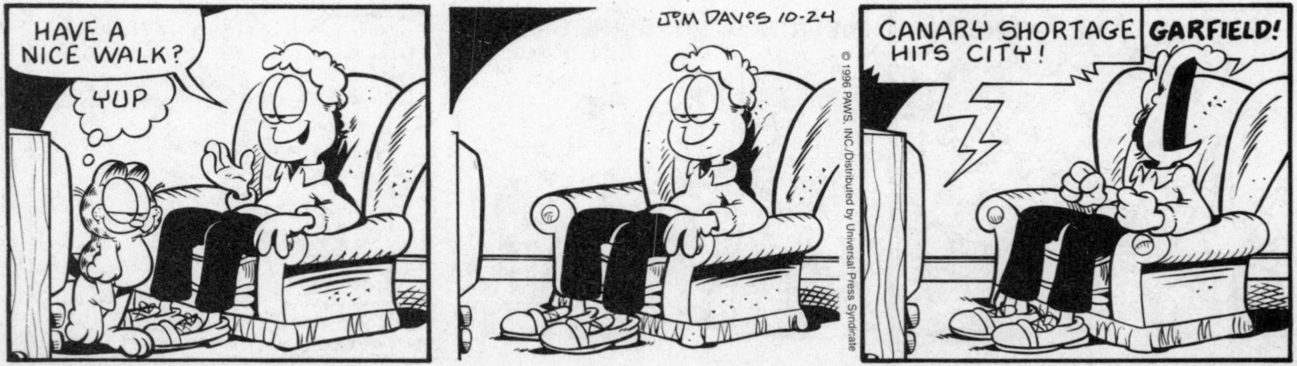
HAVE A NICE WALK?
YUP
JIM DAVIS 10-24
CANARY SHORTAGE HITS CITY!
GARFIELD!

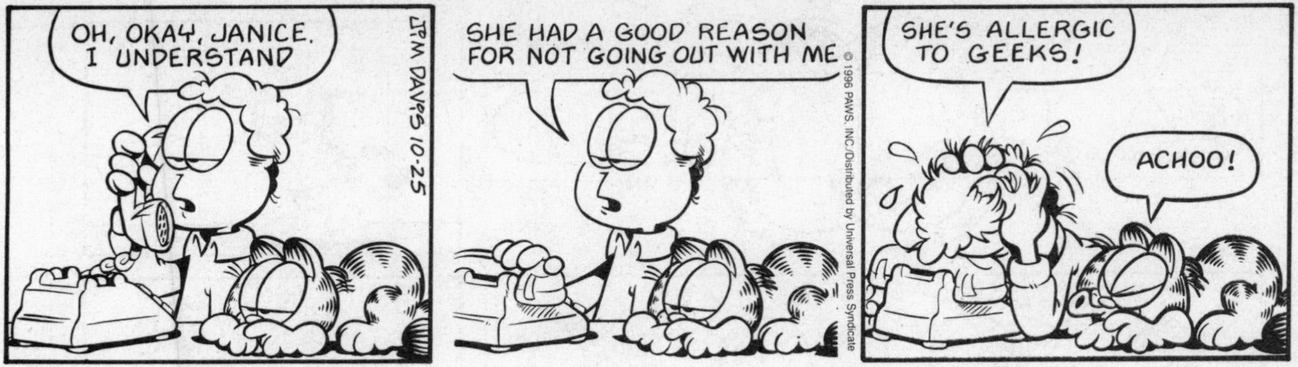
OH, OKAY, JANICE. I UNDERSTAND
JIM DAVIS 10-25
SHE HAD A GOOD REASON FOR NOT GOING OUT WITH ME
© 1996 PAWS, INC./Distributed by Universal Press Syndicate
SHE'S ALLERGIC TO GEEKS!
ACHOO!

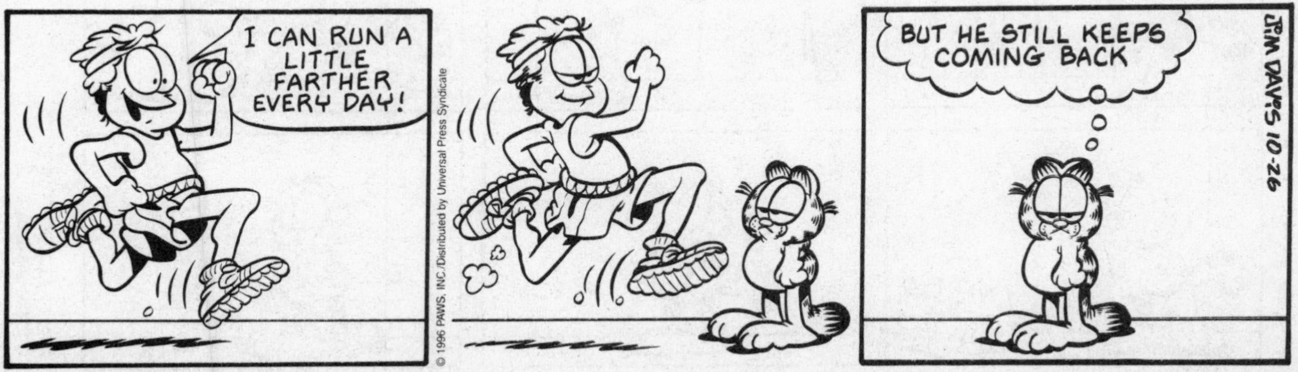
I CAN RUN A LITTLE FARTHER EVERY DAY!
© 1996 PAWS, INC./Distributed by Universal Press Syndicate
BUT HE STILL KEEPS COMING BACK
JIM DAVIS 10-26

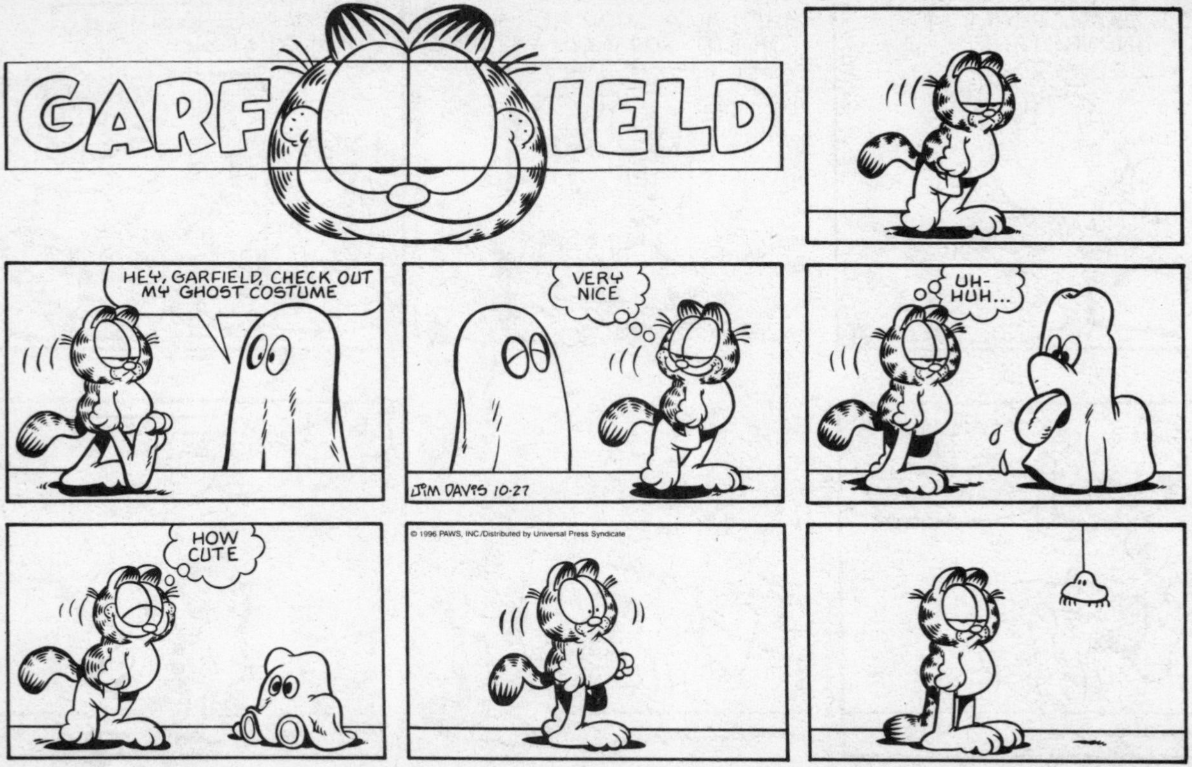
GARFIELD
HEY, GARFIELD, CHECK OUT MY GHOST COSTUME
VERY NICE
JIM DAVIS 10-27
UH-HUH...
HOW CUTE
© 1996 PAWS, INC./Distributed by Universal Press Syndicate

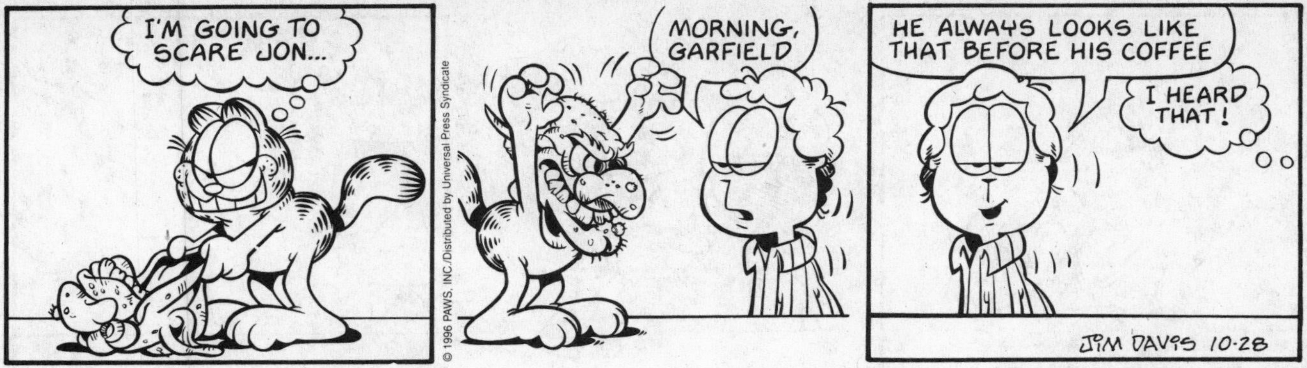
I'M GOING TO SCARE JON...
MORNING, GARFIELD
HE ALWAYS LOOKS LIKE THAT BEFORE HIS COFFEE
I HEARD THAT!
JIM DAVIS 10-28

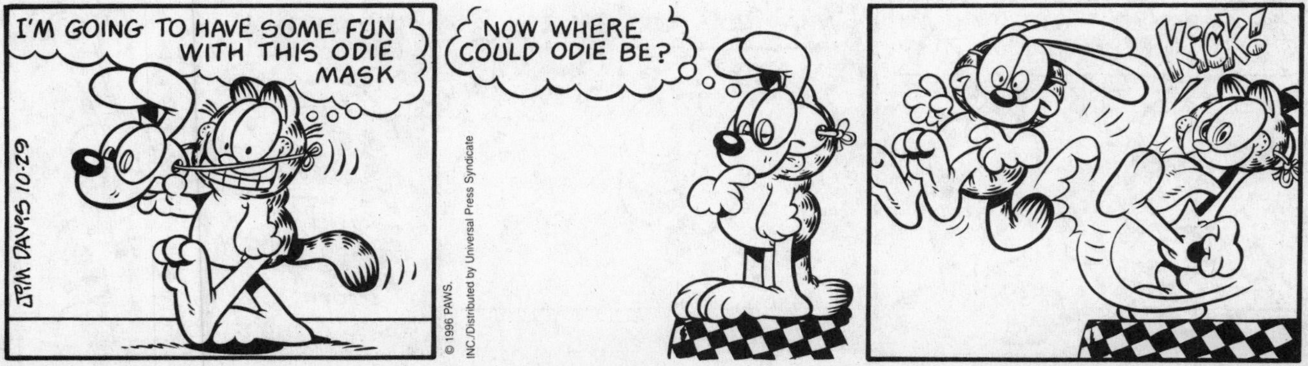
I'M GOING TO HAVE SOME FUN WITH THIS ODIE MASK
JIM DAVIS 10-29
NOW WHERE COULD ODIE BE?
KICK!

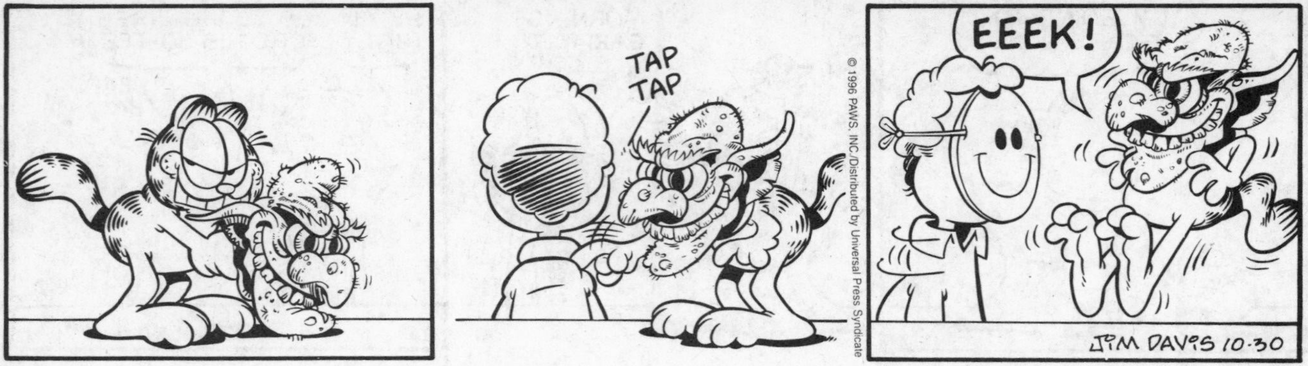
TAP
TAP
EEEK!
© 1996 PAWS, INC./Distributed by Universal Press Syndicate
JIM DAVIS 10-30

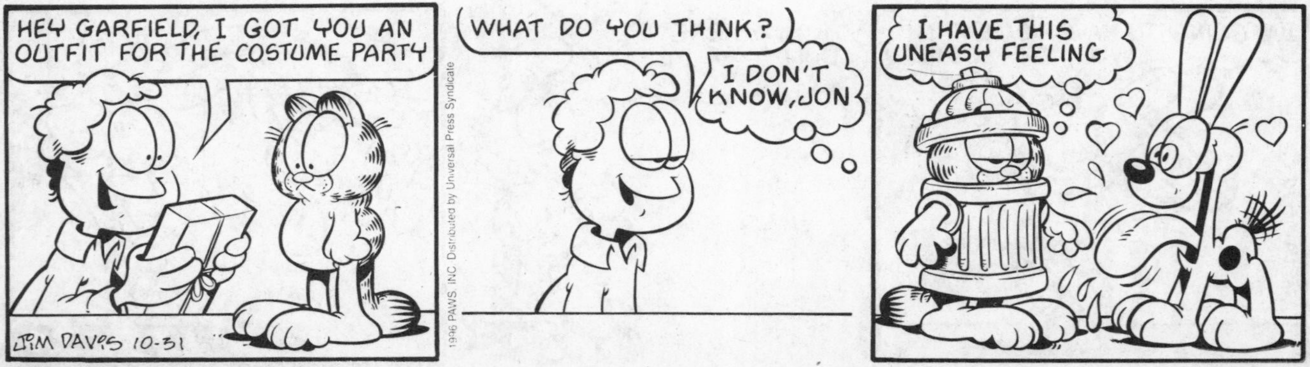
HEY GARFIELD, I GOT YOU AN OUTFIT FOR THE COSTUME PARTY
JIM DAVIS 10-31
1996 PAWS, INC. Distributed by Universal Press Syndicate
WHAT DO YOU THINK?
I DON'T KNOW, JON
I HAVE THIS UNEASY FEELING

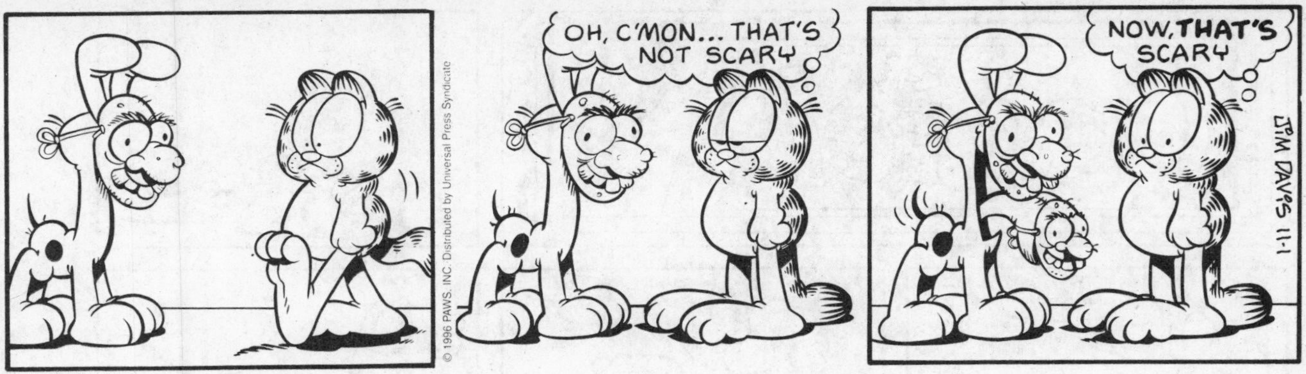
OH, C'MON... THAT'S NOT SCARY
NOW, THAT'S SCARY
JIM DAVIS 11-1

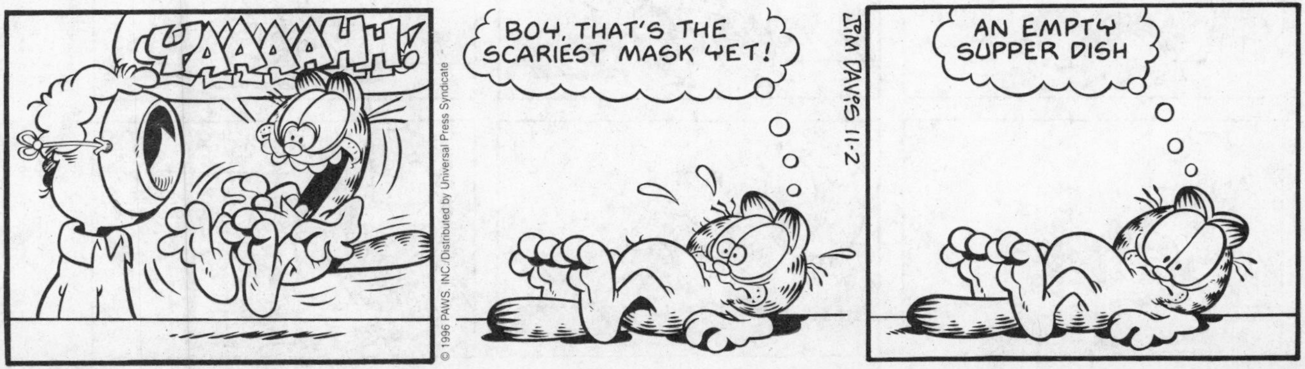
YAAAAAH!
BOY, THAT'S THE SCARIEST MASK YET!
AN EMPTY SUPPER DISH
JIM DAVIS 11-2

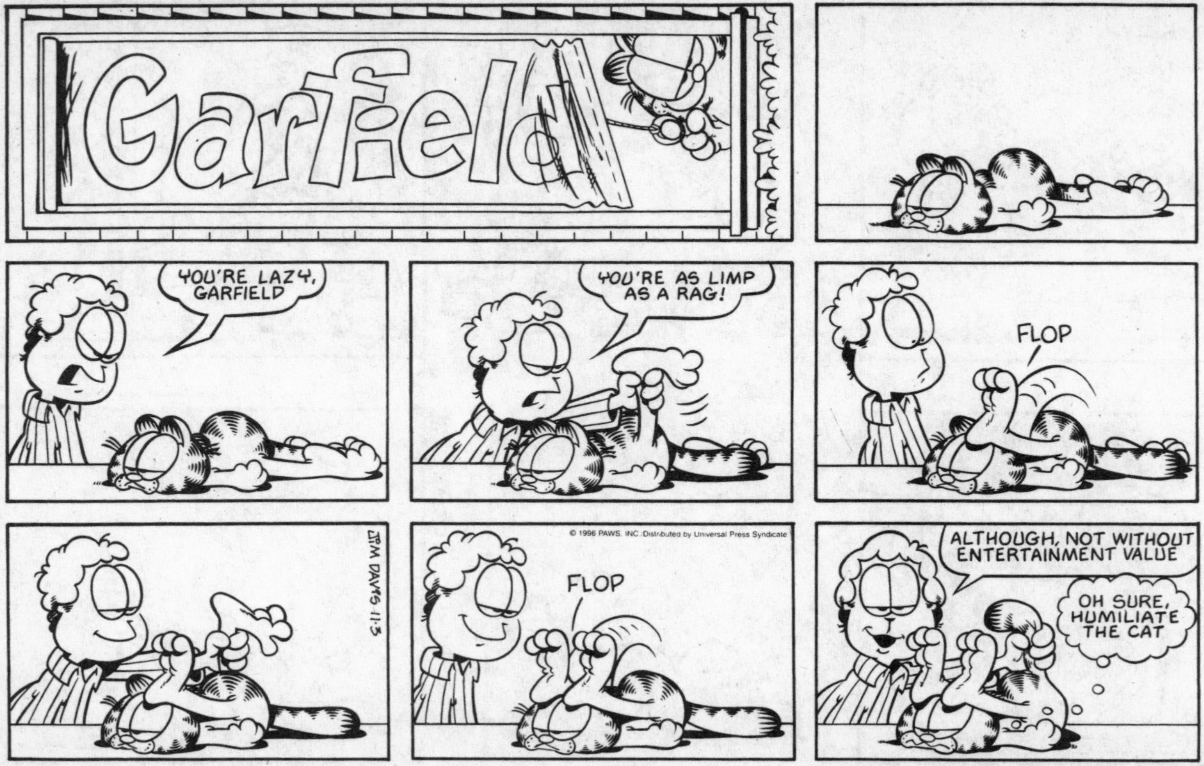
Garfield
YOU'RE LAZY, GARFIELD
YOU'RE AS LIMP AS A RAG!
FLOP
JIM DAVIS 11-3
© 1996 PAWS, INC./Distributed by Universal Press Syndicate
FLOP
ALTHOUGH, NOT WITHOUT ENTERTAINMENT VALUE
OH SURE, HUMILIATE THE CAT

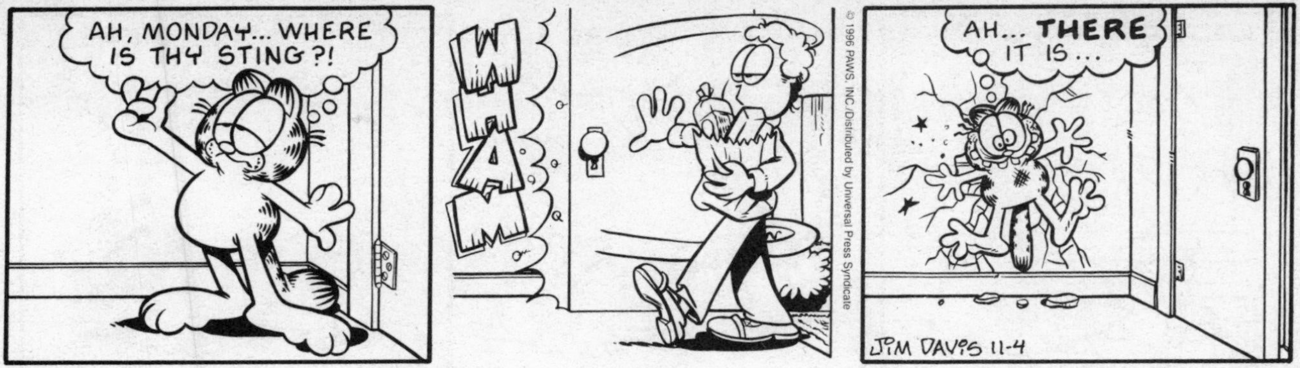
AH, MONDAY... WHERE IS THY STING?!
WHAM
AH... THERE IT IS...
© 1996 PAWS, INC./Distributed by Universal Press Syndicate
JIM DAVIS 11-4

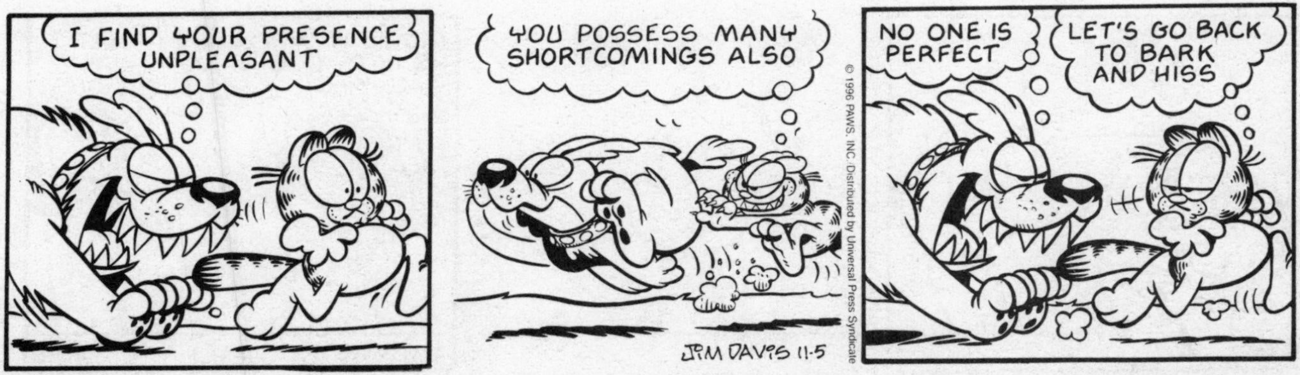
I FIND YOUR PRESENCE UNPLEASANT
YOU POSSESS MANY SHORTCOMINGS ALSO
NO ONE IS PERFECT
LET'S GO BACK TO BARK AND HISS
© 1996 PAWS, INC./Distributed by Universal Press Syndicate
JIM DAVIS 11-5

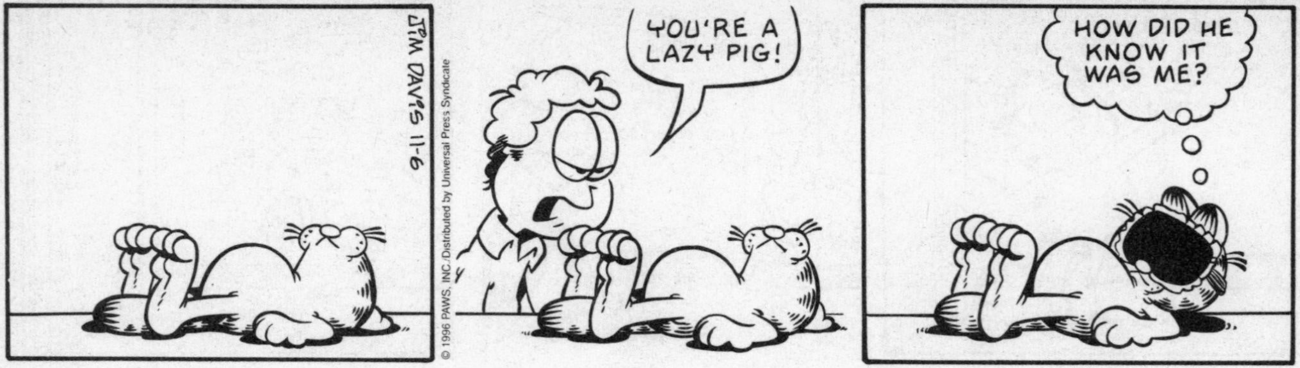
JIM DAVIS 11-6
YOU'RE A LAZY PIG!
HOW DID HE KNOW IT WAS ME?

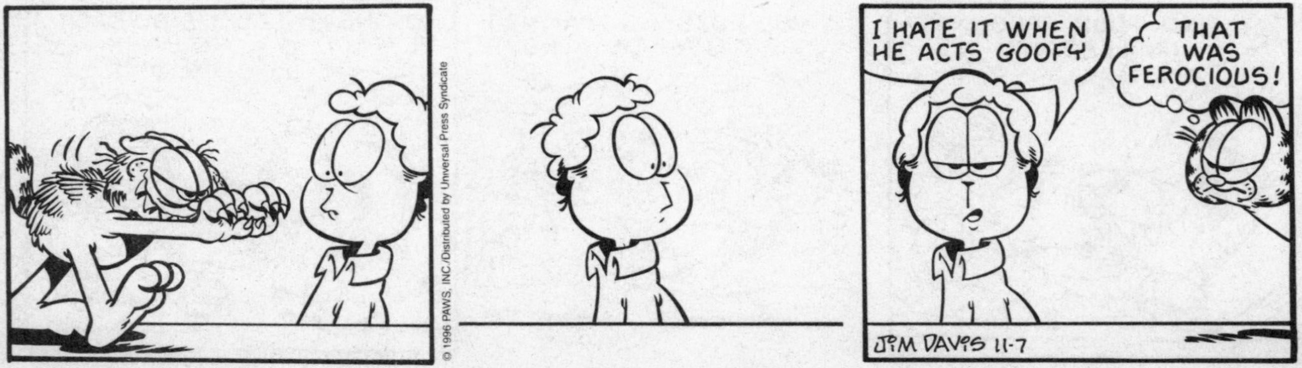
I HATE IT WHEN HE ACTS GOOFY
THAT WAS FEROCIOUS!
JIM DAVIS 11-7

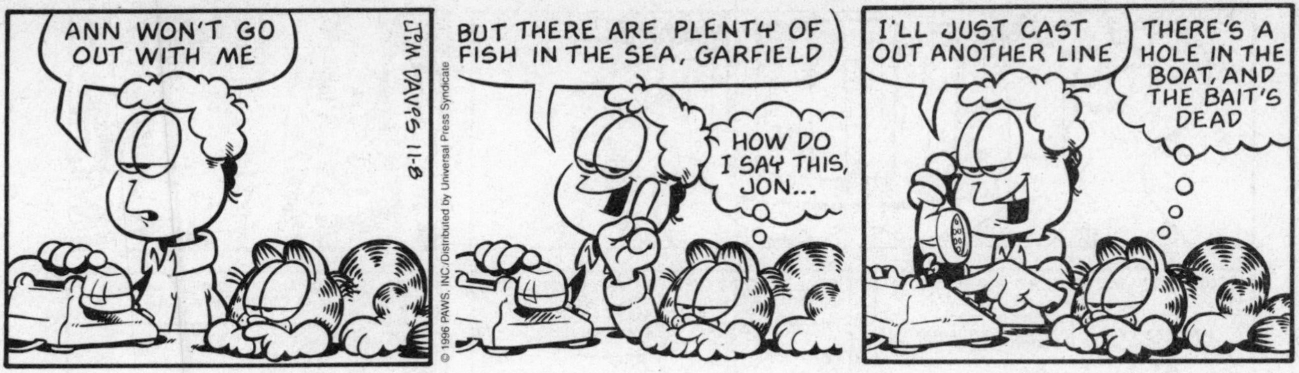
ANN WON'T GO OUT WITH ME
JIM DAVIS 11-8
© 1996 PAWS, INC./Distributed by Universal Press Syndicate
BUT THERE ARE PLENTY OF FISH IN THE SEA, GARFIELD
HOW DO I SAY THIS, JON...
I'LL JUST CAST OUT ANOTHER LINE
THERE'S A HOLE IN THE BOAT, AND THE BAIT'S DEAD

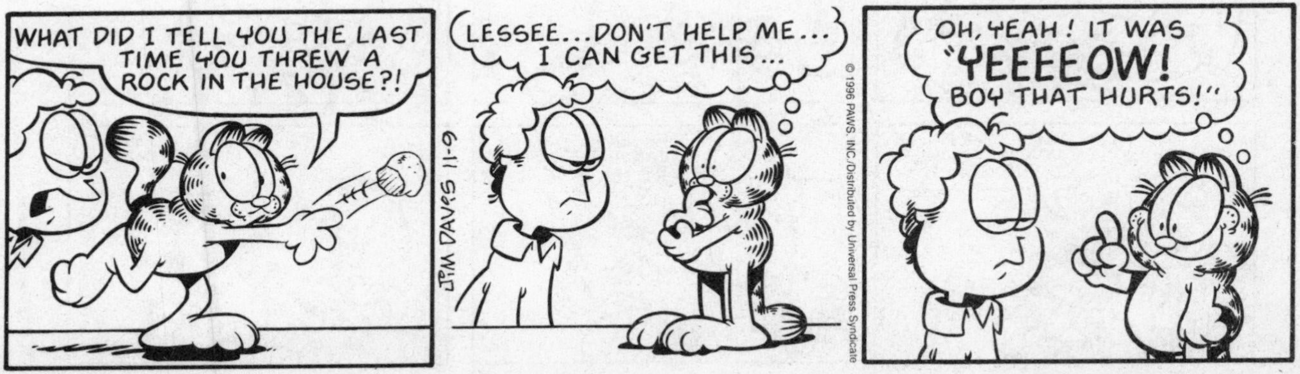
WHAT DID I TELL YOU THE LAST TIME YOU THREW A ROCK IN THE HOUSE?!
JIM DAVIS 11-9
LESSEE...DON'T HELP ME... I CAN GET THIS...
© 1996 PAWS, INC./Distributed by Universal Press Syndicate
OH, YEAH! IT WAS "YEEEEOW! BOY THAT HURTS!"

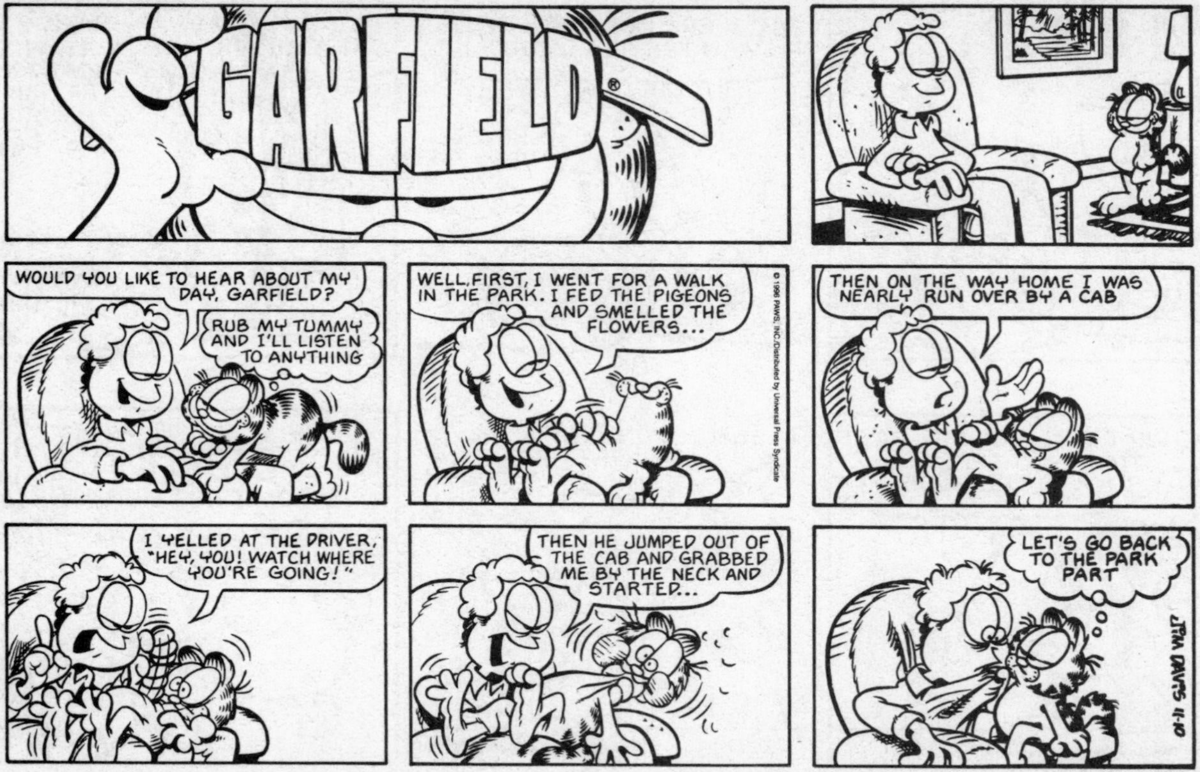
GARFIELD®
WOULD YOU LIKE TO HEAR ABOUT MY DAY, GARFIELD?
RUB MY TUMMY AND I'LL LISTEN TO ANYTHING
WELL, FIRST, I WENT FOR A WALK IN THE PARK. I FED THE PIGEONS AND SMELLED THE FLOWERS...
© 1996 PAWS, INC./Distributed by Universal Press Syndicate
THEN ON THE WAY HOME I WAS NEARLY RUN OVER BY A CAB
I YELLED AT THE DRIVER, "HEY, YOU! WATCH WHERE YOU'RE GOING!"
THEN HE JUMPED OUT OF THE CAB AND GRABBED ME BY THE NECK AND STARTED...
LET'S GO BACK TO THE PARK PART
JPM DAVIS 11-10

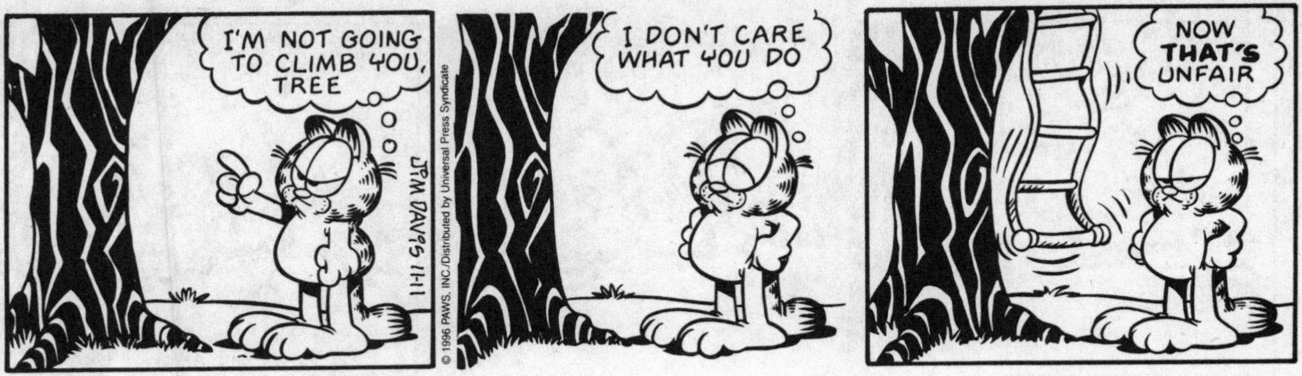
I'M NOT GOING TO CLIMB YOU, TREE
JIM DAVIS 11-11
© 1996 PAWS, INC./Distributed by Universal Press Syndicate
I DON'T CARE WHAT YOU DO
NOW THAT'S UNFAIR

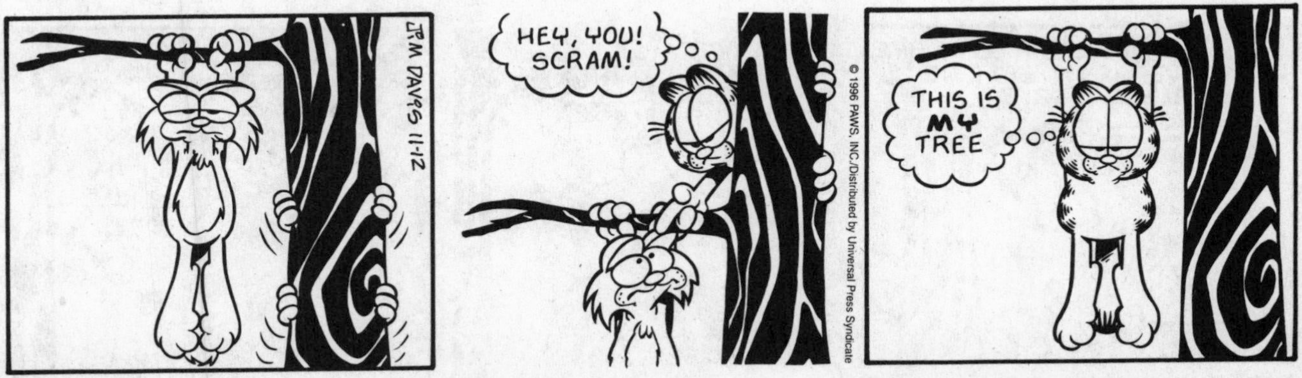
JIM DAVIS 11-12
HEY, YOU! SCRAM!
© 1996 PAWS, INC./Distributed by Universal Press Syndicate
THIS IS MY TREE

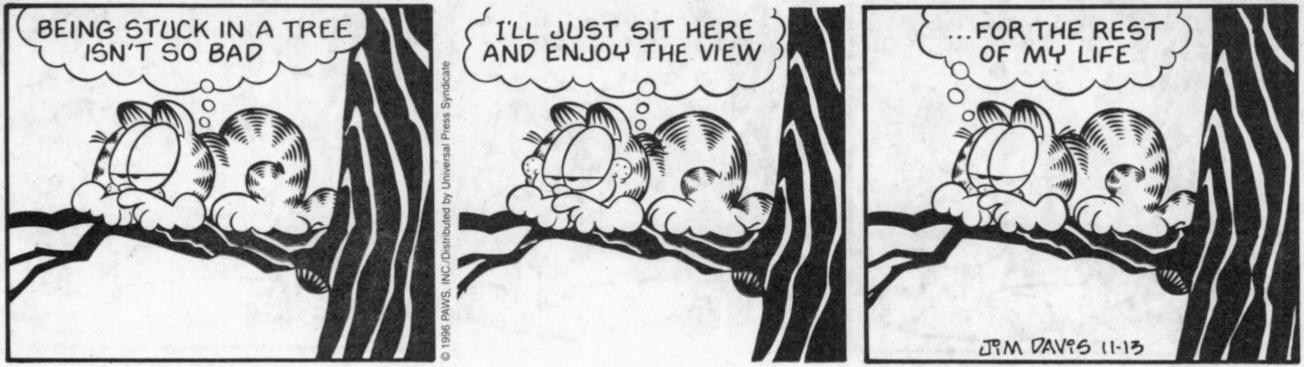
BEING STUCK IN A TREE ISN'T SO BAD
I'LL JUST SIT HERE AND ENJOY THE VIEW
...FOR THE REST OF MY LIFE
JIM DAVIS 11-13
© 1996 PAWS, INC./Distributed by Universal Press Syndicate

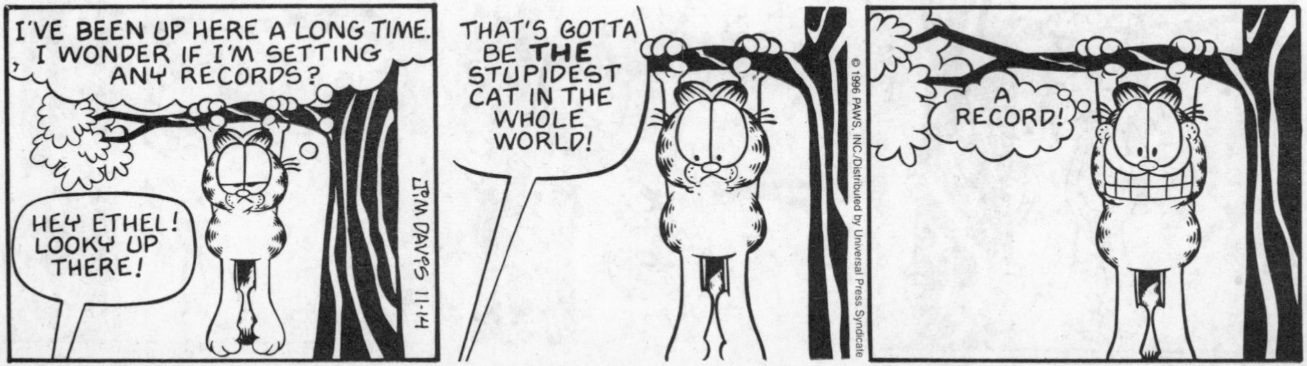
I'VE BEEN UP HERE A LONG TIME. I WONDER IF I'M SETTING ANY RECORDS?
HEY ETHEL! LOOKY UP THERE!
JIM DAVIS 11-14
THAT'S GOTTA BE **THE** STUPIDEST CAT IN THE WHOLE WORLD!
© 1996 PAWS, INC./Distributed by Universal Press Syndicate
A RECORD!

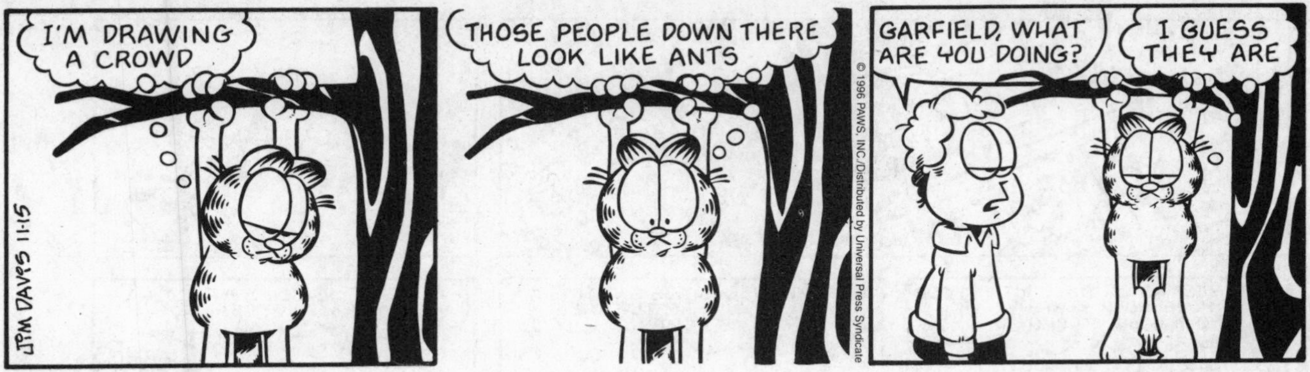
I'M DRAWING A CROWD
JIM DAVIS 11-15
THOSE PEOPLE DOWN THERE LOOK LIKE ANTS
GARFIELD, WHAT ARE YOU DOING?
I GUESS THEY ARE

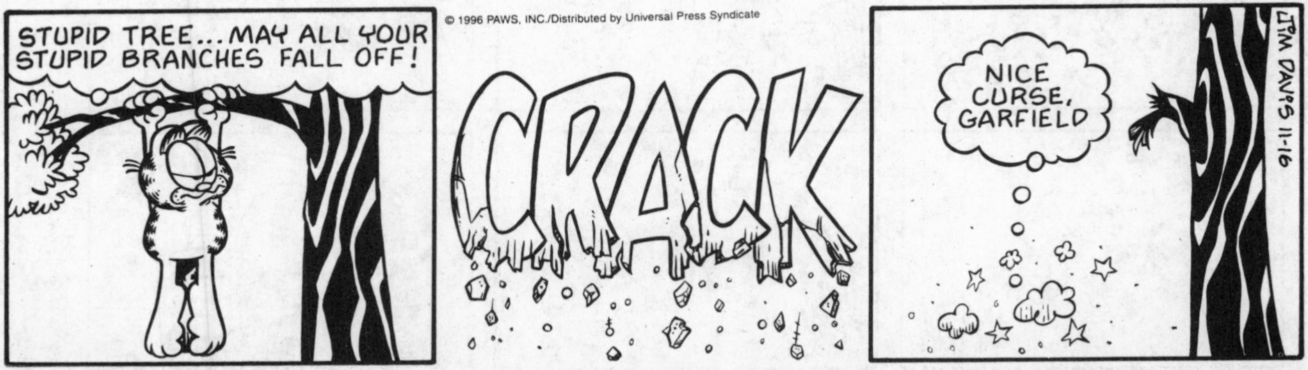
STUPID TREE... MAY ALL YOUR STUPID BRANCHES FALL OFF!
CRACK
NICE CURSE, GARFIELD
JIM DAVIS 11-16

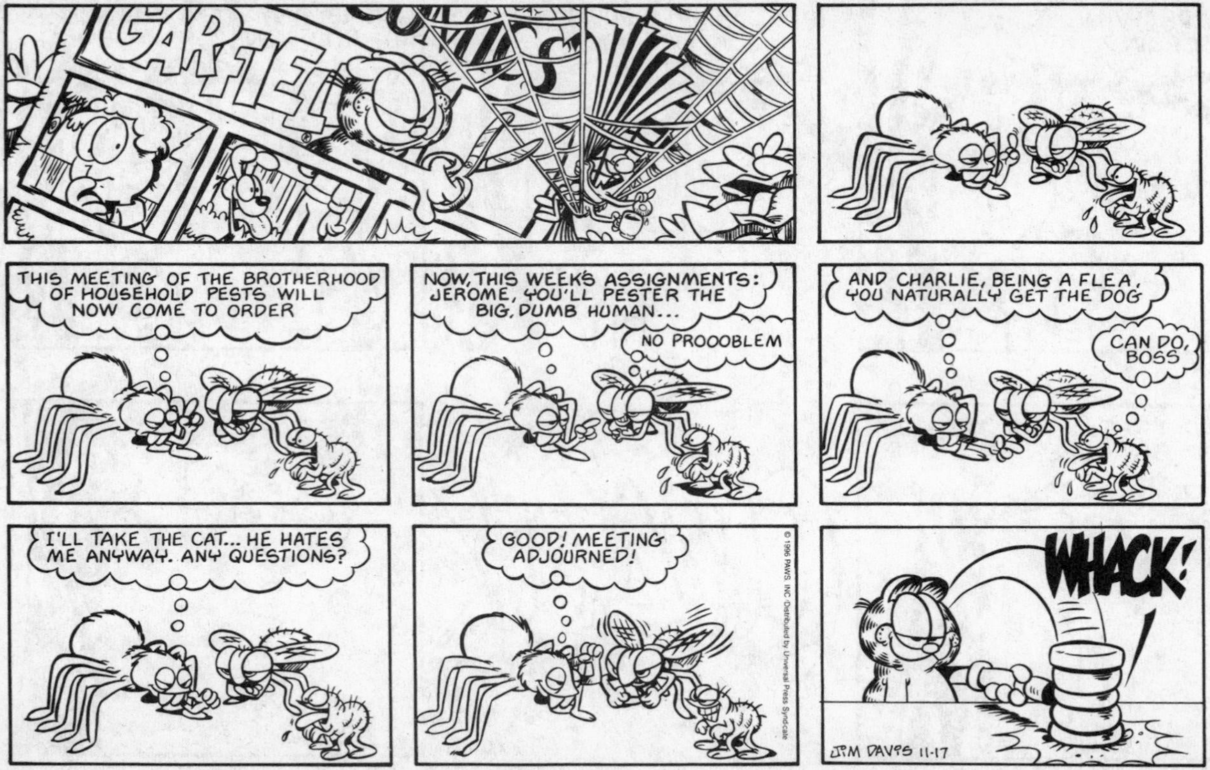
GARFIEL
THIS MEETING OF THE BROTHERHOOD OF HOUSEHOLD PESTS WILL NOW COME TO ORDER
NOW, THIS WEEKS ASSIGNMENTS: JEROME, YOU'LL PESTER THE BIG, DUMB HUMAN...
NO PROOOBLEM
AND CHARLIE, BEING A FLEA, YOU NATURALLY GET THE DOG
CAN DO, BOSS
I'LL TAKE THE CAT... HE HATES ME ANYWAY. ANY QUESTIONS?
GOOD! MEETING ADJOURNED!
© 1996 PAWS, INC. Distributed by Universal Press Syndicate
WHACK!
JIM DAVIS 11-17

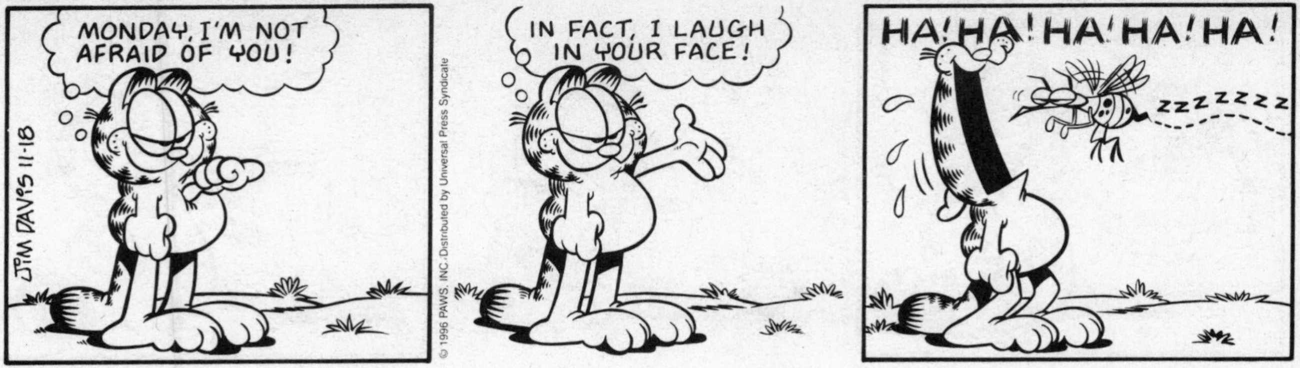
MONDAY, I'M NOT AFRAID OF YOU!
JIM DAVIS 11-18
IN FACT, I LAUGH IN YOUR FACE!
HA! HA! HA! HA! HA!
ZZZZZZZ

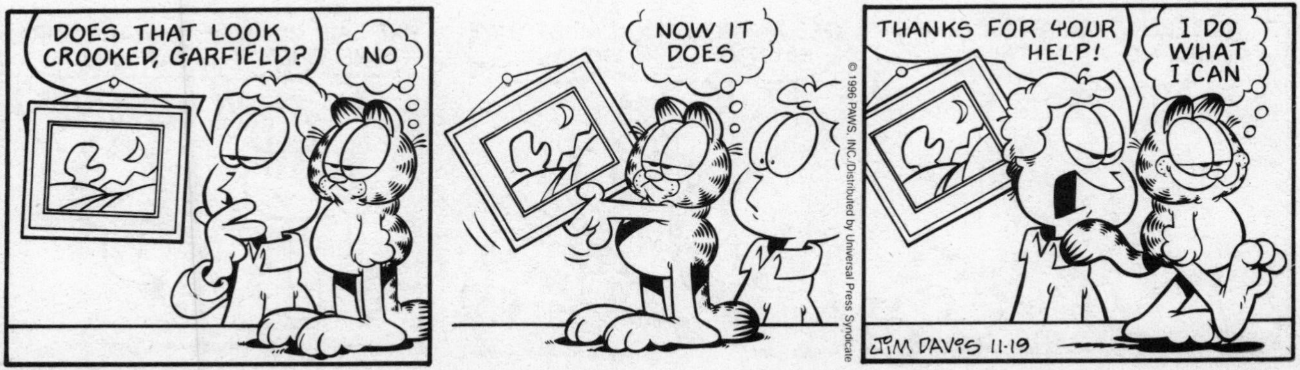
DOES THAT LOOK CROOKED, GARFIELD?
NO
NOW IT DOES
THANKS FOR YOUR HELP!
I DO WHAT I CAN
JIM DAVIS 11-19

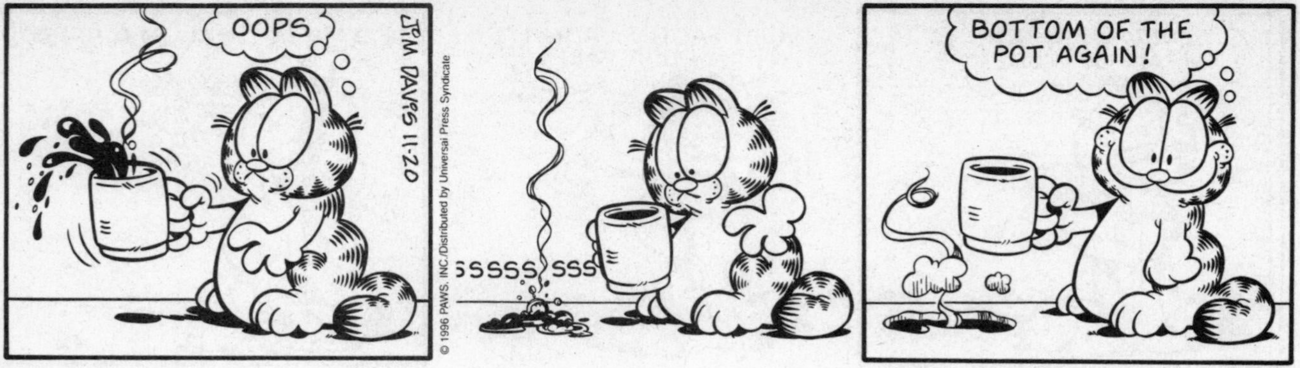
OOPS
JIM DAVIS 11-20
© 1996 PAWS, INC./Distributed by Universal Press Syndicate
SSSSS SSS
BOTTOM OF THE POT AGAIN!

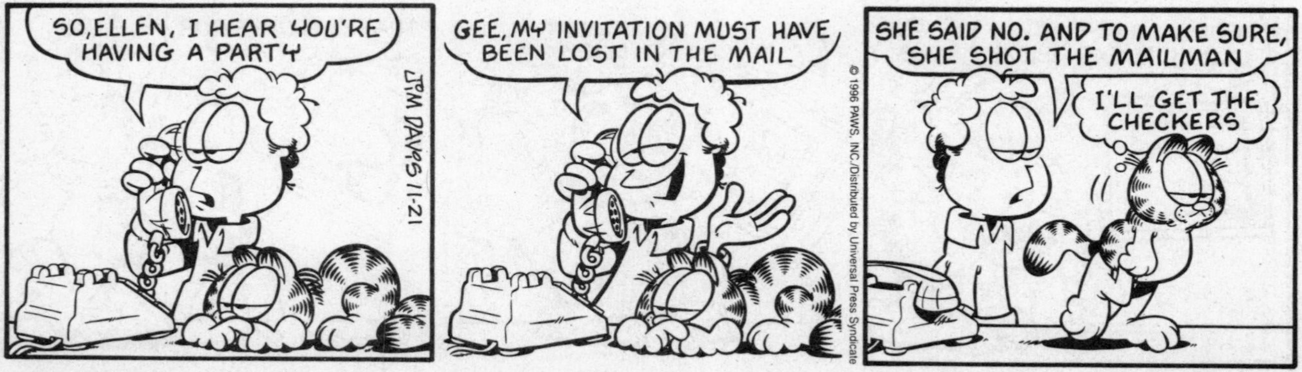
SO, ELLEN, I HEAR YOU'RE HAVING A PARTY
JIM DAVIS 11-21
GEE, MY INVITATION MUST HAVE BEEN LOST IN THE MAIL
© 1996 PAWS, INC./Distributed by Universal Press Syndicate
SHE SAID NO. AND TO MAKE SURE, SHE SHOT THE MAILMAN
I'LL GET THE CHECKERS

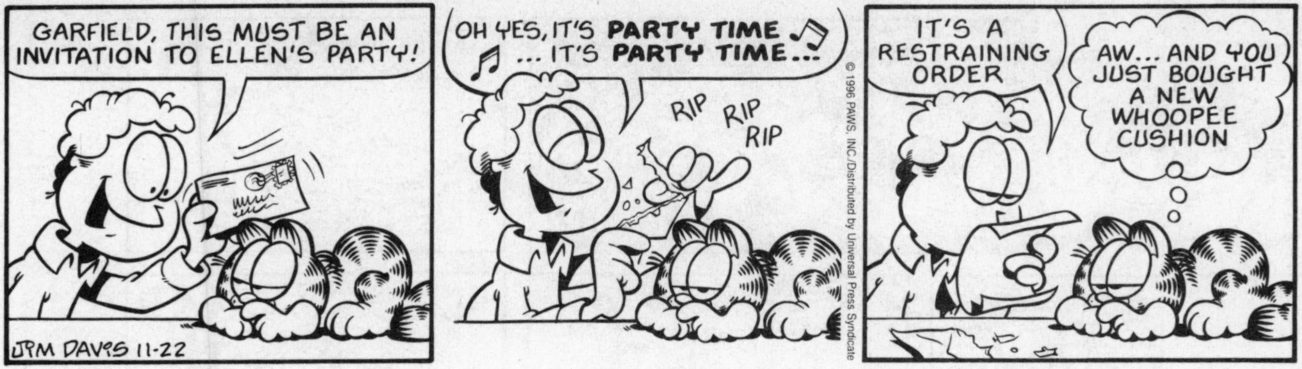
GARFIELD, THIS MUST BE AN INVITATION TO ELLEN'S PARTY!
JIM DAVIS 11-22
OH YES, IT'S **PARTY TIME** ♫ ... IT'S **PARTY TIME...**
RIP RIP RIP
© 1996 PAWS, INC./Distributed by Universal Press Syndicate
IT'S A RESTRAINING ORDER
AW... AND YOU JUST BOUGHT A NEW WHOOPEE CUSHION

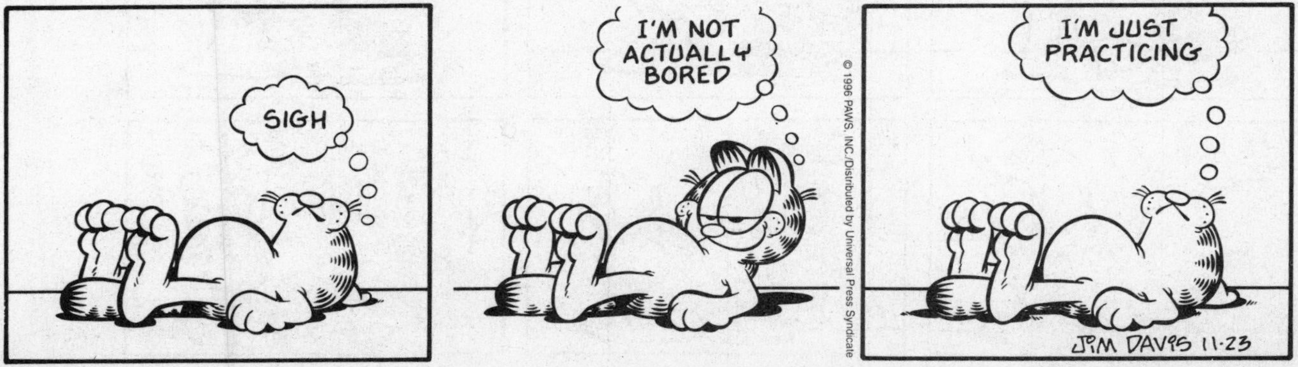
SIGH
I'M NOT ACTUALLY BORED
© 1996 PAWS, INC./Distributed by Universal Press Syndicate
I'M JUST PRACTICING
JIM DAVIS 11-23

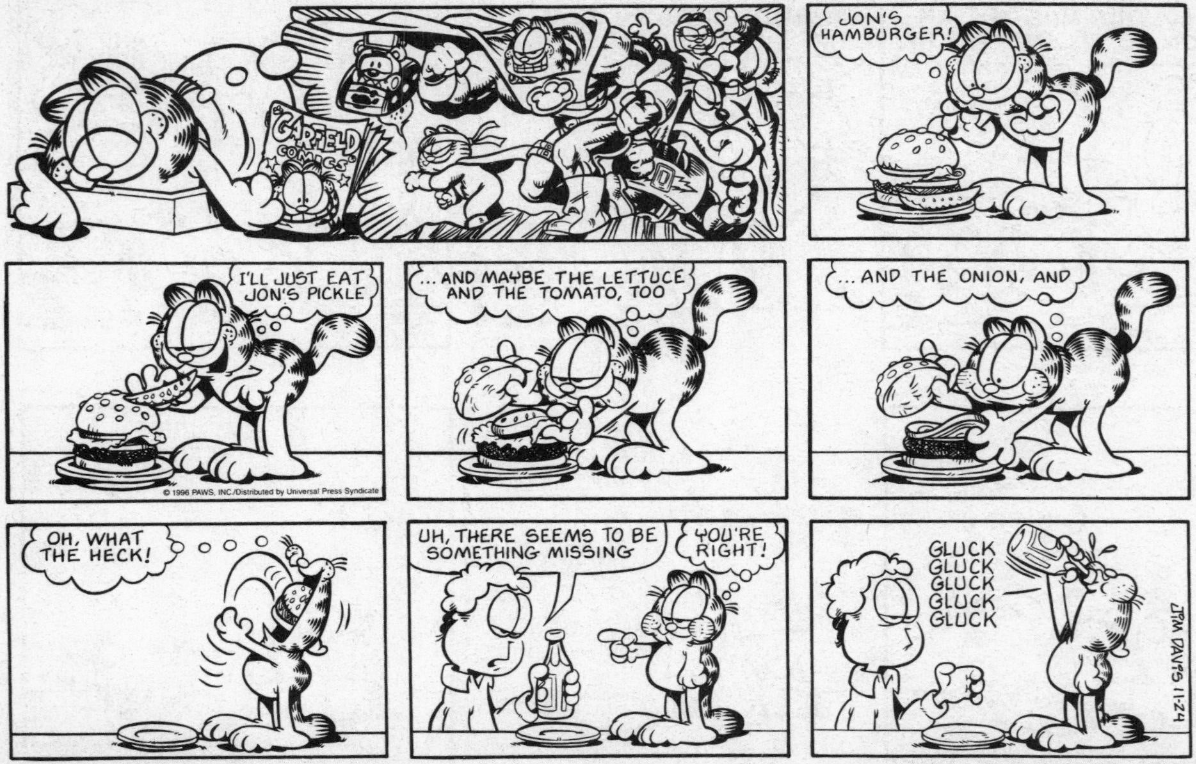
GARFIELD COMICS
JON'S HAMBURGER!
I'LL JUST EAT JON'S PICKLE
... AND MAYBE THE LETTUCE AND THE TOMATO, TOO
... AND THE ONION, AND
OH, WHAT THE HECK!
UH, THERE SEEMS TO BE SOMETHING MISSING
YOU'RE RIGHT!
GLUCK
GLUCK
GLUCK
GLUCK
GLUCK
JIM DAVIS 11-24

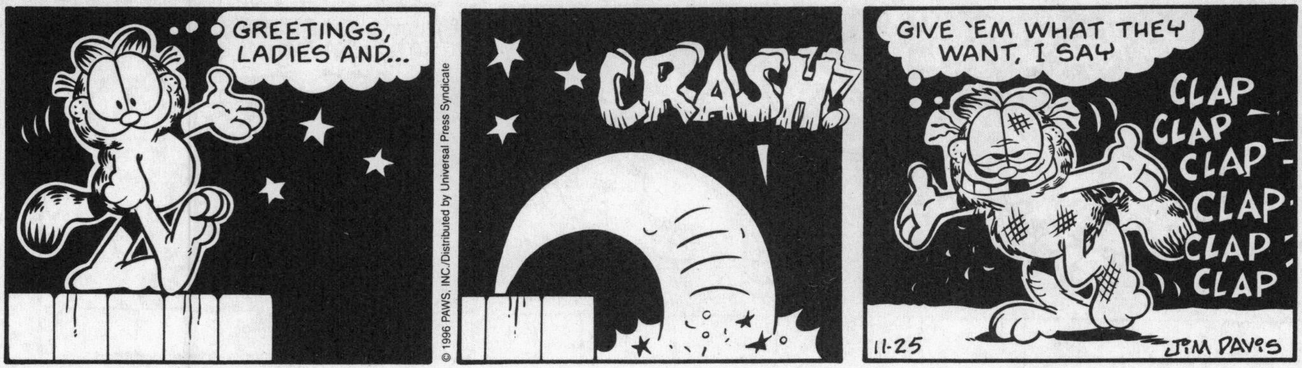
GREETINGS, LADIES AND...
© 1996 PAWS, INC./Distributed by Universal Press Syndicate
CRASH!
GIVE 'EM WHAT THEY WANT, I SAY
CLAP CLAP CLAP CLAP CLAP CLAP
11-25
JIM DAVIS

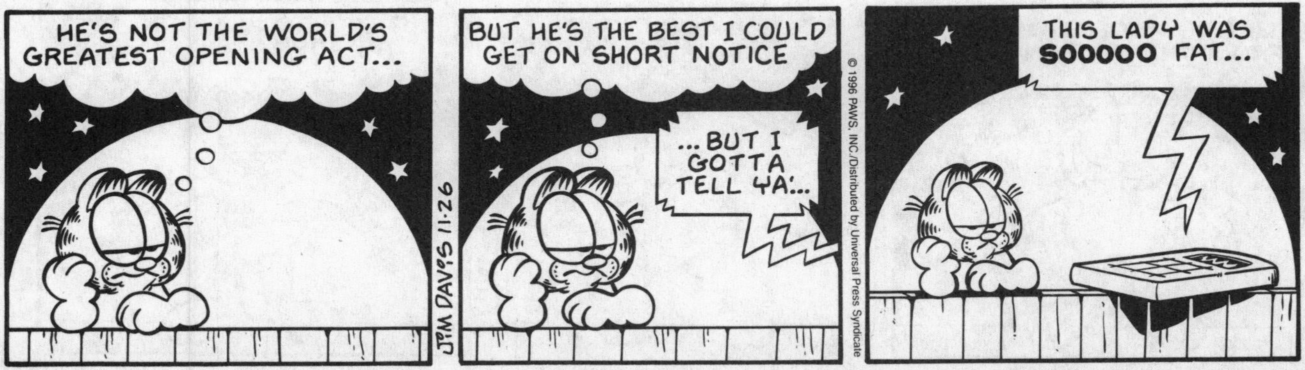
HE'S NOT THE WORLD'S GREATEST OPENING ACT...
JIM DAVIS 11-26
BUT HE'S THE BEST I COULD GET ON SHORT NOTICE
...BUT I GOTTA TELL YA'...
© 1996 PAWS, INC./Distributed by Universal Press Syndicate
THIS LADY WAS SOOOOO FAT...

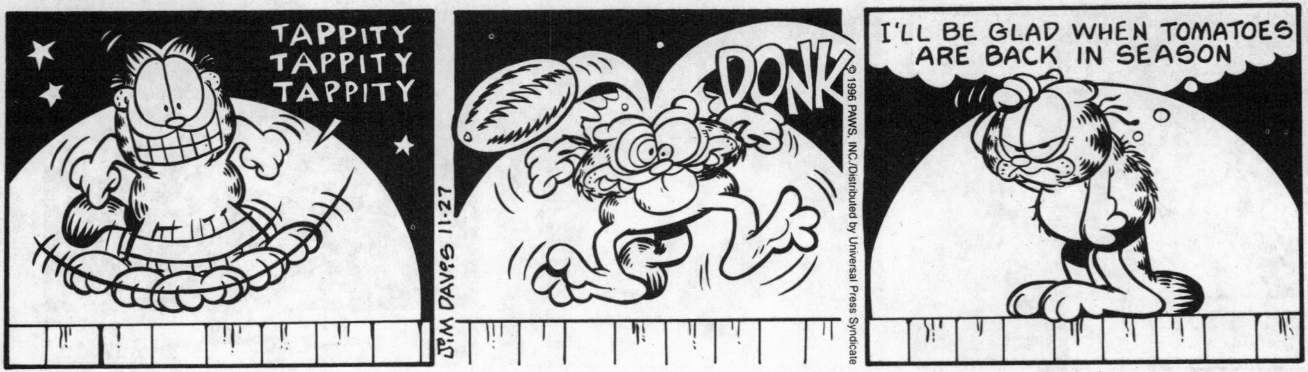
TAPPITY
TAPPITY
TAPPITY
JIM DAVIS 11-27
DONK
© 1996 PAWS, INC./Distributed by Universal Press Syndicate
I'LL BE GLAD WHEN TOMATOES ARE BACK IN SEASON

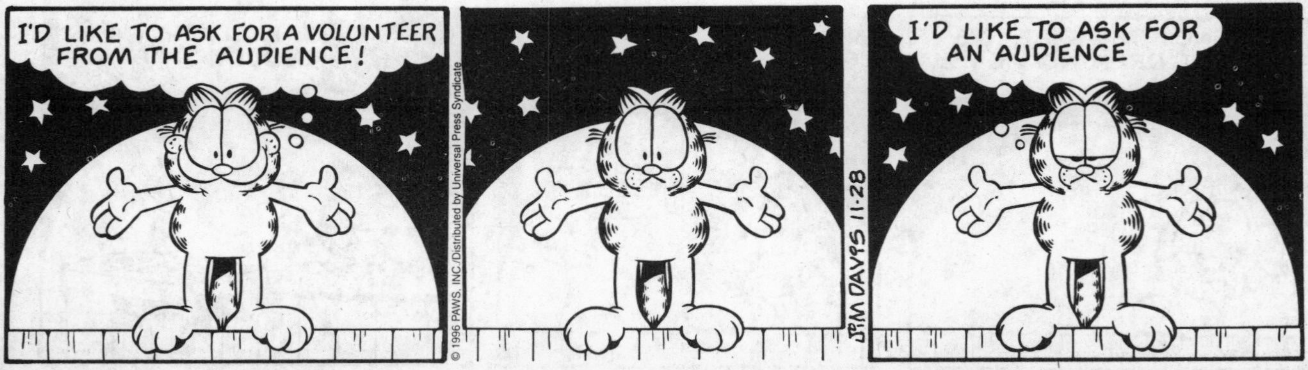
I'D LIKE TO ASK FOR A VOLUNTEER FROM THE AUDIENCE!
© 1996 PAWS, INC./Distributed by Universal Press Syndicate
JIM DAVIS 11-28
I'D LIKE TO ASK FOR AN AUDIENCE

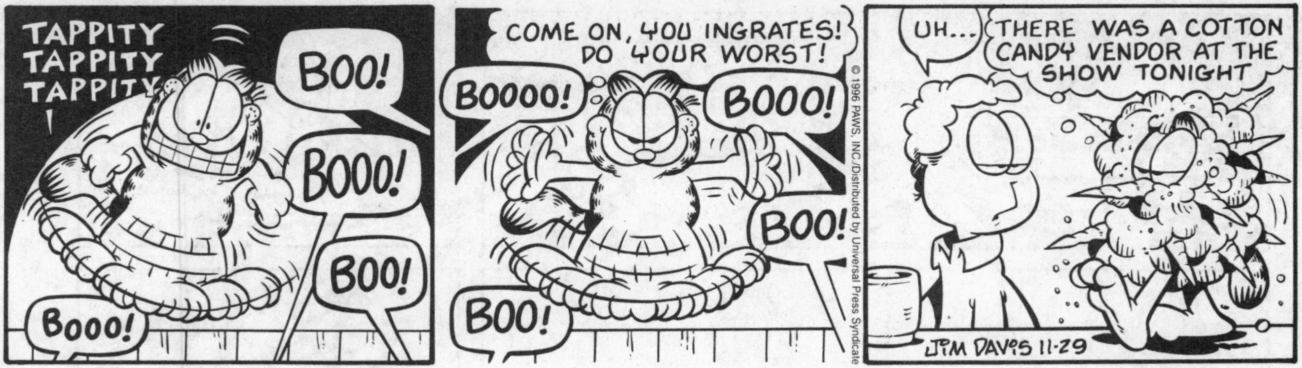
TAPPITY TAPPITY TAPPITY
BOO!
BOOO!
BOO!
Booo!
COME ON, YOU INGRATES! DO YOUR WORST!
BOOOO!
BOOO!
BOO!
BOO!
UH...
THERE WAS A COTTON CANDY VENDOR AT THE SHOW TONIGHT
JIM DAVIS 11-29

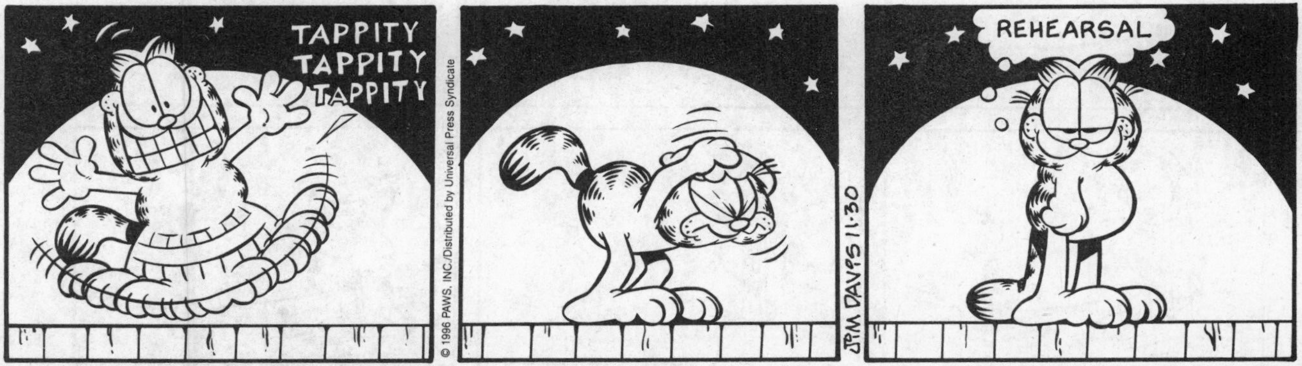
TAPPITY TAPPITY TAPPITY
REHEARSAL
JIM DAVIS 11-30

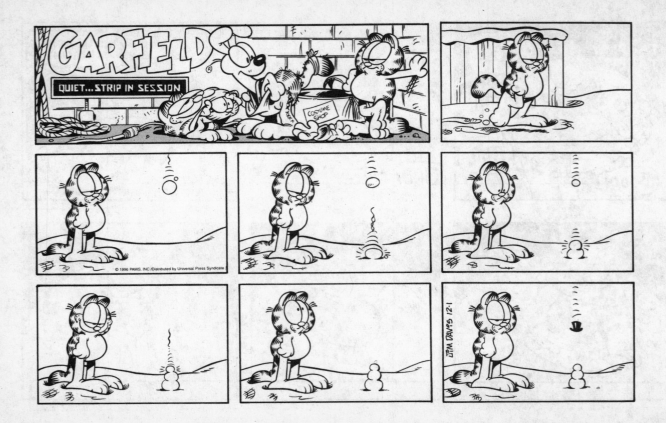

GARFIELD

QUIET... STRIP IN SESSION

COSTUME SHOP

© 1996 PAWS, INC./Distributed by Universal Press Syndicate

JIM DAVIS 12-1

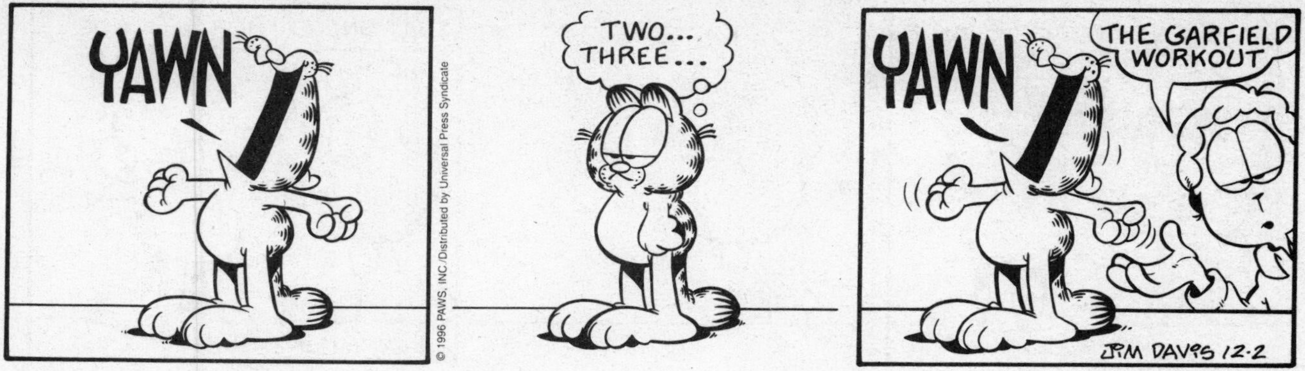
YAWN
TWO... THREE...
YAWN
THE GARFIELD WORKOUT
JIM DAVIS 12-2

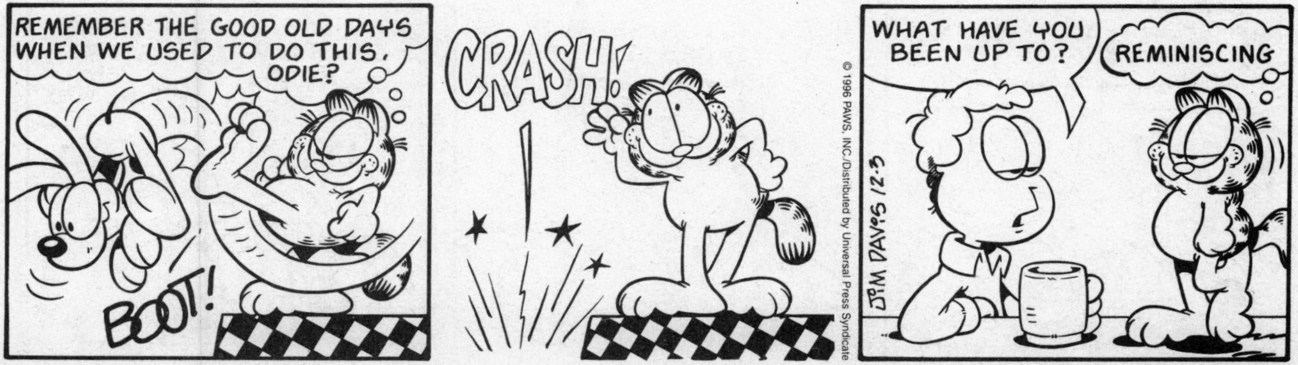
REMEMBER THE GOOD OLD DAYS WHEN WE USED TO DO THIS, ODIE?
BOOT!
CRASH!
WHAT HAVE YOU BEEN UP TO?
REMINISCING
JIM DAVIS 12-3

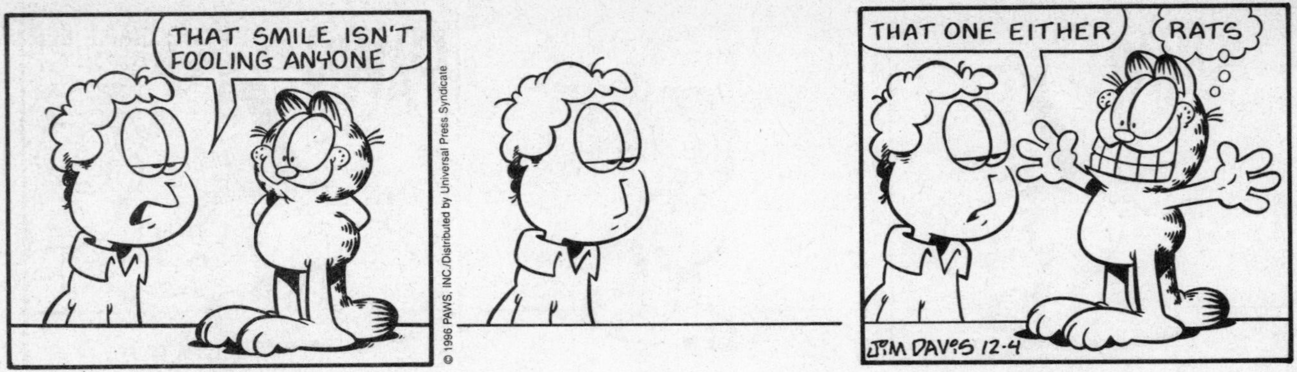
THAT SMILE ISN'T FOOLING ANYONE
© 1996 PAWS, INC./Distributed by Universal Press Syndicate
THAT ONE EITHER
RATS
JIM DAVIS 12-4

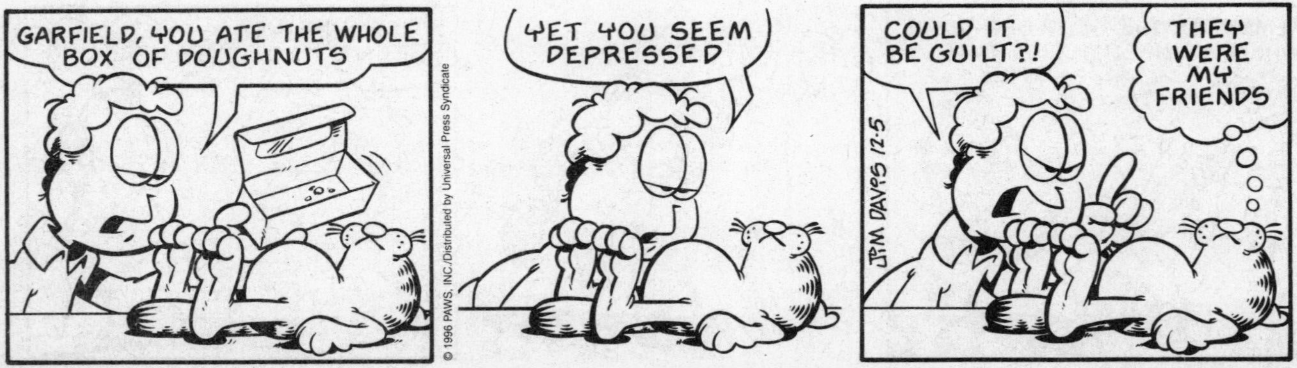
GARFIELD, YOU ATE THE WHOLE BOX OF DOUGHNUTS
© 1996 PAWS, INC./Distributed by Universal Press Syndicate
YET YOU SEEM DEPRESSED
COULD IT BE GUILT?!
THEY WERE MY FRIENDS
JIM DAVIS 12-5

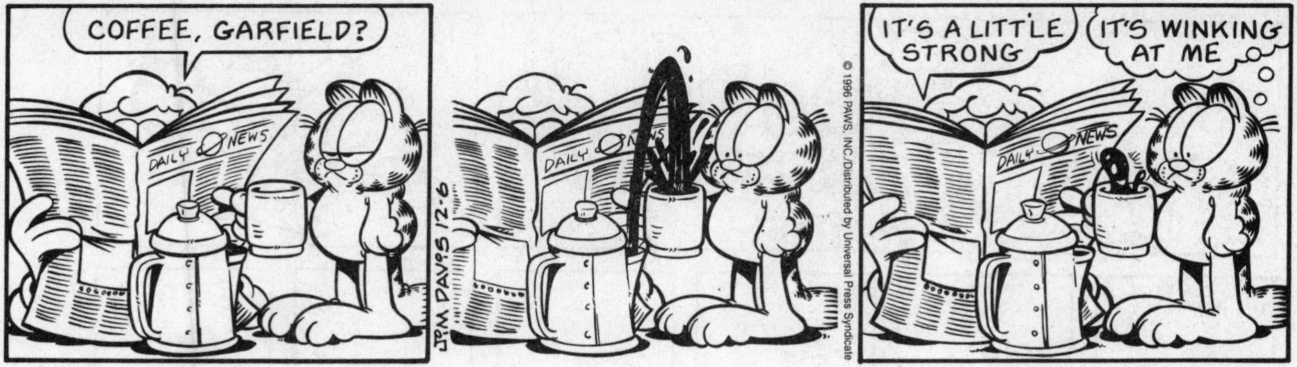
COFFEE, GARFIELD?
DAILY NEWS
IT'S A LITTLE STRONG
IT'S WINKING AT ME
JIM DAVIS 12-6

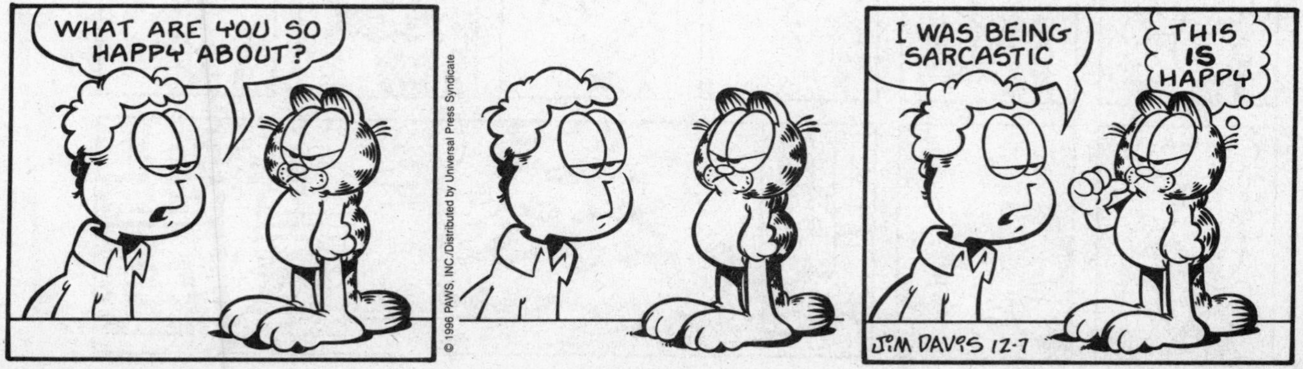
WHAT ARE YOU SO HAPPY ABOUT?
I WAS BEING SARCASTIC
THIS **IS** HAPPY
JIM DAVIS 12-7

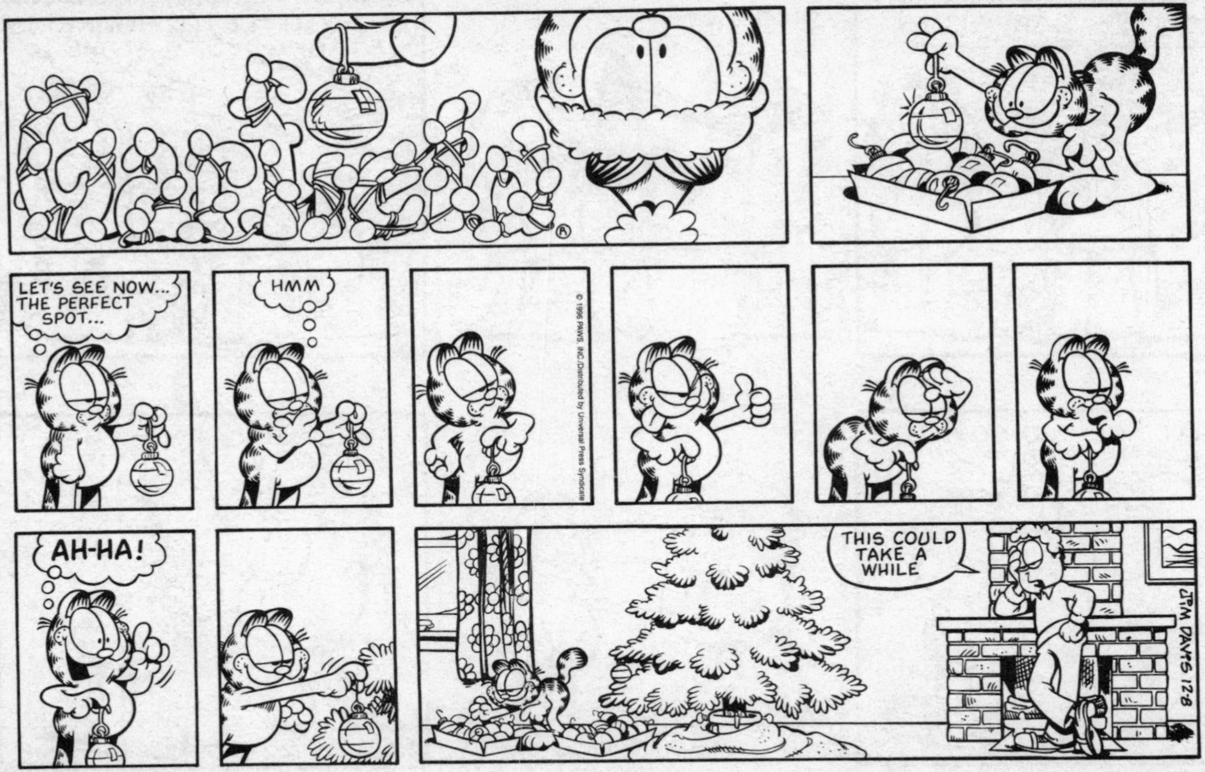
Garfield
LET'S SEE NOW... THE PERFECT SPOT...
HMM
© 1996 PAWS, INC./Distributed by Universal Press Syndicate
AH-HA!
THIS COULD TAKE A WHILE
JIM DAVIS 12-8

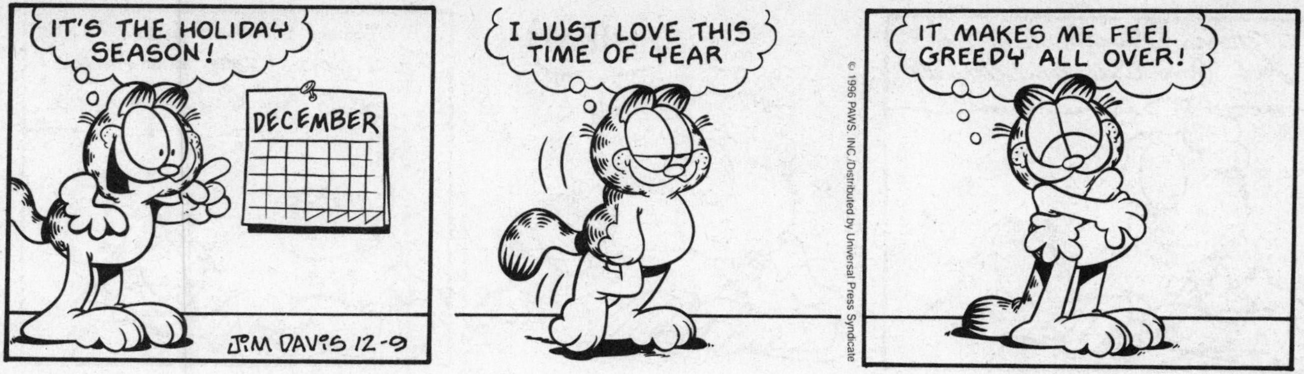
IT'S THE HOLIDAY SEASON!
DECEMBER
JIM DAVIS 12-9
I JUST LOVE THIS TIME OF YEAR
© 1996 PAWS, INC./Distributed by Universal Press Syndicate
IT MAKES ME FEEL GREEDY ALL OVER!

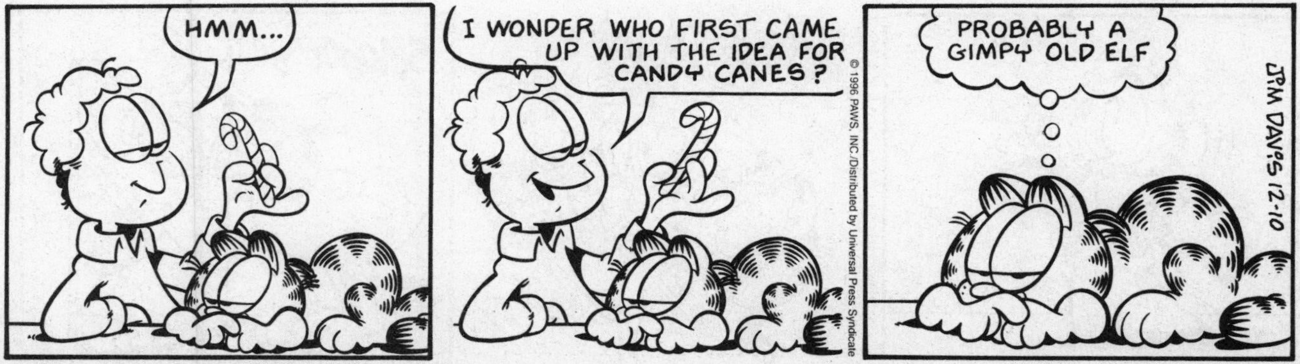
HMM...
I WONDER WHO FIRST CAME UP WITH THE IDEA FOR CANDY CANES?
© 1996 PAWS, INC./Distributed by Universal Press Syndicate
PROBABLY A GIMPY OLD ELF
JIM DAVIS 12-10

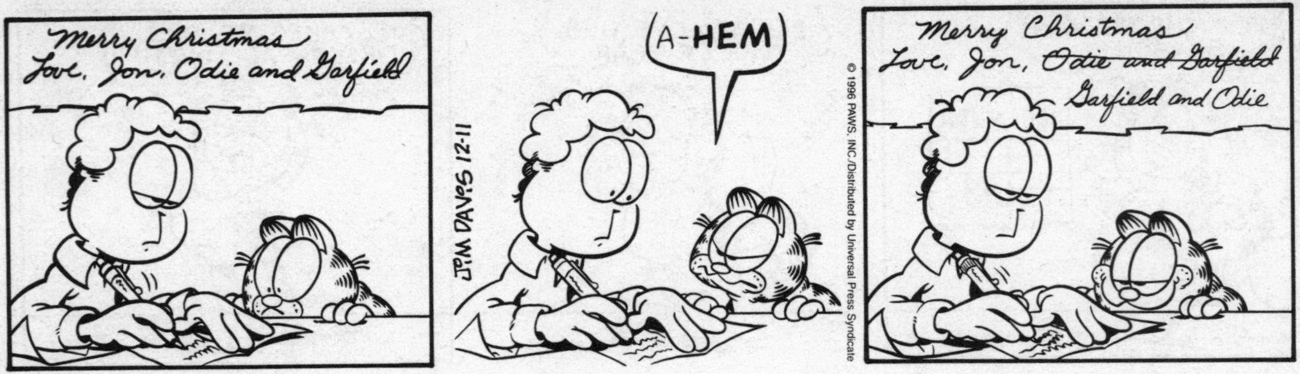
Merry Christmas
Love, Jon, Odie and Garfield
JIM DAVIS 12-11
A-HEM
© 1996 PAWS, INC./Distributed by Universal Press Syndicate
Merry Christmas
Love, Jon, ~~Odie and Garfield~~
Garfield and Odie

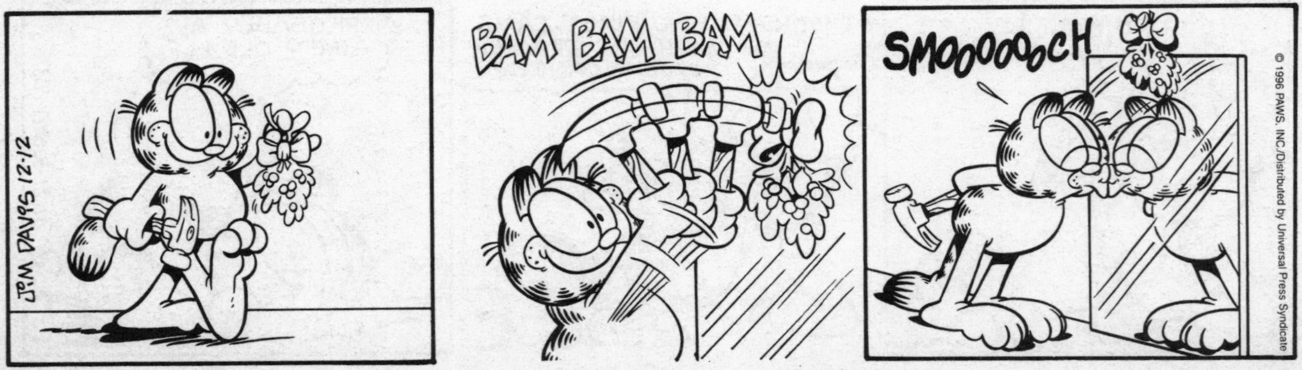
JIM DAVIS 12-12
BAM BAM BAM
SMOOOOOOCH
© 1996 PAWS, INC./Distributed by Universal Press Syndicate

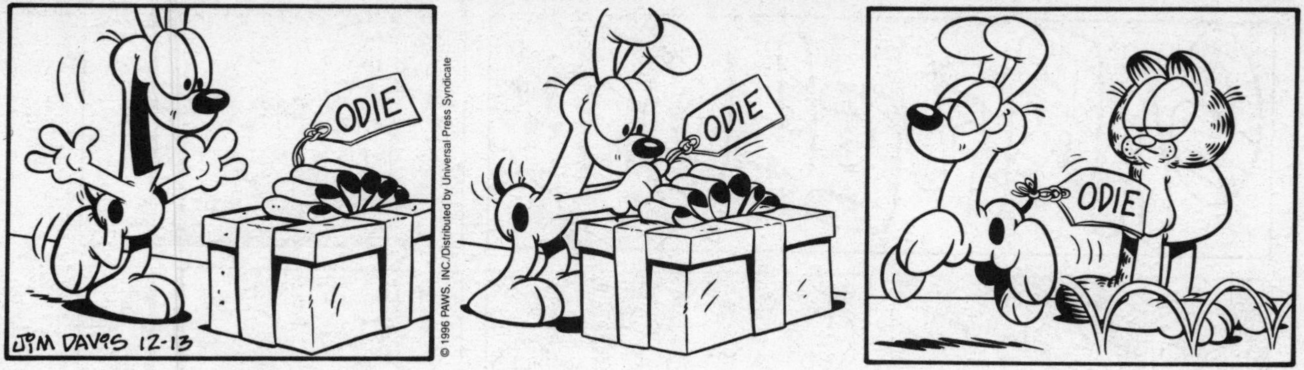
JIM DAVIS 12-13
© 1996 PAWS, INC./Distributed by Universal Press Syndicate
ODIE
ODIE
ODIE

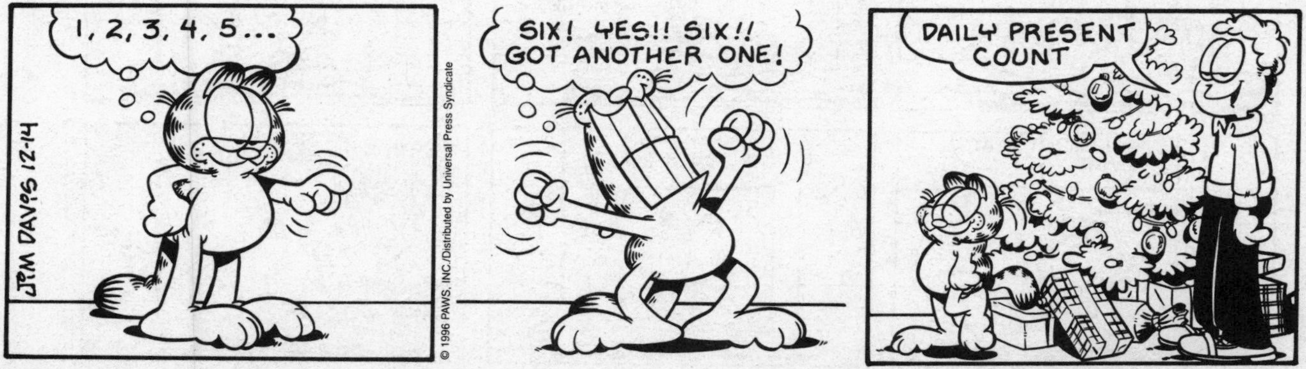
1, 2, 3, 4, 5...
JIM DAVIS 12-14
© 1996 PAWS, INC./Distributed by Universal Press Syndicate
SIX! YES!! SIX!!
GOT ANOTHER ONE!
DAILY PRESENT
COUNT

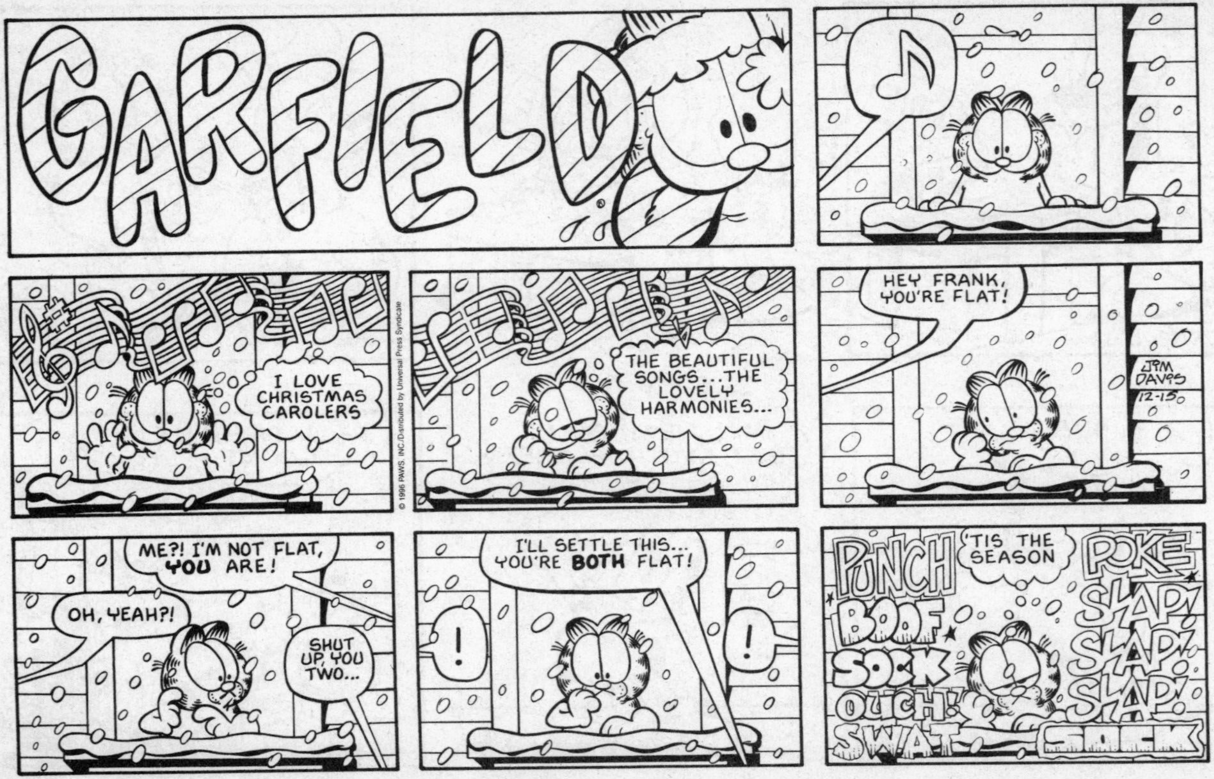
GARFIELD
I LOVE CHRISTMAS CAROLERS
THE BEAUTIFUL SONGS...THE LOVELY HARMONIES...
HEY FRANK, YOU'RE FLAT!
JIM DAVIS 12-15
ME?! I'M NOT FLAT, YOU ARE!
OH, YEAH?!
SHUT UP, YOU TWO...
I'LL SETTLE THIS... YOU'RE BOTH FLAT!
!
!
PUNCH
'TIS THE SEASON
POKE
BOOF
SLAP!
SOCK
SLAP!
SLAP!
OUCH!
SWAT
SOCK

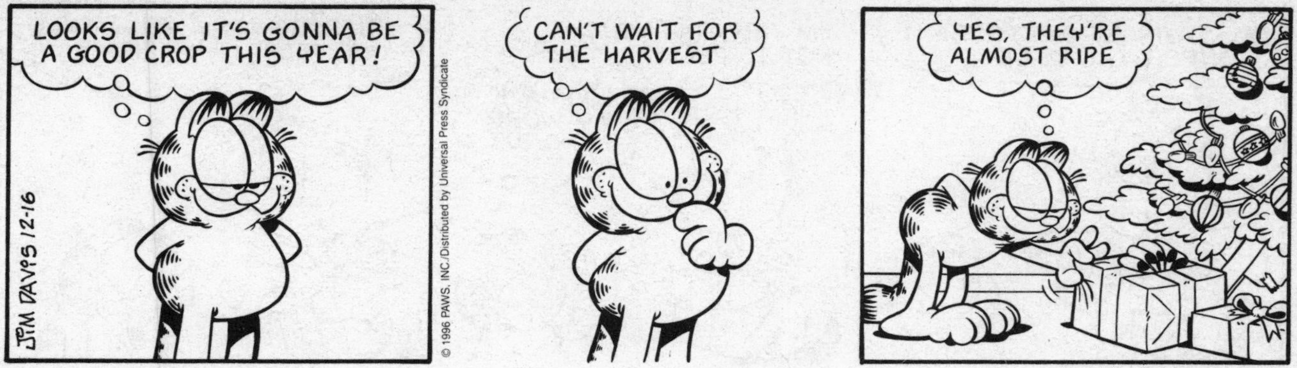
LOOKS LIKE IT'S GONNA BE A GOOD CROP THIS YEAR!
JIM DAVIS 12-16
© 1996 PAWS, INC./Distributed by Universal Press Syndicate
CAN'T WAIT FOR THE HARVEST
YES, THEY'RE ALMOST RIPE

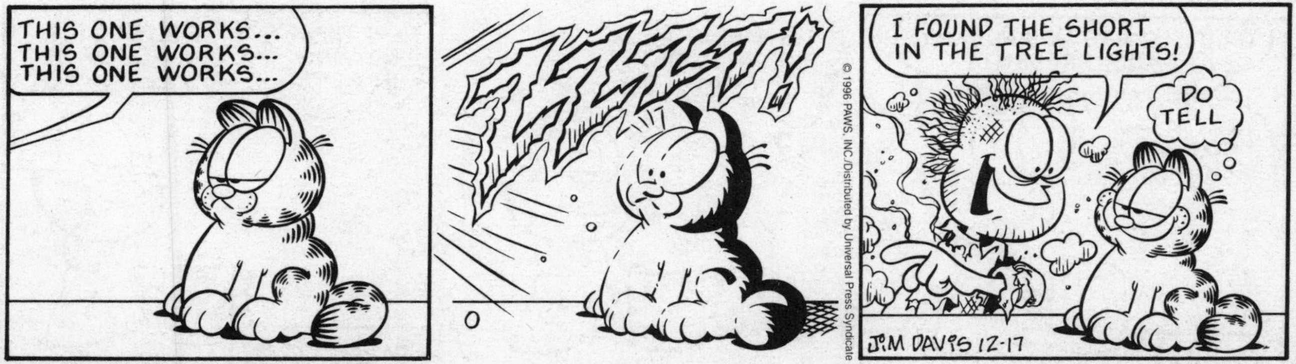
THIS ONE WORKS...
THIS ONE WORKS...
THIS ONE WORKS...
ZZZZT!
© 1996 PAWS, INC./Distributed by Universal Press Syndicate
I FOUND THE SHORT IN THE TREE LIGHTS!
DO TELL
JIM DAVIS 12-17

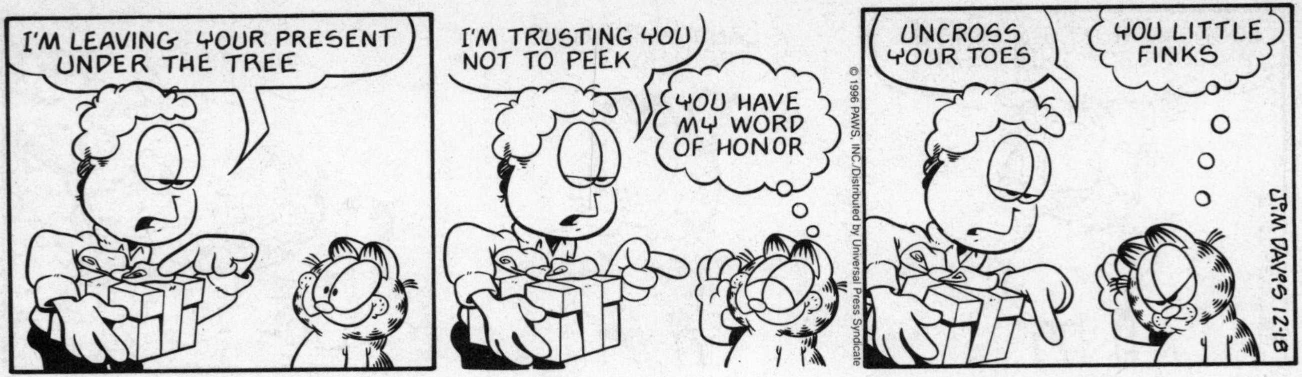
I'M LEAVING YOUR PRESENT UNDER THE TREE
I'M TRUSTING YOU NOT TO PEEK
YOU HAVE MY WORD OF HONOR
© 1996 PAWS, INC./Distributed by Universal Press Syndicate
UNCROSS YOUR TOES
YOU LITTLE FINKS
JIM DAVIS 12-18

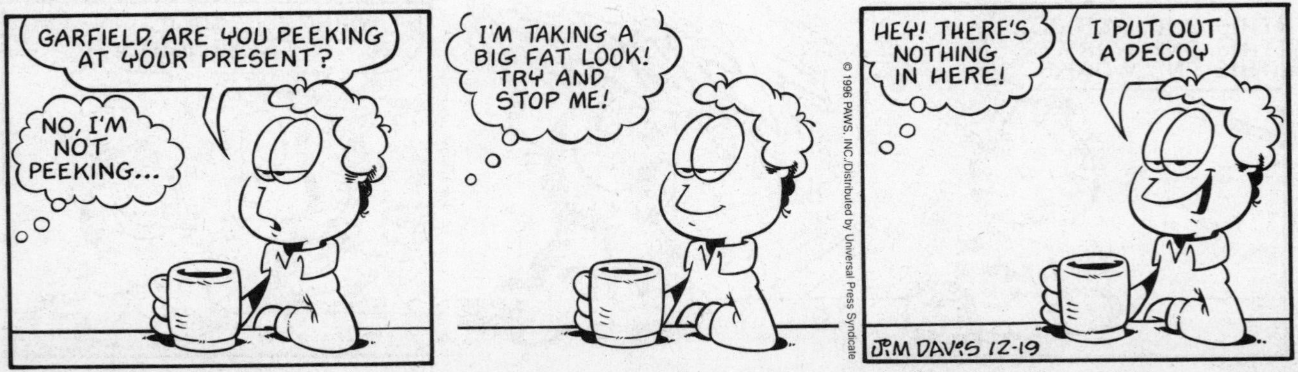
GARFIELD, ARE YOU PEEKING AT YOUR PRESENT?
NO, I'M NOT PEEKING...
I'M TAKING A BIG FAT LOOK! TRY AND STOP ME!
© 1996 PAWS, INC./Distributed by Universal Press Syndicate
HEY! THERE'S NOTHING IN HERE!
I PUT OUT A DECOY
JIM DAVIS 12-19

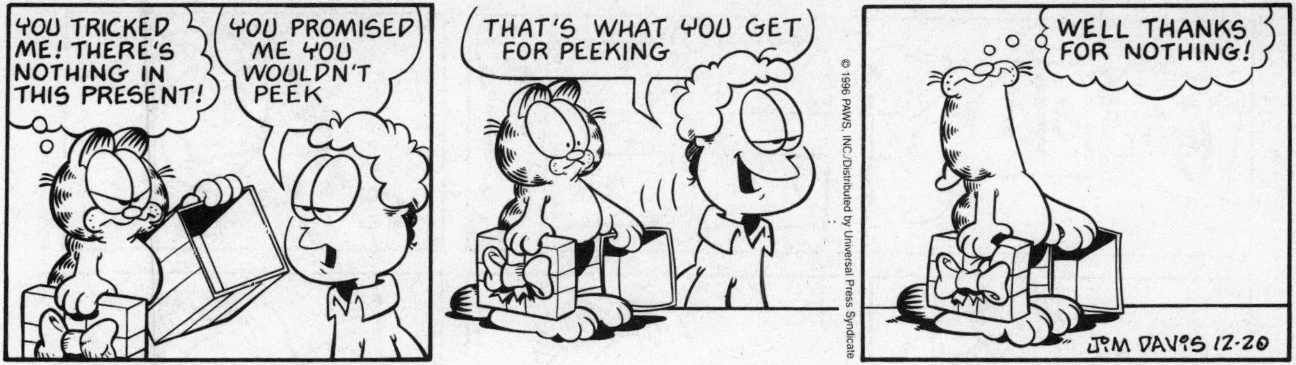
YOU TRICKED ME! THERE'S NOTHING IN THIS PRESENT!
YOU PROMISED ME YOU WOULDN'T PEEK
THAT'S WHAT YOU GET FOR PEEKING
WELL THANKS FOR NOTHING!
JIM DAVIS 12-20

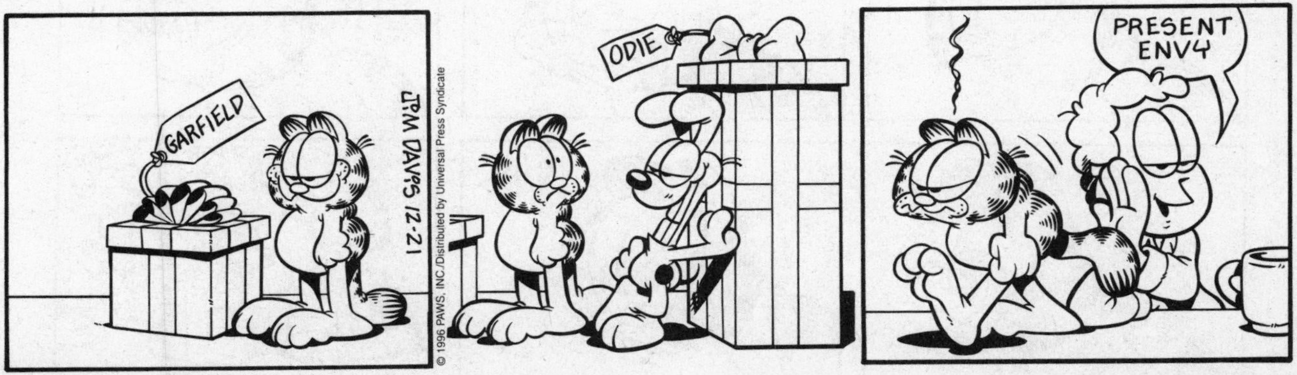
GARFIELD
JIM DAVIS 12-21
ODIE
PRESENT ENVY

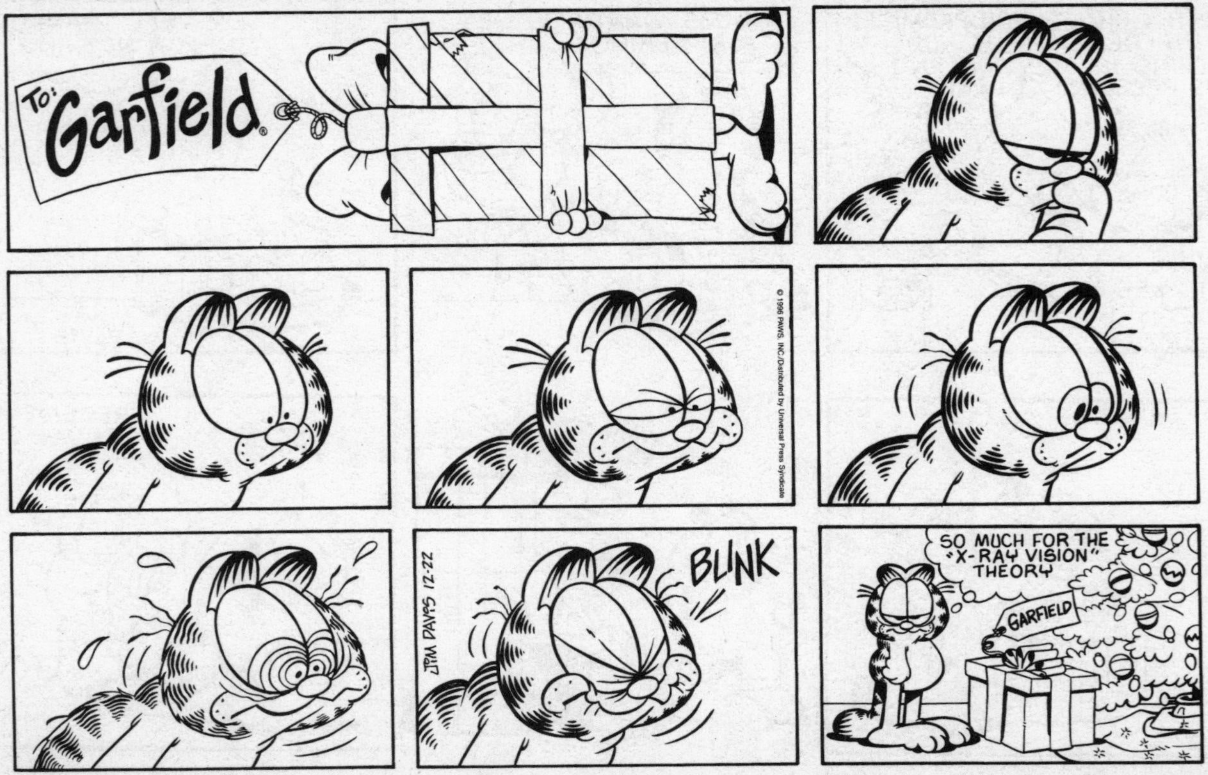
To: Garfield
© 1996 PAWS, INC./Distributed by Universal Press Syndicate
JIM DAVIS 12-22
BLINK
SO MUCH FOR THE "X-RAY VISION" THEORY
GARFIELD

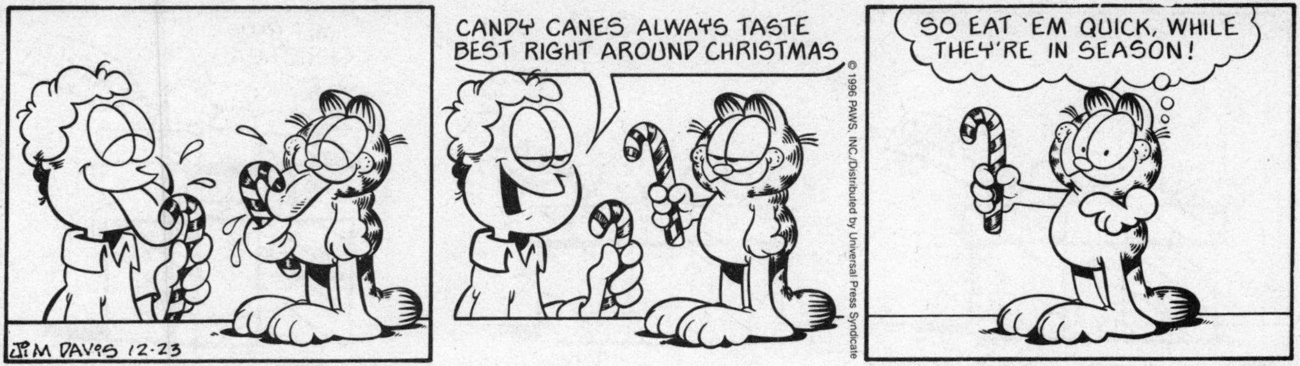
JIM DAVIS 12-23
CANDY CANES ALWAYS TASTE BEST RIGHT AROUND CHRISTMAS
© 1996 PAWS, INC./Distributed by Universal Press Syndicate
SO EAT 'EM QUICK, WHILE THEY'RE IN SEASON!

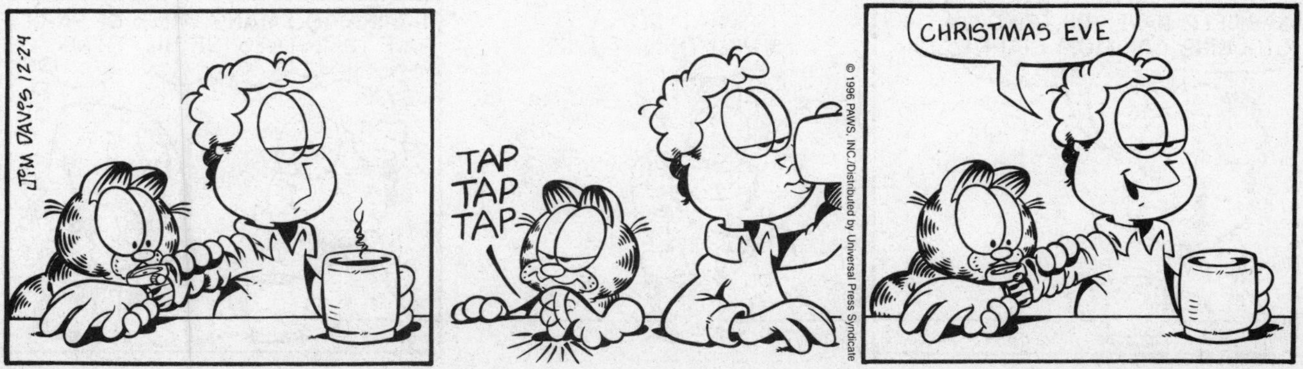
JIM DAVIS 12-24
TAP TAP TAP
© 1996 PAWS, INC./Distributed by Universal Press Syndicate
CHRISTMAS EVE

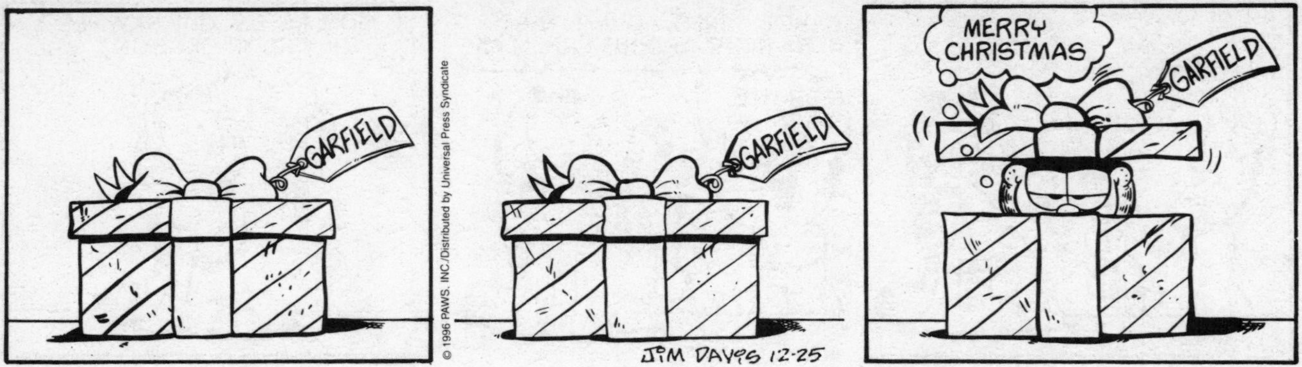
GARFIELD
GARFIELD
© 1996 PAWS, INC./Distributed by Universal Press Syndicate
JIM DAVIS 12-25
MERRY CHRISTMAS
GARFIELD

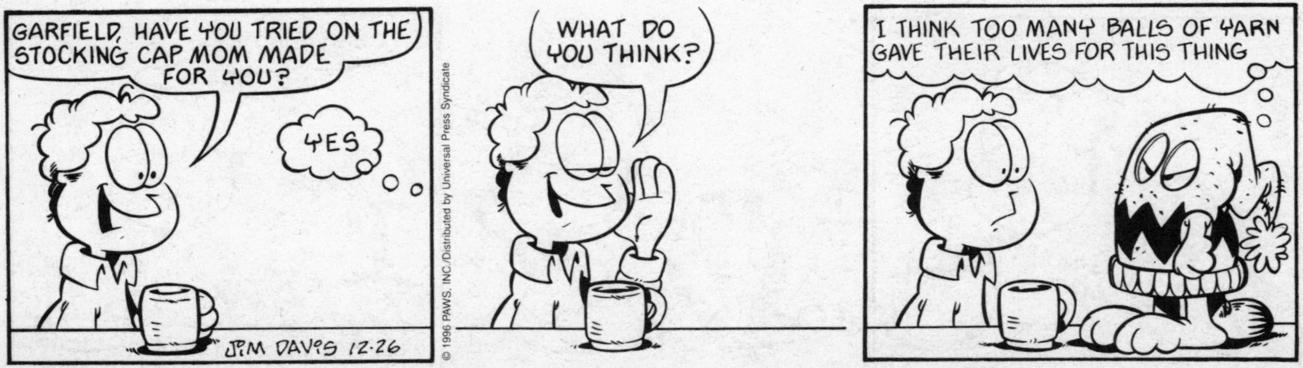
GARFIELD, HAVE YOU TRIED ON THE STOCKING CAP MOM MADE FOR YOU?
YES
JIM DAVIS 12-26
© 1996 PAWS, INC./Distributed by Universal Press Syndicate
WHAT DO YOU THINK?
I THINK TOO MANY BALLS OF YARN GAVE THEIR LIVES FOR THIS THING

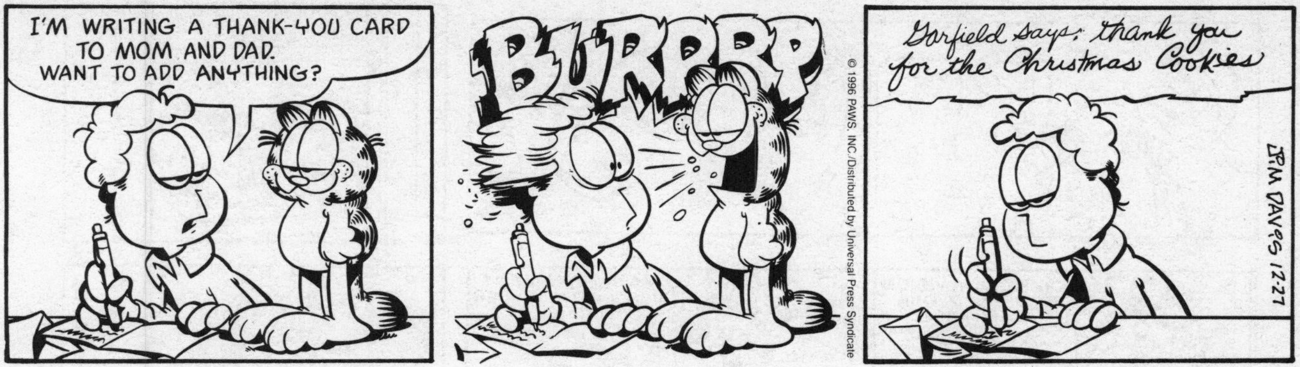
I'M WRITING A THANK-YOU CARD TO MOM AND DAD. WANT TO ADD ANYTHING?
BURPRP
Garfield says: thank you for the Christmas Cookies
© 1996 PAWS, INC./Distributed by Universal Press Syndicate
JIM DAVIS 12-27

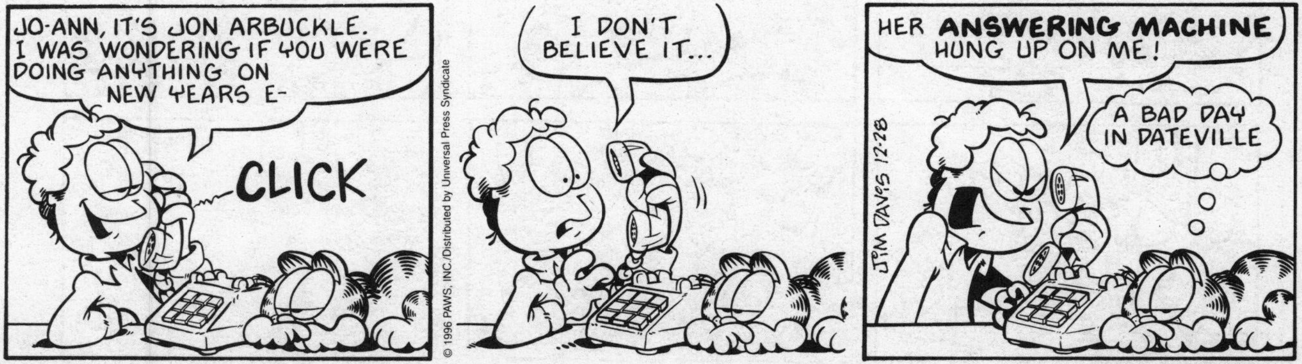
JO-ANN, IT'S JON ARBUCKLE. I WAS WONDERING IF YOU WERE DOING ANYTHING ON NEW YEARS E-
CLICK
© 1996 PAWS, INC./Distributed by Universal Press Syndicate
I DON'T BELIEVE IT...
JIM DAVIS 12-28
HER **ANSWERING MACHINE** HUNG UP ON ME!
A BAD DAY IN DATEVILLE

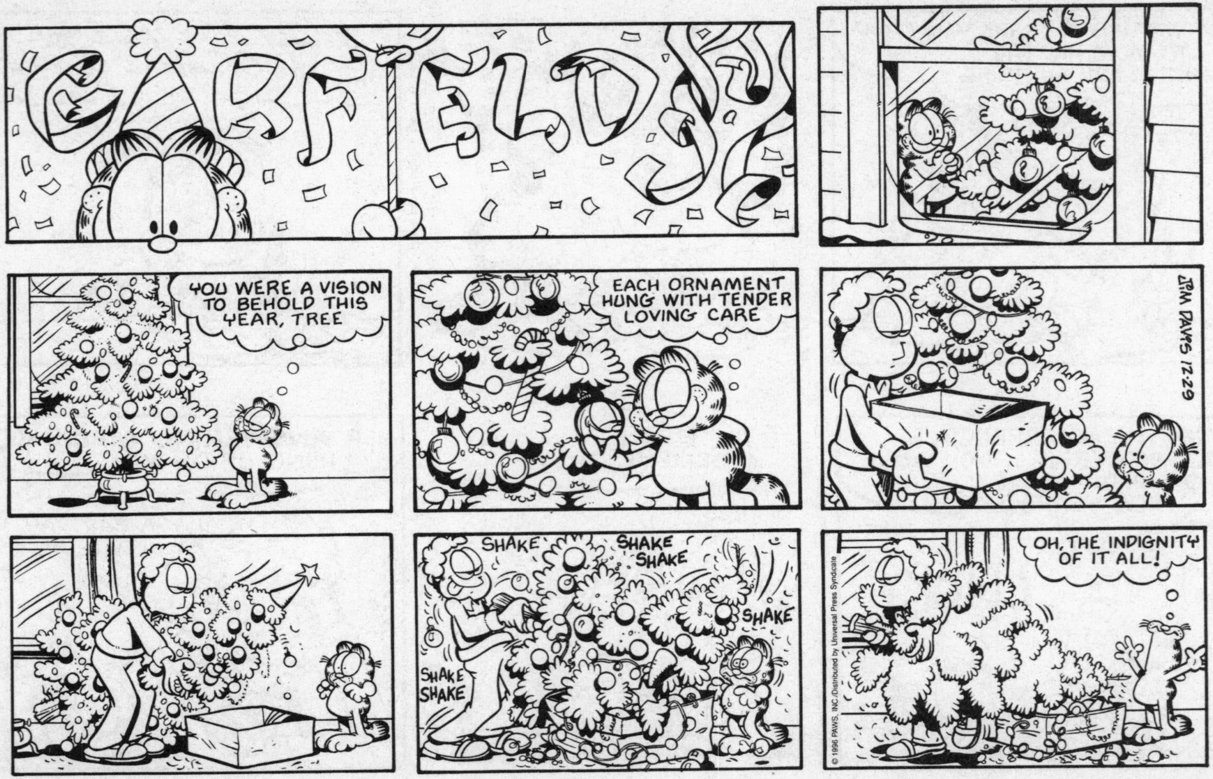
GARFIELD
YOU WERE A VISION TO BEHOLD THIS YEAR, TREE
EACH ORNAMENT HUNG WITH TENDER LOVING CARE
JPM DAVIS 12-29
SHAKE
SHAKE SHAKE
SHAKE
SHAKE SHAKE
OH, THE INDIGNITY OF IT ALL!
© 1996 PAWS, INC./Distributed by Universal Press Syndicate

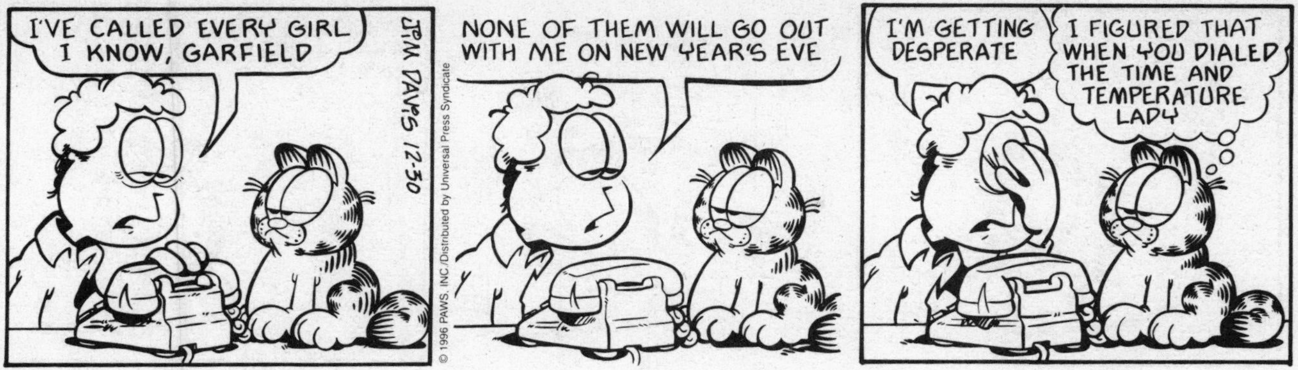
I'VE CALLED EVERY GIRL I KNOW, GARFIELD
JIM DAVIS 12-30
NONE OF THEM WILL GO OUT WITH ME ON NEW YEAR'S EVE
I'M GETTING DESPERATE
I FIGURED THAT WHEN YOU DIALED THE TIME AND TEMPERATURE LADY

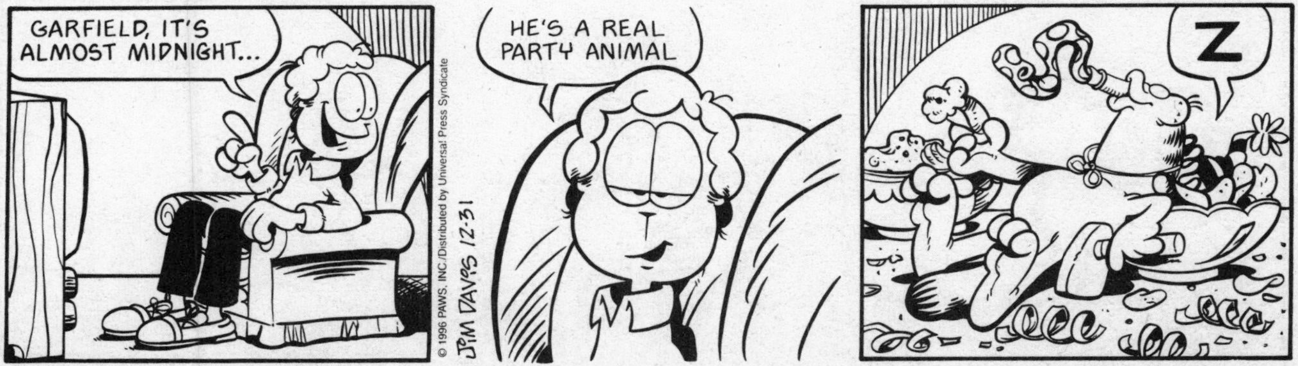
GARFIELD, IT'S ALMOST MIDNIGHT...
JIM DAVIS 12-31
HE'S A REAL PARTY ANIMAL
Z

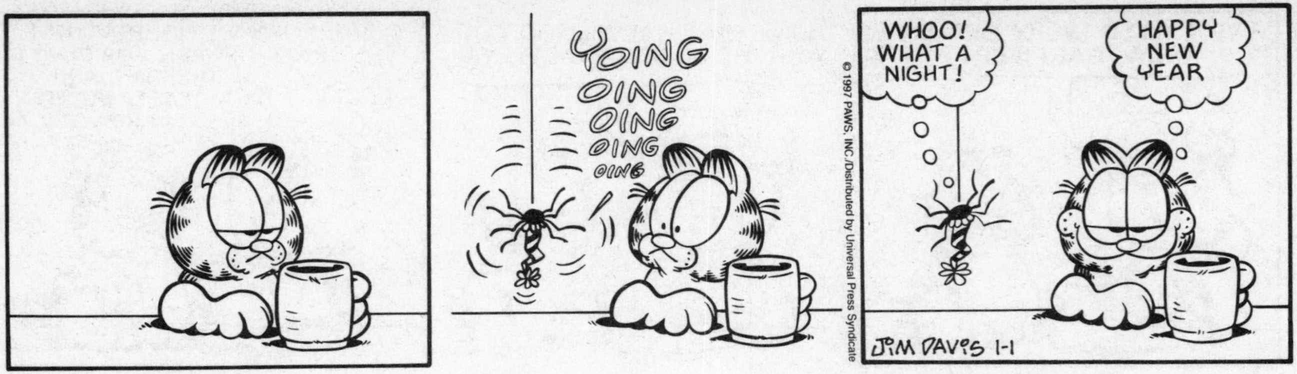
YOING
OING
OING
OING
OING
WHOO! WHAT A NIGHT!
HAPPY NEW YEAR
© 1997 PAWS, INC./Distributed by Universal Press Syndicate
JIM DAVIS 1-1

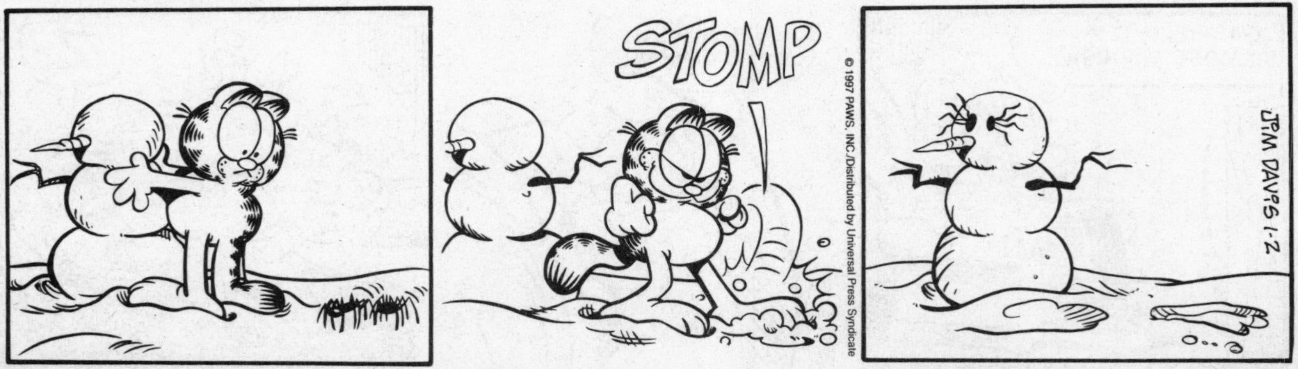
STOMP
© 1997 PAWS, INC./Distributed by Universal Press Syndicate
JIM DAVIS 1-2

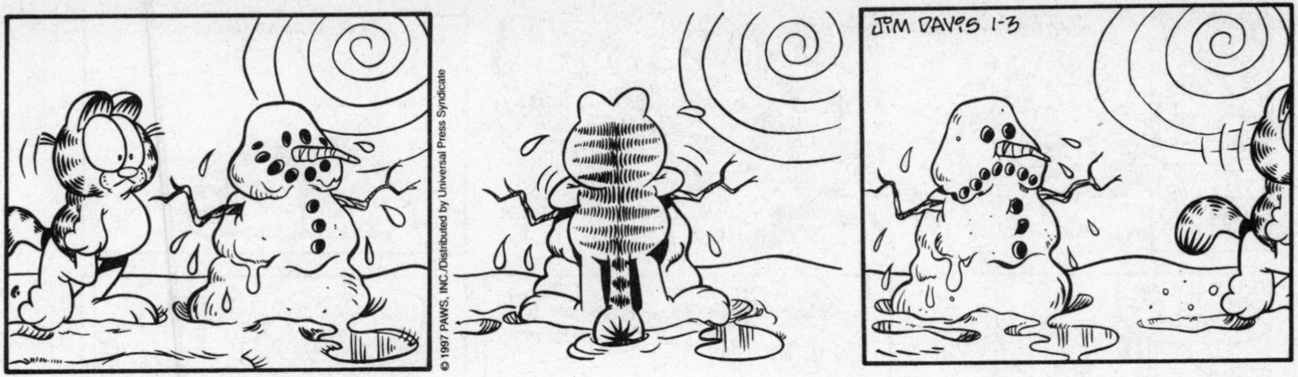
© 1997 PAWS, INC./Distributed by Universal Press Syndicate
JIM DAVIS 1-3

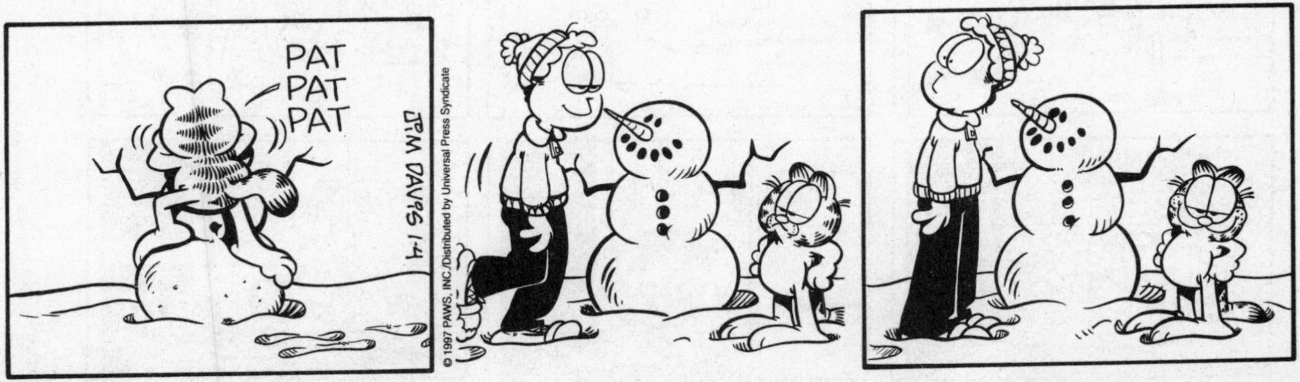
PAT
PAT
PAT
JIM DAVIS 1-4
© 1997 PAWS, INC./Distributed by Universal Press Syndicate

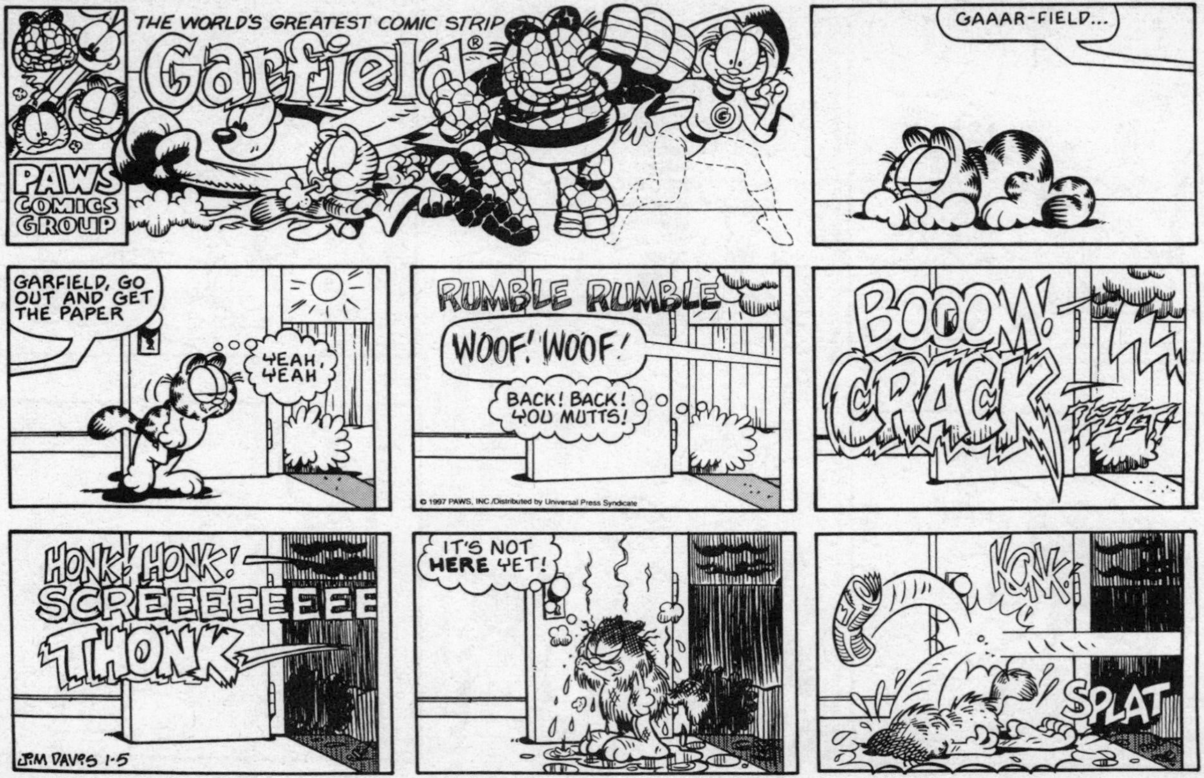
THE WORLD'S GREATEST COMIC STRIP
Garfield®
PAWS COMICS GROUP
GAAAR-FIELD...
GARFIELD, GO OUT AND GET THE PAPER
YEAH, YEAH
RUMBLE RUMBLE
WOOF! WOOF!
BACK! BACK! YOU MUTTS!
© 1997 PAWS, INC./Distributed by Universal Press Syndicate
BOOOM!
CRACK
PZZZT!
HONK! HONK!
SCREEEEEEEEE
THONK
JIM DAVIS 1-5
IT'S NOT HERE YET!
KONK!
SPLAT

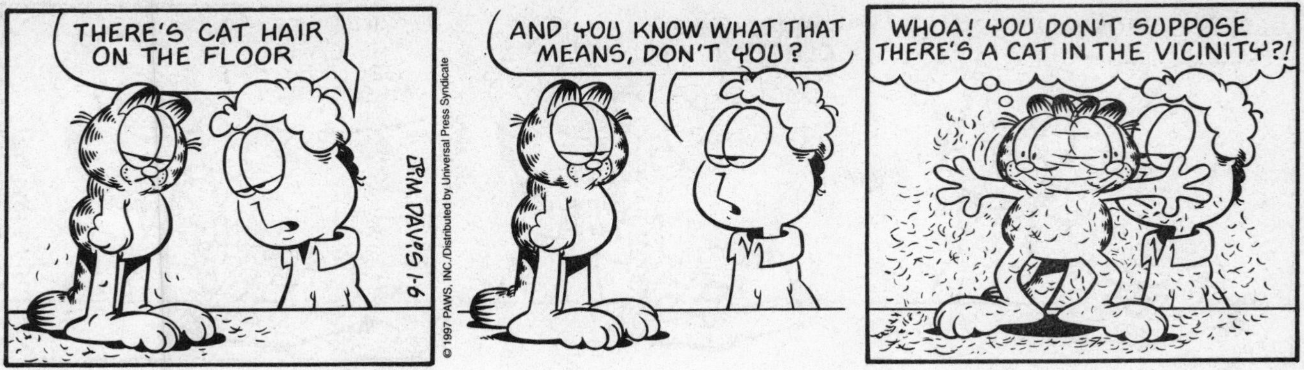
THERE'S CAT HAIR ON THE FLOOR
JIM DAVIS 1-6
© 1997 PAWS, INC./Distributed by Universal Press Syndicate
AND YOU KNOW WHAT THAT MEANS, DON'T YOU?
WHOA! YOU DON'T SUPPOSE THERE'S A CAT IN THE VICINITY?!

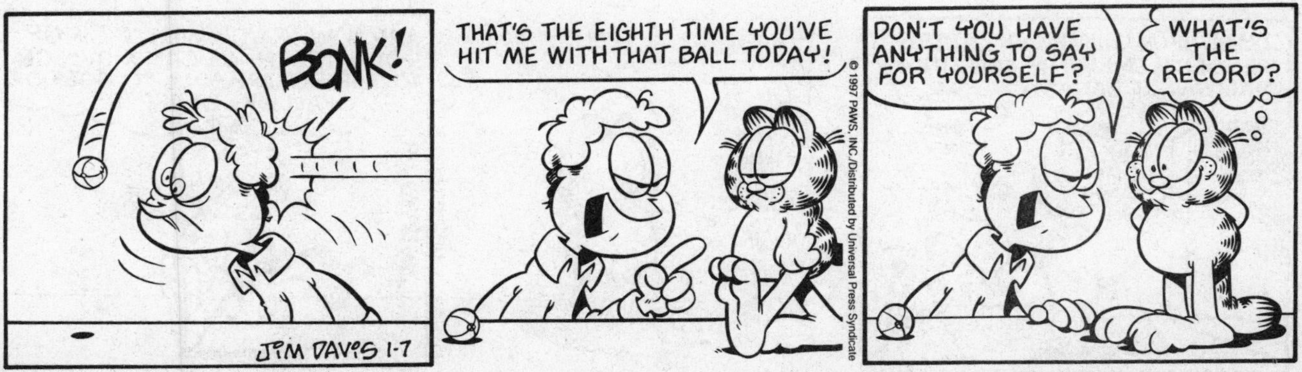
BONK!
JIM DAVIS 1-7
THAT'S THE EIGHTH TIME YOU'VE HIT ME WITH THAT BALL TODAY!
© 1997 PAWS, INC./Distributed by Universal Press Syndicate
DON'T YOU HAVE ANYTHING TO SAY FOR YOURSELF?
WHAT'S THE RECORD?

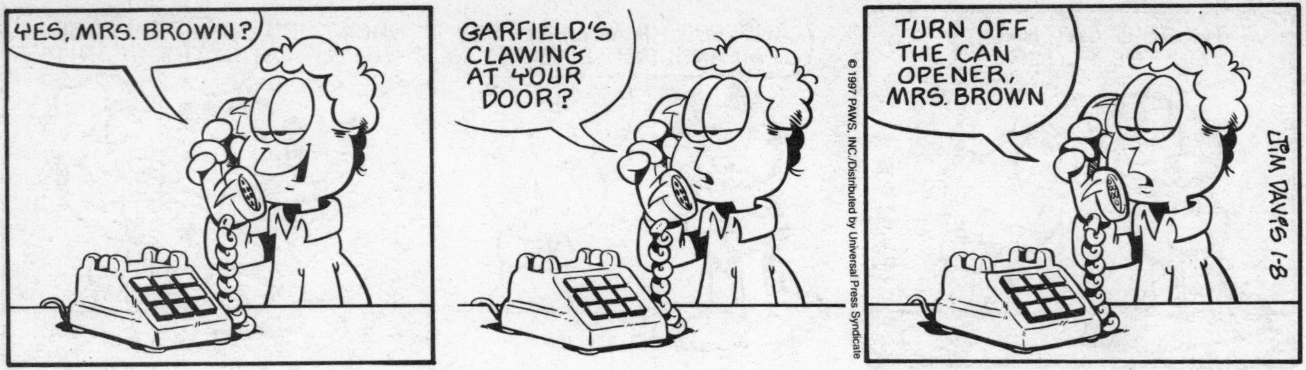
YES, MRS. BROWN?
GARFIELD'S CLAWING AT YOUR DOOR?
TURN OFF THE CAN OPENER, MRS. BROWN
JIM DAVIS 1-8
© 1997 PAWS, INC./Distributed by Universal Press Syndicate

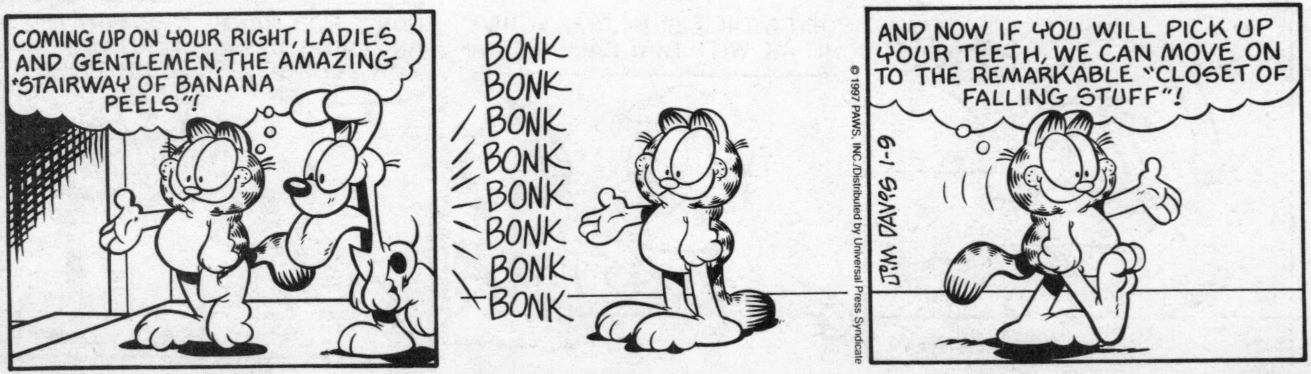
COMING UP ON YOUR RIGHT, LADIES AND GENTLEMEN, THE AMAZING "STAIRWAY OF BANANA PEELS"!
BONK BONK BONK BONK BONK BONK BONK BONK
AND NOW IF YOU WILL PICK UP YOUR TEETH, WE CAN MOVE ON TO THE REMARKABLE "CLOSET OF FALLING STUFF"!
JIM DAVIS 1-9
© 1997 PAWS, INC./Distributed by Universal Press Syndicate

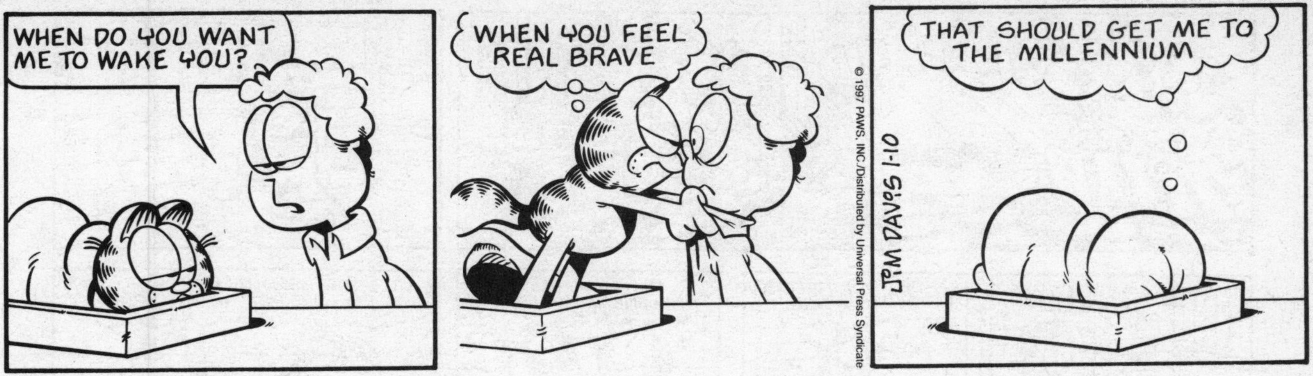
WHEN DO YOU WANT ME TO WAKE YOU?
WHEN YOU FEEL REAL BRAVE
THAT SHOULD GET ME TO THE MILLENNIUM
JIM DAVIS 1-10
© 1997 PAWS, INC./Distributed by Universal Press Syndicate

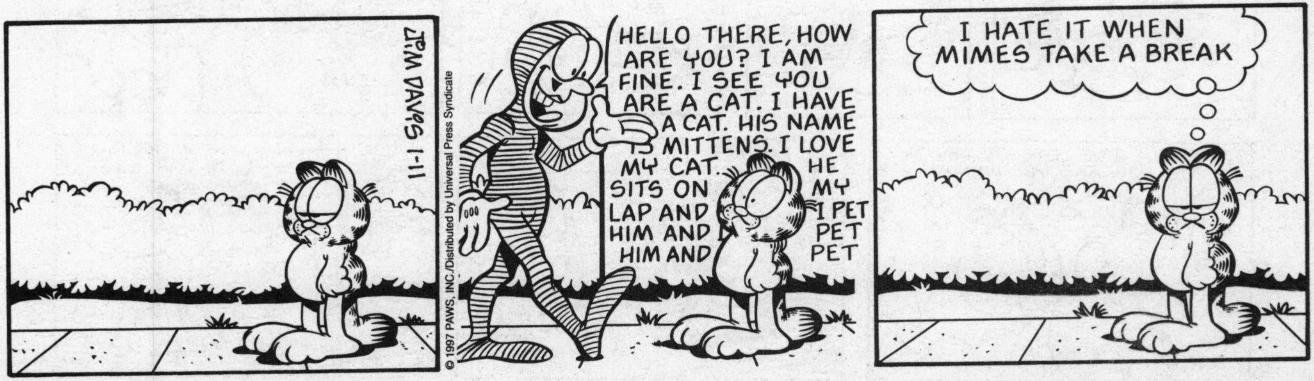
JIM DAVIS 1-11
© 1997 PAWS, INC./Distributed by Universal Press Syndicate
HELLO THERE, HOW ARE YOU? I AM FINE. I SEE YOU ARE A CAT. I HAVE A CAT. HIS NAME MITTENS. I LOVE MY CAT. HE SITS ON MY LAP AND I PET HIM AND PET HIM AND PET
I HATE IT WHEN MIMES TAKE A BREAK

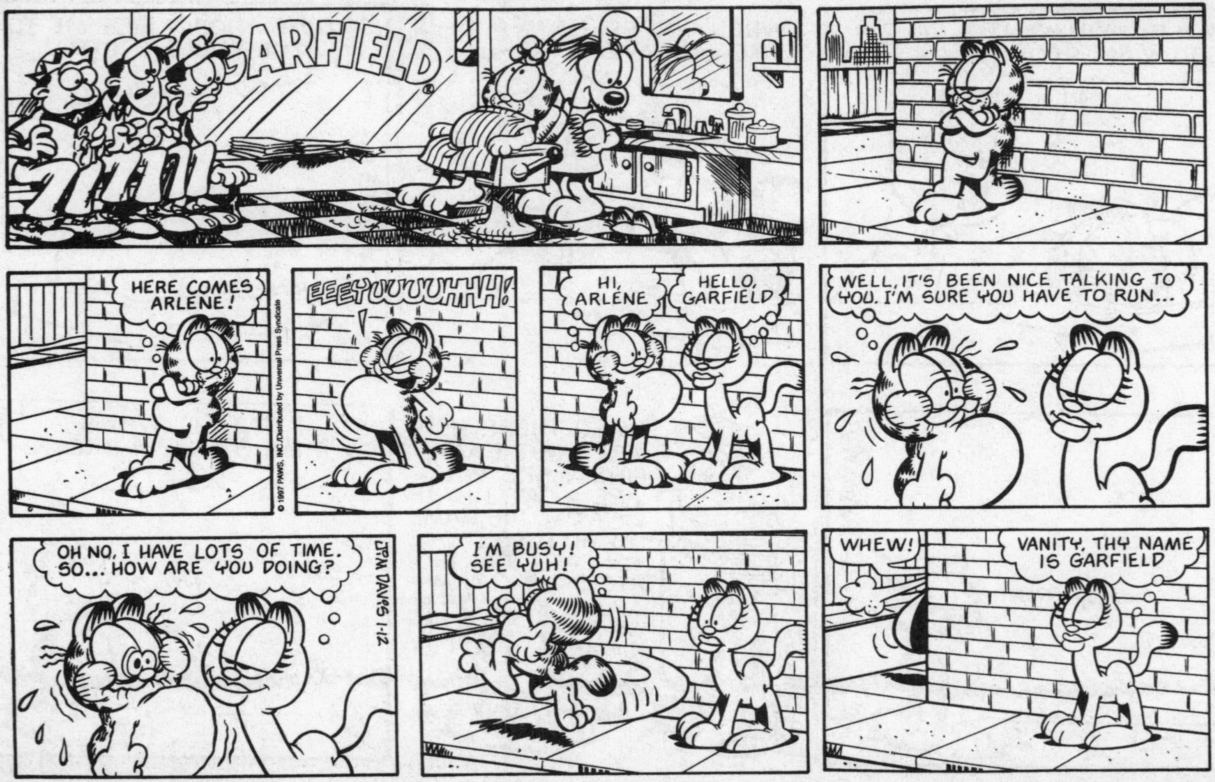
GARFIELD®
HERE COMES ARLENE!
© 1997 PAWS, INC./Distributed by Universal Press Syndicate
EEEYUUUUHHH!
HI, ARLENE
HELLO, GARFIELD
WELL, IT'S BEEN NICE TALKING TO YOU. I'M SURE YOU HAVE TO RUN...
OH NO, I HAVE LOTS OF TIME. SO... HOW ARE YOU DOING?
JPM DAVIS 1-12
I'M BUSY! SEE YUH!
WHEW!
VANITY, THY NAME IS GARFIELD

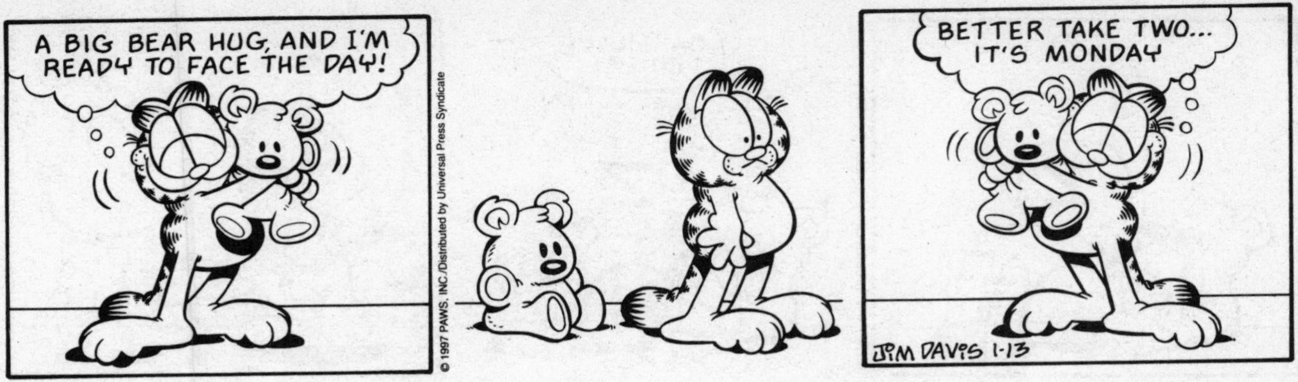
A BIG BEAR HUG, AND I'M READY TO FACE THE DAY!
© 1997 PAWS, INC./Distributed by Universal Press Syndicate
BETTER TAKE TWO... IT'S MONDAY
JIM DAVIS 1-13

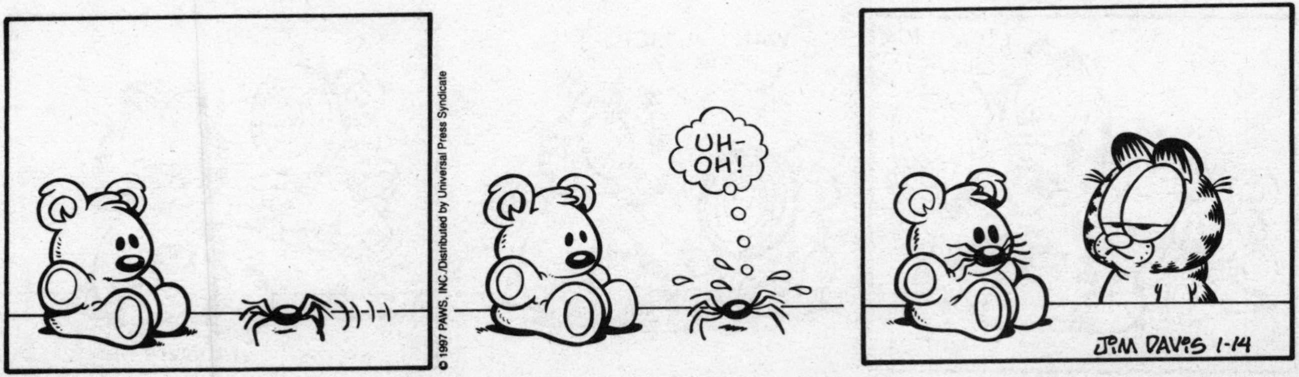
© 1997 PAWS, INC./Distributed by Universal Press Syndicate
UH-OH!
JIM DAVIS 1-14

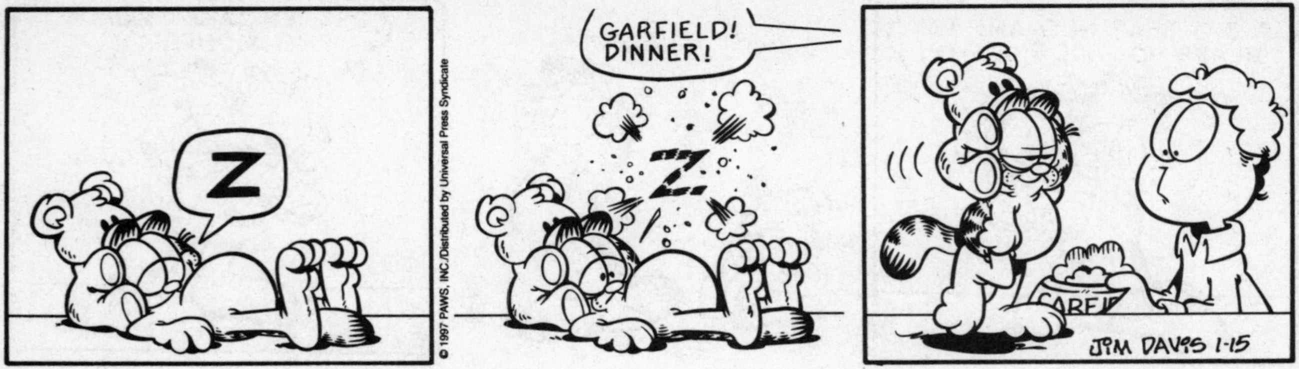
Z
Z
GARFIELD! DINNER!
JIM DAVIS 1-15

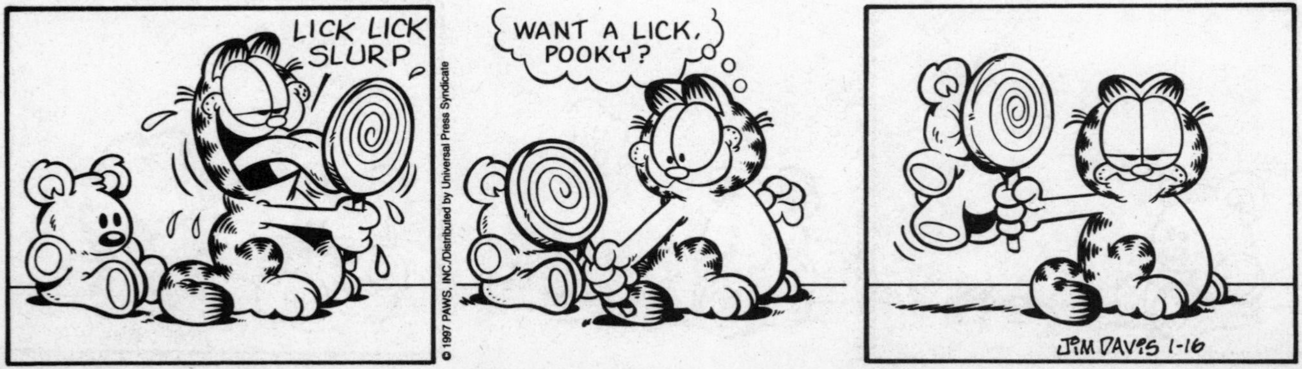
LICK LICK SLURP
WANT A LICK, POOKY?
JIM DAVIS 1-16

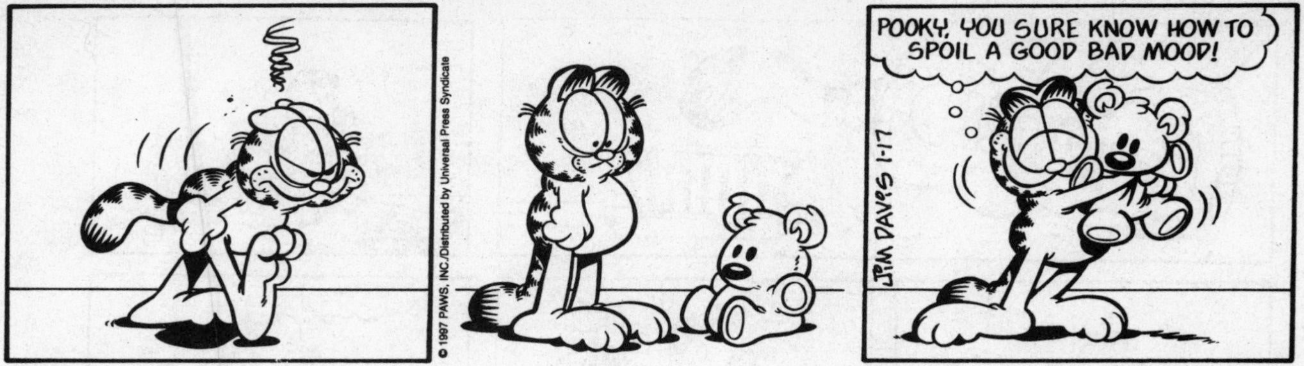
© 1997 PAWS, INC./Distributed by Universal Press Syndicate
POOKY, YOU SURE KNOW HOW TO SPOIL A GOOD BAD MOOD!
JIM DAVIS 1-17

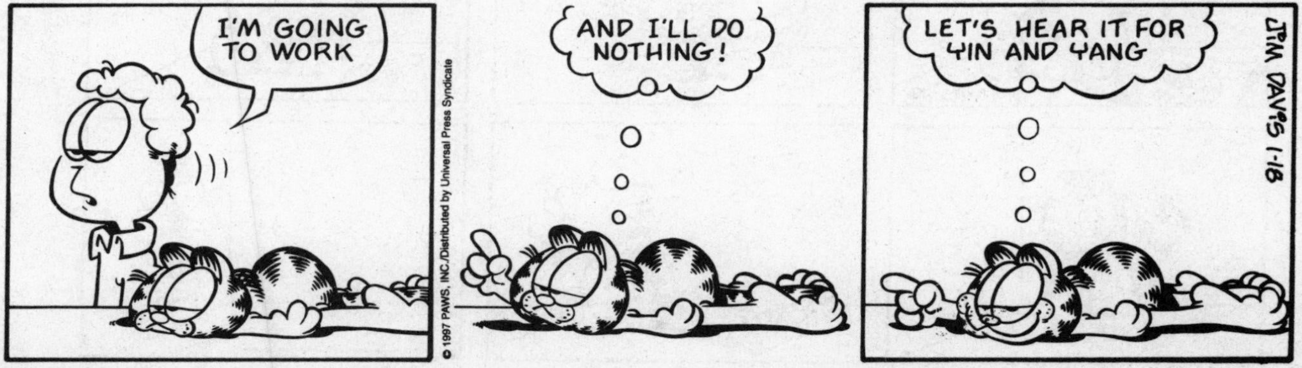
I'M GOING TO WORK
© 1997 PAWS, INC./Distributed by Universal Press Syndicate
AND I'LL DO NOTHING!
LET'S HEAR IT FOR YIN AND YANG
JIM DAVIS 1-18

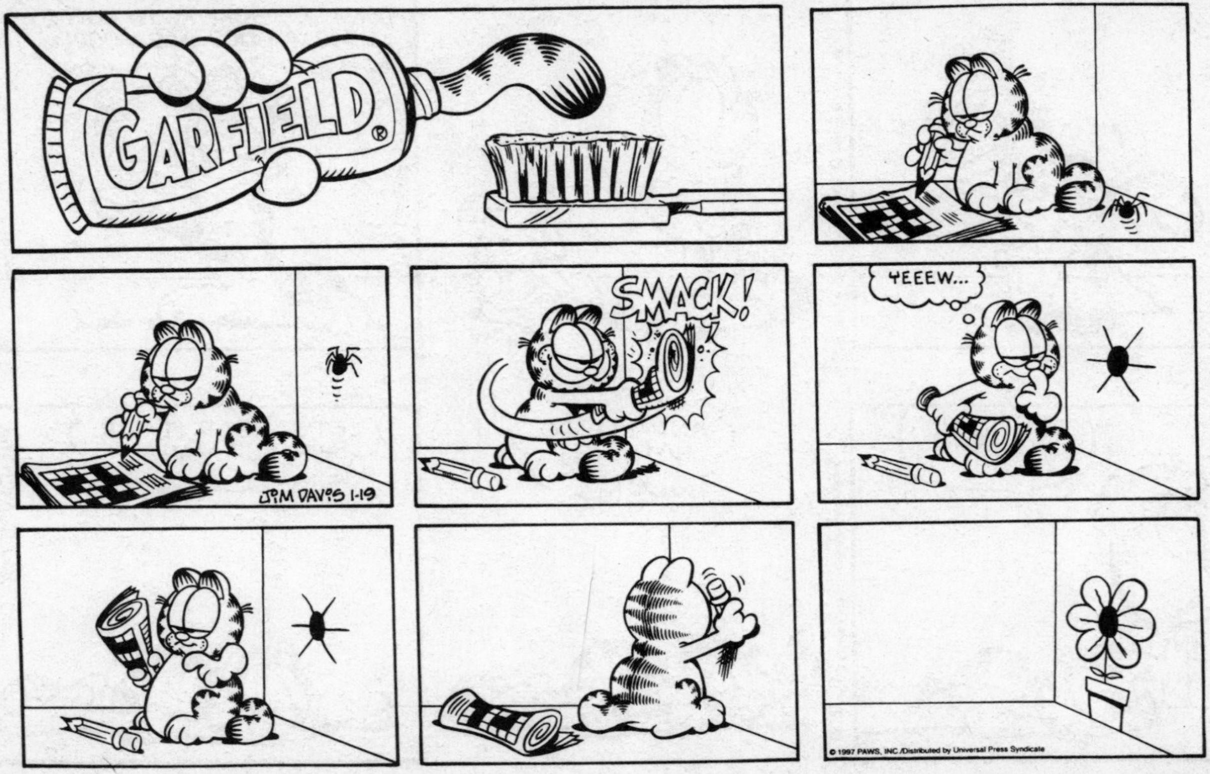
GARFIELD®
JIM DAVIS 1-19
SMACK!
YEEEW...
© 1997 PAWS, INC./Distributed by Universal Press Syndicate

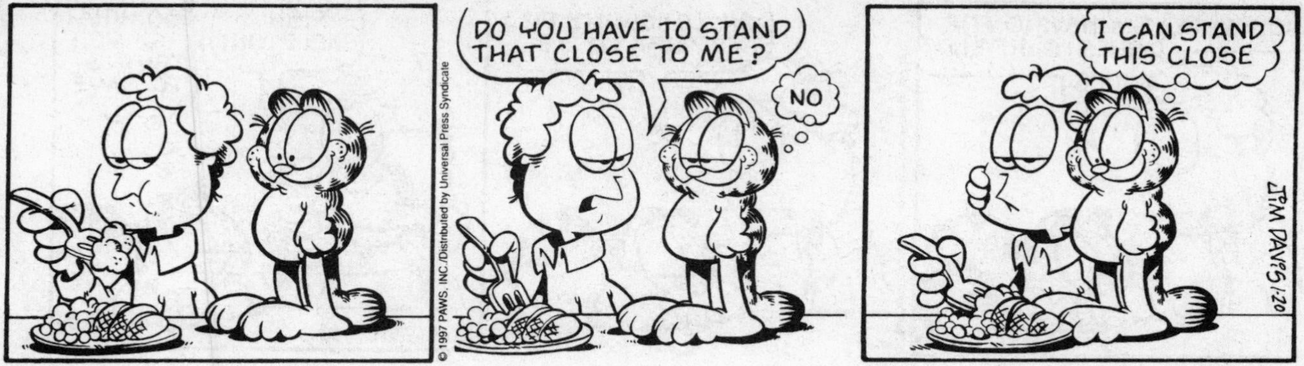
DO YOU HAVE TO STAND THAT CLOSE TO ME?
NO
I CAN STAND THIS CLOSE
JIM DAVIS 1·20

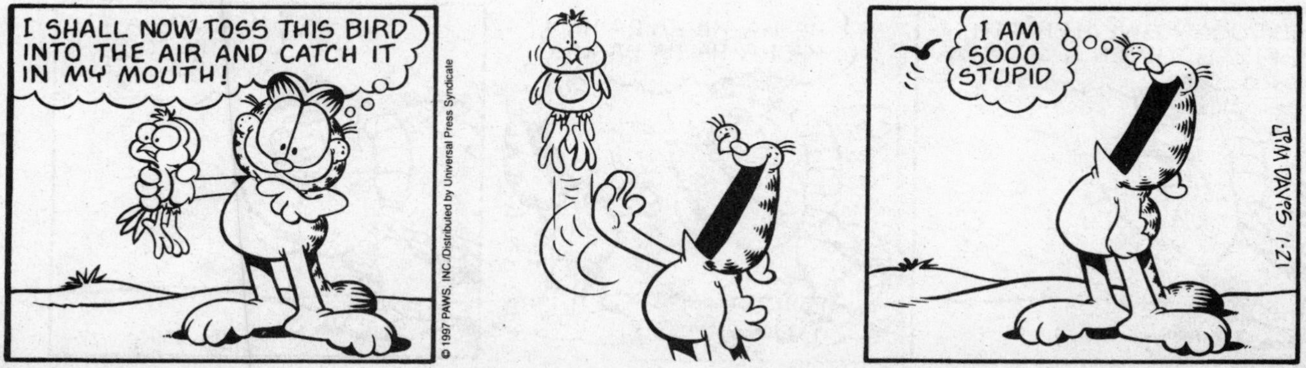
I SHALL NOW TOSS THIS BIRD INTO THE AIR AND CATCH IT IN MY MOUTH!
I AM SOOO STUPID
JIM DAVIS 1·21

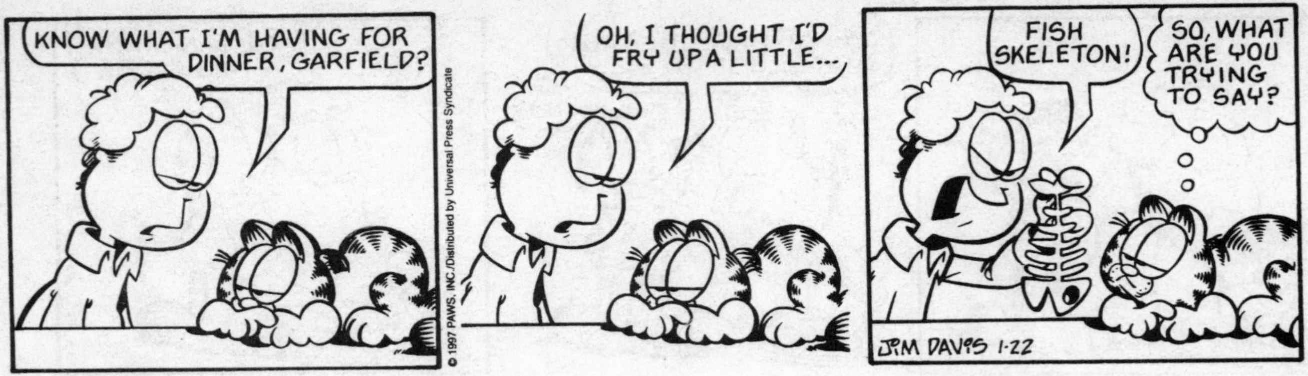
KNOW WHAT I'M HAVING FOR DINNER, GARFIELD?
© 1997 PAWS, INC./Distributed by Universal Press Syndicate
OH, I THOUGHT I'D FRY UP A LITTLE...
FISH SKELETON!
SO, WHAT ARE YOU TRYING TO SAY?
JIM DAVIS 1-22

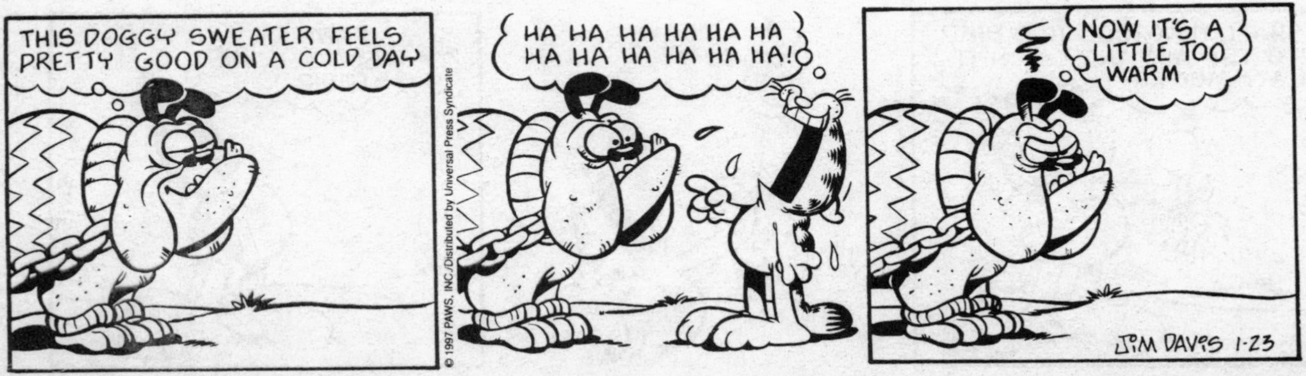
THIS DOGGY SWEATER FEELS PRETTY GOOD ON A COLD DAY
© 1997 PAWS, INC./Distributed by Universal Press Syndicate
HA HA HA HA HA HA HA HA HA HA HA HA!
NOW IT'S A LITTLE TOO WARM
JIM DAVIS 1-23

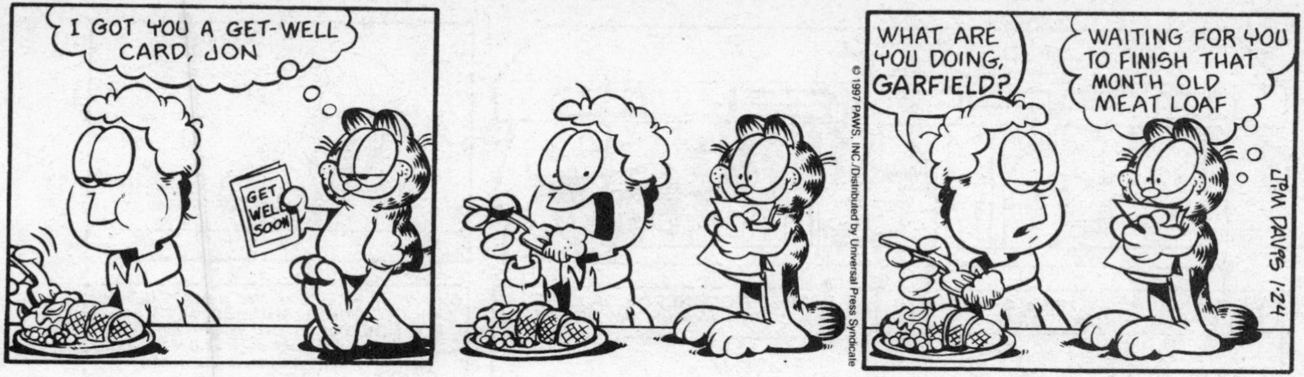
I GOT YOU A GET-WELL CARD, JON
GET WELL SOON
WHAT ARE YOU DOING, GARFIELD?
WAITING FOR YOU TO FINISH THAT MONTH OLD MEAT LOAF
JIM DAVIS 1-24
© 1997 PAWS, INC./Distributed by Universal Press Syndicate

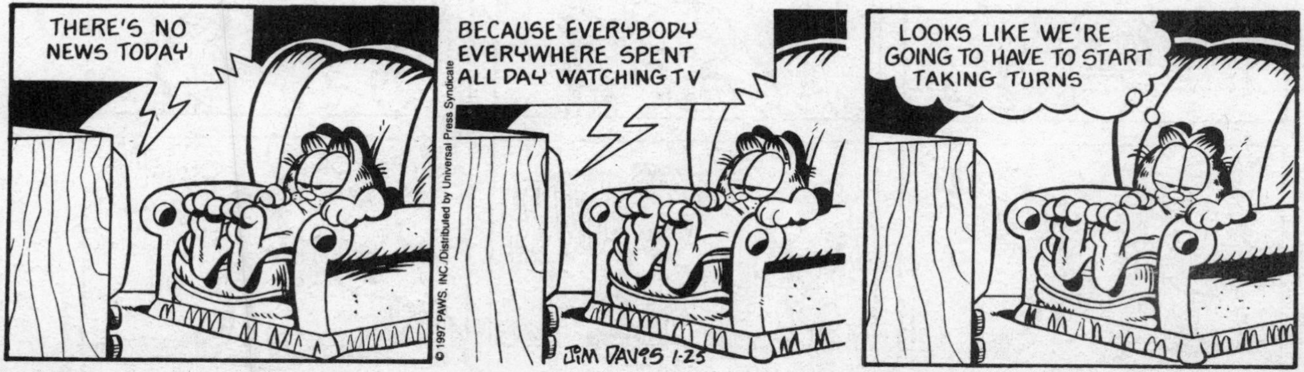
THERE'S NO NEWS TODAY
BECAUSE EVERYBODY EVERYWHERE SPENT ALL DAY WATCHING TV
LOOKS LIKE WE'RE GOING TO HAVE TO START TAKING TURNS
JIM DAVIS 1-25
© 1997 PAWS, INC./Distributed by Universal Press Syndicate

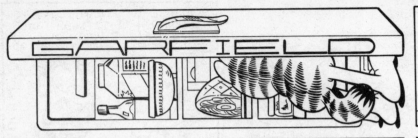

GARFIELD! DINNER!

I FIXED YOU SOMETHING SPECIAL FOR DINNER TONIGHT, GARFIELD

BROILED TOURNEDOS OF BEEF IN A BROWN MUSHROOM GRAVY...

ON A WILD RICE PILAF WITH GLAZED BABY CARROTS AND GARNISHED WITH AN ORANGE SLICE AND A SPRIG OF FRESH PARSLEY!

GULP.
SNATCH

BURRP
JIM DAVIS 1-26

I DO HOPE IT WAS SATISFACTORY

I'VE HAD FRESHER PARSLEY

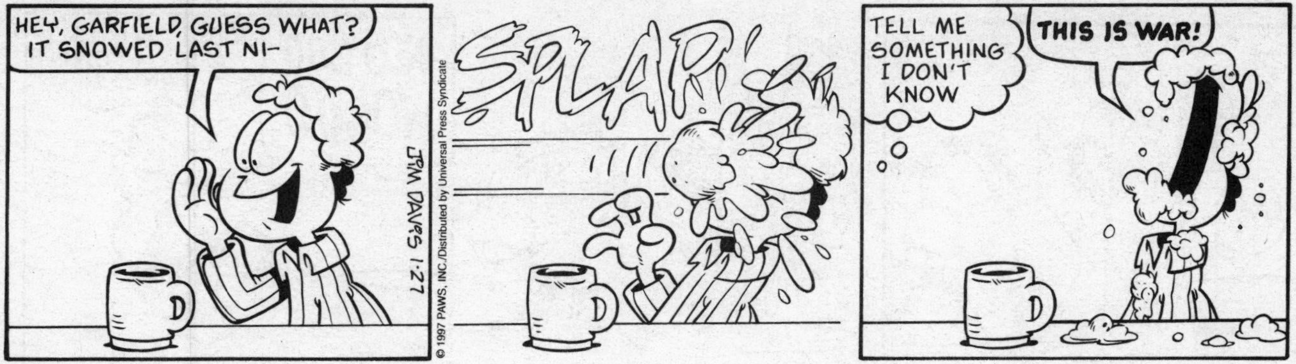
HEY, GARFIELD, GUESS WHAT? IT SNOWED LAST NI–
JIM DAVIS 1-27
© 1997 PAWS, INC./Distributed by Universal Press Syndicate
SPLAP!
TELL ME SOMETHING I DON'T KNOW
THIS IS WAR!

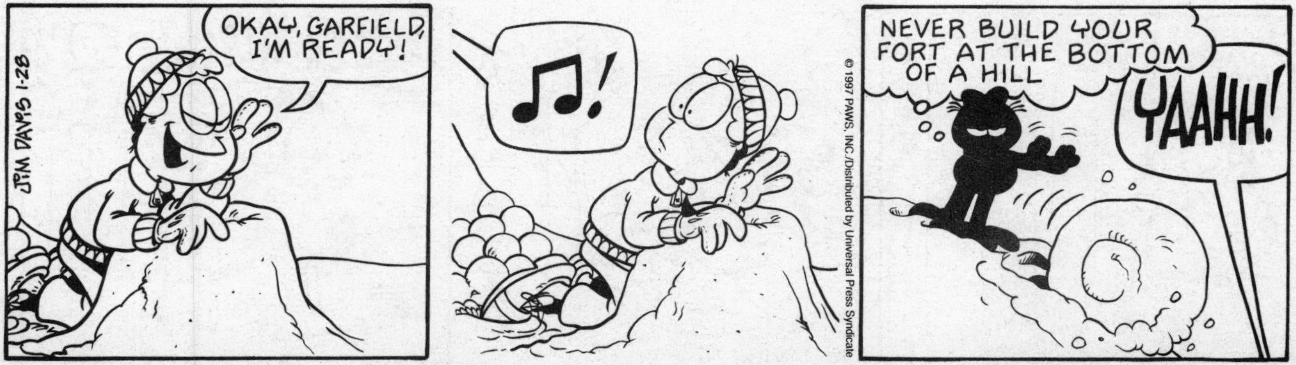
JIM DAVIS 1-28
OKAY, GARFIELD, I'M READY!
♫!
© 1997 PAWS, INC./Distributed by Universal Press Syndicate
NEVER BUILD YOUR FORT AT THE BOTTOM OF A HILL
YAAHH!

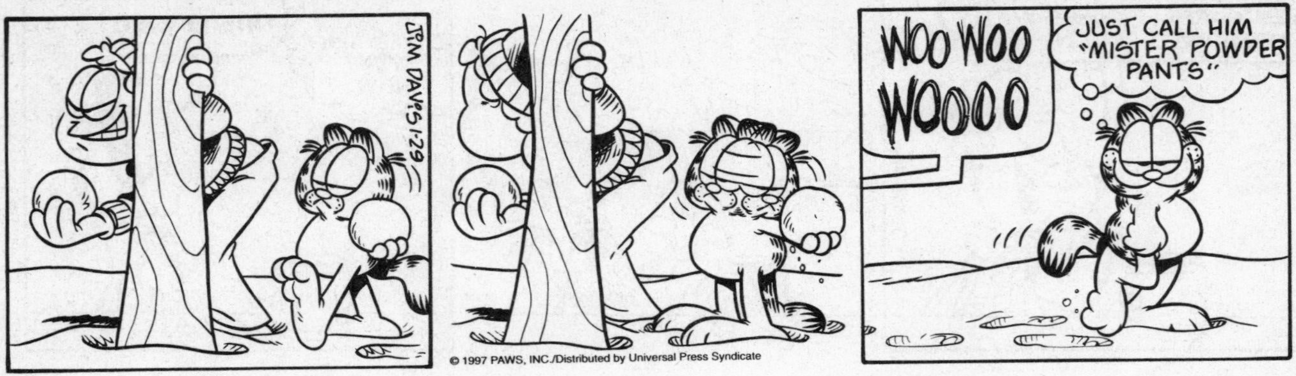
JIM DAVIS 1-29
WOO WOO WOOOO
JUST CALL HIM "MISTER POWDER PANTS"
© 1997 PAWS, INC./Distributed by Universal Press Syndicate

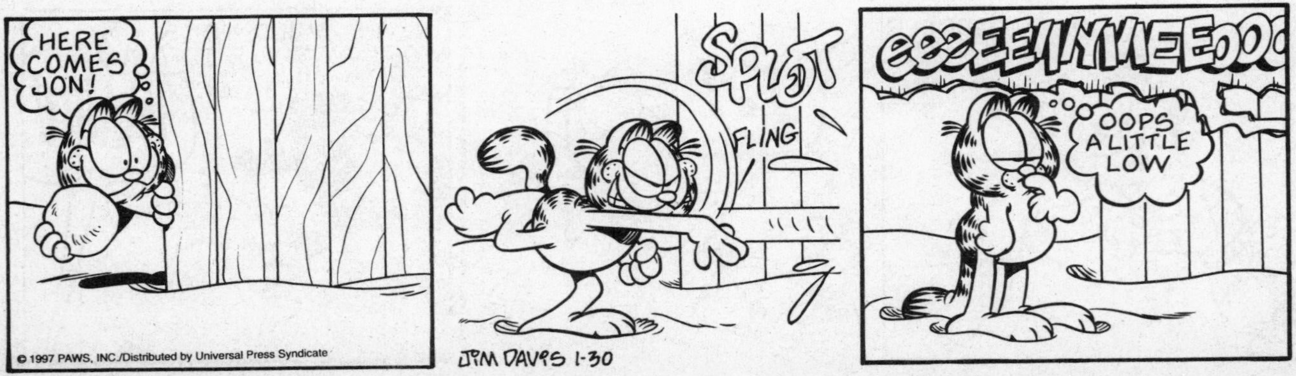
HERE COMES JON!
SPLOT
FLING
OOPS A LITTLE LOW
© 1997 PAWS, INC./Distributed by Universal Press Syndicate
JIM DAVIS 1-30

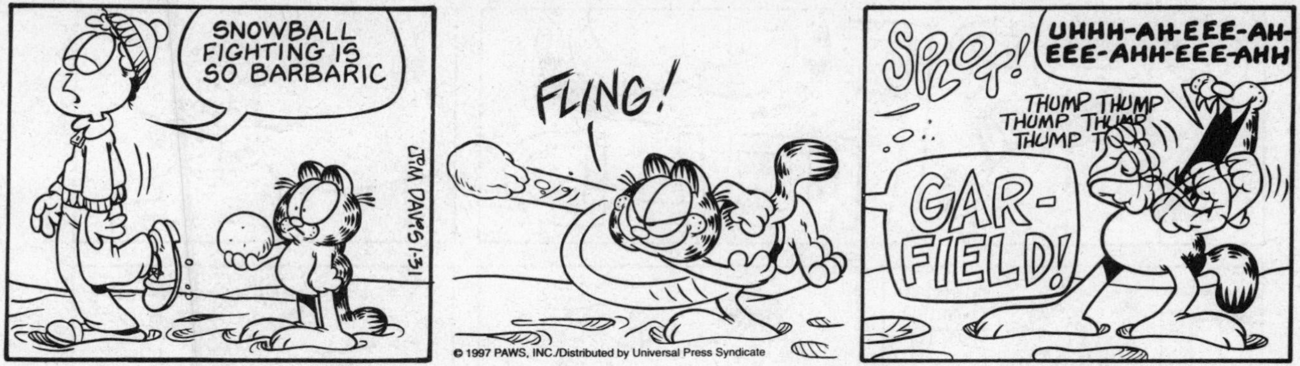
SNOWBALL FIGHTING IS SO BARBARIC
JIM DAVIS 1-31
FLING!
SPLOT!
UHHH-AH-EEE-AH-EEE-AHH-EEE-AHH
THUMP THUMP
THUMP THUMP
THUMP T
GAR-FIELD!

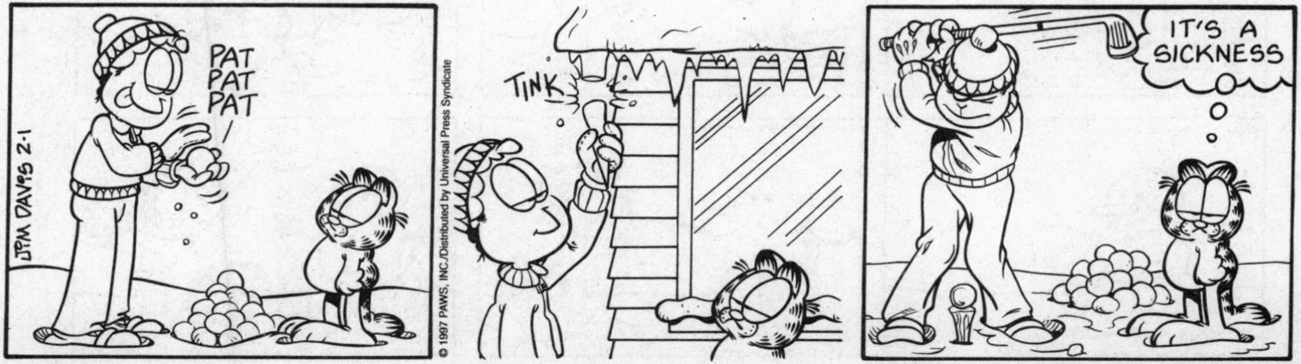
JIM DAVIS 2-1
PAT
PAT
PAT
TINK
IT'S A SICKNESS

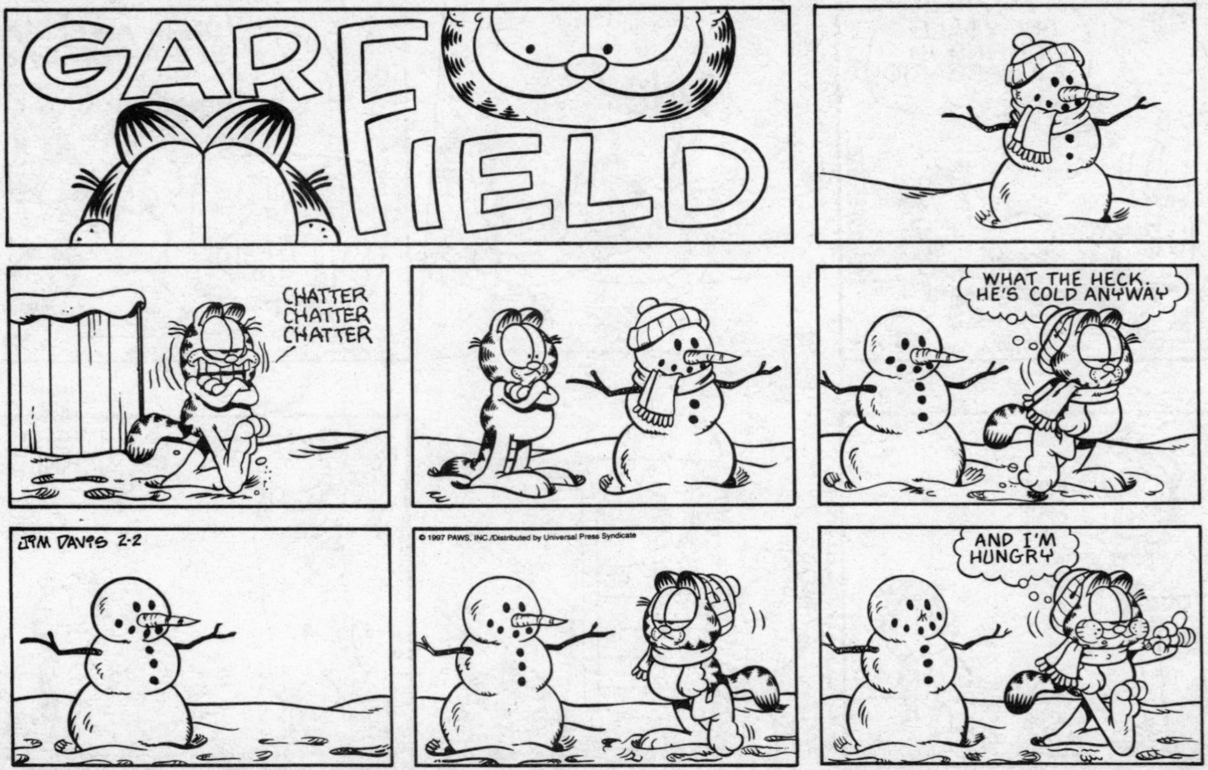
GARFIELD
CHATTER CHATTER CHATTER
WHAT THE HECK. HE'S COLD ANYWAY
JIM DAVIS 2-2
© 1997 PAWS, INC./Distributed by Universal Press Syndicate
AND I'M HUNGRY

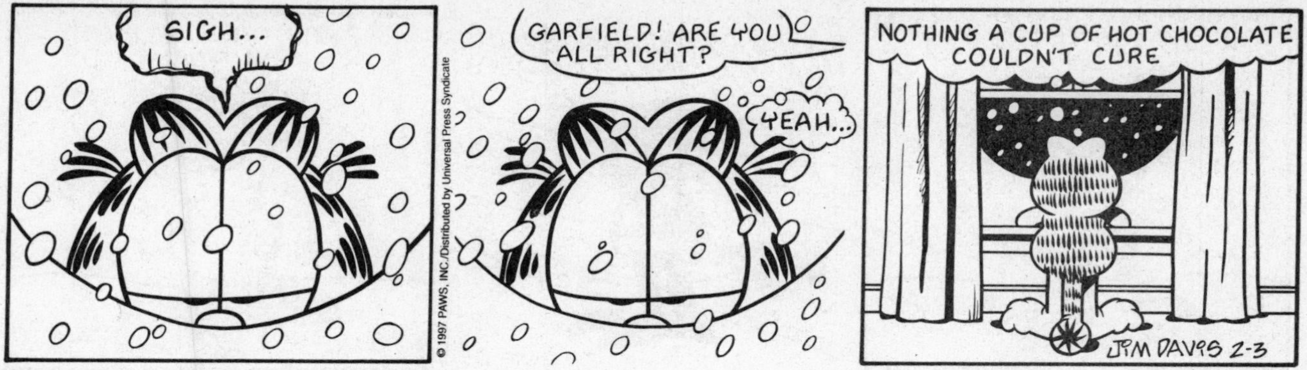

SIGH...
GARFIELD! ARE YOU ALL RIGHT?
YEAH...
NOTHING A CUP OF HOT CHOCOLATE COULDN'T CURE
JIM DAVIS 2-3

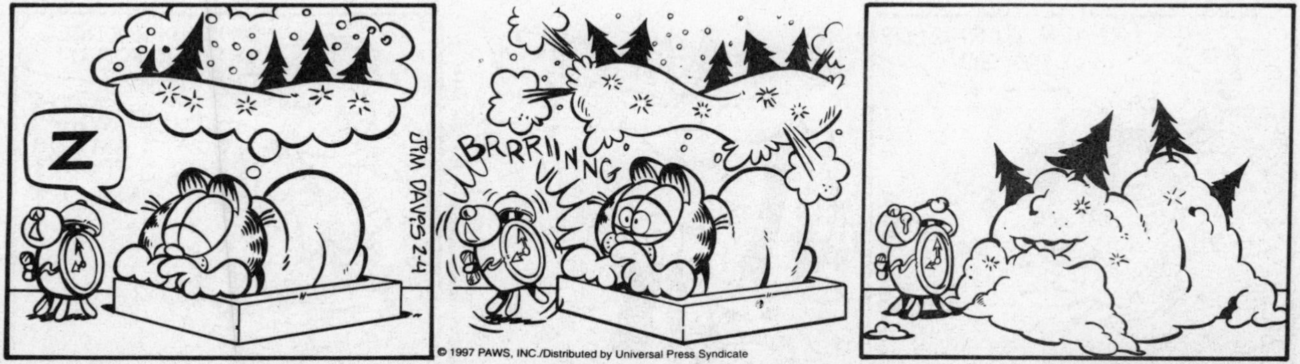

Z
JIM DAVIS 2-4
BRRRIIINNG

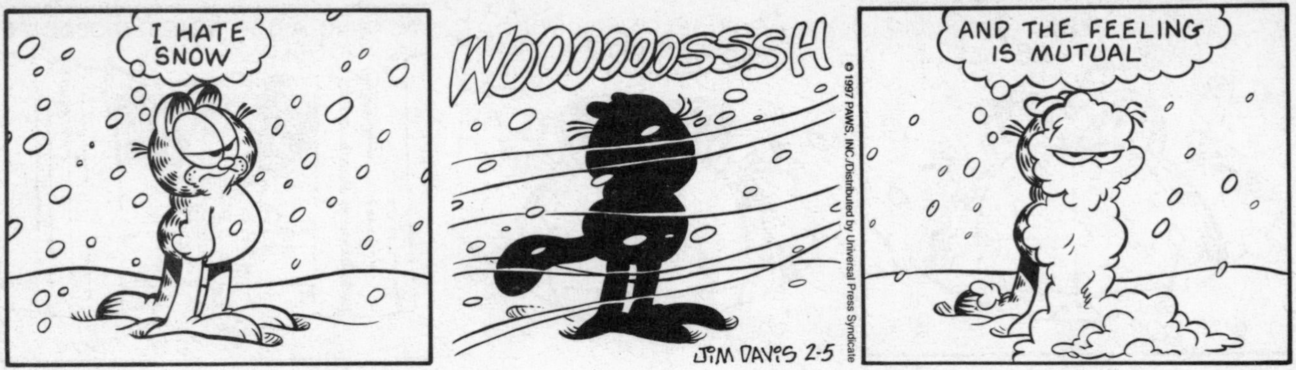
I HATE SNOW
WOOOOOOOSSSSH
JIM DAVIS 2-5
© 1997 PAWS, INC./Distributed by Universal Press Syndicate
AND THE FEELING IS MUTUAL

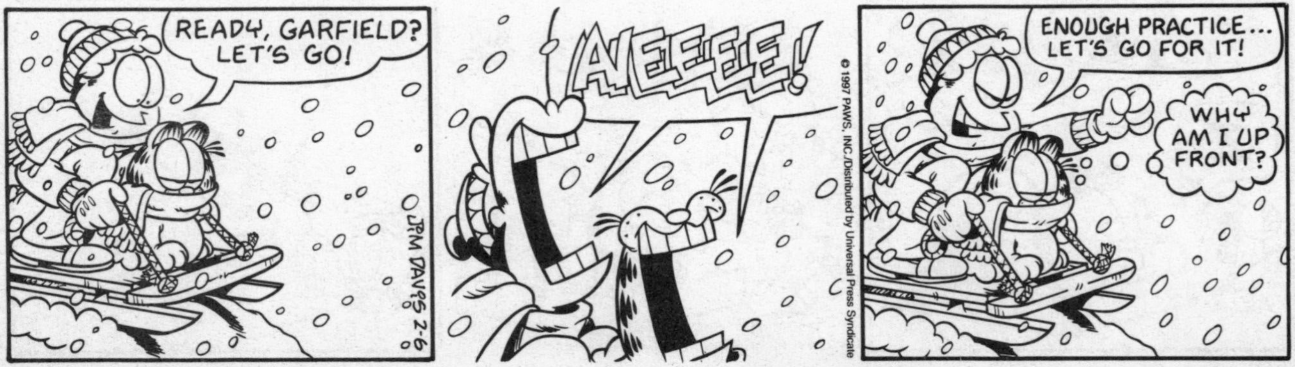
READY, GARFIELD? LET'S GO!
JIM DAVIS 2-6
AIEEEEE!
© 1997 PAWS, INC./Distributed by Universal Press Syndicate
ENOUGH PRACTICE... LET'S GO FOR IT!
WHY AM I UP FRONT?

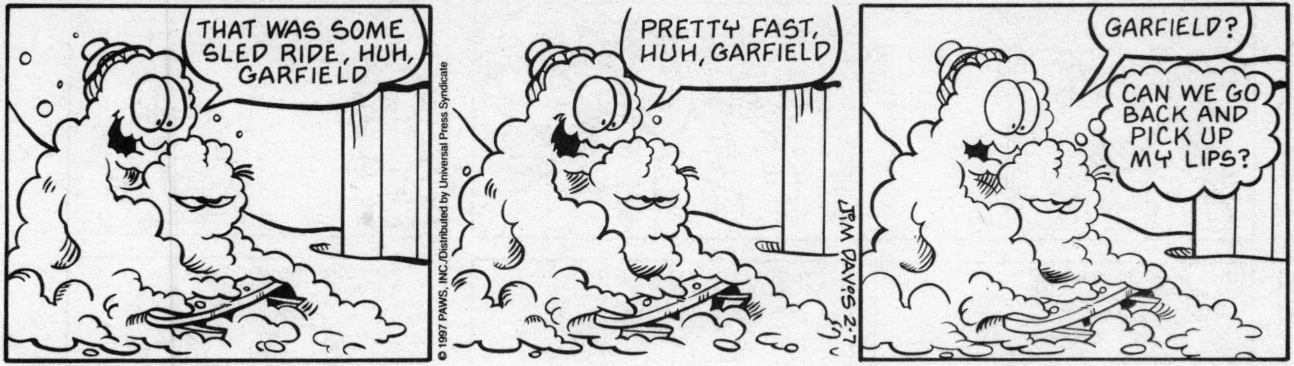
THAT WAS SOME SLED RIDE, HUH, GARFIELD
PRETTY FAST, HUH, GARFIELD
JIM DAVIS 2-7
GARFIELD?
CAN WE GO BACK AND PICK UP MY LIPS?

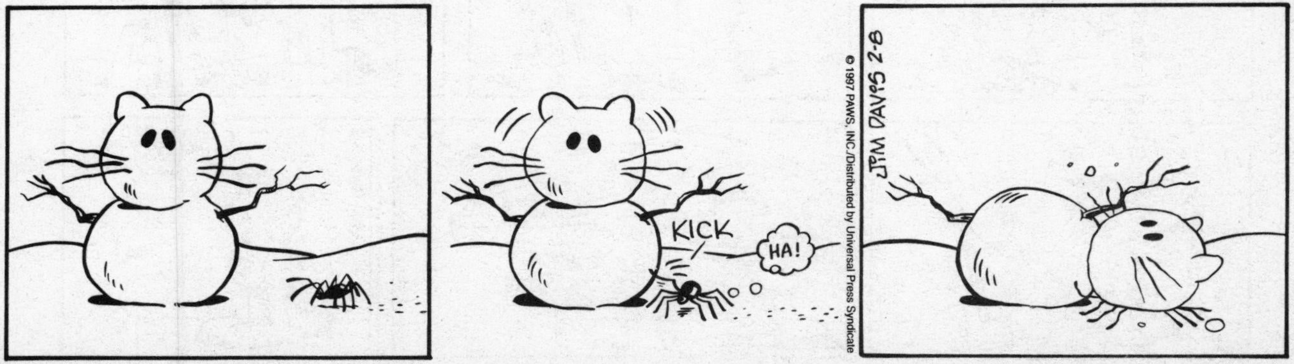
KICK
HA!
JIM DAVIS 2-8

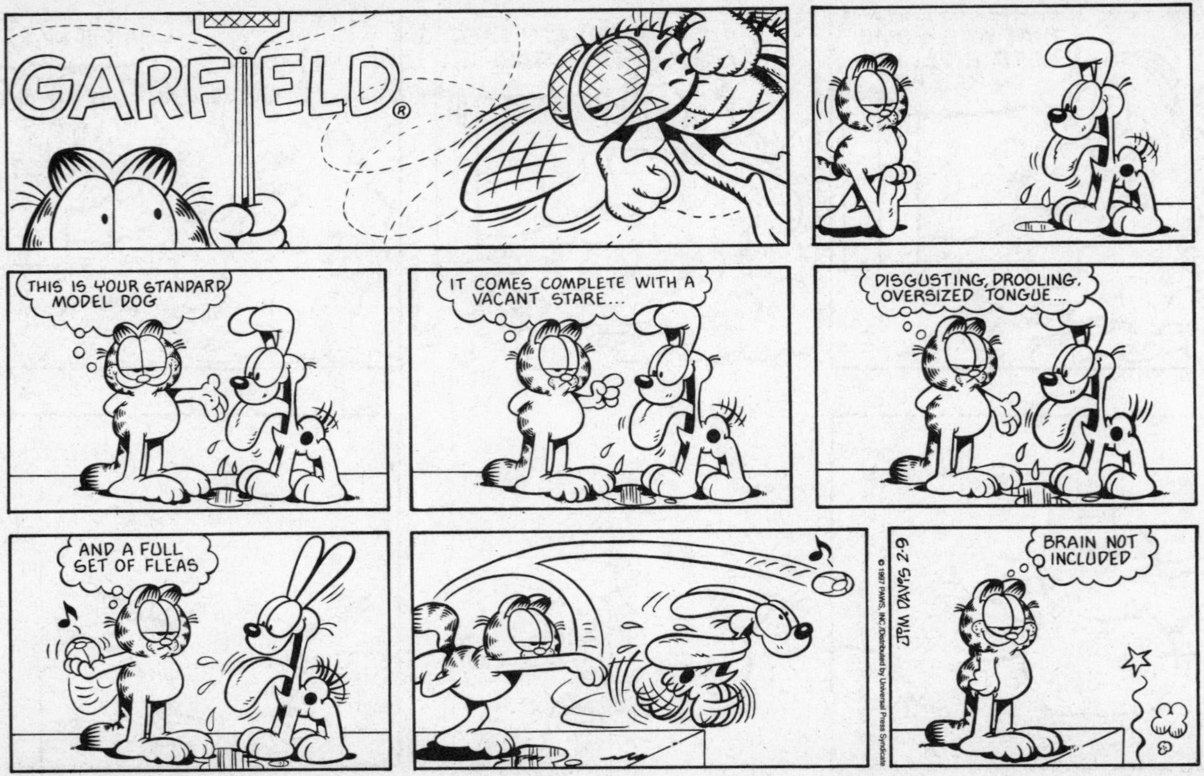
GARFIELD®
THIS IS YOUR STANDARD MODEL DOG
IT COMES COMPLETE WITH A VACANT STARE...
DISGUSTING, DROOLING, OVERSIZED TONGUE...
AND A FULL SET OF FLEAS
JPM DAVIS 2·9
© 1997 PAWS, INC./Distributed by Universal Press Syndicate
BRAIN NOT INCLUDED

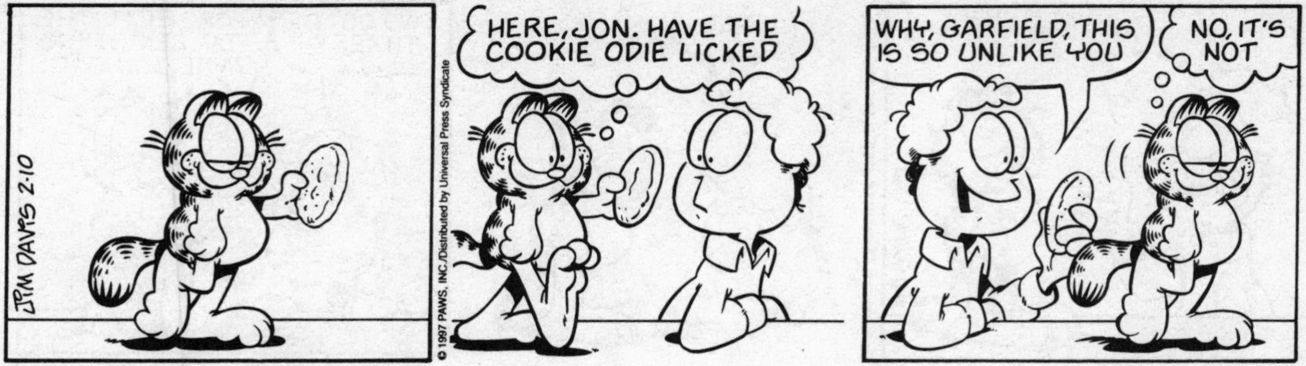
JIM DAVIS 2-10
HERE, JON. HAVE THE COOKIE ODIE LICKED
© 1997 PAWS, INC./Distributed by Universal Press Syndicate
WHY, GARFIELD, THIS IS SO UNLIKE YOU
NO, IT'S NOT

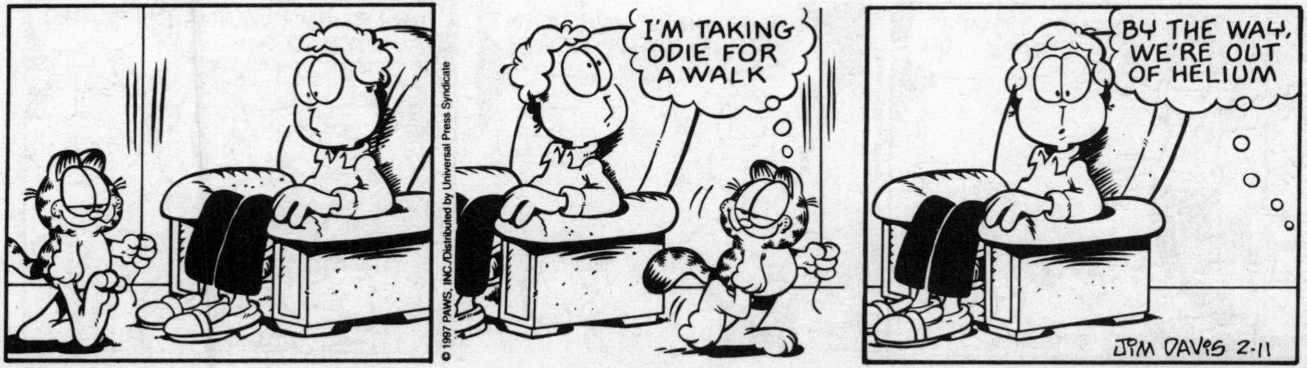
© 1997 PAWS, INC./Distributed by Universal Press Syndicate
I'M TAKING ODIE FOR A WALK
BY THE WAY, WE'RE OUT OF HELIUM
JIM DAVIS 2-11

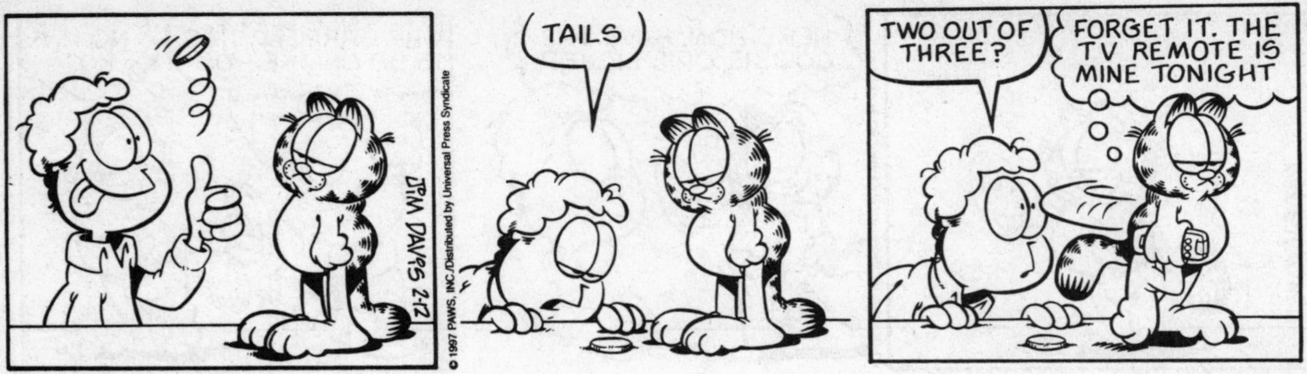
JIM DAVIS 2-12
© 1997 PAWS, INC./Distributed by Universal Press Syndicate
TAILS
TWO OUT OF THREE?
FORGET IT. THE TV REMOTE IS MINE TONIGHT

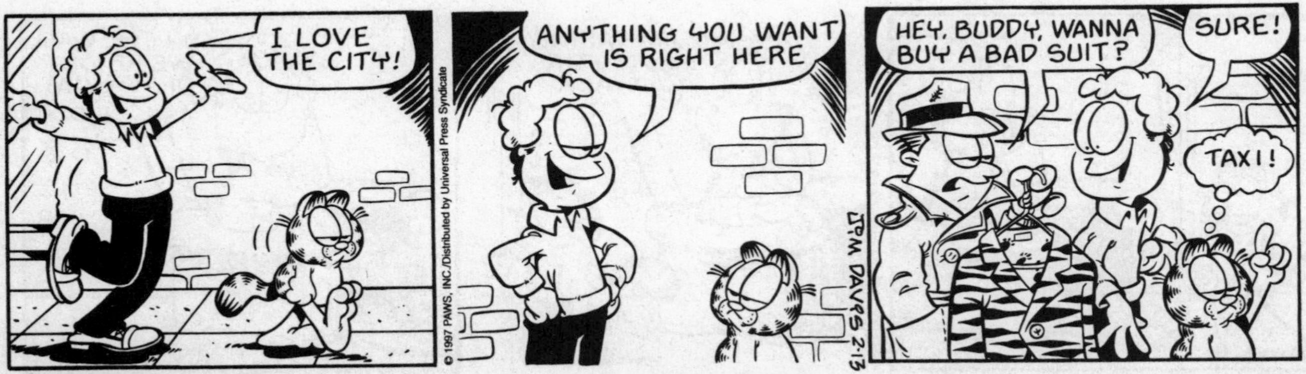
I LOVE THE CITY!
© 1997 PAWS, INC./Distributed by Universal Press Syndicate
ANYTHING YOU WANT IS RIGHT HERE
JIM DAVIS 2-13
HEY, BUDDY, WANNA BUY A BAD SUIT?
SURE!
TAXI!

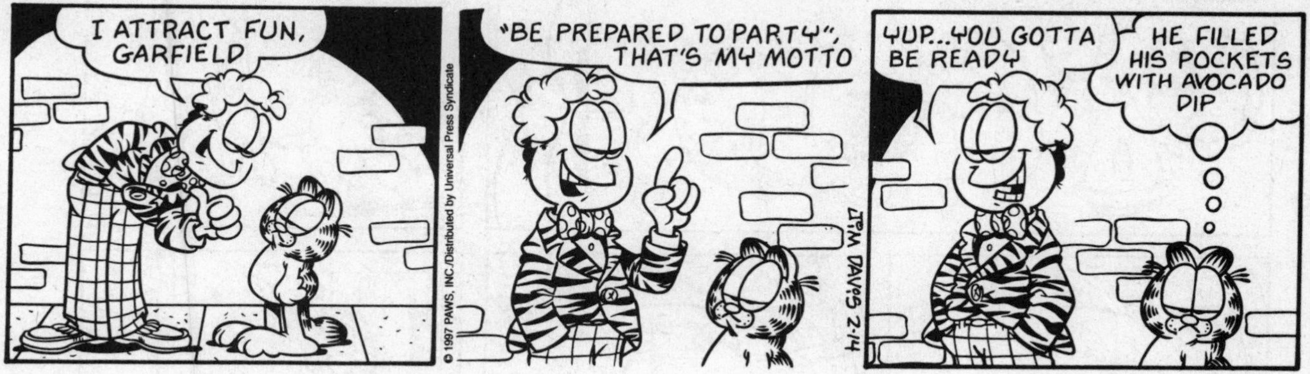
I ATTRACT FUN, GARFIELD
© 1997 PAWS, INC./Distributed by Universal Press Syndicate
"BE PREPARED TO PARTY", THAT'S MY MOTTO
JIM DAVIS 2-14
YUP...YOU GOTTA BE READY
HE FILLED HIS POCKETS WITH AVOCADO DIP

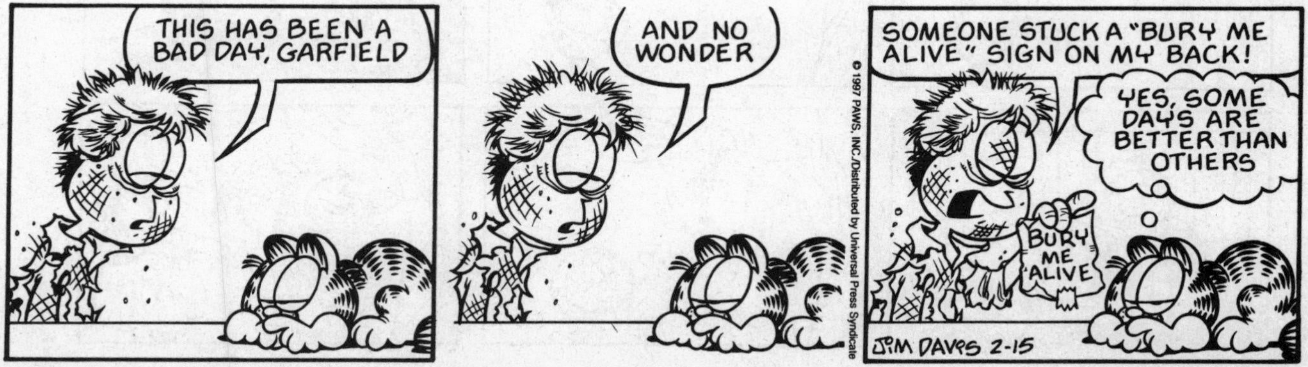
THIS HAS BEEN A BAD DAY, GARFIELD
AND NO WONDER
© 1997 PAWS, INC./Distributed by Universal Press Syndicate
SOMEONE STUCK A "BURY ME ALIVE" SIGN ON MY BACK!
BURY ME ALIVE
YES, SOME DAYS ARE BETTER THAN OTHERS
JIM DAVIS 2-15

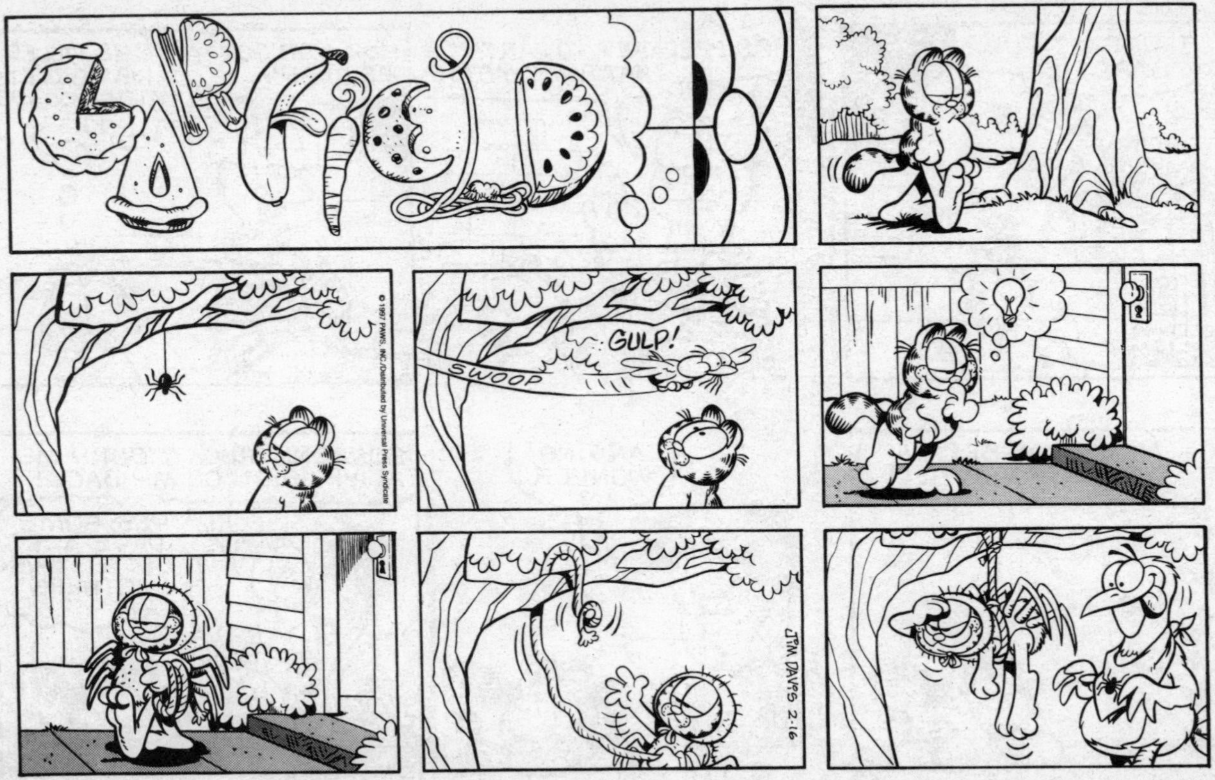
GARFIELD
© 1997 PAWS, INC./Distributed by Universal Press Syndicate
SWOOP
GULP!
JIM DAVIS 2-16

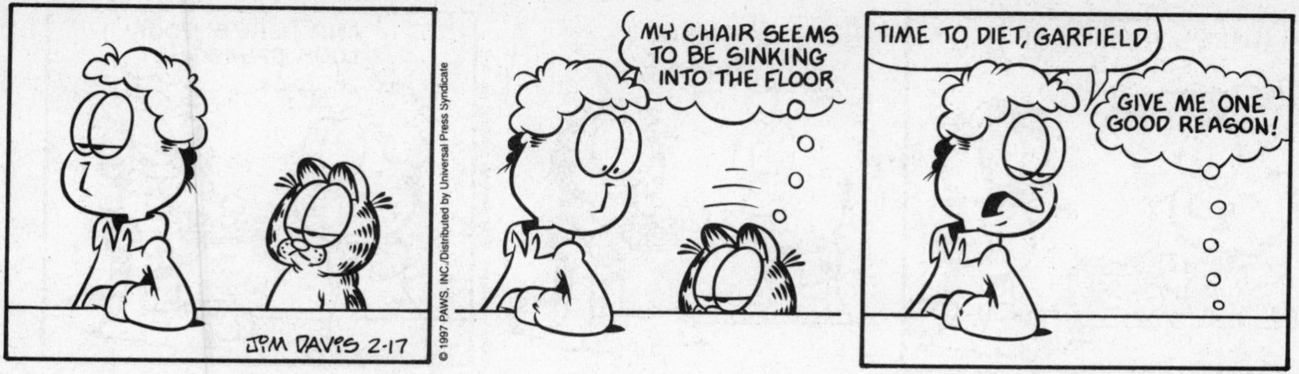

JIM DAVIS 2-17
© 1997 PAWS, INC./Distributed by Universal Press Syndicate
MY CHAIR SEEMS TO BE SINKING INTO THE FLOOR
TIME TO DIET, GARFIELD
GIVE ME ONE GOOD REASON!

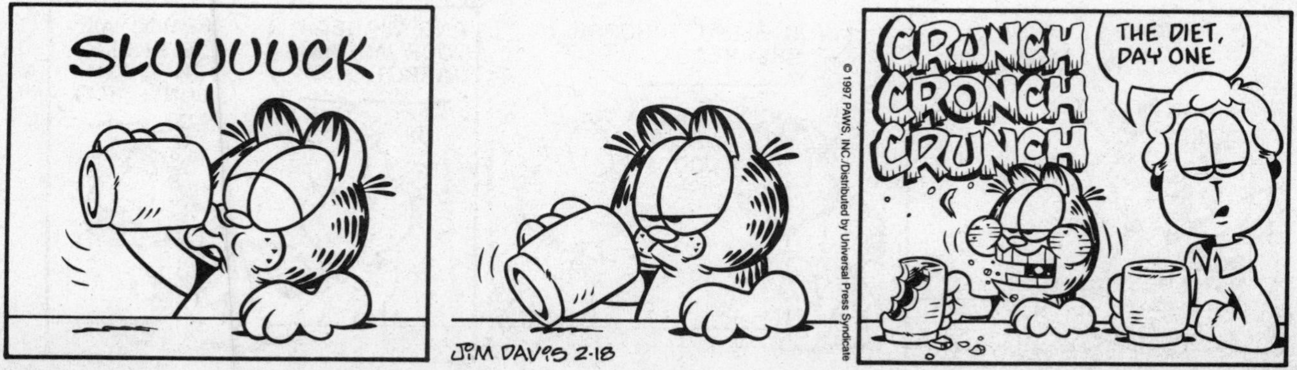

SLUUUUCK
JIM DAVIS 2-18
© 1997 PAWS, INC./Distributed by Universal Press Syndicate
CRUNCH
CRONCH
CRUNCH
THE DIET, DAY ONE

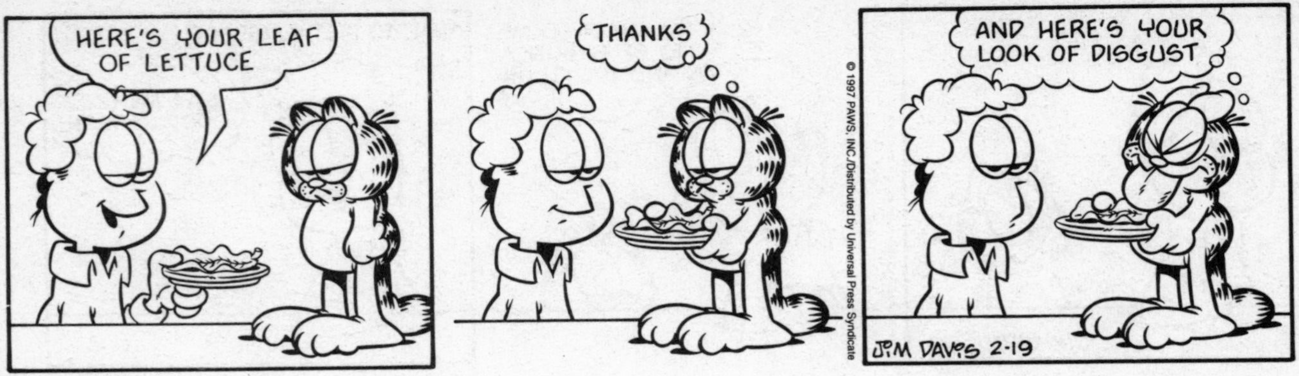
HERE'S YOUR LEAF OF LETTUCE
THANKS
AND HERE'S YOUR LOOK OF DISGUST
© 1997 PAWS, INC./Distributed by Universal Press Syndicate
JIM DAVIS 2-19

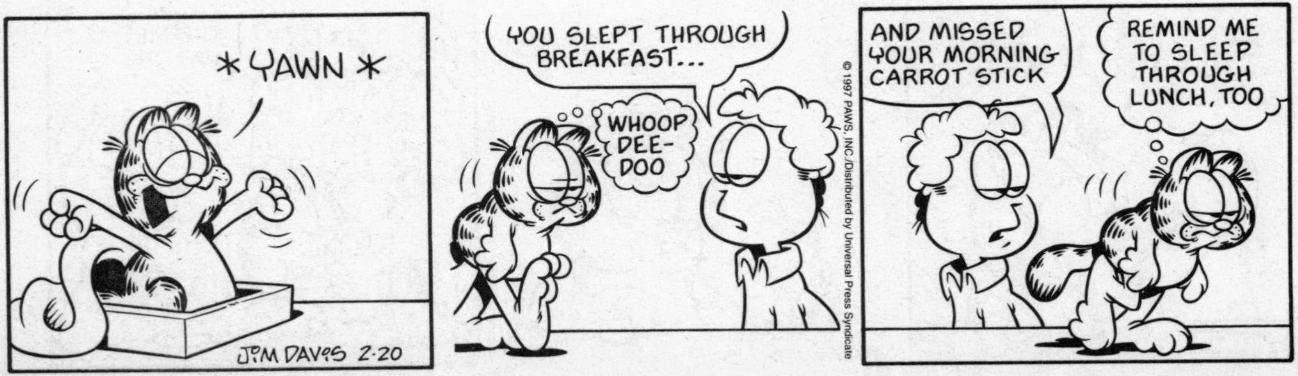
YAWN
JIM DAVIS 2-20
YOU SLEPT THROUGH BREAKFAST...
WHOOP DEE-DOO
© 1997 PAWS, INC./Distributed by Universal Press Syndicate
AND MISSED YOUR MORNING CARROT STICK
REMIND ME TO SLEEP THROUGH LUNCH, TOO

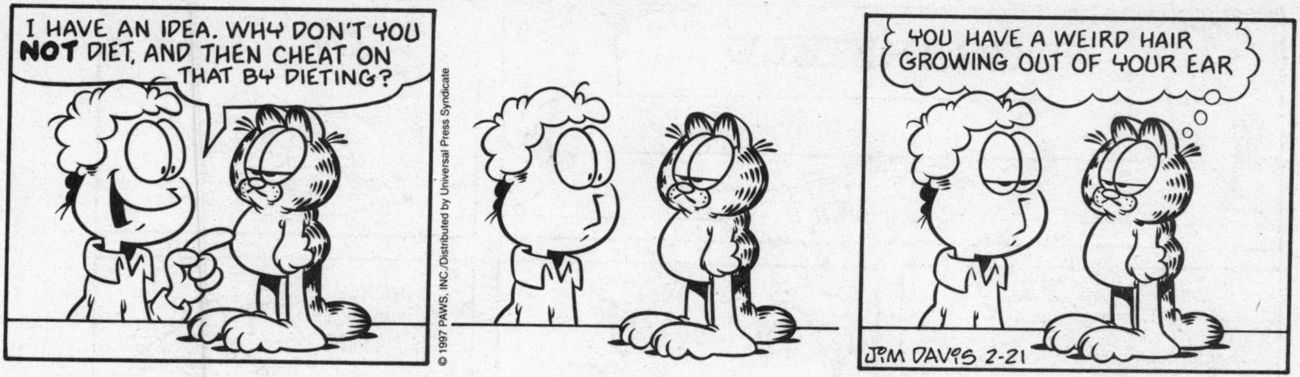
I HAVE AN IDEA. WHY DON'T YOU **NOT** DIET, AND THEN CHEAT ON THAT BY DIETING?
© 1997 PAWS, INC./Distributed by Universal Press Syndicate
YOU HAVE A WEIRD HAIR GROWING OUT OF YOUR EAR
JIM DAVIS 2-21

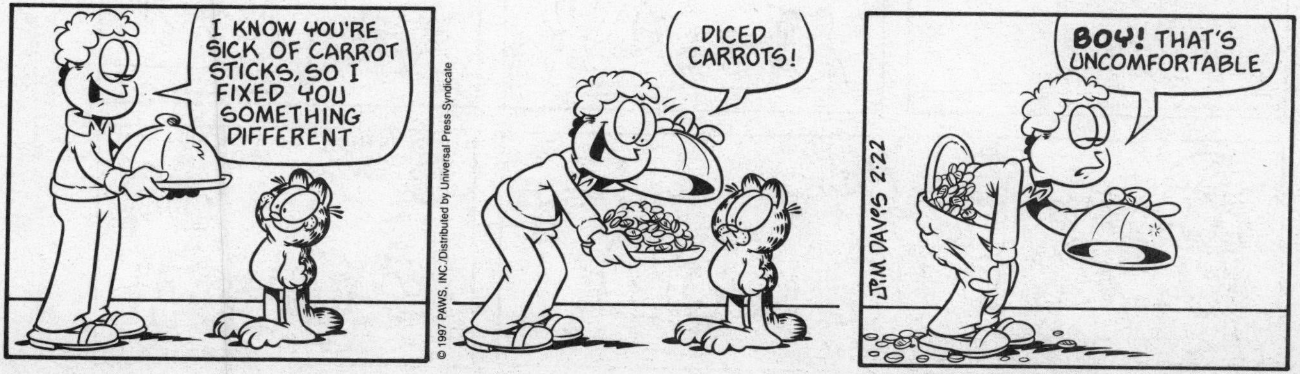
I KNOW YOU'RE SICK OF CARROT STICKS, SO I FIXED YOU SOMETHING DIFFERENT
© 1997 PAWS, INC./Distributed by Universal Press Syndicate
DICED CARROTS!
BOY! THAT'S UNCOMFORTABLE
JIM DAVIS 2-22

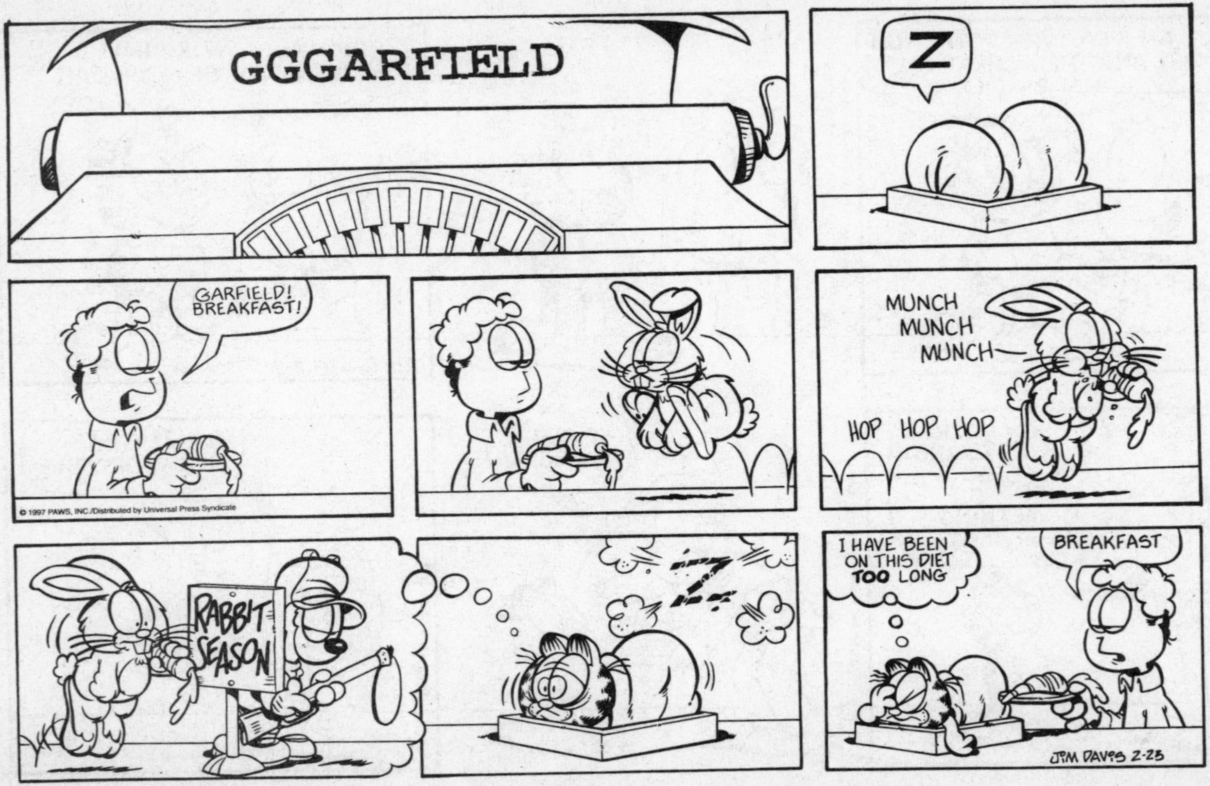
GGGARFIELD
Z
GARFIELD! BREAKFAST!
© 1997 PAWS, INC./Distributed by Universal Press Syndicate
MUNCH MUNCH MUNCH
HOP HOP HOP
RABBIT SEASON
I HAVE BEEN ON THIS DIET TOO LONG
BREAKFAST
JIM DAVIS 2-23

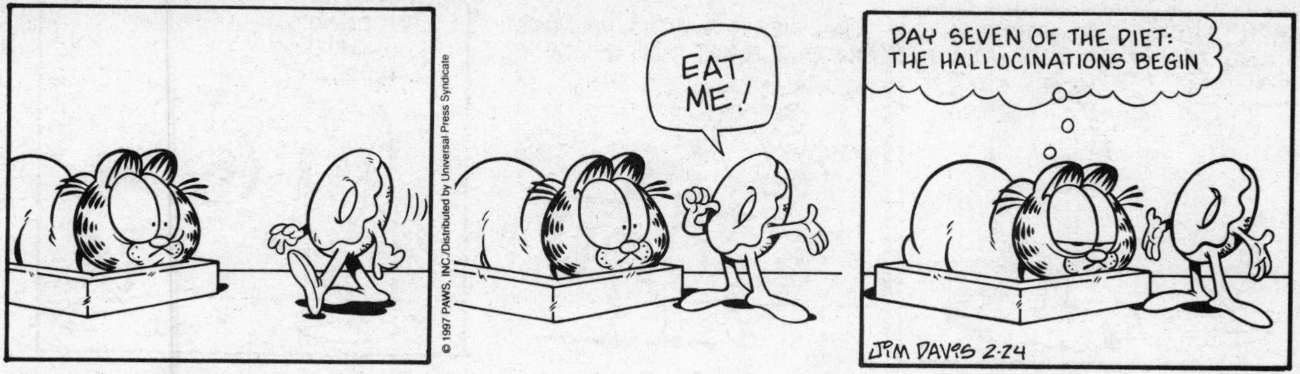

© 1997 PAWS, INC./Distributed by Universal Press Syndicate
EAT ME!
DAY SEVEN OF THE DIET: THE HALLUCINATIONS BEGIN
JIM DAVIS 2-24

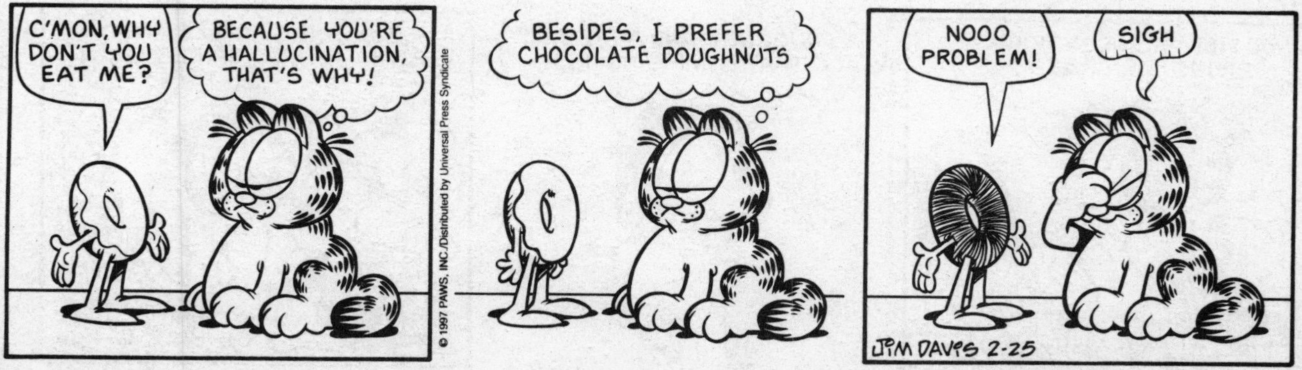

C'MON, WHY DON'T YOU EAT ME?
BECAUSE YOU'RE A HALLUCINATION, THAT'S WHY!
© 1997 PAWS, INC./Distributed by Universal Press Syndicate
BESIDES, I PREFER CHOCOLATE DOUGHNUTS
NOOO PROBLEM!
SIGH
JIM DAVIS 2-25

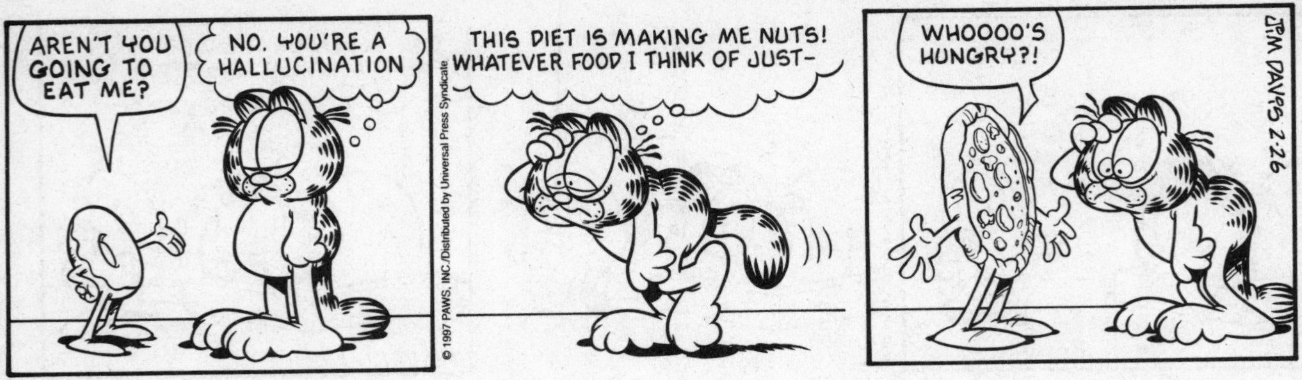
AREN'T YOU GOING TO EAT ME?
NO. YOU'RE A HALLUCINATION
© 1997 PAWS, INC./Distributed by Universal Press Syndicate
THIS DIET IS MAKING ME NUTS! WHATEVER FOOD I THINK OF JUST-
WHOOOO'S HUNGRY?!
JIM DAVIS 2-26

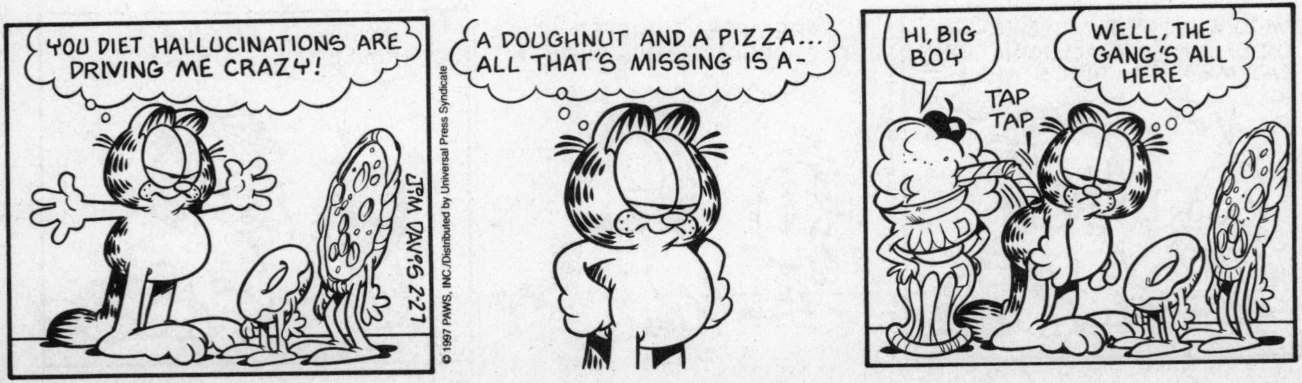
YOU DIET HALLUCINATIONS ARE DRIVING ME CRAZY!
JIM DAVIS 2-27
© 1997 PAWS, INC./Distributed by Universal Press Syndicate
A DOUGHNUT AND A PIZZA... ALL THAT'S MISSING IS A-
HI, BIG BOY
TAP TAP
WELL, THE GANG'S ALL HERE

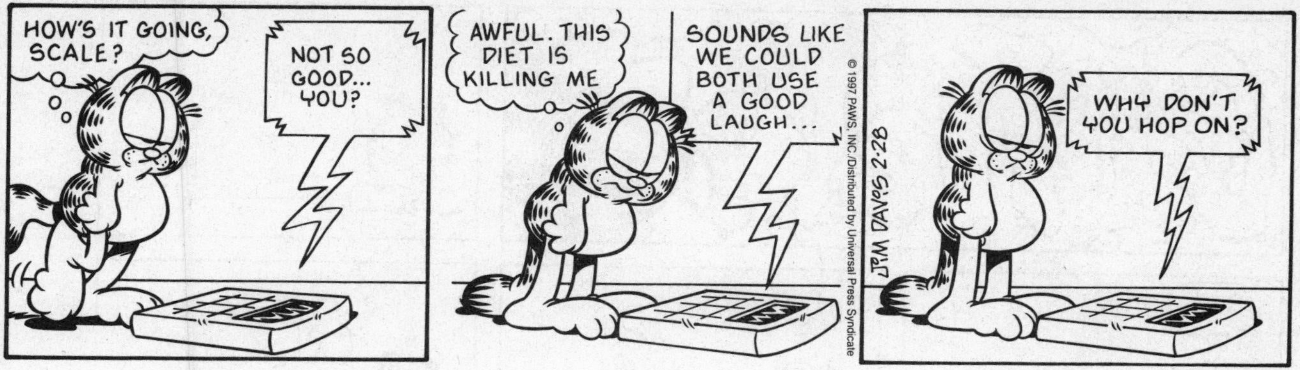
HOW'S IT GOING, SCALE?
NOT SO GOOD... YOU?
AWFUL. THIS DIET IS KILLING ME
SOUNDS LIKE WE COULD BOTH USE A GOOD LAUGH...
© 1997 PAWS, INC./Distributed by Universal Press Syndicate
JIM DAVIS 2-28
WHY DON'T YOU HOP ON?

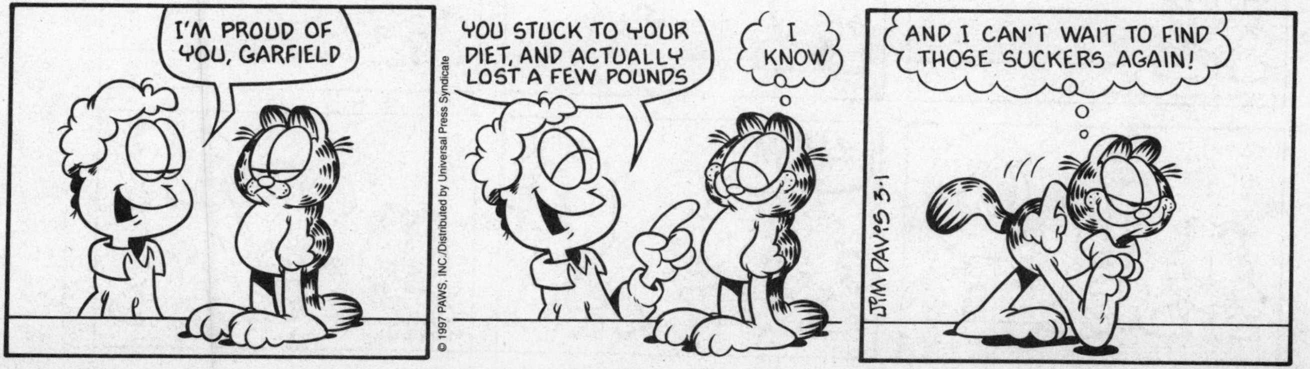
I'M PROUD OF YOU, GARFIELD
© 1997 PAWS, INC./Distributed by Universal Press Syndicate
YOU STUCK TO YOUR DIET, AND ACTUALLY LOST A FEW POUNDS
I KNOW
JIM DAVIS 3-1
AND I CAN'T WAIT TO FIND THOSE SUCKERS AGAIN!

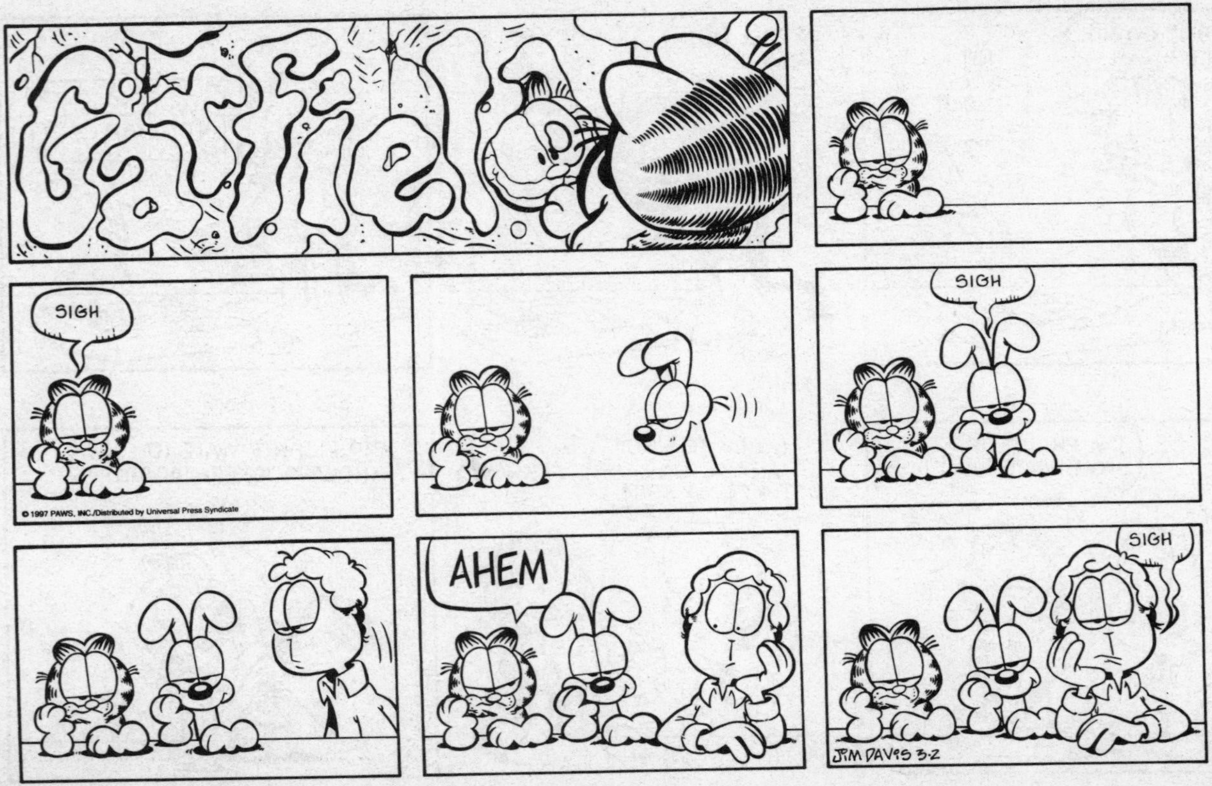
Garfield
SIGH
© 1997 PAWS, INC./Distributed by Universal Press Syndicate
SIGH
AHEM
SIGH
JIM DAVIS 3-2

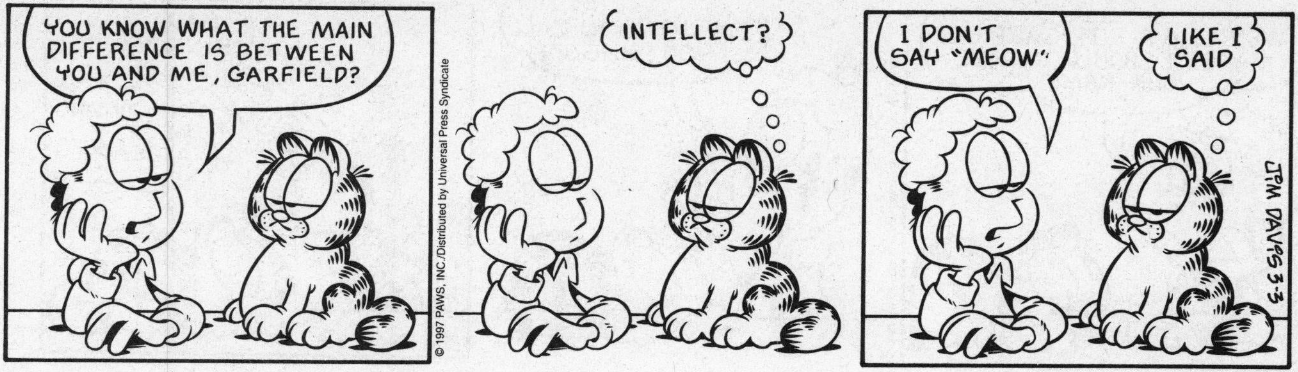
YOU KNOW WHAT THE MAIN DIFFERENCE IS BETWEEN YOU AND ME, GARFIELD?
© 1997 PAWS, INC./Distributed by Universal Press Syndicate
INTELLECT?
I DON'T SAY "MEOW"
LIKE I SAID
JIM DAVIS 3-3

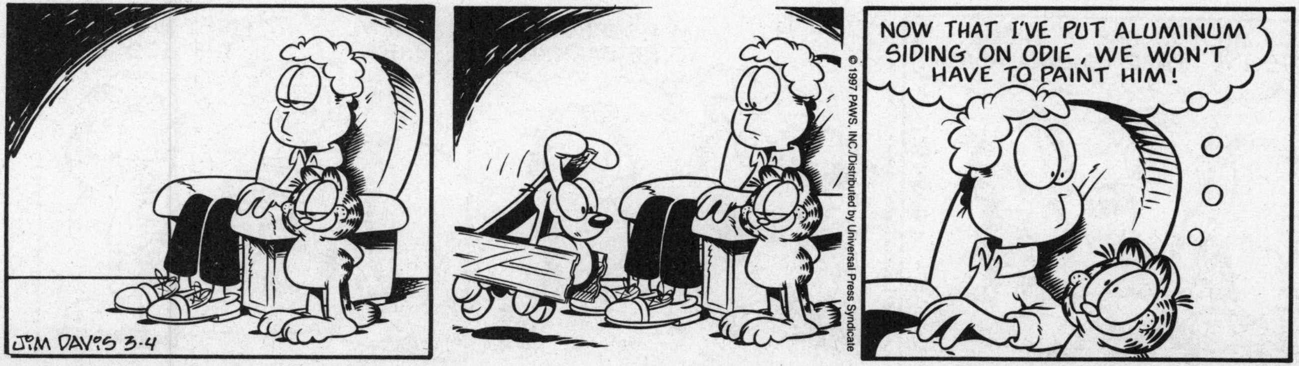
JIM DAVIS 3-4
© 1997 PAWS, INC./Distributed by Universal Press Syndicate
NOW THAT I'VE PUT ALUMINUM SIDING ON ODIE, WE WON'T HAVE TO PAINT HIM!

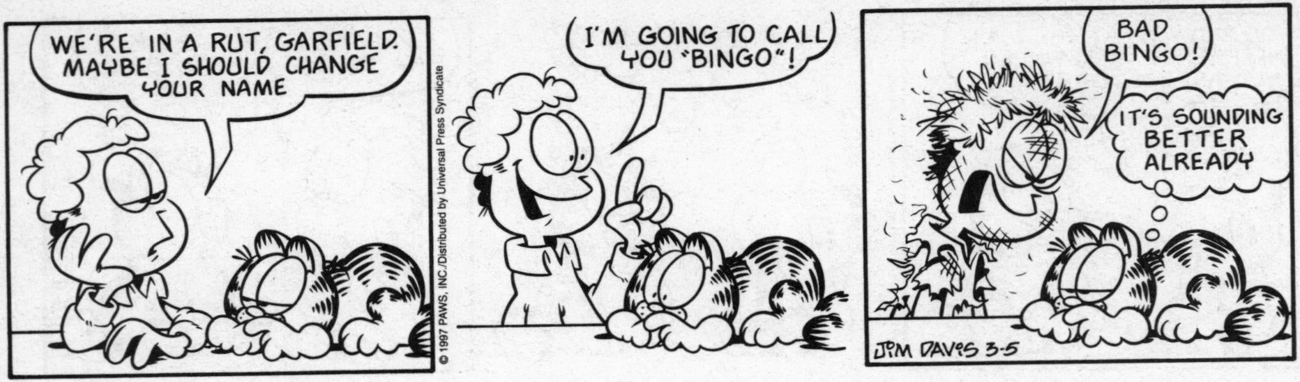
WE'RE IN A RUT, GARFIELD. MAYBE I SHOULD CHANGE YOUR NAME
I'M GOING TO CALL YOU "BINGO"!
BAD BINGO!
IT'S SOUNDING BETTER ALREADY
JIM DAVIS 3-5

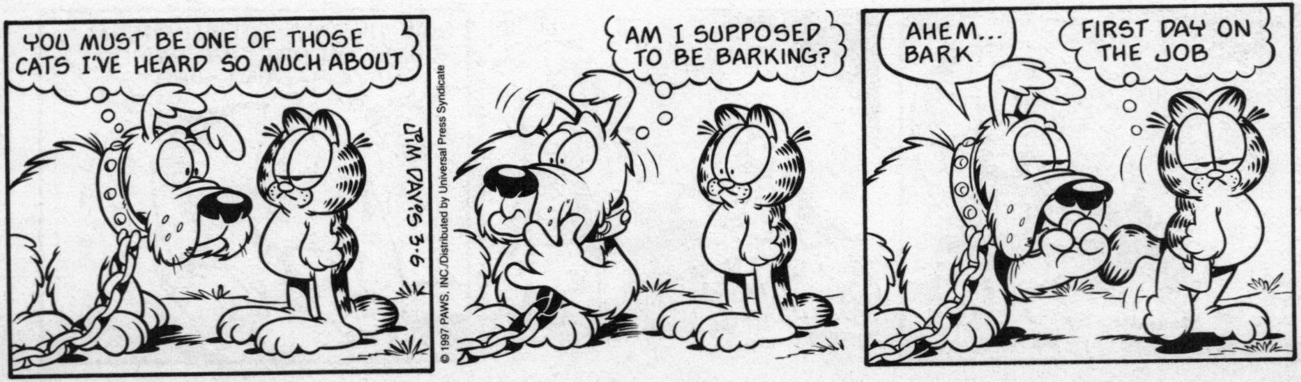
YOU MUST BE ONE OF THOSE CATS I'VE HEARD SO MUCH ABOUT
JIM DAVIS 3-6
AM I SUPPOSED TO BE BARKING?
AHEM... BARK
FIRST DAY ON THE JOB

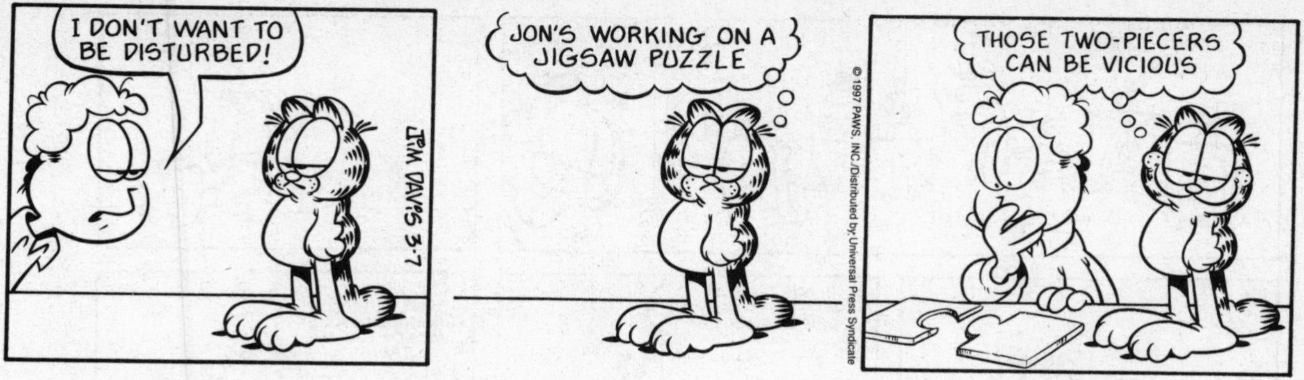
I DON'T WANT TO BE DISTURBED!
JIM DAVIS 3-7
JON'S WORKING ON A JIGSAW PUZZLE
THOSE TWO-PIECERS CAN BE VICIOUS

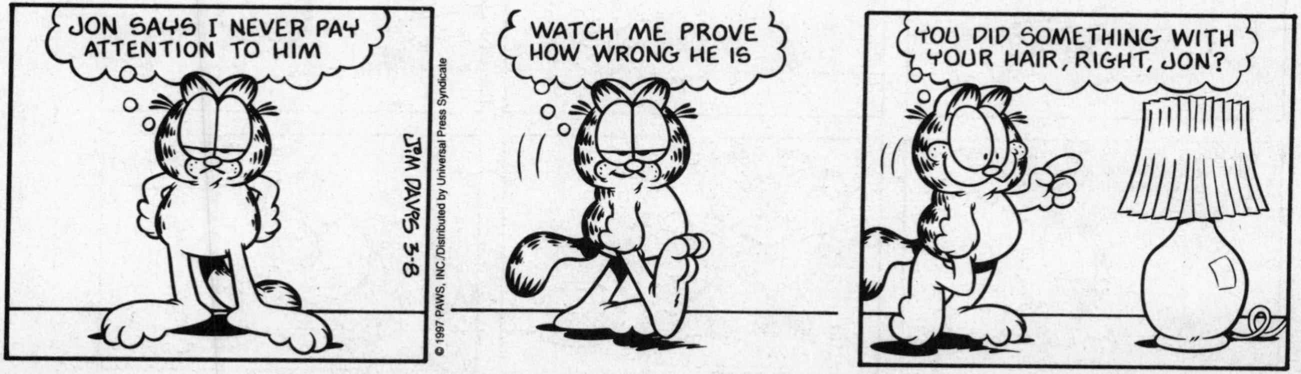
JON SAYS I NEVER PAY ATTENTION TO HIM
JIM DAVIS 3-8
WATCH ME PROVE HOW WRONG HE IS
YOU DID SOMETHING WITH YOUR HAIR, RIGHT, JON?

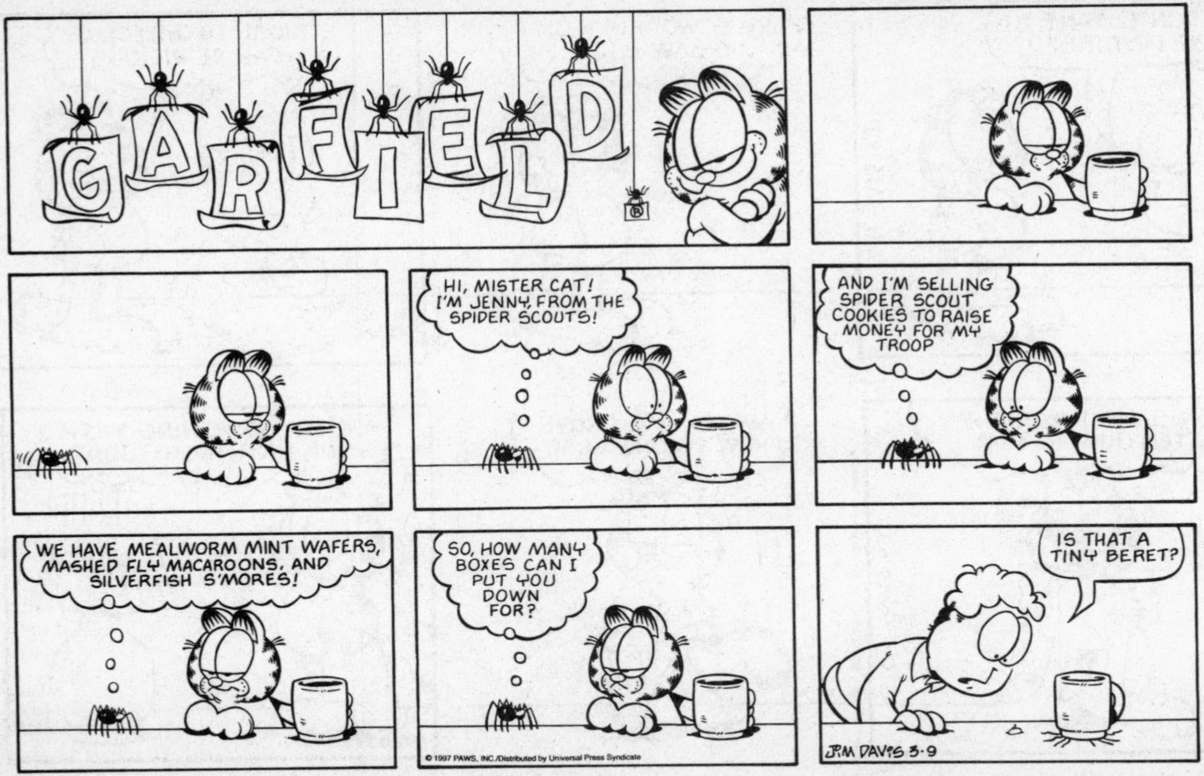
GARFIELD
HI, MISTER CAT! I'M JENNY, FROM THE SPIDER SCOUTS!
AND I'M SELLING SPIDER SCOUT COOKIES TO RAISE MONEY FOR MY TROOP
WE HAVE MEALWORM MINT WAFERS, MASHED FLY MACAROONS, AND SILVERFISH S'MORES!
SO, HOW MANY BOXES CAN I PUT YOU DOWN FOR?
IS THAT A TINY BERET?
JIM DAVIS 3-9
© 1997 PAWS, INC./Distributed by Universal Press Syndicate

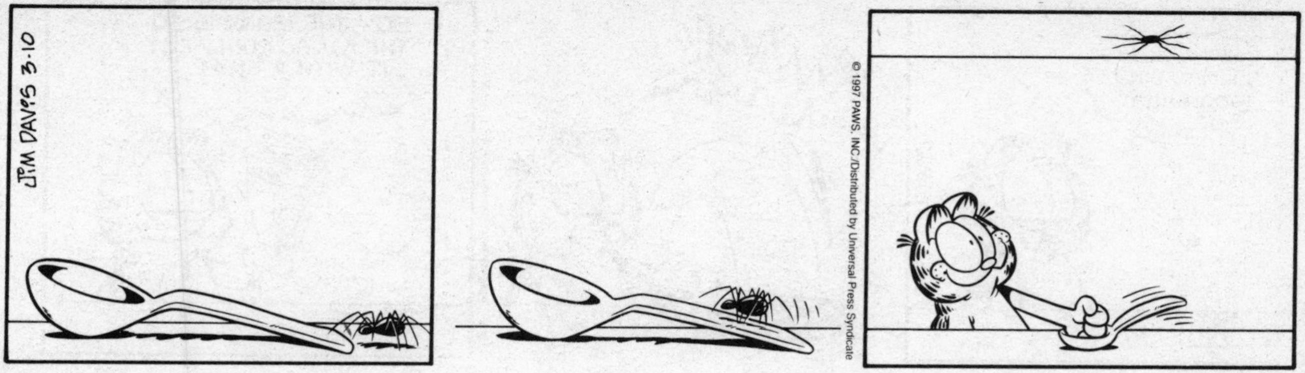
JIM DAVIS 3-10
© 1997 PAWS, INC./Distributed by Universal Press Syndicate

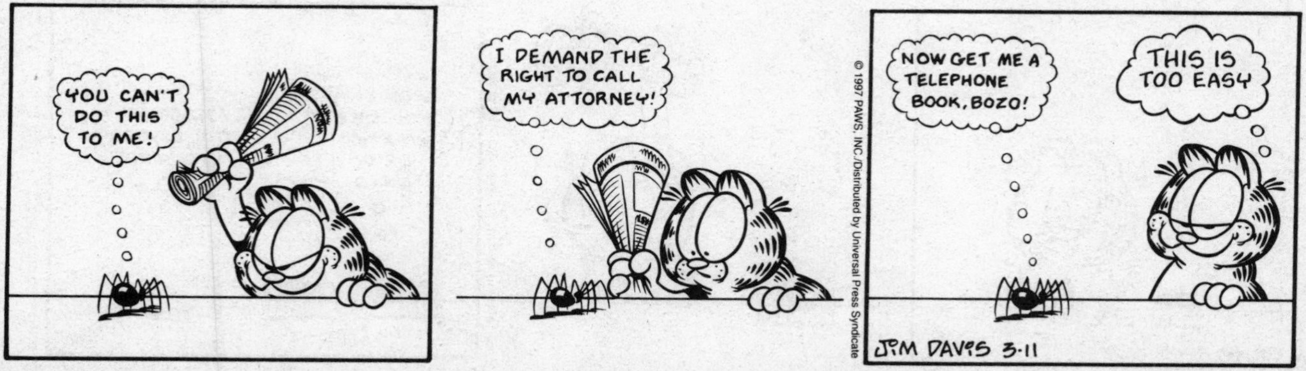
YOU CAN'T DO THIS TO ME!
I DEMAND THE RIGHT TO CALL MY ATTORNEY!
NOW GET ME A TELEPHONE BOOK, BOZO!
THIS IS TOO EASY
JIM DAVIS 3-11
© 1997 PAWS, INC./Distributed by Universal Press Syndicate

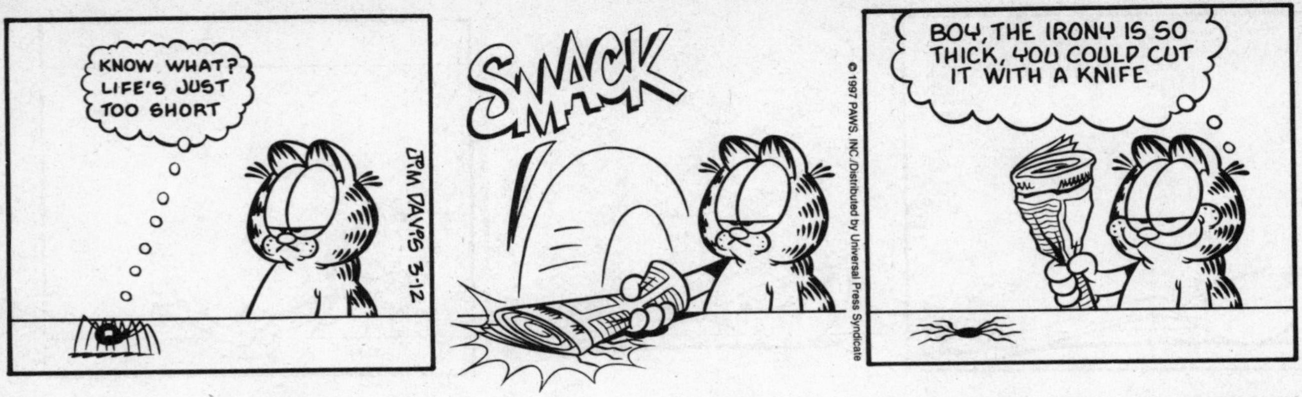
KNOW WHAT? LIFE'S JUST TOO SHORT
JIM DAVIS 3-12
SMACK
BOY, THE IRONY IS SO THICK, YOU COULD CUT IT WITH A KNIFE

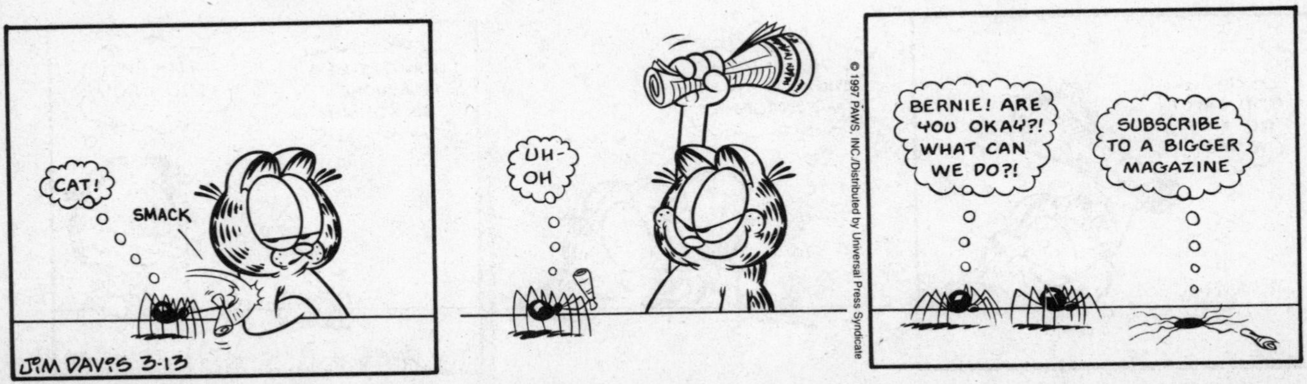
CAT!
SMACK
JIM DAVIS 3-13
UH-OH
BERNIE! ARE YOU OKAY?! WHAT CAN WE DO?!
SUBSCRIBE TO A BIGGER MAGAZINE

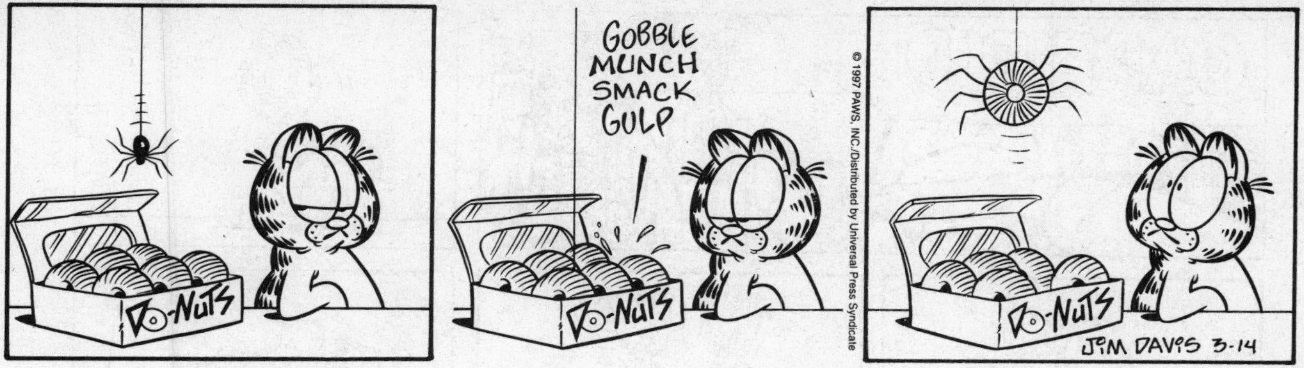
GOBBLE MUNCH SMACK GULP
DO-NUTS
JIM DAVIS 3-14

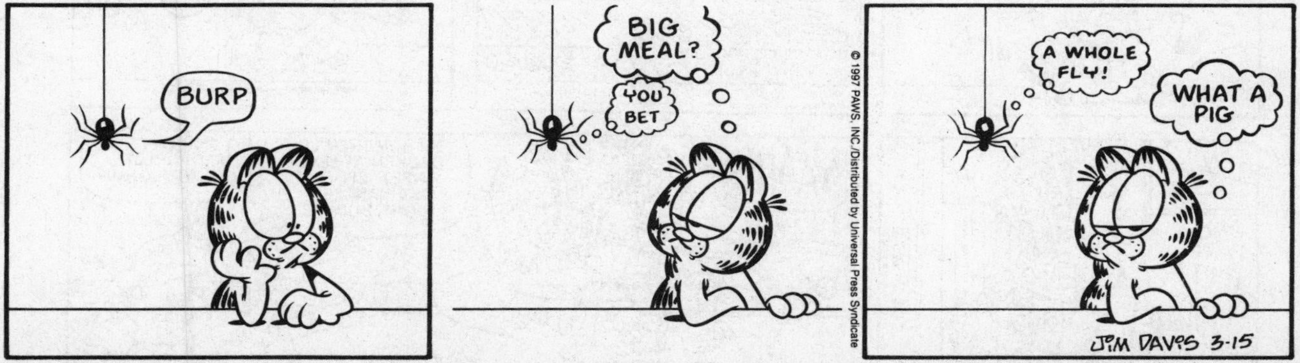
BURP
BIG MEAL?
YOU BET
A WHOLE FLY!
WHAT A PIG
JIM DAVIS 3-15

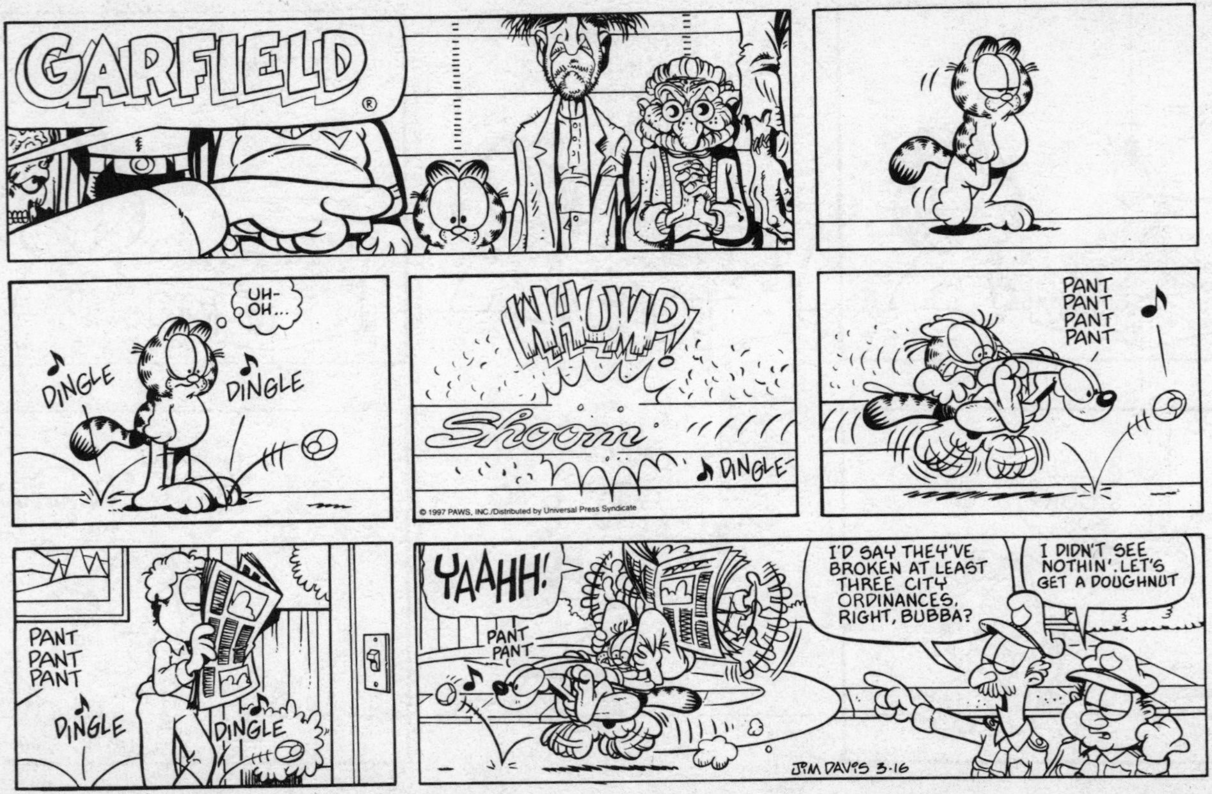
GARFIELD®
UH-OH...
DINGLE
DINGLE
WHUMP
Shoom
DINGLE
PANT PANT PANT PANT
© 1997 PAWS, INC./Distributed by Universal Press Syndicate
PANT PANT PANT
DINGLE
DINGLE
YAAHH!
PANT PANT
I'D SAY THEY'VE BROKEN AT LEAST THREE CITY ORDINANCES, RIGHT, BUBBA?
I DIDN'T SEE NOTHIN'. LET'S GET A DOUGHNUT
JIM DAVIS 3-16

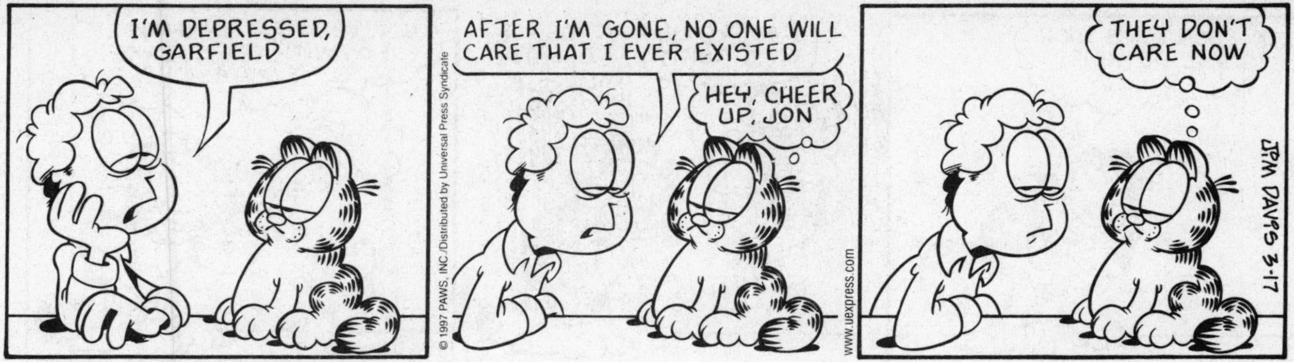
I'M DEPRESSED, GARFIELD
AFTER I'M GONE, NO ONE WILL CARE THAT I EVER EXISTED
HEY, CHEER UP, JON
THEY DON'T CARE NOW
JIM DAVIS 3-17
© 1997 PAWS, INC./Distributed by Universal Press Syndicate
www.uexpress.com

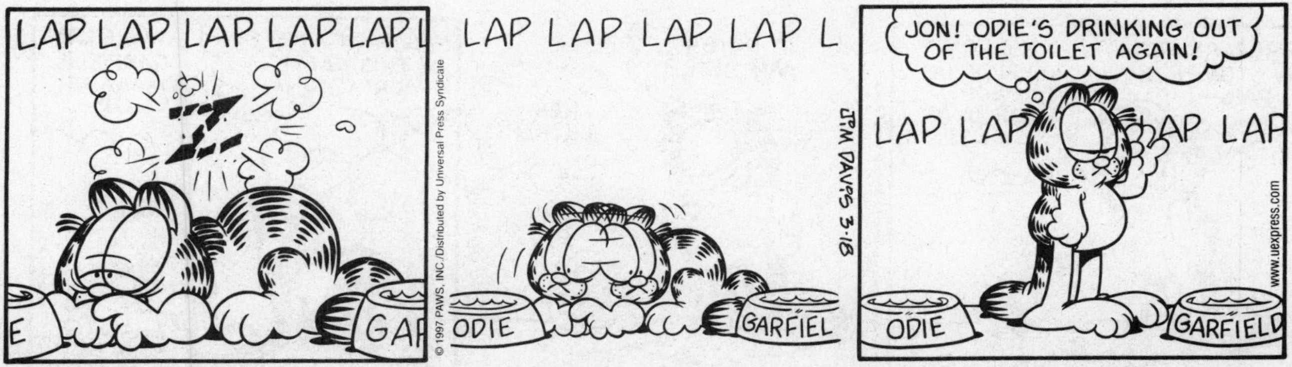
LAP LAP LAP LAP LAP L
LAP LAP LAP LAP L
GAR
ODIE
GARFIEL
JON! ODIE'S DRINKING OUT OF THE TOILET AGAIN!
LAP LAP LAP LAP
ODIE
GARFIELD
JIM DAVIS 3-18
© 1997 PAWS, INC./Distributed by Universal Press Syndicate
www.uexpress.com

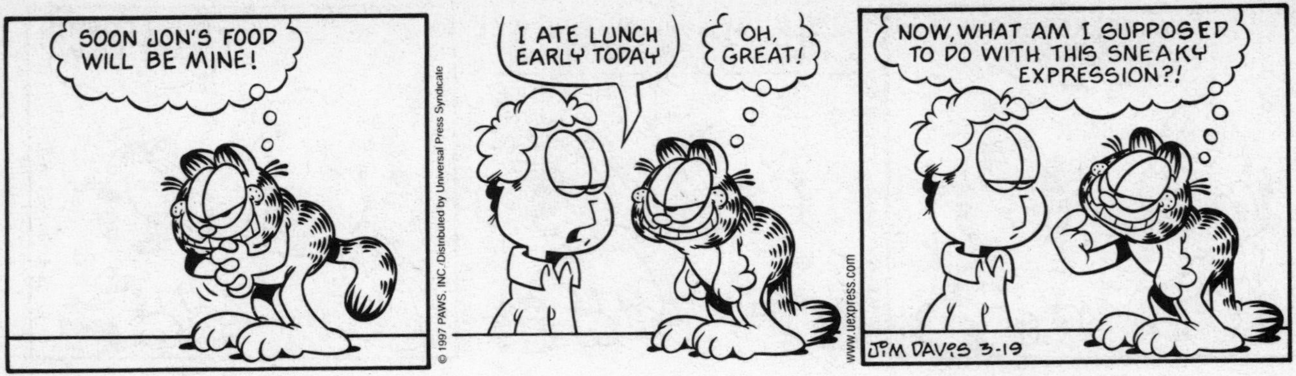
SOON JON'S FOOD WILL BE MINE!
I ATE LUNCH EARLY TODAY
OH, GREAT!
NOW, WHAT AM I SUPPOSED TO DO WITH THIS SNEAKY EXPRESSION?!
JIM DAVIS 3-19
© 1997 PAWS, INC./Distributed by Universal Press Syndicate
www.uexpress.com

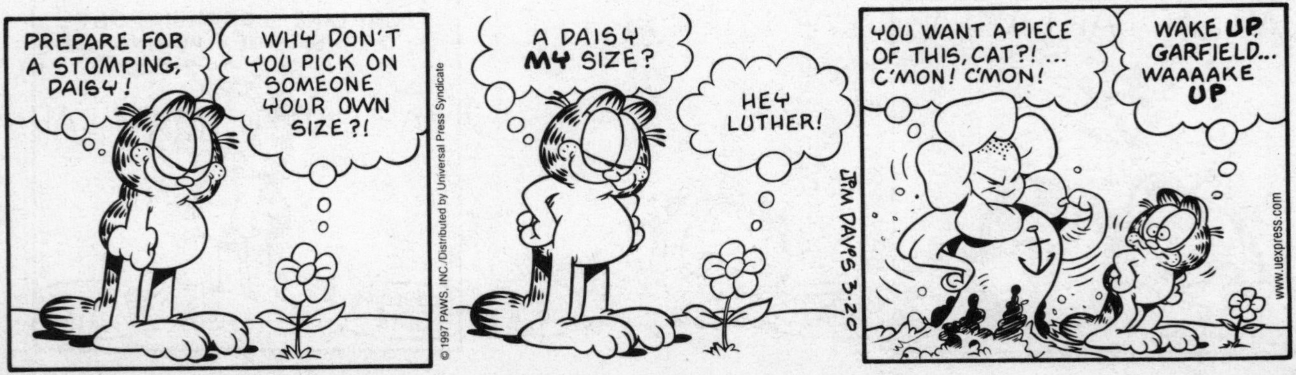
PREPARE FOR A STOMPING, DAISY!
WHY DON'T YOU PICK ON SOMEONE YOUR OWN SIZE?!
A DAISY **MY** SIZE?
HEY LUTHER!
YOU WANT A PIECE OF THIS, CAT?! ... C'MON! C'MON!
WAKE **UP**, GARFIELD... WAAAAKE **UP**
JIM DAVIS 3-20
© 1997 PAWS, INC./Distributed by Universal Press Syndicate
www.uexpress.com

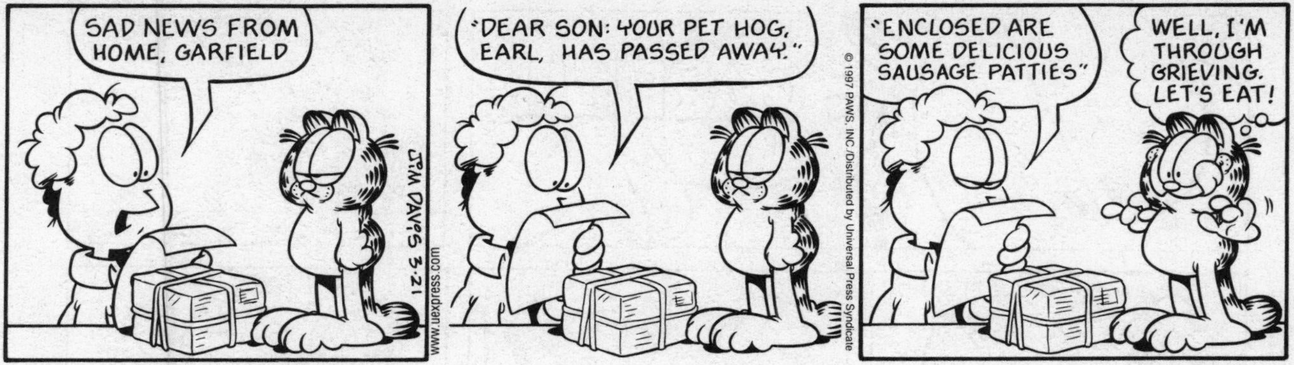
SAD NEWS FROM HOME, GARFIELD
"DEAR SON: YOUR PET HOG, EARL, HAS PASSED AWAY."
"ENCLOSED ARE SOME DELICIOUS SAUSAGE PATTIES"
WELL, I'M THROUGH GRIEVING. LET'S EAT!
JIM DAVIS 3-21
www.uexpress.com
© 1997 PAWS, INC./Distributed by Universal Press Syndicate

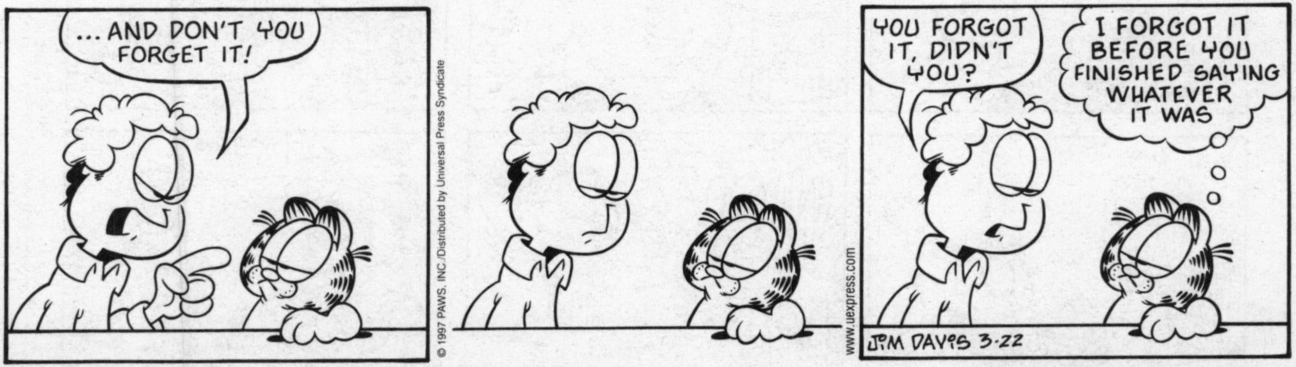
...AND DON'T YOU FORGET IT!
YOU FORGOT IT, DIDN'T YOU?
I FORGOT IT BEFORE YOU FINISHED SAYING WHATEVER IT WAS
JIM DAVIS 3-22
© 1997 PAWS, INC./Distributed by Universal Press Syndicate
www.uexpress.com

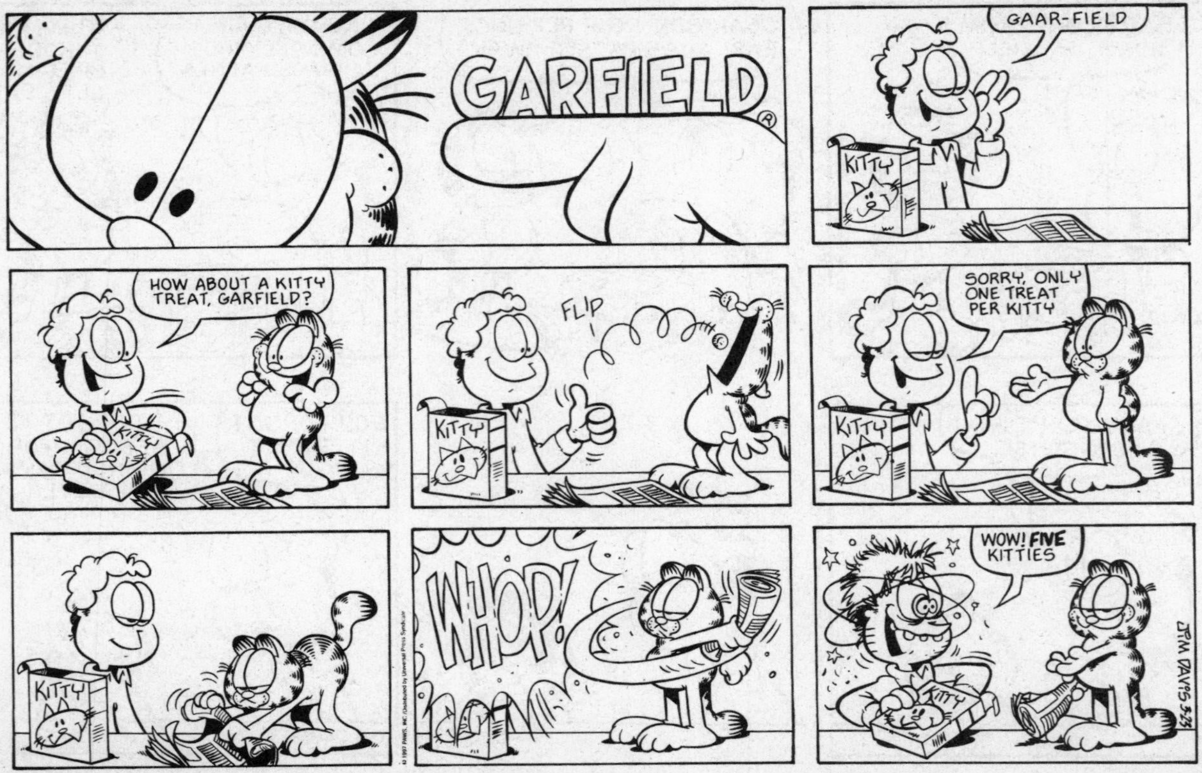
GARFIELD
GAAR-FIELD
KITTY
HOW ABOUT A KITTY TREAT, GARFIELD?
KITTY
FLIP
KITTY
SORRY, ONLY ONE TREAT PER KITTY
KITTY
KITTY
WHOP!
WOW! **FIVE** KITTIES
KITTY
JIM DAVIS 3-23

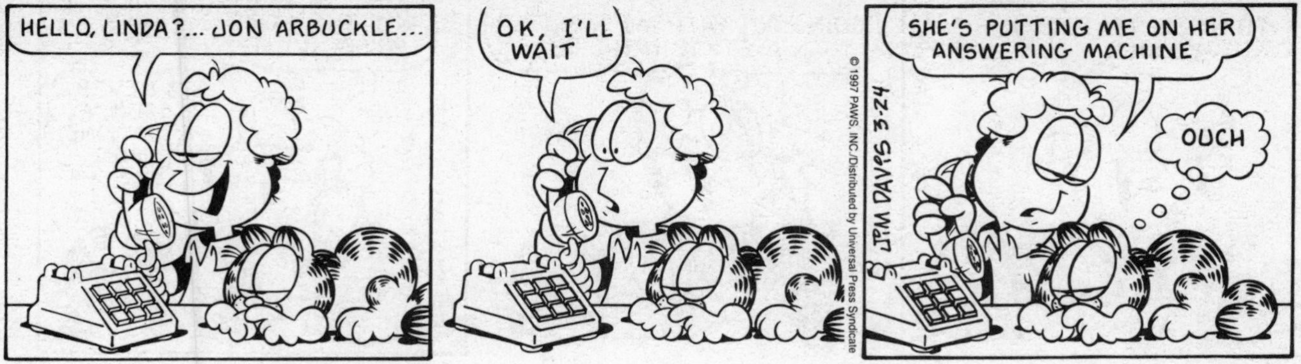
HELLO, LINDA?... JON ARBUCKLE...
OK, I'LL WAIT
© 1997 PAWS, INC./Distributed by Universal Press Syndicate
JPM DAVPS 3-24
SHE'S PUTTING ME ON HER ANSWERING MACHINE
OUCH

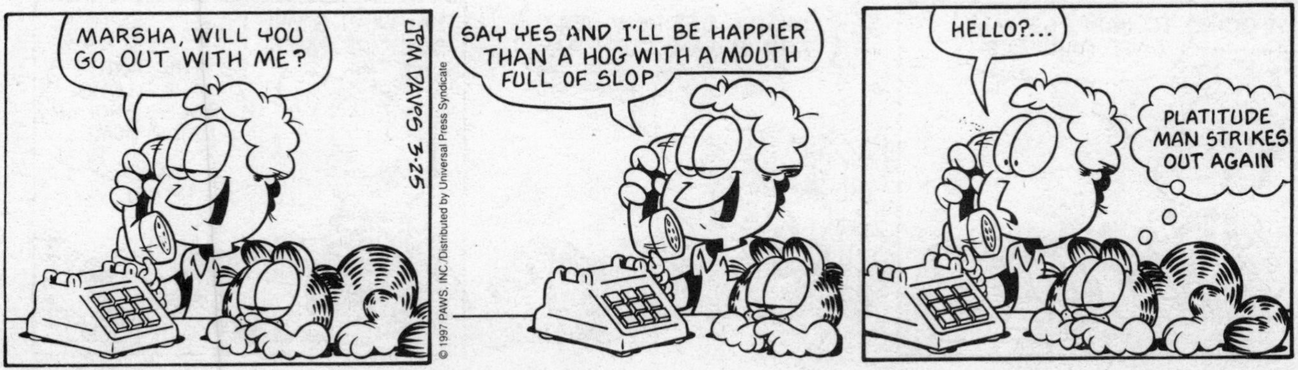
MARSHA, WILL YOU GO OUT WITH ME?
JPM DAVPS 3-25
© 1997 PAWS, INC./Distributed by Universal Press Syndicate
SAY YES AND I'LL BE HAPPIER THAN A HOG WITH A MOUTH FULL OF SLOP
HELLO?...
PLATITUDE MAN STRIKES OUT AGAIN

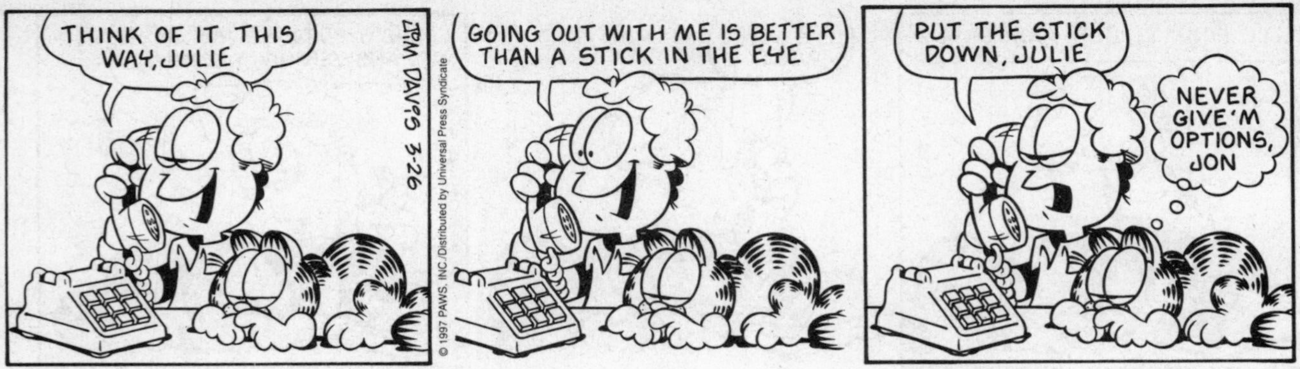
THINK OF IT THIS WAY, JULIE
JIM DAVIS 3-26
© 1997 PAWS, INC./Distributed by Universal Press Syndicate
GOING OUT WITH ME IS BETTER THAN A STICK IN THE EYE
PUT THE STICK DOWN, JULIE
NEVER GIVE 'M OPTIONS, JON

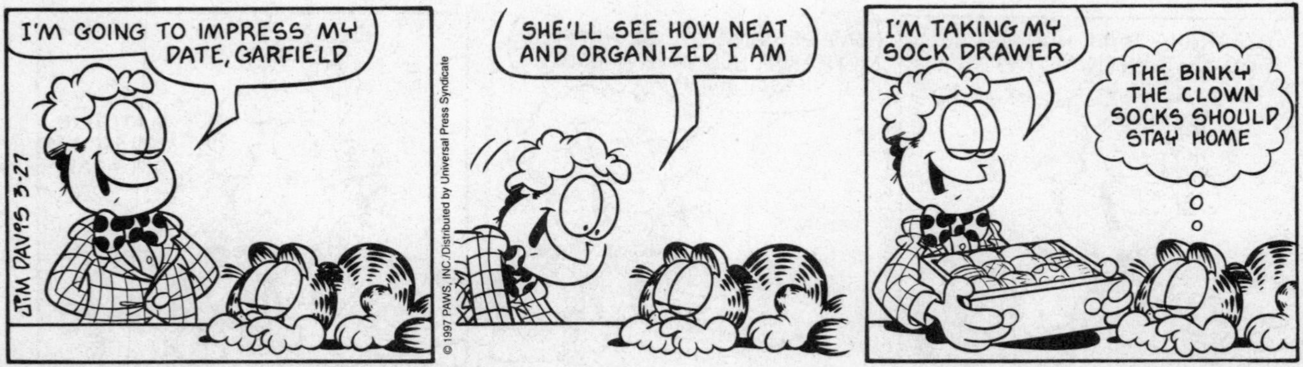
I'M GOING TO IMPRESS MY DATE, GARFIELD
JIM DAVIS 3-27
© 1997 PAWS, INC./Distributed by Universal Press Syndicate
SHE'LL SEE HOW NEAT AND ORGANIZED I AM
I'M TAKING MY SOCK DRAWER
THE BINKY THE CLOWN SOCKS SHOULD STAY HOME

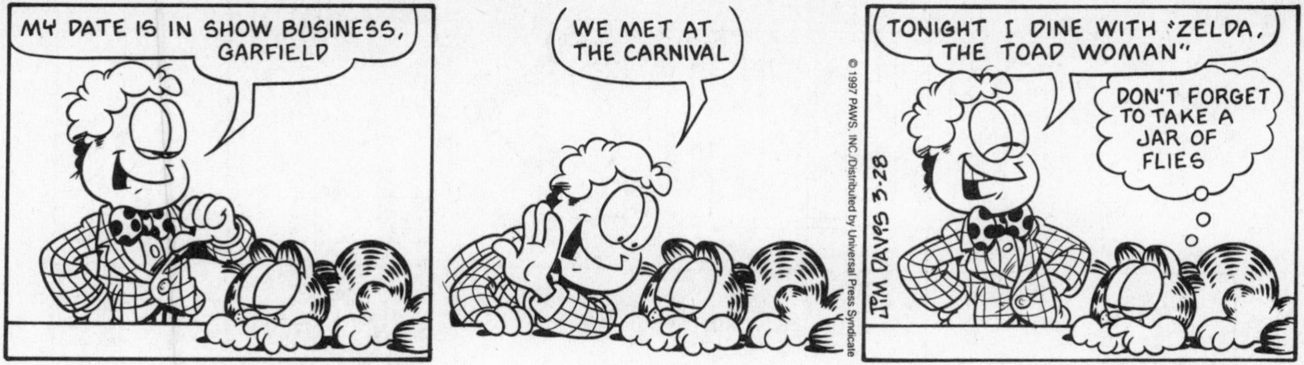
MY DATE IS IN SHOW BUSINESS, GARFIELD
WE MET AT THE CARNIVAL
© 1997 PAWS, INC./Distributed by Universal Press Syndicate
JIM DAVIS 3-28
TONIGHT I DINE WITH "ZELDA, THE TOAD WOMAN"
DON'T FORGET TO TAKE A JAR OF FLIES

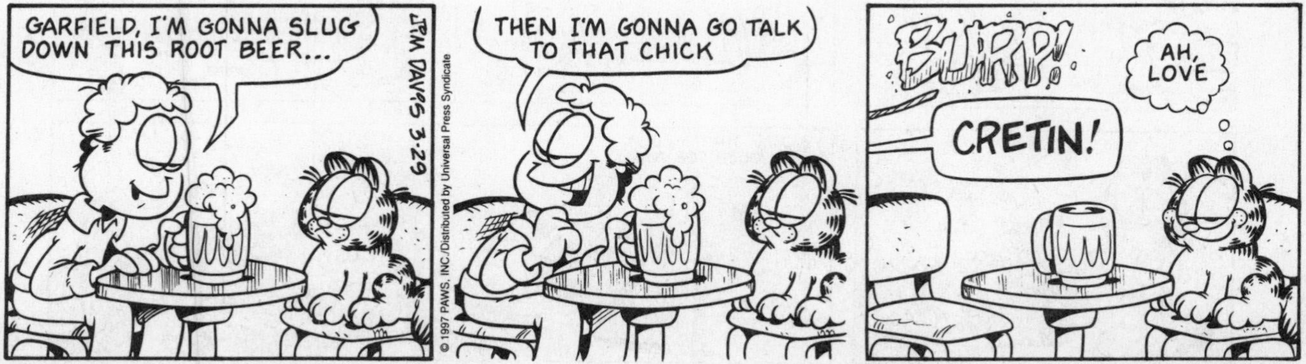
GARFIELD, I'M GONNA SLUG DOWN THIS ROOT BEER...
JIM DAVIS 3-29
© 1997 PAWS, INC./Distributed by Universal Press Syndicate
THEN I'M GONNA GO TALK TO THAT CHICK
BURP!
CRETIN!
AH, LOVE

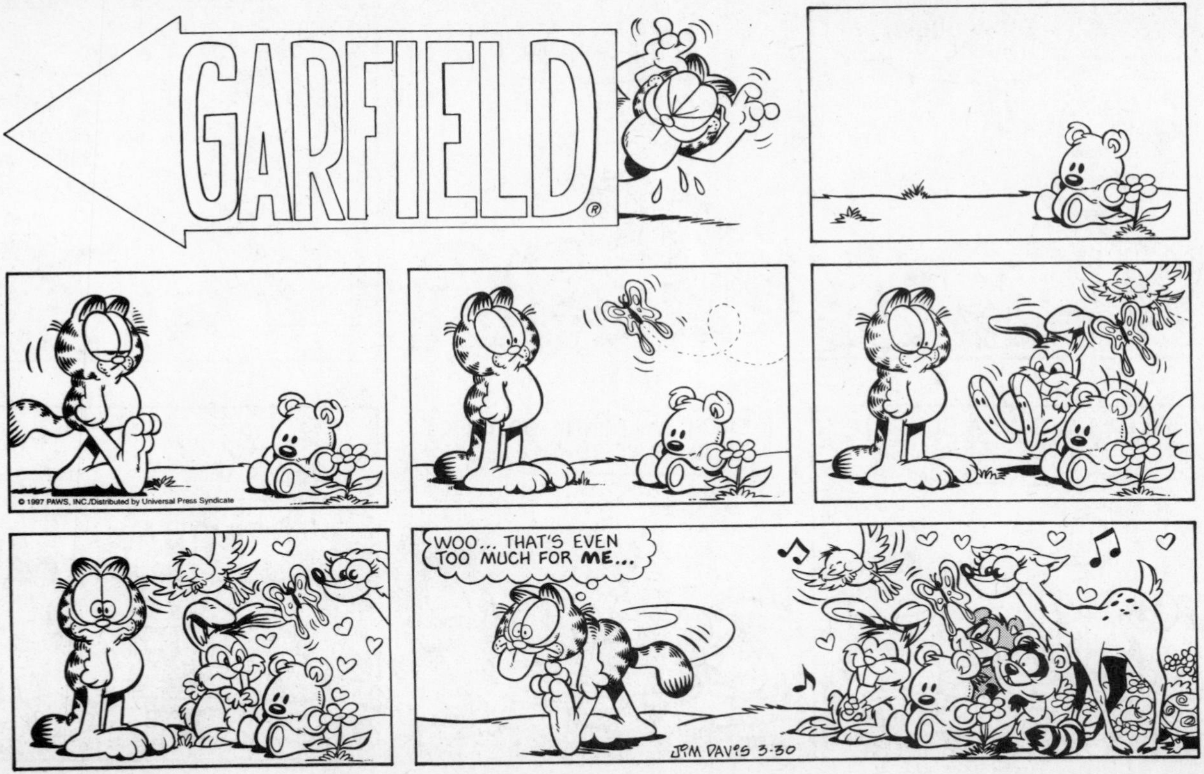
GARFIELD®
© 1997 PAWS, INC./Distributed by Universal Press Syndicate
WOO... THAT'S EVEN TOO MUCH FOR **ME**...
JIM DAVIS 3-30

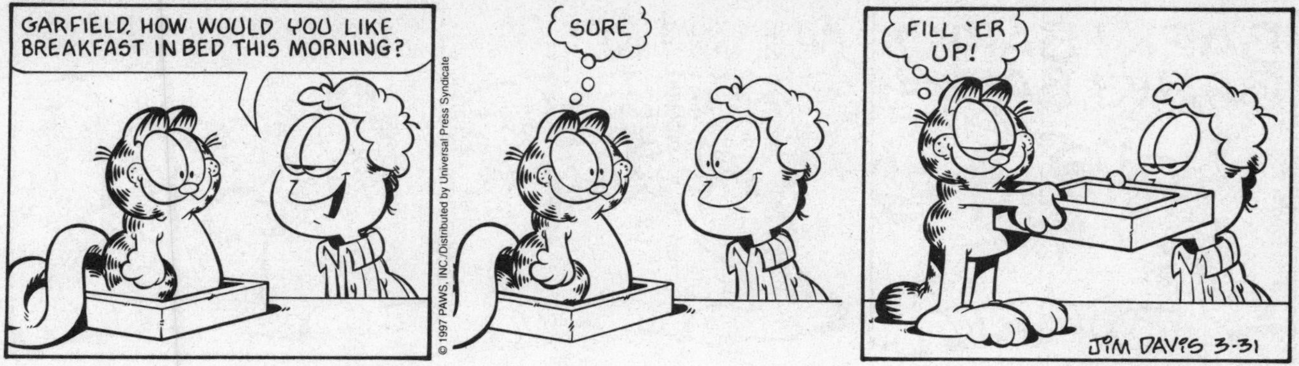
GARFIELD, HOW WOULD YOU LIKE BREAKFAST IN BED THIS MORNING?
SURE
FILL 'ER UP!
JIM DAVIS 3-31
© 1997 PAWS, INC./Distributed by Universal Press Syndicate

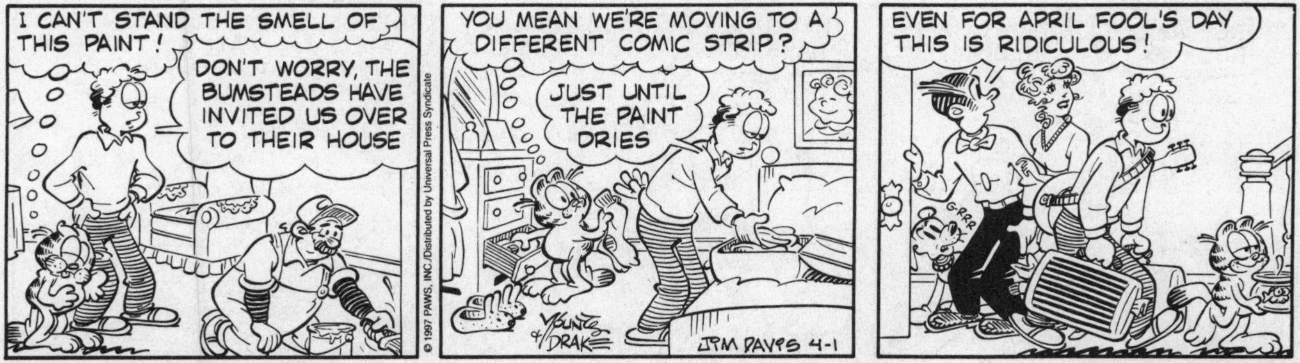
I CAN'T STAND THE SMELL OF THIS PAINT!
DON'T WORRY, THE BUMSTEADS HAVE INVITED US OVER TO THEIR HOUSE
YOU MEAN WE'RE MOVING TO A DIFFERENT COMIC STRIP?
JUST UNTIL THE PAINT DRIES
YOUNG & DRAKE
JIM DAVIS 4-1
EVEN FOR APRIL FOOL'S DAY THIS IS RIDICULOUS!
G-RRR
© 1997 PAWS, INC./Distributed by Universal Press Syndicate

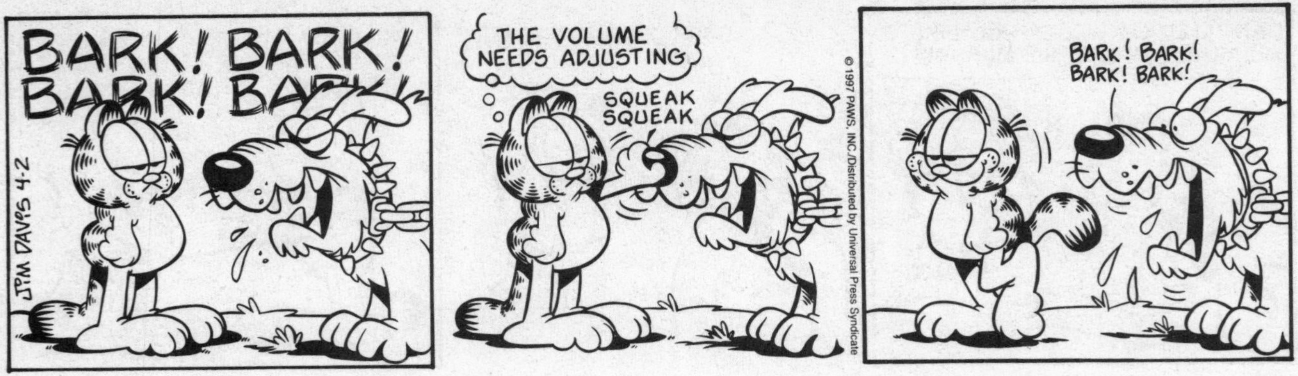
BARK! BARK! BARK! BARK!
JIM DAVIS 4-2
THE VOLUME NEEDS ADJUSTING
SQUEAK SQUEAK
© 1997 PAWS, INC./Distributed by Universal Press Syndicate
BARK! BARK! BARK! BARK!

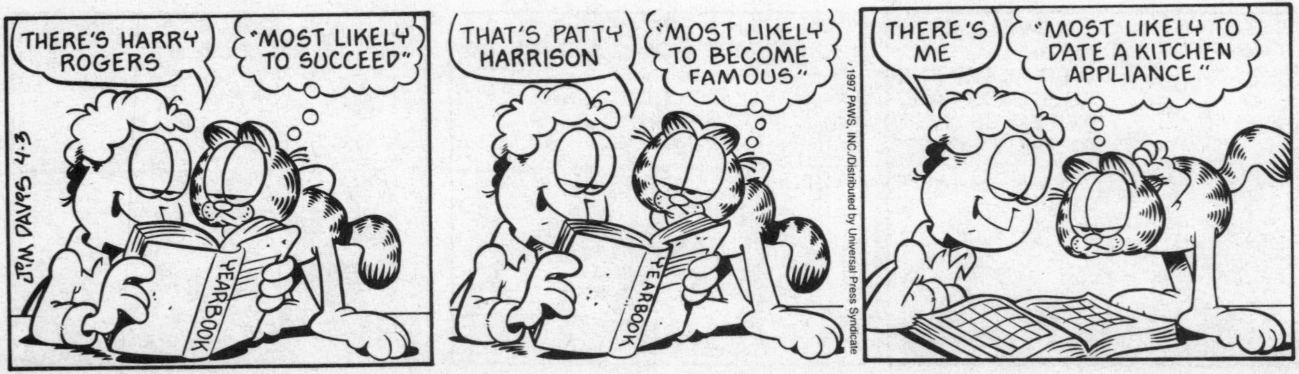
JIM DAVIS 4-3
THERE'S HARRY ROGERS
"MOST LIKELY TO SUCCEED"
YEARBOOK
THAT'S PATTY HARRISON
"MOST LIKELY TO BECOME FAMOUS"
YEARBOOK
© 1997 PAWS, INC./Distributed by Universal Press Syndicate
THERE'S ME
"MOST LIKELY TO DATE A KITCHEN APPLIANCE"

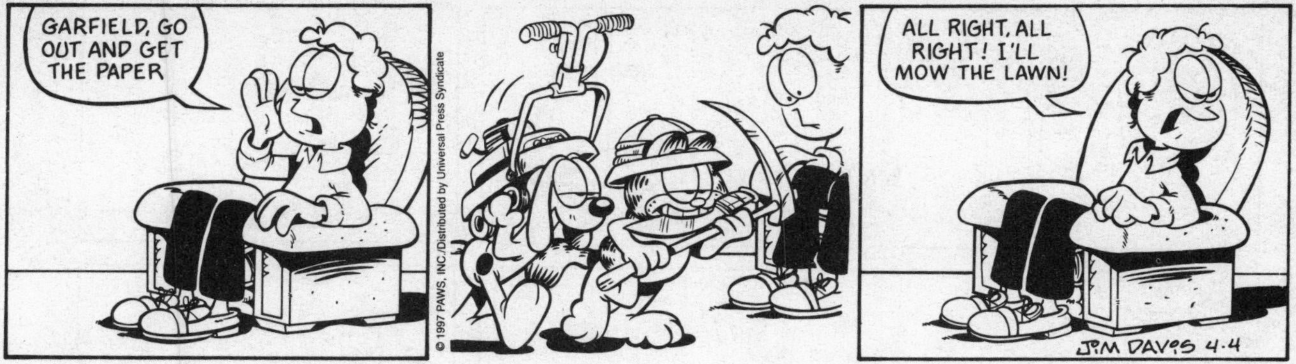
GARFIELD, GO OUT AND GET THE PAPER
© 1997 PAWS, INC./Distributed by Universal Press Syndicate
ALL RIGHT, ALL RIGHT! I'LL MOW THE LAWN!
JIM DAVIS 4-4

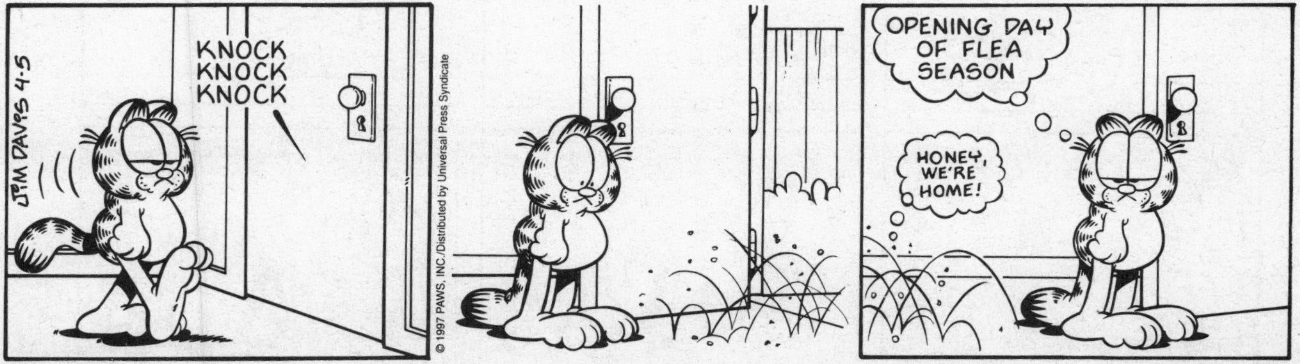
JIM DAVIS 4-5
KNOCK KNOCK KNOCK
© 1997 PAWS, INC./Distributed by Universal Press Syndicate
OPENING DAY OF FLEA SEASON
HONEY, WE'RE HOME!

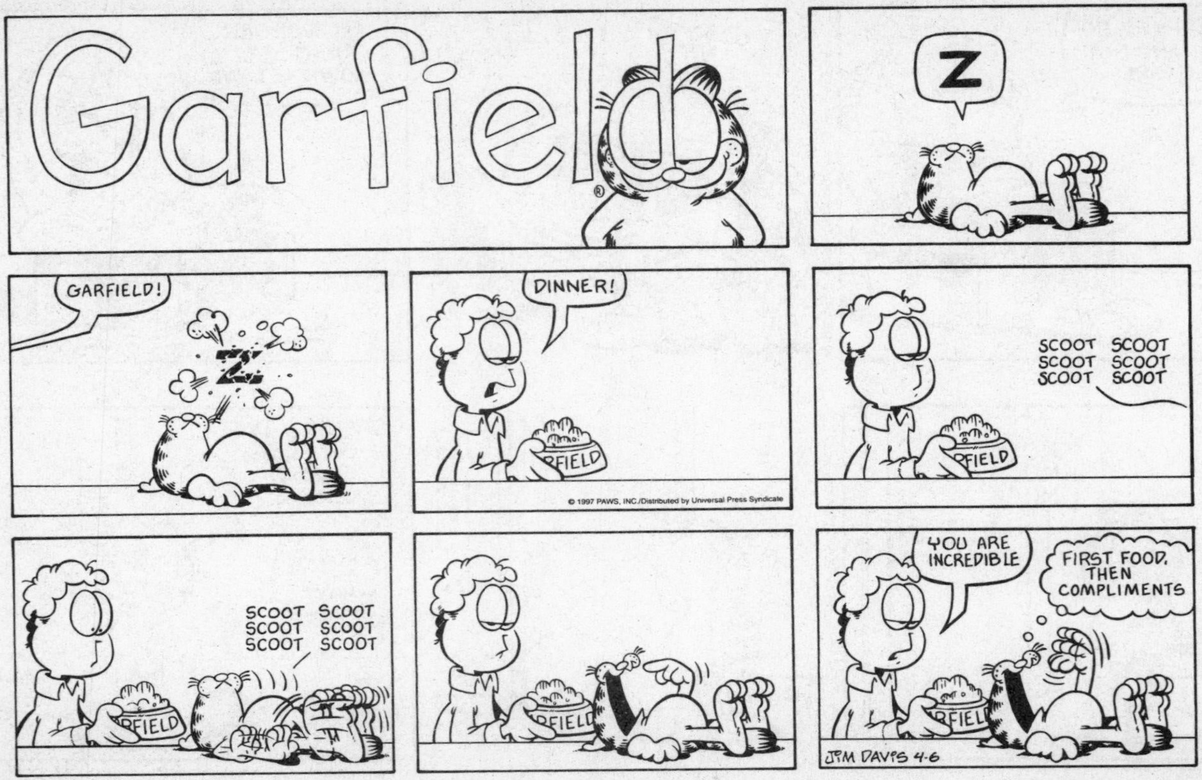
Garfield®
Z
GARFIELD!
Z
DINNER!
© 1997 PAWS, INC./Distributed by Universal Press Syndicate
SCOOT SCOOT
SCOOT SCOOT
SCOOT SCOOT
SCOOT SCOOT
SCOOT SCOOT
SCOOT SCOOT
YOU ARE INCREDIBLE
FIRST FOOD, THEN COMPLIMENTS
JIM DAVIS 4-6

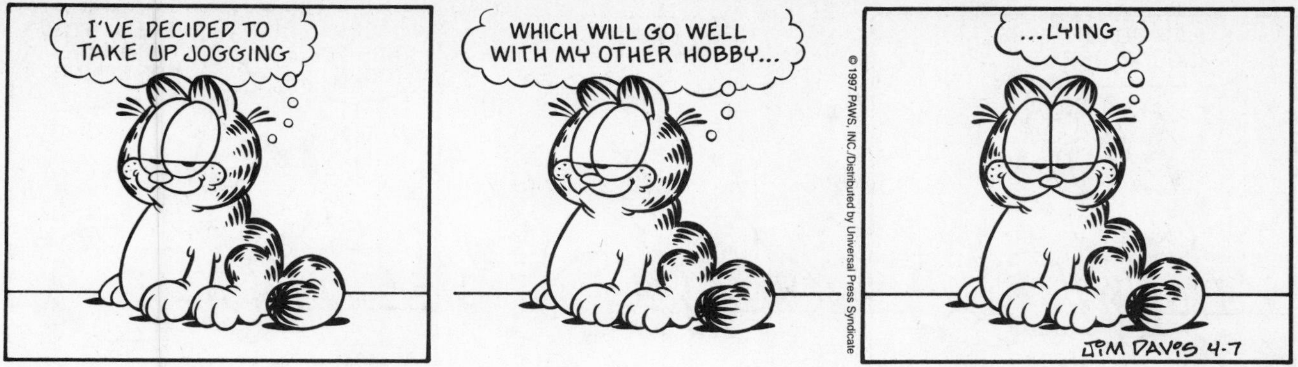
I'VE DECIDED TO TAKE UP JOGGING
WHICH WILL GO WELL WITH MY OTHER HOBBY...
...LYING
JIM DAVIS 4-7

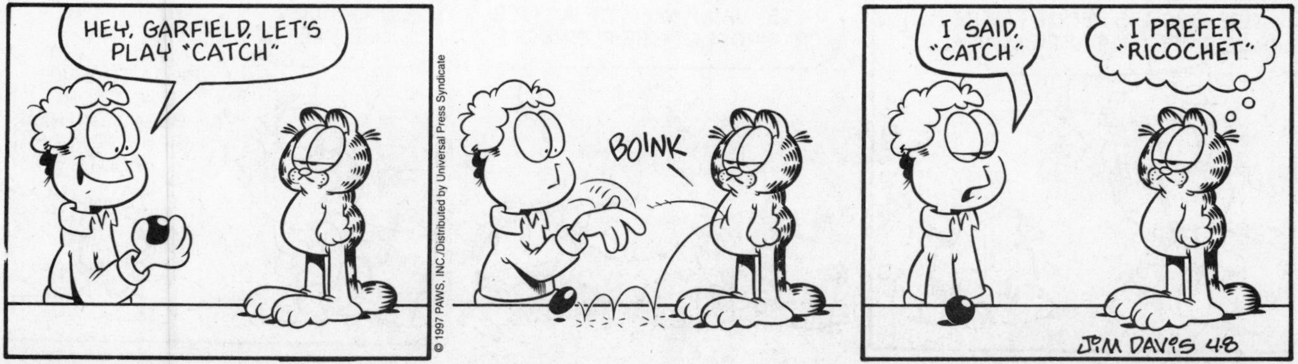
HEY, GARFIELD, LET'S PLAY "CATCH"
BOINK
I SAID, "CATCH"
I PREFER "RICOCHET"
JIM DAVIS 4-8

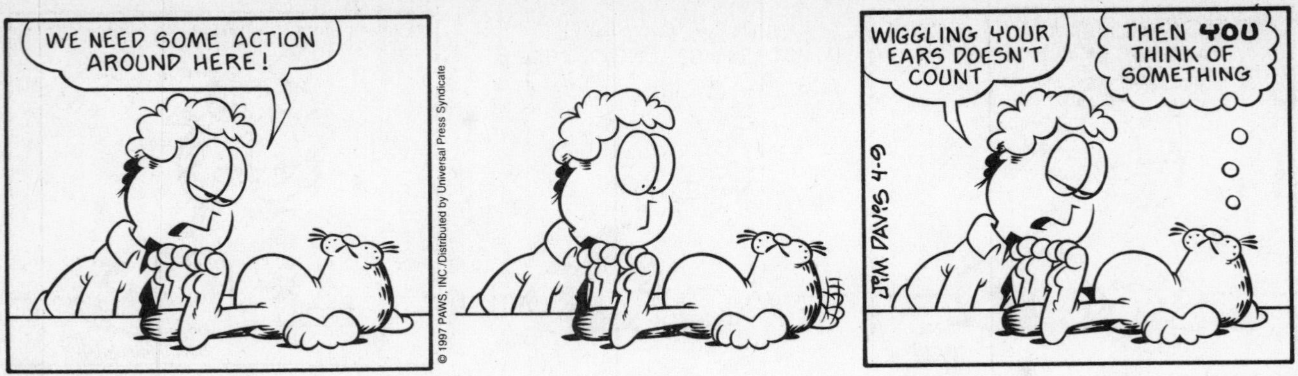
WE NEED SOME ACTION AROUND HERE!
© 1997 PAWS, INC./Distributed by Universal Press Syndicate
WIGGLING YOUR EARS DOESN'T COUNT
THEN YOU THINK OF SOMETHING
JIM DAVIS 4-9

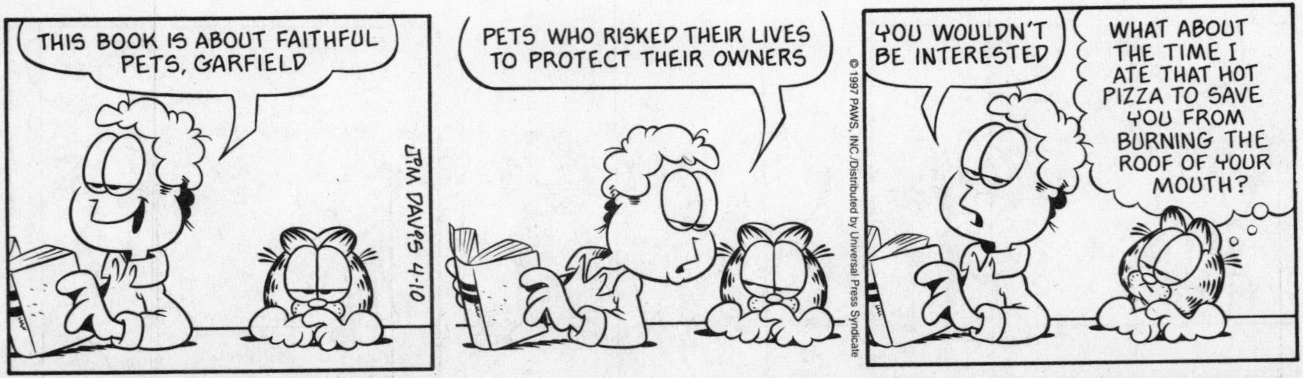
THIS BOOK IS ABOUT FAITHFUL PETS, GARFIELD
JIM DAVIS 4-10
PETS WHO RISKED THEIR LIVES TO PROTECT THEIR OWNERS
© 1997 PAWS, INC./Distributed by Universal Press Syndicate
YOU WOULDN'T BE INTERESTED
WHAT ABOUT THE TIME I ATE THAT HOT PIZZA TO SAVE YOU FROM BURNING THE ROOF OF YOUR MOUTH?

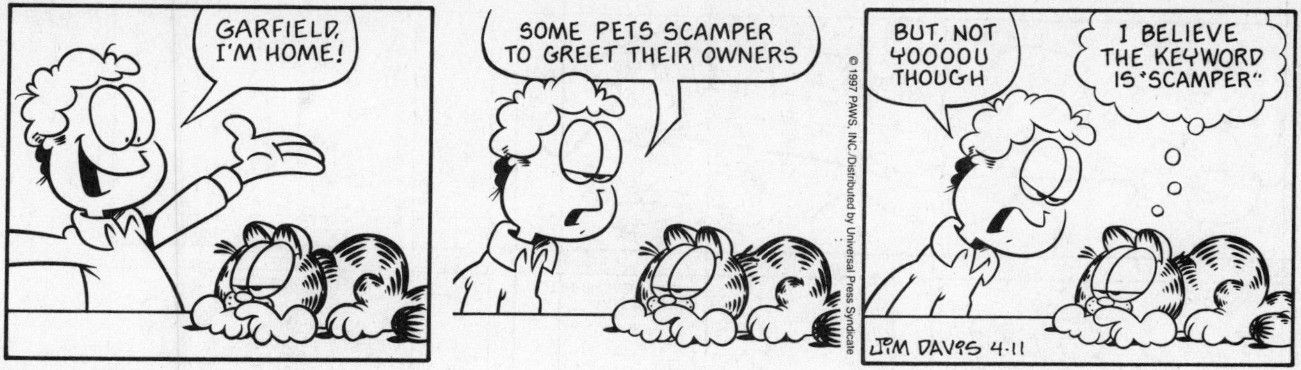
GARFIELD, I'M HOME!
SOME PETS SCAMPER TO GREET THEIR OWNERS
BUT, NOT YOOOOU THOUGH
I BELIEVE THE KEYWORD IS "SCAMPER"
JIM DAVIS 4-11

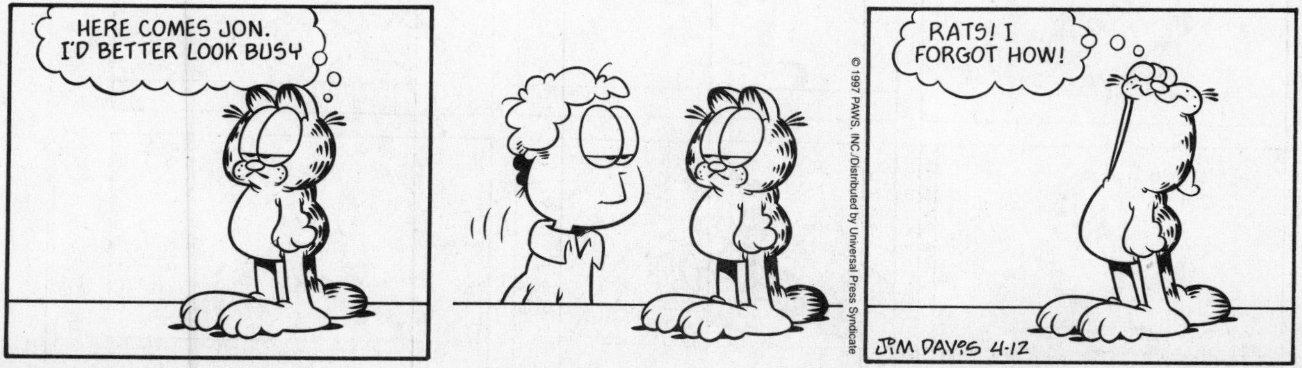
HERE COMES JON. I'D BETTER LOOK BUSY
RATS! I FORGOT HOW!
JIM DAVIS 4-12

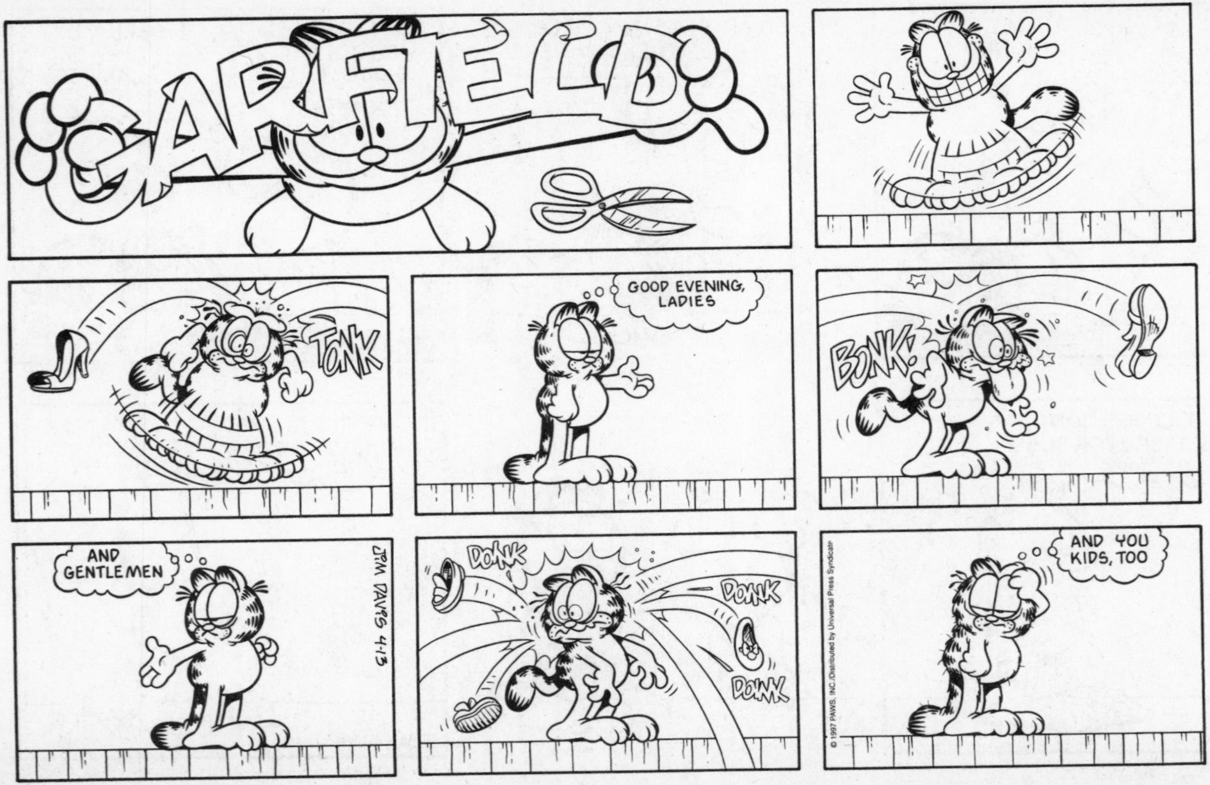
GARFIELD
TONK
GOOD EVENING, LADIES
BONK!
AND GENTLEMEN
JIM DAVIS 4-13
DONK
DONK
DONK
AND YOU KIDS, TOO
© 1997 PAWS, INC./Distributed by Universal Press Syndicate

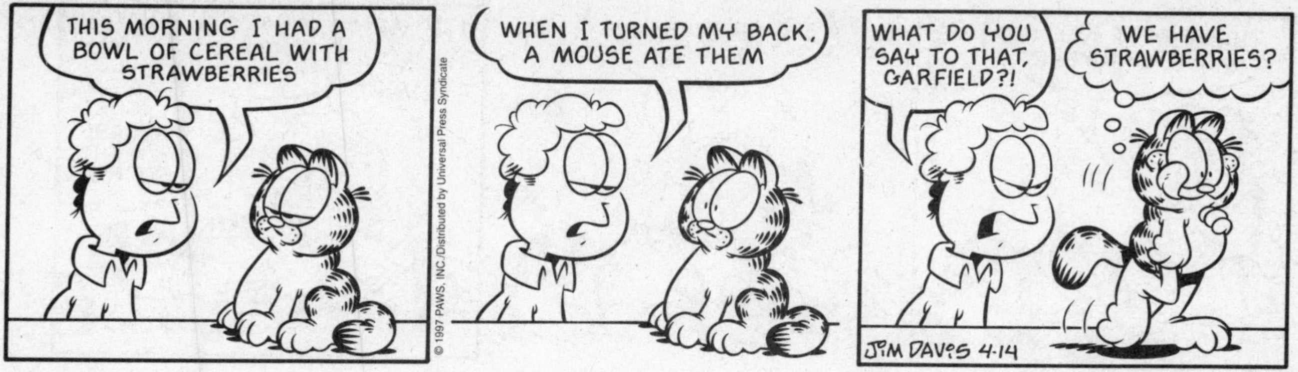
THIS MORNING I HAD A BOWL OF CEREAL WITH STRAWBERRIES
WHEN I TURNED MY BACK, A MOUSE ATE THEM
WHAT DO YOU SAY TO THAT, GARFIELD?!
WE HAVE STRAWBERRIES?
JIM DAVIS 4-14

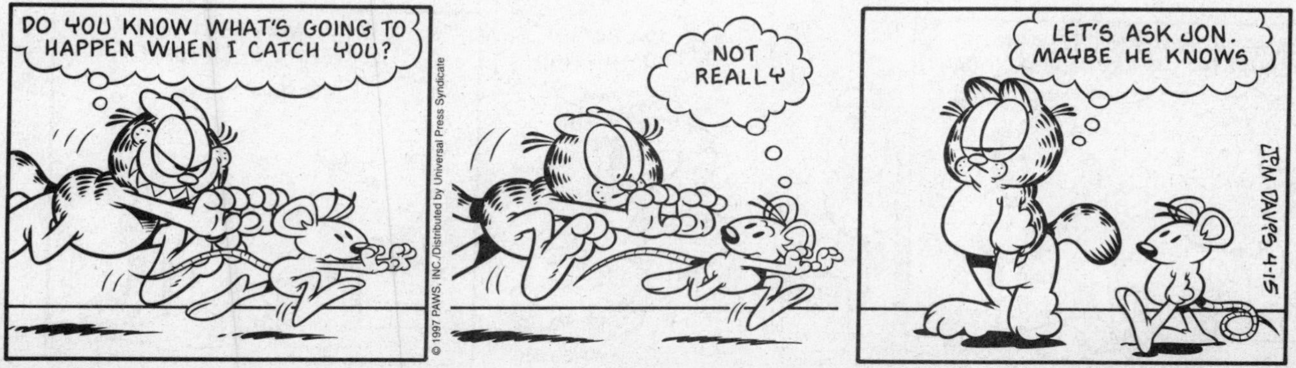
DO YOU KNOW WHAT'S GOING TO HAPPEN WHEN I CATCH YOU?
NOT REALLY
LET'S ASK JON. MAYBE HE KNOWS
JIM DAVIS 4-15

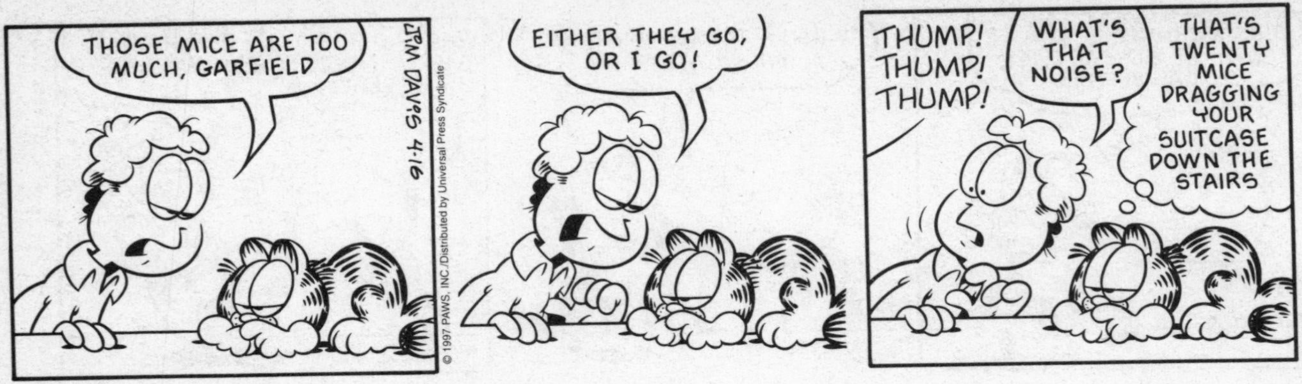
THOSE MICE ARE TOO MUCH, GARFIELD
JIM DAVIS 4-16
EITHER THEY GO, OR I GO!
THUMP! THUMP! THUMP!
WHAT'S THAT NOISE?
THAT'S TWENTY MICE DRAGGING YOUR SUITCASE DOWN THE STAIRS

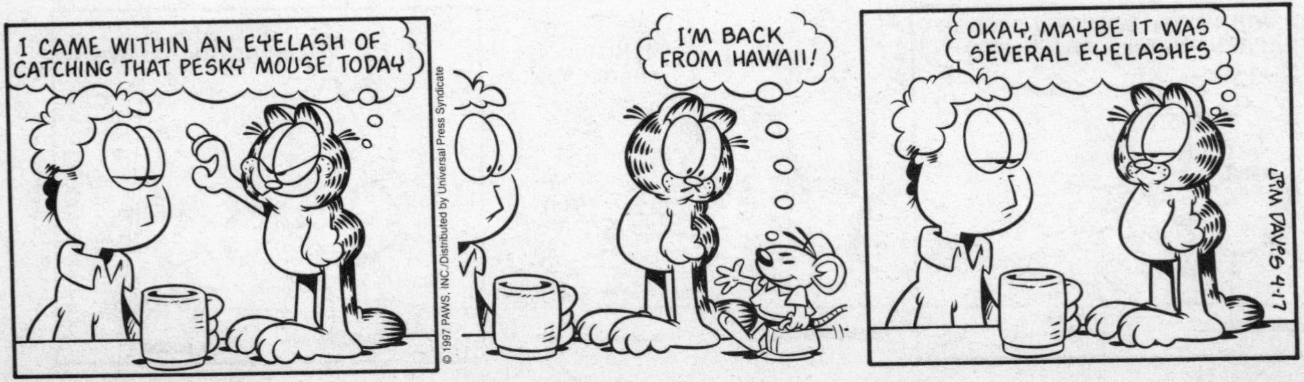
I CAME WITHIN AN EYELASH OF CATCHING THAT PESKY MOUSE TODAY
I'M BACK FROM HAWAII!
OKAY, MAYBE IT WAS SEVERAL EYELASHES
JIM DAVIS 4-17

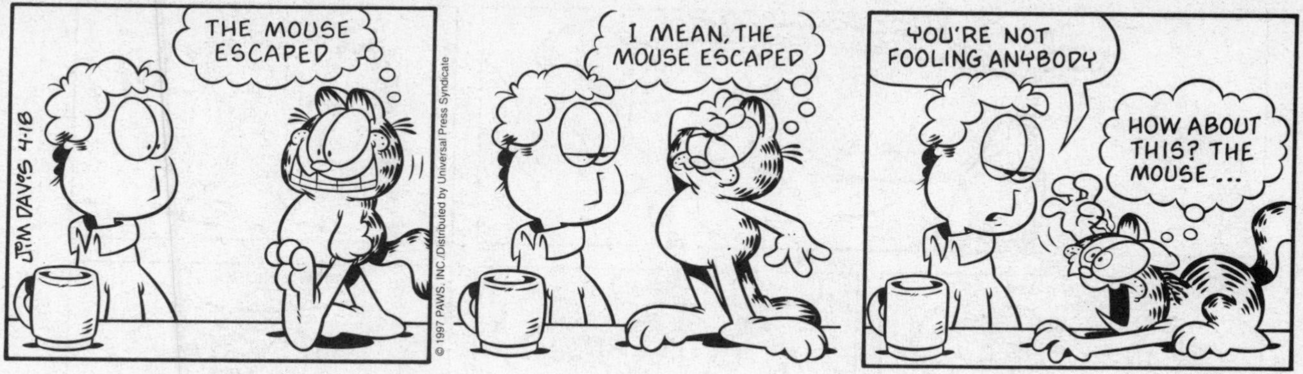
JIM DAVIS 4-18
THE MOUSE ESCAPED
I MEAN, THE MOUSE ESCAPED
YOU'RE NOT FOOLING ANYBODY
HOW ABOUT THIS? THE MOUSE ...

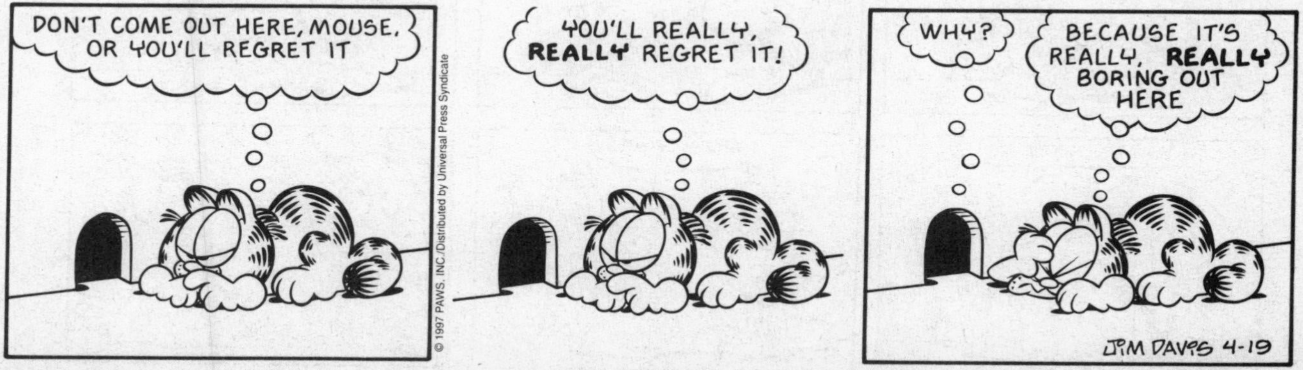
DON'T COME OUT HERE, MOUSE, OR YOU'LL REGRET IT
YOU'LL REALLY, **REALLY** REGRET IT!
WHY?
BECAUSE IT'S REALLY, **REALLY** BORING OUT HERE
JIM DAVIS 4-19

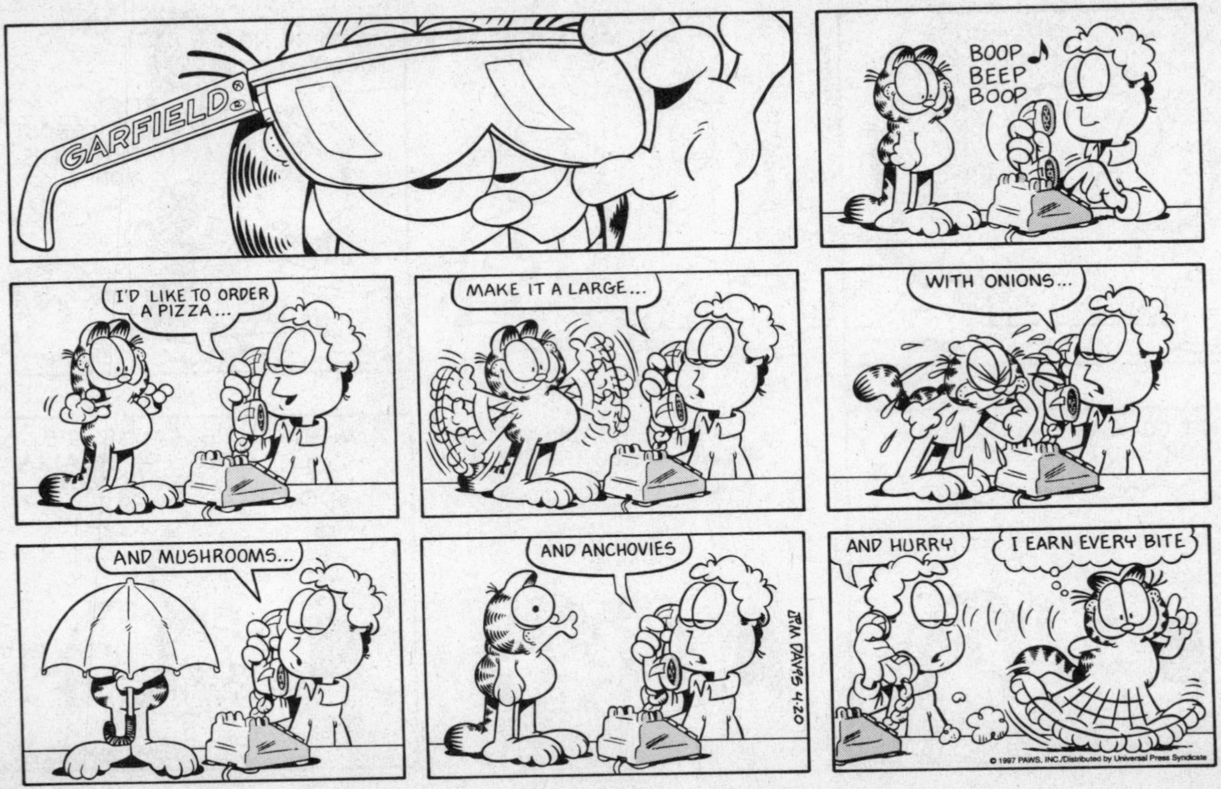
GARFIELD®
BOOP BEEP BOOP
I'D LIKE TO ORDER A PIZZA...
MAKE IT A LARGE...
WITH ONIONS...
AND MUSHROOMS...
AND ANCHOVIES
JIM DAVIS 4-20
AND HURRY
I EARN EVERY BITE
© 1997 PAWS, INC./Distributed by Universal Press Syndicate

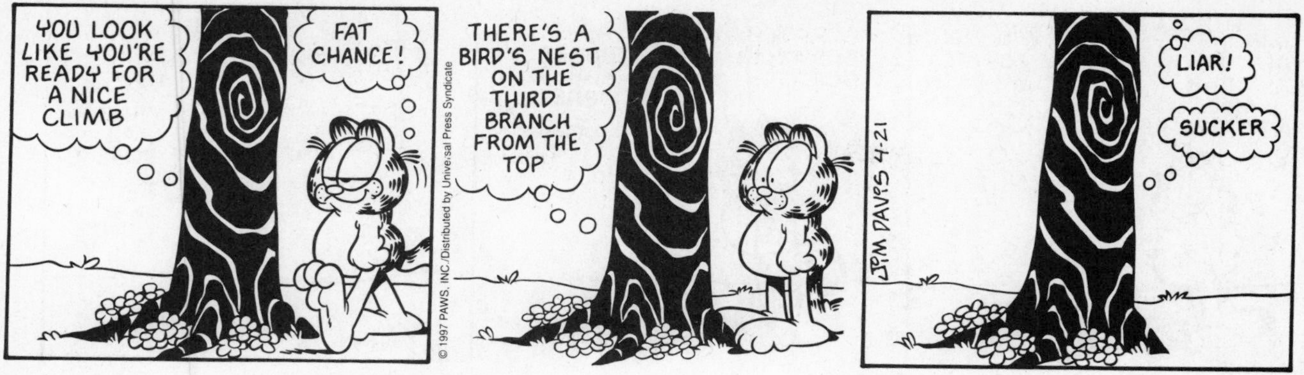
YOU LOOK LIKE YOU'RE READY FOR A NICE CLIMB
FAT CHANCE!
© 1997 PAWS, INC./Distributed by Universal Press Syndicate
THERE'S A BIRD'S NEST ON THE THIRD BRANCH FROM THE TOP
JIM DAVIS 4-21
LIAR!
SUCKER

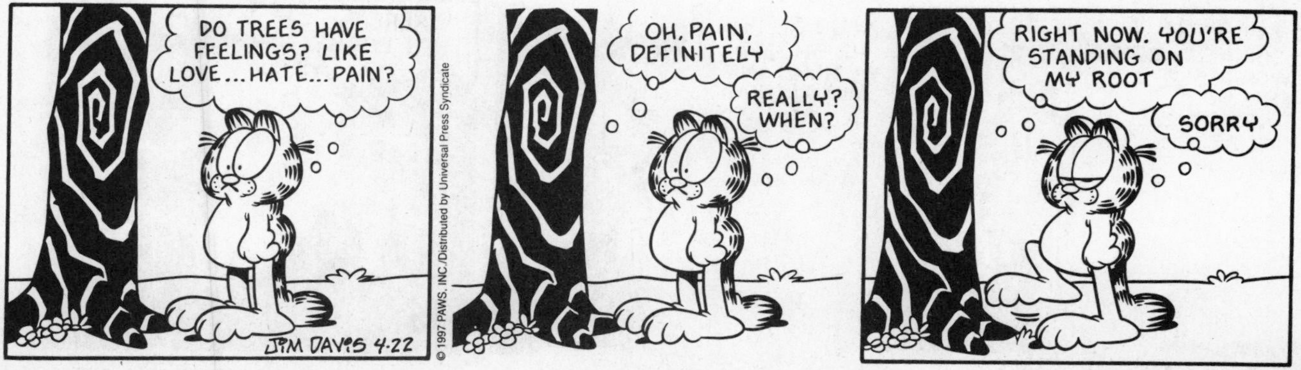
DO TREES HAVE FEELINGS? LIKE LOVE... HATE... PAIN?
JIM DAVIS 4-22
© 1997 PAWS, INC./Distributed by Universal Press Syndicate
OH, PAIN, DEFINITELY
REALLY? WHEN?
RIGHT NOW. YOU'RE STANDING ON MY ROOT
SORRY

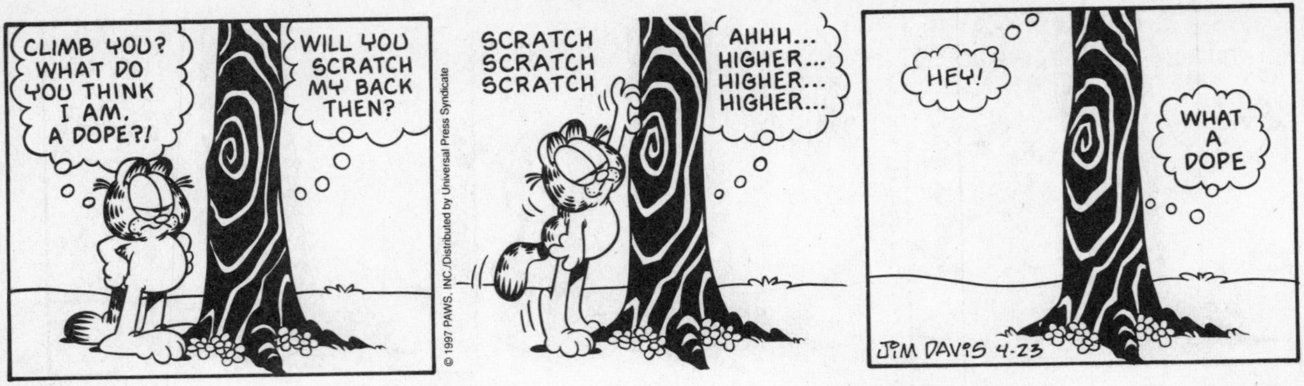
CLIMB YOU? WHAT DO YOU THINK I AM, A DOPE?!
WILL YOU SCRATCH MY BACK THEN?
© 1997 PAWS, INC./Distributed by Universal Press Syndicate
SCRATCH SCRATCH SCRATCH
AHHH... HIGHER... HIGHER... HIGHER...
HEY!
WHAT A DOPE
JIM DAVIS 4-23

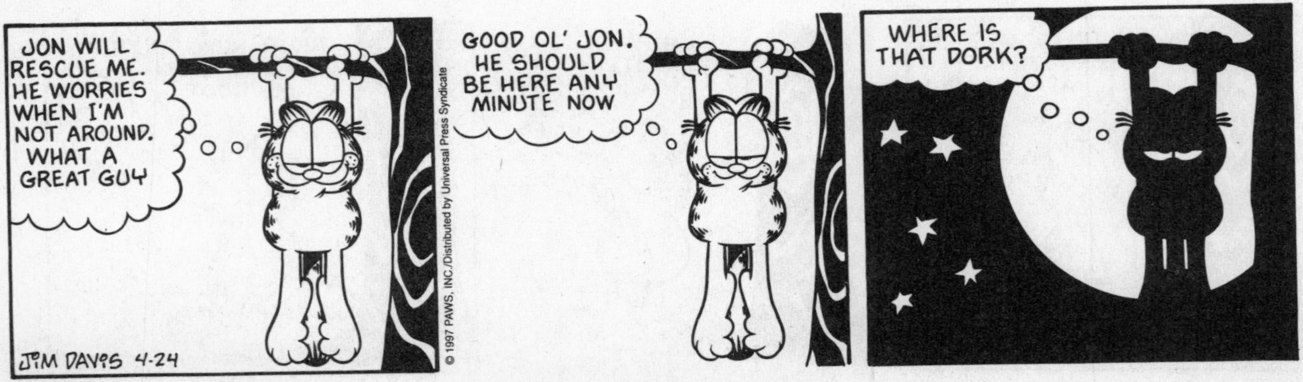
JON WILL RESCUE ME. HE WORRIES WHEN I'M NOT AROUND. WHAT A GREAT GUY
JIM DAVIS 4-24
© 1997 PAWS, INC./Distributed by Universal Press Syndicate
GOOD OL' JON. HE SHOULD BE HERE ANY MINUTE NOW
WHERE IS THAT DORK?

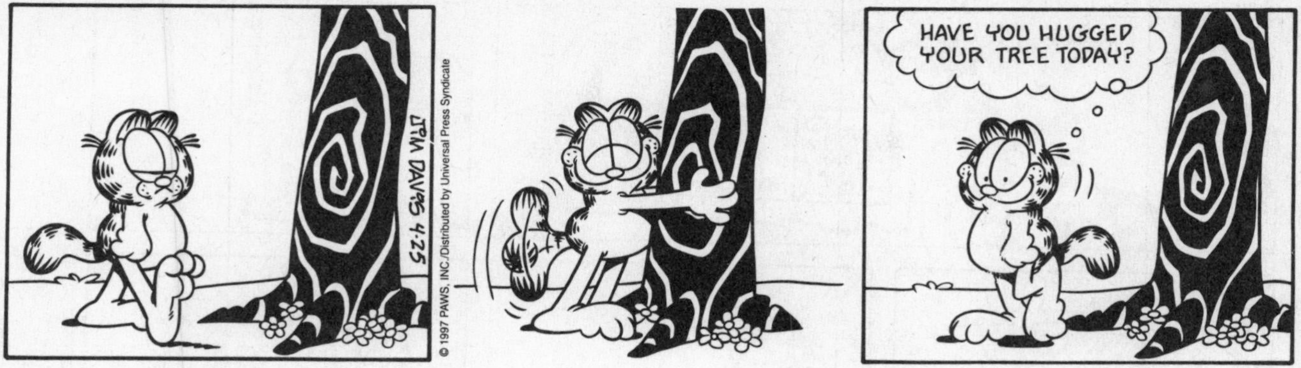
JIM DAVIS 4·25
© 1997 PAWS, INC./Distributed by Universal Press Syndicate
HAVE YOU HUGGED YOUR TREE TODAY?

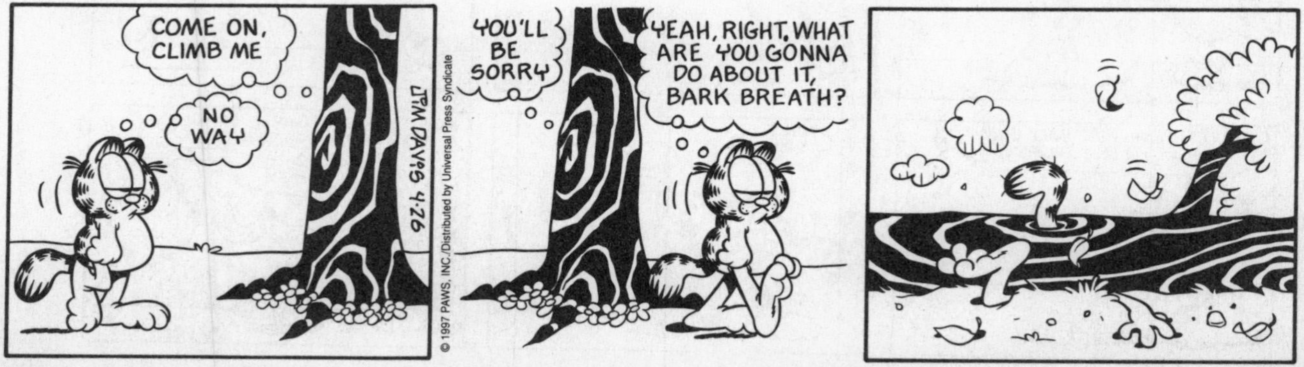
COME ON, CLIMB ME
NO WAY
JIM DAVIS 4·26
© 1997 PAWS, INC./Distributed by Universal Press Syndicate
YOU'LL BE SORRY
YEAH, RIGHT. WHAT ARE YOU GONNA DO ABOUT IT, BARK BREATH?

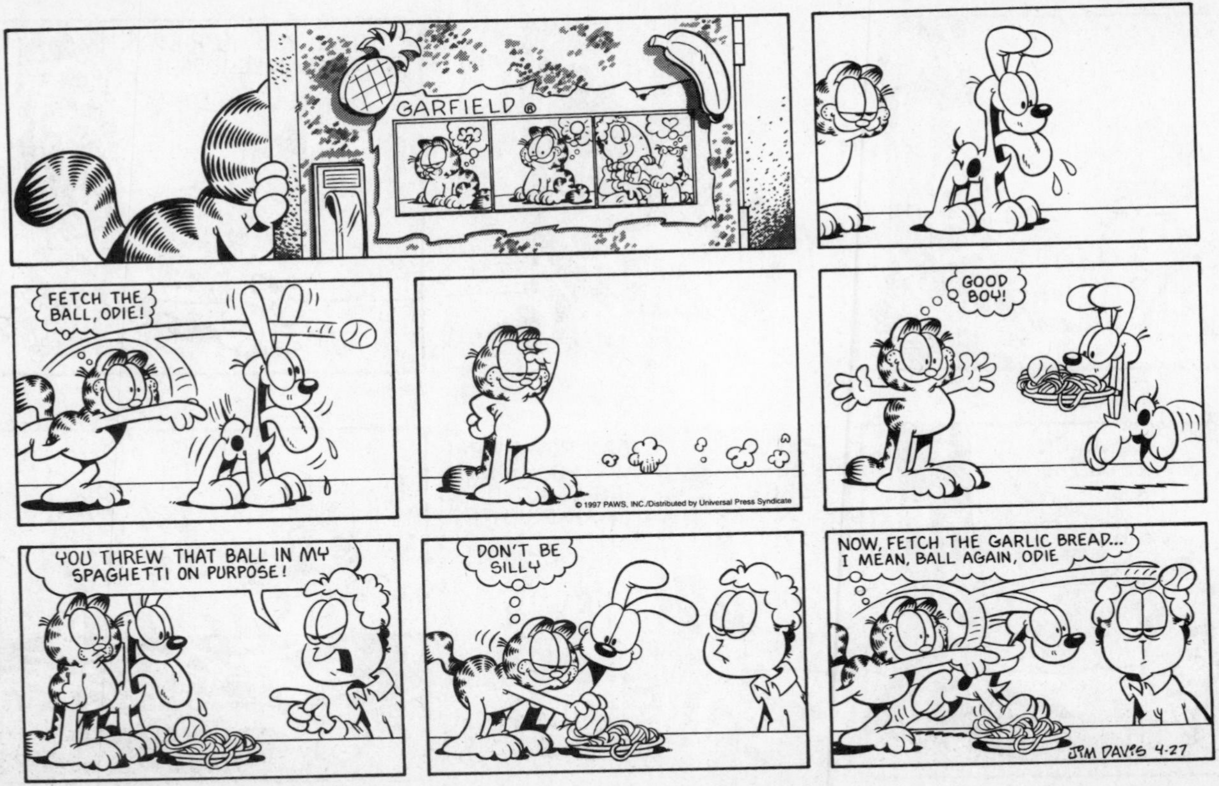
GARFIELD ®
FETCH THE BALL, ODIE!
© 1997 PAWS, INC./Distributed by Universal Press Syndicate
GOOD BOY!
YOU THREW THAT BALL IN MY SPAGHETTI ON PURPOSE!
DON'T BE SILLY
NOW, FETCH THE GARLIC BREAD... I MEAN, BALL AGAIN, ODIE
JIM DAVIS 4-27

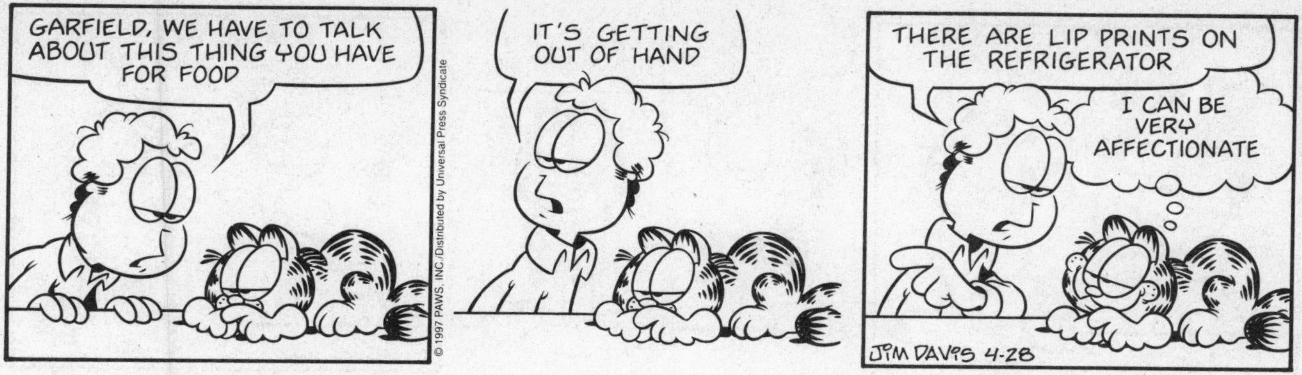
GARFIELD, WE HAVE TO TALK ABOUT THIS THING YOU HAVE FOR FOOD
IT'S GETTING OUT OF HAND
THERE ARE LIP PRINTS ON THE REFRIGERATOR
I CAN BE VERY AFFECTIONATE
JIM DAVIS 4-28

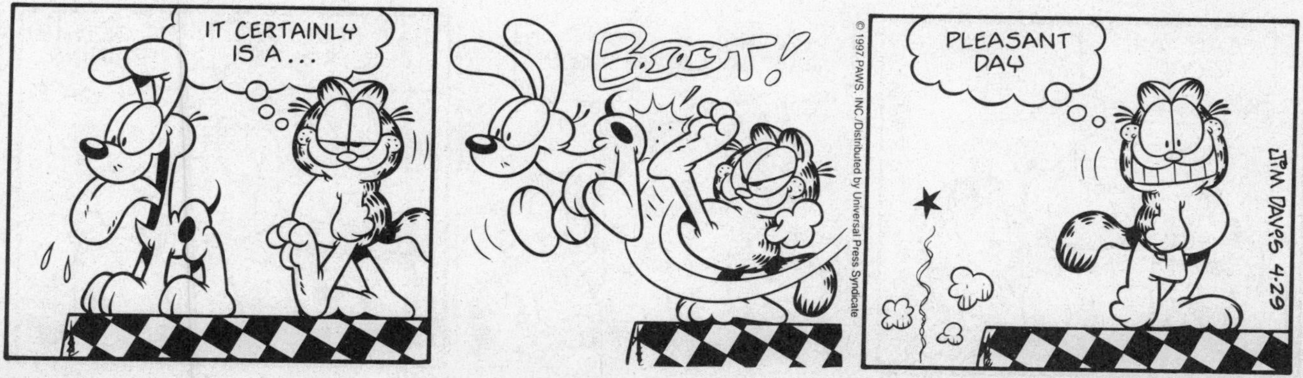
IT CERTAINLY IS A . . .
BOOT!
PLEASANT DAY
JIM DAVIS 4-29

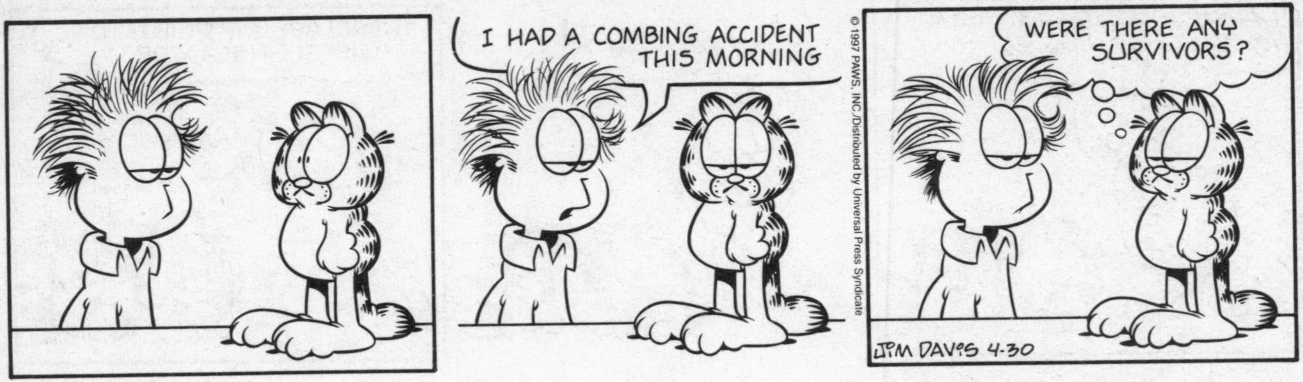
I HAD A COMBING ACCIDENT THIS MORNING
WERE THERE ANY SURVIVORS?
JIM DAVIS 4-30
© 1997 PAWS, INC./Distributed by Universal Press Syndicate

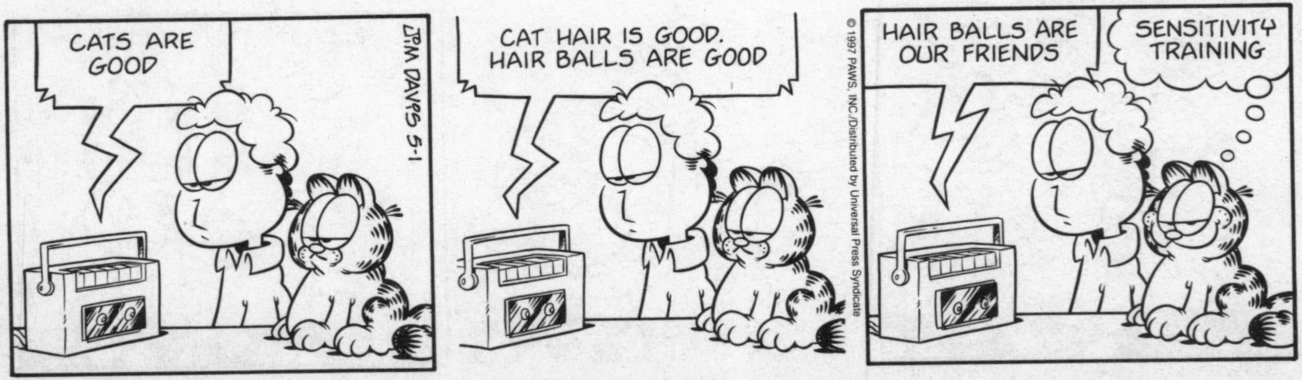
CATS ARE GOOD
JIM DAVIS 5-1
CAT HAIR IS GOOD. HAIR BALLS ARE GOOD
HAIR BALLS ARE OUR FRIENDS
SENSITIVITY TRAINING
© 1997 PAWS, INC./Distributed by Universal Press Syndicate

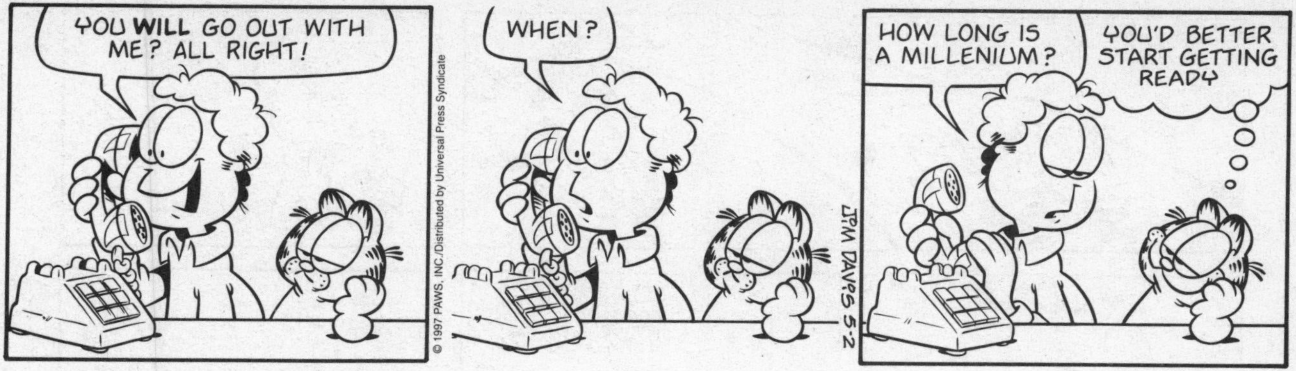
YOU WILL GO OUT WITH ME? ALL RIGHT!
WHEN?
HOW LONG IS A MILLENIUM?
YOU'D BETTER START GETTING READY

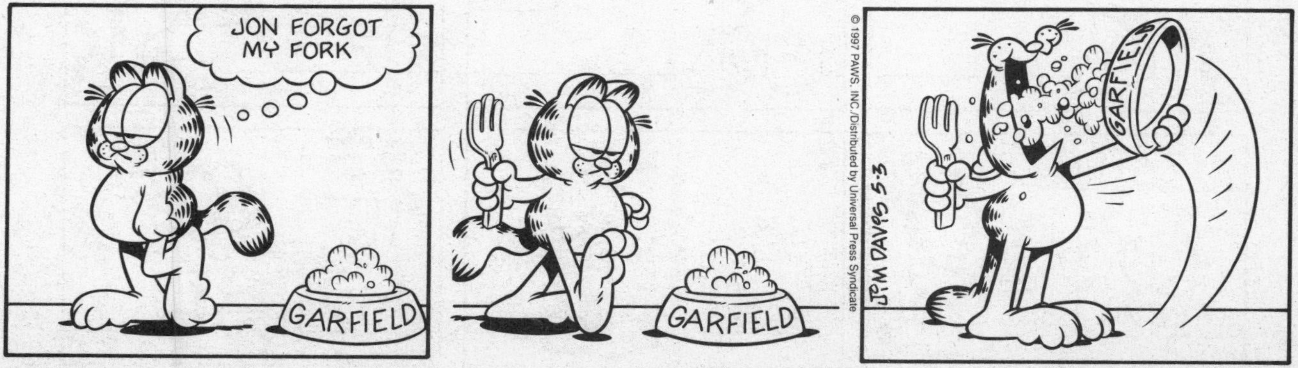
JON FORGOT MY FORK
GARFIELD
GARFIELD
GARFIELD

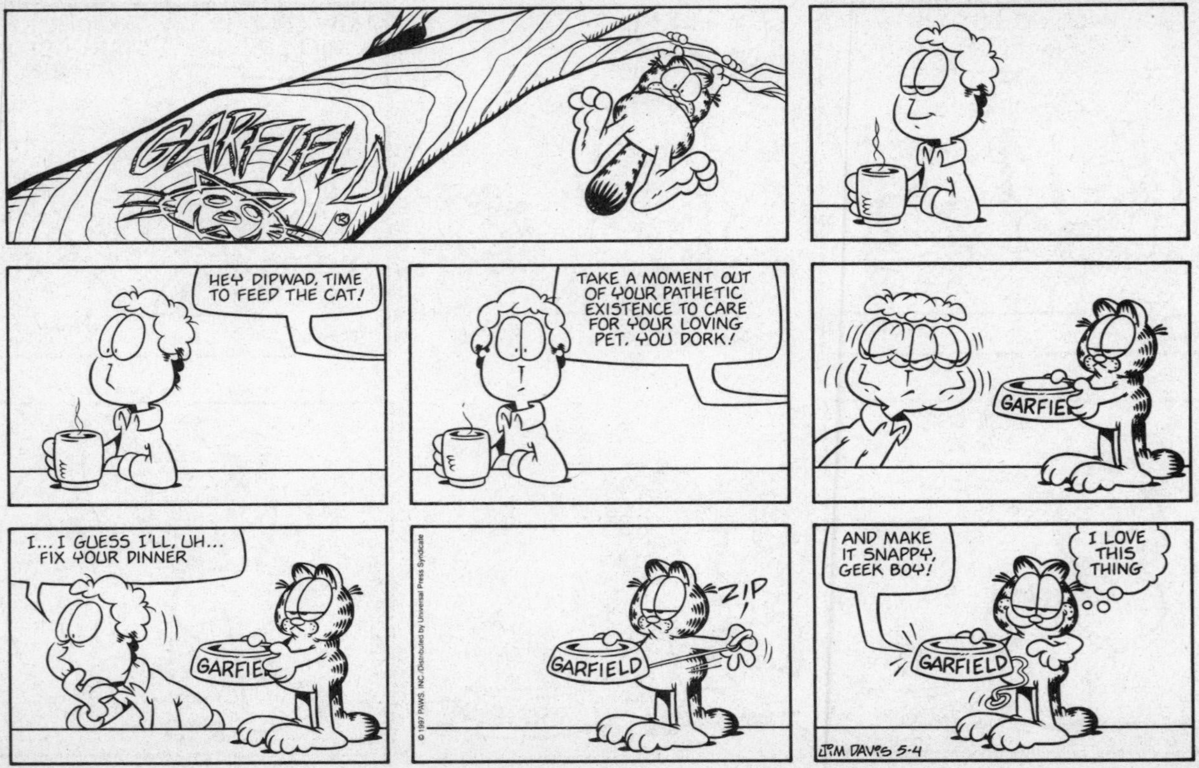
GARFIELD
HEY DIPWAD, TIME TO FEED THE CAT!
TAKE A MOMENT OUT OF YOUR PATHETIC EXISTENCE TO CARE FOR YOUR LOVING PET, YOU DORK!
GARFIE
I... I GUESS I'LL, UH... FIX YOUR DINNER
GARFIE
© 1997 PAWS, INC./Distributed by Universal Press Syndicate
GARFIELD
ZIP
AND MAKE IT SNAPPY, GEEK BOY!
I LOVE THIS THING
GARFIELD
JIM DAVIS 5-4

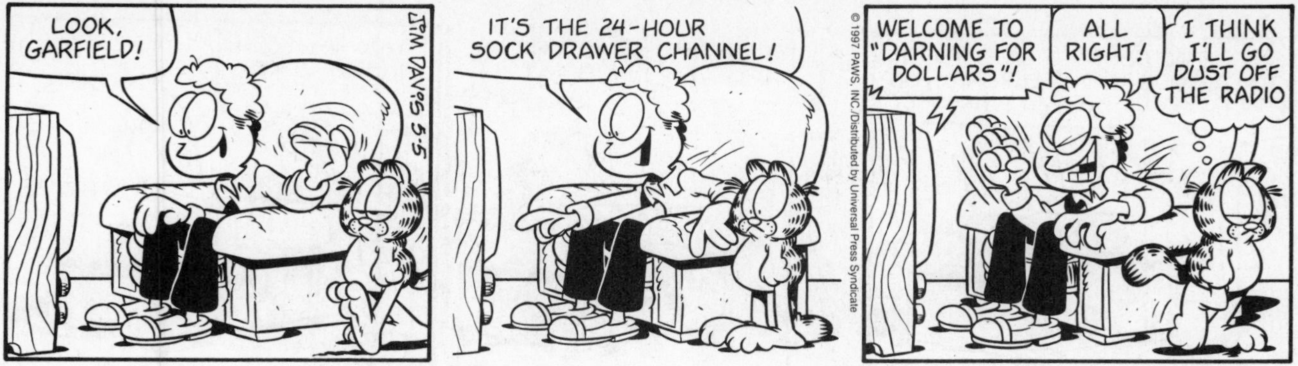
LOOK, GARFIELD!
JIM DAVIS 5-5
IT'S THE 24-HOUR SOCK DRAWER CHANNEL!
© 1997 PAWS, INC./Distributed by Universal Press Syndicate
WELCOME TO "DARNING FOR DOLLARS"!
ALL RIGHT!
I THINK I'LL GO DUST OFF THE RADIO

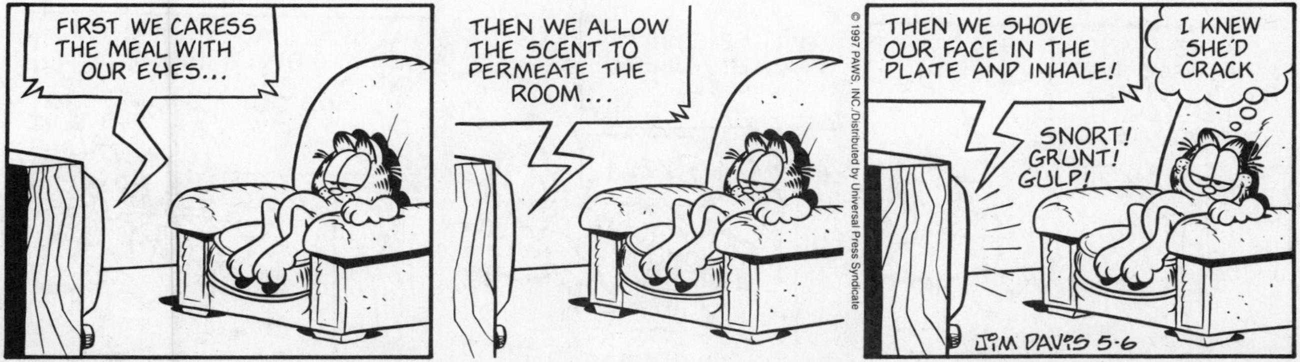
FIRST WE CARESS THE MEAL WITH OUR EYES...
THEN WE ALLOW THE SCENT TO PERMEATE THE ROOM...
© 1997 PAWS, INC./Distributed by Universal Press Syndicate
THEN WE SHOVE OUR FACE IN THE PLATE AND INHALE!
I KNEW SHE'D CRACK
SNORT! GRUNT! GULP!
JIM DAVIS 5-6

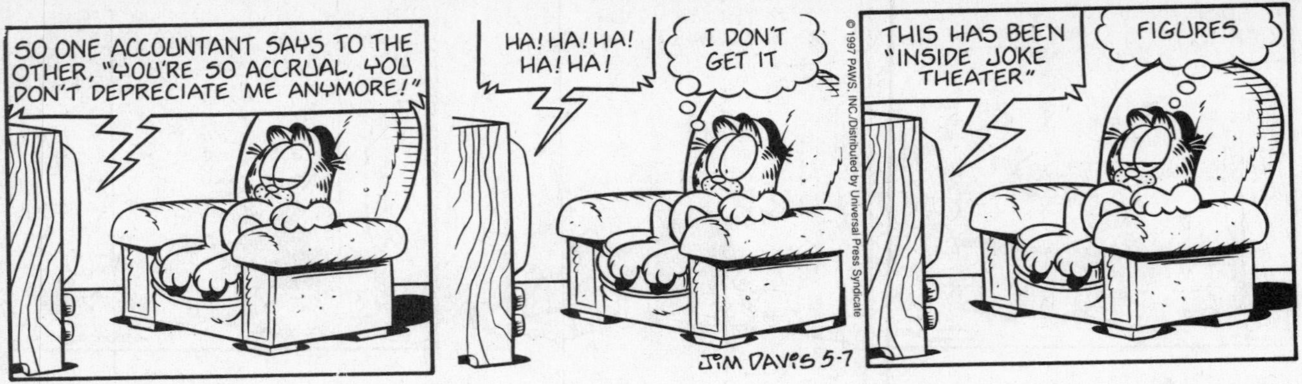
SO ONE ACCOUNTANT SAYS TO THE OTHER, "YOU'RE SO ACCRUAL, YOU DON'T DEPRECIATE ME ANYMORE!"
HA! HA! HA! HA! HA!
I DON'T GET IT
© 1997 PAWS, INC./Distributed by Universal Press Syndicate
JIM DAVIS 5-7
THIS HAS BEEN "INSIDE JOKE THEATER"
FIGURES

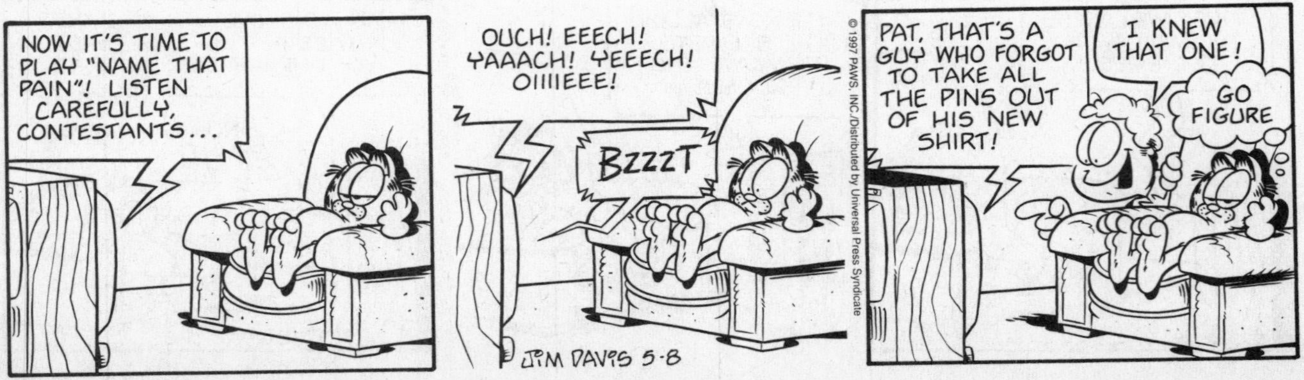
NOW IT'S TIME TO PLAY "NAME THAT PAIN"! LISTEN CAREFULLY, CONTESTANTS...
OUCH! EEECH! YAAACH! YEEECH! OIIIIEEE!
BZZZT
JIM DAVIS 5-8
© 1997 PAWS, INC./Distributed by Universal Press Syndicate
PAT, THAT'S A GUY WHO FORGOT TO TAKE ALL THE PINS OUT OF HIS NEW SHIRT!
I KNEW THAT ONE!
GO FIGURE

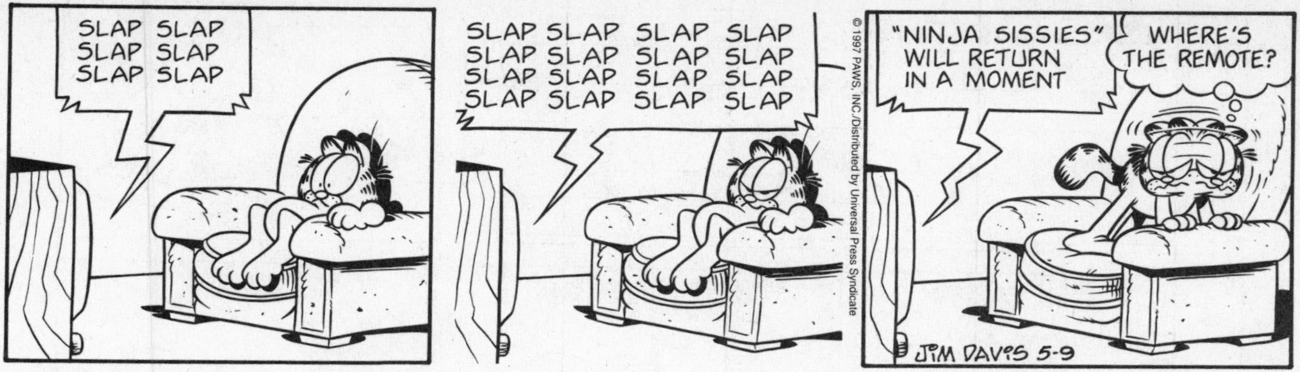
SLAP SLAP SLAP SLAP SLAP SLAP
SLAP SLAP SLAP SLAP SLAP SLAP SLAP SLAP SLAP SLAP SLAP SLAP SLAP SLAP SLAP SLAP
© 1997 PAWS, INC./Distributed by Universal Press Syndicate
"NINJA SISSIES" WILL RETURN IN A MOMENT
WHERE'S THE REMOTE?
JIM DAVIS 5-9

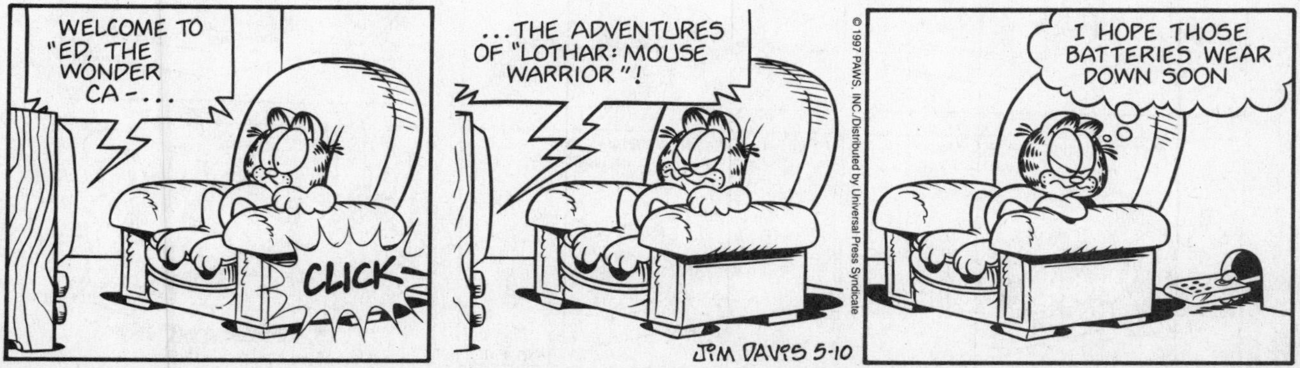
WELCOME TO "ED, THE WONDER CA-...
CLICK
...THE ADVENTURES OF "LOTHAR: MOUSE WARRIOR"!
© 1997 PAWS, INC./Distributed by Universal Press Syndicate
JIM DAVIS 5-10
I HOPE THOSE BATTERIES WEAR DOWN SOON

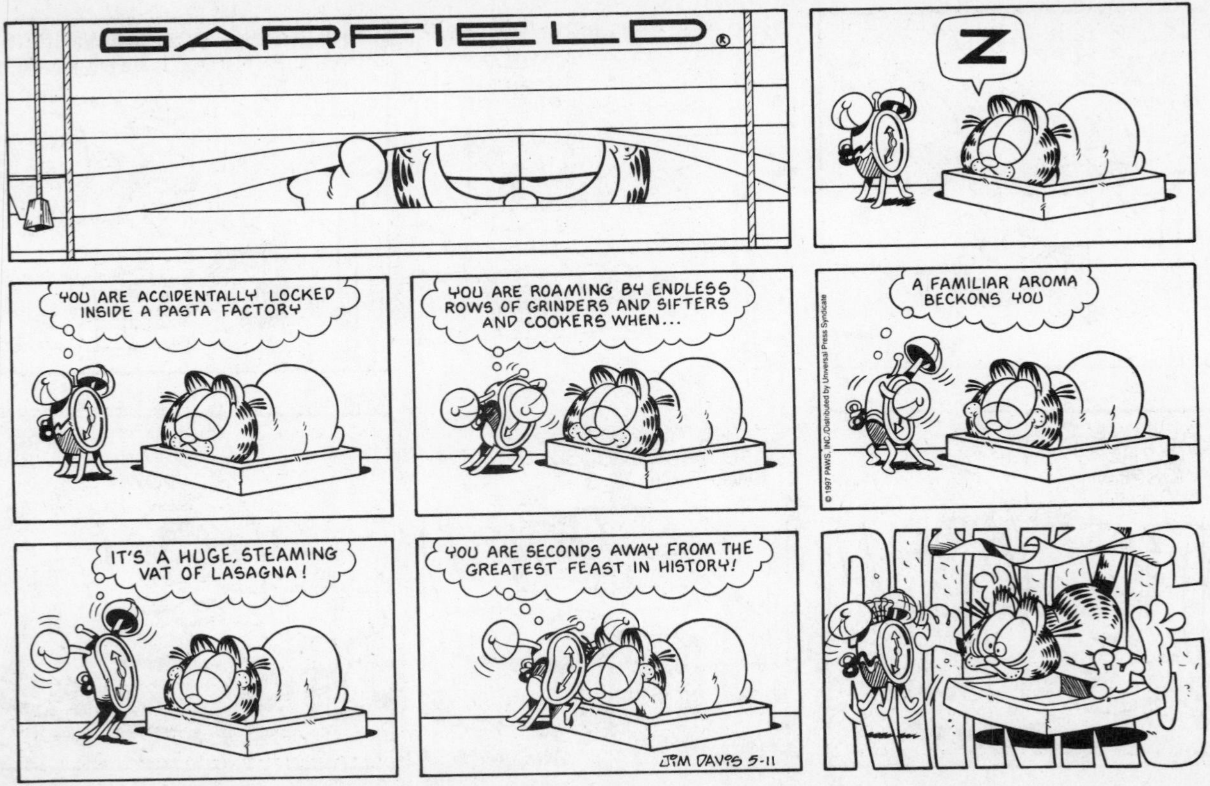
GARFIELD®
Z
YOU ARE ACCIDENTALLY LOCKED INSIDE A PASTA FACTORY
YOU ARE ROAMING BY ENDLESS ROWS OF GRINDERS AND SIFTERS AND COOKERS WHEN...
A FAMILIAR AROMA BECKONS YOU
© 1997 PAWS, INC./Distributed by Universal Press Syndicate
IT'S A HUGE, STEAMING VAT OF LASAGNA!
YOU ARE SECONDS AWAY FROM THE GREATEST FEAST IN HISTORY!
JIM DAVIS 5-11

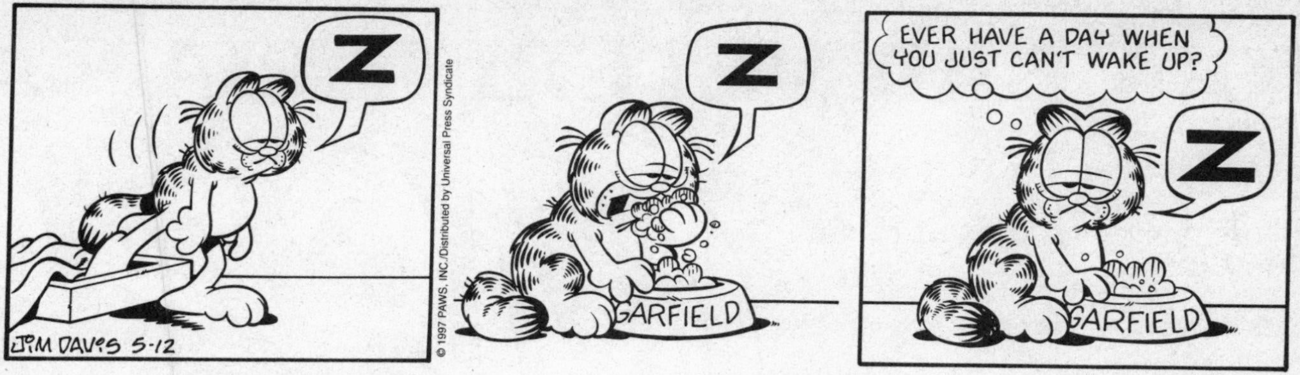
Z
JIM DAVIS 5-12
Z
GARFIELD
EVER HAVE A DAY WHEN YOU JUST CAN'T WAKE UP?
Z
GARFIELD

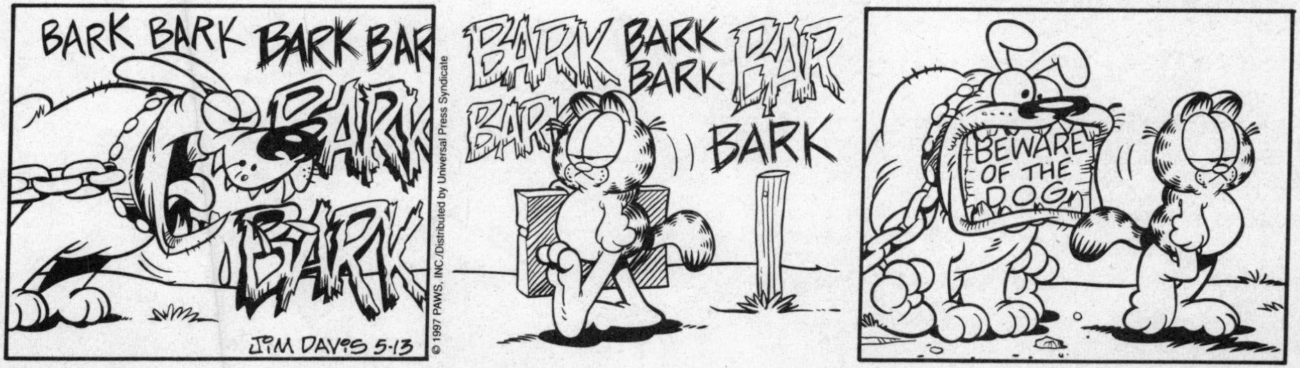
BARK BARK BARK BAR
BARK
BARK
JIM DAVIS 5-13
BARK BARK BARK BAR
BAR
BARK
BARK
BEWARE OF THE DOG

SIGNS YOU'RE GOING TO A BAD VETERINARIAN...

- moonlights as a taxidermist
- keeps excusing himself to set the traps
- can't work a "pooper scooper"
- only licensed to treat insects
- tries to floss a piranha
- was once fired for trying to put Lassie to sleep
- wears a coonskin cap
- performs surgery with a steak knife
- tries to give mouth-to-mouth to your badger

GASP!

Garfield
throws his
weight around

BY: JIM DAVIS

ODIE'S PAST LIVES

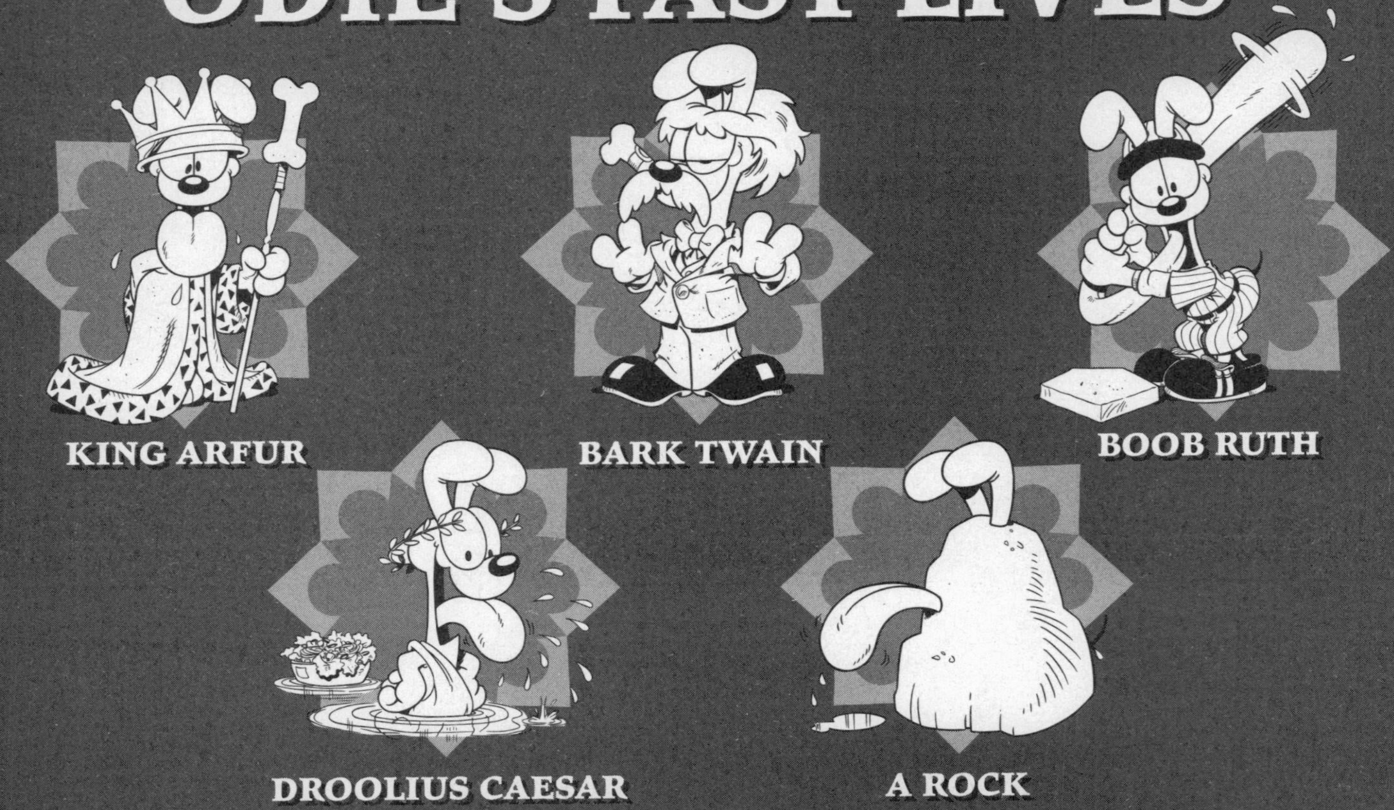
KING ARFUR
BARK TWAIN
BOOB RUTH
DROOLIUS CAESAR
A ROCK

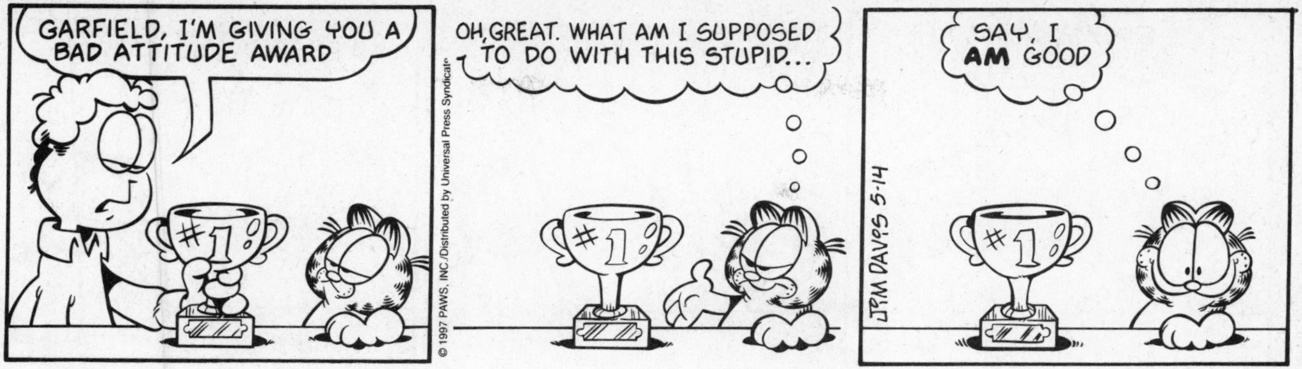
GARFIELD, I'M GIVING YOU A BAD ATTITUDE AWARD
OH, GREAT. WHAT AM I SUPPOSED TO DO WITH THIS STUPID...
SAY, I **AM** GOOD
© 1997 PAWS, INC./Distributed by Universal Press Syndicate
JIM DAVIS 5-14

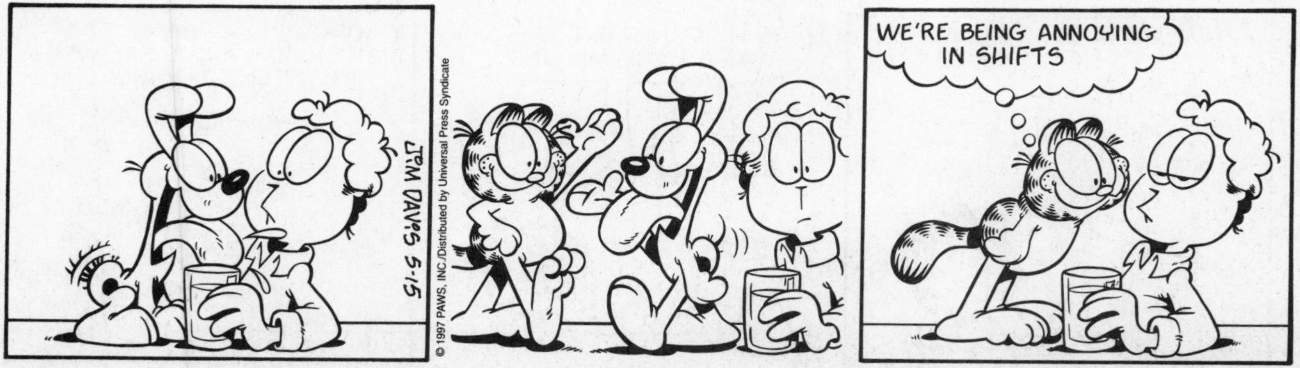
JIM DAVIS 5-15
© 1997 PAWS, INC./Distributed by Universal Press Syndicate
WE'RE BEING ANNOYING IN SHIFTS

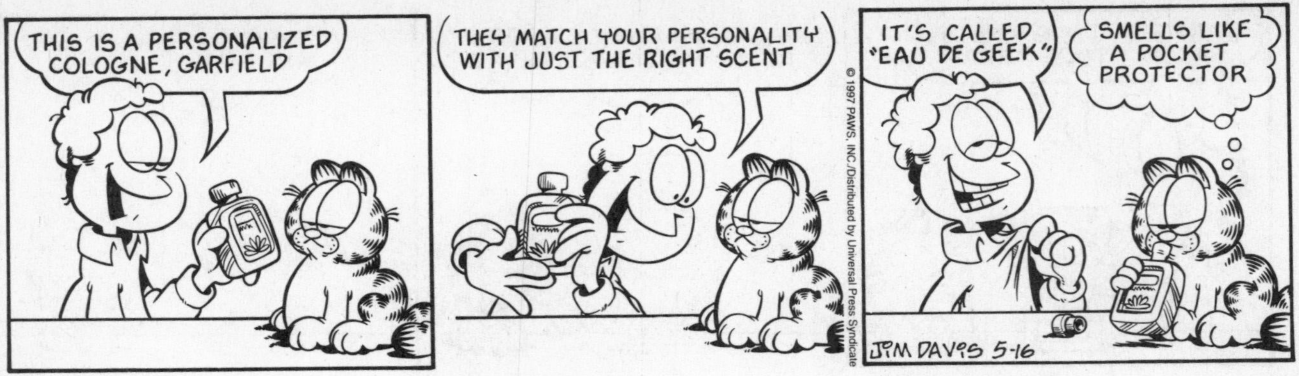
THIS IS A PERSONALIZED COLOGNE, GARFIELD
THEY MATCH YOUR PERSONALITY WITH JUST THE RIGHT SCENT
IT'S CALLED "EAU DE GEEK"
SMELLS LIKE A POCKET PROTECTOR
© 1997 PAWS, INC./Distributed by Universal Press Syndicate
JIM DAVIS 5-16

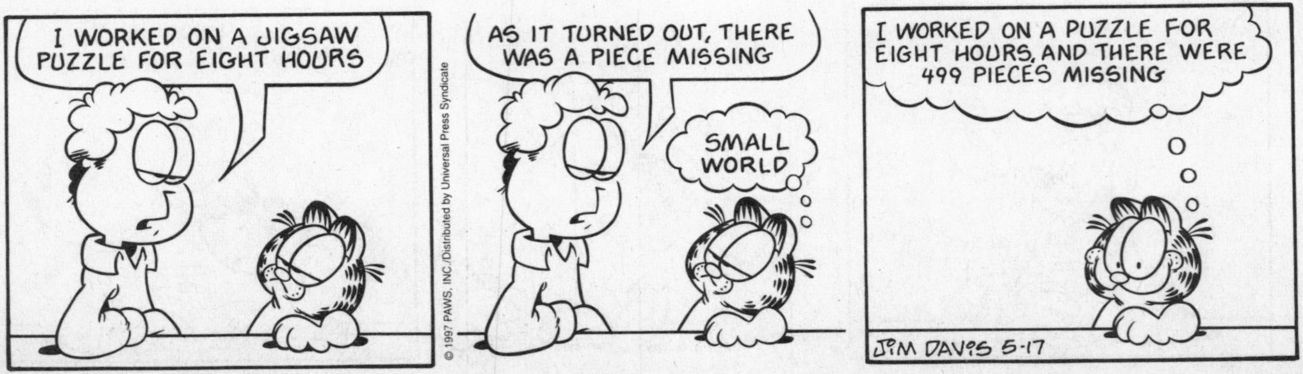
I WORKED ON A JIGSAW PUZZLE FOR EIGHT HOURS
AS IT TURNED OUT, THERE WAS A PIECE MISSING
SMALL WORLD
I WORKED ON A PUZZLE FOR EIGHT HOURS, AND THERE WERE 499 PIECES MISSING
© 1997 PAWS, INC./Distributed by Universal Press Syndicate
JIM DAVIS 5-17

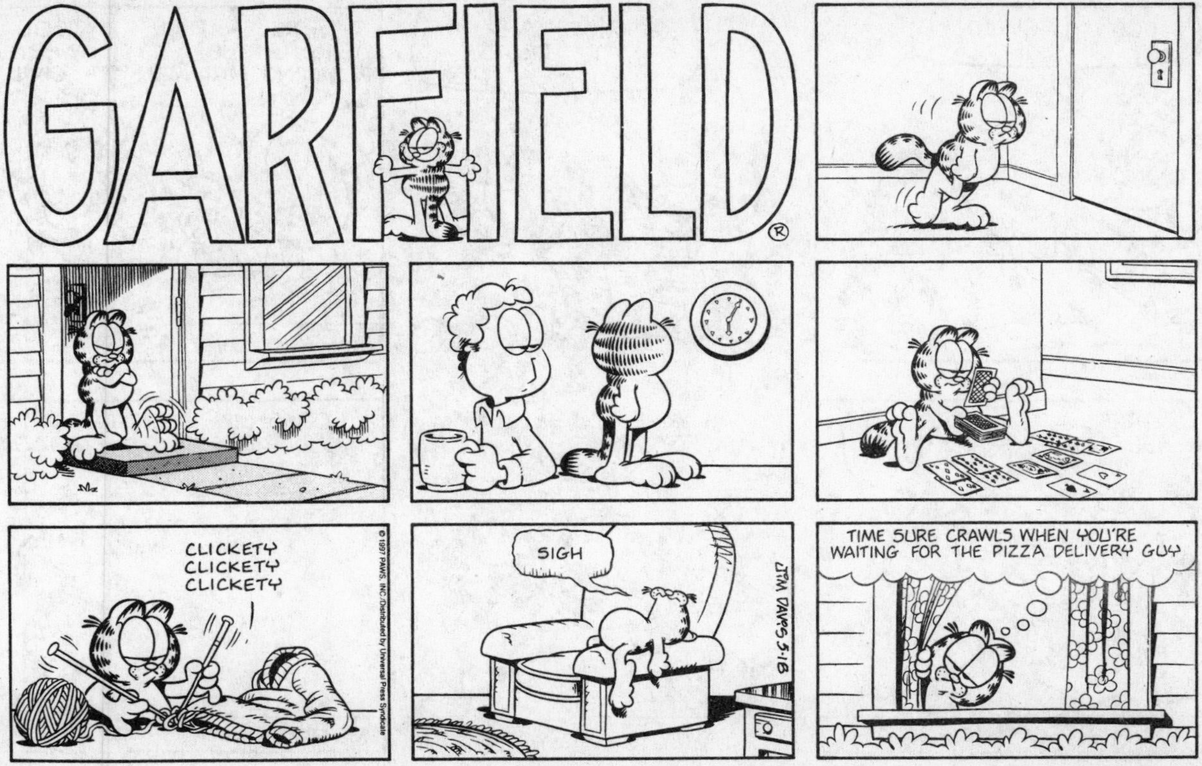
GARFIELD
CLICKETY
CLICKETY
CLICKETY
© 1997 PAWS, INC./Distributed by Universal Press Syndicate
SIGH
JIM DAVIS 5-18
TIME SURE CRAWLS WHEN YOU'RE
WAITING FOR THE PIZZA DELIVERY GUY

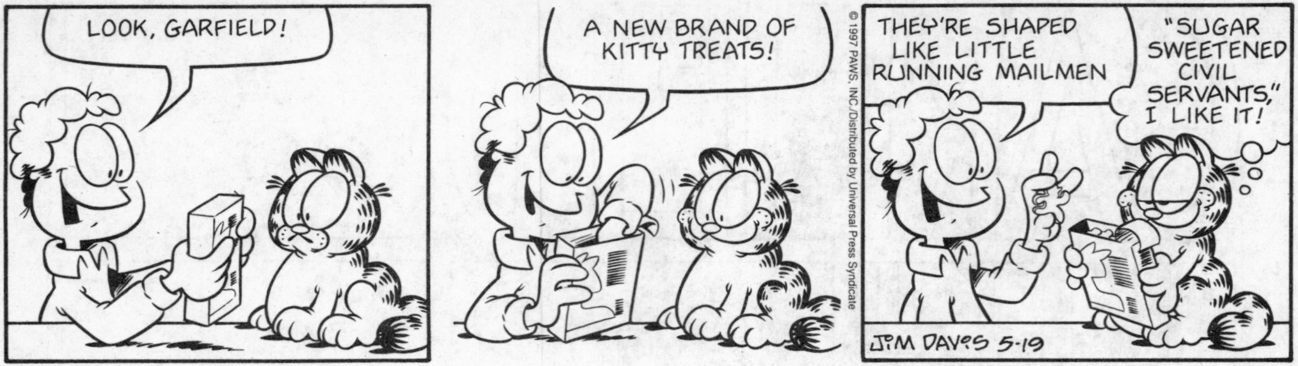
LOOK, GARFIELD!
A NEW BRAND OF KITTY TREATS!
© 1997 PAWS, INC./Distributed by Universal Press Syndicate
THEY'RE SHAPED LIKE LITTLE RUNNING MAILMEN
"SUGAR SWEETENED CIVIL SERVANTS," I LIKE IT!
JIM DAVIS 5-19

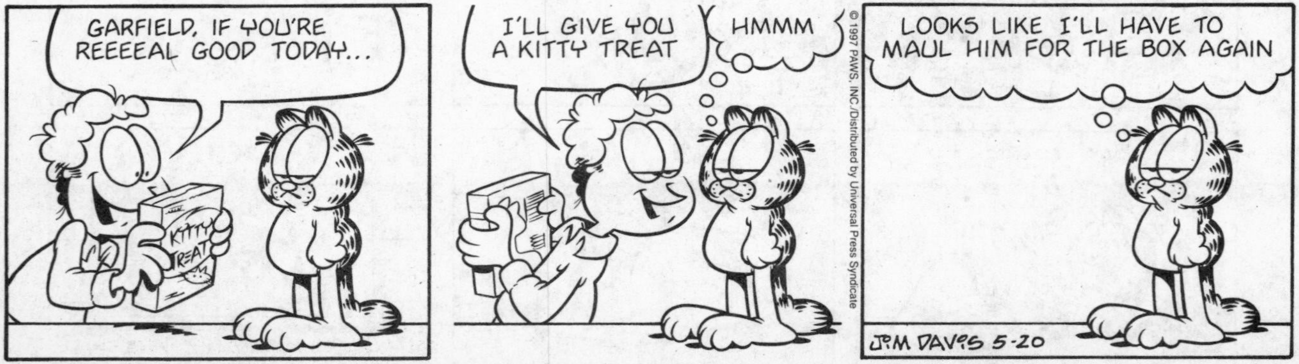
GARFIELD, IF YOU'RE REEEEAL GOOD TODAY...
KITTY TREAT
I'LL GIVE YOU A KITTY TREAT
HMMM
© 1997 PAWS, INC./Distributed by Universal Press Syndicate
LOOKS LIKE I'LL HAVE TO MAUL HIM FOR THE BOX AGAIN
JIM DAVIS 5-20

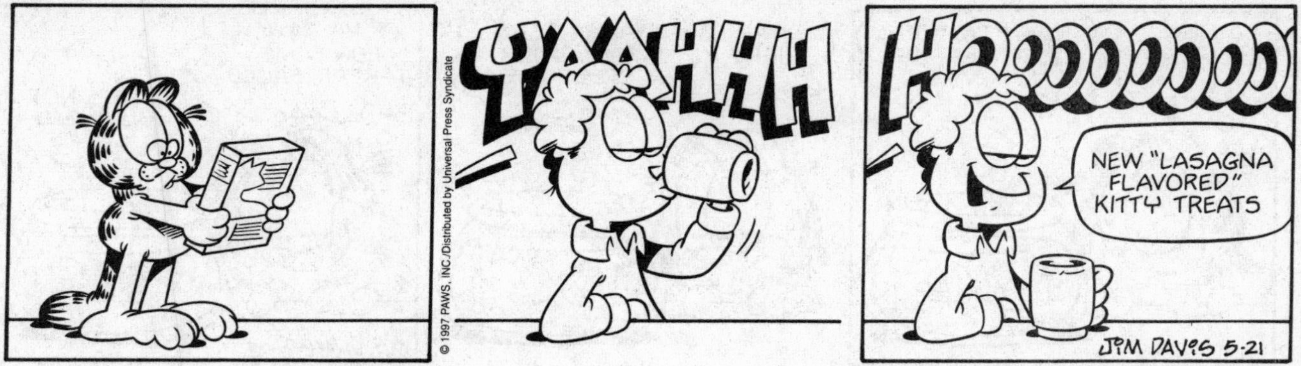
YAAHHH
HOOOOOOOO
NEW "LASAGNA FLAVORED" KITTY TREATS
JIM DAVIS 5-21
© 1997 PAWS, INC./Distributed by Universal Press Syndicate

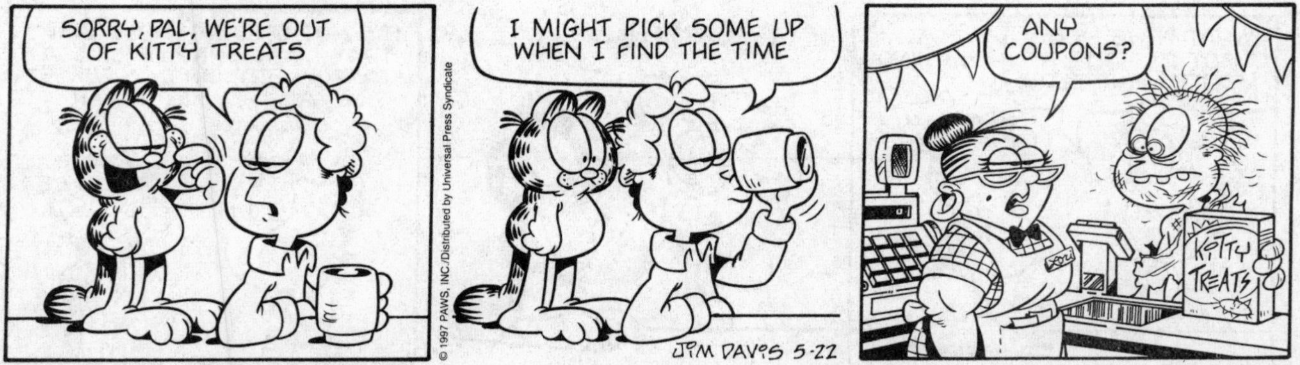
SORRY, PAL, WE'RE OUT OF KITTY TREATS
I MIGHT PICK SOME UP WHEN I FIND THE TIME
ANY COUPONS?
KITTY TREATS
JIM DAVIS 5-22
© 1997 PAWS, INC./Distributed by Universal Press Syndicate

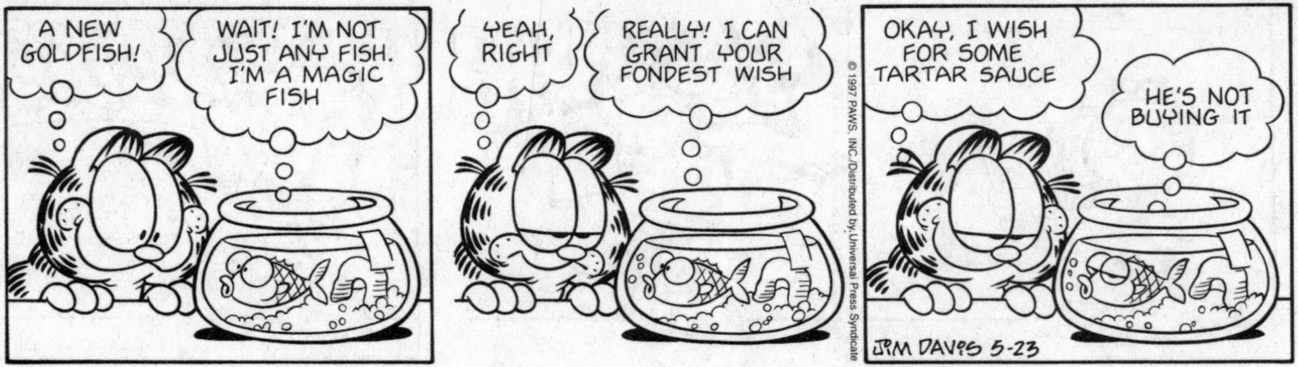
A NEW GOLDFISH!
WAIT! I'M NOT JUST ANY FISH. I'M A MAGIC FISH
YEAH, RIGHT
REALLY! I CAN GRANT YOUR FONDEST WISH
OKAY, I WISH FOR SOME TARTAR SAUCE
HE'S NOT BUYING IT
JIM DAVIS 5-23
© 1997 PAWS. INC./Distributed by Universal Press Syndicate

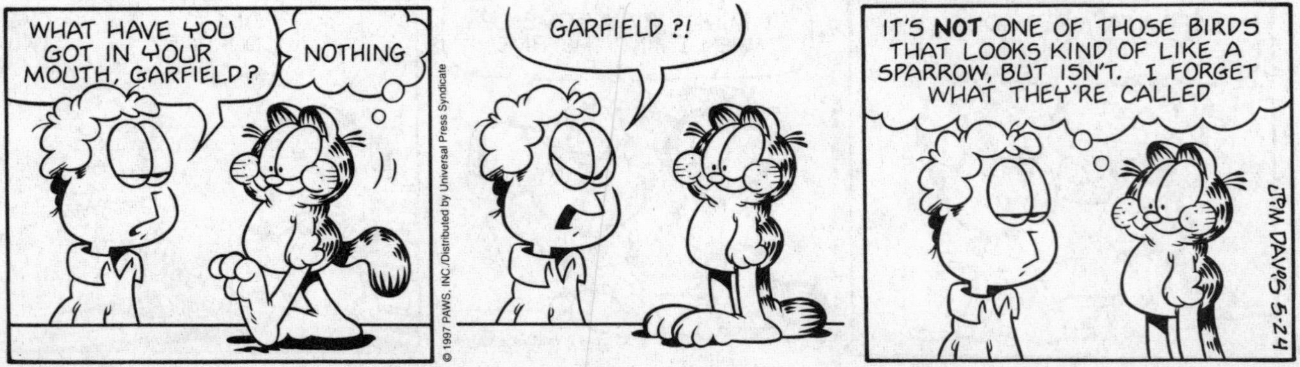
WHAT HAVE YOU GOT IN YOUR MOUTH, GARFIELD?
NOTHING
© 1997 PAWS. INC./Distributed by Universal Press Syndicate
GARFIELD?!
IT'S **NOT** ONE OF THOSE BIRDS THAT LOOKS KIND OF LIKE A SPARROW, BUT ISN'T. I FORGET WHAT THEY'RE CALLED
JIM DAVIS 5-24

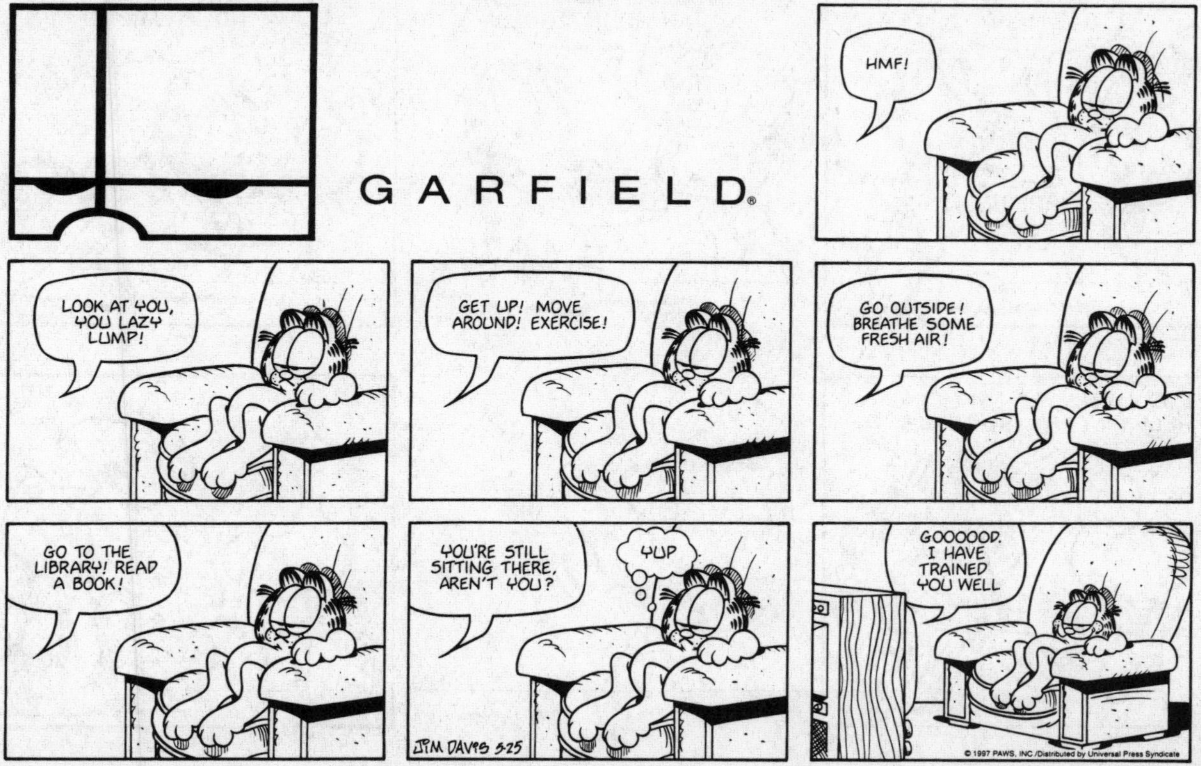
GARFIELD
HMF!
LOOK AT YOU, YOU LAZY LUMP!
GET UP! MOVE AROUND! EXERCISE!
GO OUTSIDE! BREATHE SOME FRESH AIR!
GO TO THE LIBRARY! READ A BOOK!
YOU'RE STILL SITTING THERE, AREN'T YOU?
YUP
GOOOOOD. I HAVE TRAINED YOU WELL
JIM DAVIS 5-25
© 1997 PAWS, INC./Distributed by Universal Press Syndicate

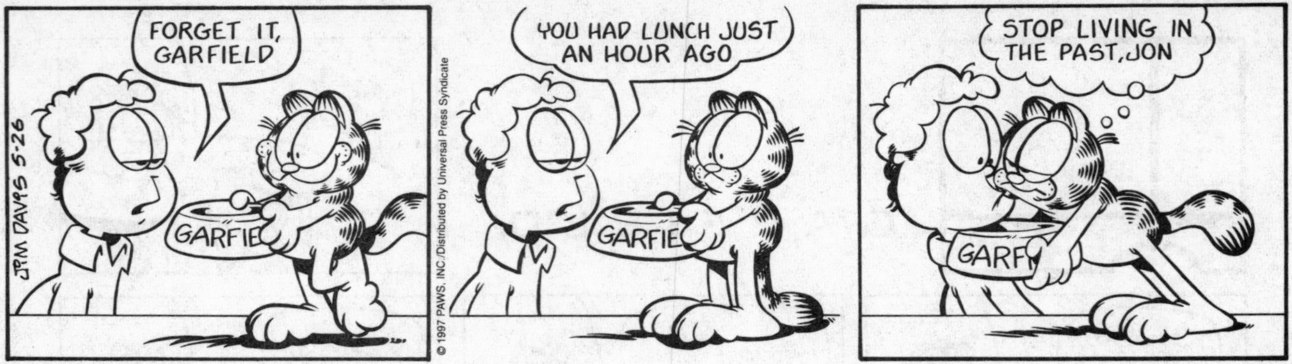
FORGET IT, GARFIELD
JIM DAVIS 5-26
GARFIE
© 1997 PAWS, INC./Distributed by Universal Press Syndicate
YOU HAD LUNCH JUST AN HOUR AGO
GARFIE
STOP LIVING IN THE PAST, JON
GARF

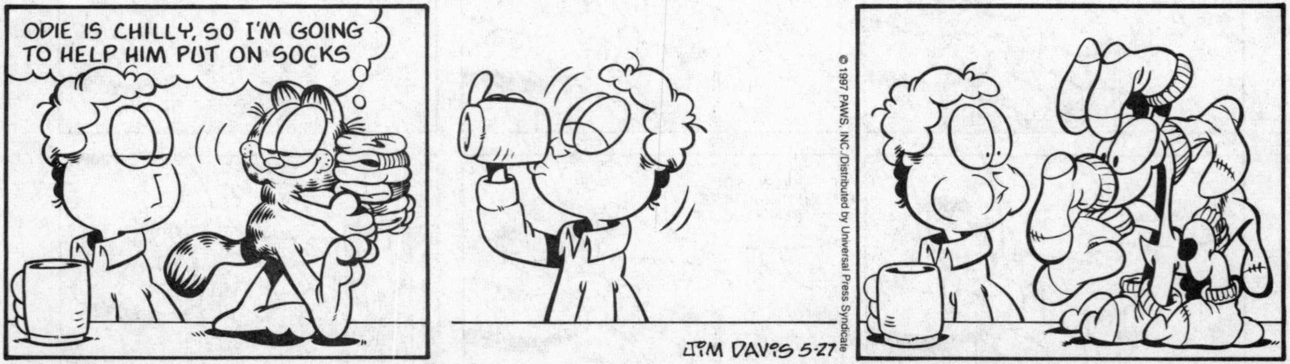
ODIE IS CHILLY, SO I'M GOING TO HELP HIM PUT ON SOCKS
JIM DAVIS 5-27
© 1997 PAWS, INC./Distributed by Universal Press Syndicate

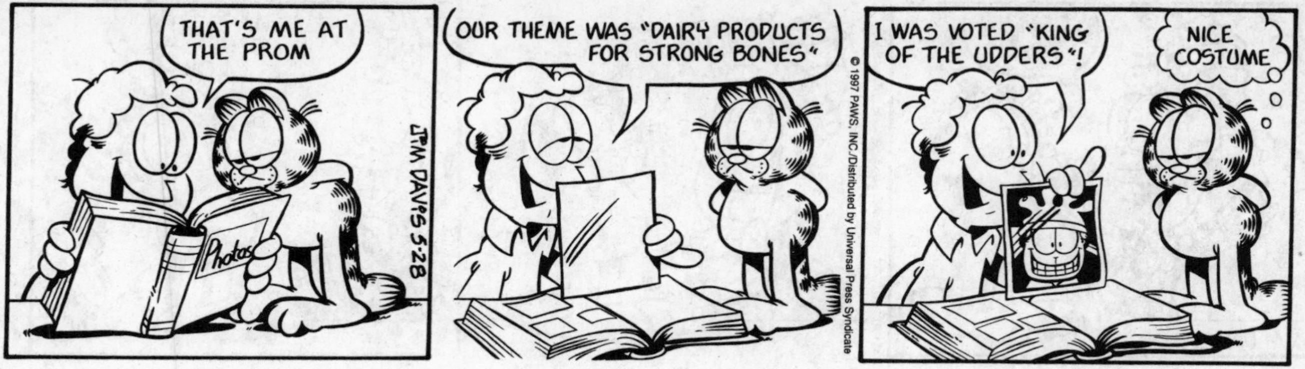
THAT'S ME AT THE PROM
Photos
JIM DAVIS 5-28
OUR THEME WAS "DAIRY PRODUCTS FOR STRONG BONES"
© 1997 PAWS, INC./Distributed by Universal Press Syndicate
I WAS VOTED "KING OF THE UDDERS"!
NICE COSTUME

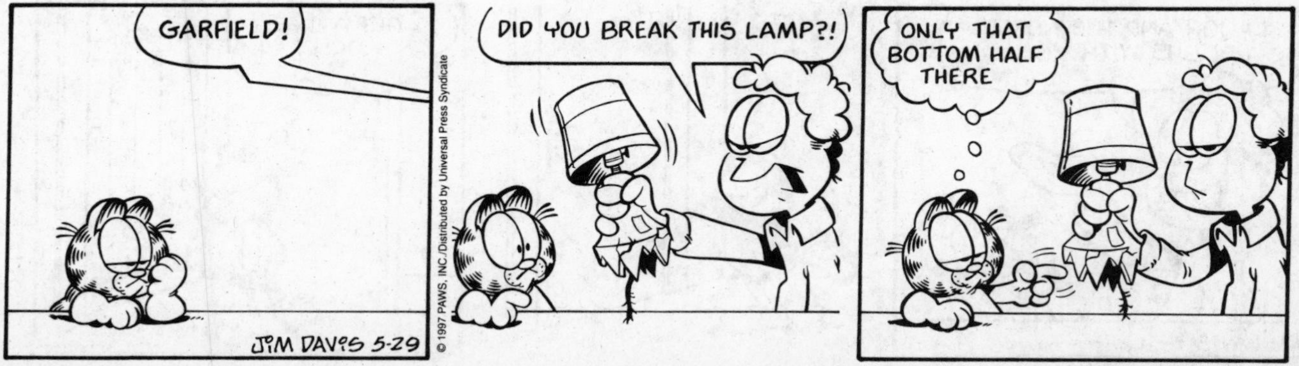
GARFIELD!
JIM DAVIS 5-29
© 1997 PAWS, INC./Distributed by Universal Press Syndicate
DID YOU BREAK THIS LAMP?!
ONLY THAT BOTTOM HALF THERE

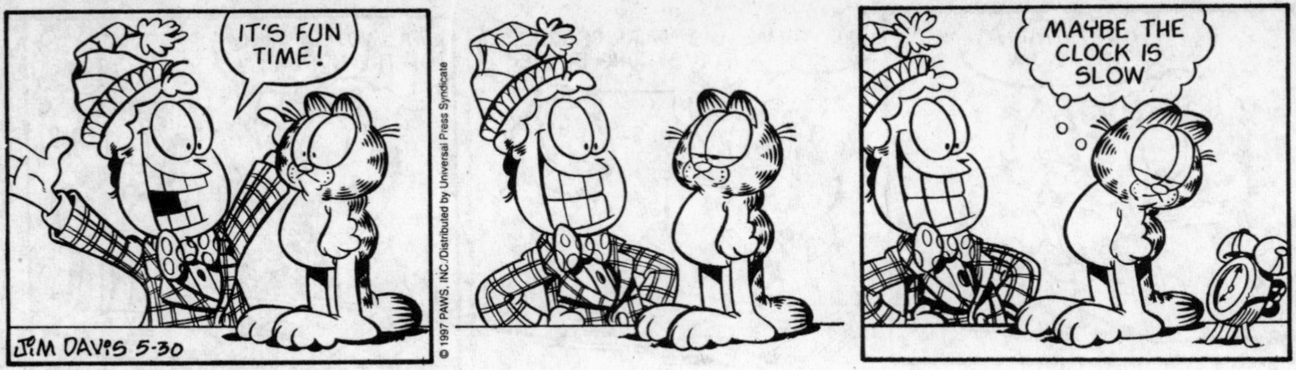
IT'S FUN TIME!
JIM DAVIS 5-30
© 1997 PAWS, INC./Distributed by Universal Press Syndicate
MAYBE THE CLOCK IS SLOW

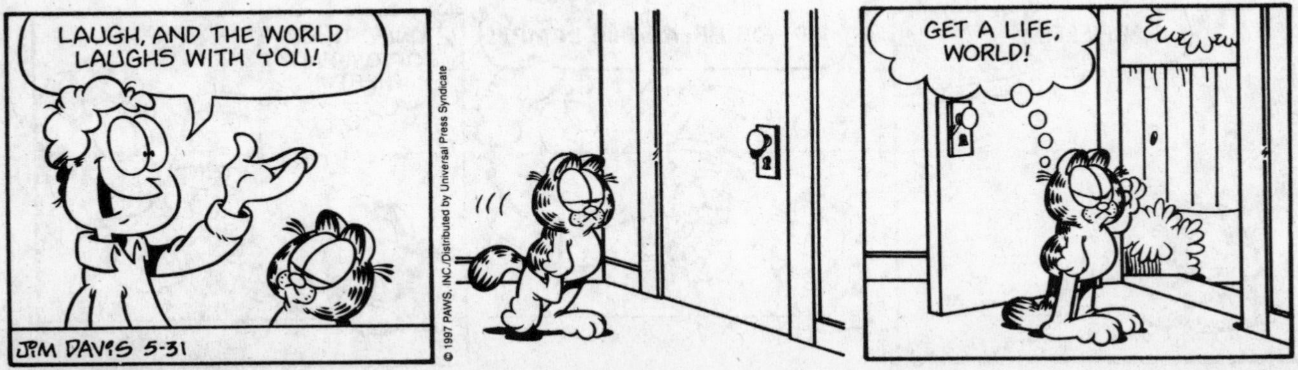
LAUGH, AND THE WORLD LAUGHS WITH YOU!
JIM DAVIS 5-31
© 1997 PAWS, INC./Distributed by Universal Press Syndicate
GET A LIFE, WORLD!

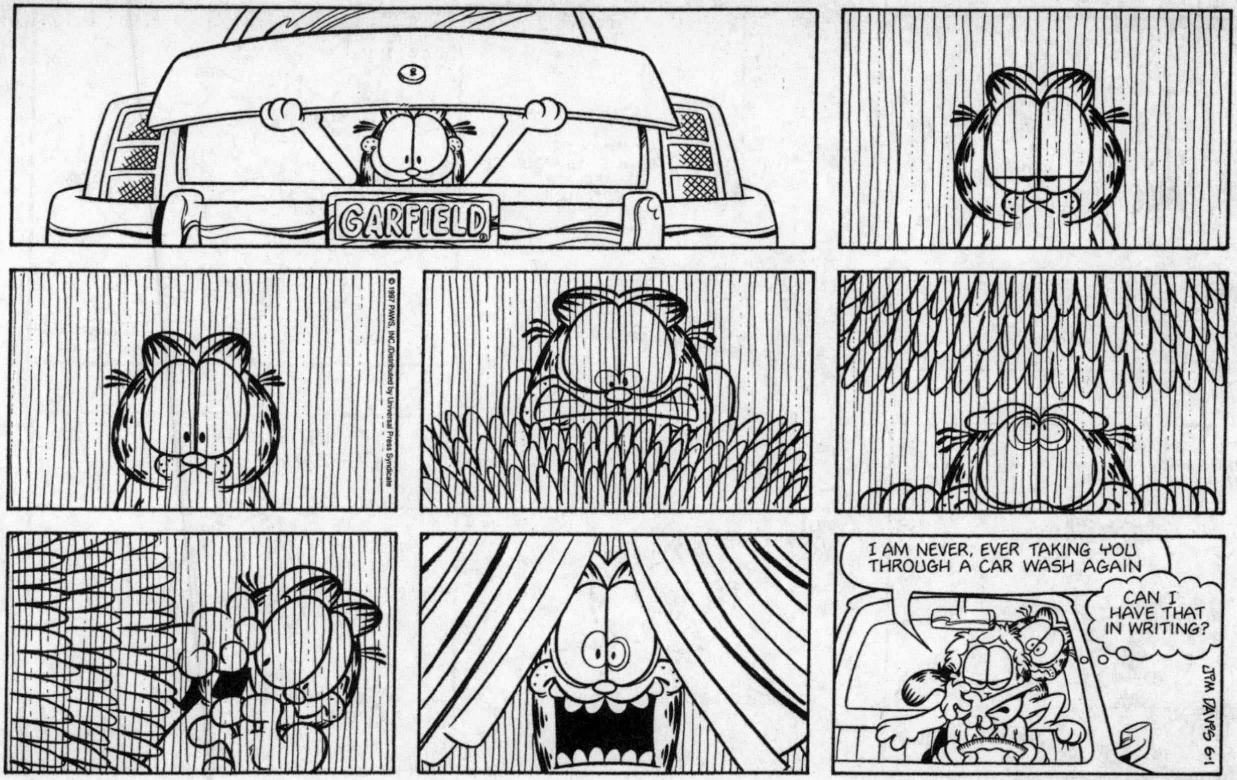
GARFIELD
© 1997 PAWS, INC./Distributed by Universal Press Syndicate
I AM NEVER, EVER TAKING YOU THROUGH A CAR WASH AGAIN
CAN I HAVE THAT IN WRITING?
JIM DAVIS 6-1

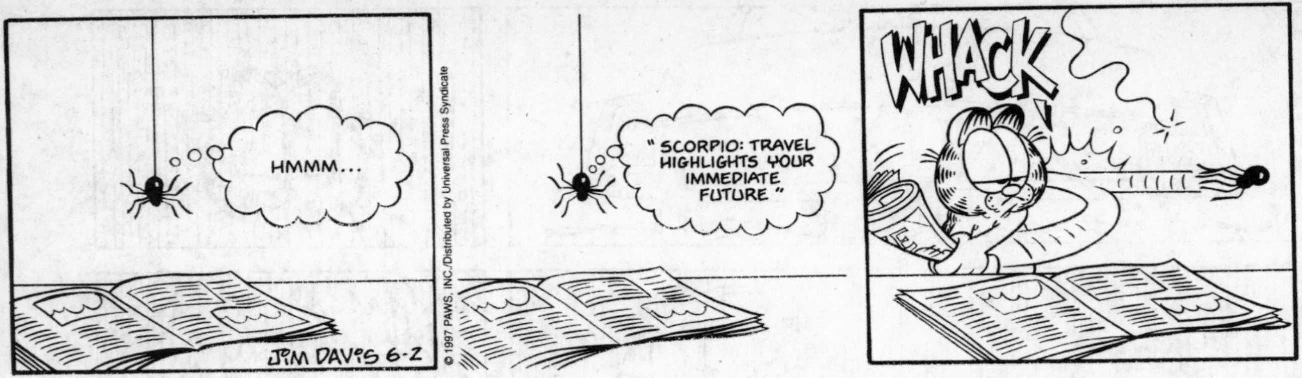
HMMM...
JIM DAVIS 6-2
© 1997 PAWS, INC./Distributed by Universal Press Syndicate
" SCORPIO: TRAVEL HIGHLIGHTS YOUR IMMEDIATE FUTURE "
WHACK

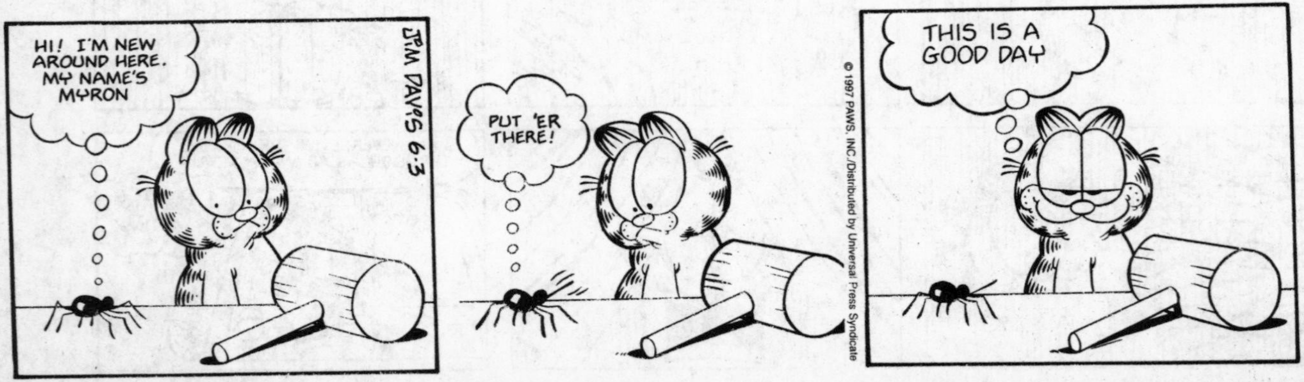
HI! I'M NEW AROUND HERE. MY NAME'S MYRON
JIM DAVIS 6-3
PUT 'ER THERE!
© 1997 PAWS, INC./Distributed by Universal Press Syndicate
THIS IS A GOOD DAY

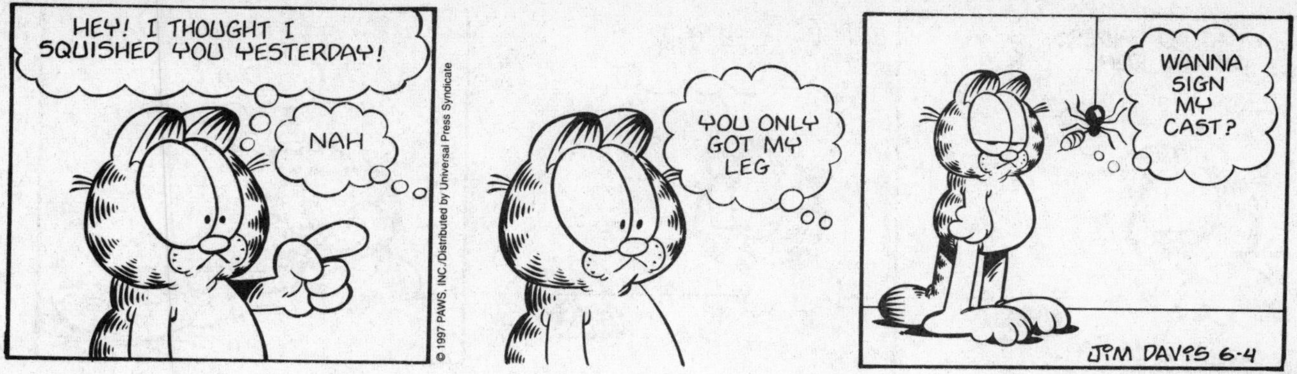
HEY! I THOUGHT I SQUISHED YOU YESTERDAY!
NAH
© 1997 PAWS, INC./Distributed by Universal Press Syndicate
YOU ONLY GOT MY LEG
WANNA SIGN MY CAST?
JIM DAVIS 6-4

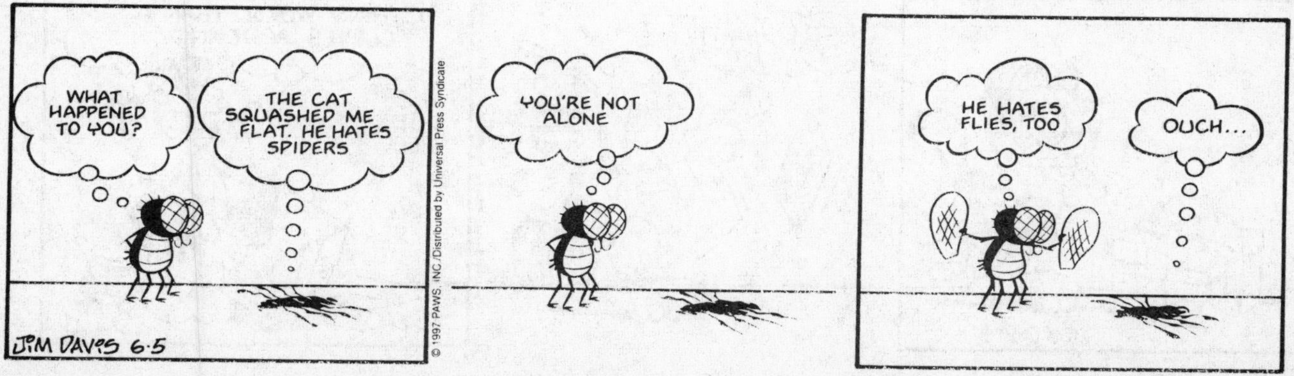
WHAT HAPPENED TO YOU?
THE CAT SQUASHED ME FLAT. HE HATES SPIDERS
JIM DAVIS 6-5
© 1997 PAWS, INC./Distributed by Universal Press Syndicate
YOU'RE NOT ALONE
HE HATES FLIES, TOO
OUCH...

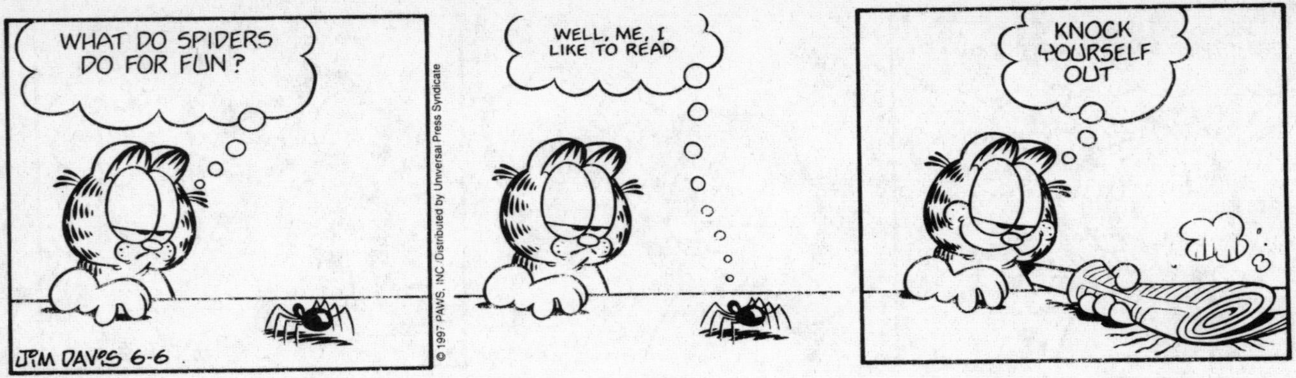
WHAT DO SPIDERS DO FOR FUN?
JIM DAVIS 6-6
© 1997 PAWS, INC./Distributed by Universal Press Syndicate
WELL, ME, I LIKE TO READ
KNOCK YOURSELF OUT

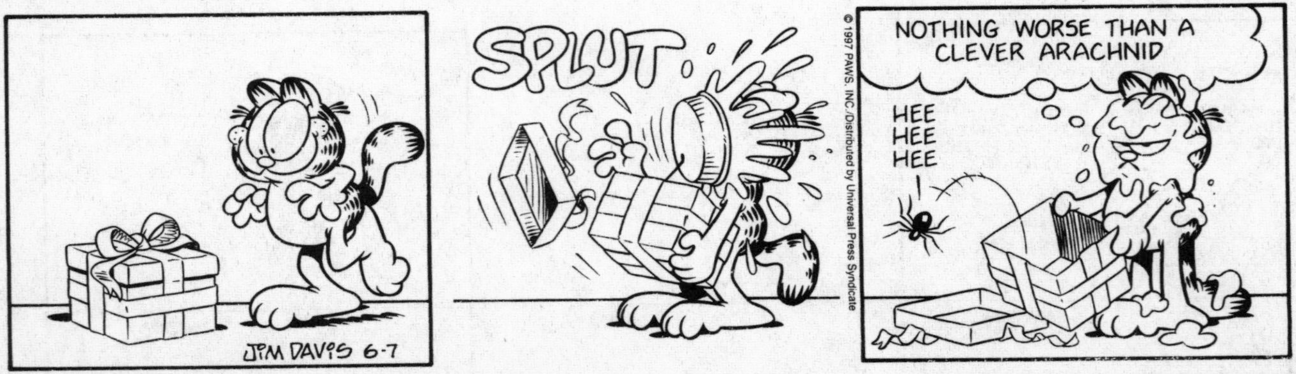
JIM DAVIS 6-7
SPLUT
© 1997 PAWS, INC./Distributed by Universal Press Syndicate
NOTHING WORSE THAN A CLEVER ARACHNID
HEE HEE HEE

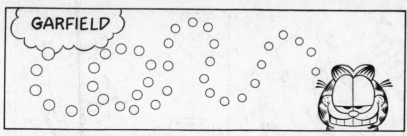

SPIDER! YOU'RE LOOKING GOOD!

YEP...

JUST HAD THE BODY CAST REMOVED YESTERDAY!

© 1997 PAWS, INC./Distributed by Universal Press Syndicate

I ALSO HAD THE STITCHES REMOVED LAST WEEK, AND I DON'T HAVE TO WEAR THAT NECK BRACE ANYMORE.

THE DOC SAYS I'M AS GOOD AS NEW. THE ONLY THING THAT HASN'T RETURNED YET IS...

SMACK!

...MY MEMORY

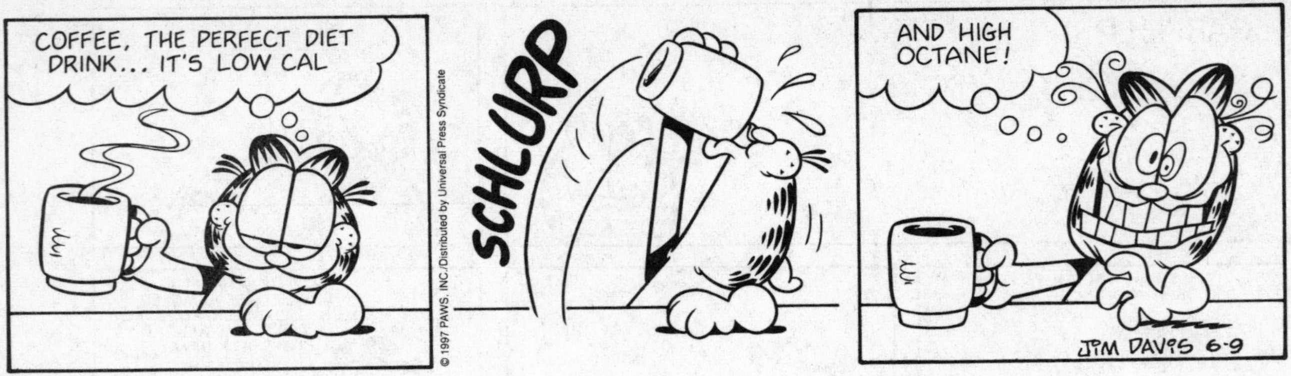
COFFEE, THE PERFECT DIET DRINK... IT'S LOW CAL
SCHLURP
AND HIGH OCTANE!
JIM DAVIS 6-9
© 1997 PAWS, INC./Distributed by Universal Press Syndicate

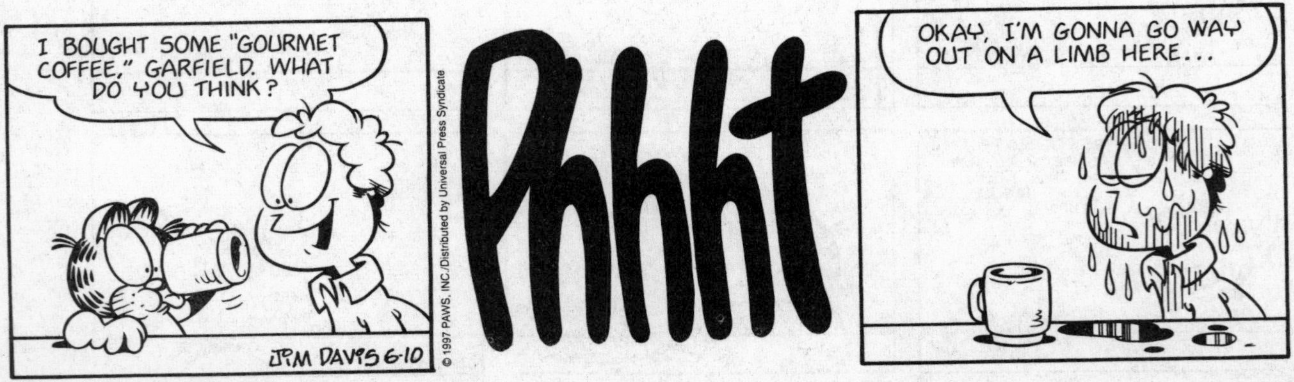
I BOUGHT SOME "GOURMET COFFEE," GARFIELD. WHAT DO YOU THINK?
JIM DAVIS 6-10
Phhht
OKAY, I'M GONNA GO WAY OUT ON A LIMB HERE...
© 1997 PAWS, INC./Distributed by Universal Press Syndicate

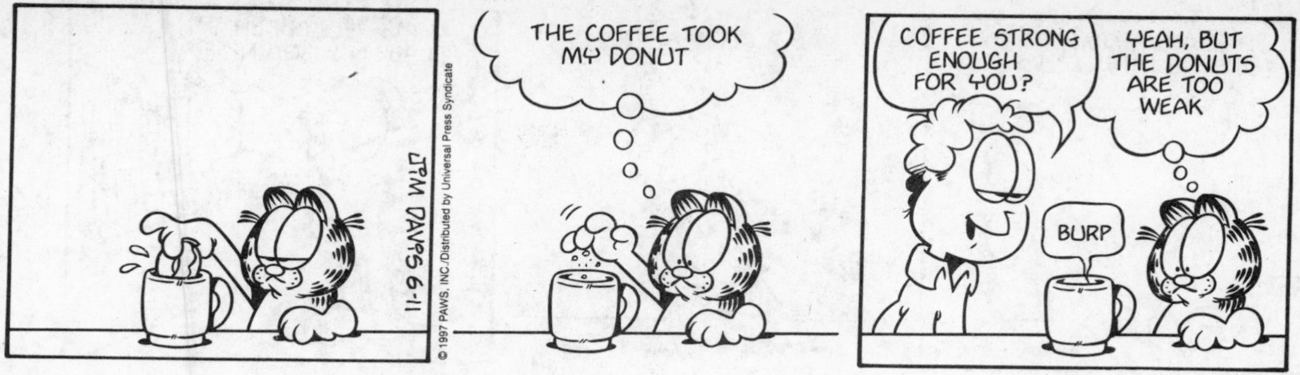
JIM DAVIS 6-11
© 1997 PAWS, INC./Distributed by Universal Press Syndicate
THE COFFEE TOOK MY DONUT
COFFEE STRONG ENOUGH FOR YOU?
BURP
YEAH, BUT THE DONUTS ARE TOO WEAK

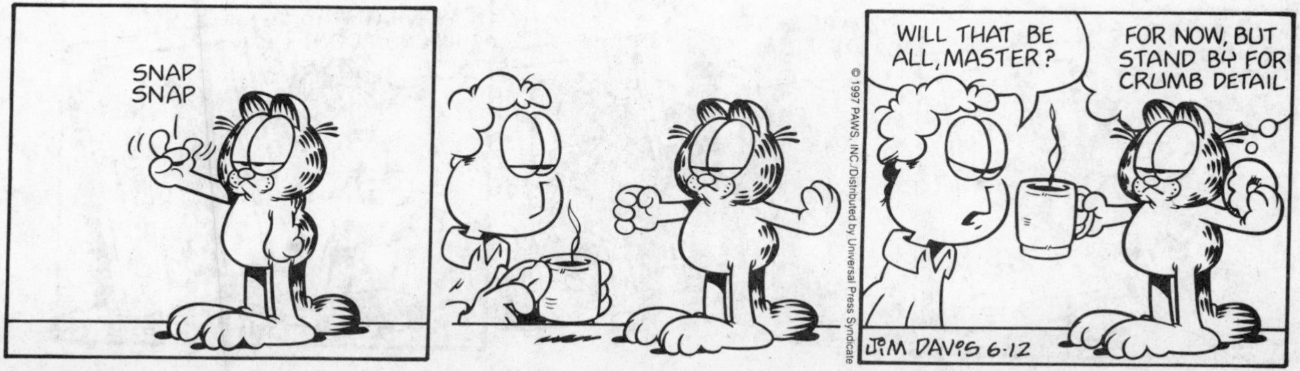
SNAP SNAP
© 1997 PAWS, INC./Distributed by Universal Press Syndicate
WILL THAT BE ALL, MASTER?
FOR NOW, BUT STAND BY FOR CRUMB DETAIL
JIM DAVIS 6-12

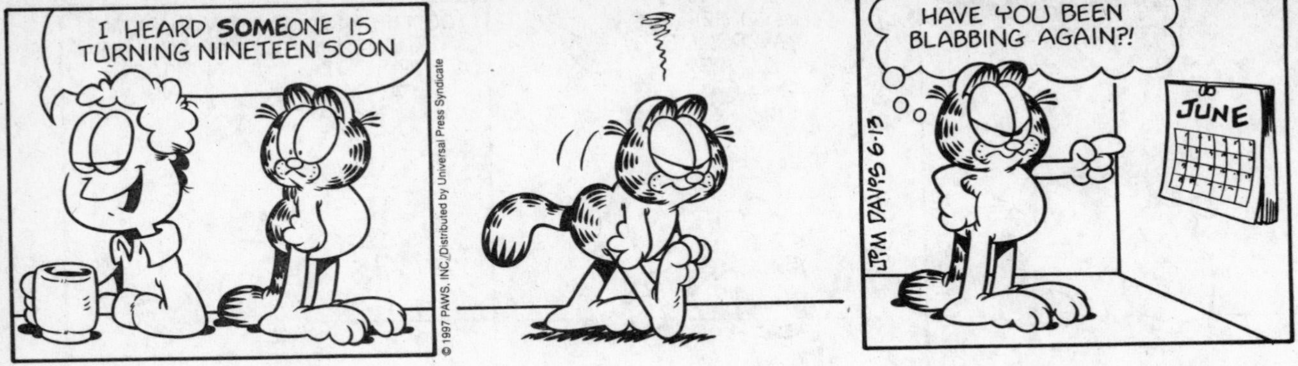
I HEARD SOMEONE IS TURNING NINETEEN SOON
HAVE YOU BEEN BLABBING AGAIN?!
JUNE
JIM DAVIS 6-13

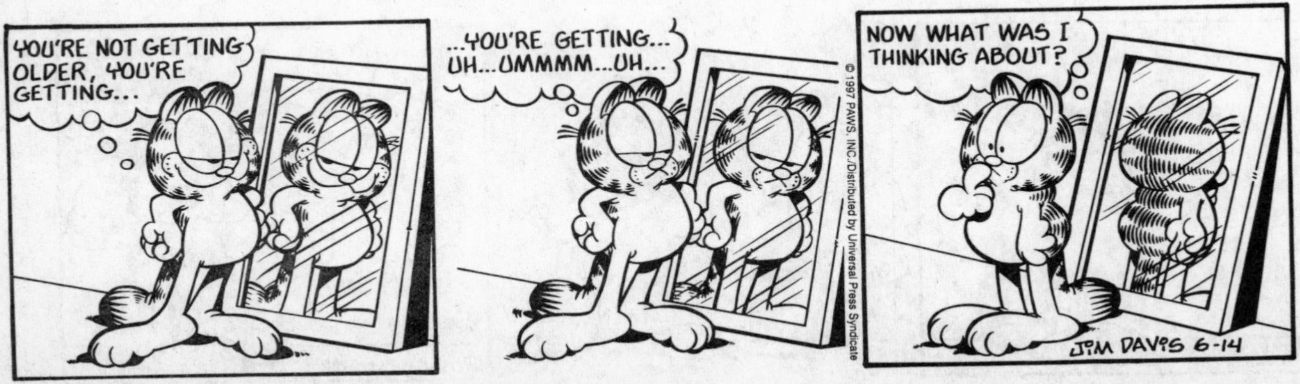
YOU'RE NOT GETTING OLDER, YOU'RE GETTING...
...YOU'RE GETTING... UH...UMMMM...UH...
NOW WHAT WAS I THINKING ABOUT?
JIM DAVIS 6-14

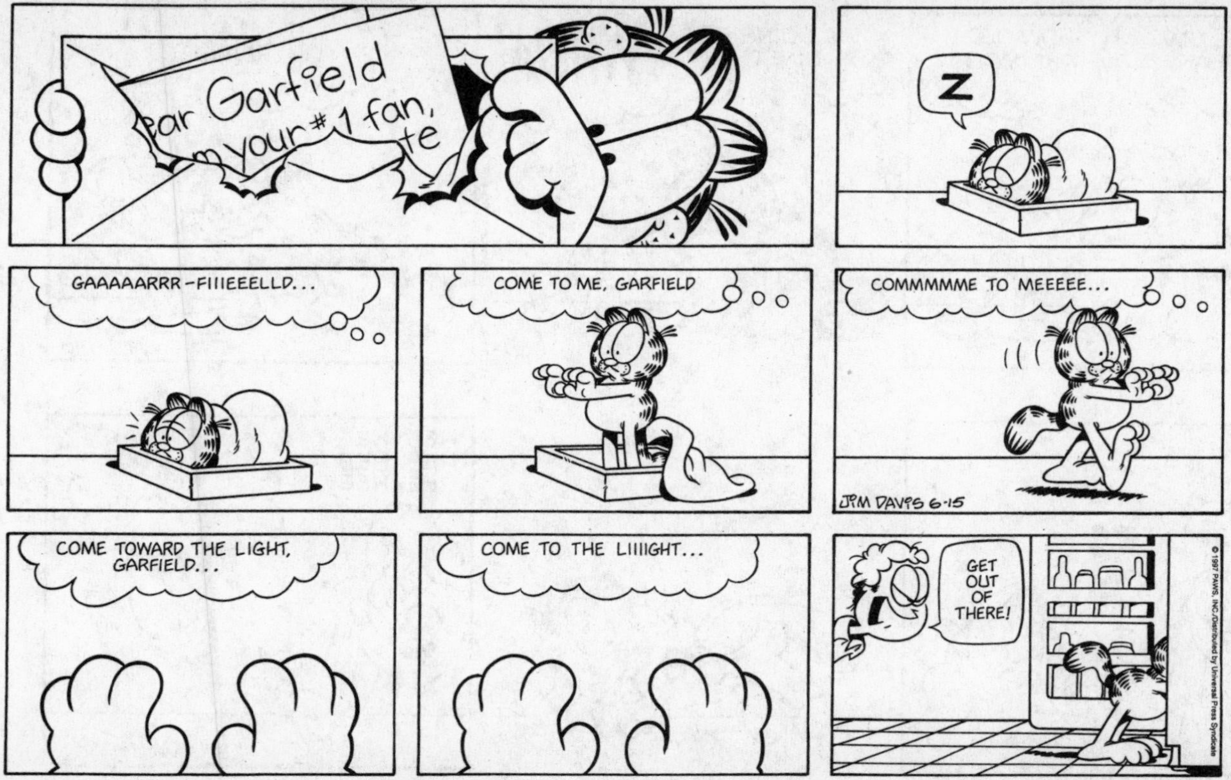

ear Garfield
m your # 1 fan,
te
Z
GAAAAARRR-FIIIEEELLD...
COME TO ME, GARFIELD
COMMMMME TO MEEEEE...
JIM DAVIS 6-15
COME TOWARD THE LIGHT, GARFIELD...
COME TO THE LIIIGHT...
GET OUT OF THERE!
© 1997 PAWS, INC./Distributed by Universal Press Syndicate

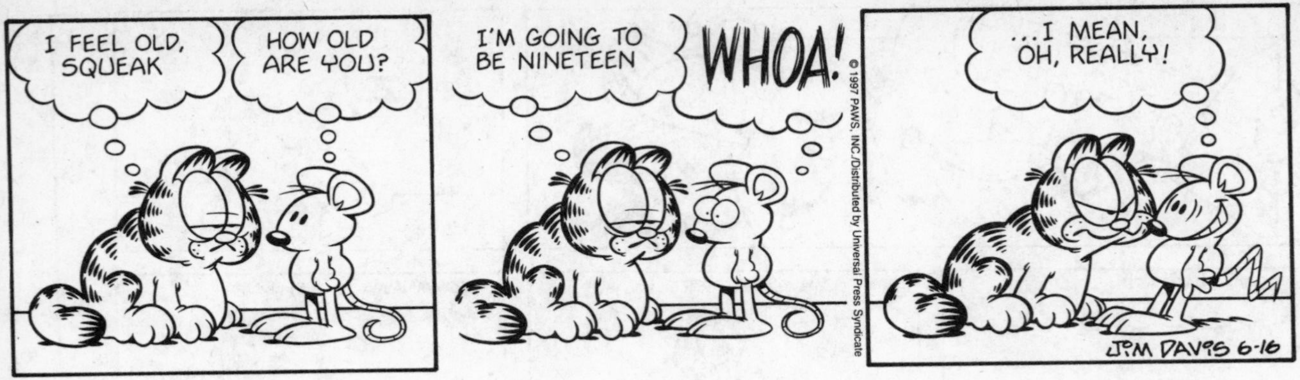
I FEEL OLD, SQUEAK
HOW OLD ARE YOU?
I'M GOING TO BE NINETEEN
WHOA!
...I MEAN, OH, REALLY!
© 1997 PAWS, INC./Distributed by Universal Press Syndicate
JIM DAVIS 6-16

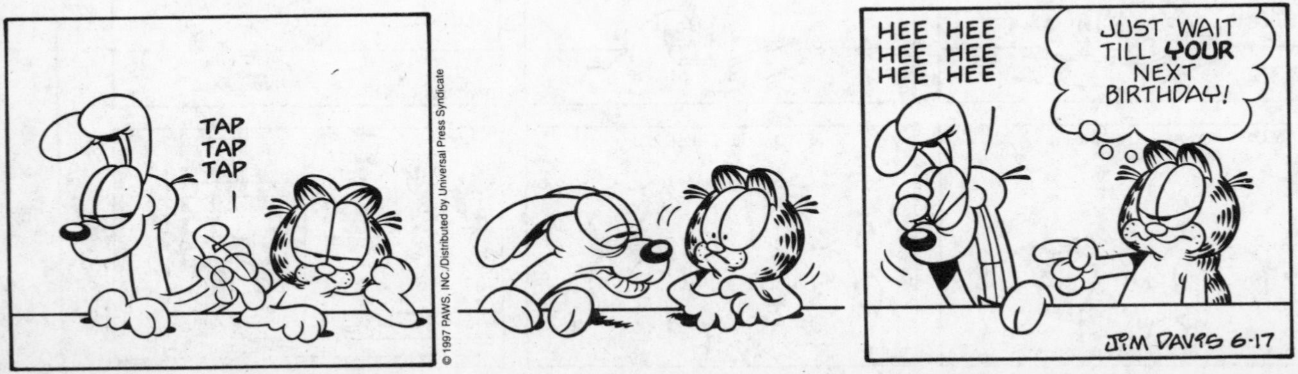
TAP TAP TAP
© 1997 PAWS, INC./Distributed by Universal Press Syndicate
HEE HEE HEE HEE HEE HEE
JUST WAIT TILL **YOUR** NEXT BIRTHDAY!
JIM DAVIS 6-17

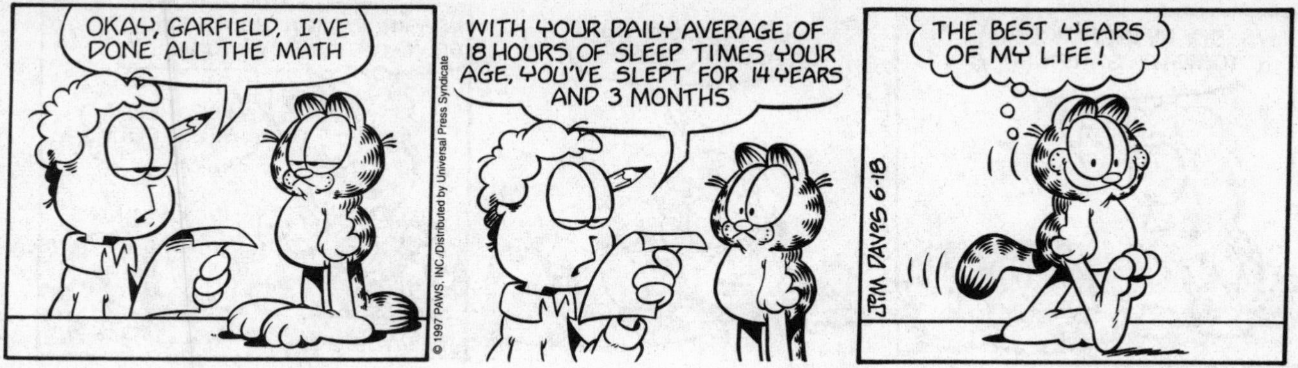
OKAY, GARFIELD, I'VE DONE ALL THE MATH
© 1997 PAWS, INC./Distributed by Universal Press Syndicate
WITH YOUR DAILY AVERAGE OF 18 HOURS OF SLEEP TIMES YOUR AGE, YOU'VE SLEPT FOR 14 YEARS AND 3 MONTHS
THE BEST YEARS OF MY LIFE!
JIM DAVIS 6-18

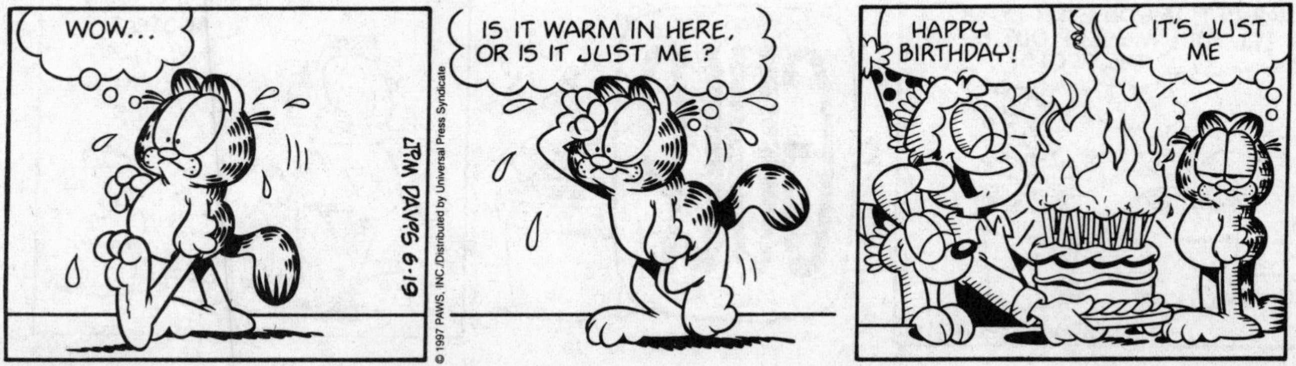
WOW...
JIM DAVIS 6-19
© 1997 PAWS, INC./Distributed by Universal Press Syndicate
IS IT WARM IN HERE, OR IS IT JUST ME ?
HAPPY BIRTHDAY!
IT'S JUST ME

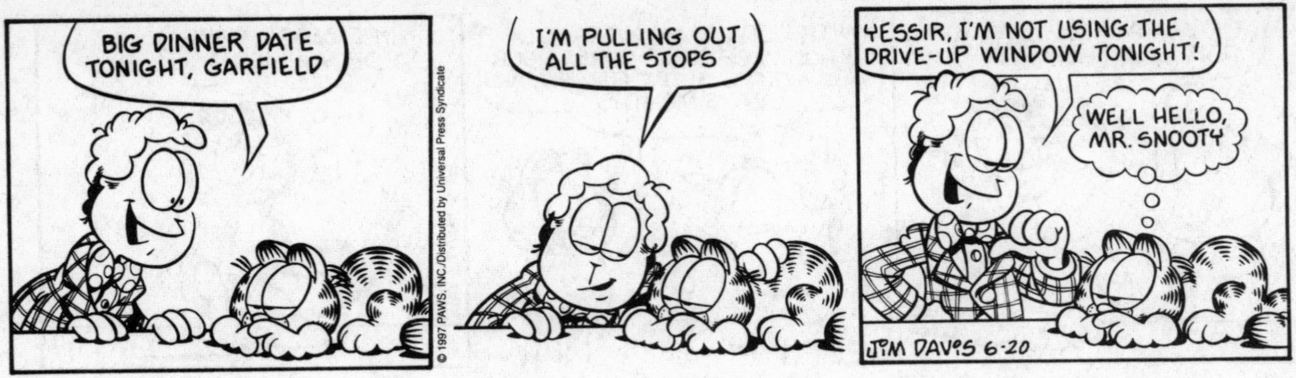
BIG DINNER DATE TONIGHT, GARFIELD
I'M PULLING OUT ALL THE STOPS
YESSIR, I'M NOT USING THE DRIVE-UP WINDOW TONIGHT!
WELL HELLO, MR. SNOOTY
JIM DAVIS 6-20
© 1997 PAWS, INC./Distributed by Universal Press Syndicate

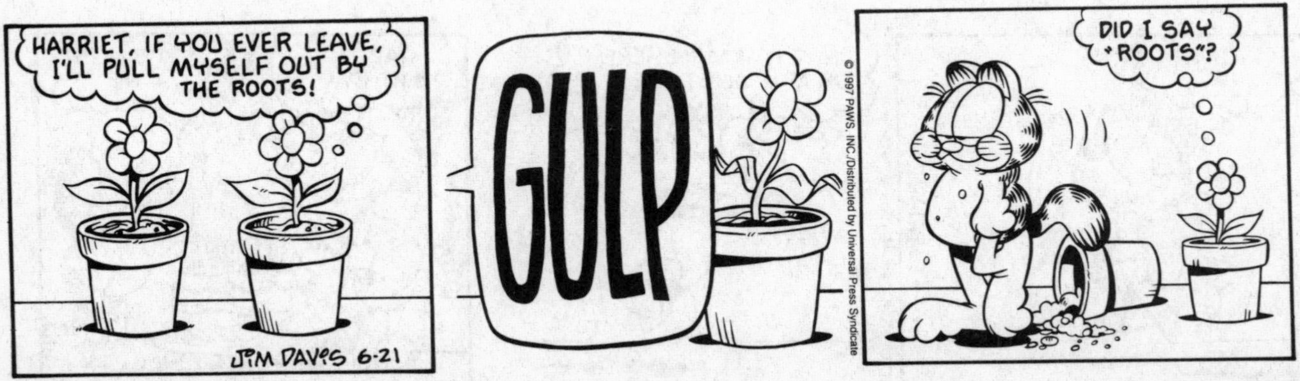
HARRIET, IF YOU EVER LEAVE, I'LL PULL MYSELF OUT BY THE ROOTS!
JIM DAVIS 6-21
GULP
DID I SAY "ROOTS"?
© 1997 PAWS, INC./Distributed by Universal Press Syndicate

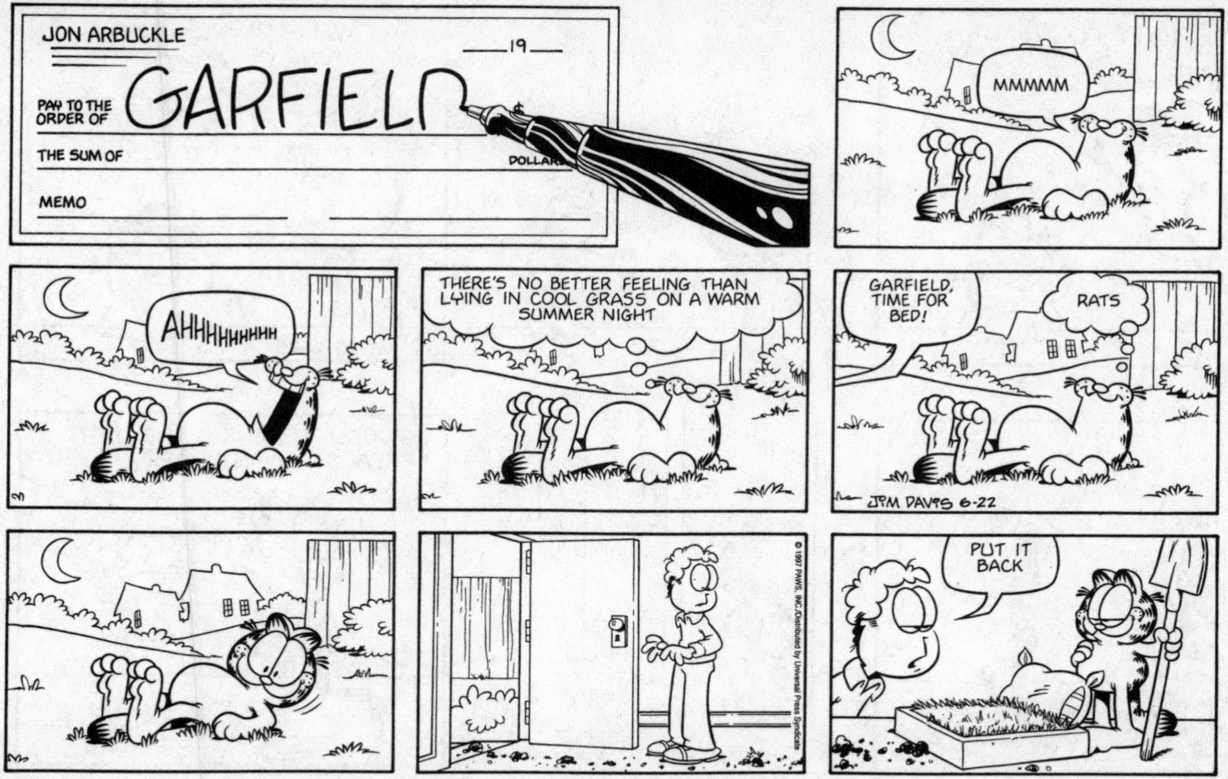
JON ARBUCKLE
19
PAY TO THE ORDER OF
GARFIELD
$
THE SUM OF
DOLLARS
MEMO
MMMMM
AHHHHHHHHHH
THERE'S NO BETTER FEELING THAN LYING IN COOL GRASS ON A WARM SUMMER NIGHT
GARFIELD, TIME FOR BED!
RATS
JIM DAVIS 6-22
© 1997 PAWS, INC./Distributed by Universal Press Syndicate
PUT IT BACK

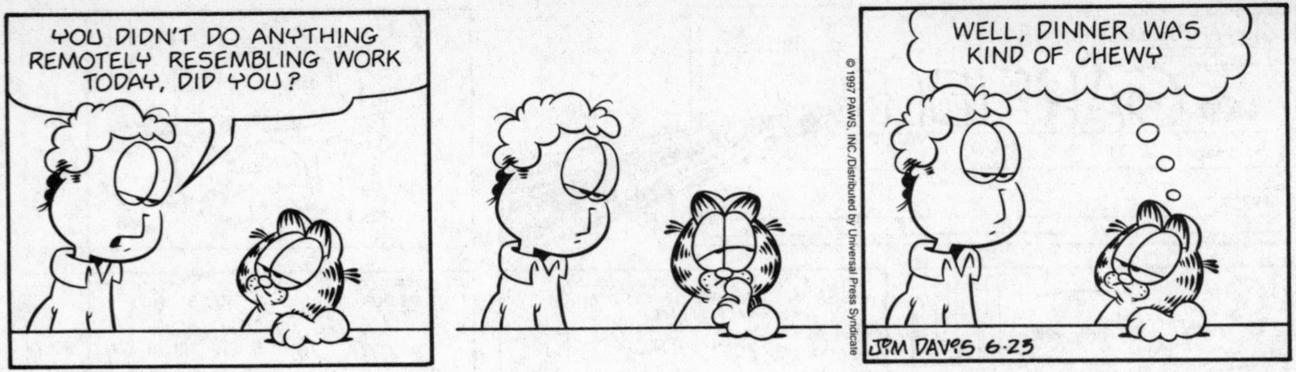
YOU DIDN'T DO ANYTHING REMOTELY RESEMBLING WORK TODAY, DID YOU?
WELL, DINNER WAS KIND OF CHEWY
© 1997 PAWS, INC./Distributed by Universal Press Syndicate
JIM DAVIS 6-23

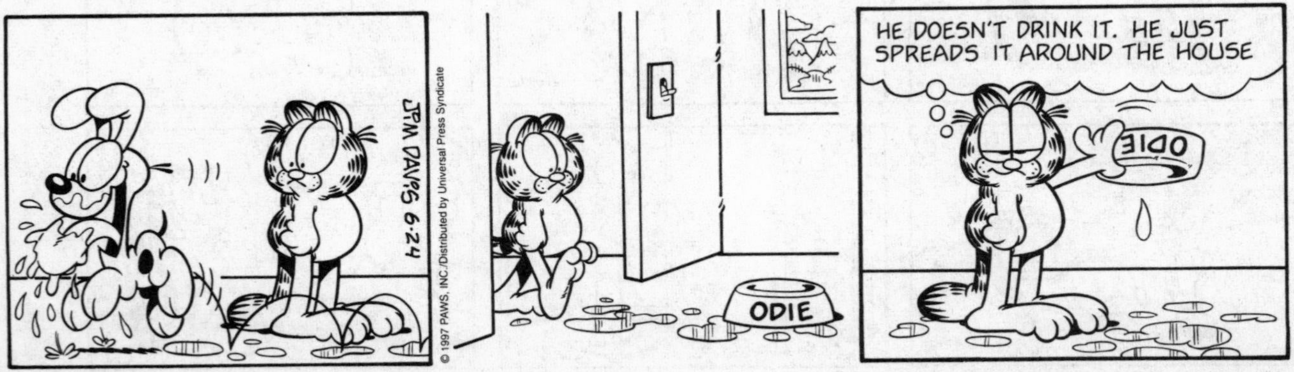
JIM DAVIS 6-24
© 1997 PAWS, INC./Distributed by Universal Press Syndicate
ODIE
HE DOESN'T DRINK IT. HE JUST SPREADS IT AROUND THE HOUSE
ODIE

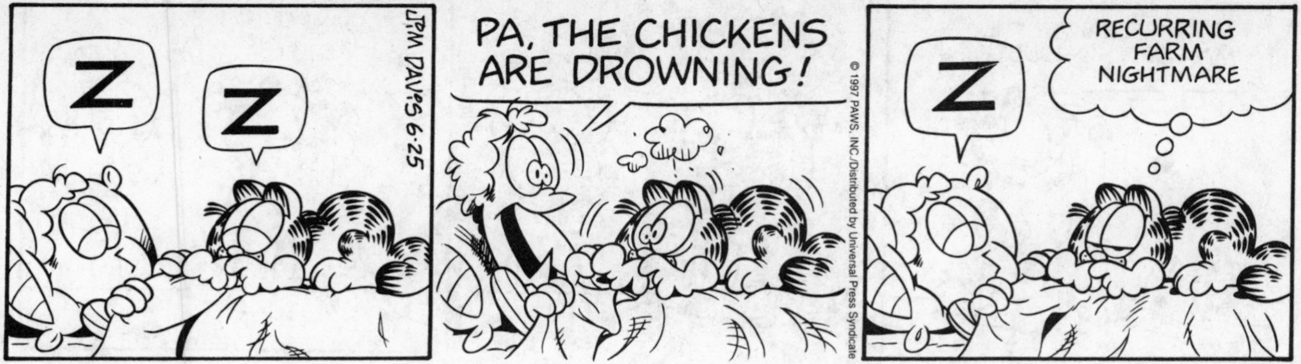

Z
Z
JPM DAVPS 6·25
PA, THE CHICKENS ARE DROWNING!
© 1997 PAWS, INC./Distributed by Universal Press Syndicate
Z
RECURRING FARM NIGHTMARE

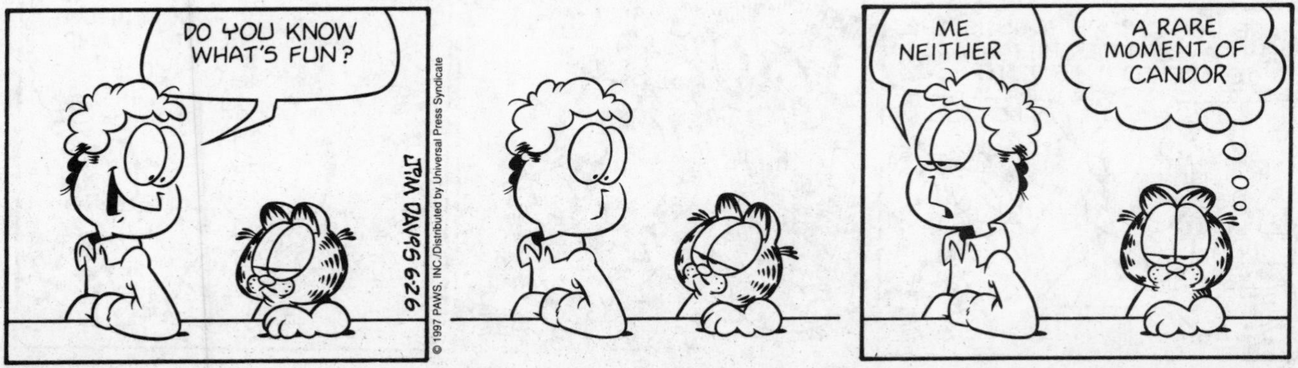

DO YOU KNOW WHAT'S FUN?
JPM DAVPS 6·26
© 1997 PAWS, INC./Distributed by Universal Press Syndicate
ME NEITHER
A RARE MOMENT OF CANDOR

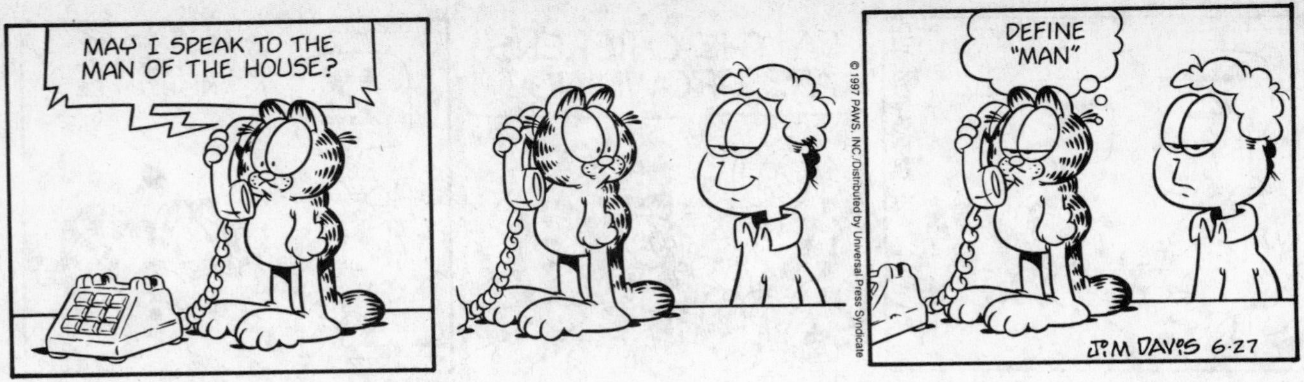
MAY I SPEAK TO THE MAN OF THE HOUSE?
DEFINE "MAN"
JIM DAVIS 6-27
© 1997 PAWS, INC./Distributed by Universal Press Syndicate

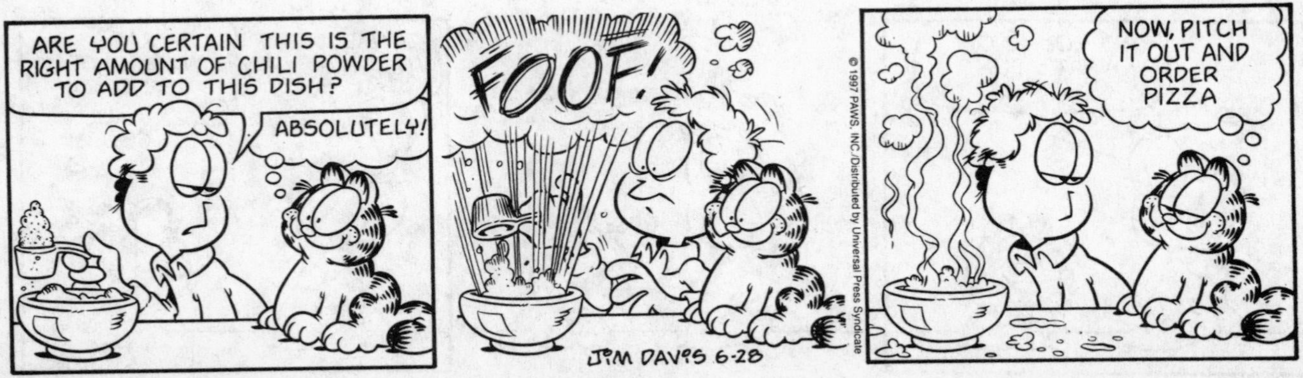
ARE YOU CERTAIN THIS IS THE RIGHT AMOUNT OF CHILI POWDER TO ADD TO THIS DISH?
ABSOLUTELY!
FOOF!
JIM DAVIS 6-28
NOW, PITCH IT OUT AND ORDER PIZZA
© 1997 PAWS, INC./Distributed by Universal Press Syndicate

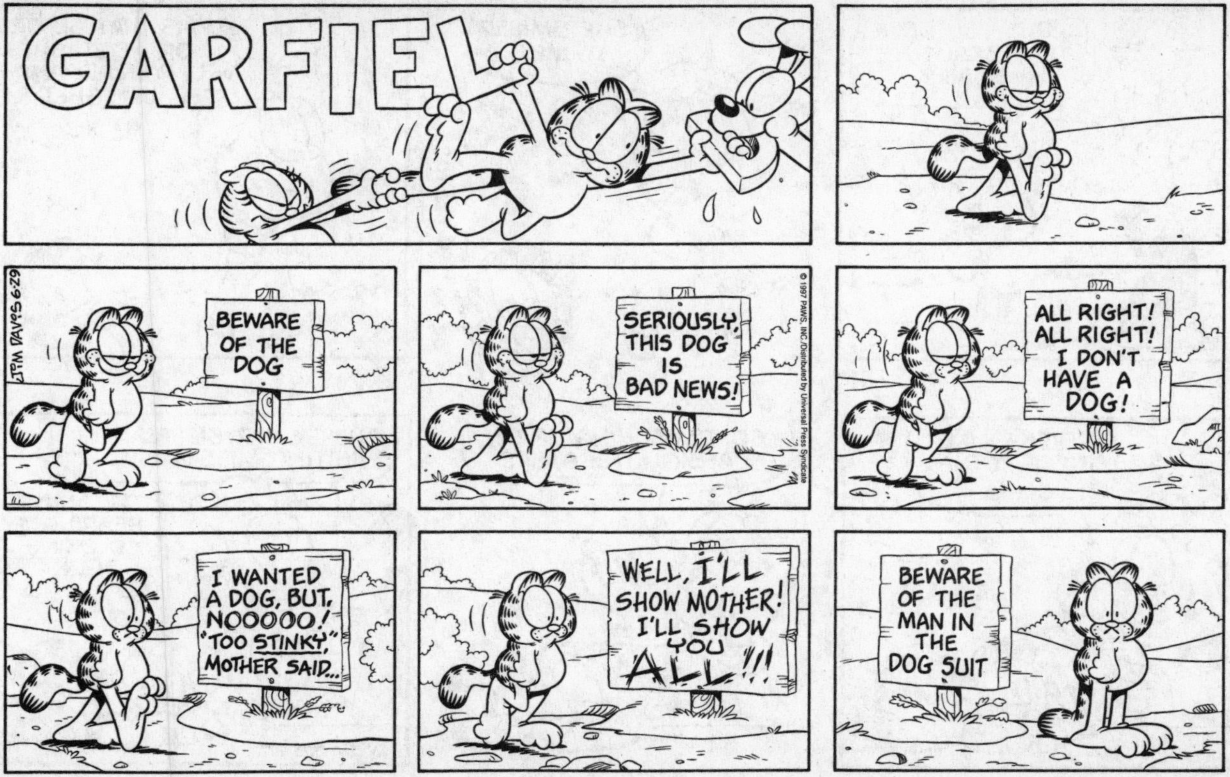
GARFIELD
JPM DAVIS 6-29
© 1997 PAWS, INC./Distributed by Universal Press Syndicate
BEWARE OF THE DOG
SERIOUSLY, THIS DOG IS BAD NEWS!
ALL RIGHT! ALL RIGHT! I DON'T HAVE A DOG!
I WANTED A DOG, BUT, NOOOOO! "TOO STINKY," MOTHER SAID...
WELL, I'LL SHOW MOTHER! I'LL SHOW YOU ALL!!!
BEWARE OF THE MAN IN THE DOG SUIT

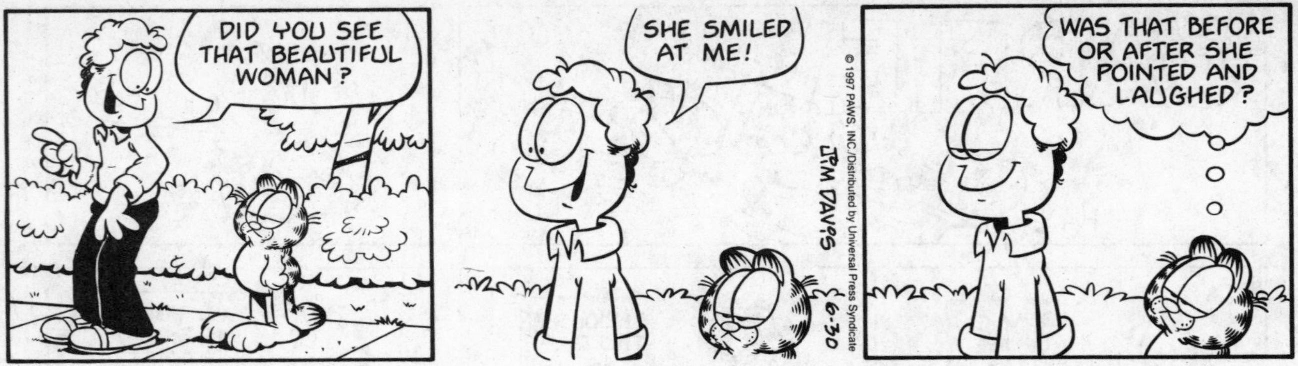
DID YOU SEE THAT BEAUTIFUL WOMAN?
SHE SMILED AT ME!
WAS THAT BEFORE OR AFTER SHE POINTED AND LAUGHED?
JIM DAVIS 6-30

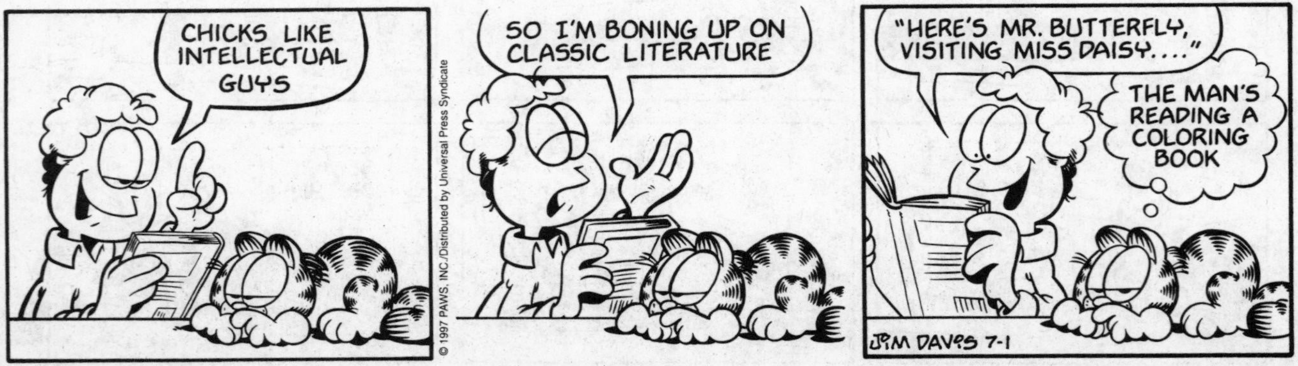
CHICKS LIKE INTELLECTUAL GUYS
SO I'M BONING UP ON CLASSIC LITERATURE
"HERE'S MR. BUTTERFLY, VISITING MISS DAISY...."
THE MAN'S READING A COLORING BOOK
JIM DAVIS 7-1

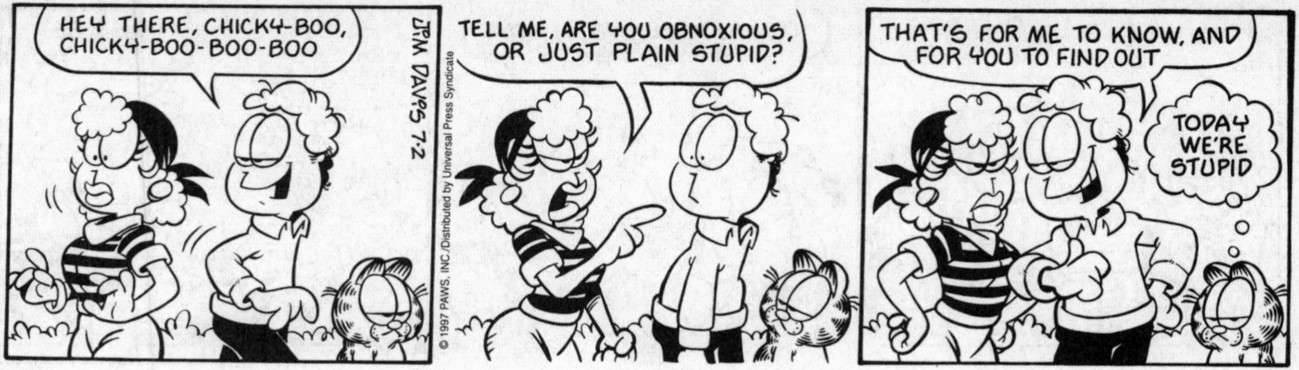
HEY THERE, CHICKY-BOO, CHICKY-BOO-BOO-BOO
JIM DAVIS 7-2
© 1997 PAWS, INC./Distributed by Universal Press Syndicate
TELL ME, ARE YOU OBNOXIOUS, OR JUST PLAIN STUPID?
THAT'S FOR ME TO KNOW, AND FOR YOU TO FIND OUT
TODAY WE'RE STUPID

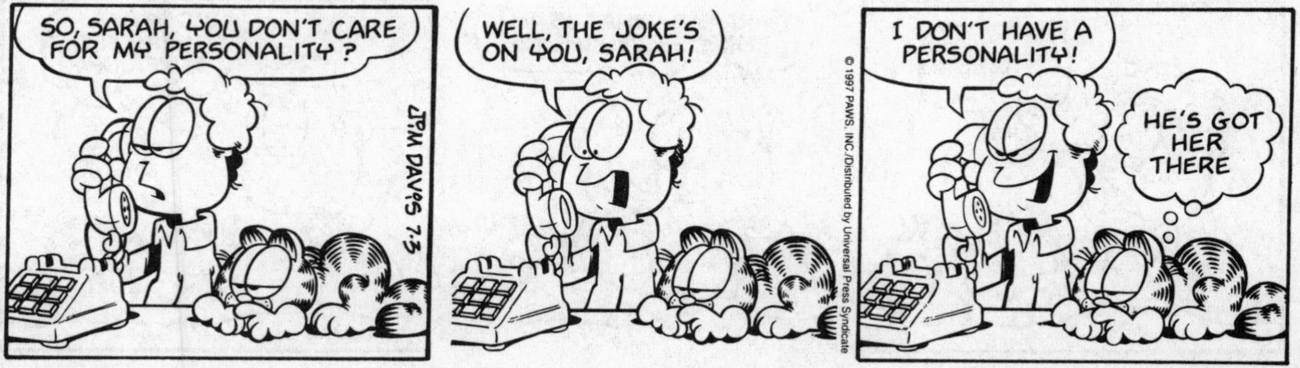
SO, SARAH, YOU DON'T CARE FOR MY PERSONALITY?
JIM DAVIS 7-3
WELL, THE JOKE'S ON YOU, SARAH!
© 1997 PAWS, INC./Distributed by Universal Press Syndicate
I DON'T HAVE A PERSONALITY!
HE'S GOT HER THERE

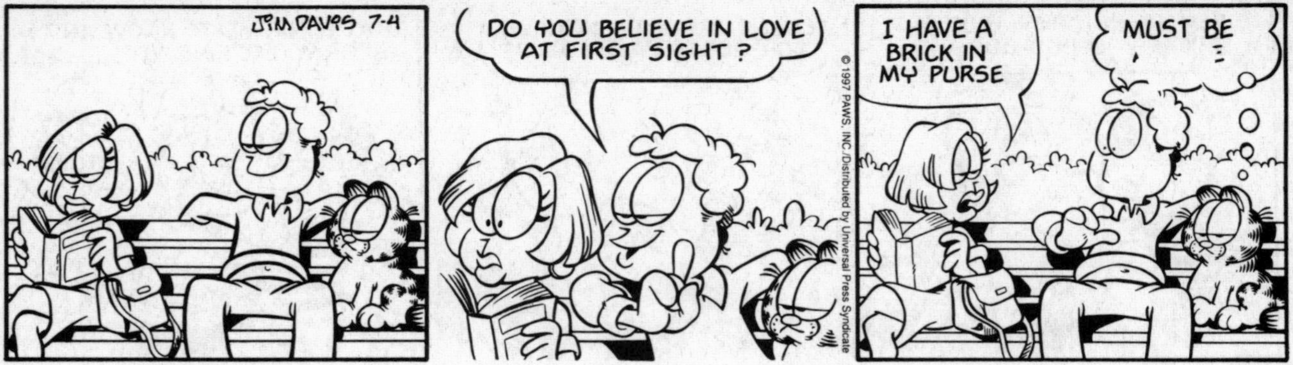
JIM DAVIS 7-4
DO YOU BELIEVE IN LOVE AT FIRST SIGHT ?
© 1997 PAWS, INC./Distributed by Universal Press Syndicate
I HAVE A BRICK IN MY PURSE
MUST BE

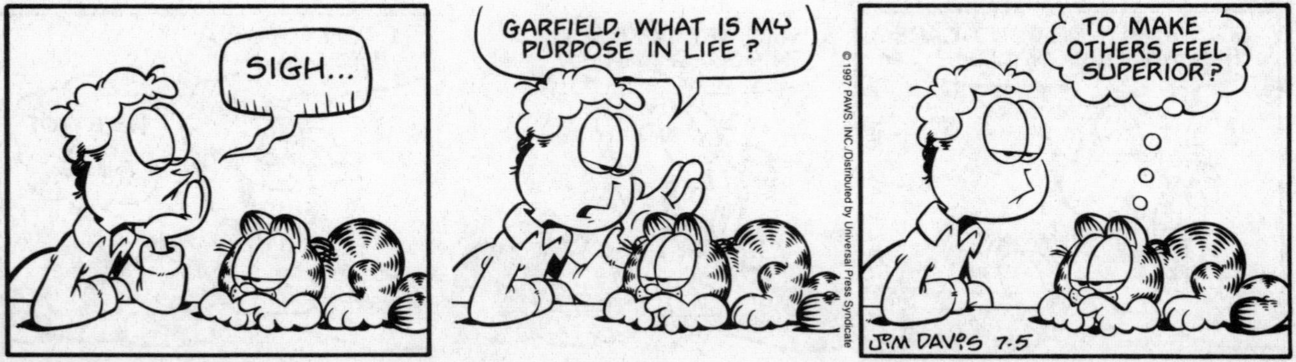
SIGH...
GARFIELD, WHAT IS MY PURPOSE IN LIFE ?
© 1997 PAWS, INC./Distributed by Universal Press Syndicate
TO MAKE OTHERS FEEL SUPERIOR ?
JIM DAVIS 7-5

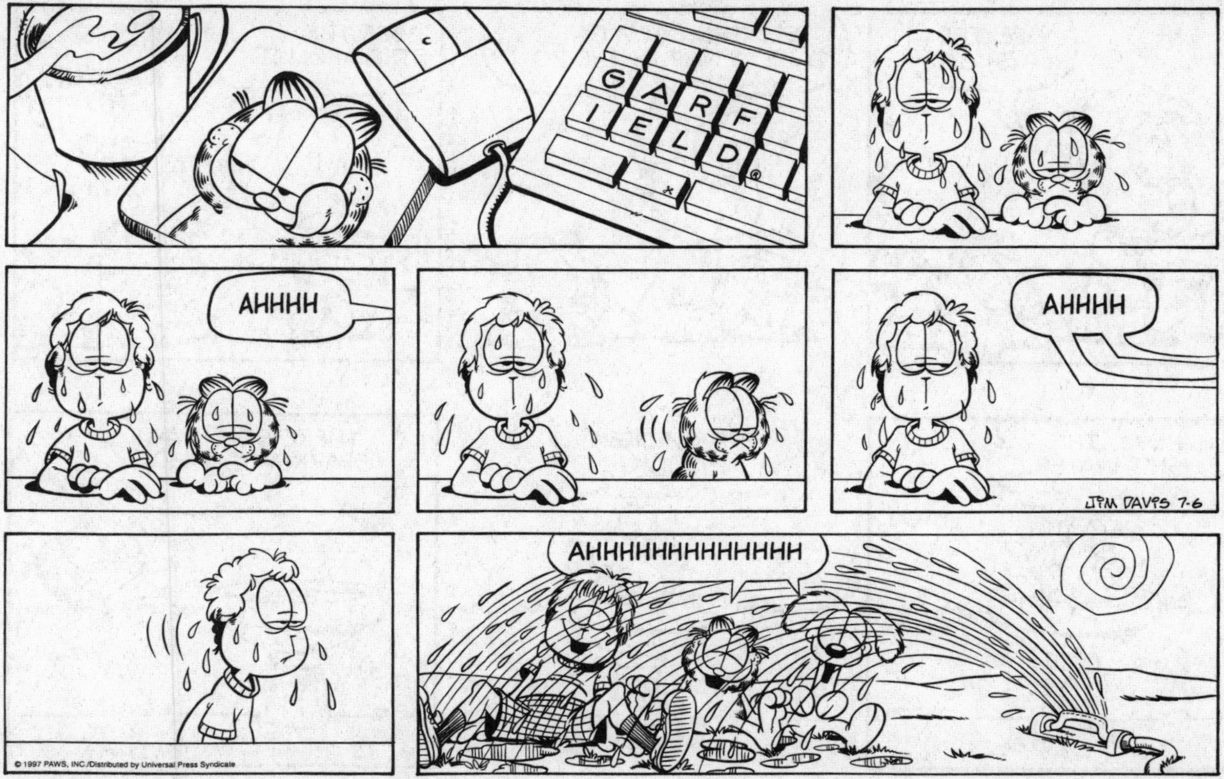
GARFIELD®
AHHHH
AHHHH
JIM DAVIS 7-6
© 1997 PAWS, INC./Distributed by Universal Press Syndicate
AHHHHHHHHHHHHH

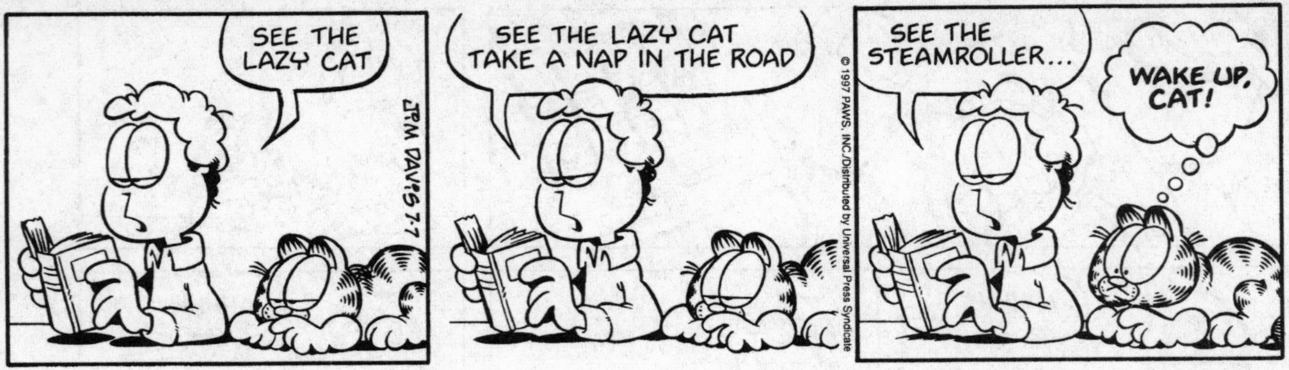
SEE THE LAZY CAT
JIM DAVIS 7-7
SEE THE LAZY CAT TAKE A NAP IN THE ROAD
© 1997 PAWS, INC./Distributed by Universal Press Syndicate
SEE THE STEAMROLLER...
WAKE UP, CAT!

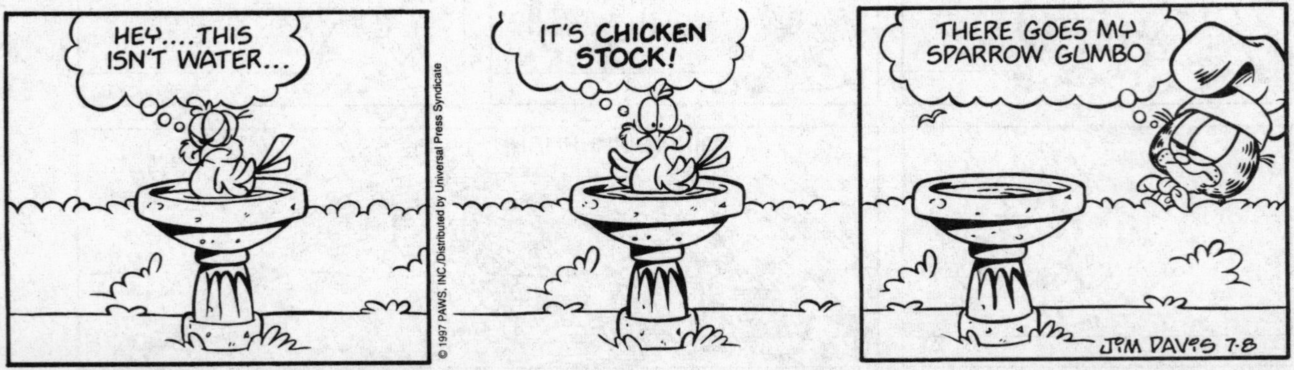
HEY....THIS ISN'T WATER...
© 1997 PAWS, INC./Distributed by Universal Press Syndicate
IT'S CHICKEN STOCK!
THERE GOES MY SPARROW GUMBO
JIM DAVIS 7-8

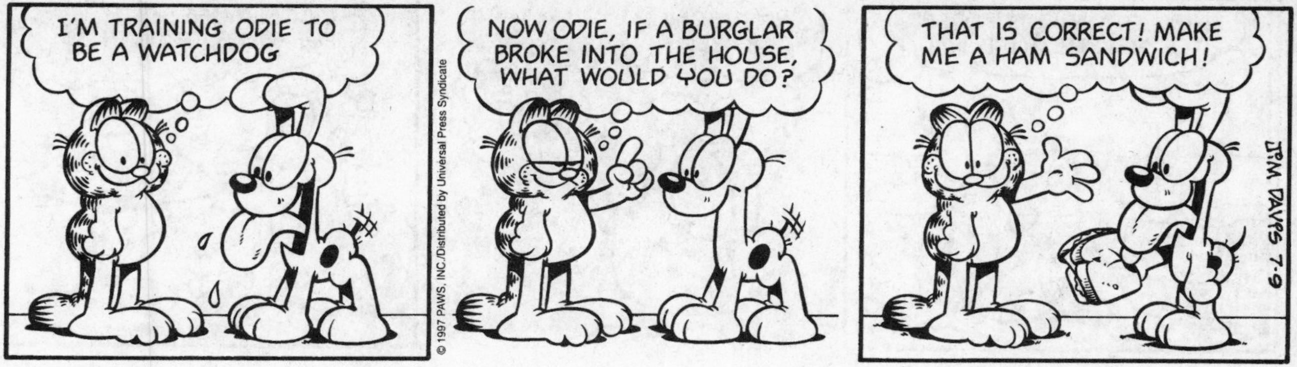
I'M TRAINING ODIE TO BE A WATCHDOG
NOW ODIE, IF A BURGLAR BROKE INTO THE HOUSE, WHAT WOULD YOU DO?
THAT IS CORRECT! MAKE ME A HAM SANDWICH!
JIM DAVIS 7-9
© 1997 PAWS, INC./Distributed by Universal Press Syndicate

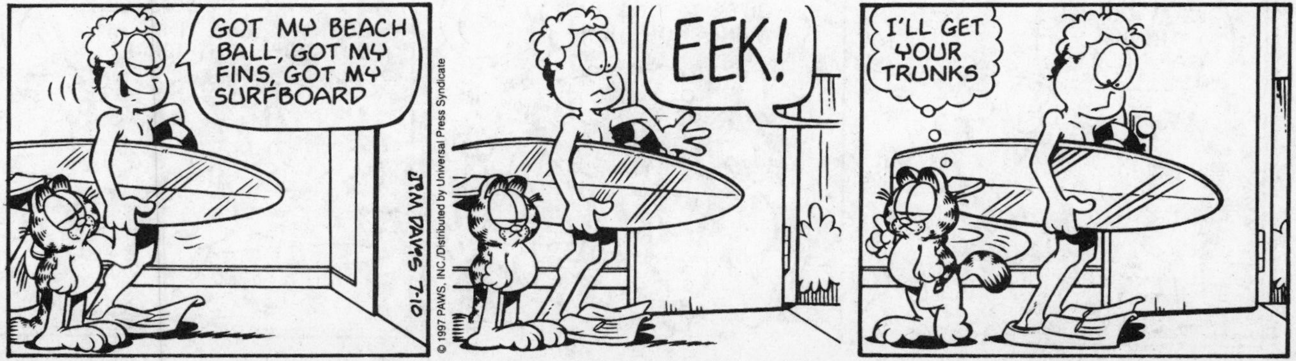
GOT MY BEACH BALL, GOT MY FINS, GOT MY SURFBOARD
EEK!
I'LL GET YOUR TRUNKS
JIM DAVIS 7-10
© 1997 PAWS, INC./Distributed by Universal Press Syndicate

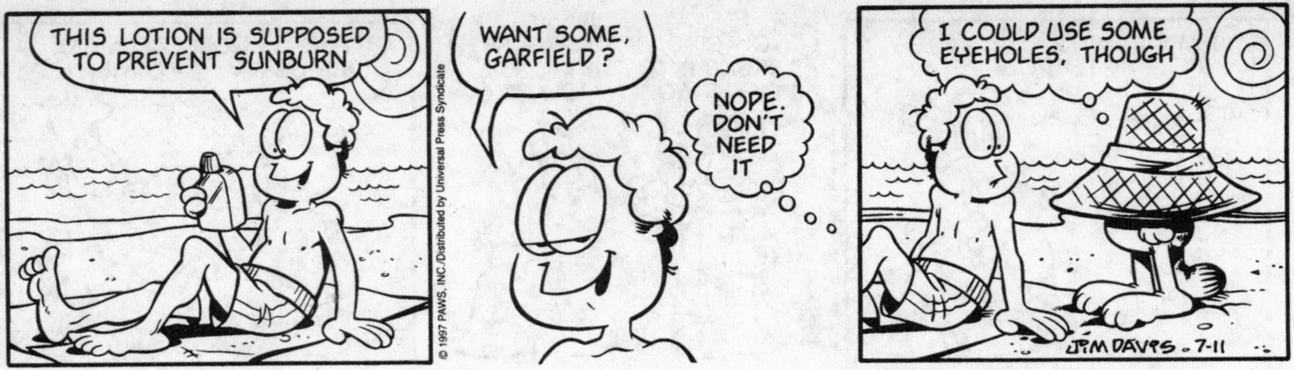
THIS LOTION IS SUPPOSED TO PREVENT SUNBURN
© 1997 PAWS, INC./Distributed by Universal Press Syndicate
WANT SOME, GARFIELD?
NOPE. DON'T NEED IT
I COULD USE SOME EYEHOLES, THOUGH
JIM DAVIS 7-11

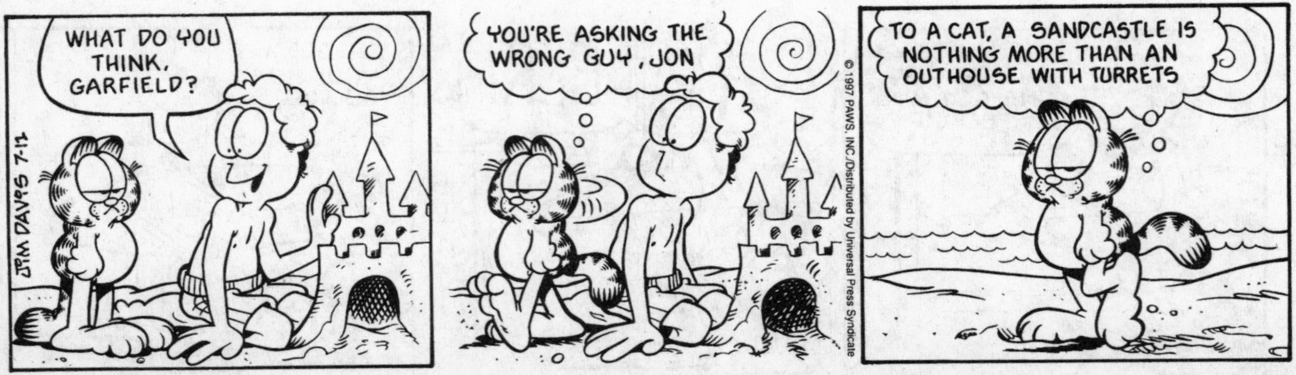
JIM DAVIS 7-12
WHAT DO YOU THINK, GARFIELD?
YOU'RE ASKING THE WRONG GUY, JON
© 1997 PAWS, INC./Distributed by Universal Press Syndicate
TO A CAT, A SANDCASTLE IS NOTHING MORE THAN AN OUTHOUSE WITH TURRETS

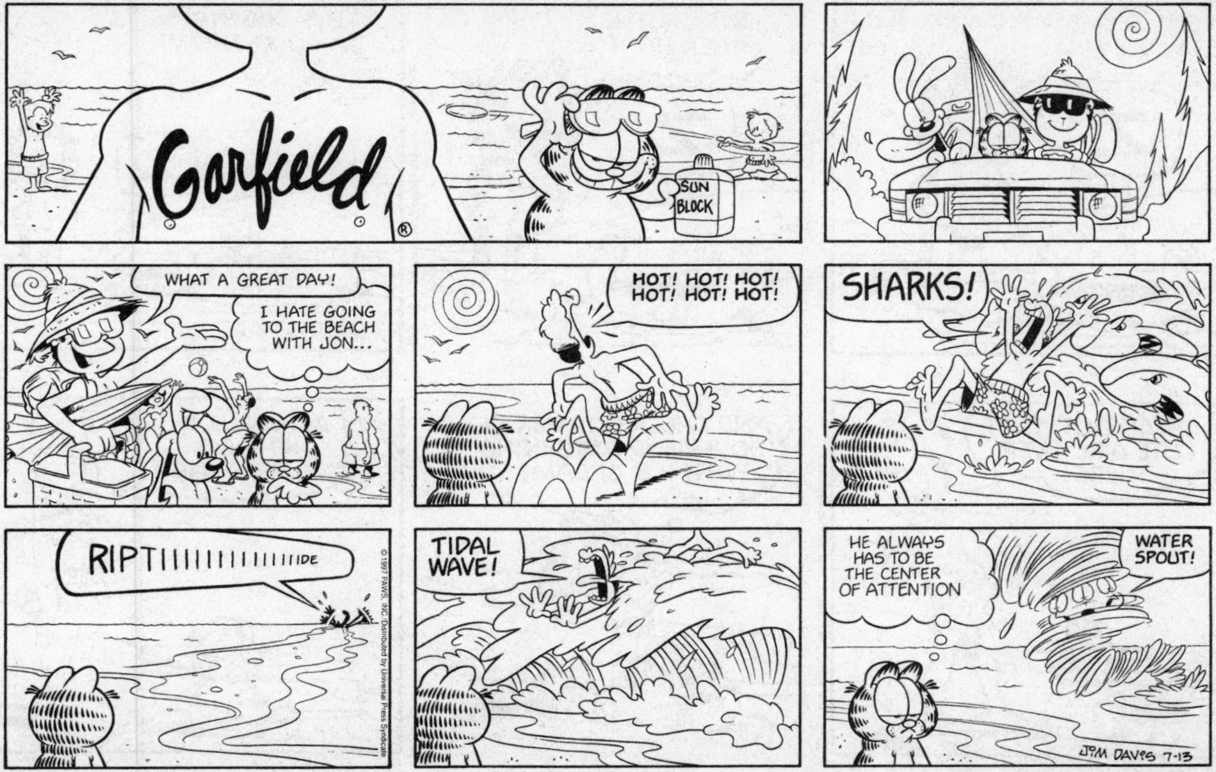
Garfield
SUN BLOCK
WHAT A GREAT DAY!
I HATE GOING TO THE BEACH WITH JON...
HOT! HOT! HOT! HOT! HOT! HOT!
SHARKS!
RIPTIIIIIIIIIIIIIIIIIDE
© 1997 PAWS, INC./Distributed by Universal Press Syndicate
TIDAL WAVE!
HE ALWAYS HAS TO BE THE CENTER OF ATTENTION
WATER SPOUT!
JIM DAVIS 7-13

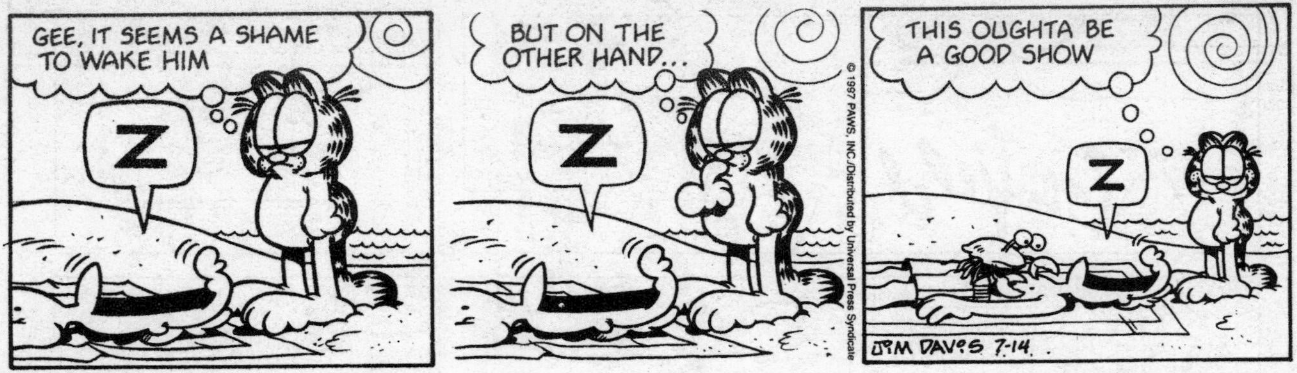
GEE, IT SEEMS A SHAME TO WAKE HIM
Z
BUT ON THE OTHER HAND...
Z
© 1997 PAWS, INC./Distributed by Universal Press Syndicate
THIS OUGHTA BE A GOOD SHOW
Z
JIM DAVIS 7-14

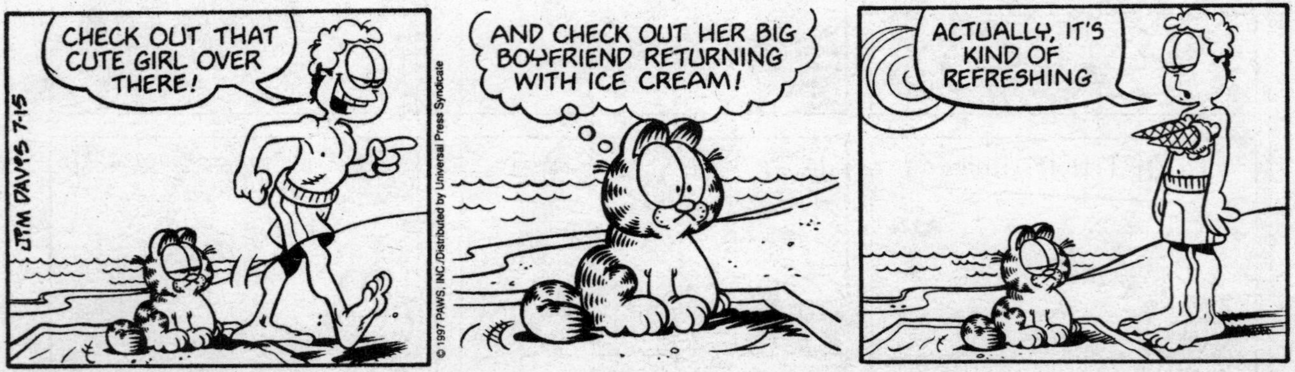
CHECK OUT THAT CUTE GIRL OVER THERE!
JIM DAVIS 7-15
© 1997 PAWS, INC./Distributed by Universal Press Syndicate
AND CHECK OUT HER BIG BOYFRIEND RETURNING WITH ICE CREAM!
ACTUALLY, IT'S KIND OF REFRESHING

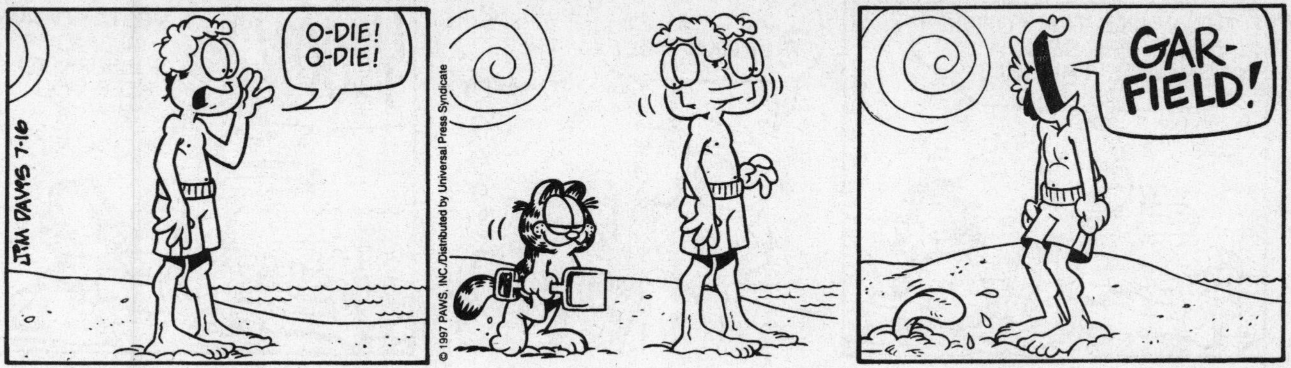
JIM DAVIS 7-16
O-DIE! O-DIE!
© 1997 PAWS, INC./Distributed by Universal Press Syndicate
GAR-FIELD!

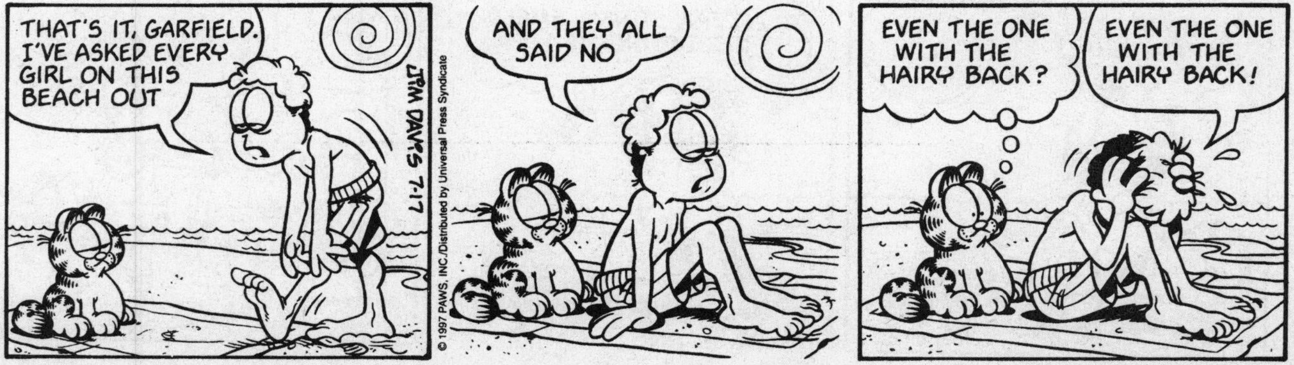
THAT'S IT, GARFIELD. I'VE ASKED EVERY GIRL ON THIS BEACH OUT
JIM DAVIS 7-17
© 1997 PAWS, INC./Distributed by Universal Press Syndicate
AND THEY ALL SAID NO
EVEN THE ONE WITH THE HAIRY BACK?
EVEN THE ONE WITH THE HAIRY BACK!

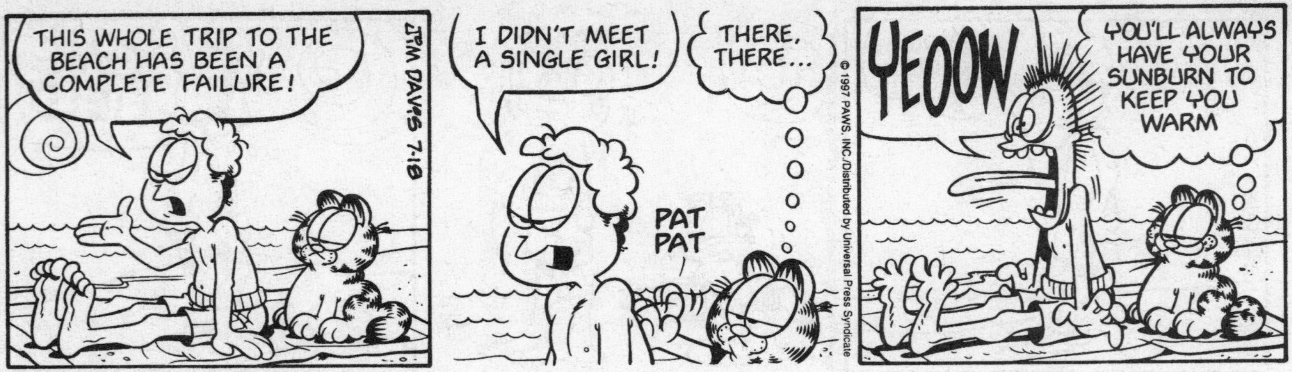
JIM DAVIS 7-18
THIS WHOLE TRIP TO THE BEACH HAS BEEN A COMPLETE FAILURE!
I DIDN'T MEET A SINGLE GIRL!
THERE, THERE...
PAT PAT
YEOOW
YOU'LL ALWAYS HAVE YOUR SUNBURN TO KEEP YOU WARM

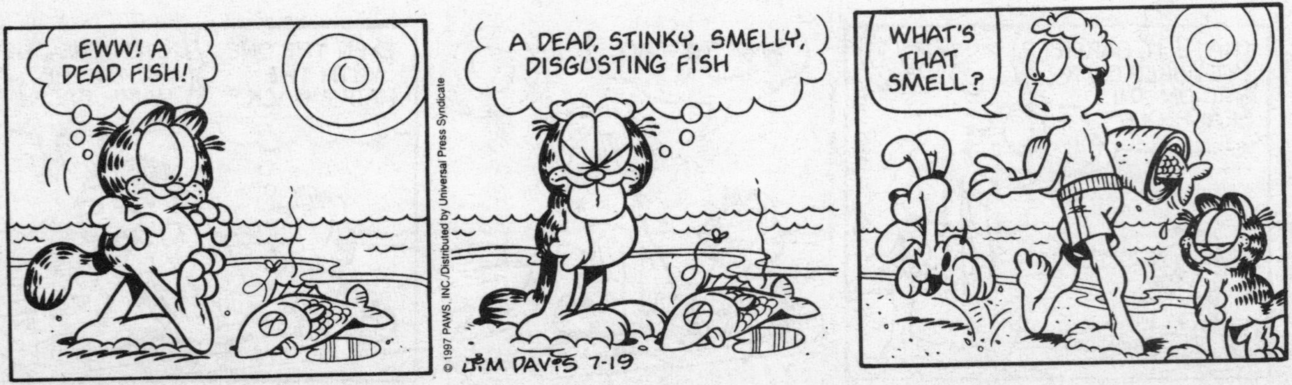
EWW! A DEAD FISH!
A DEAD, STINKY, SMELLY, DISGUSTING FISH
JIM DAVIS 7-19
WHAT'S THAT SMELL?

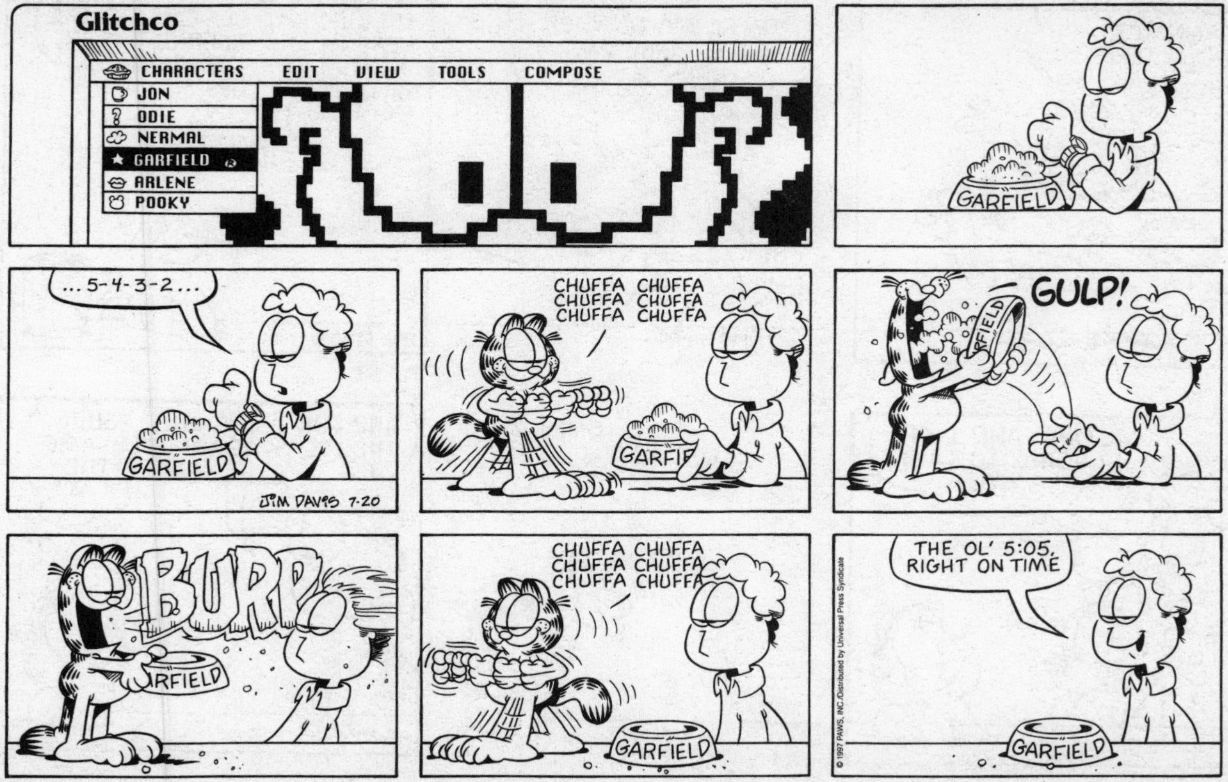
Glitchco
CHARACTERS
EDIT
VIEW
TOOLS
COMPOSE
JON
ODIE
NERMAL
GARFIELD
ARLENE
POOKY
GARFIELD
...5-4-3-2...
GARFIELD
JIM DAVIS 7-20
CHUFFA CHUFFA
CHUFFA CHUFFA
CHUFFA CHUFFA
GARFI
GULP!
RFIELD
BURP
RFIELD
CHUFFA CHUFFA
CHUFFA CHUFFA
CHUFFA CHUFFA
GARFIELD
THE OL' 5:05, RIGHT ON TIME
GARFIELD
© 1997 PAWS, INC./Distributed by Universal Press Syndicate

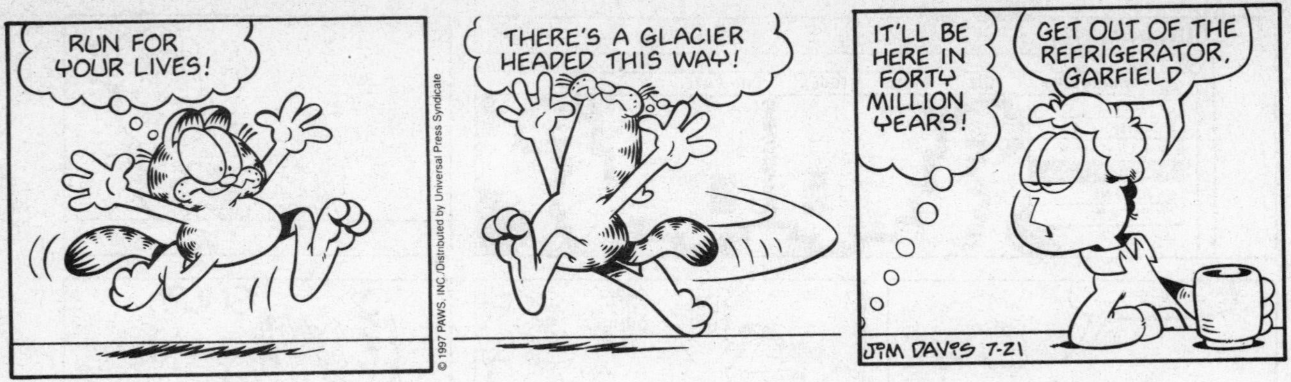

RUN FOR YOUR LIVES!
THERE'S A GLACIER HEADED THIS WAY!
IT'LL BE HERE IN FORTY MILLION YEARS!
GET OUT OF THE REFRIGERATOR, GARFIELD
JIM DAVIS 7-21
© 1997 PAWS, INC./Distributed by Universal Press Syndicate

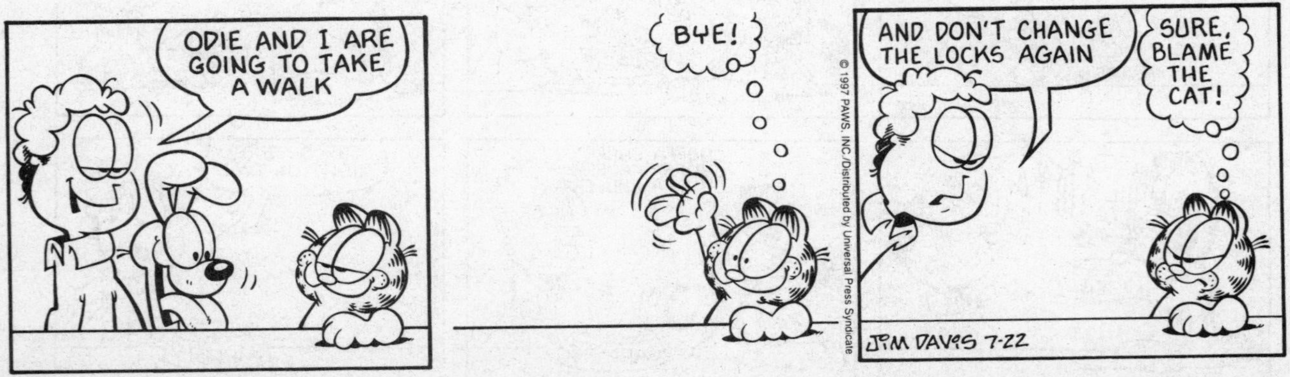

ODIE AND I ARE GOING TO TAKE A WALK
BYE!
AND DON'T CHANGE THE LOCKS AGAIN
SURE, BLAME THE CAT!
JIM DAVIS 7-22
© 1997 PAWS, INC./Distributed by Universal Press Syndicate

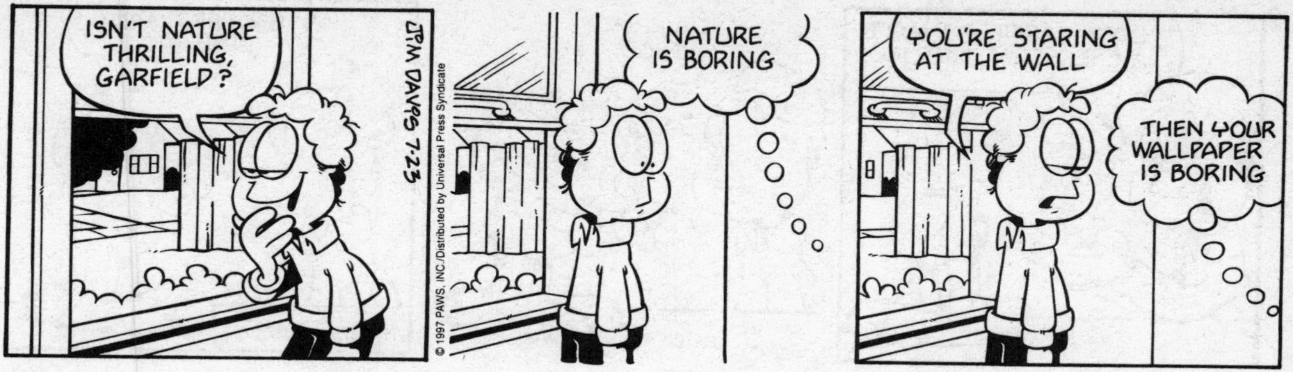
ISN'T NATURE THRILLING, GARFIELD?
JIM DAVIS 7-23
© 1997 PAWS, INC./Distributed by Universal Press Syndicate
NATURE IS BORING
YOU'RE STARING AT THE WALL
THEN YOUR WALLPAPER IS BORING

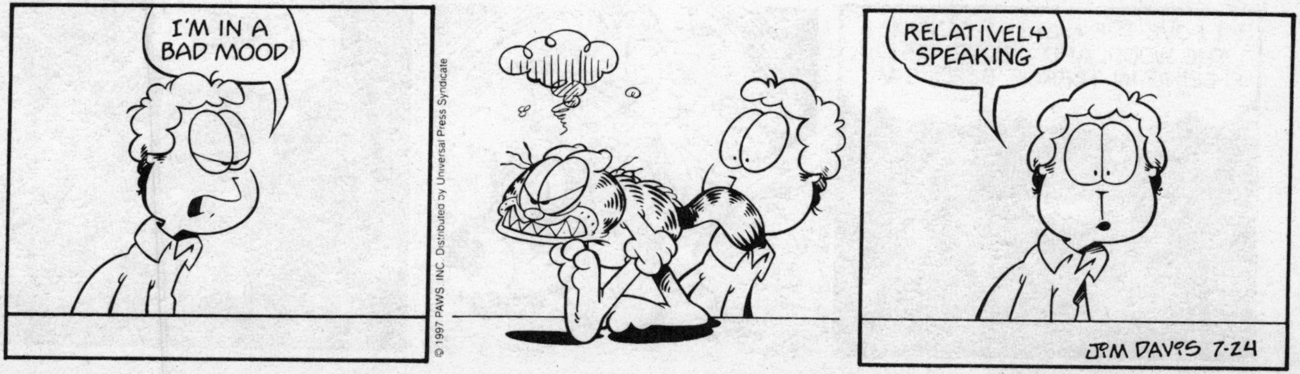
I'M IN A BAD MOOD
© 1997 PAWS, INC. Distributed by Universal Press Syndicate
RELATIVELY SPEAKING
JIM DAVIS 7-24

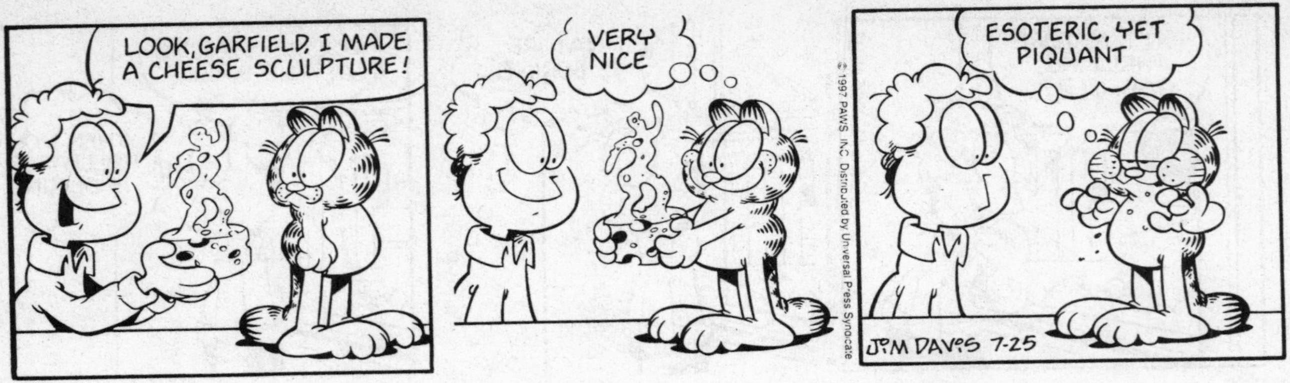
LOOK, GARFIELD, I MADE A CHEESE SCULPTURE!
VERY NICE
© 1997 PAWS, INC. Distributed by Universal Press Syndicate
ESOTERIC, YET PIQUANT
JIM DAVIS 7-25

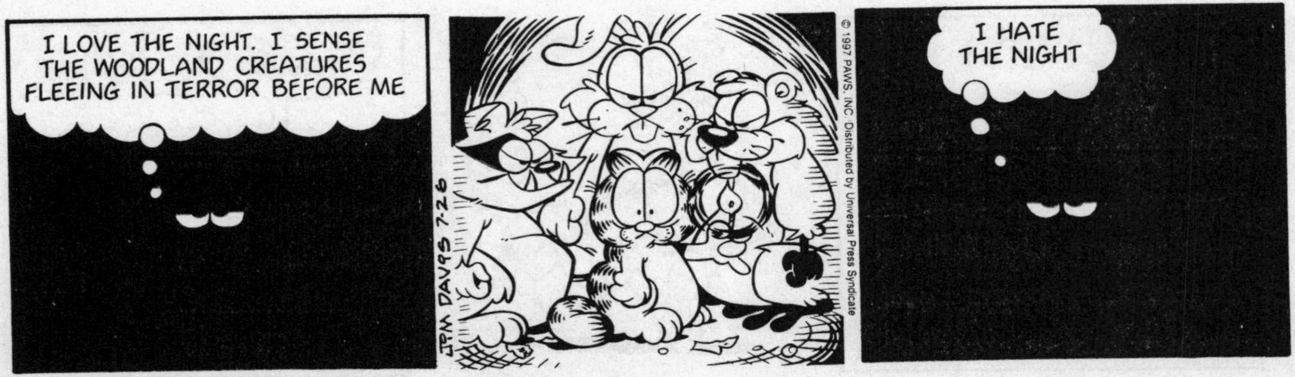
I LOVE THE NIGHT. I SENSE THE WOODLAND CREATURES FLEEING IN TERROR BEFORE ME
JIM DAVIS 7-26
© 1997 PAWS, INC. Distributed by Universal Press Syndicate
I HATE THE NIGHT

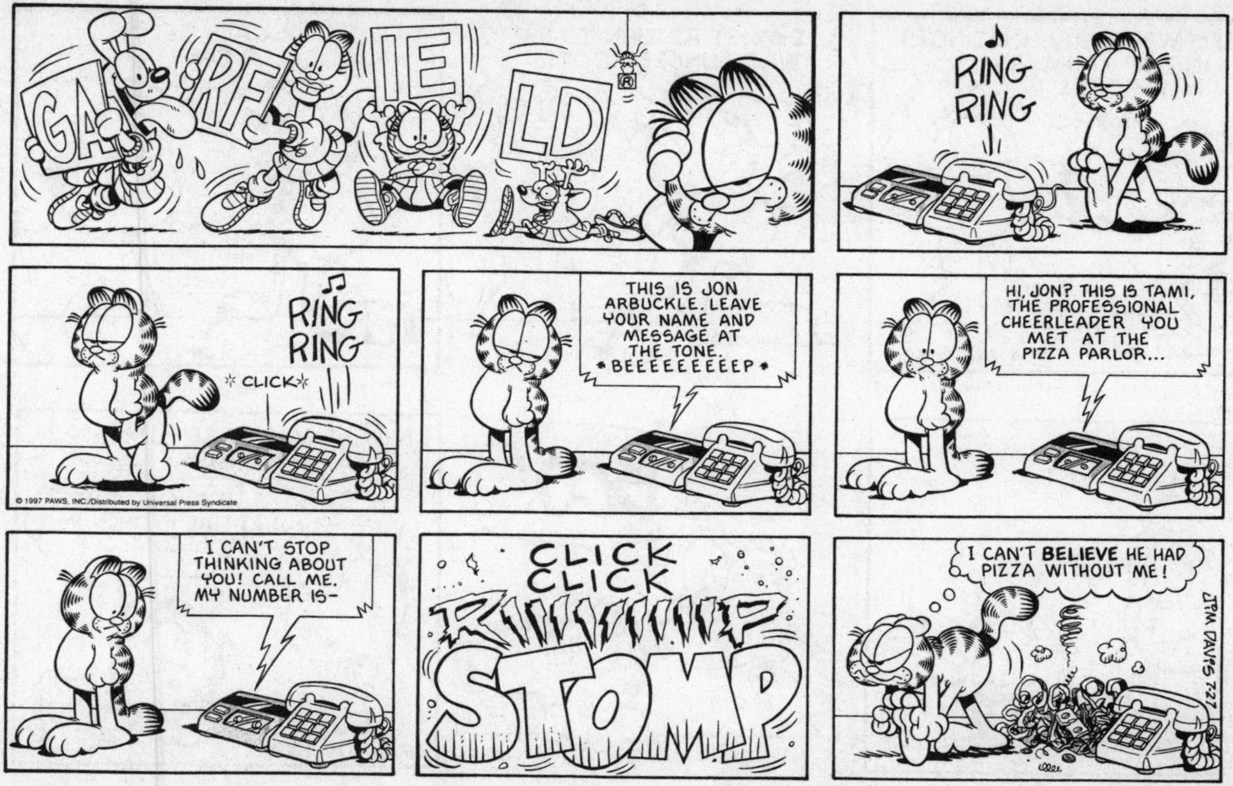
GA
RF
IE
LD
RING
RING
RING
RING
* CLICK *
© 1997 PAWS, INC./Distributed by Universal Press Syndicate
THIS IS JON ARBUCKLE. LEAVE YOUR NAME AND MESSAGE AT THE TONE. *BEEEEEEEEEP*
HI, JON? THIS IS TAMI, THE PROFESSIONAL CHEERLEADER YOU MET AT THE PIZZA PARLOR...
I CAN'T STOP THINKING ABOUT YOU! CALL ME. MY NUMBER IS–
CLICK
CLICK
RIIIIIIIP
STOMP
I CAN'T **BELIEVE** HE HAD PIZZA WITHOUT ME!
JPM DAVIS 7-27

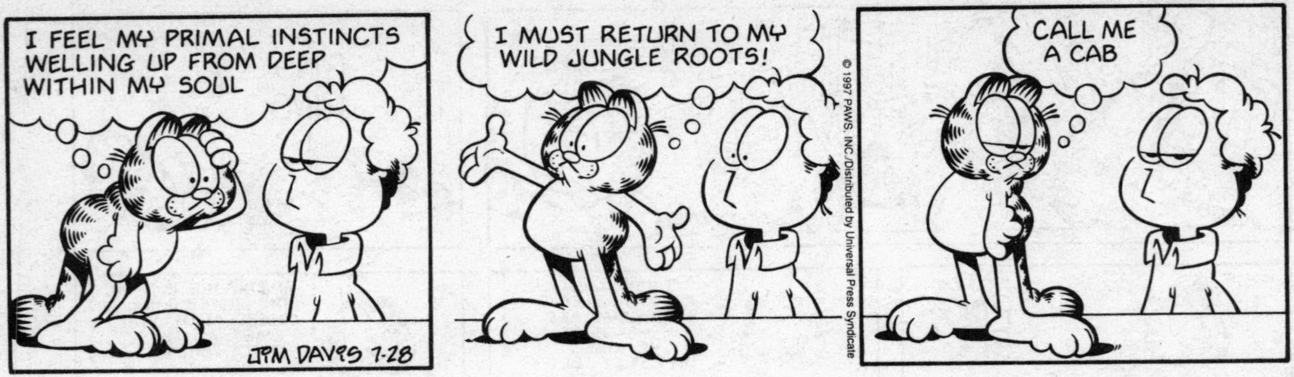
I FEEL MY PRIMAL INSTINCTS WELLING UP FROM DEEP WITHIN MY SOUL
JIM DAVIS 7-28
I MUST RETURN TO MY WILD JUNGLE ROOTS!
© 1997 PAWS, INC./Distributed by Universal Press Syndicate
CALL ME A CAB

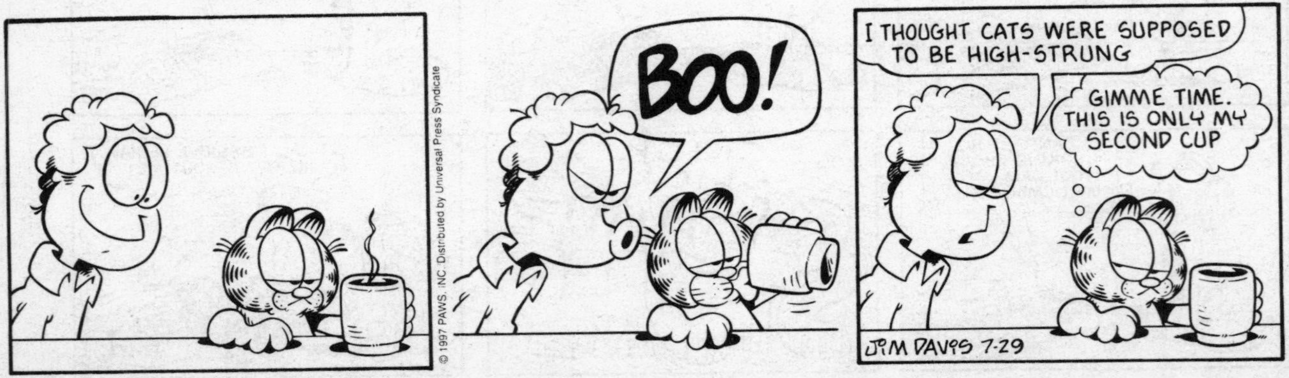
© 1997 PAWS, INC./Distributed by Universal Press Syndicate
BOO!
I THOUGHT CATS WERE SUPPOSED TO BE HIGH-STRUNG
GIMME TIME. THIS IS ONLY MY SECOND CUP
JIM DAVIS 7-29

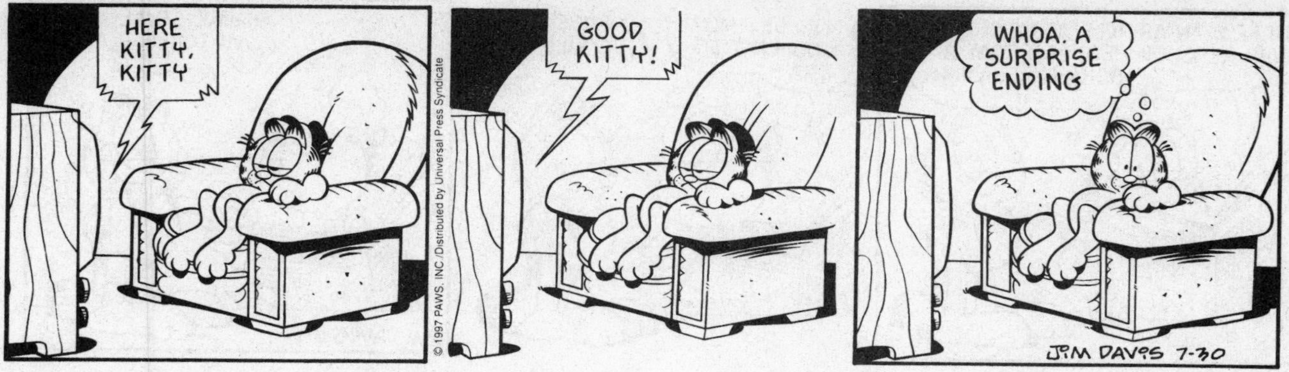
HERE KITTY, KITTY
GOOD KITTY!
WHOA. A SURPRISE ENDING
JIM DAVIS 7-30
© 1997 PAWS, INC./Distributed by Universal Press Syndicate

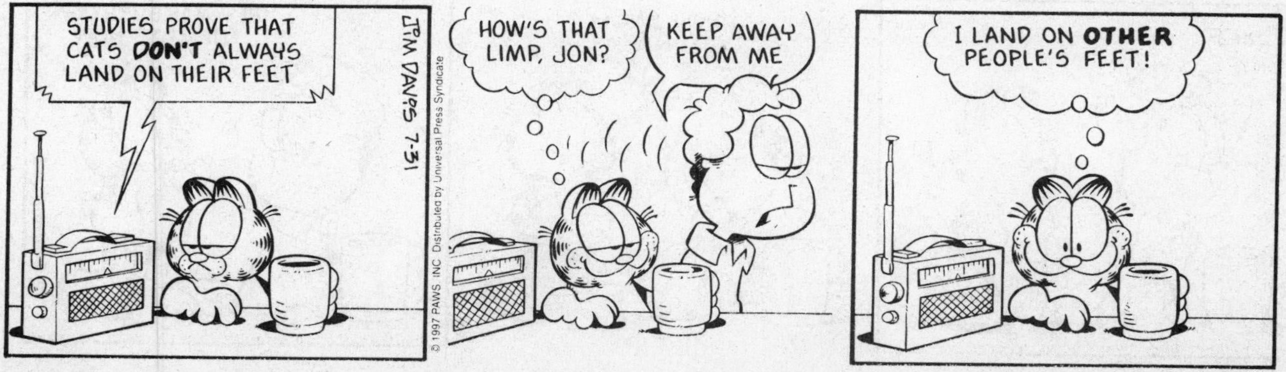
STUDIES PROVE THAT CATS **DON'T** ALWAYS LAND ON THEIR FEET
JIM DAVIS 7-31
© 1997 PAWS, INC. Distributed by Universal Press Syndicate
HOW'S THAT LIMP, JON?
KEEP AWAY FROM ME
I LAND ON **OTHER** PEOPLE'S FEET!

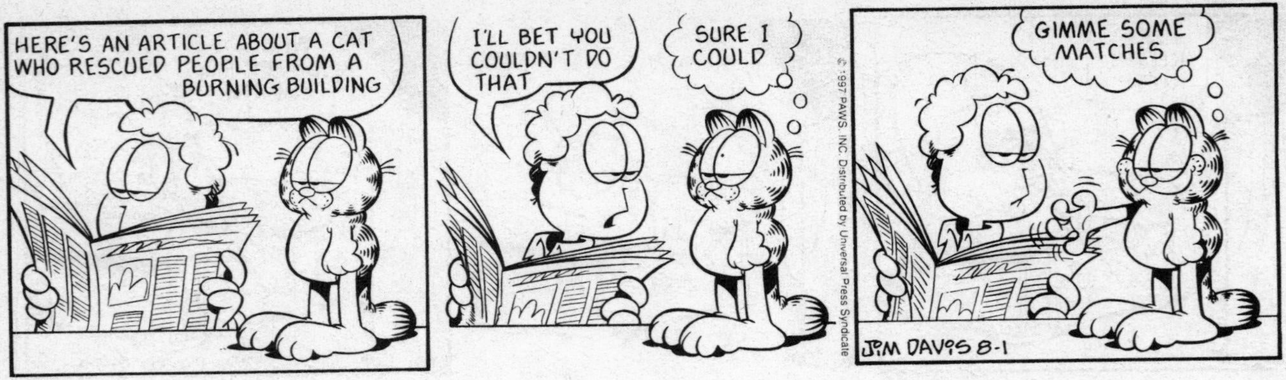
HERE'S AN ARTICLE ABOUT A CAT WHO RESCUED PEOPLE FROM A BURNING BUILDING
I'LL BET YOU COULDN'T DO THAT
SURE I COULD
GIMME SOME MATCHES
JIM DAVIS 8-1
© 1997 PAWS, INC. Distributed by Universal Press Syndicate

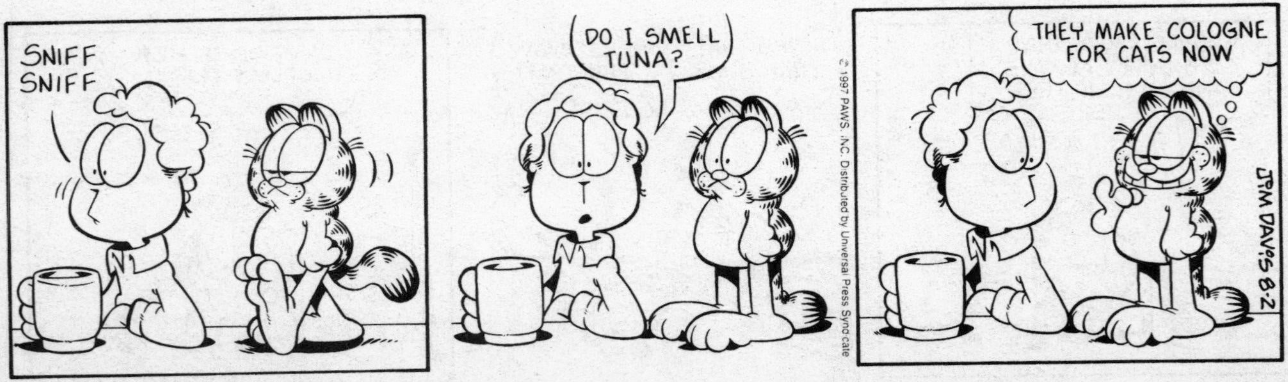
SNIFF SNIFF
DO I SMELL TUNA?
THEY MAKE COLOGNE FOR CATS NOW
JIM DAVIS 8-2
© 1997 PAWS, INC. Distributed by Universal Press Syndicate

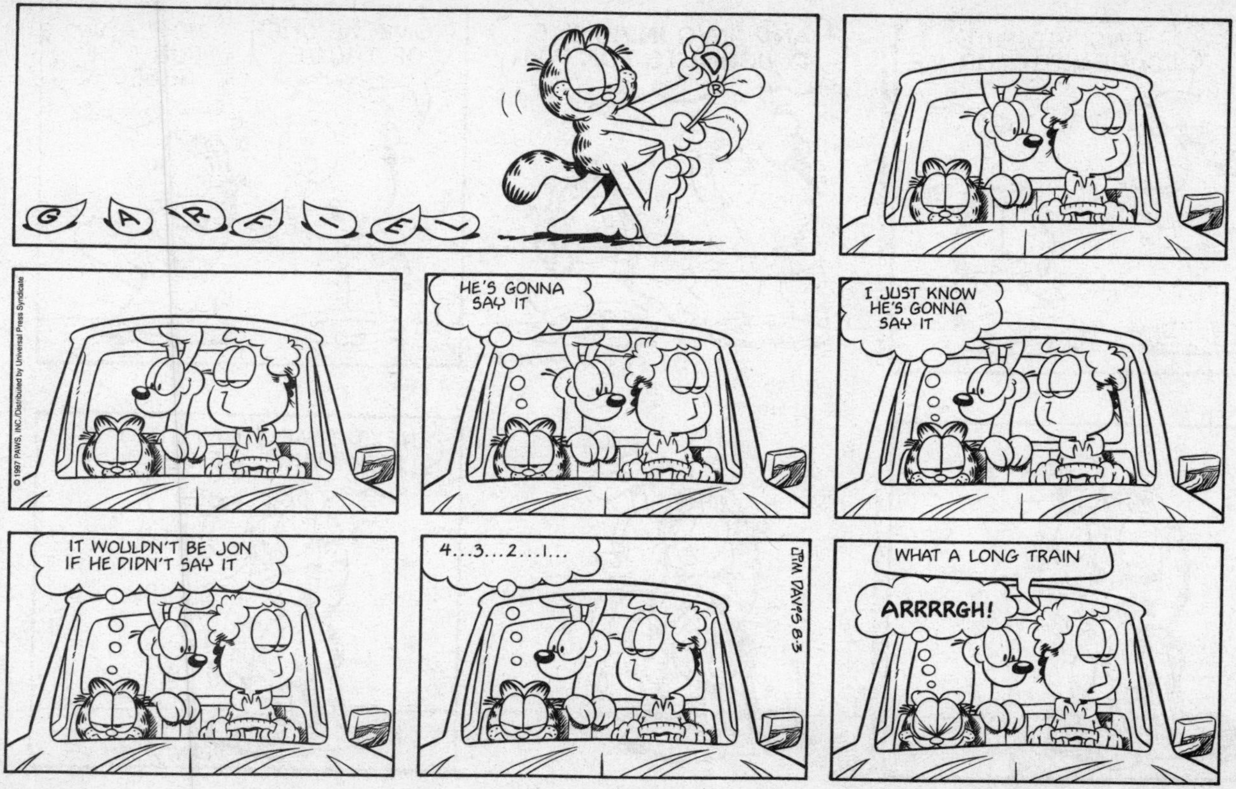

G A R F I E L D
HE'S GONNA SAY IT
I JUST KNOW HE'S GONNA SAY IT
IT WOULDN'T BE JON IF HE DIDN'T SAY IT
4...3...2...1...
WHAT A LONG TRAIN
ARRRRGH!
JIM DAVIS 8-3
© 1997 PAWS, INC./Distributed by Universal Press Syndicate

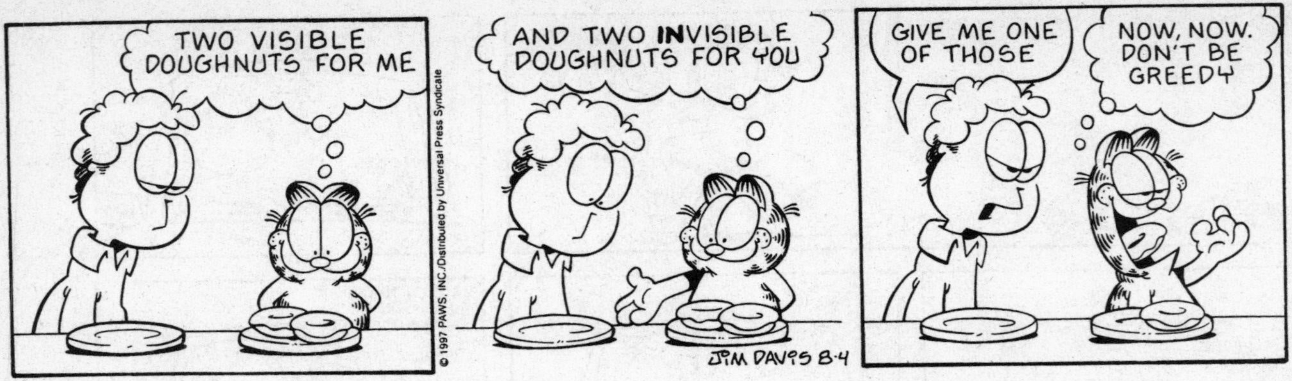
TWO VISIBLE DOUGHNUTS FOR ME
AND TWO INVISIBLE DOUGHNUTS FOR YOU
GIVE ME ONE OF THOSE
NOW, NOW. DON'T BE GREEDY
JIM DAVIS 8-4

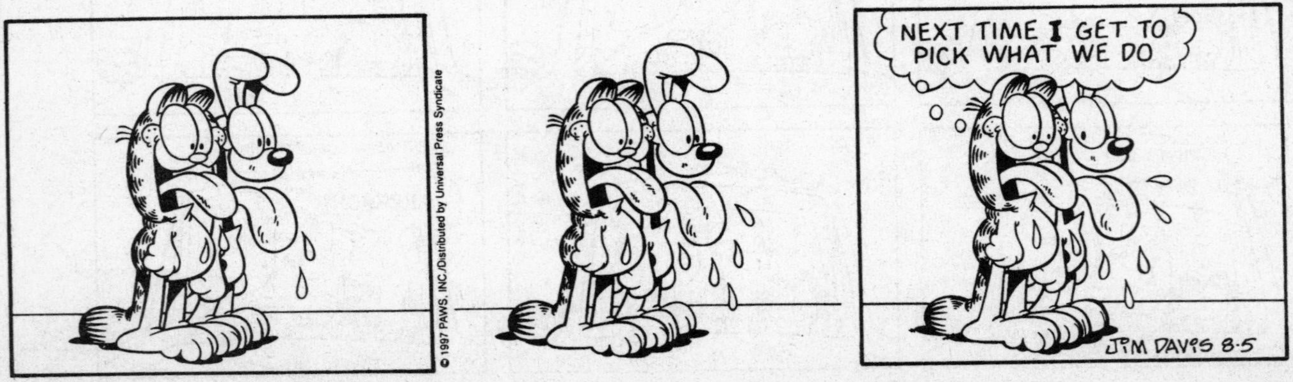
NEXT TIME I GET TO PICK WHAT WE DO
JIM DAVIS 8-5

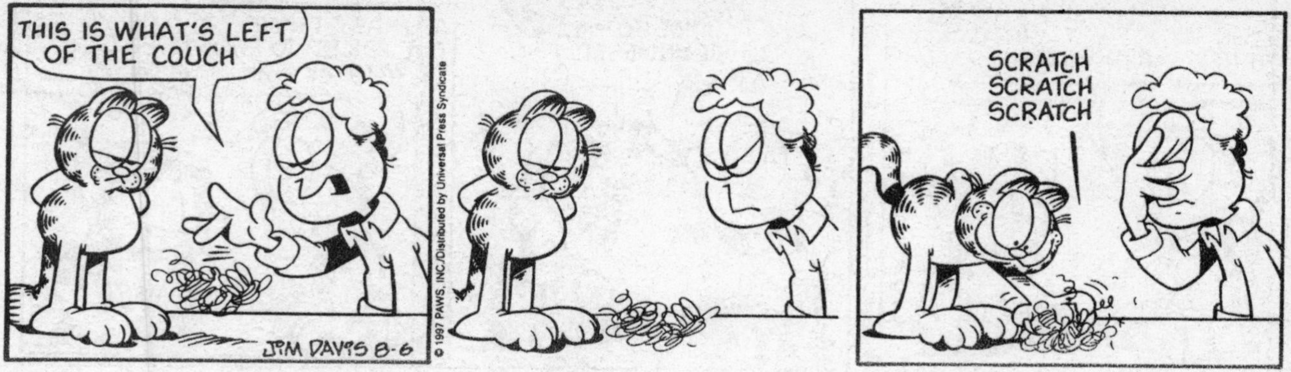
THIS IS WHAT'S LEFT OF THE COUCH
JIM DAVIS 8-6
© 1997 PAWS, INC./Distributed by Universal Press Syndicate
SCRATCH SCRATCH SCRATCH

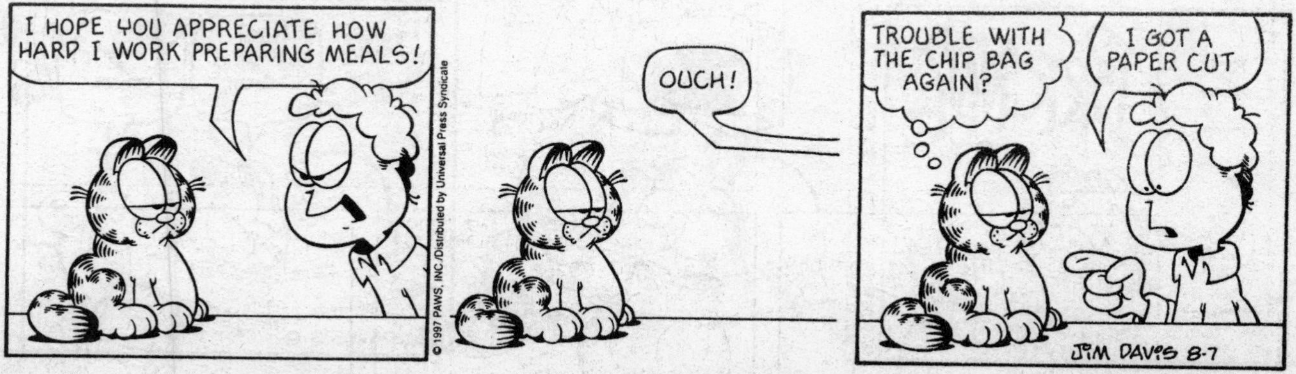
I HOPE YOU APPRECIATE HOW HARD I WORK PREPARING MEALS!
© 1997 PAWS, INC./Distributed by Universal Press Syndicate
OUCH!
TROUBLE WITH THE CHIP BAG AGAIN?
I GOT A PAPER CUT
JIM DAVIS 8-7

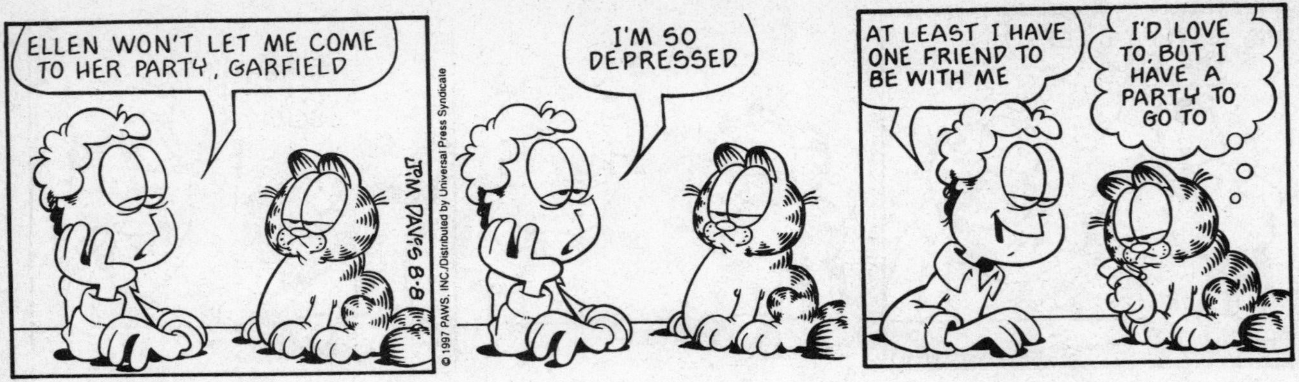
ELLEN WON'T LET ME COME TO HER PARTY, GARFIELD
JIM DAVIS 8-8
© 1997 PAWS, INC./Distributed by Universal Press Syndicate
I'M SO DEPRESSED
AT LEAST I HAVE ONE FRIEND TO BE WITH ME
I'D LOVE TO, BUT I HAVE A PARTY TO GO TO

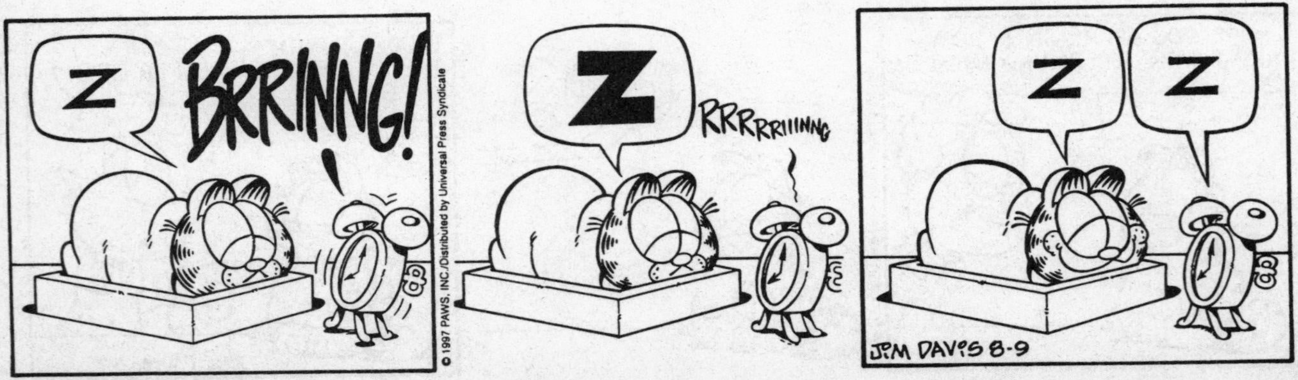
Z
BRRINNG!
© 1997 PAWS, INC./Distributed by Universal Press Syndicate
Z
RRRRRIIINNG
Z
Z
JIM DAVIS 8-9

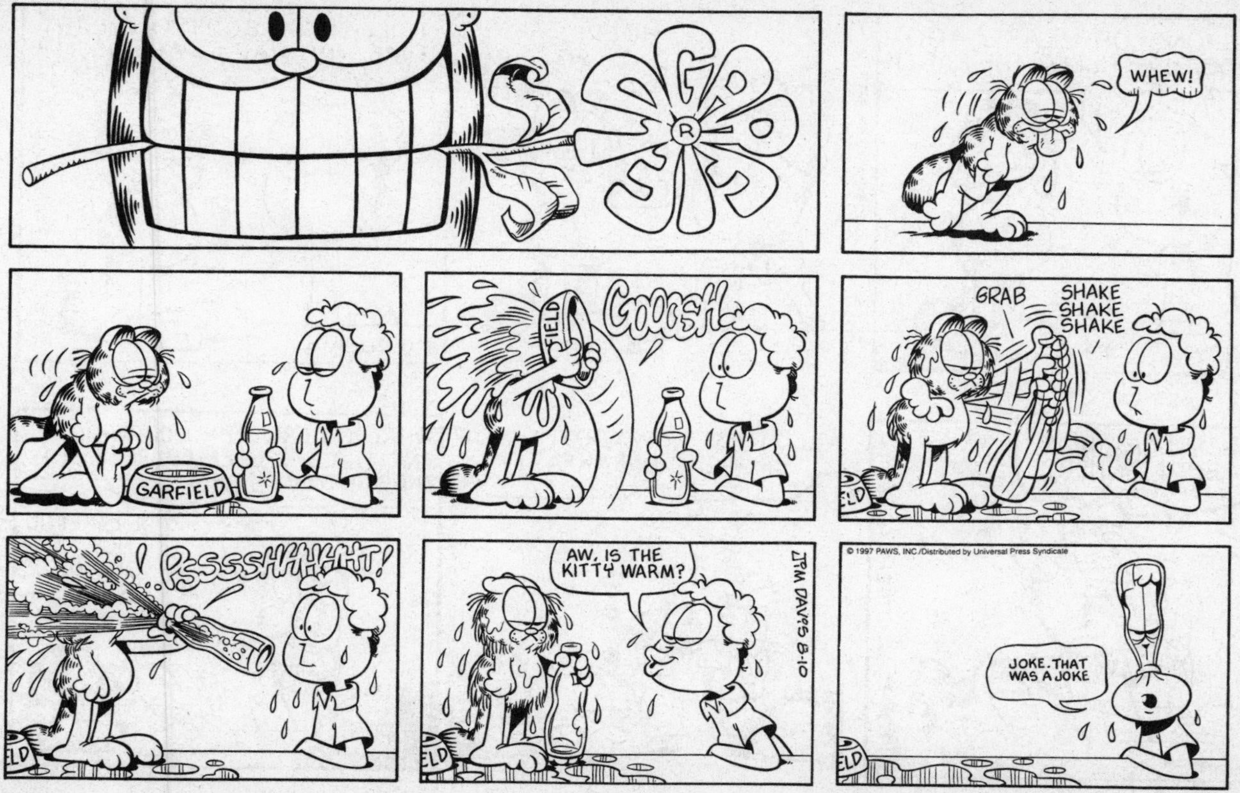

WHEW!
GAR
GOOOSH
GRAB
SHAKE SHAKE SHAKE
PSSSSHHHHHT!
AW, IS THE KITTY WARM?
JIM DAVIS 8-10
© 1997 PAWS, INC./Distributed by Universal Press Syndicate
JOKE. THAT WAS A JOKE

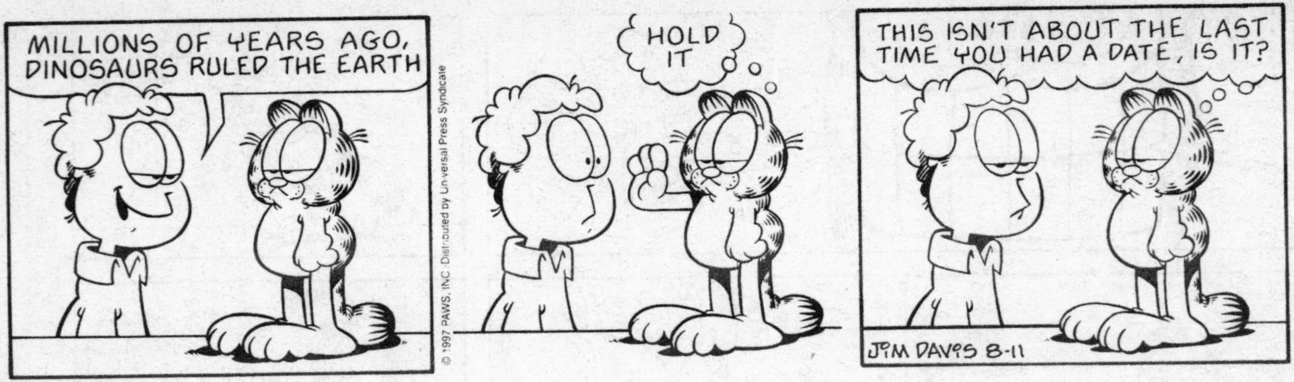
MILLIONS OF YEARS AGO, DINOSAURS RULED THE EARTH
HOLD IT
THIS ISN'T ABOUT THE LAST TIME YOU HAD A DATE, IS IT?
JIM DAVIS 8-11
© 1997 PAWS, INC./Distributed by Universal Press Syndicate

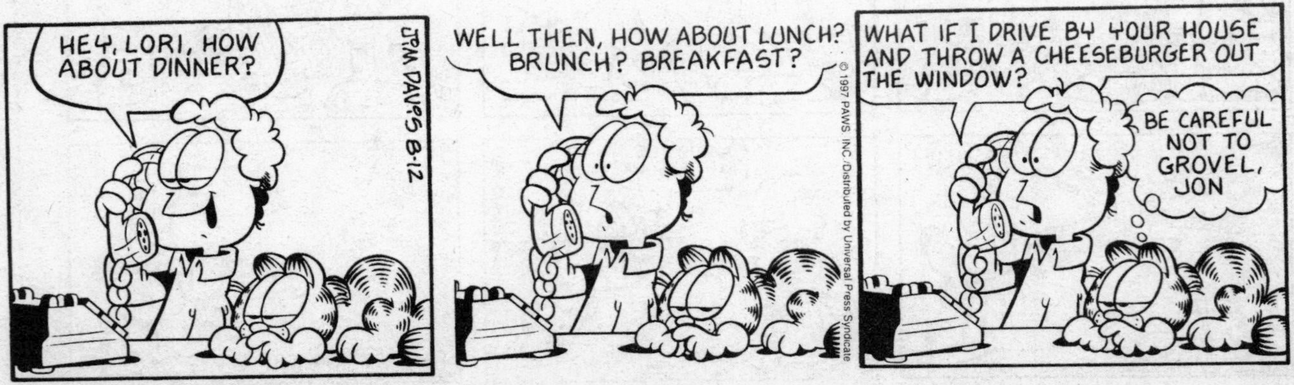
HEY, LORI, HOW ABOUT DINNER?
WELL THEN, HOW ABOUT LUNCH? BRUNCH? BREAKFAST?
WHAT IF I DRIVE BY YOUR HOUSE AND THROW A CHEESEBURGER OUT THE WINDOW?
BE CAREFUL NOT TO GROVEL, JON
JIM DAVIS 8-12
© 1997 PAWS, INC./Distributed by Universal Press Syndicate

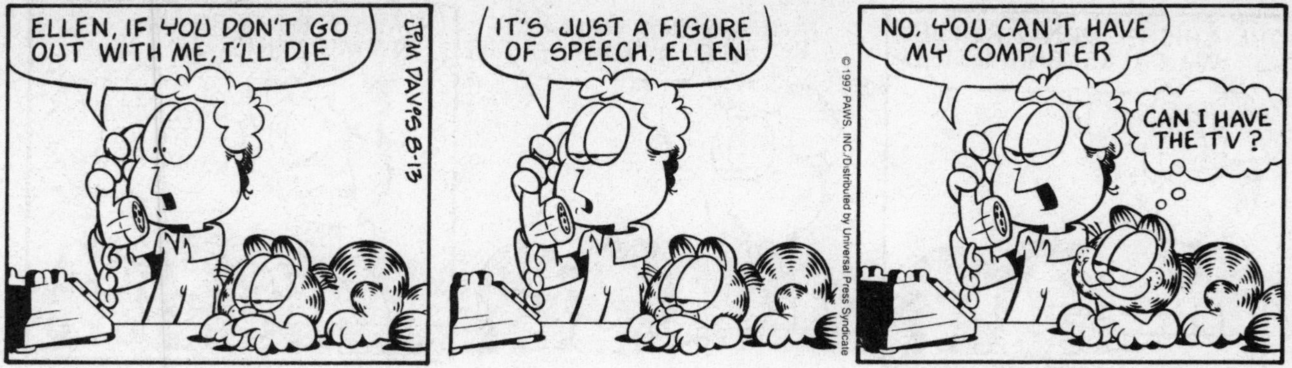
ELLEN, IF YOU DON'T GO OUT WITH ME, I'LL DIE
JIM DAVIS 8-13
IT'S JUST A FIGURE OF SPEECH, ELLEN
NO, YOU CAN'T HAVE MY COMPUTER
CAN I HAVE THE TV?

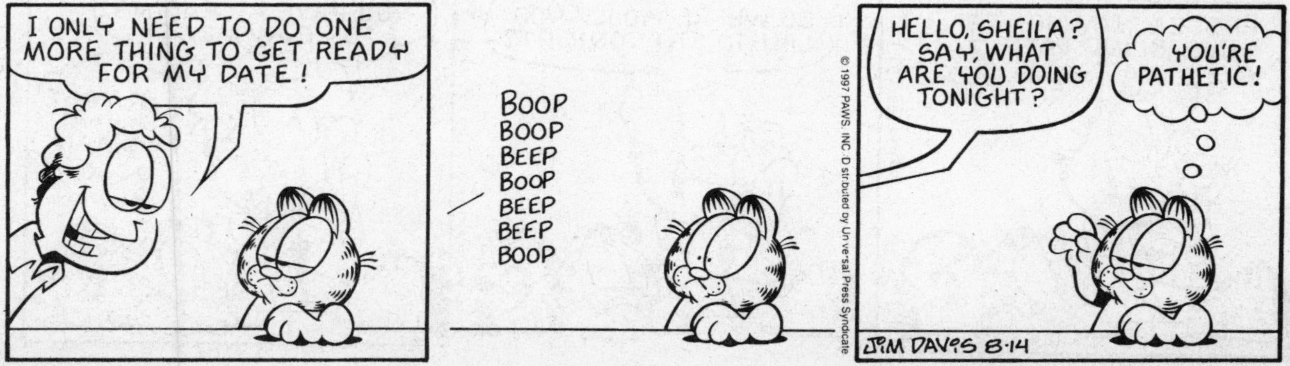
I ONLY NEED TO DO ONE MORE THING TO GET READY FOR MY DATE!
BOOP
BOOP
BEEP
BOOP
BEEP
BEEP
BOOP
HELLO, SHEILA? SAY, WHAT ARE YOU DOING TONIGHT?
YOU'RE PATHETIC!
JIM DAVIS 8-14

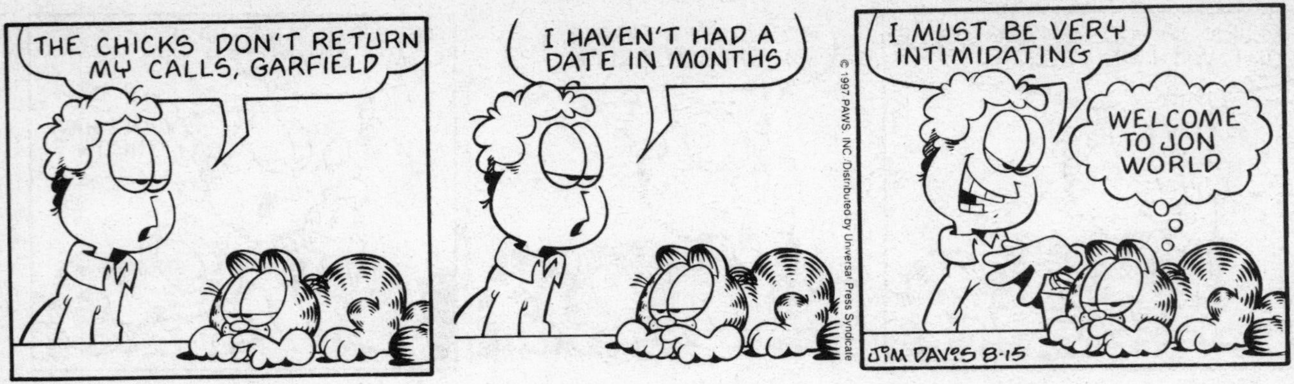
THE CHICKS DON'T RETURN MY CALLS, GARFIELD
I HAVEN'T HAD A DATE IN MONTHS
© 1997 PAWS, INC./Distributed by Universal Press Syndicate
I MUST BE VERY INTIMIDATING
WELCOME TO JON WORLD
JIM DAVIS 8-15

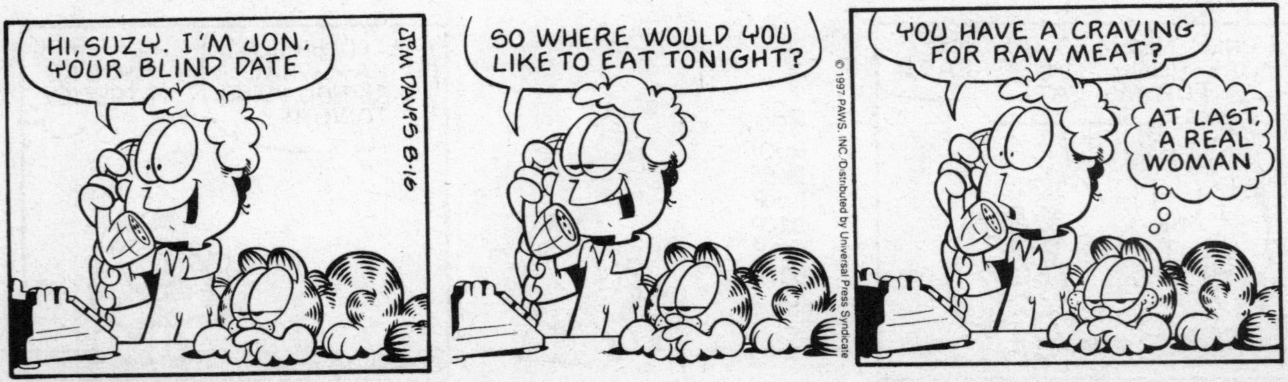
HI, SUZY. I'M JON, YOUR BLIND DATE
JIM DAVIS 8-16
SO WHERE WOULD YOU LIKE TO EAT TONIGHT?
© 1997 PAWS, INC./Distributed by Universal Press Syndicate
YOU HAVE A CRAVING FOR RAW MEAT?
AT LAST, A REAL WOMAN

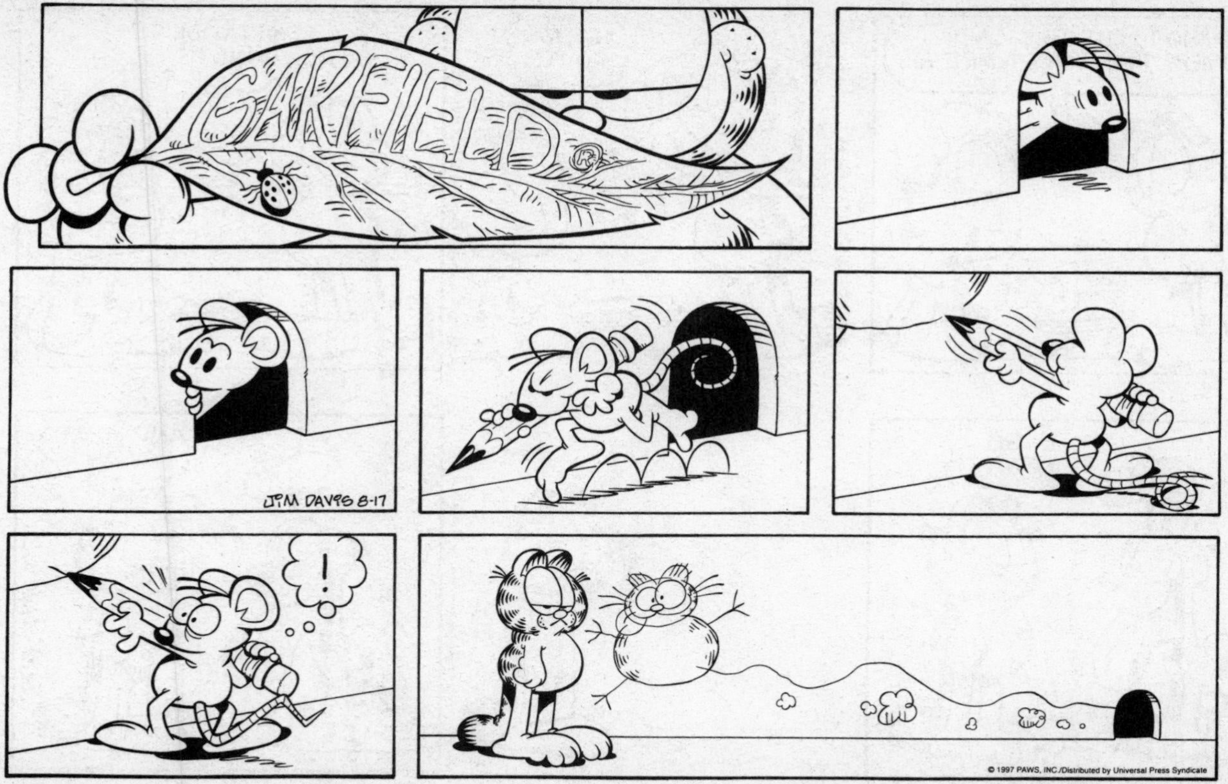
GARFIELD®
JIM DAVIS 8-17
!
© 1997 PAWS, INC./Distributed by Universal Press Syndicate

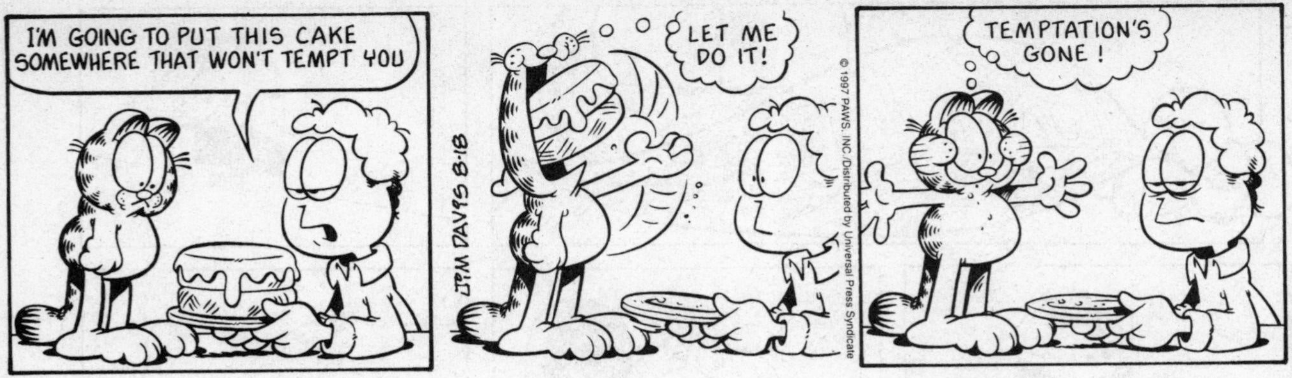
I'M GOING TO PUT THIS CAKE SOMEWHERE THAT WON'T TEMPT YOU
LET ME DO IT!
TEMPTATION'S GONE!

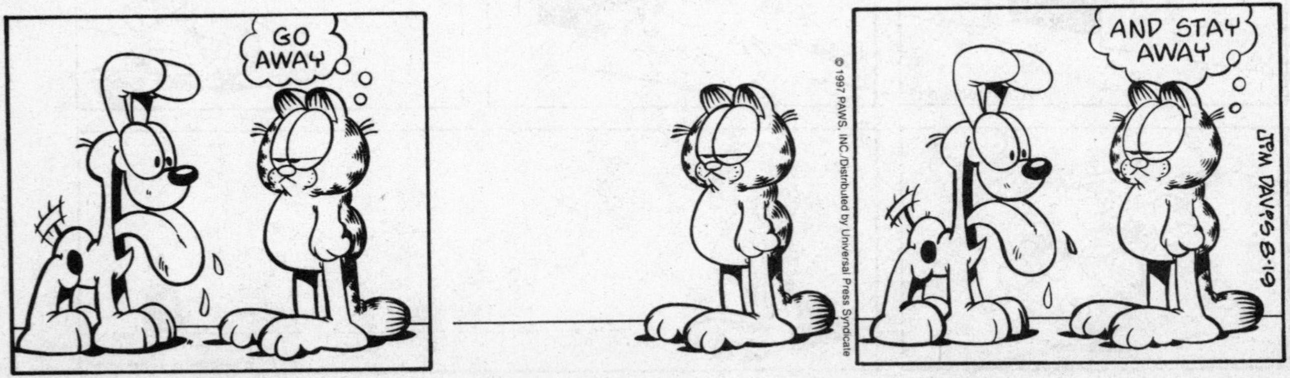
GO AWAY
AND STAY AWAY

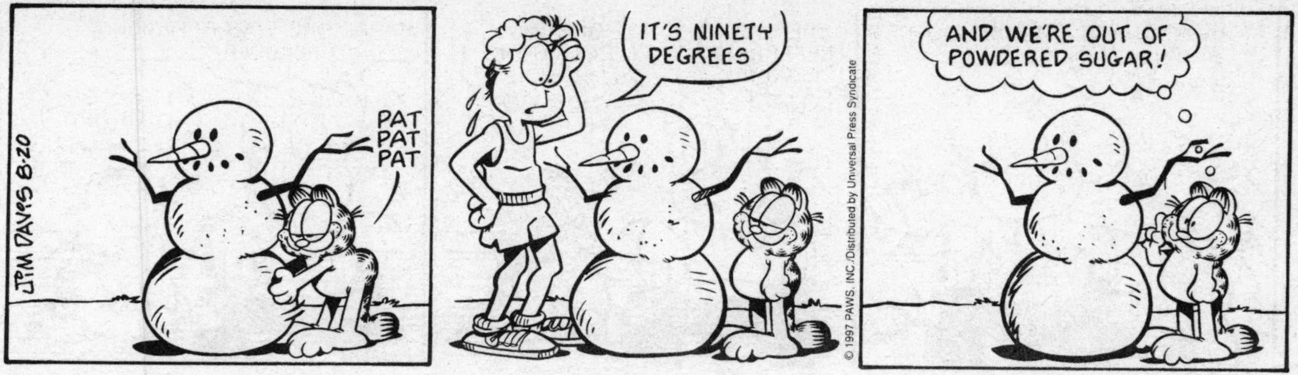
JIM DAVIS 8-20
PAT PAT PAT
IT'S NINETY DEGREES
AND WE'RE OUT OF POWDERED SUGAR!

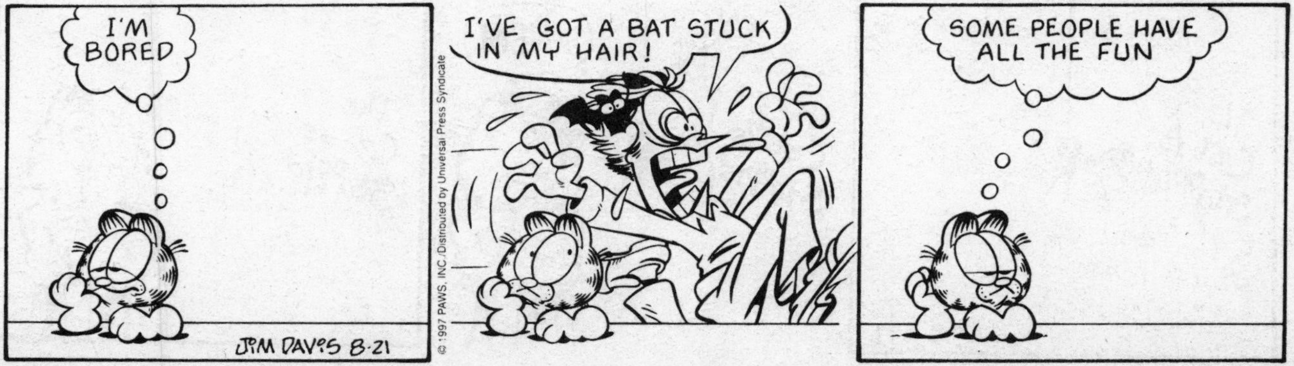
I'M BORED
JIM DAVIS 8-21
I'VE GOT A BAT STUCK IN MY HAIR!
SOME PEOPLE HAVE ALL THE FUN

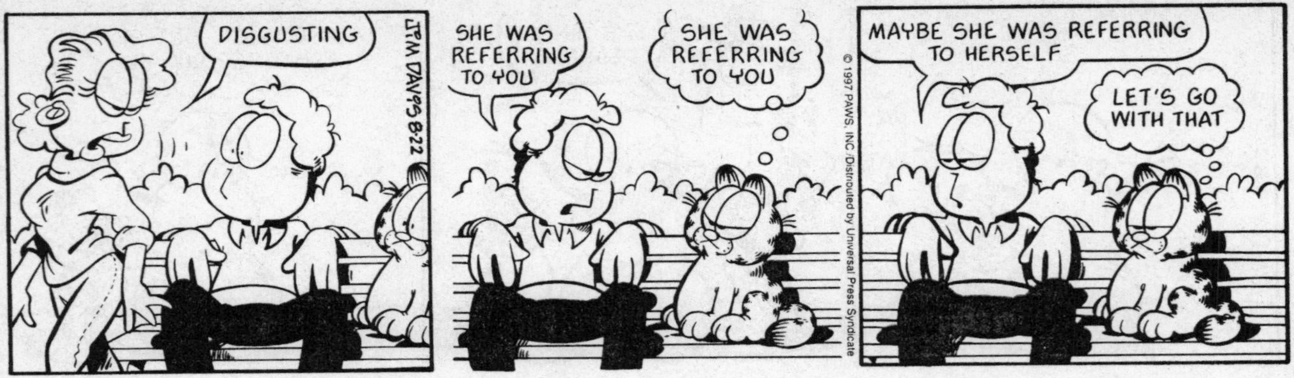
DISGUSTING
JIM DAVIS 8-22
SHE WAS REFERRING TO YOU
SHE WAS REFERRING TO YOU
© 1997 PAWS, INC./Distributed by Universal Press Syndicate
MAYBE SHE WAS REFERRING TO HERSELF
LET'S GO WITH THAT

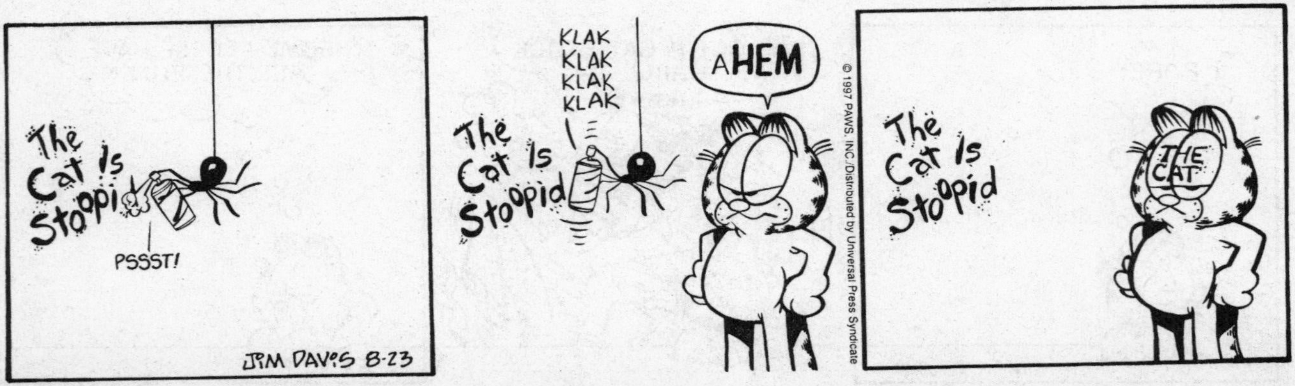
The Cat is Stoopi
PSSST!
JIM DAVIS 8-23
KLAK
KLAK
KLAK
KLAK
The Cat is Stoopid
AHEM
© 1997 PAWS, INC./Distributed by Universal Press Syndicate
The Cat is Stoopid
THE CAT

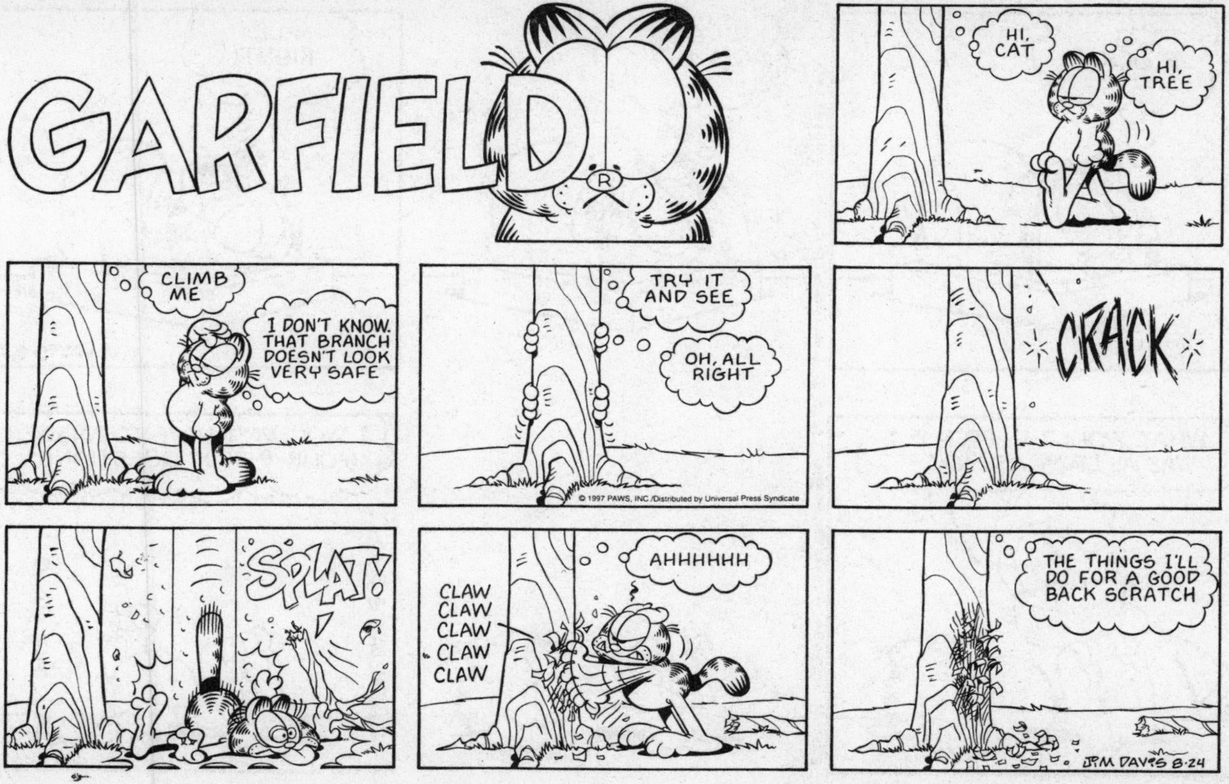
GARFIELD
HI, CAT
HI, TREE
CLIMB ME
I DON'T KNOW. THAT BRANCH DOESN'T LOOK VERY SAFE
TRY IT AND SEE
OH, ALL RIGHT
© 1997 PAWS, INC./Distributed by Universal Press Syndicate
CRACK
SPLAT!
CLAW CLAW CLAW CLAW CLAW
AHHHHHH
THE THINGS I'LL DO FOR A GOOD BACK SCRATCH
JIM DAVIS 8-24

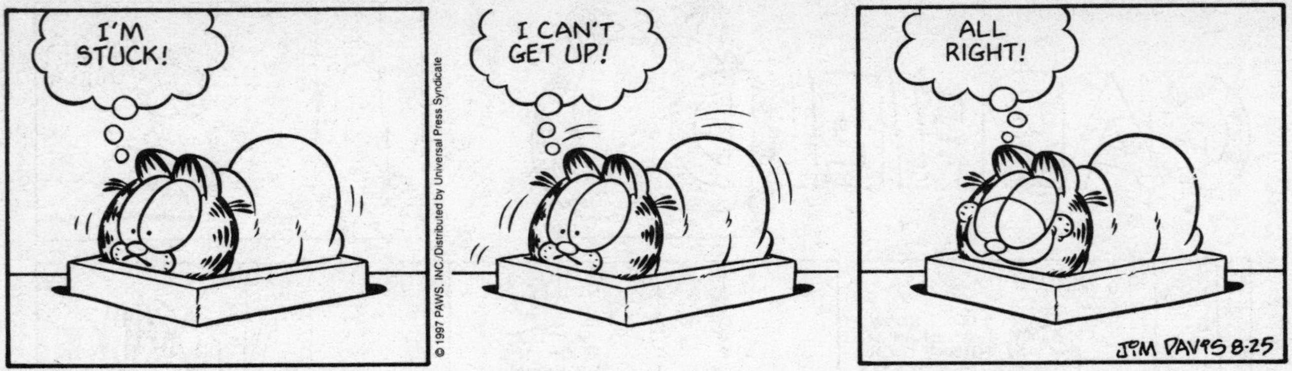
I'M STUCK!
© 1997 PAWS. INC./Distributed by Universal Press Syndicate
I CAN'T GET UP!
ALL RIGHT!
JIM DAVIS 8-25

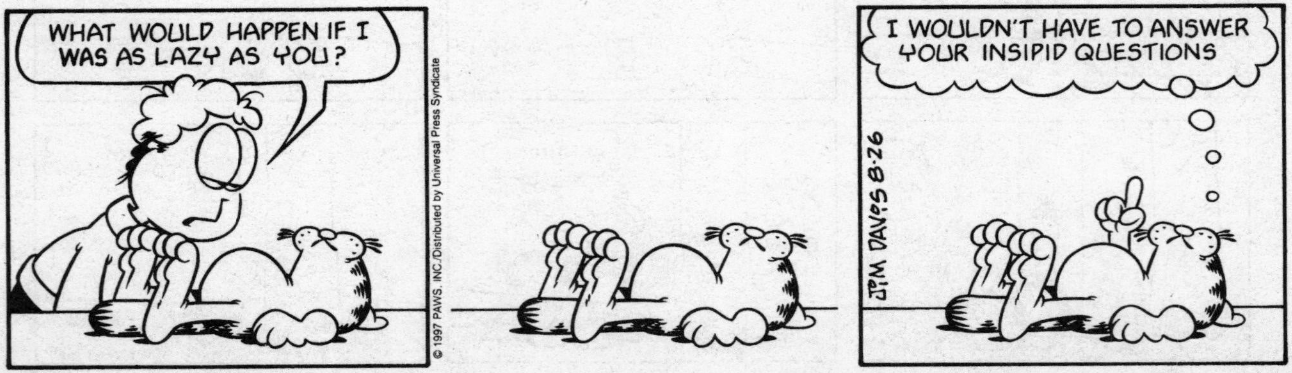
WHAT WOULD HAPPEN IF I WAS AS LAZY AS YOU?
© 1997 PAWS. INC./Distributed by Universal Press Syndicate
JIM DAVIS 8-26
I WOULDN'T HAVE TO ANSWER YOUR INSIPID QUESTIONS

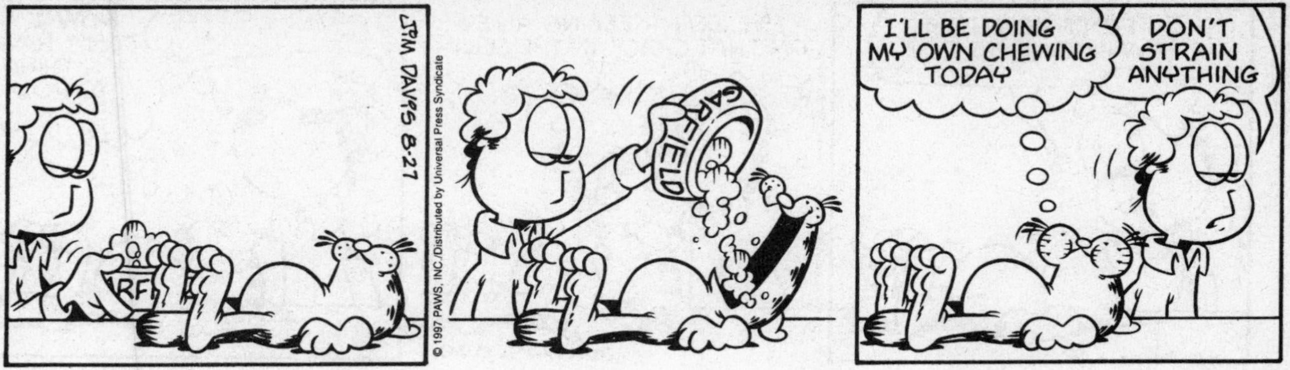
JIM DAVIS 8-27
© 1997 PAWS, INC./Distributed by Universal Press Syndicate
GARFIELD
I'LL BE DOING MY OWN CHEWING TODAY
DON'T STRAIN ANYTHING

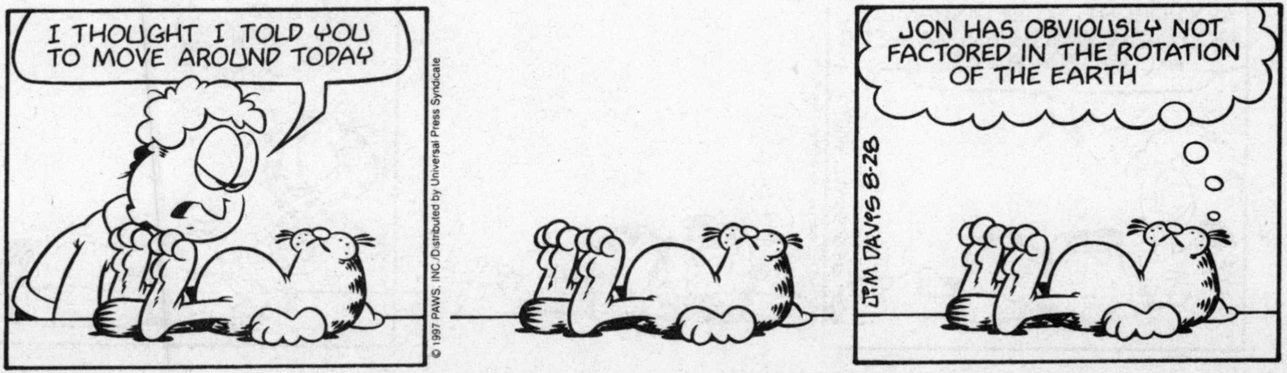
I THOUGHT I TOLD YOU TO MOVE AROUND TODAY
© 1997 PAWS, INC./Distributed by Universal Press Syndicate
JIM DAVIS 8-28
JON HAS OBVIOUSLY NOT FACTORED IN THE ROTATION OF THE EARTH

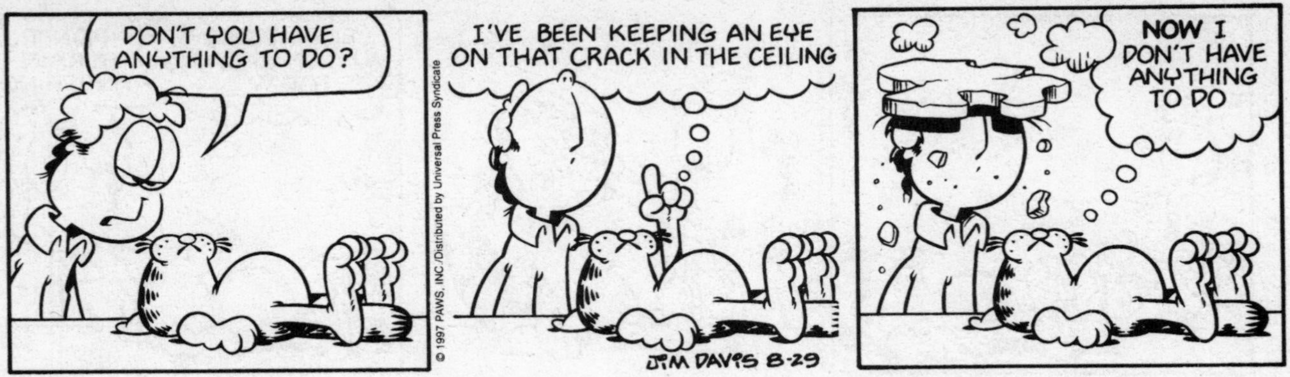
DON'T YOU HAVE ANYTHING TO DO?
I'VE BEEN KEEPING AN EYE ON THAT CRACK IN THE CEILING
NOW I DON'T HAVE ANYTHING TO DO
© 1997 PAWS, INC./Distributed by Universal Press Syndicate
JIM DAVIS 8-29

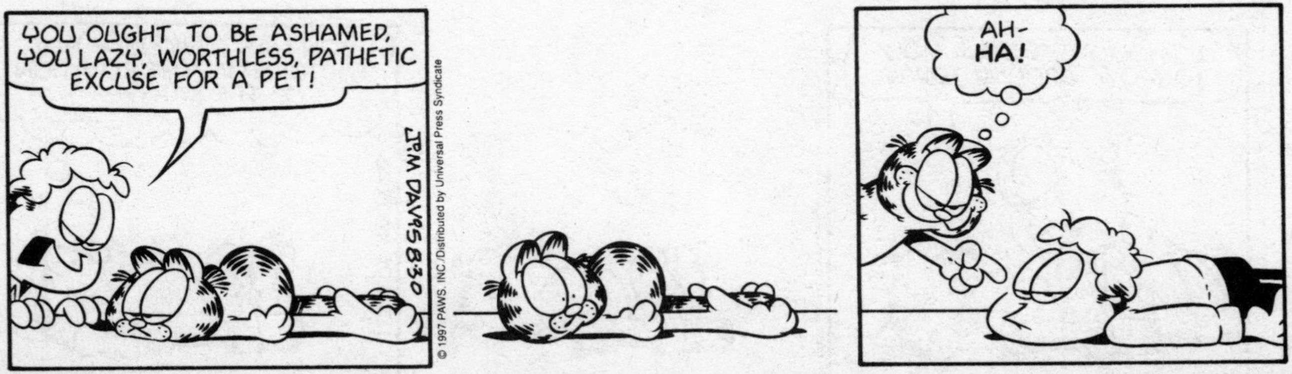
YOU OUGHT TO BE ASHAMED, YOU LAZY, WORTHLESS, PATHETIC EXCUSE FOR A PET!
AH-HA!
© 1997 PAWS, INC./Distributed by Universal Press Syndicate
JIM DAVIS 8-30

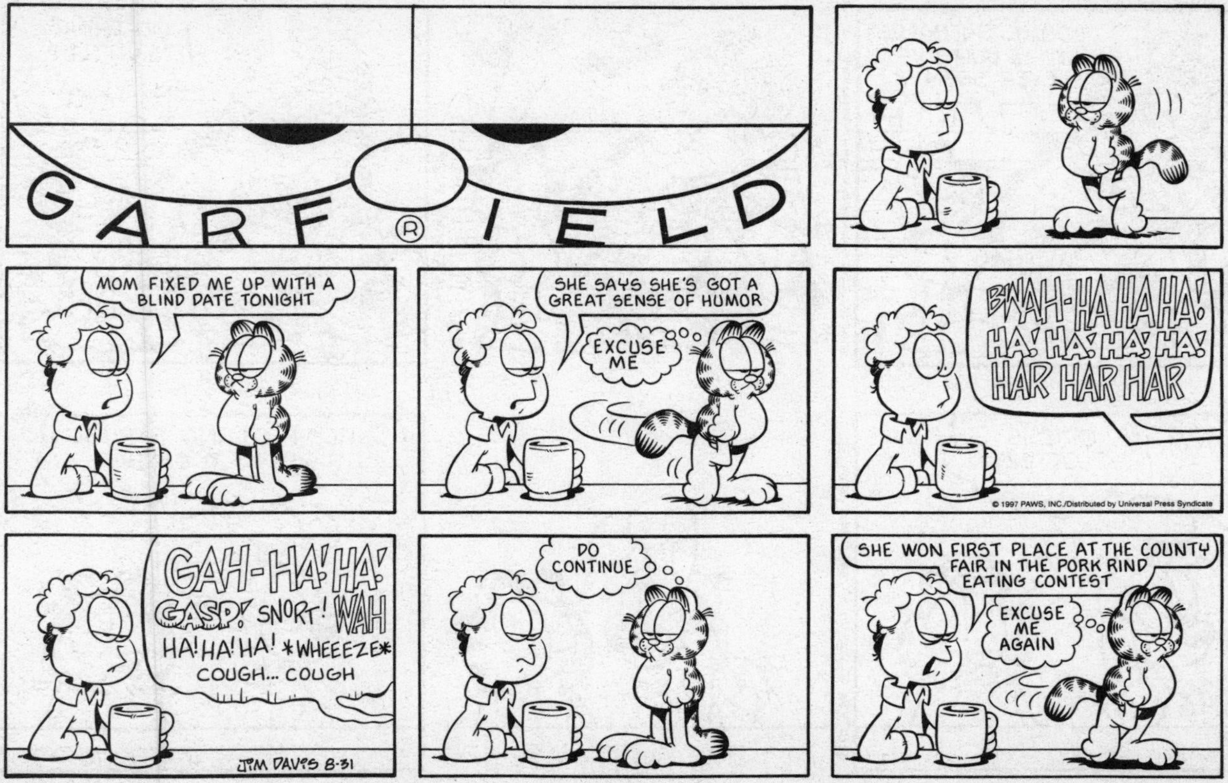
GARFIELD®
MOM FIXED ME UP WITH A BLIND DATE TONIGHT
SHE SAYS SHE'S GOT A GREAT SENSE OF HUMOR
EXCUSE ME
BWAH-HA HA HA HA!
HA! HA! HA! HA!
HAR HAR HAR
© 1997 PAWS, INC./Distributed by Universal Press Syndicate
GAH-HA! HA!
GASP! SNORT! WAH
HA! HA! HA! *WHEEEZE*
COUGH... COUGH
JIM DAVIS 8-31
DO CONTINUE
SHE WON FIRST PLACE AT THE COUNTY FAIR IN THE PORK RIND EATING CONTEST
EXCUSE ME AGAIN

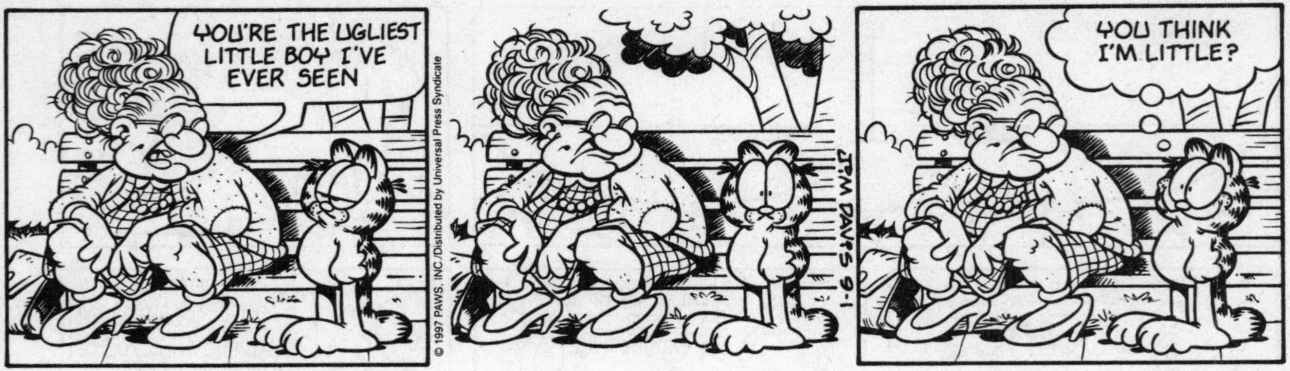
YOU'RE THE UGLIEST LITTLE BOY I'VE EVER SEEN
YOU THINK I'M LITTLE?
JIM DAVIS 9-1

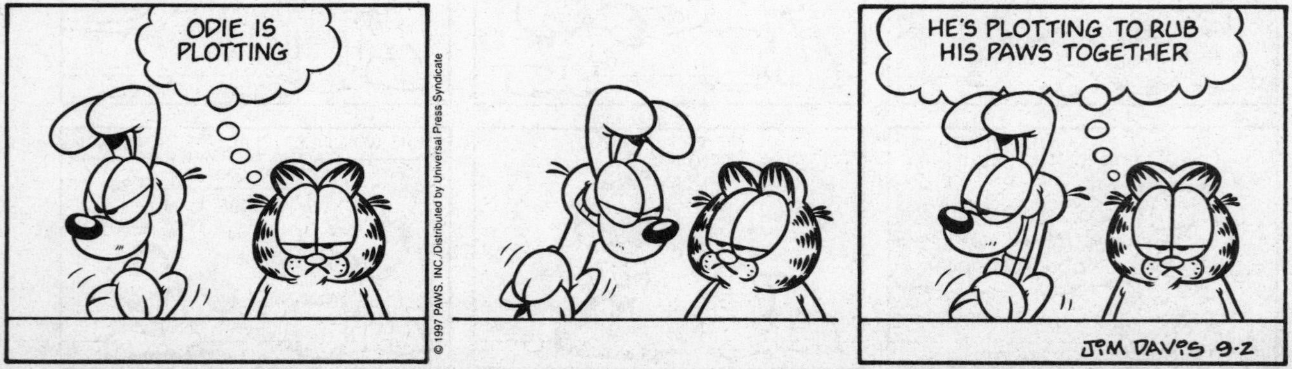
ODIE IS PLOTTING
HE'S PLOTTING TO RUB HIS PAWS TOGETHER
JIM DAVIS 9-2

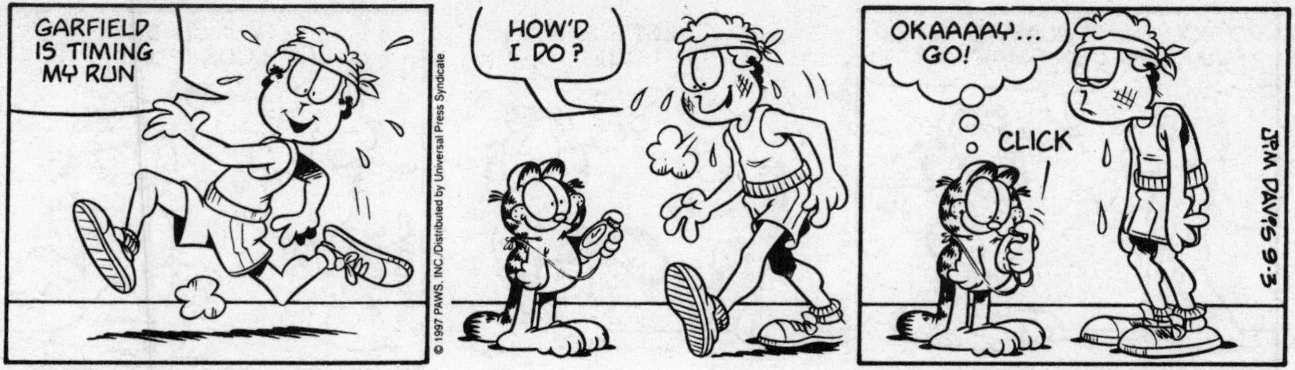
GARFIELD IS TIMING MY RUN
© 1997 PAWS. INC./Distributed by Universal Press Syndicate
HOW'D I DO?
OKAAAAY... GO!
CLICK
JIM DAVIS 9-3

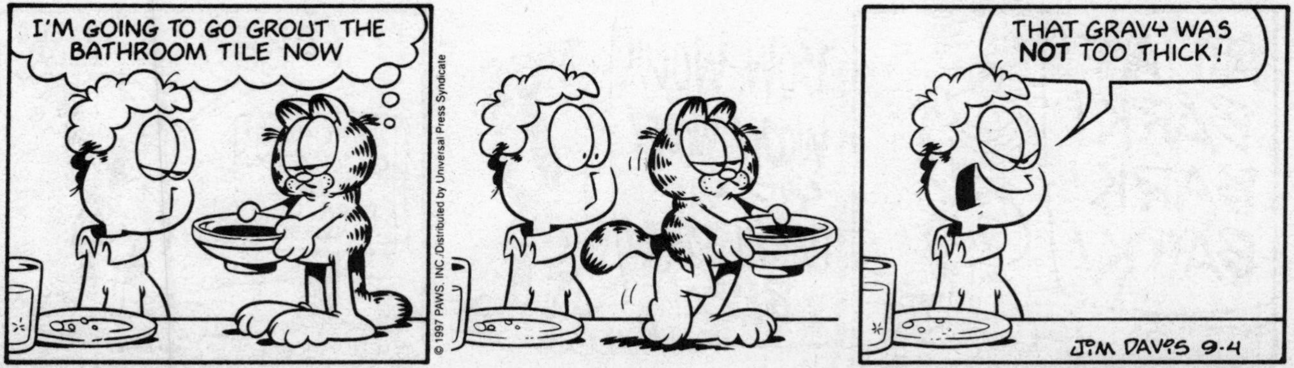
I'M GOING TO GO GROUT THE BATHROOM TILE NOW
© 1997 PAWS. INC./Distributed by Universal Press Syndicate
THAT GRAVY WAS **NOT** TOO THICK!
JIM DAVIS 9-4

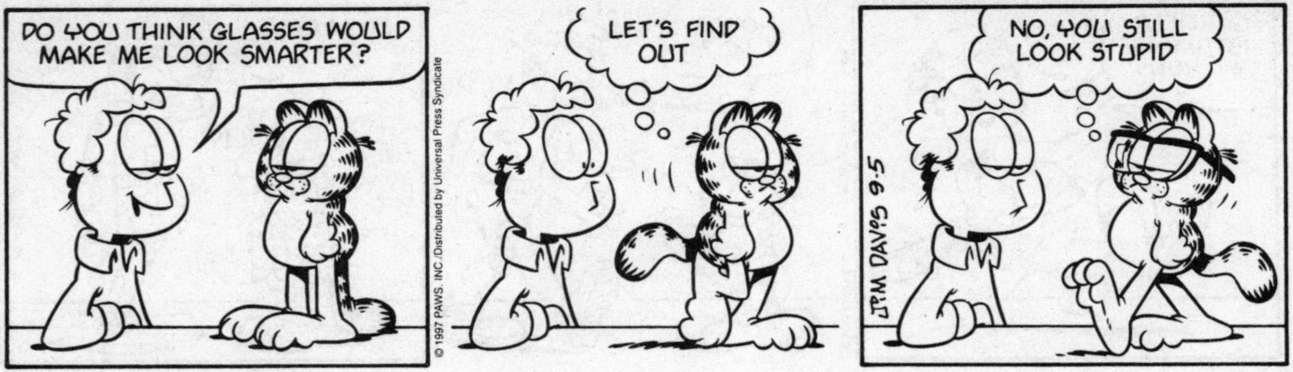
DO YOU THINK GLASSES WOULD MAKE ME LOOK SMARTER?
LET'S FIND OUT
NO, YOU STILL LOOK STUPID
JIM DAVIS 9-5

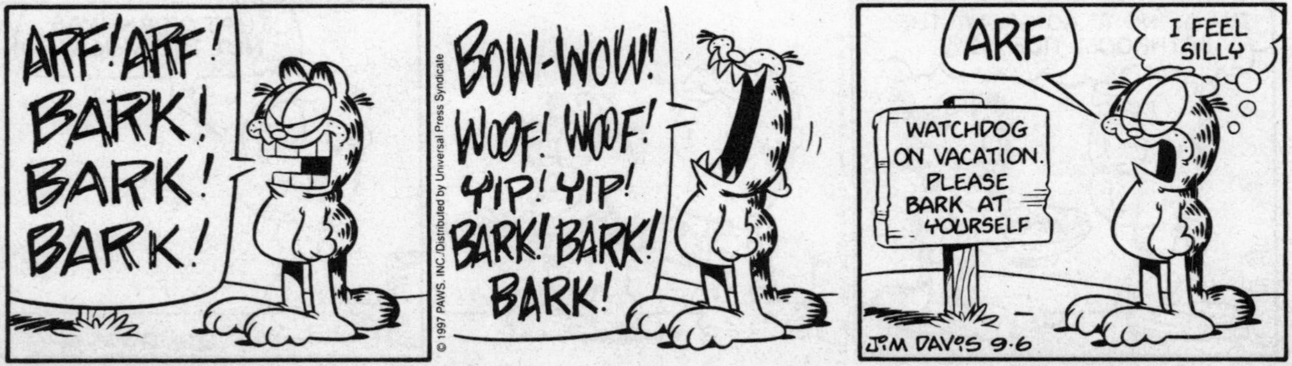
ARF! ARF! BARK! BARK! BARK!
BOW-WOW! WOOF! WOOF! YIP! YIP! BARK! BARK! BARK!
ARF
I FEEL SILLY
WATCHDOG ON VACATION. PLEASE BARK AT YOURSELF
JIM DAVIS 9-6

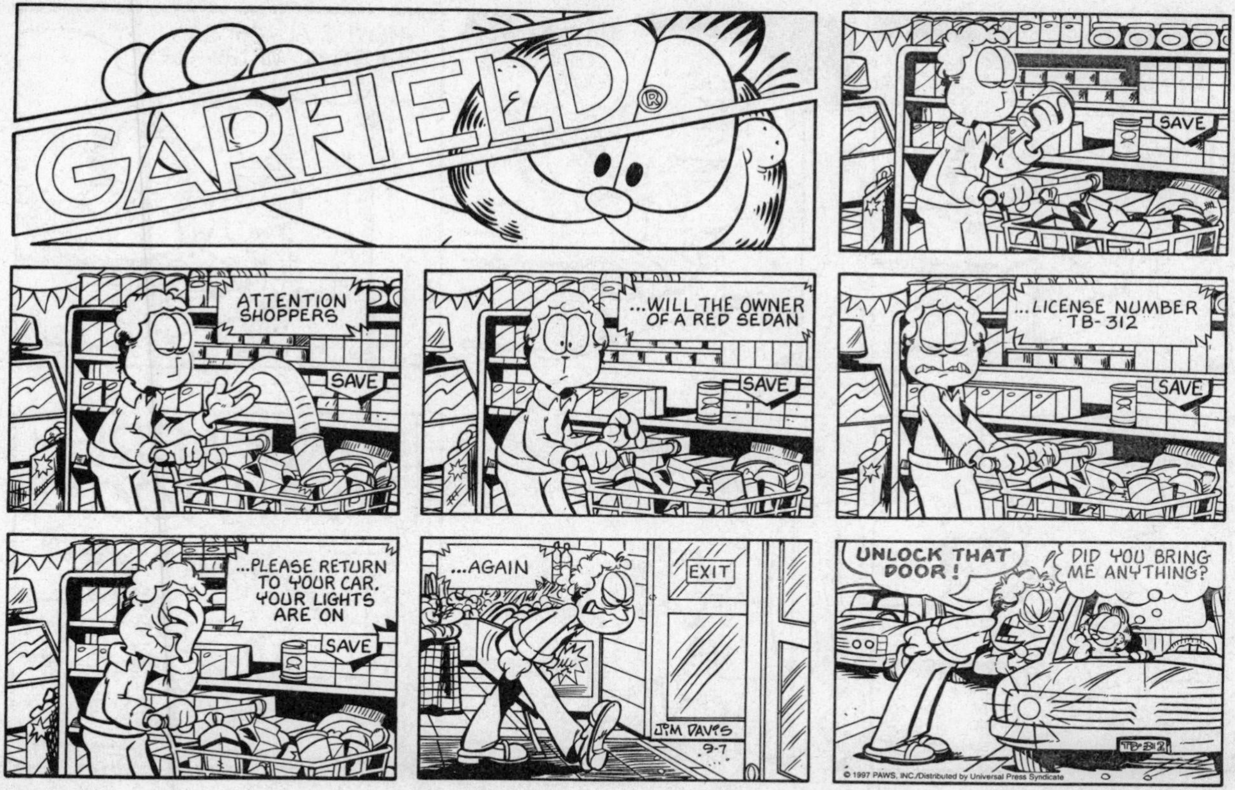
GARFIELD®
SAVE
ATTENTION SHOPPERS
SAVE
...WILL THE OWNER OF A RED SEDAN
SAVE
...LICENSE NUMBER TB-312
SAVE
...PLEASE RETURN TO YOUR CAR. YOUR LIGHTS ARE ON
SAVE
...AGAIN
EXIT
JIM DAVIS 9-7
UNLOCK THAT DOOR!
DID YOU BRING ME ANYTHING?
TB-312
© 1997 PAWS, INC./Distributed by Universal Press Syndicate

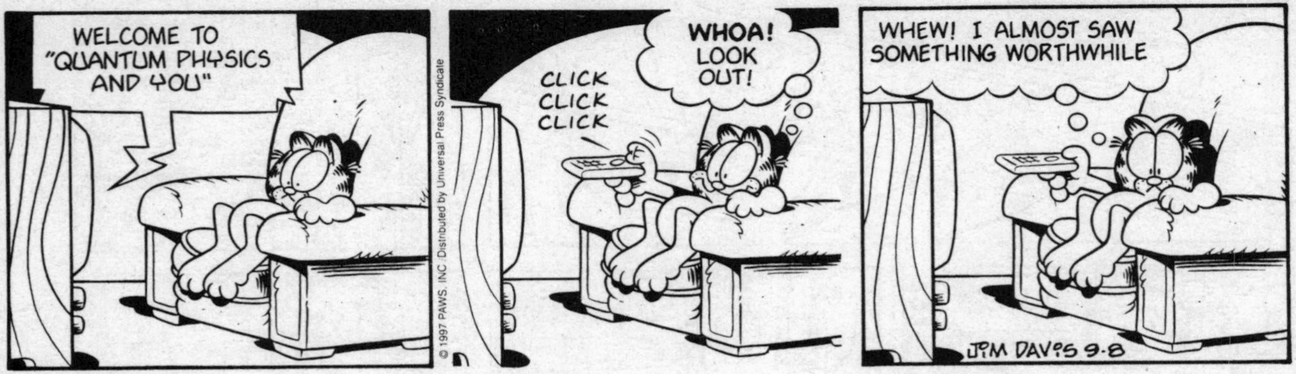
WELCOME TO "QUANTUM PHYSICS AND YOU"
CLICK CLICK CLICK
WHOA! LOOK OUT!
WHEW! I ALMOST SAW SOMETHING WORTHWHILE
JIM DAVIS 9-8

© 1997 PAWS, INC./Distributed by Universal Press Syndicate

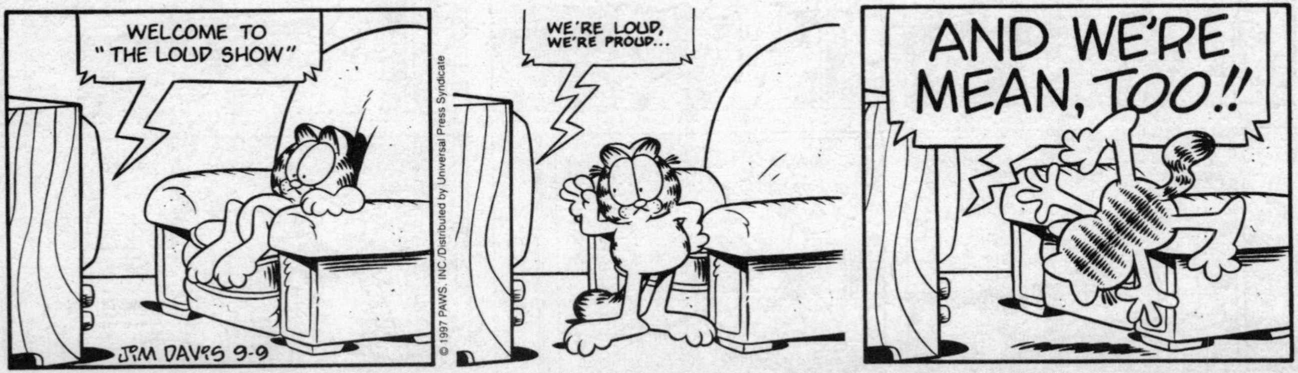
WELCOME TO "THE LOUD SHOW"
WE'RE LOUD, WE'RE PROUD...
AND WE'RE MEAN, TOO!!
JIM DAVIS 9-9

© 1997 PAWS, INC./Distributed by Universal Press Syndicate

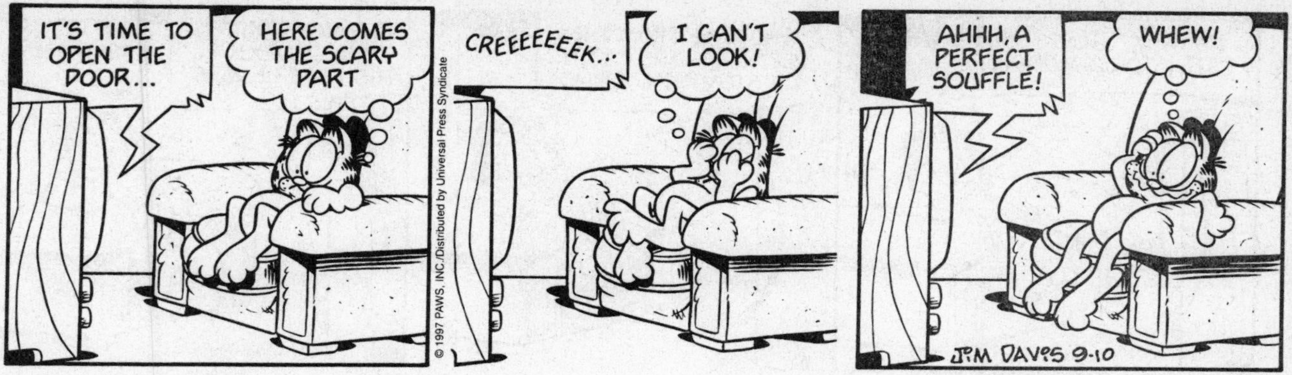
IT'S TIME TO OPEN THE DOOR...
HERE COMES THE SCARY PART
© 1997 PAWS, INC./Distributed by Universal Press Syndicate
CREEEEEEEK...
I CAN'T LOOK!
AHHH, A PERFECT SOUFFLÉ!
WHEW!
JIM DAVIS 9-10

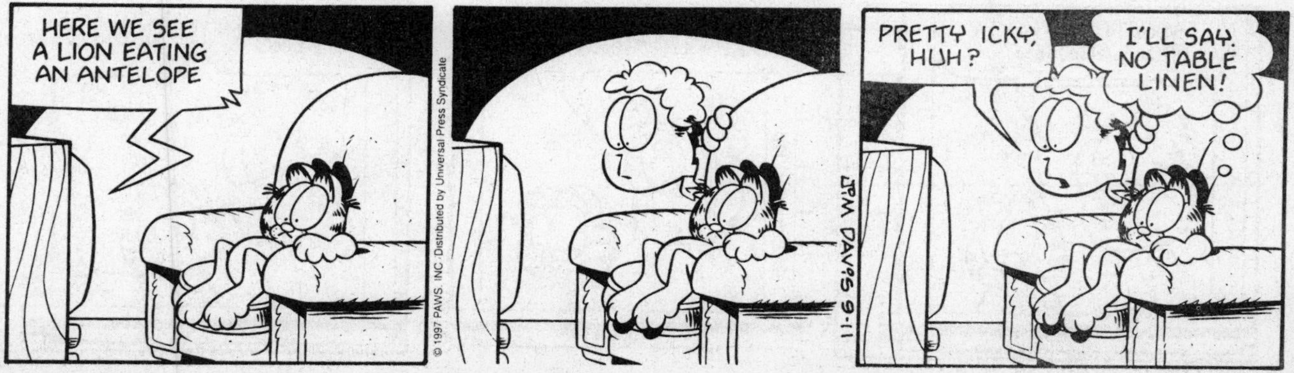
HERE WE SEE A LION EATING AN ANTELOPE
© 1997 PAWS, INC./Distributed by Universal Press Syndicate
JIM DAVIS 9-11
PRETTY ICKY, HUH?
I'LL SAY. NO TABLE LINEN!

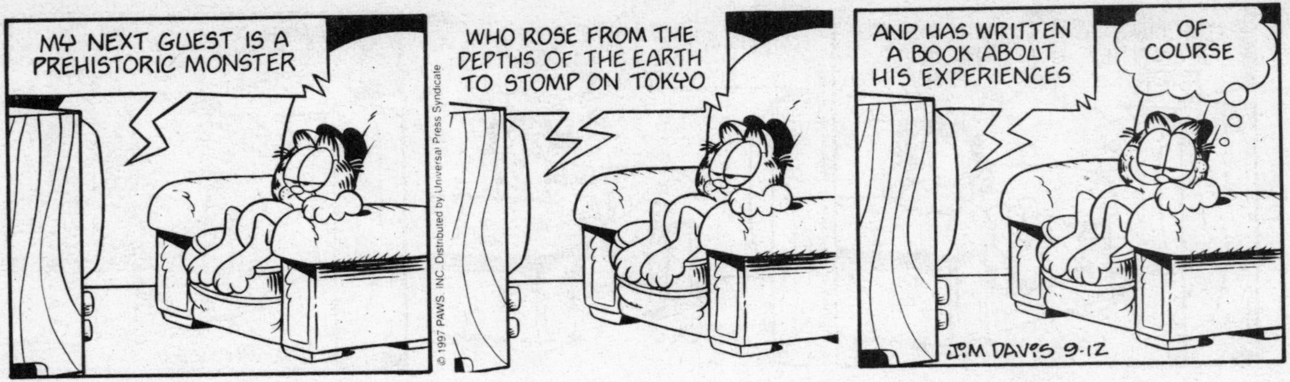

MY NEXT GUEST IS A PREHISTORIC MONSTER
© 1997 PAWS. INC. Distributed by Universal Press Syndicate
WHO ROSE FROM THE DEPTHS OF THE EARTH TO STOMP ON TOKYO
AND HAS WRITTEN A BOOK ABOUT HIS EXPERIENCES
OF COURSE
JIM DAVIS 9-12

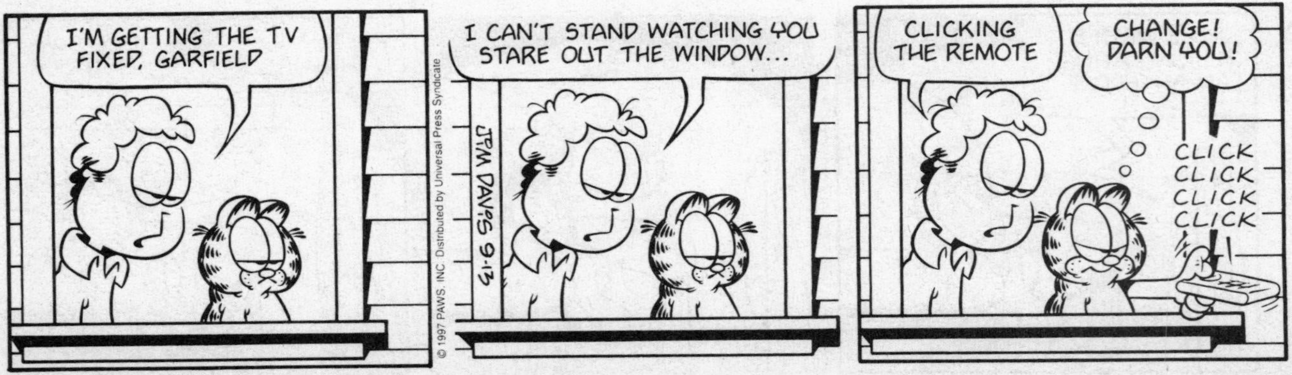

I'M GETTING THE TV FIXED, GARFIELD
© 1997 PAWS. INC. Distributed by Universal Press Syndicate
JIM DAVIS 9-13
I CAN'T STAND WATCHING YOU STARE OUT THE WINDOW...
CLICKING THE REMOTE
CHANGE! DARN YOU!
CLICK
CLICK
CLICK
CLICK

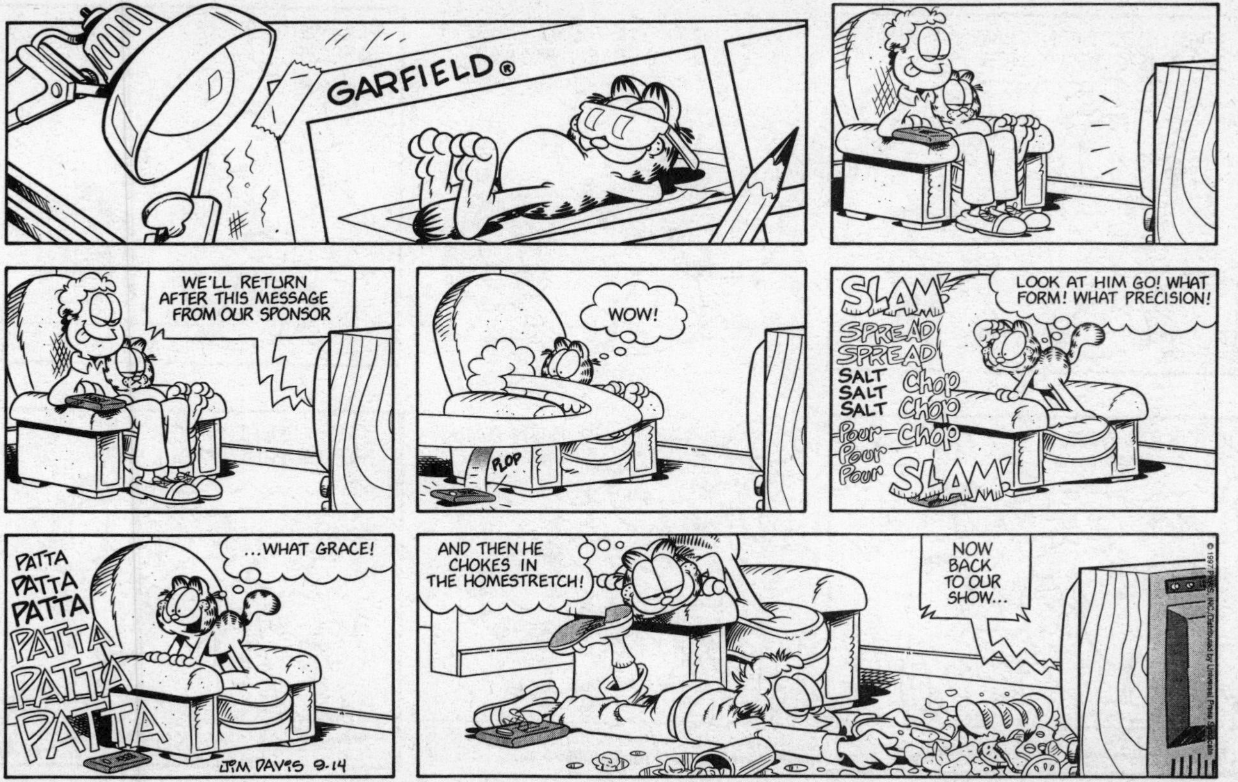
GARFIELD®
WE'LL RETURN AFTER THIS MESSAGE FROM OUR SPONSOR
WOW!
PLOP
SLAM!
SPREAD
SPREAD
SALT
SALT
SALT
Chop
Chop
Chop
Pour
Pour
Pour
SLAM!
LOOK AT HIM GO! WHAT FORM! WHAT PRECISION!
PATTA
PATTA
PATTA
PATTA
PATTA
PATTA
...WHAT GRACE!
JIM DAVIS 9-14
AND THEN HE CHOKES IN THE HOMESTRETCH!
NOW BACK TO OUR SHOW...

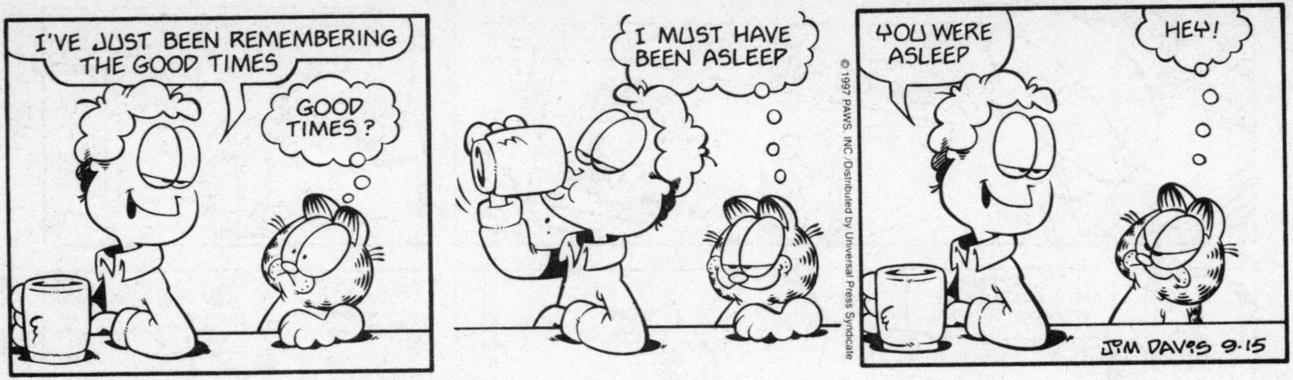
I'VE JUST BEEN REMEMBERING THE GOOD TIMES
GOOD TIMES?
I MUST HAVE BEEN ASLEEP
© 1997 PAWS, INC./Distributed by Universal Press Syndicate
YOU WERE ASLEEP
HEY!
JIM DAVIS 9-15

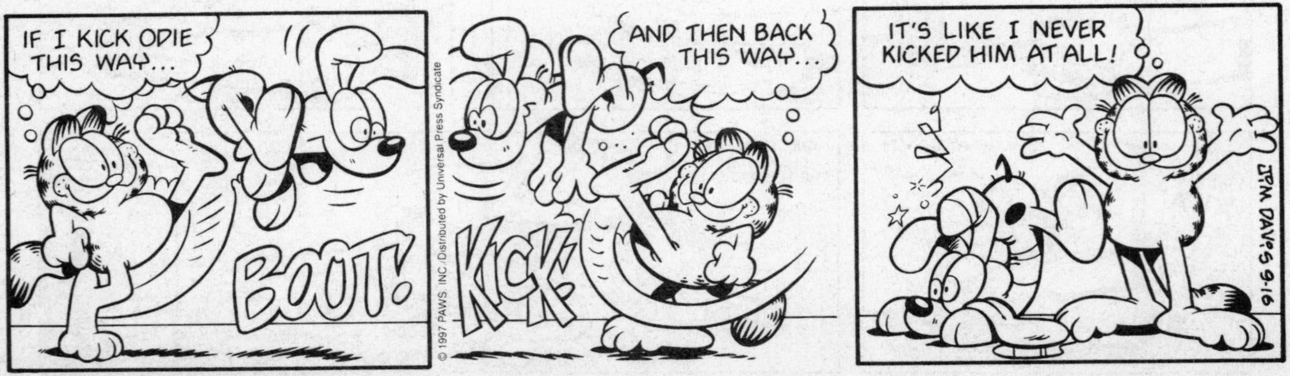
IF I KICK ODIE THIS WAY...
BOOT!
© 1997 PAWS, INC./Distributed by Universal Press Syndicate
KICK
AND THEN BACK THIS WAY...
IT'S LIKE I NEVER KICKED HIM AT ALL!
JIM DAVIS 9-16

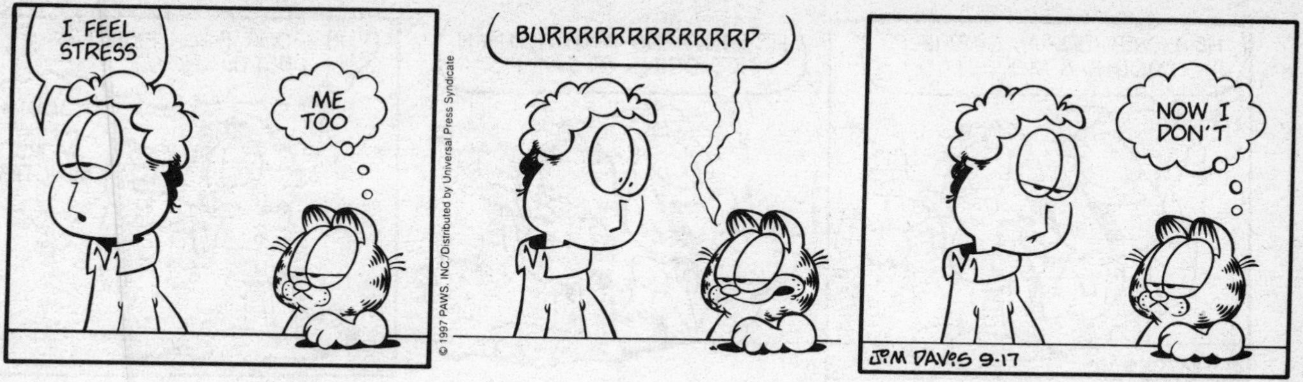
I FEEL STRESS
ME TOO
© 1997 PAWS. INC./Distributed by Universal Press Syndicate
BURRRRRRRRRRRRP
NOW I DON'T
JIM DAVIS 9-17

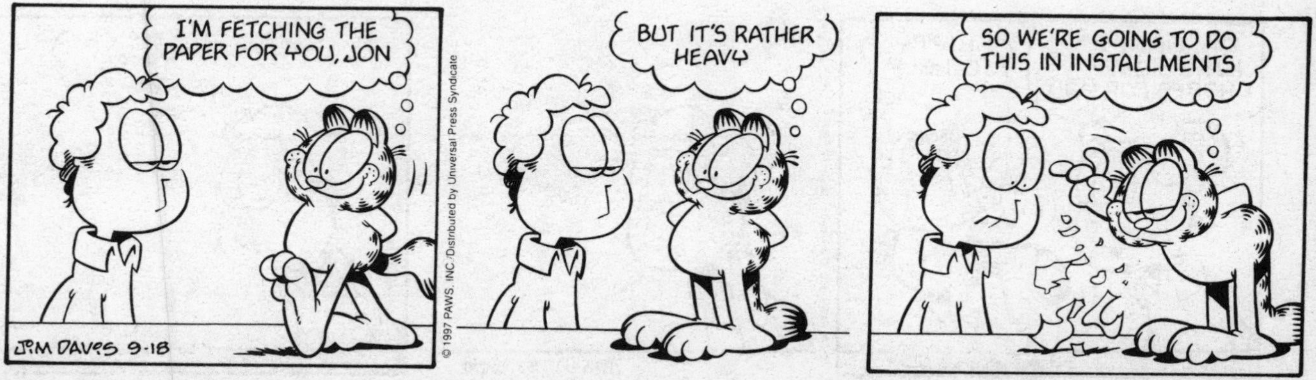
I'M FETCHING THE PAPER FOR YOU, JON
JIM DAVIS 9-18
© 1997 PAWS. INC./Distributed by Universal Press Syndicate
BUT IT'S RATHER HEAVY
SO WE'RE GOING TO DO THIS IN INSTALLMENTS

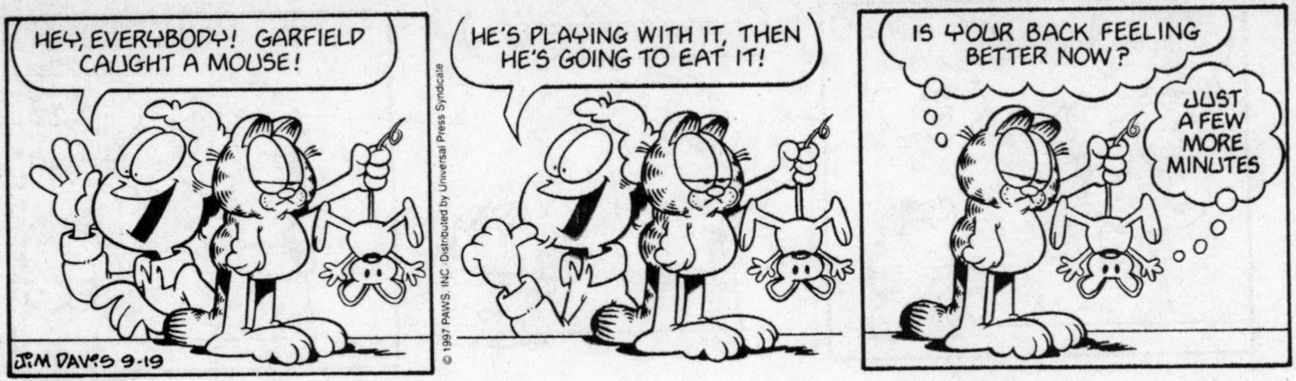
HEY, EVERYBODY! GARFIELD CAUGHT A MOUSE!
JIM DAVIS 9-19
HE'S PLAYING WITH IT, THEN HE'S GOING TO EAT IT!
IS YOUR BACK FEELING BETTER NOW?
JUST A FEW MORE MINUTES

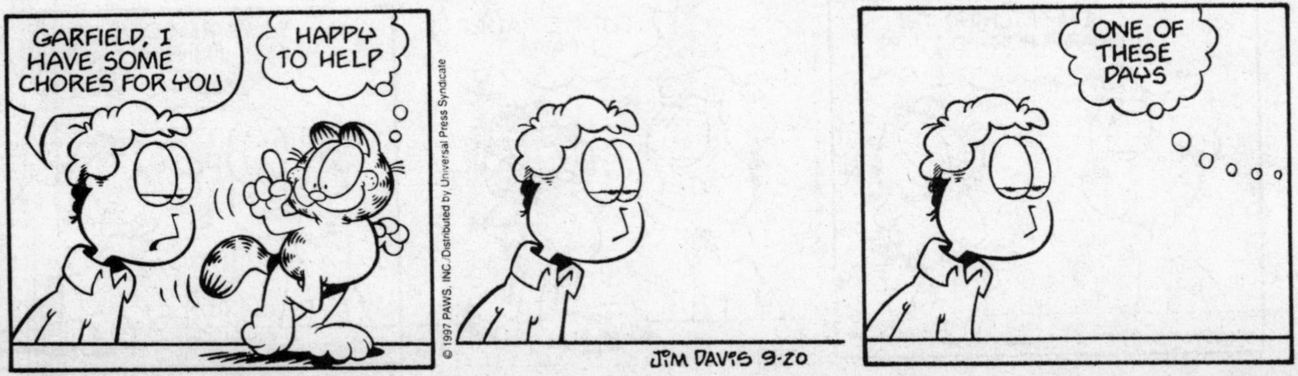
GARFIELD, I HAVE SOME CHORES FOR YOU
HAPPY TO HELP
JIM DAVIS 9-20
ONE OF THESE DAYS

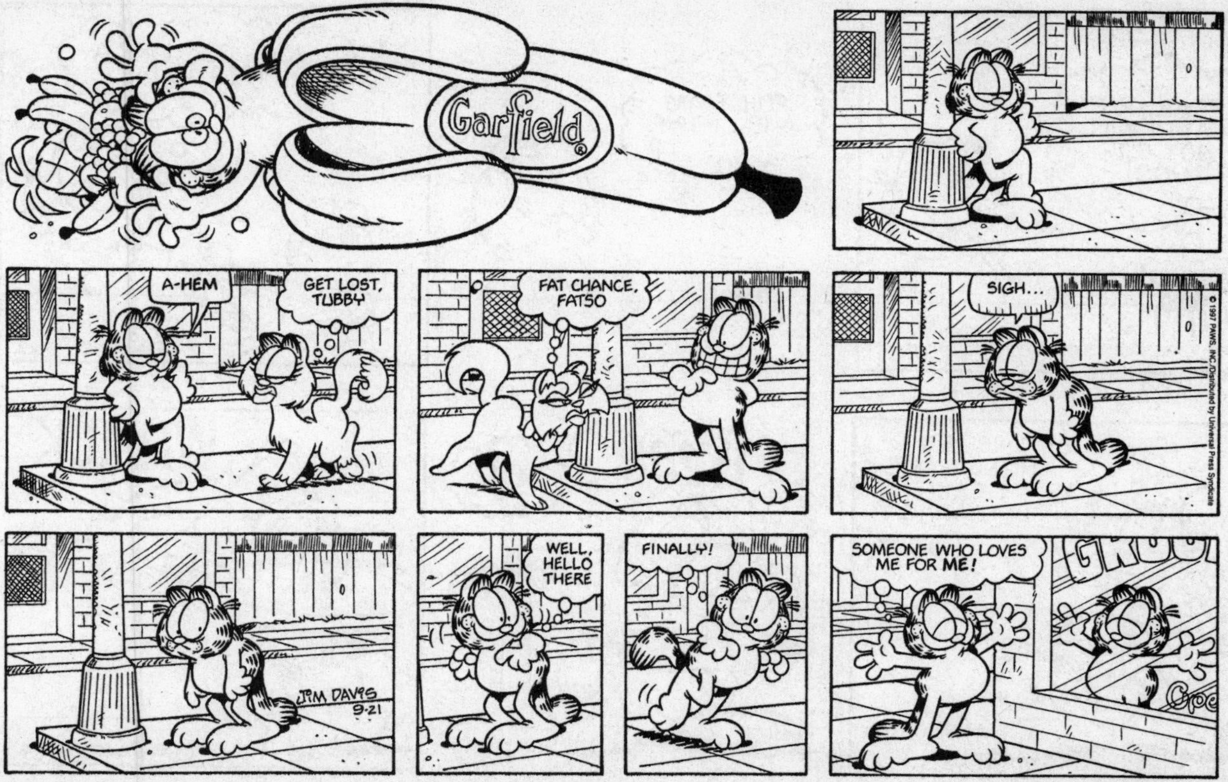
Garfield®
A-HEM
GET LOST, TUBBY
FAT CHANCE, FATSO
SIGH...
© 1997 PAWS, INC./Distributed by Universal Press Syndicate
JIM DAVIS 9·21
WELL, HELLO THERE
FINALLY!
SOMEONE WHO LOVES ME FOR ME!

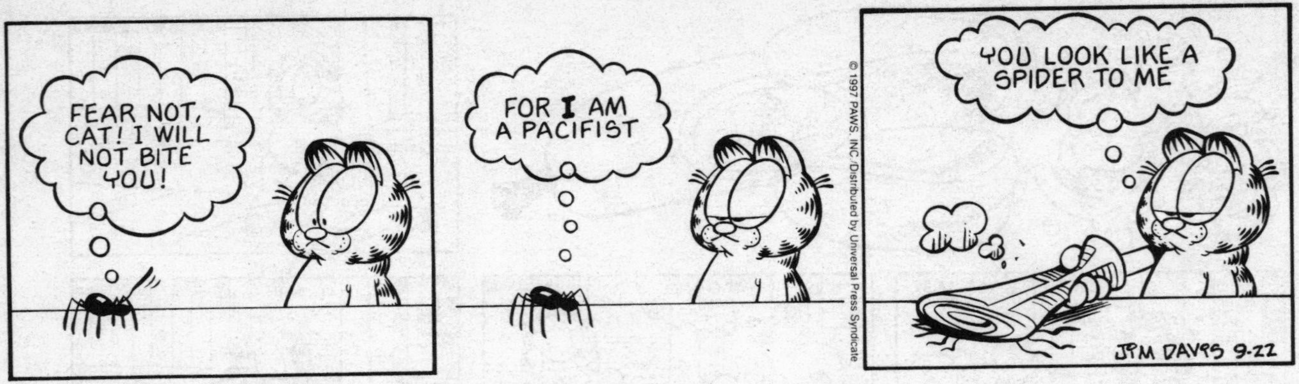
FEAR NOT, CAT! I WILL NOT BITE YOU!
FOR I AM A PACIFIST
YOU LOOK LIKE A SPIDER TO ME
JIM DAVIS 9-22

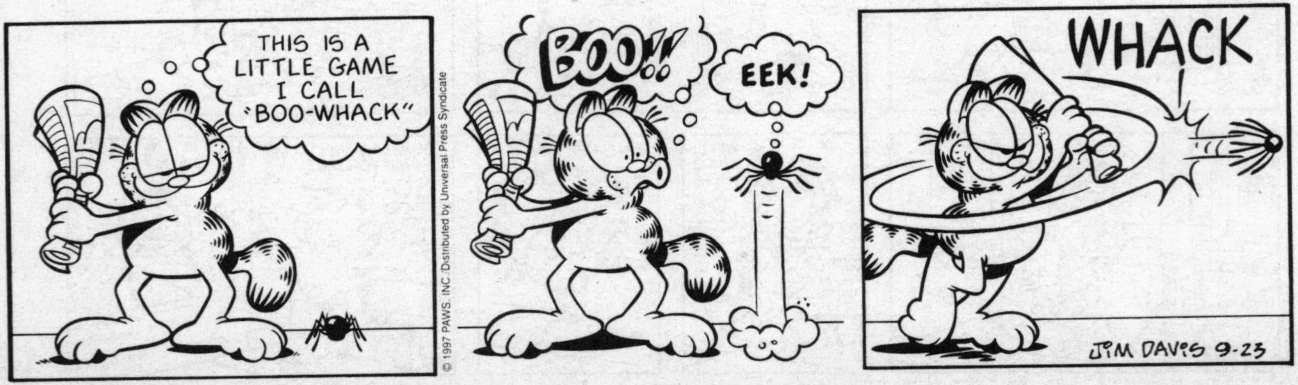
THIS IS A LITTLE GAME I CALL "BOO-WHACK"
BOO!!
EEK!
WHACK
JIM DAVIS 9-23

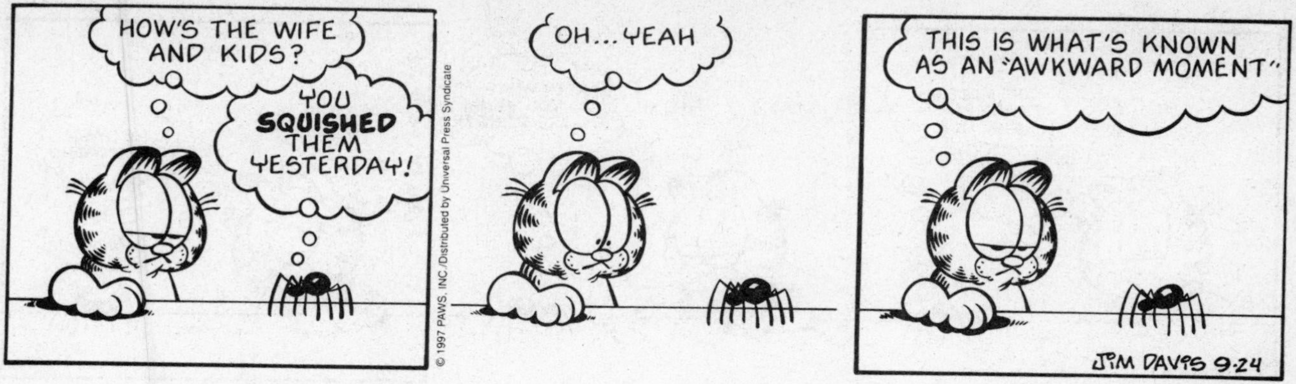
HOW'S THE WIFE AND KIDS?
YOU SQUISHED THEM YESTERDAY!
OH... YEAH
THIS IS WHAT'S KNOWN AS AN "AWKWARD MOMENT"
JIM DAVIS 9-24

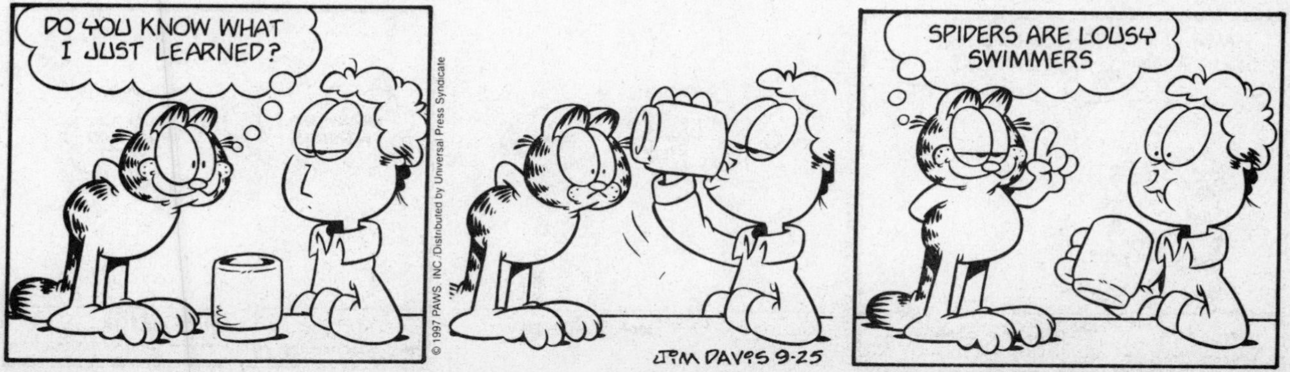
DO YOU KNOW WHAT I JUST LEARNED?
SPIDERS ARE LOUSY SWIMMERS
JIM DAVIS 9-25

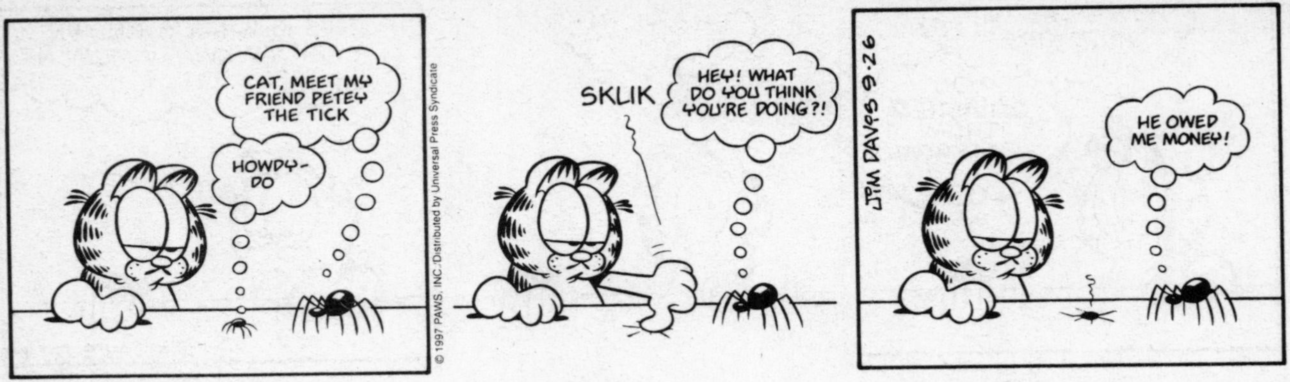
CAT, MEET MY FRIEND PETEY THE TICK
HOWDY-DO
SKLIK
HEY! WHAT DO YOU THINK YOU'RE DOING?!
JIM DAVIS 9-26
HE OWED ME MONEY!

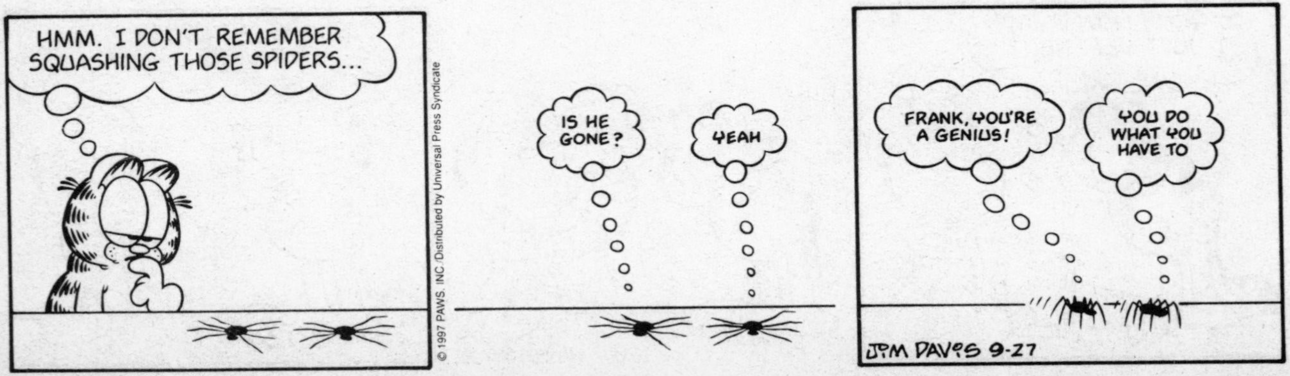
HMM. I DON'T REMEMBER SQUASHING THOSE SPIDERS...
IS HE GONE?
YEAH
FRANK, YOU'RE A GENIUS!
YOU DO WHAT YOU HAVE TO
JIM DAVIS 9-27

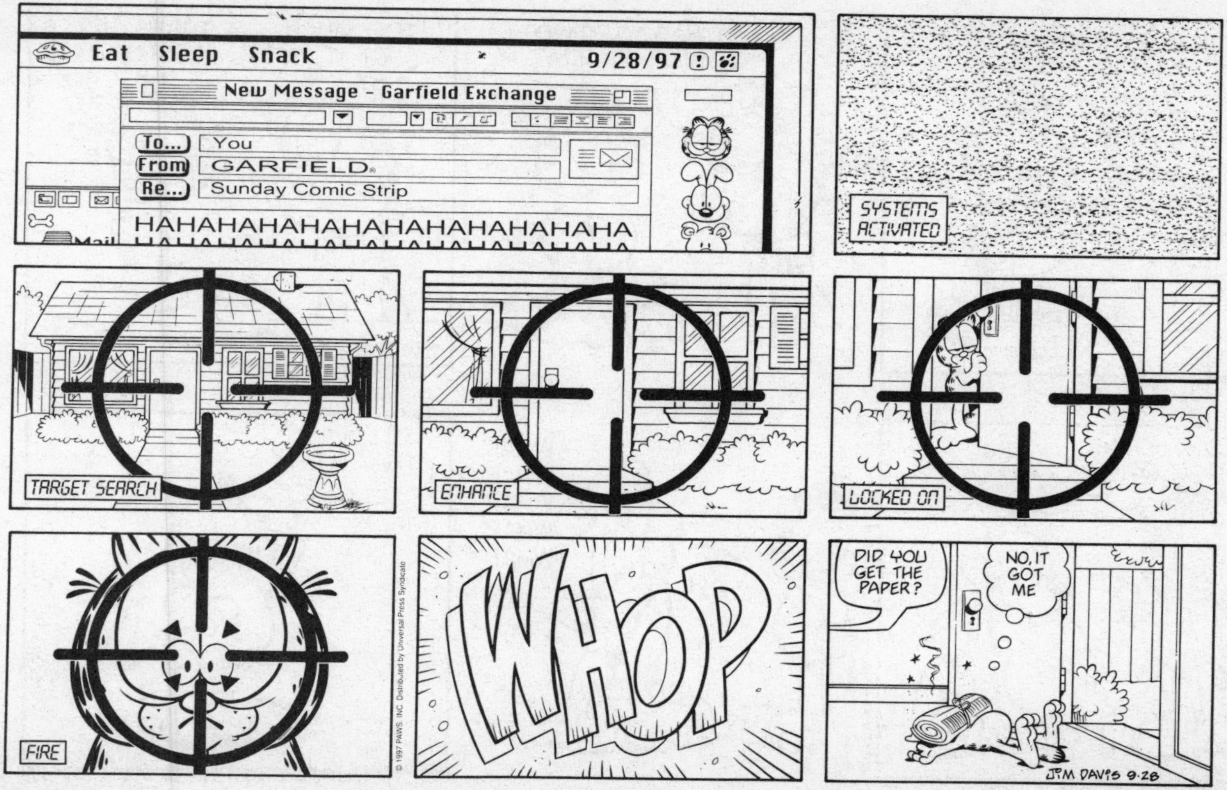

Eat Sleep Snack
9/28/97
New Message - Garfield Exchange
To... You
From GARFIELD®
Re... Sunday Comic Strip
HAHAHAHAHAHAHAHAHAHAHAHAHA
SYSTEMS ACTIVATED
TARGET SEARCH
ENHANCE
LOCKED ON
FIRE
WHOP
DID YOU GET THE PAPER?
NO, IT GOT ME
JIM DAVIS 9-28
© 1997 PAWS, INC. Distributed by Universal Press Syndicate

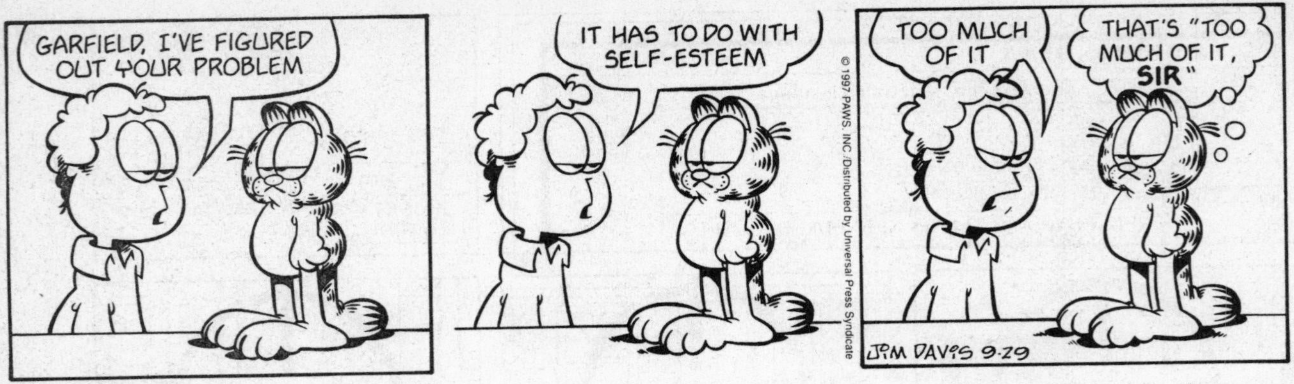
GARFIELD, I'VE FIGURED OUT YOUR PROBLEM
IT HAS TO DO WITH SELF-ESTEEM
TOO MUCH OF IT
THAT'S "TOO MUCH OF IT, SIR"
JIM DAVIS 9-29
© 1997 PAWS, INC./Distributed by Universal Press Syndicate

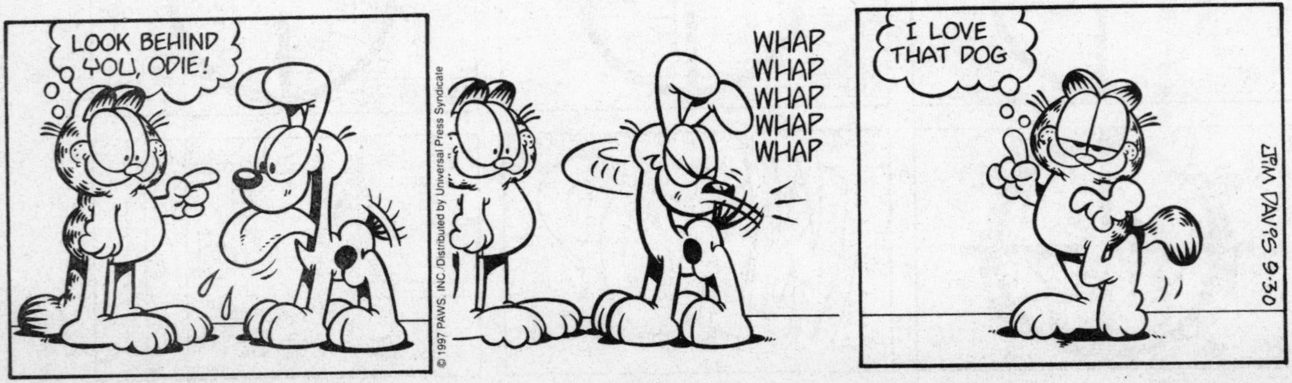
LOOK BEHIND YOU, ODIE!
WHAP WHAP WHAP WHAP WHAP
I LOVE THAT DOG
JIM DAVIS 9-30
© 1997 PAWS, INC./Distributed by Universal Press Syndicate

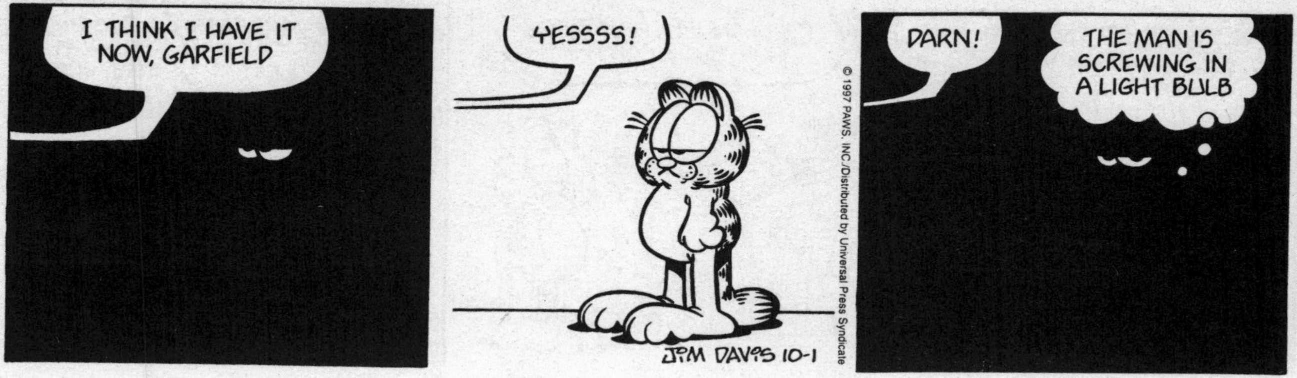
I THINK I HAVE IT NOW, GARFIELD
YESSSS!
JIM DAVIS 10-1
DARN!
THE MAN IS SCREWING IN A LIGHT BULB

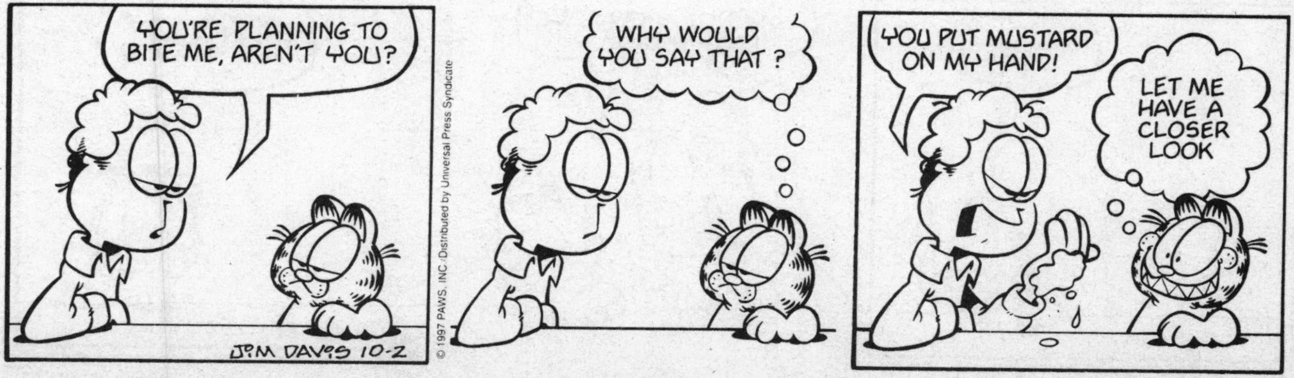
YOU'RE PLANNING TO BITE ME, AREN'T YOU?
JIM DAVIS 10-2
WHY WOULD YOU SAY THAT ?
YOU PUT MUSTARD ON MY HAND!
LET ME HAVE A CLOSER LOOK

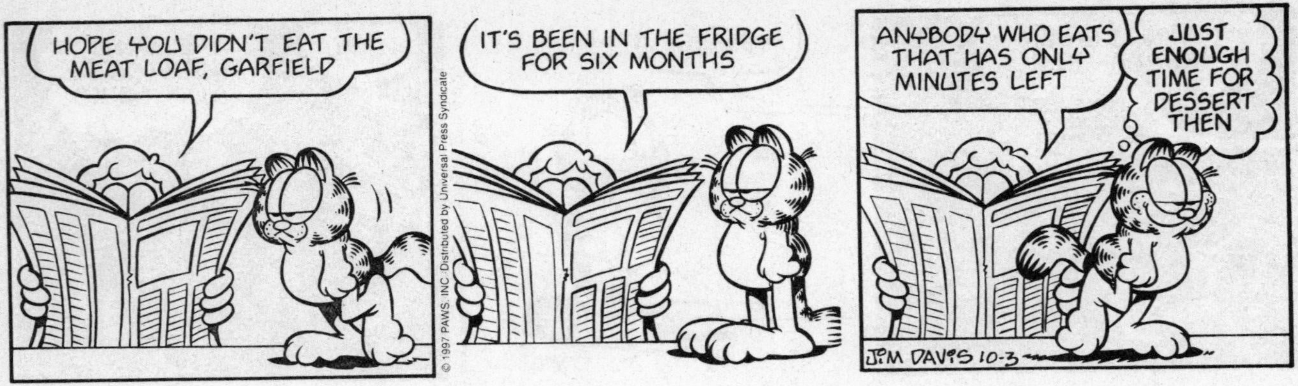
HOPE YOU DIDN'T EAT THE MEAT LOAF, GARFIELD
IT'S BEEN IN THE FRIDGE FOR SIX MONTHS
ANYBODY WHO EATS THAT HAS ONLY MINUTES LEFT
JUST ENOUGH TIME FOR DESSERT THEN
JIM DAVIS 10-3

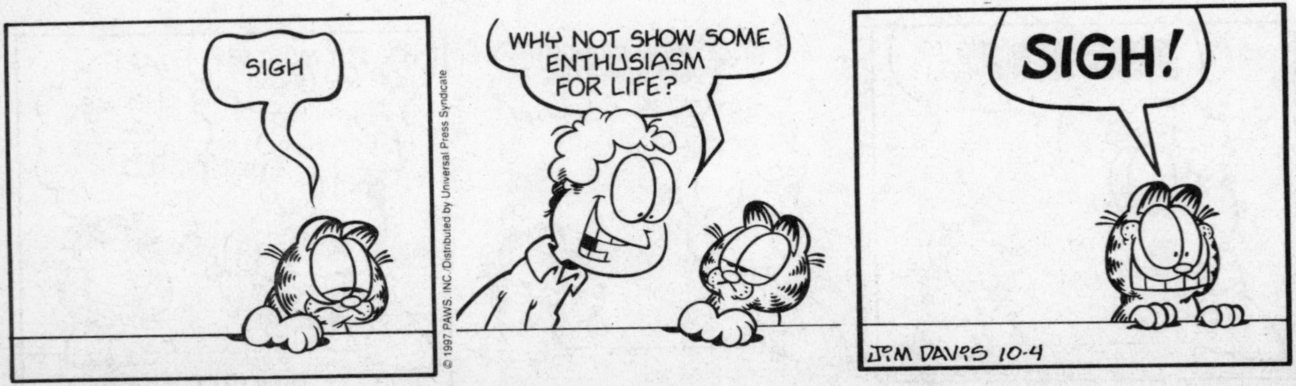
SIGH
WHY NOT SHOW SOME ENTHUSIASM FOR LIFE?
SIGH!
JIM DAVIS 10-4

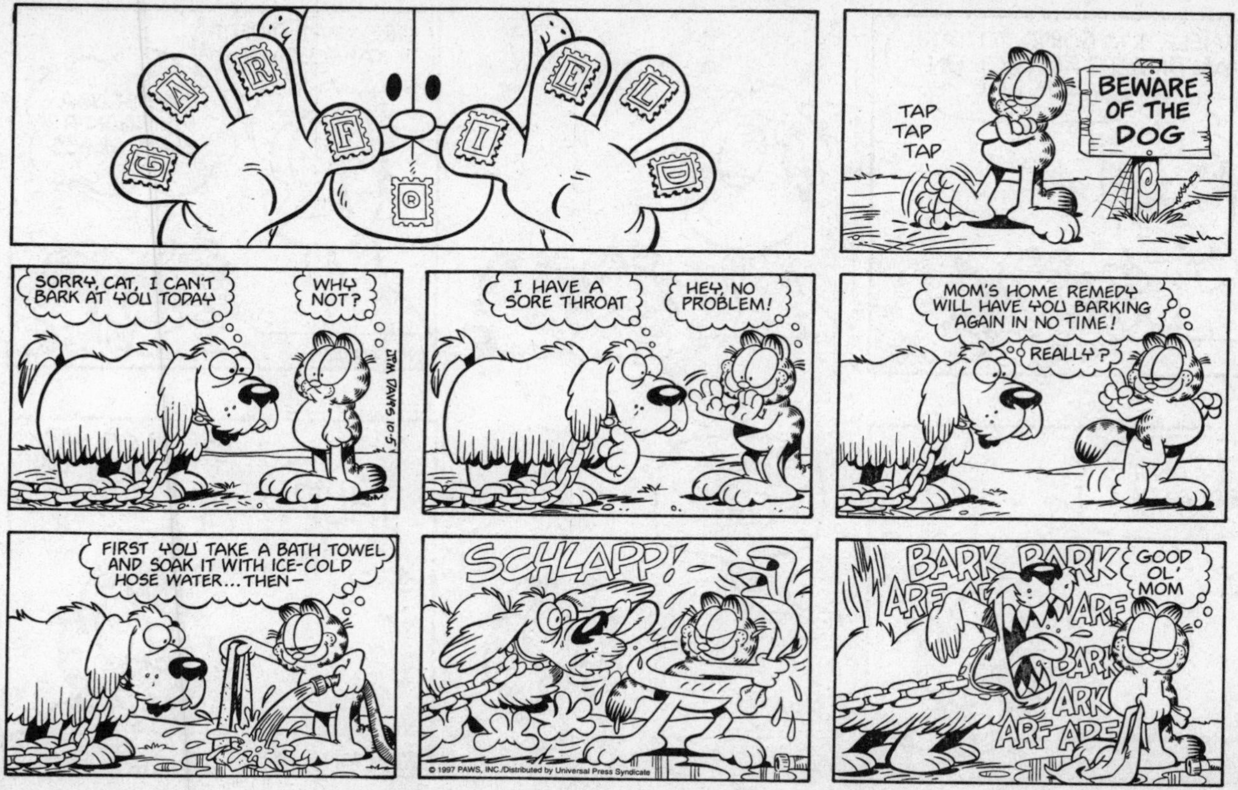
GARFIELD®
TAP TAP TAP
BEWARE OF THE DOG
SORRY, CAT, I CAN'T BARK AT YOU TODAY
WHY NOT?
JIM DAVIS 10-5
I HAVE A SORE THROAT
HEY, NO PROBLEM!
MOM'S HOME REMEDY WILL HAVE YOU BARKING AGAIN IN NO TIME!
REALLY?
FIRST YOU TAKE A BATH TOWEL AND SOAK IT WITH ICE-COLD HOSE WATER... THEN—
SCHLAPP!
BARK BARK
GOOD OL' MOM
ARF
BARK
ARK
ARF

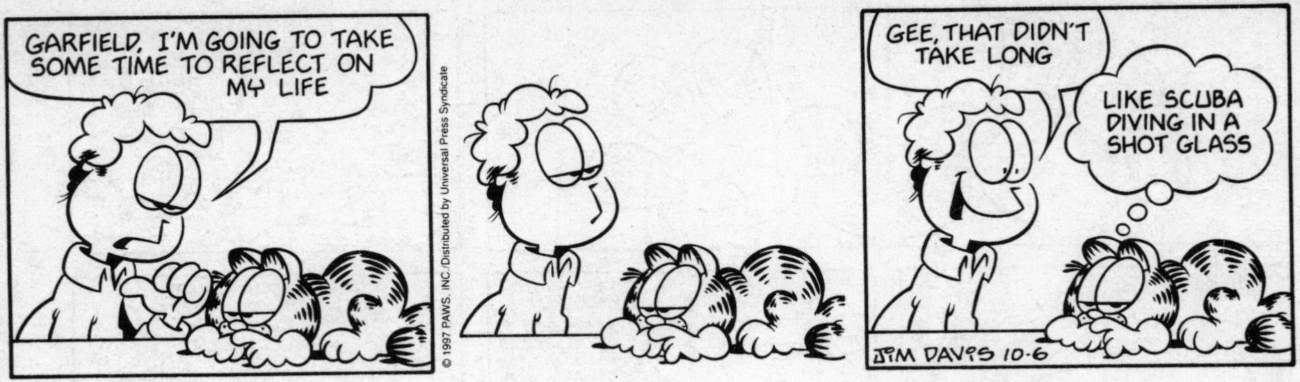
GARFIELD, I'M GOING TO TAKE SOME TIME TO REFLECT ON MY LIFE
© 1997 PAWS. INC./Distributed by Universal Press Syndicate
GEE, THAT DIDN'T TAKE LONG
LIKE SCUBA DIVING IN A SHOT GLASS
JIM DAVIS 10-6

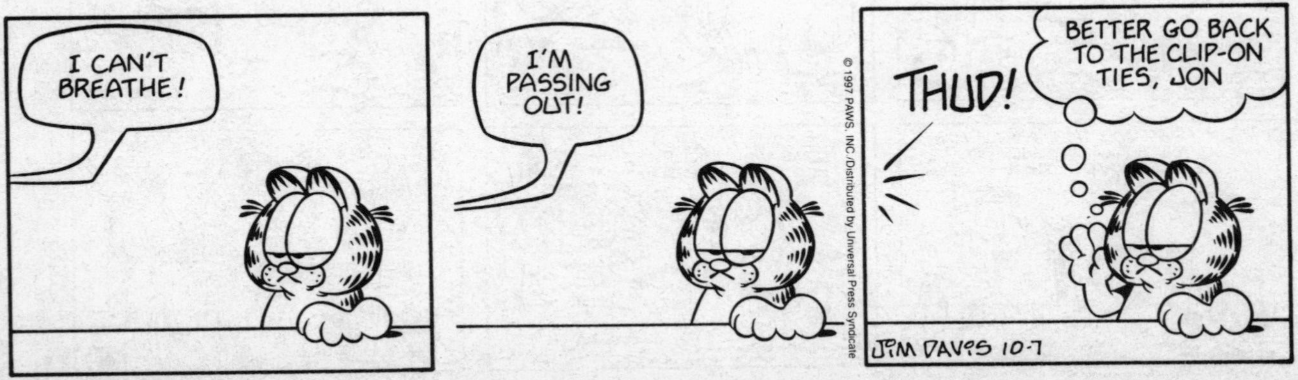
I CAN'T BREATHE!
I'M PASSING OUT!
© 1997 PAWS. INC./Distributed by Universal Press Syndicate
THUD!
BETTER GO BACK TO THE CLIP-ON TIES, JON
JIM DAVIS 10-7

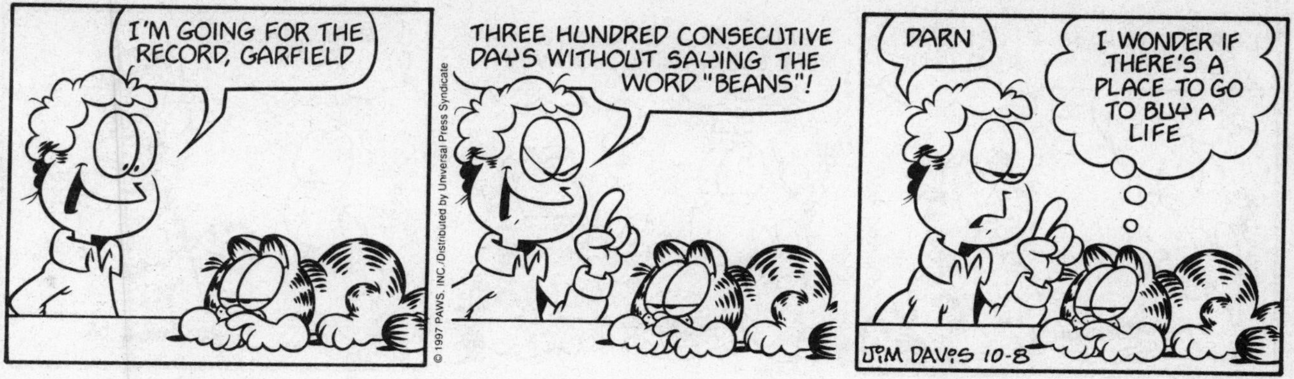
I'M GOING FOR THE RECORD, GARFIELD
THREE HUNDRED CONSECUTIVE DAYS WITHOUT SAYING THE WORD "BEANS"!
DARN
I WONDER IF THERE'S A PLACE TO GO TO BUY A LIFE
JIM DAVIS 10-8
© 1997 PAWS, INC./Distributed by Universal Press Syndicate

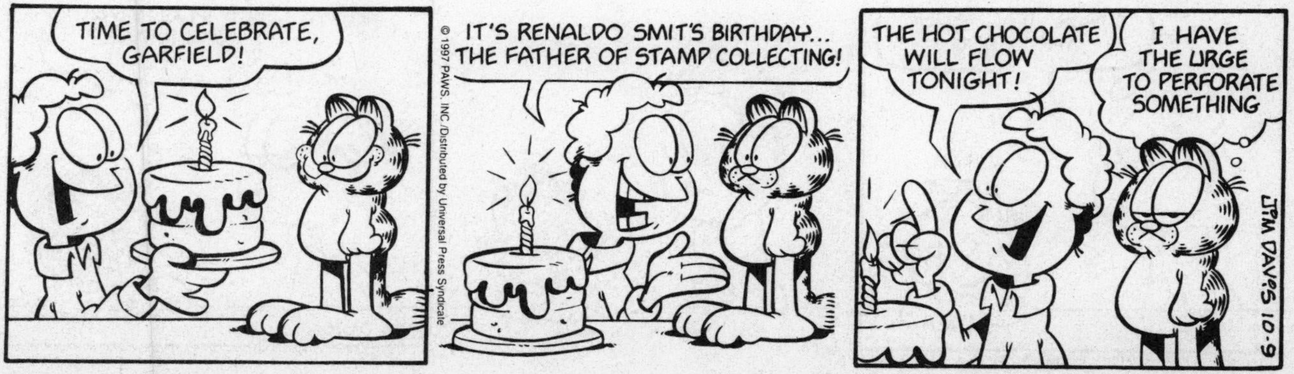
TIME TO CELEBRATE, GARFIELD!
IT'S RENALDO SMIT'S BIRTHDAY... THE FATHER OF STAMP COLLECTING!
THE HOT CHOCOLATE WILL FLOW TONIGHT!
I HAVE THE URGE TO PERFORATE SOMETHING
JIM DAVIS 10-9
© 1997 PAWS, INC./Distributed by Universal Press Syndicate

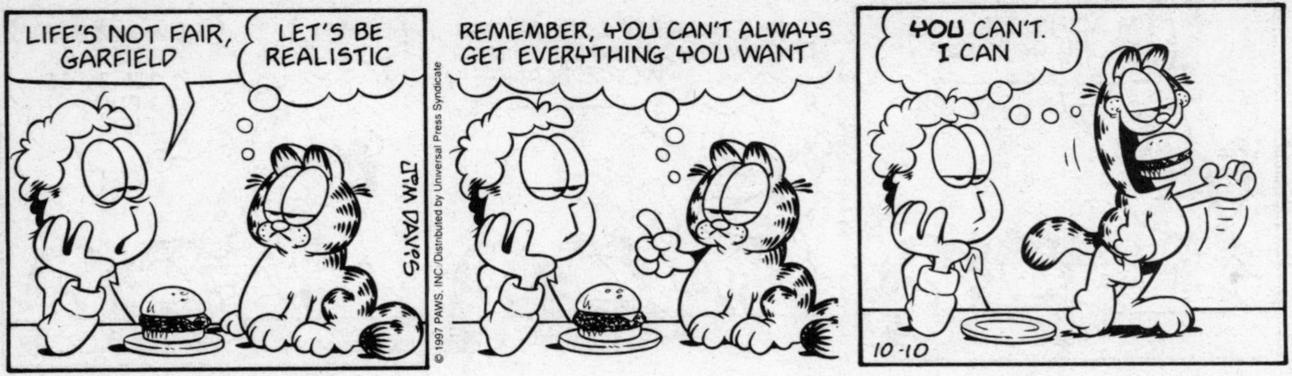
LIFE'S NOT FAIR, GARFIELD
LET'S BE REALISTIC
REMEMBER, YOU CAN'T ALWAYS GET EVERYTHING YOU WANT
YOU CAN'T. I CAN
JIM DAVIS
© 1997 PAWS. INC./Distributed by Universal Press Syndicate
10-10

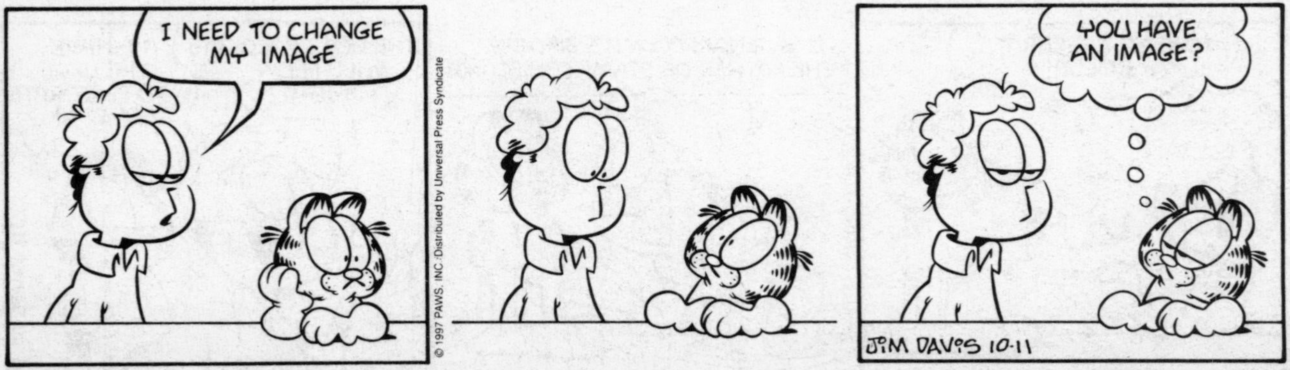
I NEED TO CHANGE MY IMAGE
YOU HAVE AN IMAGE?
© 1997 PAWS. INC./Distributed by Universal Press Syndicate
JIM DAVIS 10-11

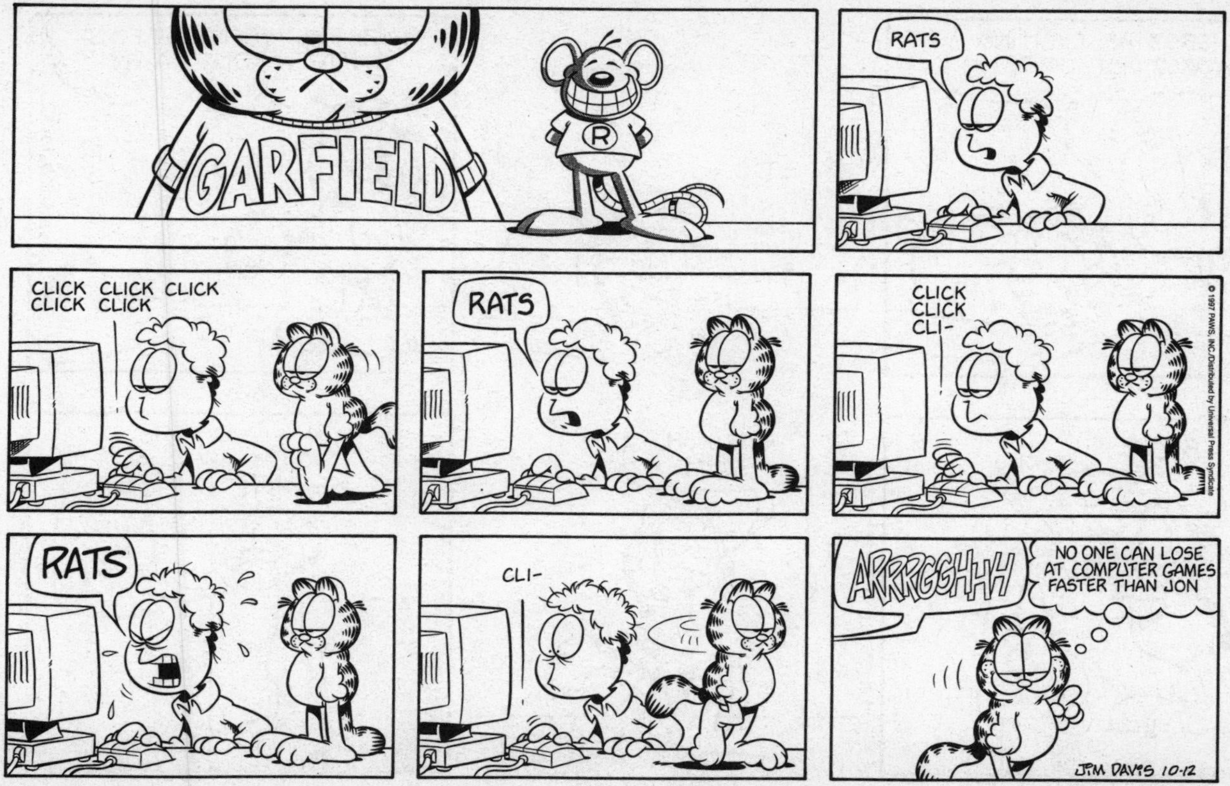

GARFIELD
R
RATS
CLICK CLICK CLICK
CLICK CLICK
RATS
CLICK
CLICK
CLI-
RATS
CLI-
ARRRGGHHH
NO ONE CAN LOSE AT COMPUTER GAMES FASTER THAN JON
JIM DAVIS 10-12
© 1997 PAWS, INC./Distributed by Universal Press Syndicate

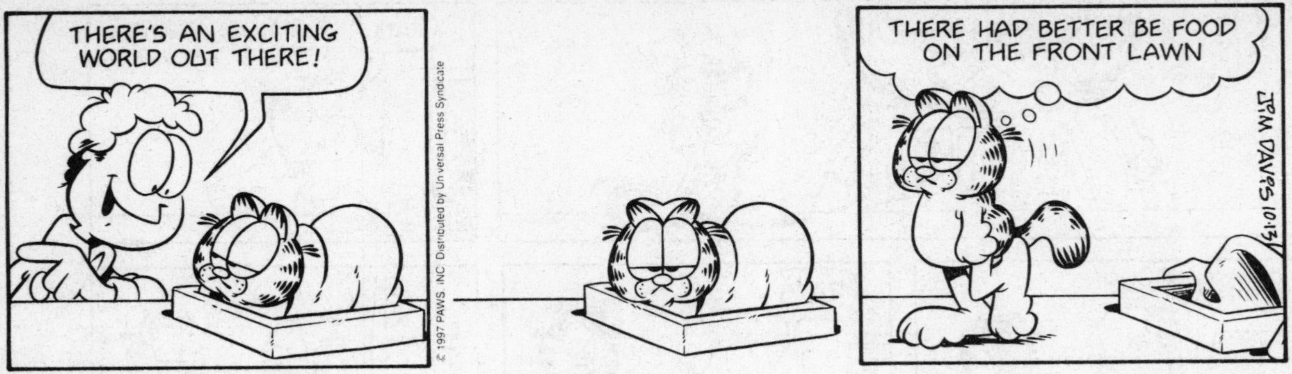
THERE'S AN EXCITING WORLD OUT THERE!
© 1997 PAWS, INC Distributed by Universal Press Syndicate
THERE HAD BETTER BE FOOD ON THE FRONT LAWN
JIM DAVIS 10-13

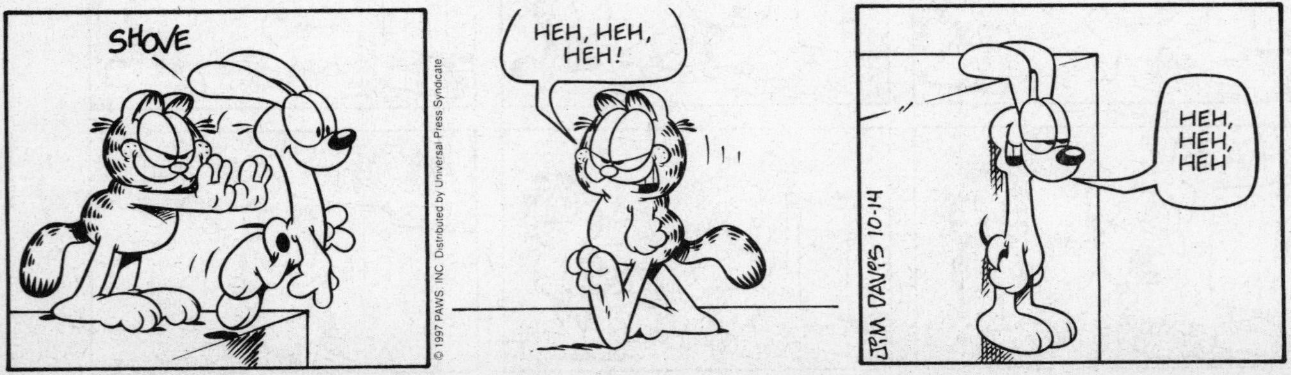
SHOVE
© 1997 PAWS, INC Distributed by Universal Press Syndicate
HEH, HEH, HEH!
HEH, HEH, HEH
JIM DAVIS 10-14

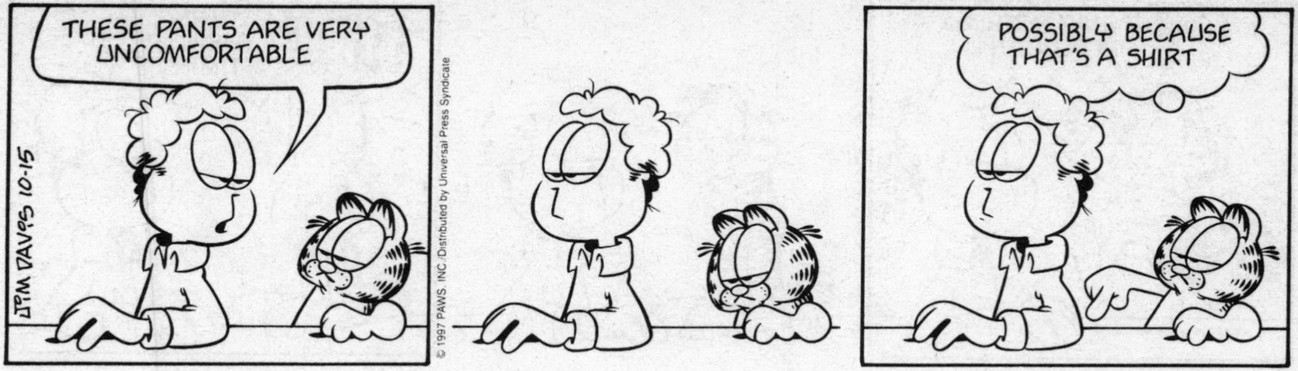
THESE PANTS ARE VERY UNCOMFORTABLE
POSSIBLY BECAUSE THAT'S A SHIRT
JIM DAVIS 10-15
© 1997 PAWS, INC./Distributed by Universal Press Syndicate

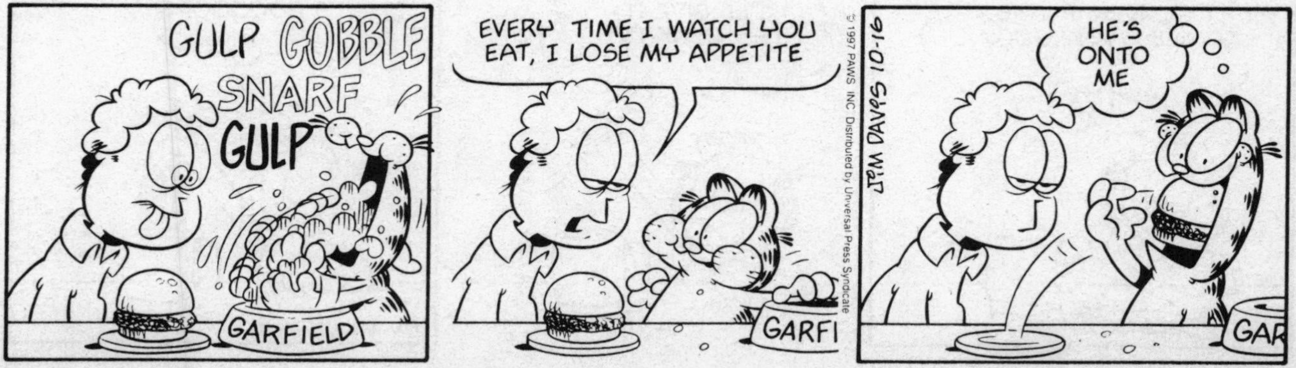
GULP GOBBLE
SNARF
GULP
GARFIELD
EVERY TIME I WATCH YOU EAT, I LOSE MY APPETITE
GARFI
HE'S ONTO ME
GAR
JIM DAVIS 10-16
© 1997 PAWS, INC. Distributed by Universal Press Syndicate

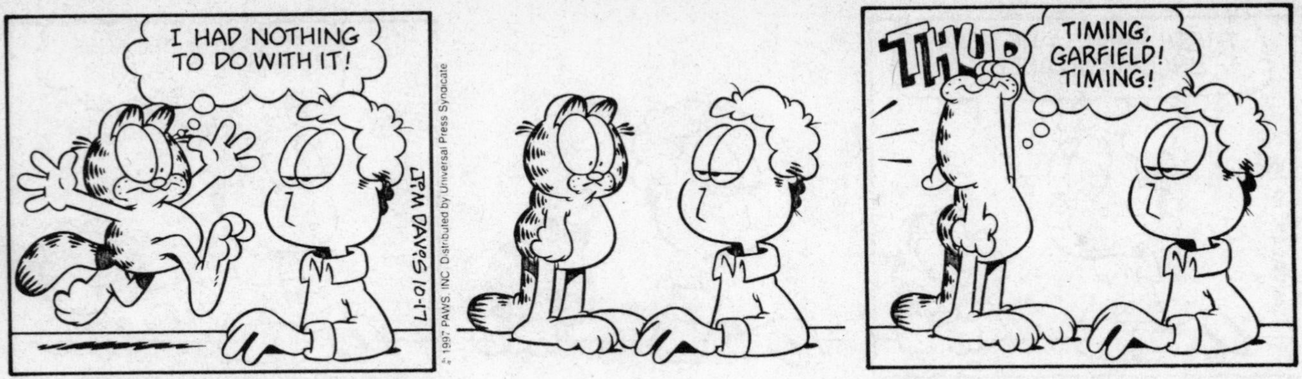
I HAD NOTHING TO DO WITH IT!
JIM DAVIS 10-17
© 1997 PAWS, INC. Distributed by Universal Press Syndicate
THUD
TIMING, GARFIELD! TIMING!

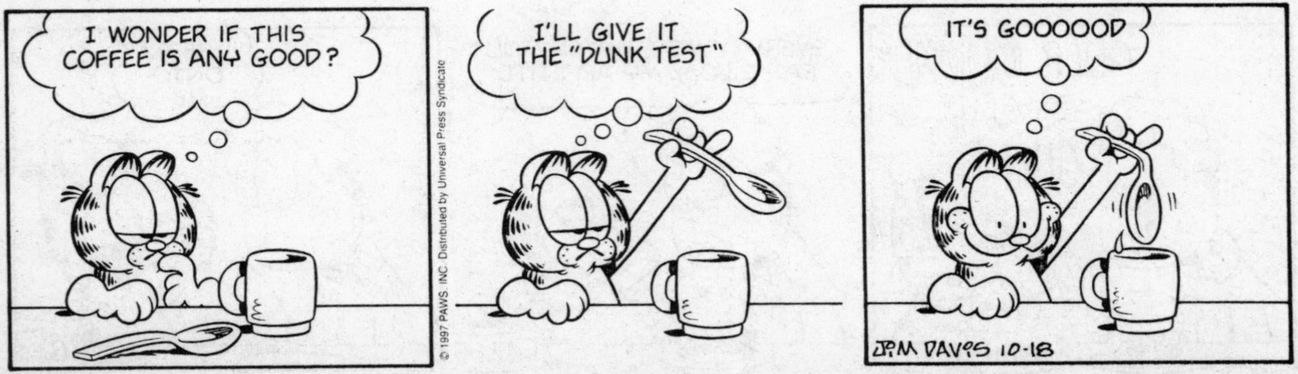
I WONDER IF THIS COFFEE IS ANY GOOD?
© 1997 PAWS, INC. Distributed by Universal Press Syndicate
I'LL GIVE IT THE "DUNK TEST"
IT'S GOOOOOD
JIM DAVIS 10-18

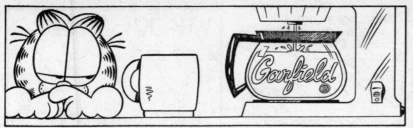

CLICK

IN THE NEWS...

GIANT BUGS INVADED A TELEVISION STATION TODAY!

GIANT, NEWS-READING BUGS

SWAT! SWAT! SWAT!
SWAT! SWAT! SWAT!

GIANT, NEWS-READING BUGS, WHO ARE MILDLY AMUSED BY ATTEMPTS TO SWAT THEM WITH A MAGAZINE...HA, HA-**HAAA**!

RESISTANCE IS FUTILE! SUBMIT, HUMANS!

COME ON, GET TO THE SPORTS SCORES

JIM DAVIS 10-19

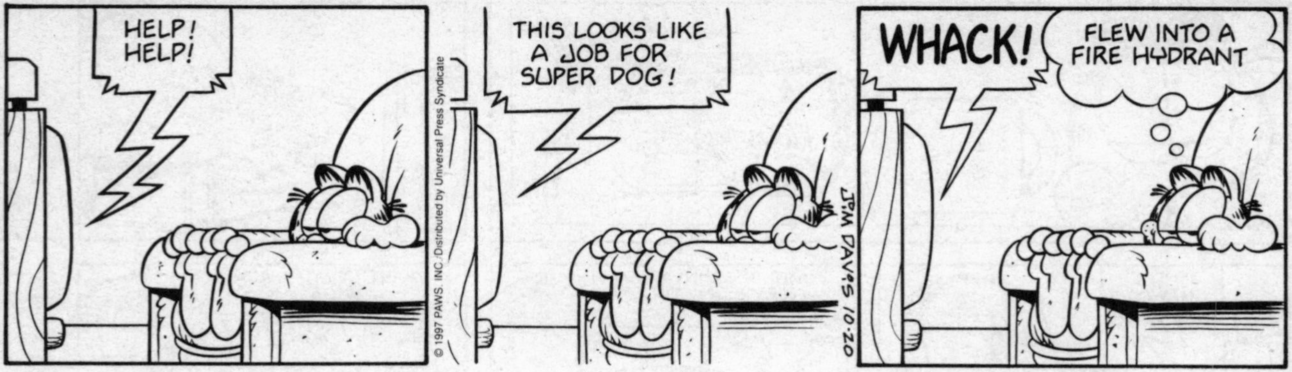
HELP! HELP!
© 1997 PAWS, INC./Distributed by Universal Press Syndicate
THIS LOOKS LIKE A JOB FOR SUPER DOG!
JIM DAVIS 10-20
WHACK!
FLEW INTO A FIRE HYDRANT

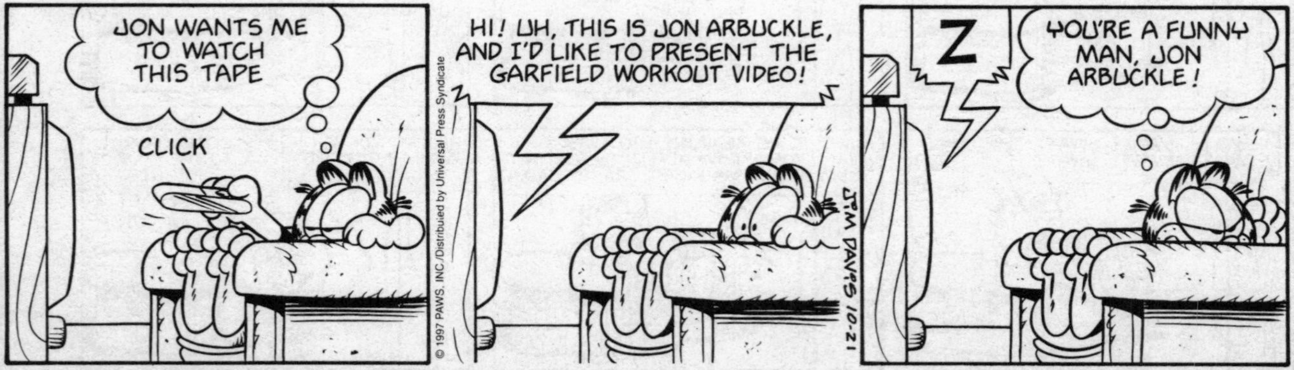
JON WANTS ME TO WATCH THIS TAPE
CLICK
© 1997 PAWS, INC./Distribuied by Universal Press Syndicate
HI! UH, THIS IS JON ARBUCKLE, AND I'D LIKE TO PRESENT THE GARFIELD WORKOUT VIDEO!
JIM DAVIS 10-21
Z
YOU'RE A FUNNY MAN, JON ARBUCKLE!

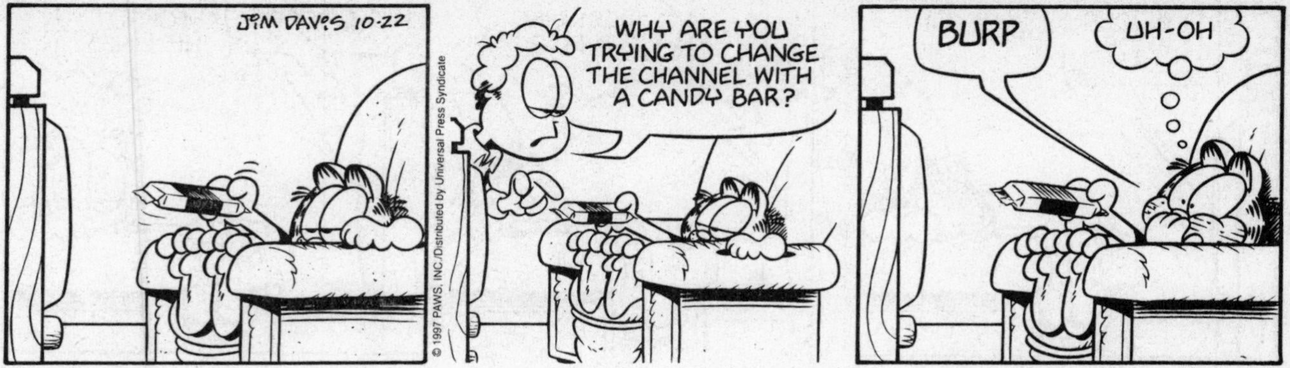
JIM DAVIS 10-22
WHY ARE YOU TRYING TO CHANGE THE CHANNEL WITH A CANDY BAR?
BURP
UH-OH
© 1997 PAWS, INC./Distributed by Universal Press Syndicate

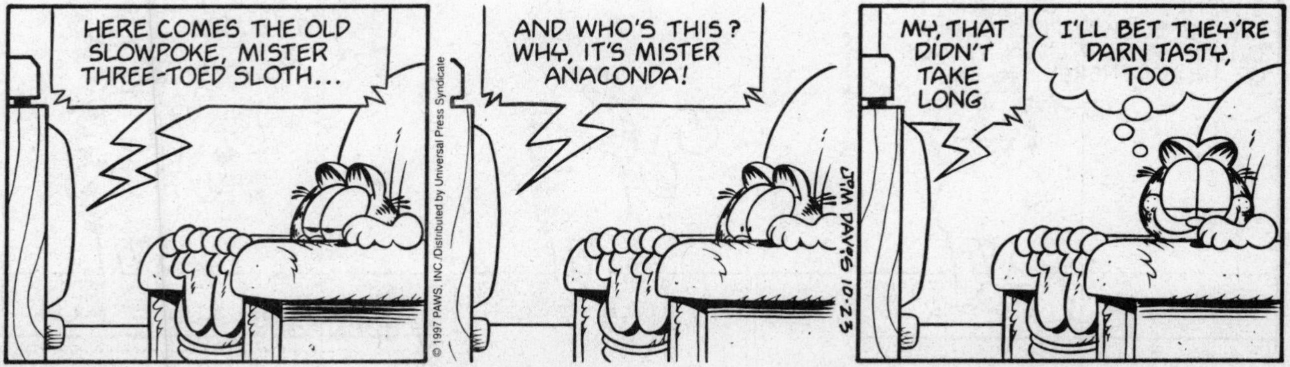
HERE COMES THE OLD SLOWPOKE, MISTER THREE-TOED SLOTH...
AND WHO'S THIS? WHY, IT'S MISTER ANACONDA!
JIM DAVIS 10-23
MY, THAT DIDN'T TAKE LONG
I'LL BET THEY'RE DARN TASTY, TOO
© 1997 PAWS, INC./Distributed by Universal Press Syndicate

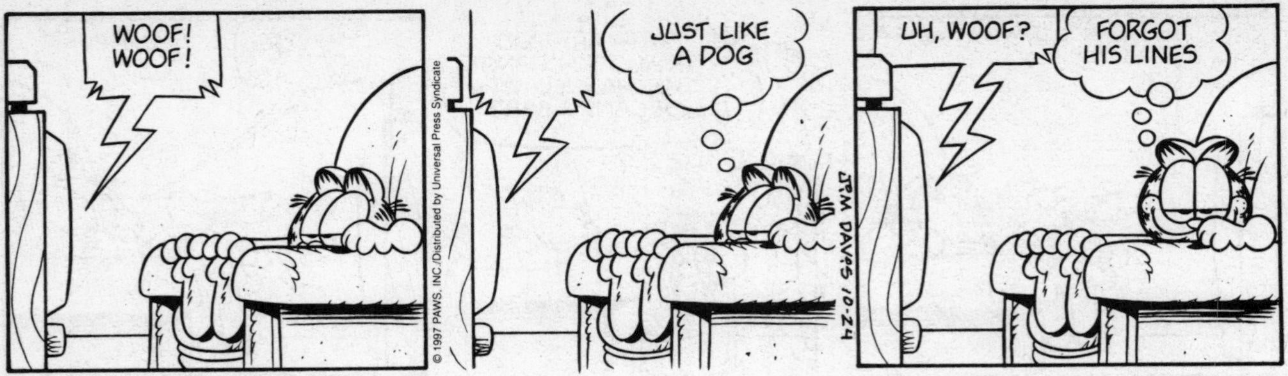
WOOF! WOOF!
JUST LIKE A DOG
UH, WOOF?
FORGOT HIS LINES
JIM DAVIS 10-24
© 1997 PAWS, INC./Distributed by Universal Press Syndicate

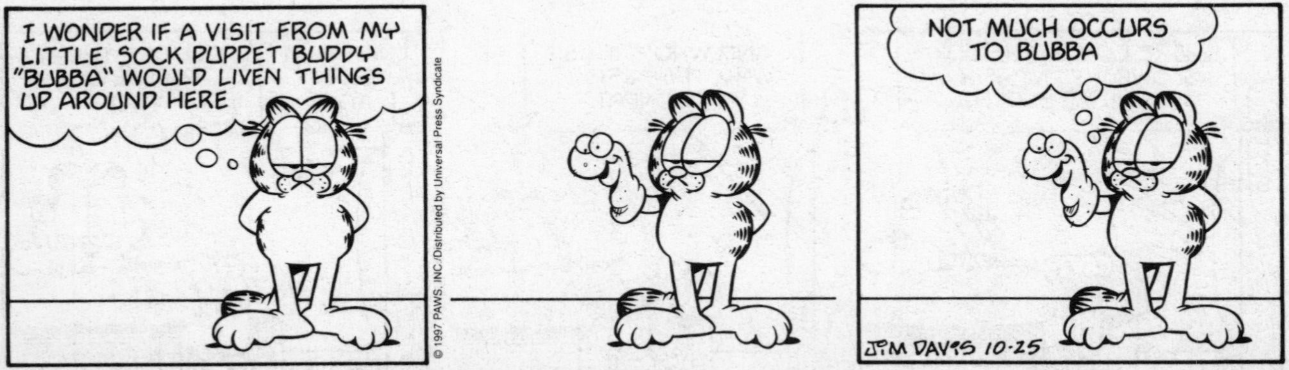
I WONDER IF A VISIT FROM MY LITTLE SOCK PUPPET BUDDY "BUBBA" WOULD LIVEN THINGS UP AROUND HERE
NOT MUCH OCCURS TO BUBBA
JIM DAVIS 10-25
© 1997 PAWS, INC./Distributed by Universal Press Syndicate

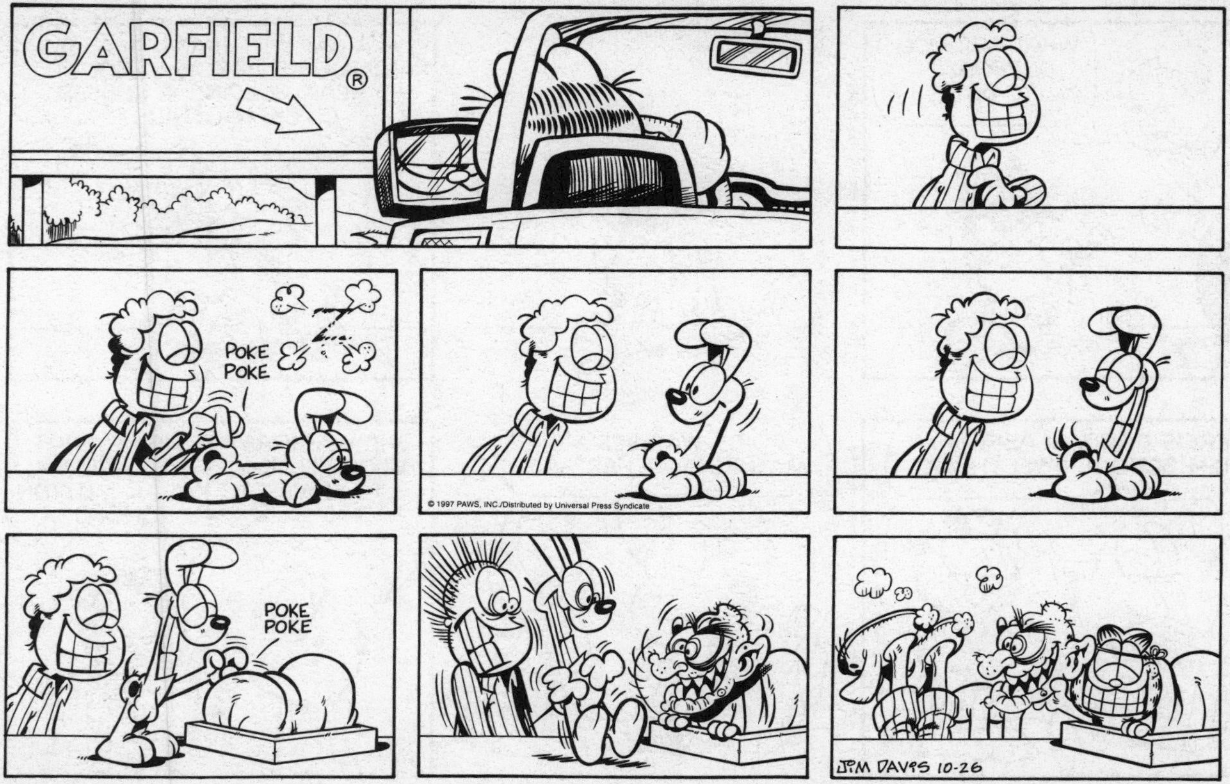
GARFIELD®
POKE POKE
© 1997 PAWS, INC./Distributed by Universal Press Syndicate
POKE POKE
JIM DAVIS 10-26

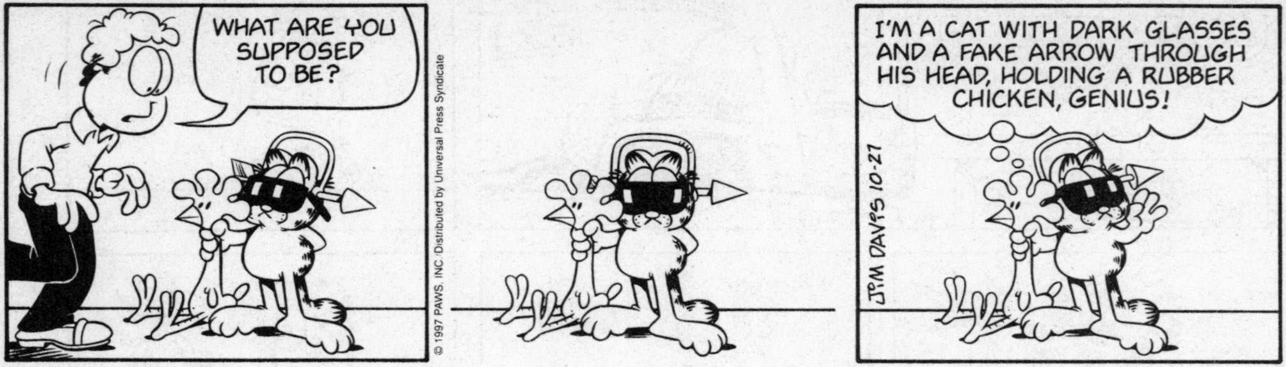
WHAT ARE YOU SUPPOSED TO BE?
I'M A CAT WITH DARK GLASSES AND A FAKE ARROW THROUGH HIS HEAD, HOLDING A RUBBER CHICKEN, GENIUS!
JIM DAVIS 10-27
© 1997 PAWS, INC./Distributed by Universal Press Syndicate

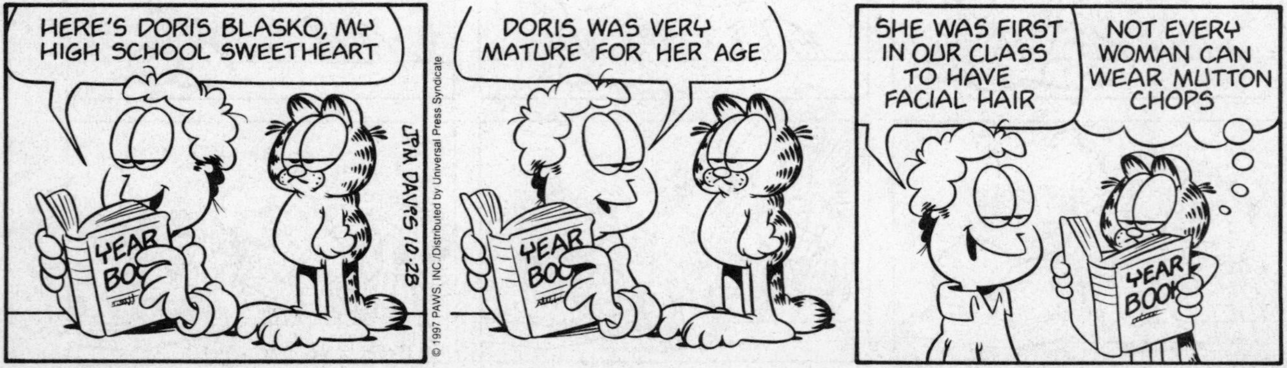
HERE'S DORIS BLASKO, MY HIGH SCHOOL SWEETHEART
DORIS WAS VERY MATURE FOR HER AGE
SHE WAS FIRST IN OUR CLASS TO HAVE FACIAL HAIR
NOT EVERY WOMAN CAN WEAR MUTTON CHOPS
YEAR BOOK
JIM DAVIS 10-28
© 1997 PAWS, INC./Distributed by Universal Press Syndicate

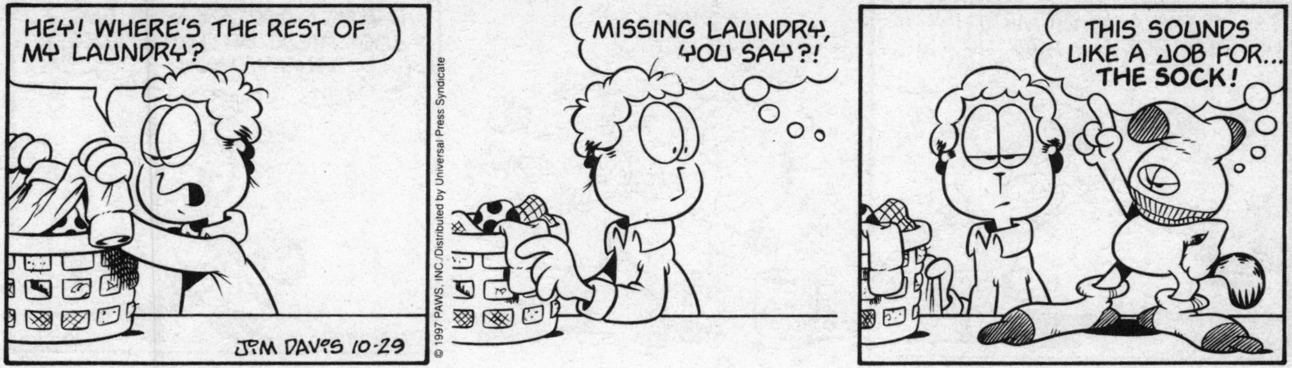
HEY! WHERE'S THE REST OF MY LAUNDRY?
JIM DAVIS 10-29
MISSING LAUNDRY, YOU SAY?!
THIS SOUNDS LIKE A JOB FOR... **THE SOCK!**

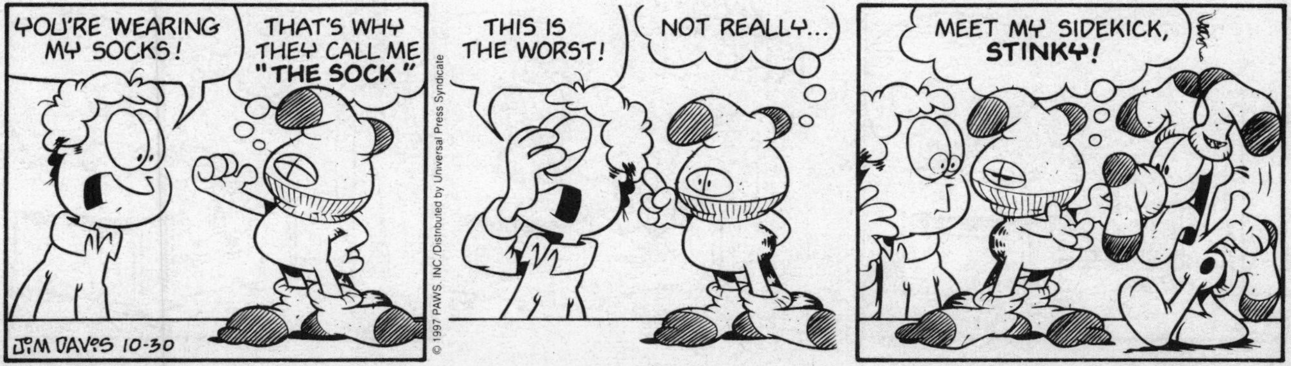
YOU'RE WEARING MY SOCKS!
THAT'S WHY THEY CALL ME "**THE SOCK**"
JIM DAVIS 10-30
THIS IS THE WORST!
NOT REALLY...
MEET MY SIDEKICK, **STINKY!**

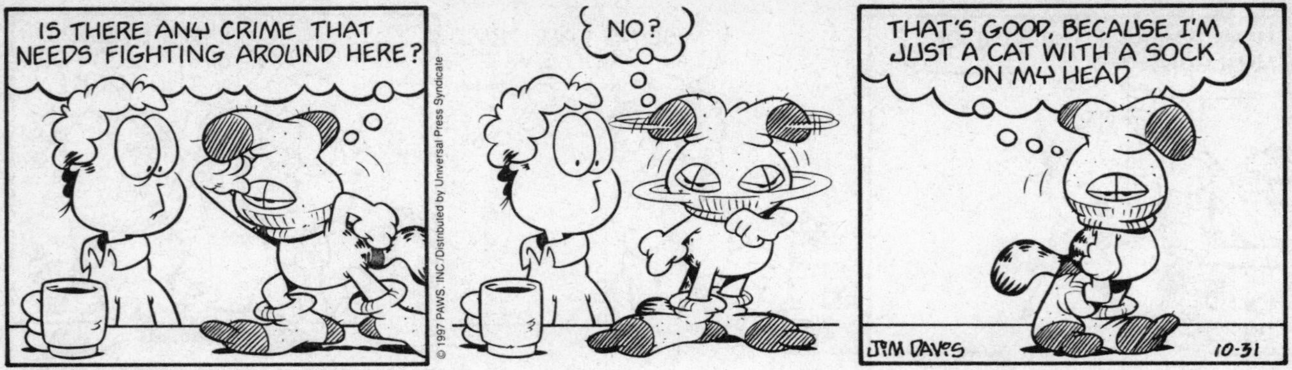
IS THERE ANY CRIME THAT NEEDS FIGHTING AROUND HERE?
NO?
THAT'S GOOD, BECAUSE I'M JUST A CAT WITH A SOCK ON MY HEAD
JIM DAVIS
10-31

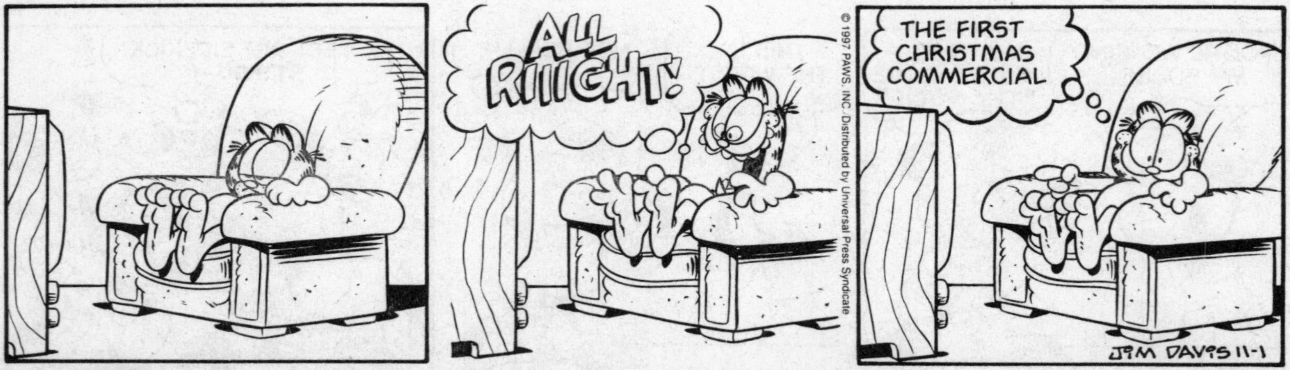
ALL RIIIGHT!
THE FIRST CHRISTMAS COMMERCIAL
JIM DAVIS 11-1

Garfield®
SIGH
THE LEAVES ARE FALLING, AND SOON I'LL BE CATCHING SNOWFLAKES ON MY TONGUE...
JPM DAVIS 11-2
!
© 1997 PAWS, INC./Distributed by Universal Press Syndicate
AMAZING
CAN I CALL 'EM, OR CAN I CALL 'EM?
PTUI! PTUI! PTUI! PTUI!

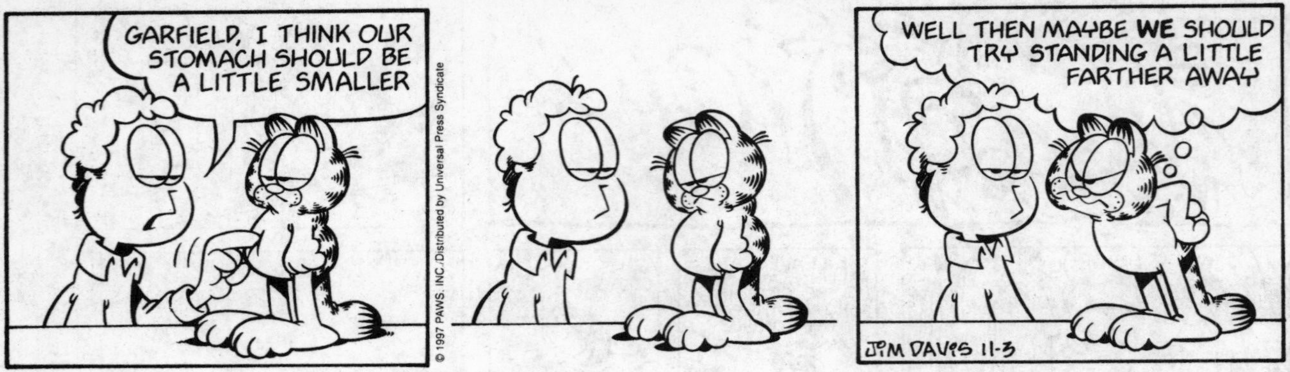
GARFIELD, I THINK OUR STOMACH SHOULD BE A LITTLE SMALLER
WELL THEN MAYBE **WE** SHOULD TRY STANDING A LITTLE FARTHER AWAY
JIM DAVIS 11-3
© 1997 PAWS. INC./Distributed by Universal Press Syndicate

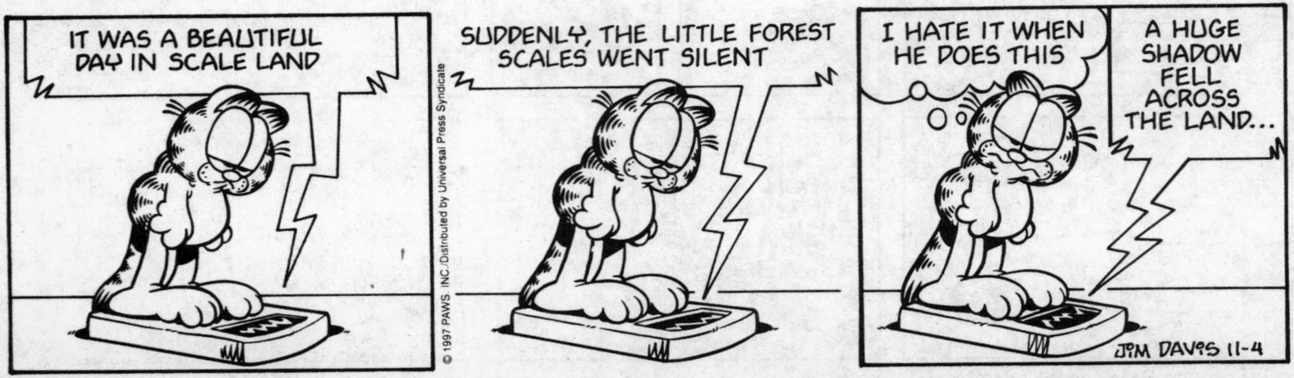
IT WAS A BEAUTIFUL DAY IN SCALE LAND
SUDDENLY, THE LITTLE FOREST SCALES WENT SILENT
I HATE IT WHEN HE DOES THIS
A HUGE SHADOW FELL ACROSS THE LAND...
JIM DAVIS 11-4
© 1997 PAWS. INC./Distributed by Universal Press Syndicate

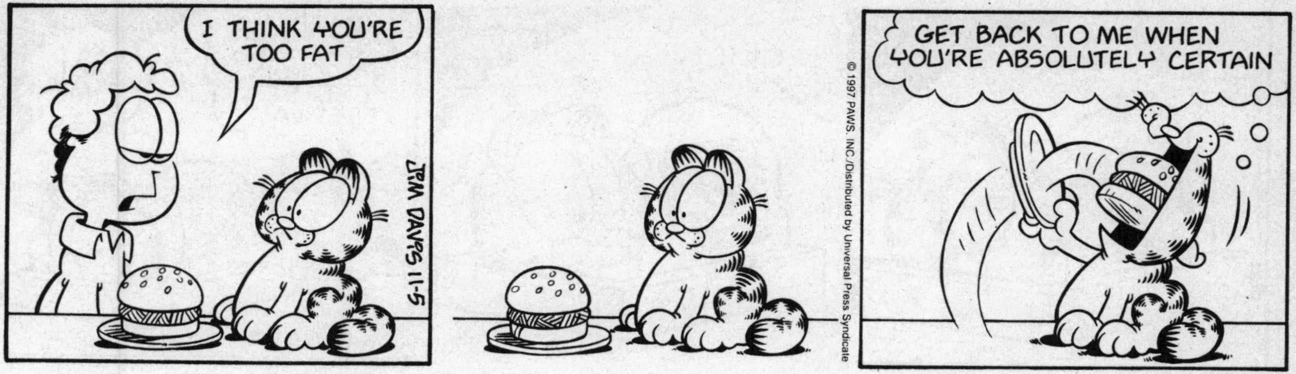
I THINK YOU'RE TOO FAT
JIM DAVIS 11-5
© 1997 PAWS. INC./Distributed by Universal Press Syndicate
GET BACK TO ME WHEN YOU'RE ABSOLUTELY CERTAIN

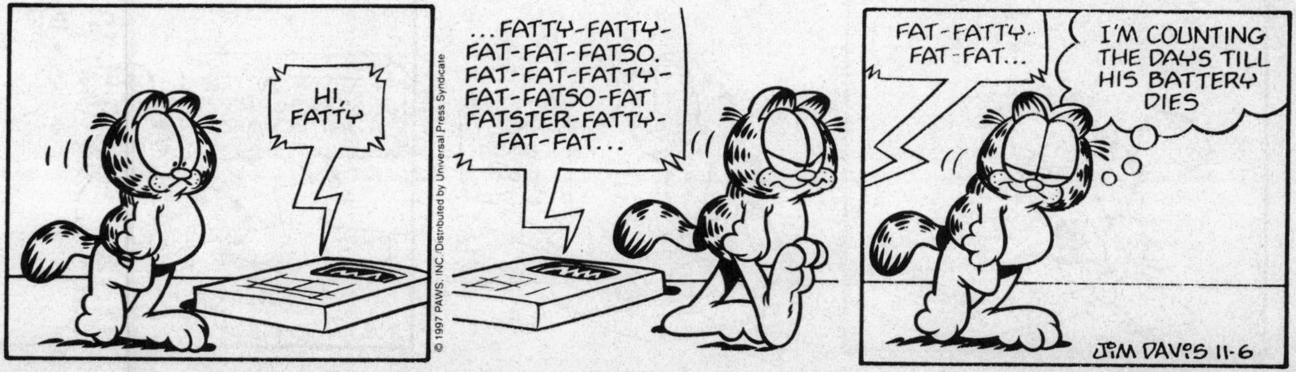
HI, FATTY
© 1997 PAWS. INC./Distributed by Universal Press Syndicate
...FATTY-FATTY-FAT-FAT-FATSO. FAT-FAT-FATTY-FAT-FATSO-FAT FATSTER-FATTY-FAT-FAT...
FAT-FATTY-FAT-FAT...
I'M COUNTING THE DAYS TILL HIS BATTERY DIES
JIM DAVIS 11-6

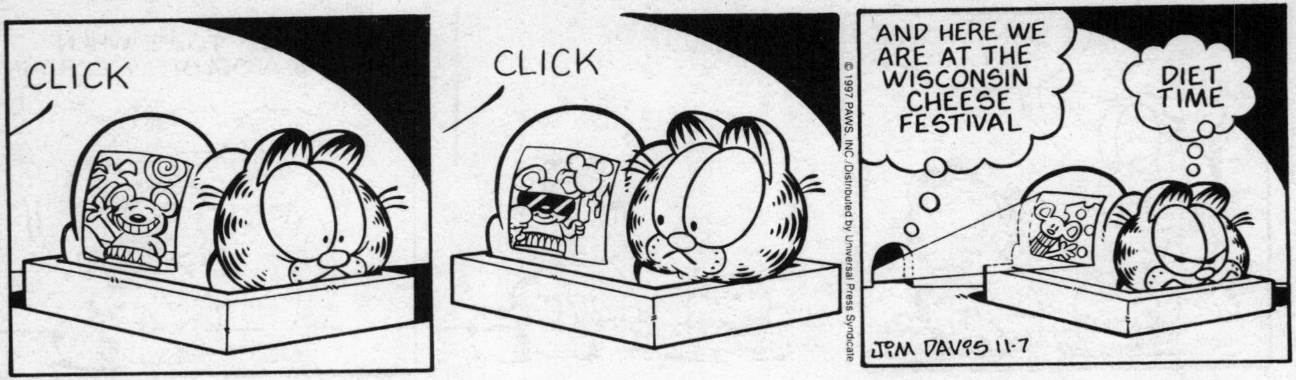
CLICK
CLICK
© 1997 PAWS, INC./Distributed by Universal Press Syndicate
AND HERE WE ARE AT THE WISCONSIN CHEESE FESTIVAL
DIET TIME
JIM DAVIS 11-7

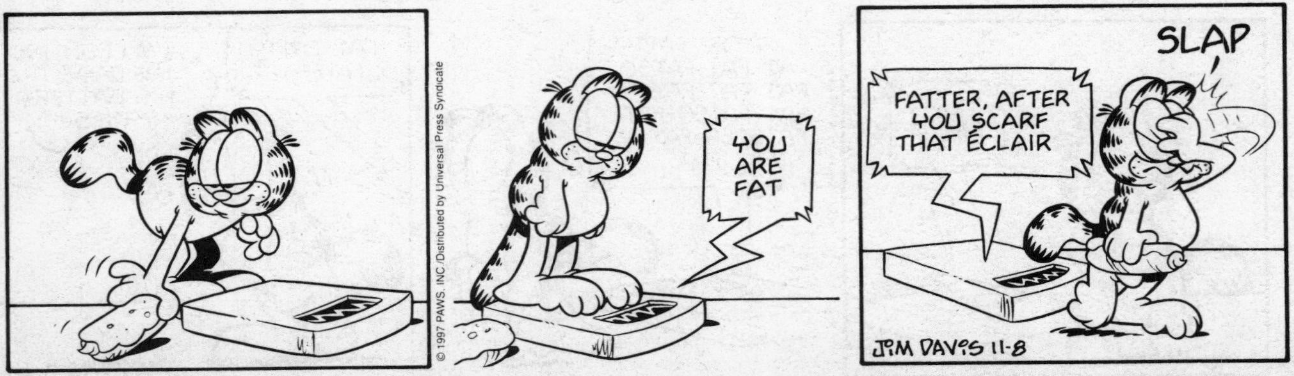
© 1997 PAWS, INC./Distributed by Universal Press Syndicate
YOU ARE FAT
SLAP
FATTER, AFTER YOU SCARF THAT ÉCLAIR
JIM DAVIS 11-8

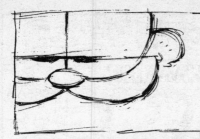

garfield ®

BOY, AM I DEPRESSED

© 1997 PAWS, INC./Distributed by Universal Press Syndicate

BZZZZ
BZZZZ
BZZZZ

JIM DAVIS 11-9

TEASE TEASE
TEASE TEASE

TEASE TEASE
TEASE TEASE

REE
REE
REE

PAINT
PAINT
PAINT

FUNNY... I FEEL BETTER

I DO WHAT I CAN

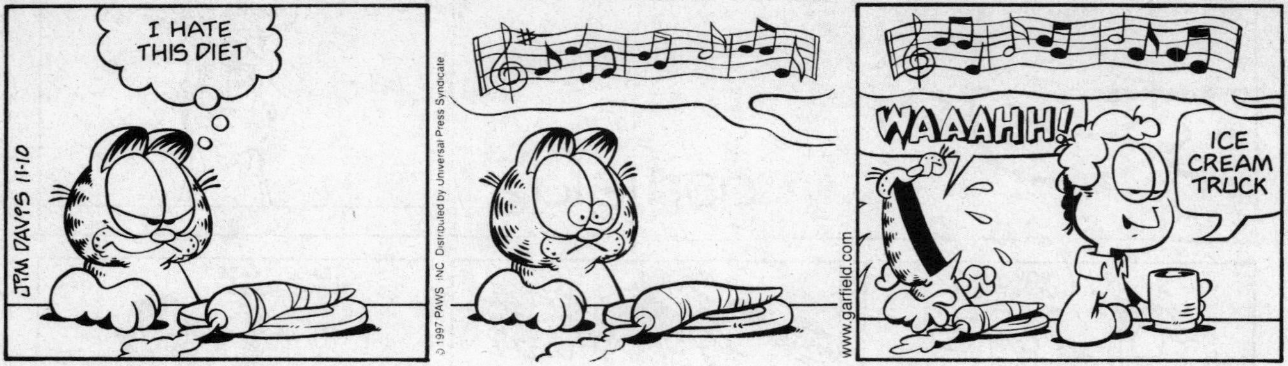
I HATE THIS DIET
JIM DAVIS 11-10
© 1997 PAWS INC Distributed by Universal Press Syndicate
WAAAHH!
ICE CREAM TRUCK
www.garfield.com

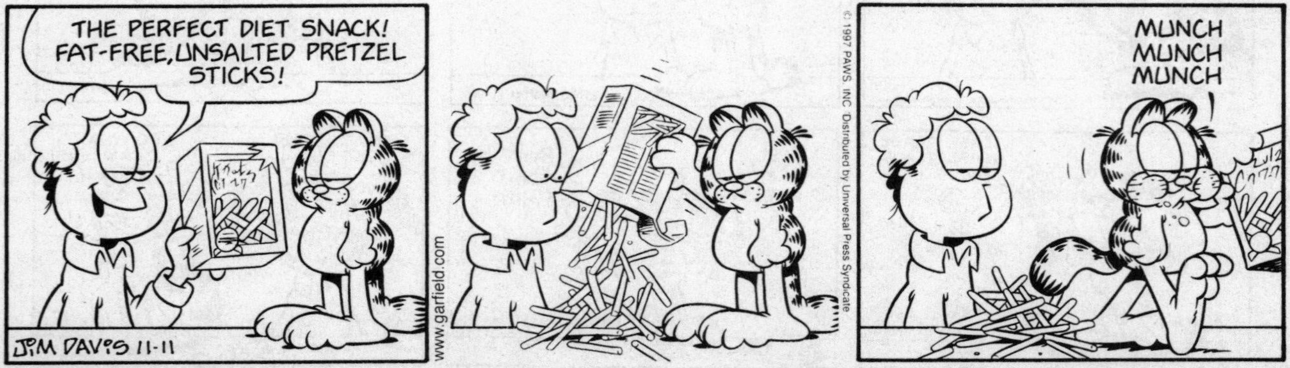
THE PERFECT DIET SNACK! FAT-FREE,UNSALTED PRETZEL STICKS!
JIM DAVIS 11-11
www.garfield.com
© 1997 PAWS INC Distributed by Universal Press Syndicate
MUNCH
MUNCH
MUNCH

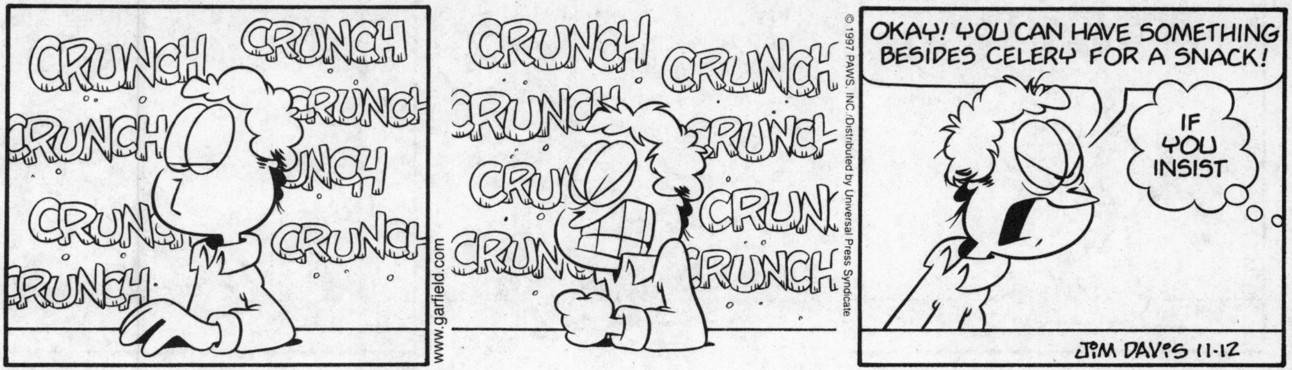
CRUNCH CRUNCH CRUNCH CRUNCH CRUNCH CRUNCH CRUNCH CRUNCH
www.garfield.com
CRUNCH CRUNCH CRUNCH CRUNCH CRUNCH CRUNCH CRUNCH
© 1997 PAWS, INC./Distributed by Universal Press Syndicate
OKAY! YOU CAN HAVE SOMETHING BESIDES CELERY FOR A SNACK!
IF YOU INSIST
JIM DAVIS 11-12

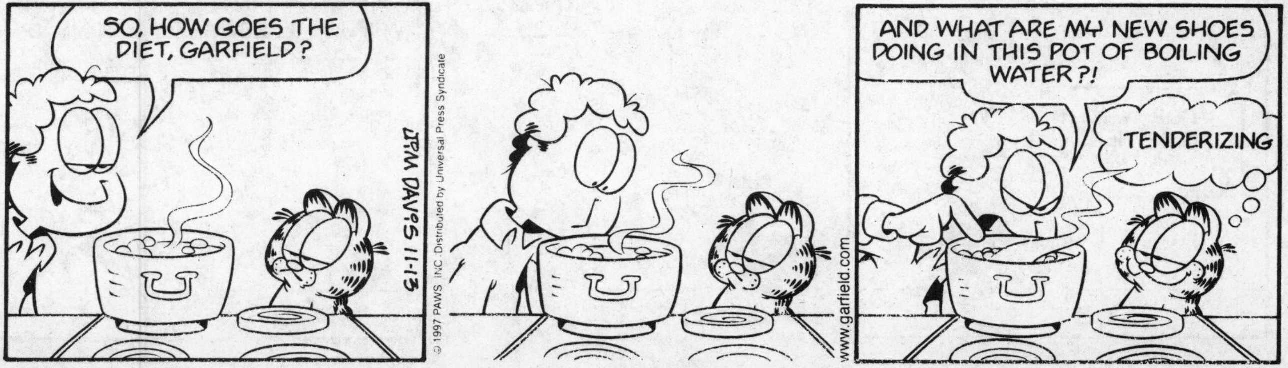
SO, HOW GOES THE DIET, GARFIELD?
JIM DAVIS 11-13
© 1997 PAWS, INC. Distributed by Universal Press Syndicate
www.garfield.com
AND WHAT ARE MY NEW SHOES DOING IN THIS POT OF BOILING WATER?!
TENDERIZING

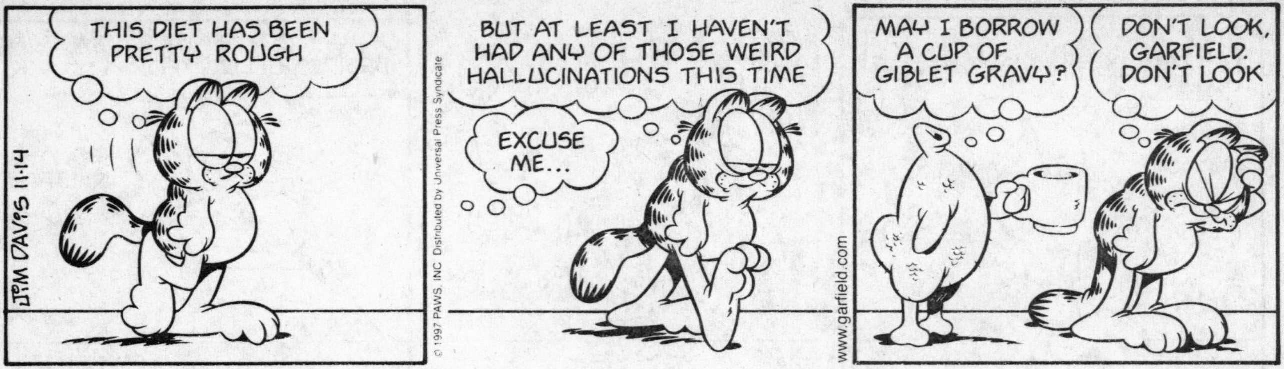
THIS DIET HAS BEEN PRETTY ROUGH
JIM DAVIS 11-14
© 1997 PAWS, INC Distributed by Universal Press Syndicate
BUT AT LEAST I HAVEN'T HAD ANY OF THOSE WEIRD HALLUCINATIONS THIS TIME
EXCUSE ME...
www.garfield.com
MAY I BORROW A CUP OF GIBLET GRAVY?
DON'T LOOK, GARFIELD. DON'T LOOK

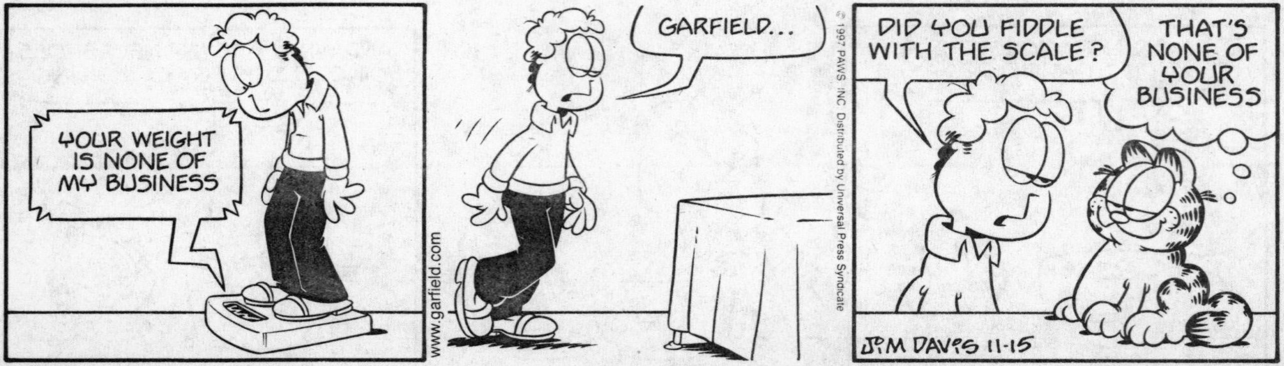
YOUR WEIGHT IS NONE OF MY BUSINESS
www.garfield.com
GARFIELD...
© 1997 PAWS, INC Distributed by Universal Press Syndicate
DID YOU FIDDLE WITH THE SCALE?
THAT'S NONE OF YOUR BUSINESS
JIM DAVIS 11-15

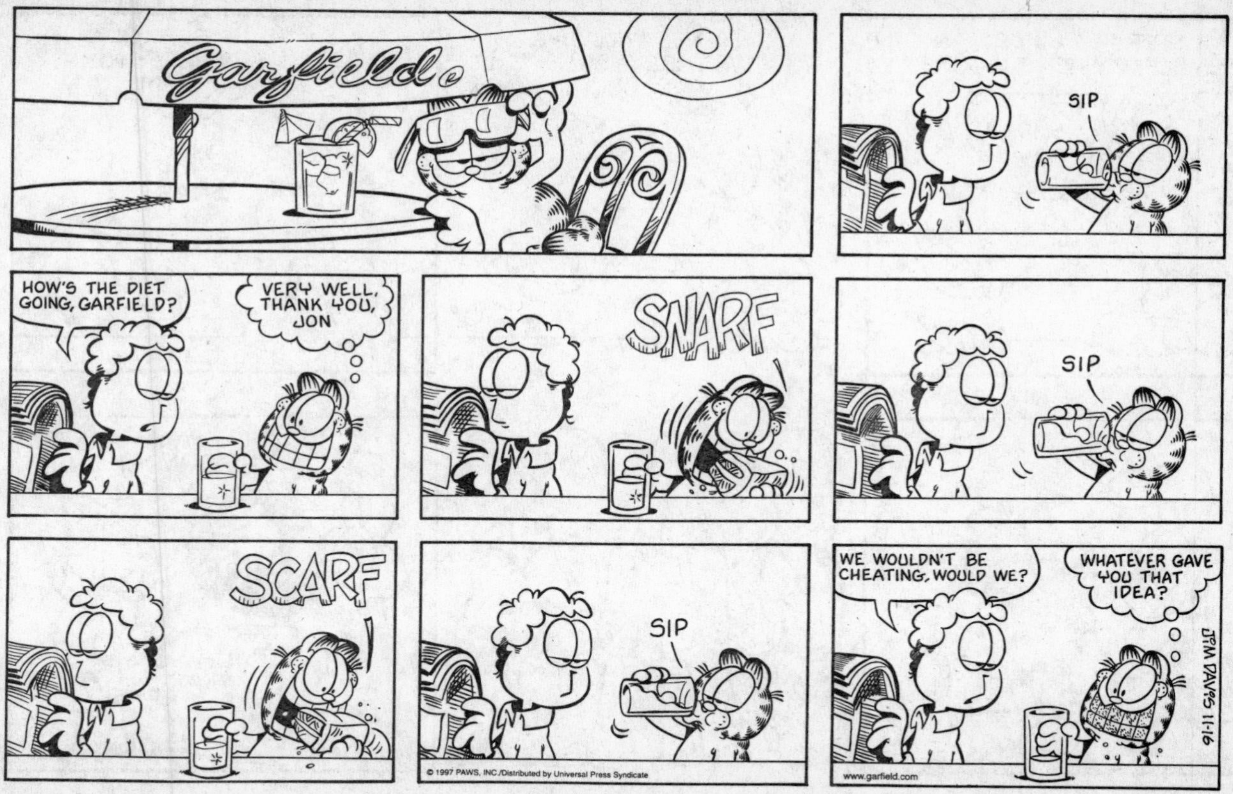
Garfield
SIP
HOW'S THE DIET GOING, GARFIELD?
VERY WELL, THANK YOU, JON
SNARF
SIP
SCARF
SIP
WE WOULDN'T BE CHEATING, WOULD WE?
WHATEVER GAVE YOU THAT IDEA?
JPM DAVPS 11-16
© 1997 PAWS, INC./Distributed by Universal Press Syndicate
www.garfield.com

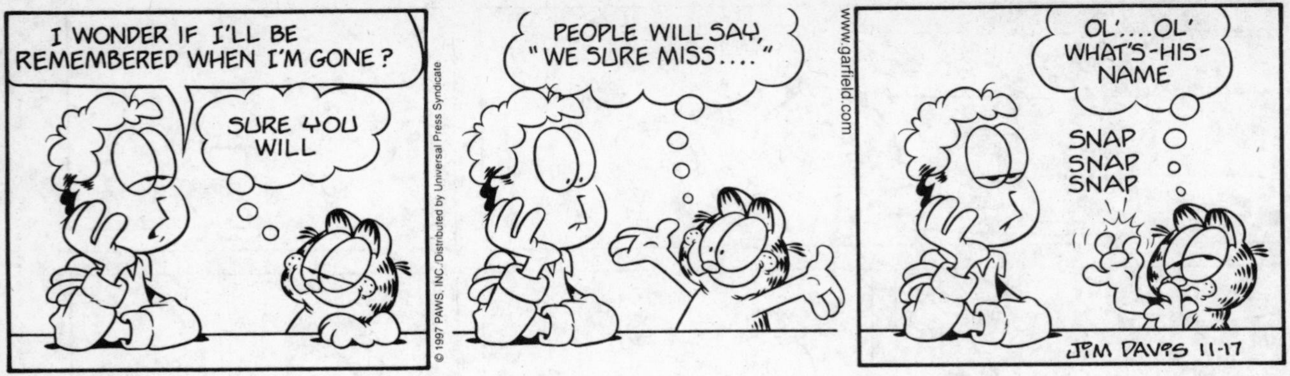
I WONDER IF I'LL BE REMEMBERED WHEN I'M GONE?
SURE YOU WILL
© 1997 PAWS, INC./Distributed by Universal Press Syndicate
PEOPLE WILL SAY, "WE SURE MISS...."
www.garfield.com
OL'....OL' WHAT'S-HIS-NAME
SNAP SNAP SNAP
JIM DAVIS 11-17

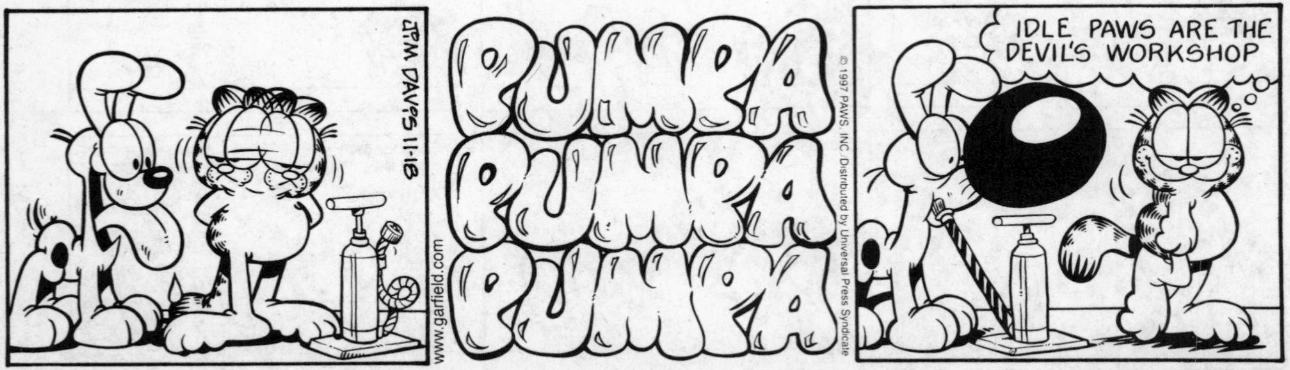
JIM DAVIS 11-18
www.garfield.com
PUMPA PUMPA PUMPA
© 1997 PAWS, INC./Distributed by Universal Press Syndicate
IDLE PAWS ARE THE DEVIL'S WORKSHOP

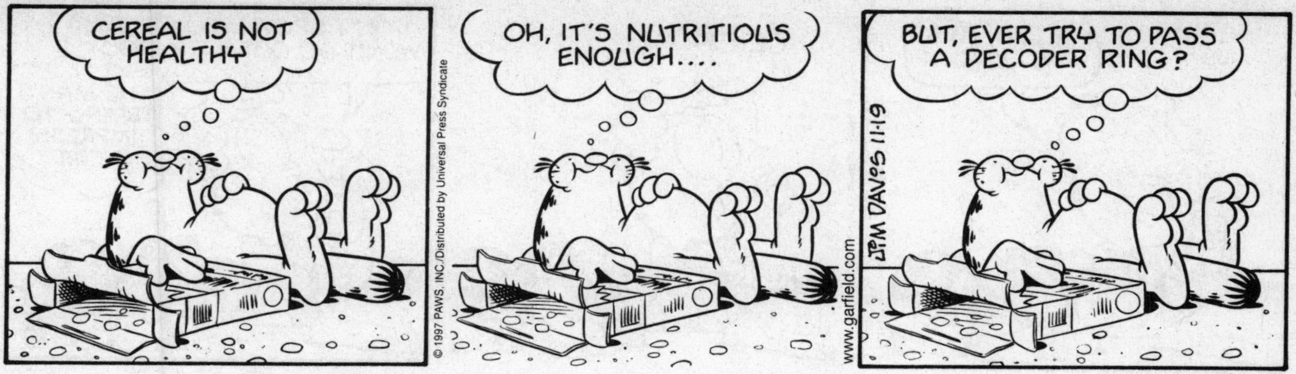
CEREAL IS NOT HEALTHY
OH, IT'S NUTRITIOUS ENOUGH....
BUT, EVER TRY TO PASS A DECODER RING?
© 1997 PAWS. INC./Distributed by Universal Press Syndicate
www.garfield.com
JIM DAVIS 11-19

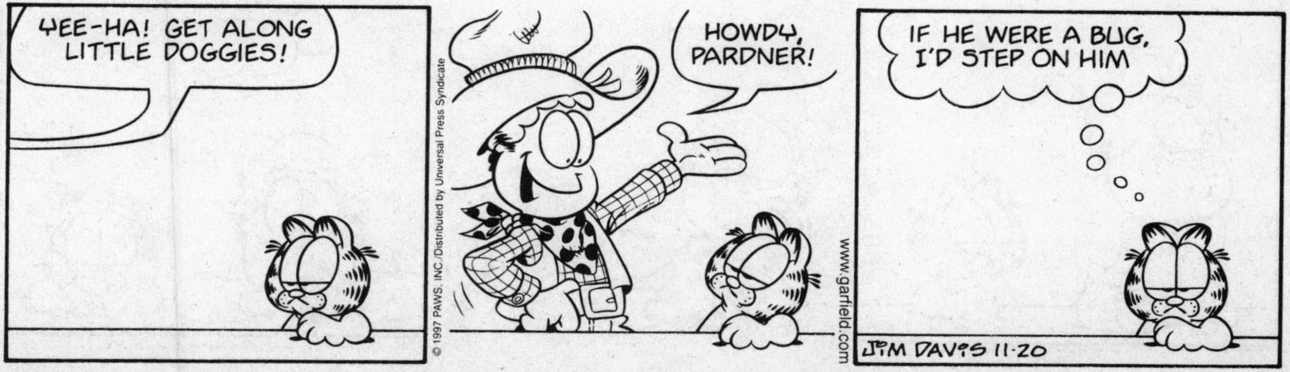
YEE-HA! GET ALONG LITTLE DOGGIES!
HOWDY, PARDNER!
IF HE WERE A BUG, I'D STEP ON HIM
© 1997 PAWS. INC./Distributed by Universal Press Syndicate
www.garfield.com
JIM DAVIS 11-20

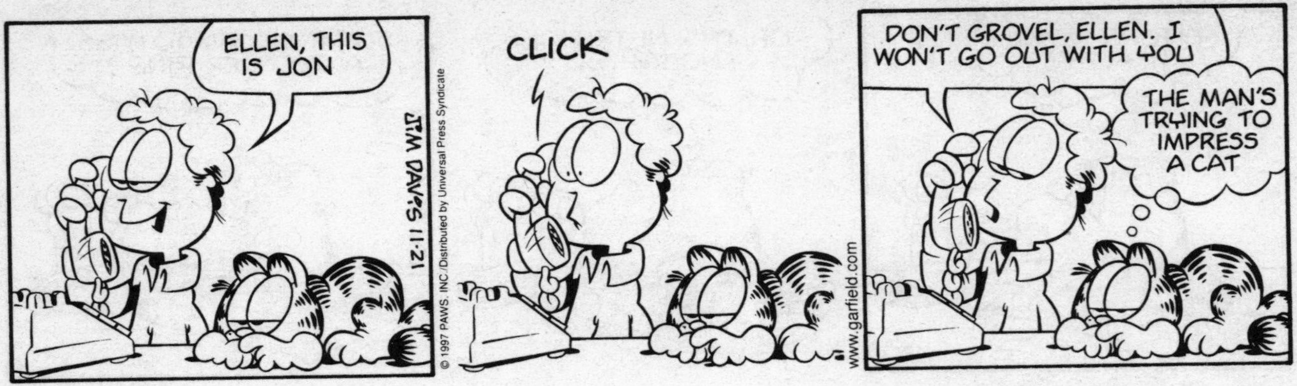
ELLEN, THIS IS JON
JIM DAVIS 11-21
© 1997 PAWS, INC./Distributed by Universal Press Syndicate
CLICK
www.garfield.com
DON'T GROVEL, ELLEN. I WON'T GO OUT WITH YOU
THE MAN'S TRYING TO IMPRESS A CAT

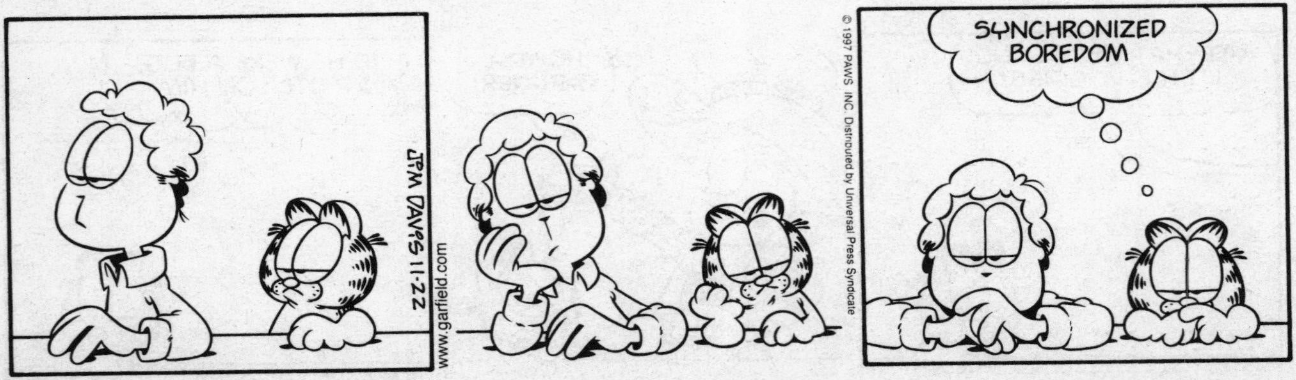
JIM DAVIS 11-22
www.garfield.com
© 1997 PAWS, INC. Distributed by Universal Press Syndicate
SYNCHRONIZED BOREDOM

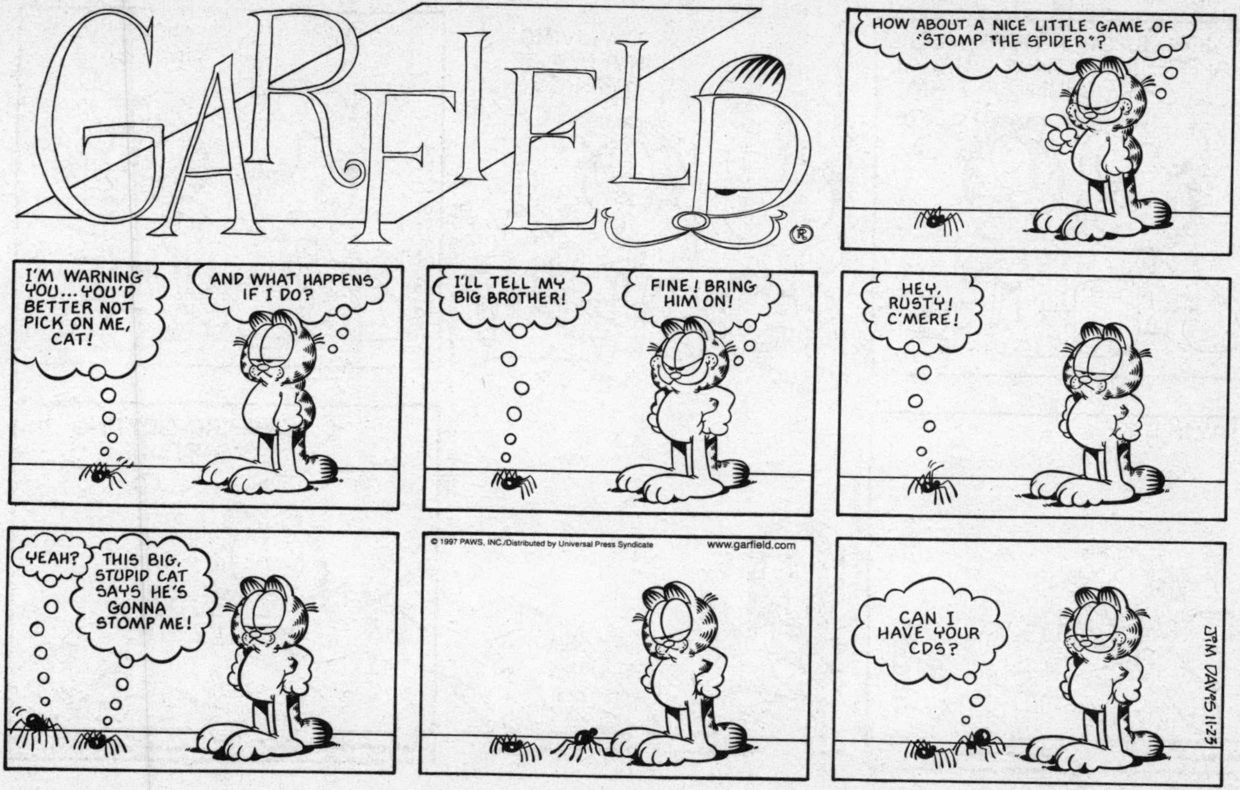
GARFIELD
HOW ABOUT A NICE LITTLE GAME OF "STOMP THE SPIDER"?
I'M WARNING YOU... YOU'D BETTER NOT PICK ON ME, CAT!
AND WHAT HAPPENS IF I DO?
I'LL TELL MY BIG BROTHER!
FINE! BRING HIM ON!
HEY, RUSTY! C'MERE!
YEAH?
THIS BIG, STUPID CAT SAYS HE'S GONNA STOMP ME!
© 1997 PAWS, INC./Distributed by Universal Press Syndicate
www.garfield.com
CAN I HAVE YOUR CDS?
JIM DAVIS 11-23

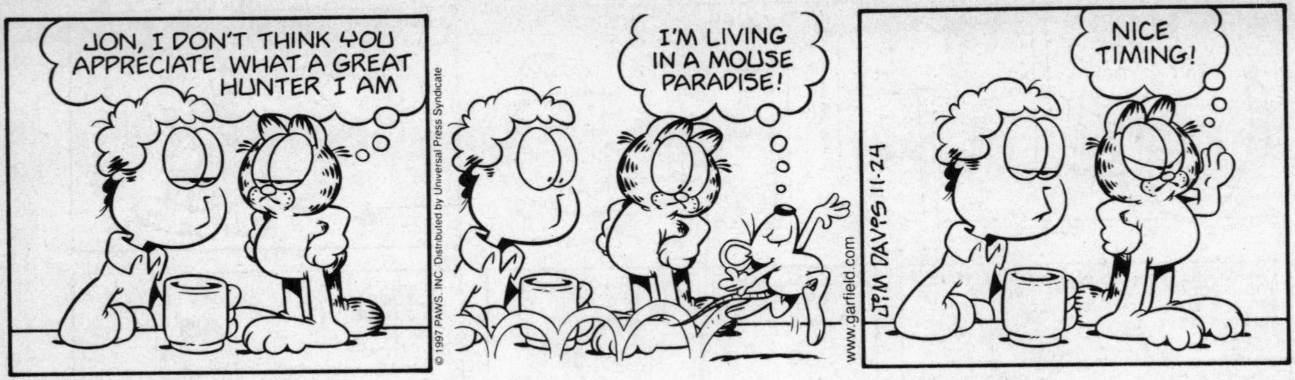
JON, I DON'T THINK YOU APPRECIATE WHAT A GREAT HUNTER I AM
© 1997 PAWS, INC. Distributed by Universal Press Syndicate
I'M LIVING IN A MOUSE PARADISE!
www.garfield.com
JIM DAVIS 11-24
NICE TIMING!

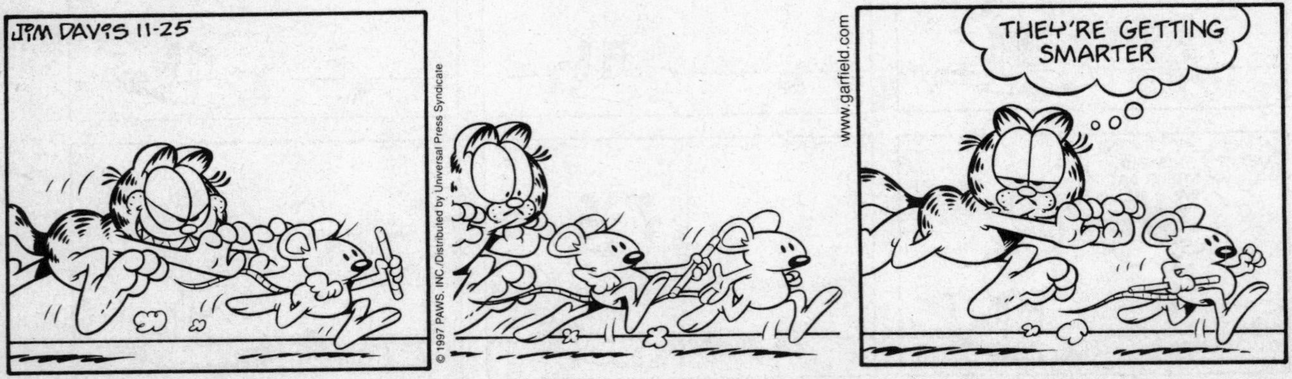
JIM DAVIS 11-25
© 1997 PAWS, INC./Distributed by Universal Press Syndicate
www.garfield.com
THEY'RE GETTING SMARTER

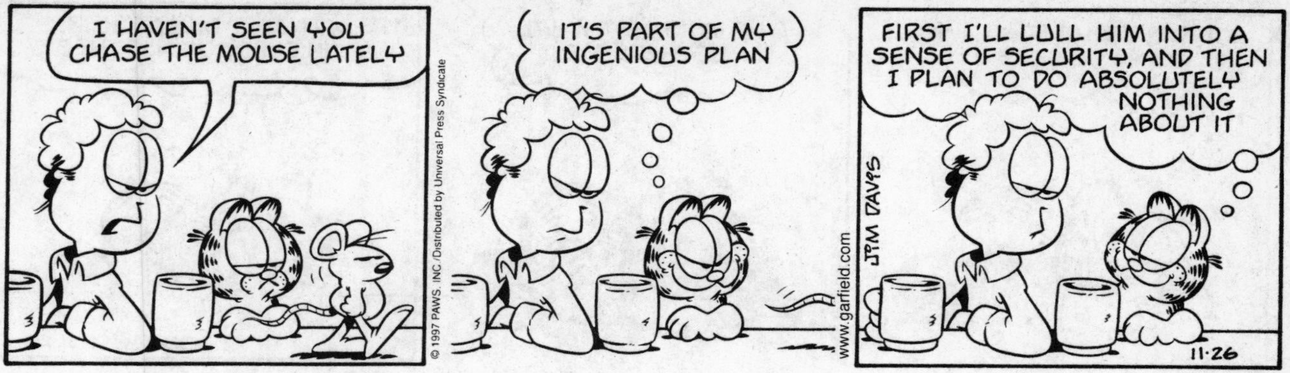
I HAVEN'T SEEN YOU CHASE THE MOUSE LATELY
IT'S PART OF MY INGENIOUS PLAN
FIRST I'LL LULL HIM INTO A SENSE OF SECURITY, AND THEN I PLAN TO DO ABSOLUTELY NOTHING ABOUT IT
© 1997 PAWS, INC./Distributed by Universal Press Syndicate
www.garfield.com
JIM DAVIS
11·26

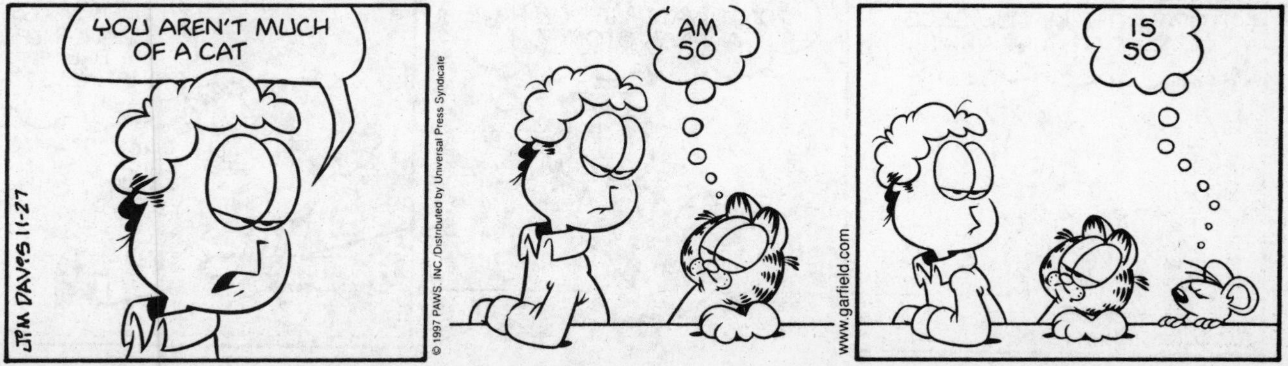
YOU AREN'T MUCH OF A CAT
AM SO
IS SO
JIM DAVIS 11-27
© 1997 PAWS, INC./Distributed by Universal Press Syndicate
www.garfield.com

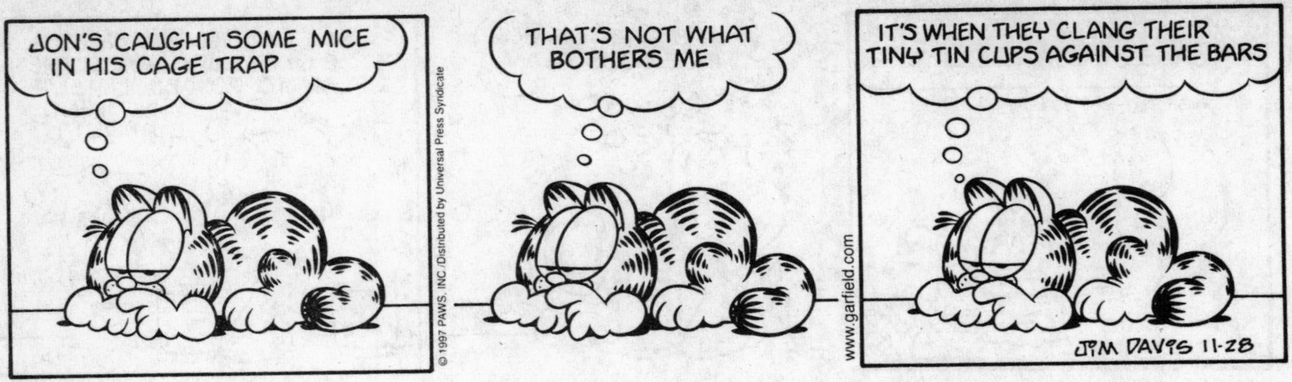
JON'S CAUGHT SOME MICE IN HIS CAGE TRAP
THAT'S NOT WHAT BOTHERS ME
IT'S WHEN THEY CLANG THEIR TINY TIN CUPS AGAINST THE BARS
JIM DAVIS 11-28
© 1997 PAWS, INC./Distributed by Universal Press Syndicate
www.garfield.com

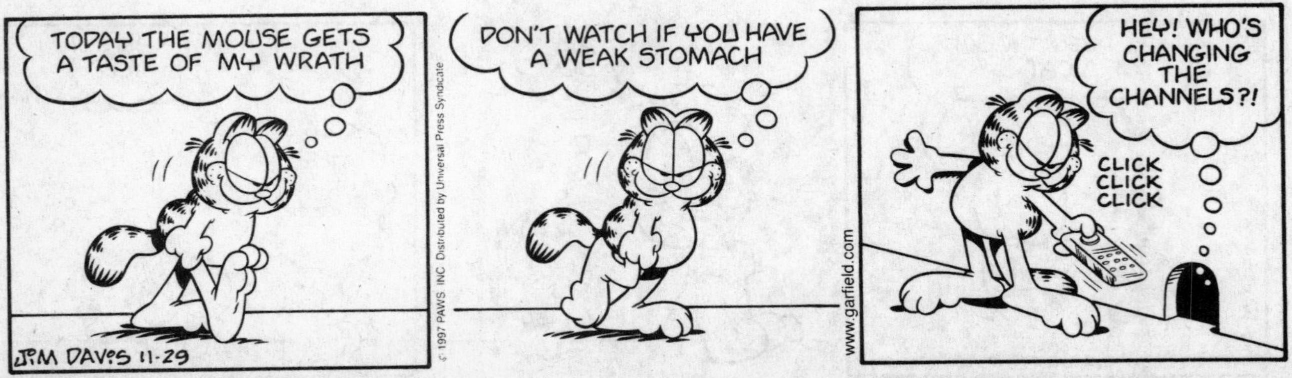
TODAY THE MOUSE GETS A TASTE OF MY WRATH
DON'T WATCH IF YOU HAVE A WEAK STOMACH
HEY! WHO'S CHANGING THE CHANNELS?!
CLICK CLICK CLICK
JIM DAVIS 11-29
© 1997 PAWS, INC. Distributed by Universal Press Syndicate
www.garfield.com

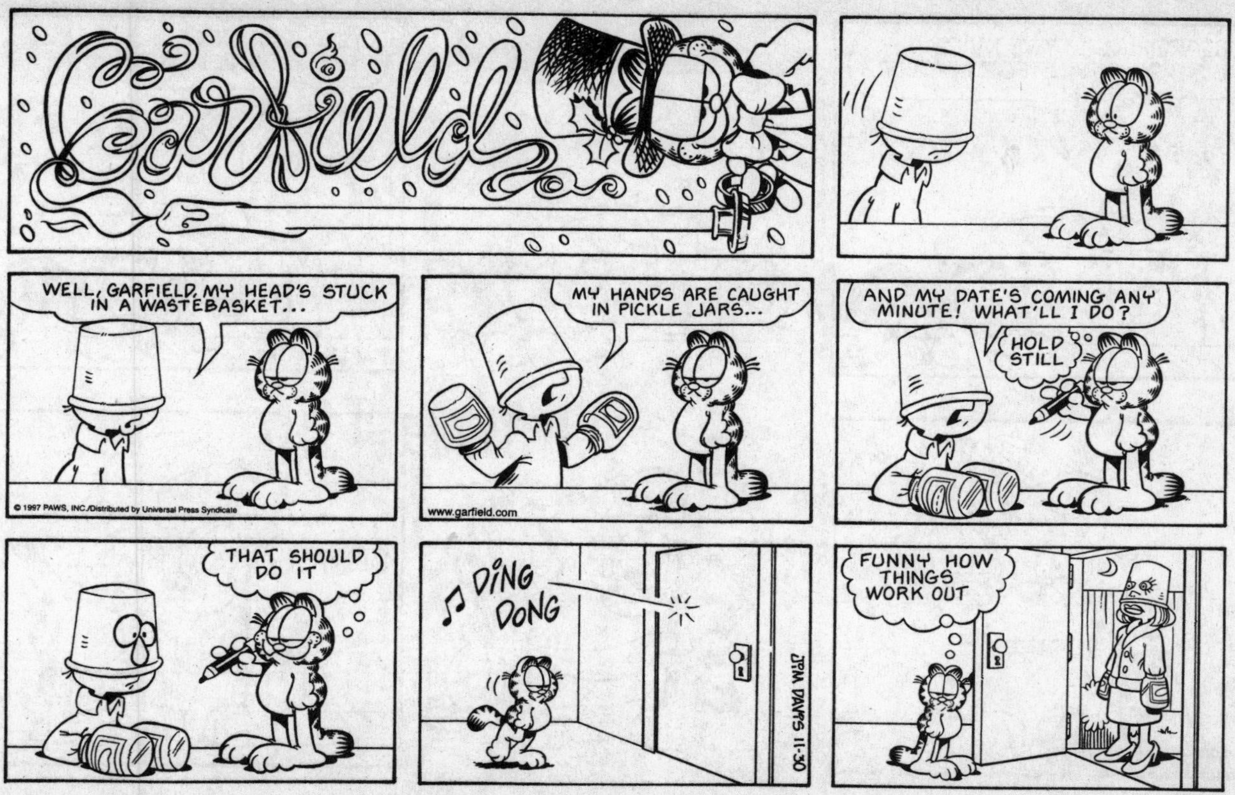
Garfield
WELL, GARFIELD, MY HEAD'S STUCK IN A WASTEBASKET...
MY HANDS ARE CAUGHT IN PICKLE JARS...
AND MY DATE'S COMING ANY MINUTE! WHAT'LL I DO?
HOLD STILL
THAT SHOULD DO IT
DING DONG
FUNNY HOW THINGS WORK OUT
JIM DAVIS 11-30
© 1997 PAWS, INC./Distributed by Universal Press Syndicate
www.garfield.com

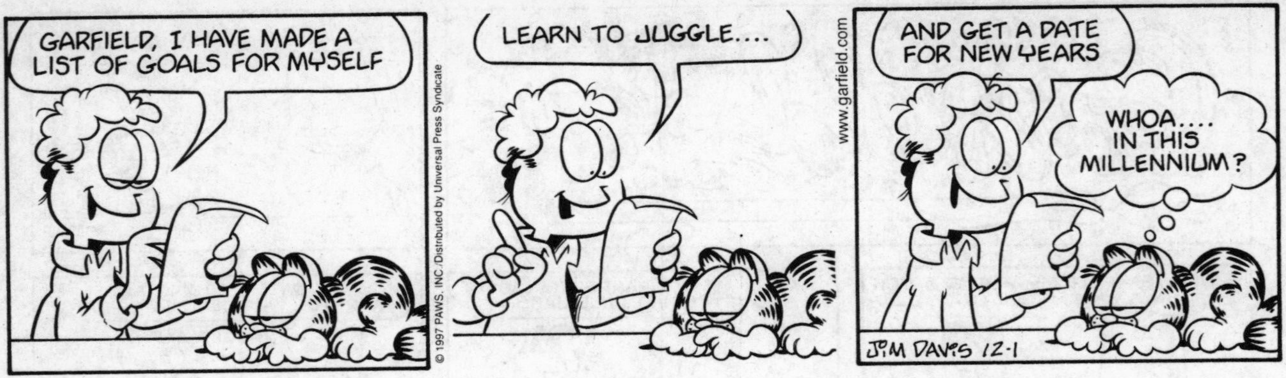
GARFIELD, I HAVE MADE A LIST OF GOALS FOR MYSELF
LEARN TO JUGGLE....
AND GET A DATE FOR NEW YEARS
WHOA.... IN THIS MILLENNIUM?
JIM DAVIS 12-1
© 1997 PAWS, INC./Distributed by Universal Press Syndicate
www.garfield.com

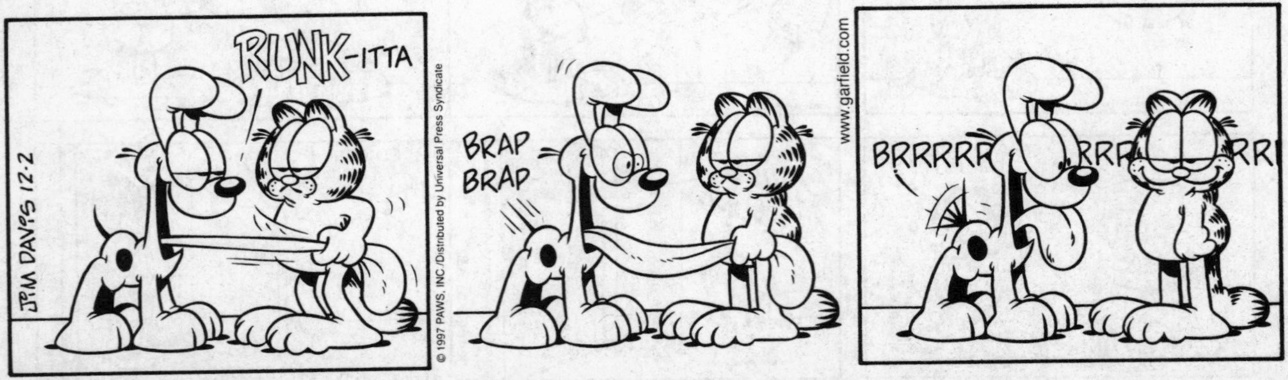
RUNK-ITTA
BRAP
BRAP
BRRRRR
JIM DAVIS 12-2
© 1997 PAWS, INC./Distributed by Universal Press Syndicate
www.garfield.com

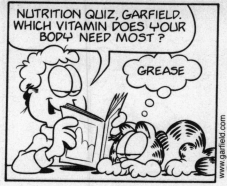

NUTRITION QUIZ, GARFIELD. WHICH VITAMIN DOES YOUR BODY NEED MOST?
GREASE
www.garfield.com
WHAT IS ENERGY FOOD?
MEAT THAT'S STILL MOVING
© 1997 PAWS. INC./Distributed by Universal Press Syndicate
JPM DAVIS 12-3
WHAT IS THE MOST IMPORTANT MEAL OF THE DAY?
4 A.M.... A BAG OF CHIPS AND A BOWL OF DIP

www.garfield.com

25

© 1997 PAWS. INC./Distributed by Universal Press Syndicate
YES, GARFIELD, I'M AWARE CHRISTMAS IS COMING
JPM DAVIS 12-4

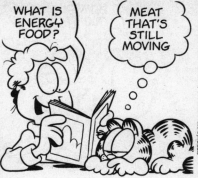

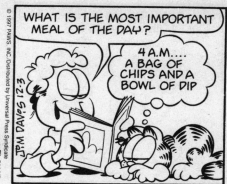

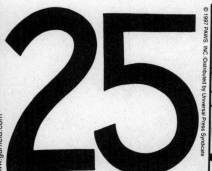

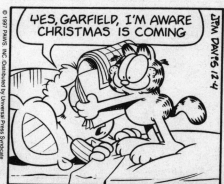

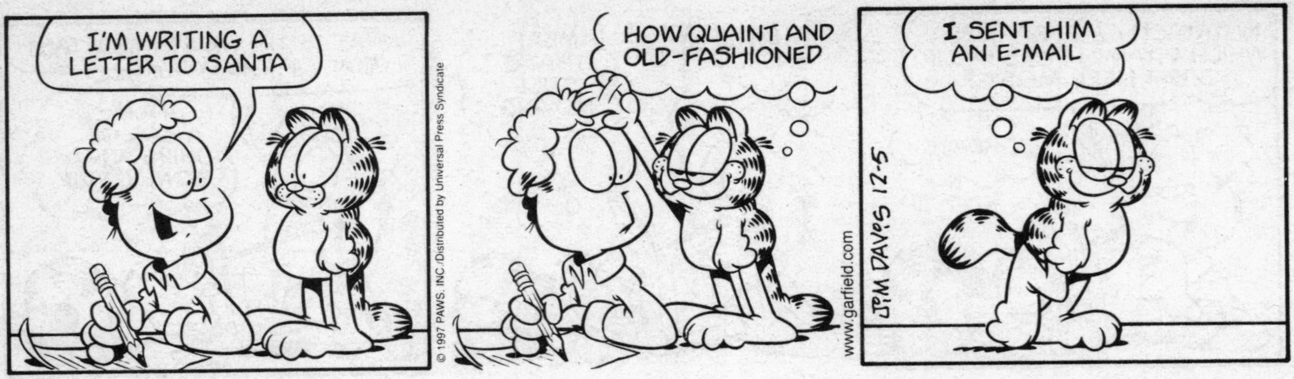
I'M WRITING A LETTER TO SANTA
HOW QUAINT AND OLD-FASHIONED
I SENT HIM AN E-MAIL
JIM DAVIS 12-5
www.garfield.com
© 1997 PAWS, INC./Distributed by Universal Press Syndicate

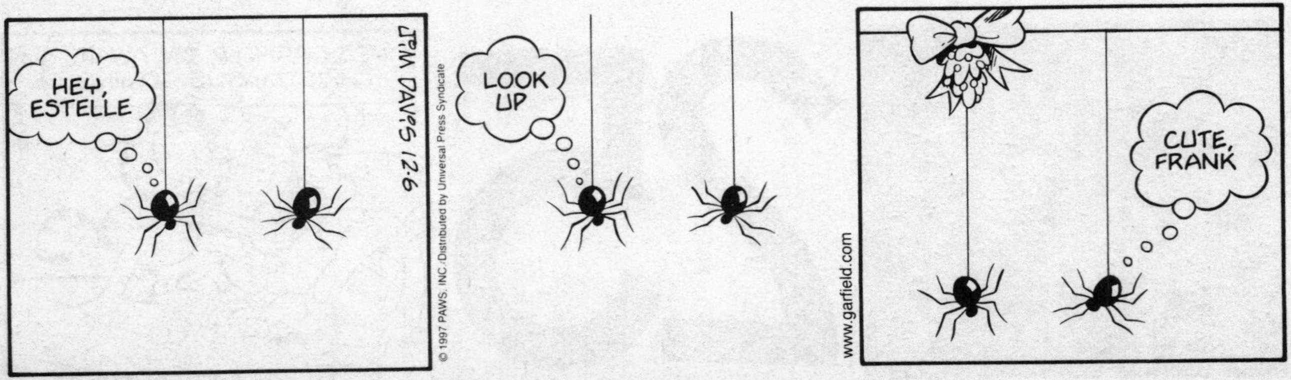
HEY, ESTELLE
LOOK UP
CUTE, FRANK
JIM DAVIS 12-6
www.garfield.com
© 1997 PAWS, INC./Distributed by Universal Press Syndicate

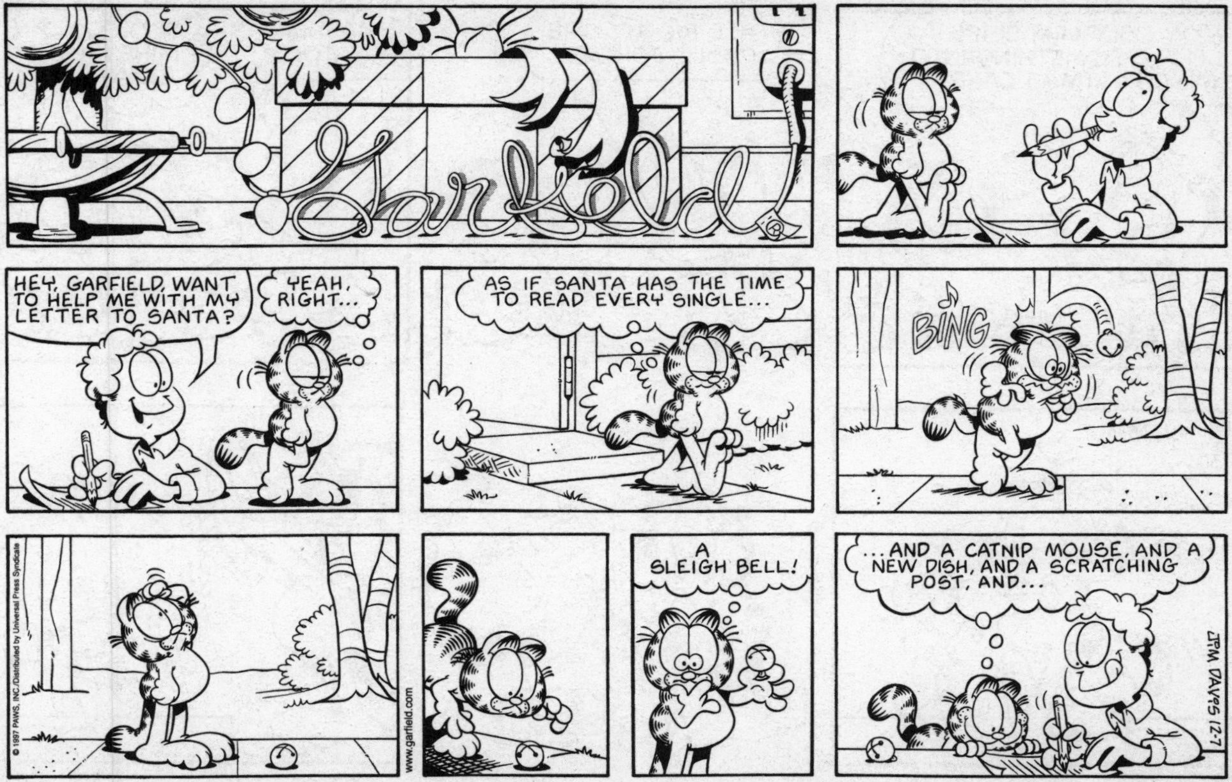
Garfield
HEY, GARFIELD, WANT TO HELP ME WITH MY LETTER TO SANTA?
YEAH, RIGHT...
AS IF SANTA HAS THE TIME TO READ EVERY SINGLE...
BING
© 1997 PAWS, INC./Distributed by Universal Press Syndicate
www.garfield.com
A SLEIGH BELL!
...AND A CATNIP MOUSE, AND A NEW DISH, AND A SCRATCHING POST, AND...
JIM DAVIS 12-7

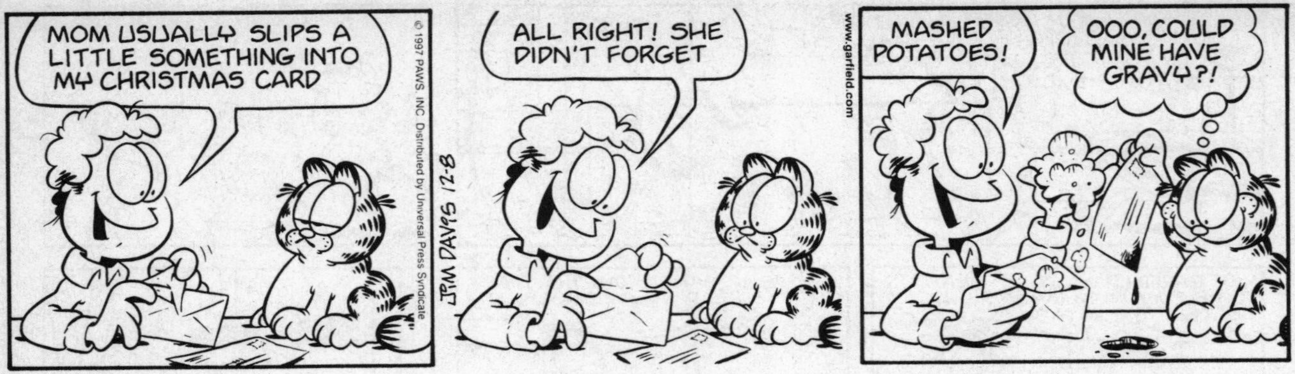
MOM USUALLY SLIPS A LITTLE SOMETHING INTO MY CHRISTMAS CARD
© 1997 PAWS, INC Distributed by Universal Press Syndicate
JPM DAVPS 12-8
ALL RIGHT! SHE DIDN'T FORGET
www.garfield.com
MASHED POTATOES!
OOO, COULD MINE HAVE GRAVY?!

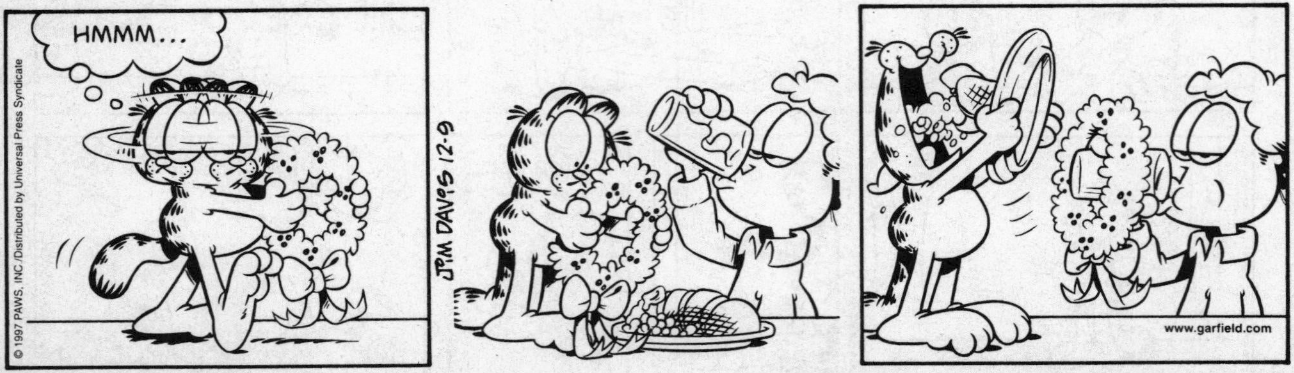
HMMM...
© 1997 PAWS, INC./Distributed by Universal Press Syndicate
JPM DAVPS 12-9
www.garfield.com

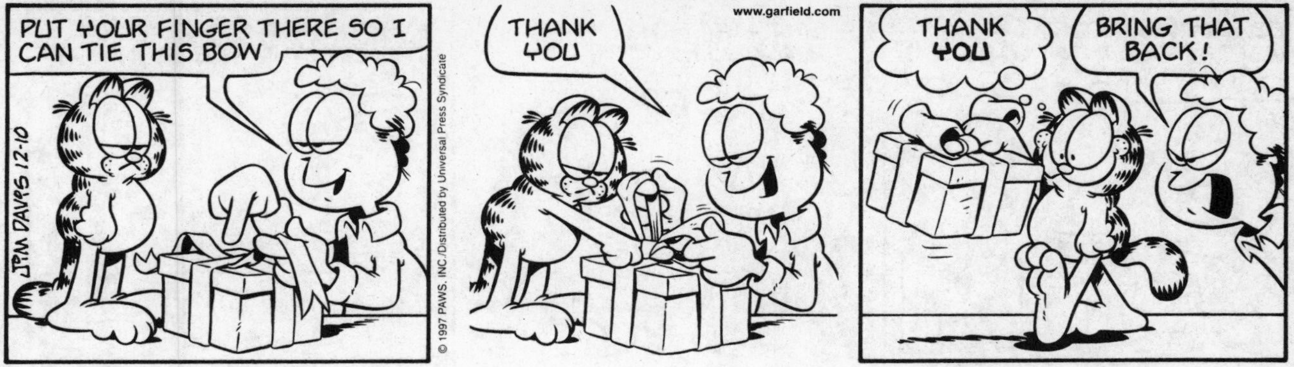
PUT YOUR FINGER THERE SO I CAN TIE THIS BOW
JIM DAVIS 12-10
© 1997 PAWS, INC./Distributed by Universal Press Syndicate
THANK YOU
www.garfield.com
THANK YOU
BRING THAT BACK!

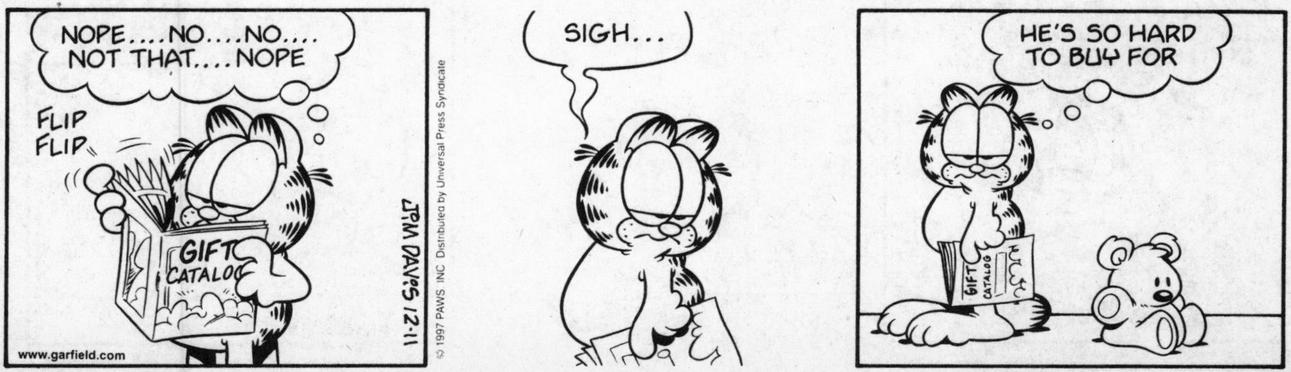
NOPE....NO....NO.... NOT THAT....NOPE
FLIP FLIP
GIFT CATALOG
www.garfield.com
© 1997 PAWS, INC. Distributed by Universal Press Syndicate
JIM DAVIS 12-11
SIGH...
HE'S SO HARD TO BUY FOR
GIFT CATALOG

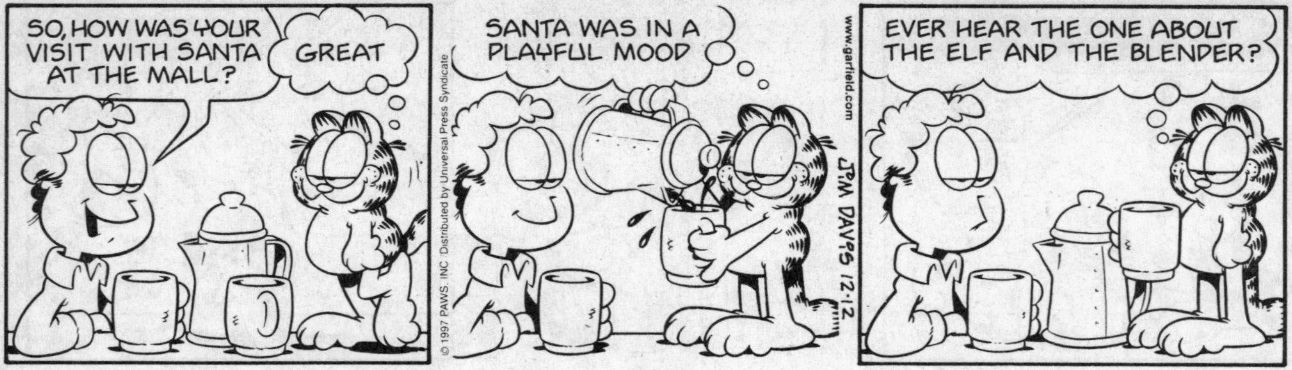
SO, HOW WAS YOUR VISIT WITH SANTA AT THE MALL?
GREAT
SANTA WAS IN A PLAYFUL MOOD
EVER HEAR THE ONE ABOUT THE ELF AND THE BLENDER?
© 1997 PAWS, INC Distributed by Universal Press Syndicate
www.garfield.com
JIM DAVIS 12-12

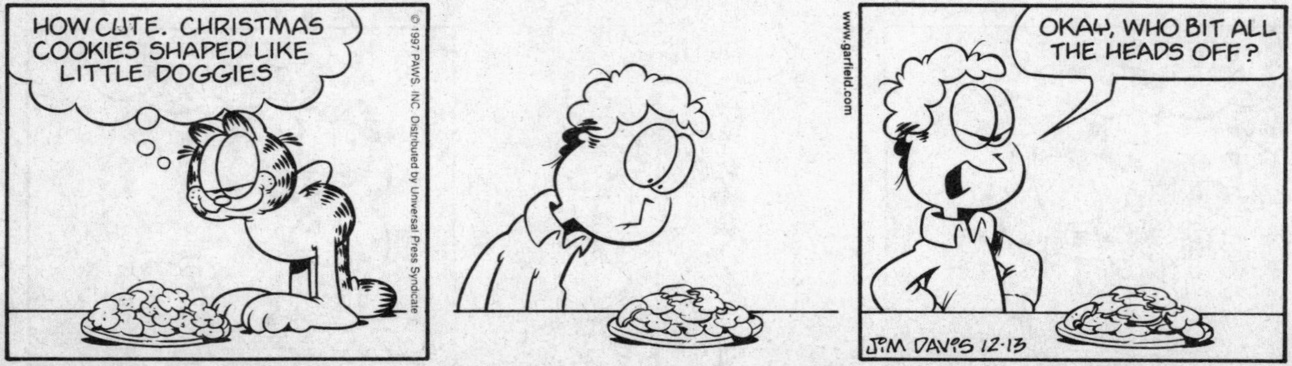
HOW CUTE. CHRISTMAS COOKIES SHAPED LIKE LITTLE DOGGIES
OKAY, WHO BIT ALL THE HEADS OFF?
© 1997 PAWS, INC. Distributed by Universal Press Syndicate
www.garfield.com
JIM DAVIS 12-13

GARFIELD'S PAST LIVES

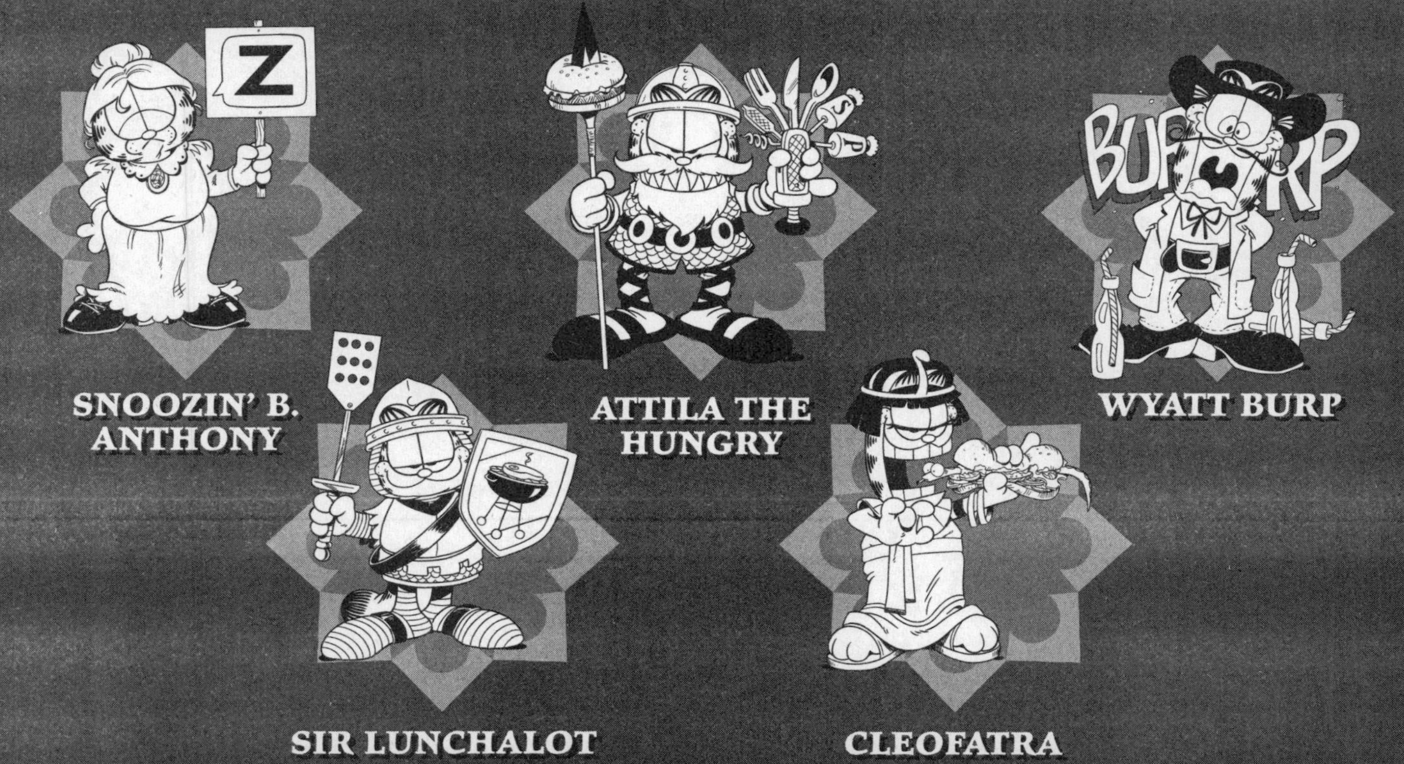
Z
SNOOZIN' B. ANTHONY
ATTILA THE HUNGRY
WYATT BURP
SIR LUNCHALOT
CLEOFATRA

Like to get a **COOL CAT**alog stuffed with great **GARFIELD** products? Then just write down the information below, stuff it in an envelope and mail it back to us....or you can fill in the card on our website - **HTTP://www.GARFIELD.com**. We'll get one out to you in two shakes of a cat's tail!

Name:
Address:
City:
State:
Zip:
Phone:
Date of Birth:
Sex:

Please mail your information to:

**Garfield Stuff Catalog
Dept.2BB38A
5804 Churchman By-Pass
Indianapolis, IN 46203-6109**

© PAWS

STRIPS, SPECIALS, OR BESTSELLING BOOKS . . .
GARFIELD'S ON EVERYONE'S MENU
Don't miss even one episode in the Tubby Tabby's hilarious series!

__GARFIELD AT LARGE (#1)   32013/$6.95
__GARFIELD GAINS WEIGHT (#2)   32008/$6.95
__GARFIELD BIGGER THAN LIFE (#3)   32007/$6.95
__GARFIELD WEIGHS IN (#4)   32010/$6.95
__GARFIELD TAKES THE CAKE (#5)   32009/$6.95
__GARFIELD EATS HIS HEART OUT (#6)   32018/$6.95
__GARFIELD SITS AROUND THE HOUSE (#7)   32011/$6.95
__GARFIELD TIPS THE SCALES (#8)   33580/$6.95
__GARFIELD LOSES HIS FEET (#9)   31805/$6.95
__GARFIELD MAKES IT BIG (#10)   31928/$6.95
__GARFIELD ROLLS ON (#11)   32634/$6.95
__GARFIELD OUT TO LUNCH (#12)   33118/$6.95
__GARFIELD FOOD FOR THOUGHT (#13)   34129/$6.95
__GARFIELD SWALLOWS HIS PRIDE (#14)   34725/$6.95
__GARFIELD WORLDWIDE (#15)   35158/$6.95
__GARFIELD ROUNDS OUT (#16)   35388/$6.95
__GARFIELD CHEWS THE FAT (#17)   35956/$6.95
__GARFIELD GOES TO WAIST (#18)   36430/$6.95
__GARFIELD HANGS OUT (#19)   36835/$6.95
__GARFIELD TAKES UP SPACE (#20)   37029/$6.95
__GARFIELD SAYS A MOUTHFUL (#21)   37368/$6.95
__GARFIELD BY THE POUND (#22)   37579/$6.95

__GARFIELD KEEPS HIS CHINS UP (#23)   37959/$6.95
__GARFIELD TAKES HIS LICKS (#24)   38170/$6.95
__GARFIELD HITS THE BIG TIME (#25)   38332/$6.95
__GARFIELD PULLS HIS WEIGHT (#26)   38666/$6.95
__GARFIELD DISHES IT OUT (#27)   39287/$6.95
__GARFIELD LIFE IN THE FAT LANE (#28)   39776/$6.95
__GARFIELD TONS OF FUN (#29)   40386/$6.95
__GARFIELD BIGGER AND BETTER (#30)   40770/$6.95
__GARFIELD HAMS IT UP (#31)   41241/$6.95
__GARFIELD THINKS BIG (#32)   41671/$6.95
__GARFIELD THROWS HIS WEIGHT AROUND (#33)   42749/$6.95
__GARFIELD LIFE TO THE FULLEST (#34)   43239/$6.95
__GARFIELD FEEDS THE KITTY (#35)   43673-/$6.95

GARFIELD AT HIS SUNDAY BEST!
__GARFIELD TREASURY   32106/$11.95
__THE SECOND GARFIELD TREASURY   33276/$10.95
__THE THIRD GARFIELD TREASURY   32635/$11.00
__THE FOURTH GARFIELD TREASURY   34726/$10.95
__THE FIFTH GARFIELD TREASURY   36268/$12.00
__THE SIXTH GARFIELD TREASURY   37367/$10.95
__THE SEVENTH GARFIELD TREASURY   38427/$10.95
__THE EIGHTH GARFIELD TREASURY   39778/$12.00
__THE NINTH GARFIELD TREASURY   41670/$12.50
__THE TENTH GARFIELD TREASURY   43674/$12.50

AND DON'T MISS...
__GARFIELD'S TWENTIETH ANNIVERSARY COLLECTION!   42126/$14.95

Please send me the BALLANTINE BOOKS I have checked above. I am enclosing $_____. (Please add $2.00 for the first book and $.50 for each additional book for postage and handling and include the appropriate state sales tax.) Send check or money order (no cash or C.O.D.'s) to Ballantine Mail Sales Dept. TA, 400 Hahn Road, Westminster, MD 21157.

To order by phone, call 1-800-733-3000 and use your major credit card.

Prices and numbers are subject to change without notice. Valid in the U.S. only. All orders are subject to availability.

Name_____

Address_____

City_____ State_____ Zip_____

BIRTHDAYS, HOLIDAYS, OR ANY DAY . . .

Keep GARFIELD on your calendar all year 'round!

GARFIELD TV SPECIALS
__GARFIELD GOES HOLLYWOOD 34580/$6.95
__GARFIELD'S HALLOWEEN ADVENTURE 33045/$6.95
   (formerly GARFIELD IN DISGUISE)
__GARFIELD'S FELINE FANTASY 36902/$6.95
__GARFIELD IN PARADISE 33796/$6.95
__GARFIELD IN THE ROUGH 32242/$6.95
__GARFIELD ON THE TOWN 31542/$6.95
__GARFIELD'S THANKSGIVING 35650/$6.95
__HERE COMES GARFIELD 32012/$6.95
__GARFIELD GETS A LIFE 37375/$6.95

ALSO FROM GARFIELD:
__GARFIELD: HIS NINE LIVES 32061/$9.95
__THE GARFIELD BOOK OF CAT NAMES 35082/$5.95
__GARFIELD: THE ME BOOK 36545/$7.95
__GARFIELD'S JUDGMENT DAY 36755/$6.95
__THE TRUTH ABOUT CATS 37226/$6.95
__GARFIELD'S JOLLY HOLIDAY 3 PACK 42042-X/$10.95